Interpersonal Relations and Social Patterns in Communication Technologies:
Discourse Norms, Language Structures and Cultural Variables

Jung-ran Park
Drexel University, USA

Eileen G. Abels
Drexel University, USA

INFORMATION SCIENCE REFERENCE

Hershey · New York

Director of Editorial Content:	Kristin Klinger
Director of Book Publications:	Julia Mosemann
Acquisitions Editor:	Lindsay Johnston
Development Editor:	Christine Bufton
Typesetter:	Gregory Snader
Production Editor:	Jamie Snavely
Cover Design:	Lisa Tosheff
Printed at:	Yurchak Printing Inc.

Published in the United States of America by
Information Science Reference (an imprint of IGI Global)
701 E. Chocolate Avenue
Hershey PA 17033
Tel: 717-533-8845
Fax: 717-533-8661
E-mail: cust@igi-global.com
Web site: http://www.igi-global.com/reference

Library of Congress Cataloging-in-Publication Data

Interpersonal relations and social patterns in communication technologies : discourse norms, language structures and cultural variables / Jung-ran Park and Eileen G. Abels, editors.
      p. cm.
   Includes bibliographical references.
   Summary: "This book provides interdisciplinary perspectives utilizing a variety of research methods to uncover the fundamental components of computer-mediated communication (i.e., language, interpersonal relations/communication and information technology) which will be discussed in the following section"- -Provided by publisher.
   ISBN 978-1-61520-827-2 -- ISBN 978-1-61520-828-9 (ebook) 1. Telecommunications--Social aspects. 2. Computer networks--Social aspects. 3. Internet--Social aspects. 4. Interpersonal relations. I. Park, Jung-ran. II. Abels, Eileen G. HM851.
I56923 2010
   303.48'33--dc22
                            2009053957

British Cataloguing in Publication Data
A Cataloguing in Publication record for this book is available from the British Library.

Table of Contents

Section 2
Interpersonal Relationships and Gendered Communication

Section 3
Language Action and Discourse Features in CMC

Section 4
Online Learning and Collaboration

Section 5
Social Support and Networking and Social Technology

Detailed Table of Contents

Section 1
Online Identity and Self Presentation

The first and second sections discuss the conceptual grounds of interpersonal relations and social discourse in CMC contexts. Chapters in the first section discuss presentations and projections of online identity and self through relational perspectives. Identity is conceptualized as socio-culturally situated and constructed. Multidimensional self and identity is presented and realized through language action and social discourse. Issues in relation to self disclosure, privacy management and anonymity are also discussed.

Chapter 1

> Lynnette G. Leonard, University of Nebraska at Omaha, USA
> Lesley A. Withers, Central Michigan University, USA
> John C. Sherblom, University of Maine, USA

Past research on the effects of computer-mediated communication (CMC) on identity has focused either on the inherent risks or opportunities it provides. The authors argue that the paradox within the nature of CMC has led to paradoxical predictions about the effects of CMC on identity. Rather than adopting a naïve perspective focusing on only one side of the paradox, the authors take a view of technological realism in which the paradox is embraced. Guided by these views, the authors analyze 59 students' papers reflecting on their identity choices in the creation and development of a Second Life avatar. Second Life is a three-dimensional (3D) multi-user virtual environment (MUVE) in which users create avatars (called "residents") to explore, interact with other residents, learn, recreate, and shop with the local currency (i.e., Linden Dollars; http://secondlife.com/whatis/). Using the constant comparative method for thematic content, themes supporting a paradox of CMC effects on identity are identified from the student papers. The implications of a view of technological realism are offered.

Chapter 2

Using Denning's model of Internet activism as a sensitizing framework, this chapter describes the manner in which Black bloggers (referred to as the 'Blackosphere') express and negotiate their ethnic identity online. We analyze discussions in the Blackosphere in response to the Jena 6 case to illustrate how the Internet has empowered Black people, changed media publicity, and served as a means of collaborative activities that support social activism. It is our hope that this chapter will encourage researchers to explore further how and why historically underserved groups engage in social activism on the Internet, and the various technologies and social practices they use to do so.

Chapter 3

This chapter adds depth to current theoretical approaches to the idea of social presence in computer-mediated communication by integrating ideas from deconstructionism, subaltern studies, phenomenological/dialogic approaches, and media ecology with current CMC perspectives on the (dis)embodied nature of CMC communication. The relation of the physical to online social environments naturally raises the question of the ways these environments inherit heteroglossic social expectations from other communication/media genres, especially from written media and from face-to-face conversational interactions. Ultimately, these inheritances, together with their ethical considerations, show that a variety of perspectives, even those that seem to be conflicting, simply serve to illuminate various aspects of the CMC environment and the ethical ramifications thereof.

Chapter 4

Use of mediated channels of communication, such as email and instant messenger, is rapidly increasing, especially with adolescents and college-aged populations. This increase may alter interpersonal relationship maintenance strategies and communication patterns. The role of mediated channels of communication in some types of relationship initiation is well documented however, research investigating use within existing relationships is more limited. Self-disclosure is an important part of relationship maintenance, both in the initial stages of development as well as in existing relationships. This chapter explores motivations for disclosure through computer mediated communication (CMC) in pre-existing relationships and describes theoretical perspectives to advance examination of this area. Examples presented indicate four primary motivations for disclose through computer mediated communication:

self, other, relationship, and situational/environmental. Further, we propose several codes within each primary reason, many of which diverged from traditional motivations for FtF disclosure. Implications and future directions for interpersonal CMC research are discussed.

Section 2
Interpersonal Relationships and Gendered Communication

The second section explores relationship development and maintenance, particularly gendered identity, in depth. Gendered identity is revealed through examination of communication styles of linguistic features. Socio-cultural variables in relation to gender and their impact on the CMC are investigated as well.

Chapter 5

Jessica L. Moore, North Carolina State University, USA
Elizabeth A. Craig, North Carolina State University, USA

This chapter presents a review of contemporary scholarship on relational communication, particularly as it relates to interpersonal relationship development and maintenance. Throughout the chapter, special attention is given to the role new technologies play in the communication process. This chapter draws together a wide array of communication research findings ranging from attraction and initial interactions to relational routines and social support. Consideration is also given to some of the methodological and conceptual issues that face contemporary communication researchers. Fundamentally, the function of this multifaceted chapter is to provide an accessible and informed introduction to relational communication and computer-mediated scholarship for both an academic and general audience. A list of recommended readings on communication scholarship concludes this chapter.

Chapter 6

Katheryn C. Maguire, Wayne State University, USA

This chapter examines the research on sex differences and gender identification in computer-mediated interaction (CMI), and presents a pilot study of synchronous, anonymous, one-to-one interactions, to understand the extent to which a person's "real life" sex can be identified in CMIs as well as the stylistic and linguistic cues that "mark" someone as "male" or "female." Although previous research has reported sex differences in a number of different variables (e.g., number of words, disagreements), analysis of the transcripts in this study revealed only one significant difference, in that men corrected themselves more often than women. Furthermore, participants correctly guessed the sex of their partner 62.5% of the time, felt approximately 65% sure of their guess, and used gender stereotypes to make their assessments. Implications for anonymity and CMI research are discussed, focusing on the conditions under which sex differences and gender stereotypes become relevant in on-line interactions.

Chapter 7

Nancy A. Burrell, University of Wisconsin, USA
Edward A. Mabry, University of Wisconsin, USA
Mike Allen, University of Wisconsin, USA

This study investigates gender differences in linguistic features of communication styles in the context of mixed public discussion groups in asynchronous, text-based CMC. The study evaluates gendered communication and language styles in situational contexts of CMC. A sample of 3000 messages from 30 Internet discussion groups was content analyzed. Results revealed gender differences in stylistic features used by discussion group participants and partially support the expectation that women's online communication style is gendered. The data did not reveal an online communication style that significantly discriminated men's communication. Findings point to the important role of gender enacted through language in the construction of social identity in the context of public discussion groups in CMC. Implications of this investigation and directions for the development of future research on gender in CMC are discussed.

Section 3
Language Action and Discourse Features in CMC

The third section of the book concerns language action and discourse features in CMC. Chapters in this section explore key characteristics of online language attributes during social interaction. These encompass the metaphoric dimension of social interactions, discourse structure and coherence, verbal and non-verbal signals and devices in relation to interpersonal discourse, (in)formal conversational practices, rhetorical acts and meaning negotiation and affective language uses.

Chapter 8

Agnès Vayreda, Open University of Catalonia (UOC), Spain
Francesc Núñez, Open University of Catalonia (UOC), Spain

This chapter focuses on the role that metaphors play in the social relationships of people who use CMC. The study analyzes the metaphors used by contributors to three different electronic fora when they refer to the process of interaction. One of our main objectives of the study is to show that the study of metaphors allows us to understand how CMC users reach agreement as to the nature of the social space that they inhabit and what behavior is considered to be appropriate or inappropriate in such a space. This chapter will show that metaphors facilitate the construction of social life and allow CMC users to propose norms of behaviour; they also facilitate the process of identification, generate confidence in a group, and orient users to the cultural contexts in which social action takes place.

Chapter 9

This chapter describes how American bloggers and Chinese bloggers from similar age and gender groups represent themselves and their identities linguistically in their blogs and explores whether and to what extent the differences in terms of the blogging language and culture affect these representations. The author adopts a corpus-based approach and focuses on the description and the comparison of the orthographic features and semantic domain preference as revealed in the blog entries. By conducting a cross-linguistic and cross-cultural comparison between American bloggers and Chinese bloggers, the author finds that bloggers' linguistic practice is closely related to their developmental stage of life, their gender, and the cultural environment they are immersed in. Meanwhile, bloggers' linguistic practice is also constrained by the internal system of the language they use for blogging.

Chapter 10

This chapter investigates discourse features in asynchronous Nigerian discussion forums, which is now becoming a popular medium for discussing issues of interest to many Nigerians. The sample was based on extracts from CONCOMED, a corpus of Nigerian Computer-mediated English Discourse compiled by this researcher between 2006 and 2009. Four threads, one for each year were subjected to analysis based on Herring's (2004) Computer Mediated Discourse Analysis (CMDA) framework. Analysis focused on interaction features of turn-taking, topic focus and coherence. Turn-taking process in the threads was a complex phenomenon characterized by non-sequential turns and adjacency disruptions. Interactants typically self-selected and used Quoting as turn tracking device. Global topics often split into sub-topics to address details. Despite the limitations of messaging systems on sequential turn-taking and referencing, interactional and topical coherence was established in the threads, as participants were able to logically connect their ideas in this complex virtual conversational context through Quoting, Addressivity and topic focus.

Chapter 11

Building on the research produced by early and current computers and writing scholars, this chapter looks at the results of an analysis of both virtual- and classroom-based texts produced by nine first-year writers, five from composition I and four from composition II courses at a mid-sized, Midwestern, public university. The research included in this chapter explores the results of how blogging affected student writing in the first-year writing classroom. Specifically, this chapter focuses on the results of this study in relation to the explicit and implicit textual signals and how these textual signals complicate communication in computer mediated environments.

Chapter 12

Kris M. Markman, University of Memphis, USA

This chapter presents an analysis of interaction in computer-mediated group meetings. Five undergraduate students used a quasi-synchronous chat interface to conduct four virtual team meetings. Using the framework of conversation analysis, the author describes how self-initiated self repair of minor errors such as typos was used by team members as a vehicle for group norm development. The norms for typing style (punctuation, correcting typos and spelling mistakes) vary widely across computer-mediated communication (CMC) contexts. The author shows how the main function of the repair attempts was not to clarify meaning, but rather to help team members, particularly in their first meeting, work out an agreed-upon set of typing conventions for their subsequent interactions, thus contributing to the development of a norm of informality.

Section 4
Online Learning and Collaboration

The fourth section focuses on the online learning community and group collaboration. Chapters in this section discuss the psycho-social and interpersonal dynamics of online learning and group collaboration and implications to online education. Owing to richness of emerging information technology, stakeholders of online learning communities reflect the diverse geographic and language backgrounds as well as various socio-cultural values and norms. Such contexts foreground interpersonal communication as a key factor in facilitating group involvement and collaboration (Park, 2007). Through examining social presence, along with teaching and cognitive presence of discourse participants, chapters in this section uncover complex and intricate process of online learning and collaboration and construction of online groups and communities in virtual as well as blended contexts.

Chapter 13

Sharon Stoerger, Indiana University, USA

Much of the literature argues that educational initiatives that take place in three-dimensional virtual worlds such as *Second Life* (SL) enable students to construct their knowledge and take ownership for their learning. The notion of a more student-centered learning environment is not new; in fact, similar claims were made about text-based MUD environments and to some extent, educational chat spaces. This study is an attempt to more rigorously examine some of the claims made about the democratic nature of communication in virtual worlds such as SL and the potential for these electronic spaces beyond social exchanges. The findings support the notion that deep learning is possible in virtual worlds using synchronous text chat. However, evidence to suggest that the structure of the educational activities is student-centered is lacking. Contrary to the claims, instructional activities used in the SL courses under investigation relied heavily on a teacher-centered model.

Chapter 14

S. Annese, University of Bari, Italy

M. Traetta, University of Bari, Italy

P. F. Spadaro, University of Bari, Italy

Blended learning communities are defined by specific learning and psychosocial processes based on the multilayered sense of belonging of the group's members, related to the merging of both virtual and real interactive contexts. This chapter focuses on the psychosocial dynamics of blended communities, in order to identify some specific participation strategies and identity dynamics, which both vary with the double interactive context. The study used a qualitative variant of Social Network Analysis to analyse the interactions of two blended student communities, identifying various participation trajectories and identity positionings of the group members. The results revealed that the blending of two communication contexts generates different psychosocial dynamics from those activated by the same community in a wholly on- or offline context. The combination of interactive environments results in participation strategies in which members can choose distinctive trajectories, shaping their original identity positionings.

Chapter 15

Blurring Boundaries with Computer-Mediated Communication:

Kayla D. Hales, Pennsylvania State University, USA

Stephanie Troutman, Pennsylvania State University, USA

The authors survey the landscape of CMC and education by relating it to increasingly popular hybrid course structures. This chapter maps findings associated with academic learning and subjective knowledge in a graduate course assignment: the "electronic palimpsest". This became a vehicle for the exploration of embodiment, identity, and virtual learning. Within the electronic palimpsest these themes were sustained, complicated, and evaluated from multiple standpoints, as demonstrated through content analysis of postings. Ultimately, this case study contributes to and supports the belief that case-specific accounts of alternative CMC projects are highly valuable in providing future directions for the requisite evolution of technologies associated with hybrid learning. The electronic palimpsest challenges typical assumptions of learning communities, as well as assessments and outcomes of learning in virtual environments. This study promotes possibilities for different pedagogical approaches to the question: *what is the relationship between knowledge production and the development of learning communities?*

Chapter 16

J. A. McArthur, Queens University of Charlotte, USA

This chapter focuses on an interpersonal approach to understanding small group development in mediated environments. Whereas much of the literature in this area has emerged in the study of workplace and organizational development, this chapter is grounded in small group development theory and folds in relevant studies of virtual communication in groups. This approach is designed to complement a larger work based in interpersonal communication by providing students of interpersonal communication with a basic introduction to small groups and the impact of communication technology on small group development.

Chapter 17

In a climate of increasing globalization with calls for the development of online learning communities that thrive on diversity, it is important to consider how diversity might influence the nature of interpersonal action and the dynamics of collaboration in computer-mediated education. This chapter considers the case of problematic collaboration in an online graduate program. Discourse analysis grounded in Systemic Functional Linguistics is applied to illustrate how various aspects of stakeholders' identities can be traced in the discourse related to online collaborative processes. A model of situated multidimensional identity is used to consider how localized constructions of identity may be linked to broader frames of reference. Findings suggest that when stakeholders from a range of backgrounds are drawn together, online collaboration becomes a complex social practice.

Section 5
Social Support and Networking and Social Technology

There is a lack of research on cultural manifestations in the CMC and online networking behavior across cultures. The fifth section addresses this research gap by exploring the impact of communication technologies in seeking and sharing information through online social support and social networking beyond cultural boundaries. It also presents communication patterns of online social support and networking while taking cultural differences into account. Cultural representations on web interface and usability issues are also discussed in depth.

Chapter 18

Taking a culture-centered approach within the uses and gratifications theoretical framework, a quantitative content analysis was conducted to analyze the support messages of two online message boards: the Dear Baby message board created and moderated mainly by overseas Chinese prenatal and postnatal women, and the BabyCenter message board created and moderated mainly by USAmerican prenatal and postnatal women. Both similarities and differences of the two message boards were identified in message type (seek or give support), content, support type and support behavior. Constructed narratives were produced to qualitatively analyze the voices within the context of both USAmerican and overseas Chinese online communities. The results can help researchers and practitioners to better understand how cultural characteristics of Chinese and USAmerican groups influence the patterns of women's online social support seeking/giving behaviors, enabling them to customize specific communication programs and services to meet the needs of members of those two cultural groups.

Chapter 19

Devan Rosen, University of Hawaii, USA
Michael A. Stefanone, University at Buffalo, USA
Derek Lackaff, University of Texas at Austin, USA

People from distinct cultural backgrounds communicate and manage their interpersonal relations in systematically different ways. The current chapter utilizes a survey of young adults to examine the social patterns of culturally influenced differences in online behavior. Results show that individuals that identify with individualistic cultural backgrounds have larger networks of friends on social network sites (SNSs), have a larger proportion of these friends that they have not actually met face-to-face, and share more photos online, opposed to individuals that identify with less individualistic cultural backgrounds. The size of an individuals' offline social support network size was a significant predictor of satisfaction with life, while SNS network size was not. Findings suggest that individuals who identify with more individualistic cultural backgrounds tend to be better connected, self-promote, and are more satisfied with their social lives.

Chapter 20

Rowena Li, Bayside High School Library, New York, USA

The purpose of this chapter is to explore the representation of national political freedom on Web interface design by using power distance, one of the culture dimensions identified by Geert Hofstede, as a measurement. It also aims to determine if there are any differences between government-based Web sites and business-oriented Web sites in representing national political freedom. This study applied seven indicators validated from previous study (Li, 2009) in coding 312 Web sites selected from 39 countries and analyzed national political freedom represented on these Web sites with content analysis method. The result of two-way analysis of variance (ANOVA) indicated that large differences exist in Web interface design, which in turn reflects the aforementioned national political freedom. The research showed that the mean effect of freedom level between free-country group, partly-free-country group and not-free-country group was statistically significant (p = .003). So was the mean effect of Web site type between government-based and business-oriented Web sites (p = .000). Furthermore, the interaction between the freedom level and Web site type was also significant (p = .041). Therefore, the study concludes that Web interface design correlates with a country's political freedom level and government-based Web sites embody more of a nation's authority and supremacy than business-oriented Web sites do. It is expected that this study furthers our exploration in culture dimensions on Web interface design and advances our knowledge in sociological and cultural studies of the Web.

Chapter 21

Paula M. Bach, Pennsylvania State University, USA
Hao Jiang, Pennsylvania State University, USA
John M. Carroll, Pennsylvania State University, USA

This chapter investigates the social and communication challenges surrounding usability information sharing. Our objective is to investigate a communication paradox: software development teams, consisting of usability engineers, software developers, and project managers, chose communication channels to use every day that are not channels they prefer to use. This paradox was discovered in a survey and explored further in interviews with software development teams. Results indicated that challenges with common ground and work coupling affect the extent to which the affordances of different communication channels can be taken advantage of. The value of this study highlights and explains the paradox from a time-space perspective and provides insight to usability information sharing among software engineering teams. Future work includes investigating the effect of social capital on communication channel preference along with understanding how important usability issues can be discussed in complex teams.

Preface

INTRODUCTION

The development of information and communication technologies has enabled dynamic social interaction through a computer-mediated communication (CMC) channel. Human interaction in a dyadic (one-on-one), public or group context through networked computers constitutes computer-mediated communication. A survey of internet use revealed phenomenal growth (132%, totaling over 250 million users) of internet usage in just North America between 2000 and 2008 (Internetworldstats, 2009). Accordingly, there has been rapid growth in CMC genres and applications of social interaction encompassing online message boards and discussion lists, newsgroups, digital reference, instant messaging, multi-user dimensions, blogs, social support groups and social networking sites.

The proliferation of CMC applications calls for new perspectives, methods and tools for research and practice in order to broaden our understanding of communication patterns and augment our understanding of the theoretical underpinnings of communication in CMC contexts. Also necessitated is an understanding of online social interaction and an analysis of interpersonal relations and social discourse in order to facilitate effective and dynamic interaction and building a sustainable online community. In daily interaction, it is inevitable that one will be involved in speech acts such as requests, disagreements, apologies, acknowledgment or thanks. Daily interaction is therefore anchored in interpersonal relations and social discourse involving communication in a dyadic, public or small-group context.

The impact of information and communication technologies vis-à-vis interpersonal relations and online social discourse has been relatively unexplored. This book addresses these issues by looking into conceptual foundations of computer-mediated interaction, language action and discourse features in various CMC contexts. The authors explore the manifestations of communicative and networking behavior of participants engaged in online discourse and address interpersonal relations and social discourse in the building of online communities and virtual teams for online learning and collaboration. In addition, online social support and networking across cultures and social technology are discussed in relation to social discourse and information technologies.

There is a rapidly growing body of literature in the area of CMC; however, there remains a dearth of literature dealing with CMC topics from interdisciplinary perspectives. This book provides interdisciplinary perspectives utilizing a variety of research methods to uncover the fundamental components of CMC (i.e., language, interpersonal relations/communication and information technology) which will be discussed in the following section.

Authors present data that are drawn from a wide range of sources including surveys, interview transcripts, personal blogs, online message boards and student discussion forums, health support groups, social network sites including Facebook and three-dimensional multi-user virtual environments such as Second Life. Data sources represent local and global CMC interaction.

FUNDAMENTALS IN CMC: LANGUAGE, SOCIAL INTERACTION, AND INFORMATION AND COMMUNICATION TECHNOLOGIES

Language confers humanity. Acquisition of a mother tongue is one of the most prominent characteristics of human beings. Language enables us to communicate, organize and access information and knowledge beyond the boundaries of time, space, and media. It is the cornerstone of socio-cultural experiences and the fundamental means for the embodiment and inheritance of intellectual and cultural heritages and values.

Studies of online language usage vis-à-vis face-to-face language usage are critical for understanding social interaction and interpersonal relations through CMC channels. Face-to-face communication makes use of a number of discourse features that facilitate an efficient process for encoding and decoding linguistic and paralinguistic elements that convey interpersonal and affective meanings among participants. Paralinguistic features are supra-linguistic cues that are added to linguistic elements. For instance, prosodic features such as high pitch intonation, pause and accent, together with non-verbal signals such as gesture and facial expressions function to convey interpersonal and affective meanings as well as to modify semantic meanings delivered by the linguistic elements.

Users of text-based CMC by and large lack these contextual cues. In contrast to a face-to-face setting, text-based CMC does not afford discourse participants opportunities for communicating meanings through the above mentioned paralinguistic cues. However, studies show that that CMC employs a high degree of interpersonally-oriented language (e.g., Park, 2007). Online discourse participants employ a variety of creative linguistic and paralinguistic devices to signal non-verbal communication cues that serve to build interpersonal solidarity and rapport. As well, by seeking common ground and by expressing agreement, online participants may build mutual understanding and harmonious social interaction. Communication based on shared interest and common ground facilitates dynamic interaction (Park, 2008).

The text-based real-time synchronous communication channel enables discourse participants to engage in spontaneous interaction. This allows discourse participants to experience online social interaction similar to communication achieved through spoken language. Rapid feedback is possible and online discourse participants are able to develop rapport. Such rapid feedback and rapport enhances social presence among discourse participants and engenders the building of social cohesion. On the other hand, the text-based asynchronous communication channel affords discourse participants time for reflecting on the message before transfer and allows them to preserve and revisit messages. These characteristics of CMC are to some degree analogous to written language and contribute to enrich the depth and quality of asynchronous social interaction. Accordingly, this may engender online social support, learning and group collaboration.

The advancement of information and communication technologies has brought to the fore social interaction across languages and cultures. Geospatial boundaries are no longer barriers to social interaction, which enables stakeholders of online communities from diverse cultural backgrounds to interact with each other. However, there is still a lack of studies on cultural representation and manifestations in CMC (Herring ed., 1996). Several studies in this volume begin to fill this research gap (e.g., Mao et al.; Rosen et al.; Li).

The Web page, a new form of communication system and information technology, can be seen to represent a society's original cultural and social attributes. It constructs and reproduces both social and cultural inequality. The chapter by Li in this volume looks at the impact of cultural representation on web interface design. Through language representation, Li examines the relationship between interpersonal relations and online communications from a cultural perspective. The chapter provides insights and implications regarding human-computer interaction and usability within culture. Interpersonal as well as the emotional and affective aspects of communication have been studied as critical factors in designing interactive systems of social technologies (Sharp, 2007). Issues of interactive system design, social technology and social interface need to be further examined in relation to intercultural dimension.

ORGANIZATION OF THE BOOK

This volume consists of five sections consisting of a total of twenty-one chapters: 1) Online identity and self presentation; 2) Interpersonal relationships and gendered communication; 3) Language action and discourse features in the CMC; 4) Online learning and collaboration; 5) Social support and networking and social technology. The section topics are not mutually exclusive and there is some overlap. Some chapters could have been placed in multiple sections. For instance, most of the studies in this volume deal with language in one way or another; although not grouped in section three, language action and discourse features in CMC

The first and second sections of the book discuss the conceptual grounds of interpersonal relations and social discourse in CMC contexts. Chapters in the first section discuss presentations and projections of online identity and self through relational perspectives. Identity is conceptualized as socio-culturally situated and constructed. Multidimensional self and identity are presented and realized through language action and social discourse. Issues related to self disclosure, privacy management and anonymity are also discussed. The second section explores relationship development and maintenance, particularly gendered identity, in depth. Gendered identity is revealed through examination of communication styles of linguistic features. Socio-cultural variables in relation to gender and their impact on the CMC are investigated as well.

The third section of the book concerns language action and discourse features in CMC. Chapters in this section explore key characteristics of online language attributes during social interaction. These encompass the metaphoric dimension of social interactions, discourse structure and coherence, verbal and non-verbal signals and devices in relation to interpersonal discourse, (in) formal conversational practices, rhetorical acts and meaning negotiation and affective language uses.

The first three sections are further extended and applied to elements of sections four and five; namely, online learning and developing online community through group collaboration and virtual teams and online social support and networking across cultures and social technology.

The fourth section focuses on the online learning community and group collaboration. Chapters in this section discuss the psycho-social and interpersonal dynamics of online learning and group collaboration and implications to online education. Owing to richness of emerging information technology, stakeholders of online learning communities reflect the diverse geographic and language backgrounds as well as various socio-cultural values and norms. Such contexts foreground interpersonal communication as a key factor in facilitating group involvement and collaboration (Park, 2007). Through examining social presence, along with teaching and cognitive presence of discourse participants, chapters in this section uncover complex and intricate process of online learning and collaboration and construction of online groups and communities in virtual as well as blended contexts.

The fifth section explores the impact of communication technologies in seeking and sharing information through online social support and social networking beyond cultural boundaries. This section addresses the lack of research on cultural manifestations in the CMC and online networking behavior across cultures. It also presents communication patterns of online social support and networking while taking cultural differences into account. Cultural representations on web interface and usability issues are also discussed in depth.

OVERVIEW OF THE CHAPTERS

Each chapter contains an introduction, background/literature review, research findings and discussion, future trends/research directions and a conclusion and references.

Section 1: Online Identity and Self Presentation

Leonard, Withers, and Sherblom integrate theoretical frameworks and empirical research on both the negative and positive effects of the CMC on identity into a perspective of technological realism that embraces paradoxical predictions. Guided by this perspective, the authors analyze student papers reflecting on their identity choices in the creation and development of a Second Life avatar. Some users described developing avatars that mirrored their perceptions of self; others reported exploring creative identities ranging from the fictional to the fantastic. This chapter highlights the need to view the relationship between identity and CMC as complex and reflective, taking into account our motivations and intentions when communicating with others.

The chapter by Kvasny, Payton, and Hales uses ethnic identity labels as a sensitizing framework to explore the relationships among CMC, language, and social interaction. By looking into an online community composed of people of African descent, the study presents how Web forums serve as a narrative space for negotiating and representing a shared African Diaspora Identity. The discussions taking place on the forum (re)construct symbols of identity (labels) that reflect positive images that result from reflective identity politics. Black selfhood is (re)constituted through both deference and opposition to dominant constructions such as whiteness, nationality and colonialism that have historically serve to subjugate people of African descent.

Using examples primarily drawn from the social networking site Facebook, Leiter and Dowd interpretively highlight the axiological affordances of media platforms and how they intersect with social expectations surrounding media and the genres they afford. By looking at the ethical dimensions in and around digital sites that stand at the intersection of the expectations of written communication and face-to-face conversation, the authors investigate how these hybrid spaces and their inherited social expectations variously represent identity and (dis)embodiment.

Information and communication technologies have affected the way people both build and maintain interpersonal relationships. Self-disclosure has been investigated by scholars because of the important role it plays in relationships, yet we know little about decisions to disclose through the CMC outside of relationship initiation (e.g., dating services). To date, limited research has explored the influence of CMC on disclosure and relationships. However, much of this research has been lacking in integrative interpersonal theory and assumes marked differences in interaction patterns using CMC (as compared to face-to-face communication). The chapter by Greene and Magsamen-Conrad offers a theory-driven approach to the exploration of an important aspect of communication decision-making, self-disclosure and privacy management, as it relates to how people maintain existing interpersonal relationships through CMC interaction.

Section 2: Interpersonal Relationships and Gendered Communication

Moore and Craig demonstrate how CMC technologies play a key role in the development and maintenance of interpersonal relationships. A review of contemporary scholarship on relational communication in relation to interpersonal relationship development and maintenance are provided while drawing on a wide array of communication research findings covering initial interactions to relational routines and social support.

For some CMC users, the ability to interact anonymously with other people online allows them the freedom to say or be whatever they want without fear of retribution. Yet, this level of anonymity can also lead to consternation for others who want to know more about their interaction partners--including their "real life" gender (RLG). The chapter by Maguire explores these issues in-depth and examines the extent to which a CMC user's RLG can often be determined by language use, interaction style and message content. She concludes that motivated users will rely on gender stereotypes to make their gender assessments and are often accurate at a rate greater than chance. Yet, whereas some research has found that gender differences do emerge when gender is made a salient aspect of the interaction, other studies show that these differences practically disappear when the RLG of users is not an issue.

The chapter by Burrell, Mabry and Allen investigates gendered communication and language styles in the context of mixed public discussion groups in asynchronous, text-based CMC. It presents similarities and differences in language use of men and women participating in online groups in order to discern the presence and empirical distinctness of gender markers that emerge during CMC. The authors analyze 3000 messages from 30 Internet discussion groups. The study provides evidence of gender differences in the linguistic stylistic features embedded in CMC. Results highlight the important role of gender in language employed in the construction of social identity in the CMC.

Section 3: Language Action and Discourse Features in the CMC

In order to understand the nature of the CMC, it is essential to take into account the diversity of circumstances that give meaning to the uses made of various information technologies. In this process, metaphors play an important role. The chapter by Vayreda and Núñez analyzes the role of metaphors in the interpersonal discourse of online forums. By examining a health-related social support community and a students' online forum, the study presents the mediating role of metaphors in four fundamental CMC dimensions: metaphors play a prominent role in the construction of social reality; metaphors are a source of social norms in the CMC; metaphors generate confidence and identity at an individual and group level; metaphors contextualize, both historically and culturally, the reality constructed by the CMC.

The chapter by Gong adopts a sociolinguistic perspective in exploring the language, social interaction and information and communication technology constituting personal blogs. The study presents the linguistic strategies that bloggers from two different linguistic and cultural backgrounds (i.e., American and mainland Chinese bloggers) employ to express themselves and their identities in their blog entries. By examining differences and similarities in bloggers' employment of linguistic strategies, this chapter offers insights into the influence of language, culture and information technology on the expression of online self and identity.

Taiwo examines the discursive practices of Nigerians as they engage in social interaction through online forums. The chapter demonstrates that despite non-sequential turn-taking patterns, participants are still able to achieve interactional and topical coherence with their choice of quoting as a turn-tracking device and addressivity as a means of sustaining interpersonal relations. The study identifies how the features of discourse were manipulated in the complex social interaction system of the asynchronous mode to achieve coherence in discourse. It also identifies the building of a dynamic online community of Nigerians who through their interpersonal discourse look at Web forums as a public space for agitating for social reforms.

To study the affects of information technology on language use, the chapter by Cottrill examines the differences in texts created for traditional classroom assessment and in CMC environments, specifically blogs. This comparative study looks at how student writing differs in traditional essays and assigned blogs and explores how students demonstrate rhetorical acts such as how students convey meaning, express emotion and elicit reader response. The results of this study demonstrate how space complicates communication and the understanding of language and conventions.

Ending this section, Markman explores the relationship between language and conversational practices and small group dynamics in her chapter on computer-mediated team meetings. By examining one specific conversational practice, the repair of minor errors and typos, she is able to document empirically the emergence of a group norm of informality. She discusses how the affordances and constraints of synchronous chat inform the need for this particular interactional norm and shape how repair is deployed as a resource for norm development in group meetings. In addition to contributing to our understanding of group development, Markman's chapter provides further evidence for the ways that the technical infrastructure of online group discussion spaces shape conversational practices.

Section 4: Online Learning and Collaboration

In her chapter on student-instructor interactions, Stoerger begins section four by examining the computer-mediated communication that takes place in continuing education classes based in the three-dimensional virtual world Second Life. This discussion is situated within theoretical frameworks used to investigate early virtual worlds such as Multi-user Dungeons as well as synchronous educational chat. A discourse analysis approach was used to analyze these virtual classroom interactions. In contrast to the literature that suggests SL classes are often more student-centered and have the potential to disrupt physical world hierarchies, her study revealed that the virtual world classes were teacher-centered. Instructors wishing to create a more student-centered and egalitarian learning space may need to reflect upon their teaching methods and the ways in which those techniques translate in a virtual world.

Annese, Traetta, and Spadaro's chapter focuses on social features of the CMC by comparing interpersonal relations and social interaction in the virtual and real environments of "blended" communities. The authors explore the psychosocial dynamics of participation (Lave & Wenger, 1991) and identity (Hermans, 1996) in learning communities interacting both online and offline. Their research helps to explain the increasing diffusion of this new model of community and its successful learning process. Research findings show specific participation dynamics developing in virtual and real contexts, deriving from special intertwinings of individual and social identity. The authors suggest that blending virtual and real contexts allows community members to construct a sense of belonging based on intersubjective negotiations.

Hales and Troutman contribute a unique perspective to CMC-based social interactions that inform learning. In the case of the electronic palimpsest, the study highlights interpersonal, technology-based relations to reveal the way higher education continues to evolve with respect to changing -- and as a result "blurred"-- boundaries between the academic and the personal domains. The study demonstrates the complexity of hybridized courses with special attention paid to student interactions therein. It also demonstrates how the advantages of an electronic environment provide individuals with a multitude of opportunities and new ways of self-expression. The chapter illustrates varying viewpoints regarding the hybrid course approach and how it may change the realm of education and learning.

The chapter by McArthur examines the developmental processes of groups and teams in interpersonal and social interaction contexts. By intertwining group development theories with a discussion of emerging research in group interaction technologies, this chapter addresses the impact of the use of communication technologies on issues including group cohesion, conflict, verbal and nonverbal communication patterns, group interaction and task performance. These issues shape an understanding of the means whereby groups develop in online communities, in virtual meeting spaces and through other social networking technologies.

Section four ends with the chapter by Kristjánsson which presents a snapshot of the outworking of diversity in the context of online collaboration. Through discourse analysis and a model of situated multidimensional identity, the study demonstrates the complex social practice of online collaboration in the context of computer mediated learning especially when stakeholders from a range of backgrounds are drawn together. The manner in which collaboration or the lack thereof is understood, interpreted and evaluated, can be linked to perceptions of self, constructions of identity and frames of reference that merge online together with offline situations.

Section 5: Social Support and Networking beyond Cultures and Social Technology

In the era of new information technology, the Internet provides an avenue for individuals with special health needs to interact with and provide social support to each other, share personal narratives and experiences and exchange information. The first chapter in this section by Mao, Qian and Starosta focuses on comparing online social interactions of American prepartum and postpartum women with those of overseas Chinese prepartum and postpartum women. Both quantitative and qualitative data were collected from two popular online message boards maintained by American women and overseas Chinese women. The results show both similarities and differences between those two online communities in content and types of social interactions. A culture-centered approach was applied to understand the differences. The findings of this study are well positioned to help both researchers and practitioners tailor health messages to cultural characteristics of the audience and to better serve the unique needs of cultural minorities in the prepartum and postpartum period.

The chapter by Rosen, Stefanone and Lackaff compare behavioral patterns in social-networking sites and social-psychological measures of satisfaction among people who identify with two distinct cultural backgrounds. The findings suggest that people who identify with different cultural backgrounds behave in systematically different ways when networking online and have significantly different levels of satisfaction with their social lives. Taking a social networking approach, findings also suggest that one's offline social support network size is more closely associated with satisfaction than one's online network size.

Li presents culture dimensions represented on Web interface design through the use of power distance, one of the culture dimensions identified by Geert Hofstede (2001), by examining government-based and business-oriented web sites. The aim is to determine any appreciable differences in the representation of national political freedom in those websites. This study investigates the representation of social and interpersonal relations in online communications and contributes to the advance of knowledge in sociological and cultural studies of online communities.

The final chapter in section five and in the volume by Bach, Jiang, and Carroll examines computer-mediated communication practices in a large software company. In an empirical study surveying these practices, the authors found that challenges arose using information and communication technologies and revealed the paradox that participants actually wanted drastically different communication mechanisms than what they were practicing. The explanations for this paradox include a rich web of social and interpersonal interconnections that make electronic communication much more challenging than face-to-face communication. Furthermore, the authors explain the challenges through a theoretical framework from Computer-Supported Cooperative Work that includes looking at common ground, coupling of work, collaboration readiness and technology readiness. The paradox can be explained mainly in terms of common ground and coupling of work. The study provides insight to usability information sharing among software engineering teams.

SUMMARY

Through systematic research findings, using various perspectives and research methods, all twenty-one chapters in this volume address key ingredients of the CMC (language, social interaction and information/ communication technologies) and future research directions. We hope that this volume provides a bridge between the fundamental components of CMC and serves to bring together academic disciplines engaged in CMC research and practice. The reader is provided with a broad interdisplinary view of emerging CMC research as well as in-depth discussion of areas associated with specific disciplines. Readers may also benefit from practical perspectives and applications of interpersonal relations and social discourse for online interaction across CMC applications. We hope that this volume stimulates new avenues of research and engenders the development of a better understanding of online social interaction.

Jung-ran Park, Drexel University, USA
Eileen G. Abels, Drexel University, USA

REFERENCES

Hermans, H. J. M., & Kempen, H. J. G. (1993). *The dialogical self: meaning as movement.* San Diego, CA: Academic Press.

Herring, S. (1996). *Computer-mediated communication: Linguistic, social and cross-cultural perspectives.* Amsterdam: John Benjamins Pub.

Hofstede, G. (2001). *Culture's consequences: Comparing values, behaviors, institutions, and organizations across nations* (2nd. Ed.). Thousand Oaks, CA: Sage Publications.

Lave J., & Wenger E. (1991). *Situated learning: Legitimate peripheral participation.* Cambridge, UK: Cambridge University Press.

Miniwatts Marketing Group. (2009). *Internet world stats: Usage and population statistics.* Retrieved July 2009, from http://www.internetworldstats.com/stats.htm

Park, J.-R (2007). Interpersonal and affective communication in synchronous online discourse. In S. Talja and P.J. McKenzie (eds.), *Library Quarterly, 77*(2), 133-155. (Special Issue on Discursive Approaches to Information Seeking in Context.

Park, J.-R. (2008). Linguistic politeness and face-work in computer mediated communication, part 1: A theoretical framework. *Journal of the American Society for Information Science and Technology 59*(13), 2051-2059.

Park, J.-R. (2008). Linguistic politeness and face-work in computer mediated communication, part 2: An application of the theoretical framework. *Journal of the American Society for Information Science and Technology 59*(14), 2199-2209.

Sharp, H., Rogers, Y. & Preece, J. (2007). *Interaction design: Beyond human-computer interaction.* New York: John Wiley & Sons.

Section 1
Online Identity and
Self Presentation

Chapter 1
The Paradox of Computer–Mediated Communication and Identity:
Peril, Promise and Second Life

Lynnette G. Leonard
University of Nebraska at Omaha, USA

Lesley A. Withers
Central Michigan University, USA

John C. Sherblom
University of Maine, USA

ABSTRACT

Past research on the effects of computer-mediated communication (CMC) on identity has focused either on the inherent risks or opportunities it provides. The authors argue that the paradox within the nature of CMC has led to paradoxical predictions about the effects of CMC on identity. Rather than adopting a naïve perspective focusing on only one side of the paradox, the authors take a view of technological realism in which the paradox is embraced. Guided by these views, the authors analyze 59 students' papers reflecting on their identity choices in the creation and development of a Second Life avatar. Second Life is a three-dimensional (3D) multi-user virtual environment (MUVE) in which users create avatars (called "residents") to explore, interact with other residents, learn, recreate, and shop with the local currency (i.e., Linden Dollars; http://secondlife.com/whatis/). Using the constant comparative method for thematic content, themes supporting a paradox of CMC effects on identity are identified from the student papers. The implications of a view of technological realism are offered.

INTRODUCTION

Past research on the effects of the use of computer-mediated communication (CMC) on identity tends to fall into one of two polarized camps: either the use of CMC will fracture the self in ways that threaten the very fabric of humanity, or CMC offers users a virtual utopia of self-disclosure, self-discovery, and self-actualization. However, to assume that

DOI: 10.4018/978-1-61520-827-2.ch001

the use of CMC will result in only positive or negative identity outcomes is to underestimate the complexity of the relationship between these constructs. A step into the world of one of CMC's newest technologies – Second Life – reveals that the future is neither as bleak nor as rosy as past research has predicted.

Second Life is a three-dimensional (3D) multi-user virtual environment (MUVE) in which users create avatars (called "residents") to explore, interact with other residents, learn, recreate, and shop with the local currency (i.e., Linden Dollars; http://secondlife.com/whatis/). Second Life is described by its creator, Linden Labs, as "a free online virtual world imagined and created by its Residents. From the moment you enter Second Life, you'll discover a fast-growing digital world filled with people, entertainment, experiences and opportunity (http://secondlife.com/whatis/). As of February 15, 2009, approximately 1,444,530 people logged into Second Life with approximately 60,000 logged in at any given time. An avatar is "an interactive, social representation of the user" (Meadows, 2008, p. 13). Residents initially choose between male and female 3D animated forms. However, once in Second Life, these "starter avatars" are modified by a series of identity choices limited only by a resident's imagination. For this reason, the Second Life environment is a rich area for the exploration of both CMC and identity issues.

To facilitate a more critical understanding of CMC and identity, the chapter explores the paradoxes revealed by research on CMC and identity. First, we explore the paradoxical nature of CMC, guided by competing theoretical explanations. Second, we examine how changes in the conceptualization of the self (from premodern, to modern, to postmodern) have lead to paradoxical predictions about identity in computer-mediated contexts. Finally, we posit that the naïve past conceptualizations of the effect of CMC use on identity must be replaced by a more realistic understanding of the complex relationship between these concepts. The

advantages of adopting a view of technological realism are revealed in the analysis of students' attitudes toward Second Life (SL) avatars and identity in a hybrid Face to Face (FtF)/Second Life course. By understanding the paradoxes of CMC and identity through an exploration of the empirical research, we seek to establish a greater recognition of and appreciation for the complex relationship between CMC and identity.

THE PARADOXICAL NATURE OF CMC CHARACTERISTICS

The many advantages and disadvantages characteristic of the CMC process create the unique paradoxical nature of the Internet (Joinson, 2005). The same CMC characteristics that comprise CMC's advantages – the perception of anonymity, the ability to communicate efficiently across time and geographical distance, the chance to experiment with self-presentation and identity – also pose the greatest risks to CMC users.

One key feature that distinguishes CMC from FtF is anonymity, or the inability to confirm through visual cues the identity of the person(s) with whom users communicate via CMC (Gurak, 2001). The paradox lies in the fact that the perception of anonymity can free users to share their honest opinions without the fear of retribution (Joinson, 1999, 2001; McKenna, Green, & Gleason, 2002), but can also allow users to deceive (Joinson & Dietz-Uhler, 2002), harass (Barak, 2005), or mistreat others without fearing reprisal. For online predators, the anonymity of CMC offers a new, expansive hunting ground (Denegri-Knott & Taylor, 2005), leading to aversive interpersonal behaviors such as cybercheating (Joinson, 2005; Whitty, 2005), cyberstalking (Joseph, 2003), cyberteasing (Madlock & Westerman, 2009), and cyberbullying (Hinduja & Patchin, 2008; Li, 2006; Patchin & Hinduja, 2006; Smith, et al., 2008).

A second key feature of CMC is speed, which refers to the changing expectations about and perceptions of time and space with CMC. Users often expect quick responses to email or IMs, perceive the length of time between a message and a response more keenly, and do not consider the geographical distance traveled by the message in those expectations and perceptions. A third key CMC feature is reach, or CMC users' ability to communicate with many people at once, anywhere in the CMC-accessible world, and absent many of the traditional gatekeepers (Gurak, 2001). These two features also illustrate the paradoxical nature of CMC. Although the ability of CMC users to communicate easily, quickly, and relatively inexpensively from nearly anywhere, at any time, can create opportunities for communication and collaboration that might otherwise be impossible (Janssen, Erkens, Kirschner, & Kanselaar, 2009), those same CMC characteristics also allow users to enact asocial, antisocial, and deviant behaviors (Denegri-Knott & Taylor, 2005) that alienate and harm others – and to do so more easily and with considerably less perceived risk than might occur with FtF communication (Joinson, 2005).

CMC allows users the opportunity to experiment with self-presentation and identity in ways that can lead to discovery and self-growth including: gender play and experimentation, the performance of multiple identities, and even the expression of a "true self" (Bargh, McKenna, & Fitzsimons, 2002; Curtis, 19997; Danet, 1998; McKenna, Green, & Gleason, 2002; Taylor, 1999). However, CMC also allows users the means by which they can exaggerate or idealize (Turkle, 1995), fabricate, conceal, and steal identities (Finch, 2003; Suler, 1999) or hurt individuals or groups – directly or indirectly – by flaming (Collins, 1992; Dyer, Green, Pitts, & Millward, 1995; Joinson, 2003; Riva, 2001; Sproull & Kiesler, 1991), using cyberhate speech (Douglas, McGarty, Bliuc, & Lala, 2005), or encouraging others to harm themselves (Adler & Adler, 2007, 2008; Davies & Lipsey, 2003; Force, 2005).

Competing theories offer explanations for the paradoxical nature of CMC. The first theory, the

Social Identity Model of Deindividuation Effects (SIDE), explains and predicts both the positive and negative effects of CMC use (Lea, Spears, & deGroot, 2001). SIDE theorists argue that anonymity, group immersion, and/or interaction via a computer cause deindividuation—a state of reduced awareness or loss of self (Postmes, Spears, & Lea, 1998). Deindividuation in CMC resulting from visual anonymity and fewer social contextual cues can lower self-awareness and reduce self-regulation (Sassenberg & Boos, 2003). This outcome can increase strategic freedom in the identity choices beyond social boundaries, increase the power of existing social boundaries/ expectations, or create new ones (Postmes, Spears, & Lea, 1998; Spears & Lea, 1994). Depending on the context, SIDE predicts different outcomes. Postmes, Spears, and Lea (1998) conclude that in circumstances where social identity and norms are readily available, "a deindividuating encounter in a group may divert attention away from the individual level of interaction and focus attention on the social level"(p. 708). Therefore, rather than creating the conditions for a lawless, deviant, or dangerous community, the characteristics of CMC can increase conformity through the formation of social norms. According to SIDE theorists, in cases where there is not a strong group identity, there will not be a rise in social conformity. The issue of increased conformity can be viewed as both positive and negative: positive in that it may reduce disruptive behavior such as flaming if that behavior goes against the norms of the group. However, this controlling influence can also be seen as negative in that it can limit the freedom of expression, the ability to challenge boundaries, and the ability to create new boundaries and expectations.

Contrary to the argument in SIDE that technology use, within group contexts, can reduce self-awareness (Sassenberg & Boos, 2003), Shedletsky (1993) offers another theoretical perspective. Shedletsky argues that the characteristics of CMC technologies bring our communication choices to our attention in a way that FtF communication does not. With FtF communication, we most often use a first person perspective, aware of the world and those with whom we communicate, but not often as aware of ourselves and our choices in the communication act. We may employ a second or dual perspective if we take the other person/people with whom we communicate into consideration, evaluating our intentions and presentations through their expectations and perceptions before, during, and after communicating (Barnes, 2003). However, in CMC use, we continually confront our identity presentation choices as we read the text scrolling up the screen in an online chat, as we type and re-read an email, or as we watch our avatars smile and laugh. This visualization of our communication choices provides a third perspective, revealing our communication choices as we make them (Meadows, 2008).

Communicating from this third perspective raises several issues. First, we see in advance the choices we make. This perspective, coupled with an unfamiliarity or discomfort with communicating via CMC, can increase self-consciousness (Spears & Lea, 1994). This self-consciousness may lead the user to self-censor or use negative spontaneity in order to "carefully craft their message to create the 'right' impression" (Barnes, 2003, p. 352). Second, if self-conscious, we may make more strategic choices in our presentation of self. Goffman's (1959) work on identity facilitates the exploration of our choices in presentation of identity online. Presentation of identity includes the expression of individual identity by what they "give" (verbal symbols) and what they "give off" (nonverbal symbols). When applying these concepts to our online communication, users "give" expressions of their identity through their writing, screen names, nicknames, pseudonyms, profiles, and signature files. Users "give off" expressions of their identity through use of emoticons, language style, and choices of presentation on personal websites (e.g., pictures, fonts, colors, clip art).

Interpersonal Discourse Concerns: The Paradoxical Nature of CMC Identity

Within the CMC literature exists a paradox around the issue of identity. On one hand, empirical results support the argument that CMC use breaks down identity constraints and allows, even facilitates, deviant (non-normative) behavior that may have negative consequences for both individual and society. On the other hand, there is also an body of research supporting the argument that CMC use facilitates an individual's ability to articulate a new identity and safely explore new ways of being, leading to personal growth. These contradictions begin with the philosophical positions on the construction of identity.

Constructing Identity

Traditional definitions of identity that involve a stable, fixed self-concept have given way to more modern understandings that allow for identities that are "mobile, multiple, personal, self-reflexive, and subject to change" (Barnes, 2003, p. 117). This shift, documented in part by Richardson, Rogers, and McCarroll (1998), moves from the traditional or premodern self, to the modern self, and finally, to the decentered or postmodern self. Working from the premodern construction of identity, a stable or fixed sense of self emerges from playing the role required by the community and the larger cosmic design. By this conceptualization, the character of an individual is constructed by following ethical and religious teachings that focus on reaching for a better life. In the modern conceptualization of self, which followed the rise of science in the 17th century, the self is an autonomous, rational individual free of the constraints and commitments of the premodern self. Richardson, Rogers, and McCarroll (1998) conceptualized a decentered or postmodern self as a pragmatic response to the influences of language and culture absent an objective reality or truth. In the postmodern conceptualization, identity is fluid, multiple, contingent, created, and recreated.

Much of the scholarship regarding the effects of technology on identity is based on—or argues against—one or more of these conceptualizations and as a result, describes paradoxical predictions for the effects of CMC use on society and identity. When these competing conceptualizations of identity are explored within the CMC context, theorists disagree about the effects of CMC use on users' identities. A paradox of CMC identity emerges in which theorists predict that CMC use will fragment identity and facilitate identity development.

Effects of CMC on Identity

Gergen (2000) argues that technology use stops us from constructing the self as a stable identity; this argument reflects a premodern conception of identity. We construct a solid sense of self through our interaction with others and the rules and norms of our culture; therefore, our identity is dependent on stable relationships and trust in cultural authority. Technology use undermines these forces in two ways: first, by increasing mobility, allowing for a wider range of relationships, and eroding the strong bonds between people in the community; and second, by removing certainty through information overload or access to multiple truths, leading to a loss of faith, distrust, confusion, self-interest, and suspicion. Increasing conflict is a negative repercussion of this erosion of the self. This conflict is based in a retrenchment of traditional ideologies, defensive reactions, and increased group identification leading to persistent state of culture war.

However, rather than ending with this dystopian prediction for society, Gergen (2000) acknowledges the possibility of a second, more positive outcome. The multiple, weak, and distrustful bonds created through technology use could also lead to more temporary loyalties and increase our interdependency, creating a distaste

for aggressive behaviors. This outcome would then provide an opportunity to remake our society based on new relational concepts such "as interdependence, conjoint construction of meaning, mutually interacting entities, and systemic process"(Gergen, 2000, p. 212). Whether the outcomes of technology use are ultimately positive or negative, Gergen predicts that technology use will change our fundamental constructions of the self—resulting in a fractured and unstable identity with no basis in the real, embodied self.

Taking issue with conceptualizations of the self that focus on its deconstruction in modern society, Wynn and Katz (1997) argue that we must consider contributions from social theory that define the self as a product and process of social forces, negotiations over meaning and manners, and struggles for social dominance. Although the argument is similar to the postmodern conception of identity, Wynn and Katz disagree with the focus on deconstruction present in postmodern approaches to the study of identity in CMC. They stop short of advocating a premodern or modern conception of identity. Rather, their analysis of Internet home pages and discourse supports a socially-constructed view of CMC identity that allows for co-creation and questions the reality of online anonymity and a virtual existence separate from our bodies (Wynn & Katz, 1997). They concluded that CMC use allows us to see the nature of identity in a modern world. Rather than fragmenting self and identity, CMC use allows us to construct new presentations of the self that may show different sides of the self, but still represent a consistent overall "authentic" identity.

Therein lies the paradox of the effects of CMC use on identity; it is predicted to both fragment the self and offer new possibilities for self-growth and actualization. This paradox leads to polarized predictions about CMC behavior, as the ways in which users communicate through CMC is influenced by the users' understandings of their identity and their perceptions of others. However, to focus predominantly on the positive effects of CMC use or the negative outcomes seems shortsighted and unrealistic; CMC use neither assures the user of self-actualized perfection, nor of becoming a cybervillain's victim. Rather, given CMC's paradoxical nature and effects, it is time to recognize the complex relationship between CMC use and identity, to acknowledge both the positive and negative elements, and ultimately, to embrace the risks and opportunities.

SECOND LIFE AND IDENTITY: EMBRACING THE PARADOX

In order to explore the complex relationship between CMC use and identity, a research project was undertaken at two mid-sized Midwestern universities[1]. Students in a virtual class, composed of 30 students (12 male and 18 female) from a CMC class at one university and 29 students (7 male and 22 female) from an interpersonal communication class at a second university, opened free Second Life accounts, created and developed avatars, and used their avatars to interact with others in this virtual world.

Creating and Developing Avatars

Three-dimensional avatars, such as those created and developed in Second Life, expand the choices for the visual, nonverbal expression of identity in CMC by resembling the cues available in FtF communication (e.g., gestures, appearance, artifacts). However, unlike the self-presentation choices available in FtF communication, SL users can assume any body, shape, or form they choose. They are not limited by the intrinsic nonverbal codes that reflect age, biological sex, race, or physical ability. Instead, the nonverbal codes employed in SL are iconic in nature; users can modify their avatars to resemble humans of any age, biological sex, or race, or can choose to be any non-human animal or object. These choices further complicate and challenge our

understanding of identity and change perceptions of visual anonymity.

As users "give" and "give off" expressions of identity as they interact through their avatars with others, they may experience their communication through the third perspective (Goffman, 1959). This perspective facilitates self-reflection and analysis—a key component of experiential learning.

Reflecting on Identity Choices

After creating and developing avatars, students used their avatars to interact with one another through a series of individual and dyadic class activities. After this interaction, students reflected upon their identity choices and communication experiences in an assigned analysis paper. The analysis paper assignment is based on Kolb's (1984) *experiential learning theory*, utilizing Kolb's four categories to direct the students' essays into four sections: concrete experience (i.e., doing/having an experience), reflective observation (i.e., reviewing/reflection on the experience), abstract conceptualization (i.e., learning from the experience), and active experimentation (i.e., planning for the future) which has been modified to address enduring ideas from the experience of creating an avatar in Second Life.

In order to explore issues related to CMC and identity in virtual environments, the concrete experience and reflective observation sections of the analysis papers were analyzed with the constant comparative method for thematic content (Strauss, 1987; Strauss & Corbin, 1990). The first section (concrete experience) required students to objectively describe the experience, focusing on the choices that they made in creating and developing their avatar, and to subjectively describe their feelings, perceptions, and thoughts that occurred while creating and interacting through their avatar. Specifically, they were asked to explain how their avatar represented their identity. The second section (reflective observations) required students to describe their experience from different points of view by explaining how other people reacted to their avatar. Students were also asked to describe how other avatars looked. They were then instructed to explain their reactions to others' expressions of identity through their avatars and to speculate on others' motivations for their identity choices.

Complete thoughts were the unit of analysis, as a single sentence or paragraph could have multiple thoughts representing several themes, or a complete thought could extend over several sentences or paragraphs, depending on the writing style of the student (Krippendorff, 2004). When a unique theme emerged, a new thematic category was created. As additional themes emerged from a complete thought, they were compared with existing thematic categories. If the theme did not fit within the previous thematic categories, a new category was created (Creswell, 1998). The thematic categories were refined as the comparison continued throughout the analysis of the data set.

The analysis of the papers revealed nine thematic categories concerned with presentation of identity in CMC. These thematic categories are listed in order of frequency, with the thematic category with the most examples listed first: avatar characteristics (chosen and observed), chosen presentations similar to users' physical appearance, others' presentations as interesting and/or fun, chosen presentation similar to users' personality, reluctance to speculate on choices, chosen presentations different from users' physical appearance (fictional character, exploration, and alter ego), others' presentations as strange and/or dangerous, others' presentations as similar to users' physical appearance and/or personality, and others' presentations as ideal self. Table 1 lists these categories with a brief description. More in-depth description and examples of these categories are presented below.

Avatar Characteristics

Chosen Characteristics. Students overwhelmingly chose or created avatars with human forms. Forty avatars were described as female; seventeen avatars were described as male, and two did not designate gender. However, two students chose the animal form known as "furry." One chose a male fox avatar and the other chose a female avatar with squirrel features. Two avatars were neither human nor animal, with one student instead choosing to be a dragon and another Star Wars' Yoda. When describing their avatar choices, most students described physical body features such as height, weight, color of hair and eyes, breast size (female), and shoulder width and musculature (male), as well as clothing choices. One student described himself as "just another regular guy in jeans and a t-shirt and a comfortable pair of shoes" (participant 6). Finally, some students mentioned representing ethnicity in the creation of their avatar—Caucasian, African-American, Middle Eastern, and Italian. The students with African-American and Middle Eastern ethnicity expressed concern at the choices for presenting non-white in Second Life. Two African-American students expressed concern over how they would be treated by others if they chose to present black skin; one student chose to present as African-American and the other student chose to present as Caucasian.

Observed Characteristics. Similar to their own avatar choices, when observing others' avatars, students reported observing a majority of human forms, except that female and male were more evenly represented, and some did just refer to the human form without identifying biological sex. Students reported observing eight furries in Second Life with only two being identified in terms of biological sex (one male and one female). There were several object avatar choices mentioned in the papers. Students observed a dragon, more Star Wars characters (a Storm Trooper, Yoda, and Darth Vader), an anime cartoon, a talking yak, a

Table 1. Thematic categories with descriptions (in order of frequency)

Name of Category	Brief Descriptions
Avatar characteristics	Avatar characteristics chosen by the students in the creation of their avatar and those observed as the students interacted with others in Second Life
Chosen presentation similar to users' physical appearance	Students' presentations of identity through their avatars were described as similar to their physical appearance
Others' presentations as interesting and/or fun	Students described others' presentations of identity as interesting and/or fun
Chosen presentation similar to users' personality	Students' presentations of identity through their avatars were described as similar to their personality
Reluctance to speculate on choices	Students' reflections demonstrated reluctance to speculate on their identity choices or the identity choices of others
Chosen presentations different from users' physical appearance or personality (fictional character, exploration, alter ego)	Students' presentations of identity through their avatars were described as different from their physical appearance or personality • Fictional character subcategory indicates the choice to perform a fictional identity that was already scripted. • Exploration subcategory indicates the choice to explore a new identity. • Alter ego subcategory indicates the choice to create a new version of themselves writing their own "scripts" rather than relying on characters that had already been created by others.
Others' presentations as strange and/or dangerous	Students described others' presentations of identity as strange and/or dangerous
Others' presentations as similar to users' physical appearance and/or personality	Students' reflections on others' identity choices explained them as likely to be similar to the users' actual physical appearance and/or personality
Others' presentations as ideal self •	Students' reflections on others' identity choices explained them as likely to represent the others' ideal self

man made entirely of glowing squares, an alien, mutants, werewolves, vampires, angels, demons, and an avatar that was part man/part robot. Reported observations of these other avatars tended to center on physical or clothing attributes, though several students mentioned a concern for the lack of ethnic diversity.

Chosen Presentation Similar to Users' Physical Appearance

The most frequent descriptions of choices for avatar characteristics focused on changing the avatar's appearance so that it matched the student's own physical appearance. Students tended to characterize that identity choice as more honest or appropriate than choosing a presentation that differed from their own. One student explained, "I wanted to be as true as possible, creating an avatar that looked just like me and wore the same

kind of clothes that I might wear... [otherwise] it feels wrong and gives me a strange sense of anxiety" (participant 6). Another student described her choices thusly, "I knew from the beginning that I wanted her to look like me; someone from the Middle East, with darker skin and eye color. Then I started to make her tall and chubby, exactly how I look" (participant 17). This student also expressed concern that she could not find clothing that reflected her choice to wear hijab in her "real" life, "Hijab shows my identity as a Muslim and a modest woman; and this is how I like to appear in any virtual or real world" (participant 17).

One student had difficulty separating him/herself from his/her avatar. "I found myself sometimes referring to [my avatar's] experience in first person account. Her body was my body. The people she met were people I met" (participant 19). The description of this avatar further reflects the student's connection to the avatar: "I wanted to make [my avatar] thicker and heavier like me. If I chose to make a skinny avatar, I felt I was denying myself and saying how I exist in my first life was not good enough" (participant 19). Finally, one student initially started with an avatar different from herself in terms of biological sex, but once in Second Life, "it dawned on me that I was not just playing a game, but this was something more realistic... This was a virtual world, almost as real as the one in which I was sitting. I immediately began to edit my avatar's appearance, changing 'him' to a 'her'. ... I adjusted every little detail to make my avatar as similar to my 'real life' appearance as possible and I did not even realize I was doing so" (participant 41).

Again, descriptions coded in this category discussed how choices in avatar physical appearance were similar to their real life appearance and how important it was to many students that their avatars stay "true" to the students' physical appearance.

Others' Presentations as Interesting, Fun

In students' reflections, some others' avatar identity presentations were perceived as different, but not negative; instead, they were described as interesting. When describing Darth Vader and animal avatars one student remarked, "I found these avatars very interesting choices... This is what makes our world and Second Life an exciting place to be a member" (participant 16). One student admitted, "I thought I was being creative when I switched gender identity for my avatar. While I am certain that other users have done likewise, I must admit that I have found it very difficult to determine whether or not I am having a conversation with a male or female in real life, despite appearances and attitudes" (participant 56). However, the student did not express much discomfort at this uncertainty, instead concluding that the other users "often adopt an identity that is appropriate to the Second Life communities

they frequent. I found this to be an interesting facet of Second Life" (participant 56). Another mentioned seeing an avatar that "wore cat ears and had a tail and paws. In between words she would type 'meow' as if she were a cat. At first I was a little taken aback, but after I got to know her I realized that there was no difference between her living out her Second Life fantasy with mine" (participant 26). The student concluded that the ability to enact one's fantasies was a fun part of Second Life.

Chosen Presentation Similar to Users' Personality

Presenting the personality of the user was the focus of some descriptions of the physical features, clothing, and communication behavior students chose for their avatars. One of the students who chose a furry avatar explained her choice as representing aspects of her personality stated,

I wanted [my avatar] to appear friendly, carefree, approachable, and fun-loving. These are my personality characteristics that I wanted her to show. That is why I decided she should have big eyes to suggest open-mindedness. She had big ears to suggest metaphorically that she is open and ready to listen at any moment. These are all choices I made with careful calculation (participant 9).

Having fun and expressing that fun in the creation of the avatar as well as presentation of identity was the focus of the other student who chose a furry avatar. An avid gamer, this student reflected on his choices to go "against convention, and chose a fox (at first I thought it was a wolf). The fox was dressed in shorts, a nice polo type shirt, and hiking boots, which seemed to be a must since I didn't see any cars or bicycles in Second Life. I figured [my avatar] would be doing a lot of walking" (participant 4). In describing the choice, the student explained

I tried not to take myself too seriously, so the creation of some handsome, broad shouldered, muscular avatar that walks around trying to impress the world with his appearance never crossed my mind. My avatar is representative of both my ability to laugh at myself and a deep introspective nature that I possess to constantly challenge the way I think and function in the world and with myself (participant 5).

For several students, their avatars' clothing represented their personality. One stated, "I wanted to wear bright and vibrant colors because my personality is loud and outgoing.. ... The red dress matches my personality nearly perfectly" (participant 38). Another student tied her avatar's clothing and communication behavior to her "true" self:

[My avatar] has two outfits that I change periodically that both represent the fun, carefree persona I think she represents. I dress her in black skinny hot pants, and a red leather jacket with heels, or a baby blue halter-top and itty-bitty shorts with a lot of shiny jewelry.. ... She has a unique personality that reminds me of my true self.. ... My true identity is seen in the ways she talks and gets to know others (participant 22).

These are just a few of the descriptions focused on avatars' clothing choices, but represent other students' descriptions of their choices to visually represent their positive personality traits -- such as being fun-loving, friendly, and open -- in the creation of the avatar.

Reluctance to Speculate on Choices

Despite the instructions of the assignment, some students were reluctant or openly refused to speculate on their avatar identity choices or the choices of others. Many said that it could be any number of reasons why someone would make those choices and others said that it would depend on what that person wanted out of the game. In explaining their choices as well as the choices of other users one student explained "The perception of others does not matter in Second Life. Creators might make judgments of other avatars but it does not matter

because avatars are a creation from own personal thoughts and a person can never have thoughts that are right or wrong" (participant 52). Another stated, "I could guess why [the avatar] made these appearance choices, but I wish to not do this type of observation," ultimately concluding that those appearance choices could be made for any number of reasons (participant 55).

Chosen Presentation Different from Users' Physical Appearance or Personality

Descriptions of choices to create avatars that were different from their real life physical appearance or personality comprise this category. While representing the least frequent thematic category choice, these students' descriptions explain the full range of choices available in Second Life, as well as the potential motivations for creating an avatar. These choices were characterized as: creating a fictional character to play, creating an avatar for exploration, creating an alter ego, and as interesting.

Fictional character. Two students chose to create an avatar that resembled a character from a movie (James Bond from Ian Fleming's series) and a book series (Alice from Stephenie Meyer's *Twilight* series). The James Bond avatar was described as an "old gentleman that enjoys fine suits, exquisite scotch, and high class cigars.. ... I myself couldn't be different; I don't smoke cigars, I hate the taste of scotch, and I can barely afford a decent sweater not to mention finely tailored suits" (participant 26). In creating this avatar, the student fulfilled a wish. "I wanted an avatar that could do all of the things that I would never do in my first life" (participant 26).

The choice of vampire avatar was explained as re-creating the description of the character Alice Cullen. While the student recognized some elements of her own identity in the choice -- "I wanted her to almost represent me in the sense of being a petite woman" (participant 43) -- the majority of the explanation focused on creating an accurate semblance of the fictional character. After discussing how others might see her avatar as an attempt to be something she is afraid to be in real life, she refutes this possible interpretation. "I choose how I looked as a vampire because of my inspirations from the books I read. The complete opposite of the actual reality of my identity" (participant 43).

Another student framed the entire act of creating an avatar as creating a character in a fictional story. In creating the avatar, the student stated, "after careful consideration I decided that I already exist and there did not need to be another me... The decision making process to creating an avatar is much like writing a fictional story and creating characters that exist in the new world" (participant 52). The student discussed creating an avatar that had elements similar to her own, but did not provide specific examples of how those parts were presented. Instead, the student explained, "It is interesting to think that in another world that might not be real, there are parts of me that exist and nobody really knows about it but me" (participant 52).

Exploration. One student discussed avatar choices as an exploration focused on non-human form avatars. He chose to create an avatar that resembled the Star Wars character Yoda to take a self-defined "intellectual approach" to identity that focused on how others world react. The implications of this choice was described as follows: "I liked the respect and way people interacted with Yoda [in the films], so I thought I would try out the avatar and see how people responded.. ... in RL [real life] I want respect. I want to be seen as an intellectual person and someone with a great deal of wisdom. I found that within the persona of Yoda" (participant 49). The need for respect carried from the student's "real" life to the virtual one, and was reflected in his avatar choices.

Another chose to explore an avatar of the opposite biological sex for his interactions in Second Life. A male student described the act of creating

an avatar as creating an "alternate identity.. ... I decided to create a female avatar so that I could fully explore the concept of identity in Second Life. I wanted something that would draw attention, so I decided to name my avatar. .. after an American pornographic actress" (participant 56). The student went on to describe the physical appearance of the avatar: "my avatar's appearance is what society would refer to as sexy and sophisticated. She is tall and slender with long black hair and a dark complexion... The appearance that I chose for my avatar was my attempt to manifest a sense of confidence. I wanted to observe whether or not other users would be drawn to the avatar" (participant 56).

Alter Ego. The creation of an alter ego based on elements of the personality, but someone separate from themselves and anything else, was the focus for one student: "I wanted to use Second Life as a place where I could be the person I would never allow myself to be in the real world" (participant 55). This alter ego was discussed in terms of the avatar's name, which reflected a combination of "my two high school sweetheart's [sic] names" (participant 55). The physical appearance also reflected the alter ego: "I chose to be blonde. I have a fascination with blondes. I made myself tall, skinny, and somewhat muscular. I chose these personal appearances from a picture of the ideal me locked away in my mind" (participant 55).

Others' Presentations as Strange and/or Dangerous

Students did not describe their own choices of presentation as deceptive or dangerous, but often described other avatars' appearance as such. This description was especially common for alternative presentations of identity; those most often mentioned were punks and Goths. One student described an avatar's appearance as making him/her "leery. I wasn't sure if I wanted to approach him. He was bald with facial hair, and dressed like a punk rocker" (participant 55). Another student mentions the over sexualized appearance of avatars as strange and potentially dangerous, however, once she interacted with the avatar she concluded that she "was actually nice and helpful.. .. The interaction reminded me of the stereotypes I have of people in my first life who look a certain way.. .. It made me feel wrong for thinking that way" (participant 19).

Others' Presentation as Similar to Users' Physical Appearance and/or Personality

In terms of discussing others' choices, only a few assumed that the avatars they saw were similar to the user. One student remarked, "I think that there was a fair amount of people that created their avatar. .. to resemble themselves, like I did" (participant 7). In reflecting on other users' presentation of identity, students would discuss personality characteristics of the avatar as a likely match for the user. One student commented, "I met a woman on the island that was very interesting and considerate.. .. Talking with this avatar allowed for me to see that she entered Second Life with the hope to explore her creative side.. .. Her appearance was creative much like her personality and mind" (participant 55). Another student commented that one avatar "appeared to be part fox and part human being. At least someone had a sense of humor" (participant 1). If the student acknowledged that it was unlikely that the users looked like their avatars, they would extract personality cues from the avatar characteristics to support their claim for similarity.

Others' Presentation as Ideal Self

A few students explained other's choices that were not likely to represent the user's actual physical appearance or personality as that user wanting to present an ideal self. One student explained, "When I really stop to think about the way these people chose to have their avatars, they could

have made their avatar represent their ideal self" (participant 42). Another said "I believe that most avatar creator's use Second Life to become someone they wish they could be in real life" (participant 57). The category is further represented in the comments that explained other's choices as improving themselves or trying to be what they couldn't be in real life.

DISCUSSION

Our study of students' reflections about avatars and identity demonstrates their ability to reflect on communication choices relating to presentation of identity through the creation of a Second Life avatar and interactions with others in Second Life. In creating their avatars, students described their choice to create an avatar similar to their own physical appearance or personality. This focus on being "true" to their "real" selves (their words) was a bit surprising given the preponderance of negative evidence from research that would suggest an increased likelihood of deceptive identity choices. Additionally, students who described their choices as different from their offline identity chose to characterize their choices in positive terms such. Even when discussing others' strange and dangerous choices, students were reluctant to call these choices "deceptive," often explaining that all was well once they got to know the strange avatar. The reluctance or refusal to speculate on their or others' choices was surprising given the nature of the reflection activity, but demonstrates that students did not feel forced to analyze identity choices.

These findings provide further support for the paradoxical nature of CMC and identity. First, there is evidence of the positive or optimistic predictions about the effects of CMC use on identity. Consistent with Wynn and Katz's (1997) assertions, many students' papers claimed that their avatar choices represented a true self and consistency in identity presentation. Though it is possible that the context of the classroom discouraged most students from exploring and experimenting with identity, as discussed in Bayne (2005) and Monroe (1999), students' descriptions of choosing avatars similar to their own physical and personality characteristics would still support Wynn and Katz's predictions that the variety of CMC identity choices will lead to more consistency in presentation of identity. The data also support Gergen's (2000) more positive concession that despite the fact that CMC use is likely to fracture the self, after some societal difficulty, these different choices could break down social boundaries. Students descriptions of strange and or dangerous avatars supports Gergen's (2000) predictions; while they were nervous, most approached these strange avatars and learned something new and different about someone they would never approach in "real" life. It is possible that CMC's lack of physical presence removed some students' fear, for while there are socio-emotional consequences to our online behavior, the threat of physical injury is largely removed by CMC's perceived anonymity and geographical distance.

In addition to evidence supporting the positive/optimistic predictions about the effects of CMC use on identity, the data also support the more negative or pessimistic predictions. Students did make choices that can be characterized as deceptive in that the choices did not align with their physical appearance, gender, and/or personality, although the students did not acknowledge their choices as being deceptive. Their initial, negative reactions to shun others who they perceived as dissimilar from themselves could indicate evidence of what Gergen's (2000) calls tribalization—grouping around similarities and then shunning those who are different. While most students were able to overcome these initial, negative reactions, their first instinct was to stay away from dissimilar others. Finally, students' reluctance or refusal to speculate on their identity choices or others' choices support Spears and Lea's (1994) claim

that CMC can reduce or lower self-awareness, a key component for reflection.

To reconcile these paradoxical findings, a perspective of technological realism is required. This perspective acknowledges that, based on the paradoxical characteristics of the technology and on the communication choices and motivations of the users, the use of technology must result in both negative and positive outcomes. This perspective supports Postmes, Spears, and Lea's (1998) description of their research on SIDE. As they explain, "according to this model, the characteristics of a communication medium interact with characteristics of the social context and with the particular social definition of self to produce media effects" (Postmes, Spears, & Lea, 1998, p. 690). This approach helps to identify the conditions required for the results that, in turn, affect the explanations and predictions.

FUTURE RESEARCH DIRECTIONS

Further research needs to embrace the paradoxical effects of CMC use on identity in order to understand the complexity of the relationship between these constructs. To embrace the paradox requires recognition of the different assumptions underlying our definitions of identity and of the nature of CMC. Once recognized, future research findings need to be interpreted in ways that incorporate theories on both sides of the paradox: both the positive and the negative possible outcomes of the use of CMC on identity. Similarly, when presenting research limitations, these competing explanations should be acknowledged.

In terms of empirical research, there needs to be a continued investigation of the changing CMC characteristics as reflected in 3D virtual worlds with interactive avatars. Characteristics such as the addition of voice chat in Second Life can potentially reduce anonymity, rendering useless its effects as previously discovered with text-only CMC. Additionally, in exploring the variation of human communication choices and motivations, the offline expectations influencing online behavior should be explored more fully. As evidenced in students' analysis papers, users report similar choices and motivations for communicating in CMC as they have for FtF communication. There needs to be further research into which of our offline communication norms, roles, rules, and expectations apply to our online communication and how those behaviors affect individuals, groups, and communities communicating in CMC.

CONCLUSION

Research on CMC and its effects on identity have revealed the paradoxical nature of the constructs; competing approaches and assumptions support a theoretical view that recognizes the complexity of the relationship between concepts. There is not a monolithic understanding of the process of constructing and presenting identity, nor of the meaning of the self (Richardson, et al., 1998). The same is true for CMC, a label that comprises many different technologies with characteristics that simultaneously offer users advantages and disadvantages, risks and opportunities (Spears & Lea, 1994). Although assumptions about technology driving change abound in the literature, there is literature with a focus on how humans socially construct our online communication behavior. This perspective also explains how each person can experience CMC in a different way (Shedletsky, 1993).

The results of this analysis support much of the past research on CMC and identity. There is evidence of the positive or optimistic side of the paradox predicting that CMC use will result in a true self, consistency, or even the ability to break down boundaries. But this evidence is tempered by choices that could be characterized as deceptive and by negative reactions to others perceived as dissimilar. Finally, the opportunity for self-reflec-

tion appeared to be facilitated by characteristics of Second Life that allowed users to take a third perspective and see their communication choices in a new light. However, this outcome can be partially explained by the reflection-based design of the assignment. Additionally, the reluctance of some students to reflect on identity choices shows support for SIDE theorists' predictions of a lack of or reduced self-awareness on the part of the user. These contradictory results demonstrate the paradox of the effects CMC use on identity. The evidence provided to date, both in this study as well in others, supports both a positive, optimistic view of CMC and identity, as well as a negative, pessimistic view. This paradox highlights the need to approach the use of CMC from a perspective of technological realism that takes into account the complex and reflexive relationship between identity and CMC, as well as the infinite variety that is humanity, including our motivations and intentions when communicating with others.

Ultimately, we cannot resolve these paradoxes; we cannot have the darkness without the light. Instead, we must accept and even embrace the paradoxical nature of these concepts. To gain a more complete understanding, we must first recognize their complexity, leaving behind the more naïve characterizations and predictions of CMC use and effects as entirely positive or negative, and focusing instead on a more realistic view of both the nature of CMC and the effects of its use on identity.

REFERENCES

Adler, P. A., & Adler, P. (2007). The demedicalization of self-injury: From psychopathology to sociological deviance. *Journal of Contemporary Ethnography*, *36*(5), 537–570. doi:10.1177/0891241607301968

Adler, P. A., & Adler, P. (2008). The cyber worlds of self-injurers: Deviant communities, relationships, and selves. *Symbolic Interaction, 31*, 33–56. doi:10.1525/si.2008.31.1.33

Barak, A. (2005). Sexual harassment on the Internet. *Social Science Computer Review, 23*, 77–92. doi:10.1177/0894439304271540

Bargh, J. A., McKenna, K. Y. A., & Fitzsimons, G. M. (2002). Can you see the real me? Activation and expression of the "true self" on the Internet. *The Journal of Social Issues, 58*, 33–48. doi:10.1111/1540-4560.00247

Barnes, S. (2003). *Computer-mediated communication: Human-to-human communication across the Internet*. Boston, MA: Allyn & Bacon.

Bayne, S. (2005). Deceit, desire and control: the identities of learners and teachers in cyberspace. In Land, R., & Bayne, S. (Eds.), *Education in cyberspace* (pp. 26–42). London: Routledge Falmer.

Collins, M. (1992). *Flaming: The relationship between social context cues and uninhibited verbal behavior in computer mediated communication*. Retrieved February 13, 2009, from http://www.emoderators.com/papers/flames.html

Creswell, J. W. (1998). *Qualitative inquiry and research design: Choosing among five traditions*. Thousand Oaks, CA: Sage.

Curtis, P. (1997). Mudding: Social phenomena in text-based virtual realities. In Kiesler, S. (Ed.), *Culture of the Internet* (pp. 121–142). Mahwah, NJ: Lawrence Erlbaum.

Danet, B. (1998). Text as mask: Gender, play and performance on the Internet. In Jones, S. G. (Ed.), *Cybersociety 2.0: Computer-mediated communication and community revisited* (pp. 129–158). Thousand Oaks, CA: Sage.

Davies, P., & Lipsey, Z. (2003). Ana's gone surfing: A look at the disturbing rise of pro-anorexic websites. *The Psychologist, 16*(8), 424–425.

Denegri-Knott, J., & Taylor, J. (2005). The labeling game: A conceptual exploration of deviance on the Internet. *Social Science Computer Review, 23*, 93–107. doi:10.1177/0894439304271541

Douglas, K. M., McGarty, C., Bliuc, A., & Lala, G. (2005). Cyberhate: Social competition and social creativity in online white supremacist groups. *Social Science Computer Review, 23*, 68–76. doi:10.1177/0894439304271538

Dyer, R., Green, R., Pitts, M., & Millward, M. (1995). What's the flaming problem? or Computer mediated communication—Deindividuating or disinhibiting? In A. J. Dix, J. E. Finlay, & M. A. R. Kirby (Eds.), *People and computers X: Proceedings of HCI'95 conference* (pp. 289-302). Cambridge, UK: Cambridge University Press.

Finch, E. (2003). What a tangled web we weave: Identity theft and the Internet. In Jewkes, Y. (Ed.), *Dot.cons: Crime, deviance, and identity on the Internet* (pp. 86–104). Portland, OR: Willan.

Force, W. R. (2005, February). There are no victims here: Determination versus disorder in pro-anorexia. Paper presented at the *Couch-Stone Symposium of the Society for the Study for Symbolic Interaction*, Boulder, CO.

Gergen, K. J. (2000). The self in the age of information. *The Washington Quarterly, 23*(1), 201–214. doi:10.1162/016366000560656

Goffman, E. (1959). *The presentation of self in everyday life*. New York: Doubleday & Company.

Gurak, L. J. (2001). *Cyberliteracy: Navigating the Internet with awareness*. New Haven, CT: Yale University.

Hinduja, S., & Patchin, J. W. (2008). Cyberbullying: An exploratory analysis of factors related to offending and victimization. *Deviant Behavior, 29*, 129–156. doi:10.1080/01639620701457816

Janssen, J., Erkens, G., Kirschner, P. A., & Kanselaar, G. (2009). Influence of group member familiarity on online collaborative learning. *Computers in Human Behavior, 25*, 161–170. doi:10.1016/j.chb.2008.08.010

Joinson, A. N. (1999). Anonymity, disinhibition, and social desirability on the Internet. *Behavior Research Methods, Instruments, & Computers, 31*, 433–438.

Joinson, A. N. (2001). Self-disclosure in CMC: The role of self-awareness and visual anonymity. *European Journal of Social Psychology, 31*, 177–192. doi:10.1002/ejsp.36

Joinson, A. N. (2003). *Understanding the psychology of Internet behaviour, virtual worlds, real lives.* Basingstoke, UK: Palgrave-Macmillan.

Joinson, A. N. (2005). Deviance and the Internet: New challenges for social science. *Social Science Computer Review, 23*, 5–7. doi:10.1177/0894439304271527

Joinson, A. N., & Dietz-Uhler, B. (2002). Explanations for the perpetration of and reactions to deception in a virtual community. *Social Science Computer Review, 220*, 275–289.

Joseph, J. (2003). Cyberstalking: An international perspective. In Jewkes, Y. (Ed.), *Dot.cons: Crime, deviance, and identity on the Internet* (pp. 105–125). Portland, OR: Willan.

Kolb, D. A. (1984). *Experiential learning experience as a source of learning and development.* Upper Saddle River, NJ: Prentice Hall.

Krippendorff, K. (2004). *Content analysis: An introduction to its methodology.* Thousand Oaks, CA: Sage.

Lea, M., Spears, R., & de Groot, D. (2001). Knowing me, knowing you: Anonymity effects on social identity processes within groups. *Personality and Social Psychology Bulletin, 27*, 526–537. doi:10.1177/0146167201275002

Li, Q. (2006). Cyberbullying in schools: A research of gender differences. *School Psychology International, 27*(2), 157–170. doi:10.1177/0143034306064547

Madlock, P. E., & Westerman, D. (2009). *Cyberteasing as a component of cyberbullying in romantic relationships: Who's LOL?* Unpublished manuscript.

McKenna, K. Y. A., Green, A. S., & Gleason, M. E. J. (2002). Relationship formation on the Internet: What's the big attraction? *The Journal of Social Issues, 58*, 9–31. doi:10.1111/1540-4560.00246

Meadows, M. S. (2008). *I, avatar: The culture and consequences of having a second life.* Berkeley, CA: New Riders.

Monroe, B. (1999). Re-membering Mama: The female body in embodied and disembodied communication. In Blair, K., & Takayoshi, P. (Eds.), *Feminist cyberscapes: Mapping gendered academic spaces* (pp. 63–82). Stamford, CT: Ablex.

Patchin, J. W., & Hinduja, S. (2006). Bullies move beyond the schoolyard: A preliminary look at cyberbullying. *Youth Violence and Juvenile Justice, 4*(2), 148–169. doi:10.1177/1541204006286288

Postmes, T., Spears, R., & Lea, M. (1998). Breaching or building social boundaries? *Communication Research, 25*(6), 689–715. doi:10.1177/009365098025006006

Postmes, T., Spears, R., & Lea, M. (2000). The formation of group norms in computer-mediated communication. *Human Communication Research, 26*(3), 341–372. doi:10.1111/j.1468-2958.2000.tb00761.x

Richardson, F. C., Rogers, A., & McCarroll, J. (1998). Toward a dialogical self. *The American Behavioral Scientist, 41*, 496–514. doi:10.1177/0002764298041004004

Riva, G. (2001). Communicating in CMC: Making order out of miscommunication. In Anolli, L., Ciceri, R., & Riva, G. (Eds.), *Say not to say: New perspectives on miscommunication* (pp. 204–230). Amsterdam: IOS Press.

Sassenberg, K., & Boos, M. (2003). Attitude change in computer-mediated communication: Effects of anonymity and category norms. *Group Processes & Intergroup Relations, 6*, 405–422. doi:10.1177/13684302030064006

Scott, C. R. (2007). Communication and social identity theory: Existing and potential connections in organization identification research. *Communication Studies, 58*(2), 123–138. doi:10.1080/10510970701341063

Shedletsky, L. J. (1993). Minding computer-mediated communication: CMC as experiential learning. *Educational Technology, 33*(12), 5–10.

Smith, P. K., Mahdavi, J., Carvalho, M., Fisher, S., Russell, S., & Tippett, N. (2008). Cyberbullying: Its nature and impact in secondary school pupils. *Journal of Child Psychology and Psychiatry, and Allied Disciplines, 49*(4), 376–385. doi:10.1111/j.1469-7610.2007.01846.x

Spears, R., & Lea, M. (1994). Panacea or Panopticon? The hidden power in computer-mediated communication. *Communication Research, 21*(4), 427–459. doi:10.1177/009365094021004001

Sproull, L., & Kiesler, S. (1991). *Connections: New ways of working in the networked organization*. Cambridge, MA: MIT Press.

Strauss, A. (1987). *Qualitative analysis for social scientists*. New York: Cambridge University Press. doi:10.1017/CBO9780511557842

Strauss, A., & Corbin, J. (1990). *Basics of qualitative research: Grounded theory procedures and techniques*. Newbury Park, CA: Sage.

Suler, J. (1999). *The psychology of cyberspace*. Retrieved February 13, 2009, from http://www.rider.edu/users/suler/psycyber/psycyber.html.

Taylor, T. L. (1999). Life in virtual worlds: Plural existence, multimodalities, and other online research challenges. *The American Behavioral Scientist, 43*(3), 436–449. doi:10.1177/00027649921955362

Turkle, S. (1995). *Life on the screen*. New York: Simon & Schuster.

Whitty, M. (2005). The realness of cybercheating: Men's and women's representations of unfaithful internet relationships. *Social Science Computer Review, 23*, 57–67. doi:10.1177/0894439304271536

Wynn, E., & Katz, J. E. (1997). Hyperbole over cyberspace: Self-presentation and social boundaries in Internet home pages and discourse. *The Information Society, 13*, 297–327. doi:10.1080/019722497129043

ENDNOTE

[1]   This research was sponsored in part by a grant from the Center for Collaboration Science at the University of Nebraska at Omaha.

Chapter 2
Social Activism in the 'Blackosphere':
The Jena 6 Case

Lynette Kvasny
Pennsylvania State University, USA

Fay Cobb Payton
North Carolina State University, USA

Kayla D. Hales
Pennsylvania State University, USA

ABSTRACT

Using Denning's model of Internet activism as a sensitizing framework, this chapter describes the manner in which Black bloggers (referred to as the 'Blackosphere') express and negotiate their ethnic identity online. We analyze discussions in the Blackosphere in response to the Jena 6 case to illustrate how the Internet has empowered Black people, changed media publicity, and served as a means of collaborative activities that support social activism. It is our hope that this chapter will encourage researchers to explore further how and why historically underserved groups engage in social activism on the Internet, and the various technologies and social practices they use to do so.

INTRODUCTION

Personally, I'm interested in what made the plight of the Jena 6 so compelling that it moved Black students across this country to turn off BET, pull up their pants, reach into their wallets, and travel to Jena to defend six of their own.[1]

DOI: 10.4018/978-1-61520-827-2.ch002

In this chapter, we examine how and why black[2] bloggers express ethnic identity through an analysis of computer-mediated communication (CMC) that supported social activism in response to the Jena 6 case. The Jena 6 case began in August 2006 when black students at the local high school in Jena, Louisiana sat under a tree that was known to be a place where white students usually congregated. White students took offense and responded by hanging three nooses in the tree. In following months, racial tensions escalated. There were confrontations between black and white students, and there was a fire that destroyed the central wing of the Jena High School. On December 4, 2006, black students heard a white student (Justin Barker, 17) bragging about a racial assault his friend had made. Six black students (Robert Bailey, 17; Mychal Bell, 16; Carwin Jones, 18; Bryant Purvis, 17; Jesse Ray Beard, 14; and Theo Shaw, 17) responded by assaulting Barker. Barker was treated in the local emergency room. The injuries were minor as he was able to attend a party later that same evening.

The white local officials responsible for handling the incident judged the nooses as a youthful prank, and punished the white offenders with a few brief school suspensions. The six black juvenile offenders, however, were expelled from school, arrested and charged as adults with felony offenses, including attempted murder and aggravated assault (Robinson, 2007). Later, the charges were reduced to battery for all but one the offenders, Mychal Bell. "Civil rights advocates, who have called the punishment of the arrested youths disproportionate, say the case has raised the questions of how much race still plays a part in the workings of the legal system in the South" (Newman, 2007).

On September 22, 2007, fifteen to twenty thousand people from across the nation traveled to Jena to attend peaceful rallies to protest this disparity in the justice system and show their support for the six black defendants known as the Jena 6. According to Younge (2007), "These incidents have turned Jena into a national symbol of racial injustice. As such, it is both a potent emblem… because it shines a spotlight on how race and class conspire to deny black people equality before the law…and a convenient whipping boy because it allows the rest of the nation to dismiss the incidents as the work of Southern redneck backwoodsmen without addressing the systemic national failures it showcases".

In what follows, we briefly describe the Blackosphere and Denning's five modes of using the Internet for activism. Our conceptualization of the Blackosphere as well as the five modes of Internet activism will be used to inform a textual analysis of how ethnic identity emerged in the blog entries and comments that helped to bring the Jena 6 case to the attention of the mainstream media. While the events in Jena happened in 2006, they were not reported nationally until 2007. As Robinson (2007, p. A19) notes, "We still might not know about what was happening in Jena if the case hadn't been noticed by bloggers, who sounded the alarm". As African Americans increasingly use social media, such as blogs and social networks, to produce their own content and foster virtual communities that serve their collective interests, there is potential for new modes of social activism to materialize.

BACKGROUND

Ethnic Identity and Computer-Mediated Communication

African Americans are not a monolithic group; they are distinguishable along gender, class, age, regional, and socio-economic lines. However, ethnic identity acts as a "tie that binds" this group cohesively. Identity development has been described as a cognitive process by which an individual establishes a relationship with a reference group, with the group being capable of influencing the individual's worldview through the adoption of group values and goals (Greenwald, 1988; Thompson & Akbar, 2003). For African Americans, ethnic identity is developed from a longstanding struggle against white domination marked by slavery, segregation, the great migration, the civil rights movement, and the black power movement. Throughout this history, African Americans became aware of their oppression within US society, and their attitudes towards themselves, their ethnic group, and members of other ethnic groups crystallized to form a core sense of identity (Crawford, Allison, Zamboni, & Soto, 2002; Sellers, Smith, Shelton, Rowley, & Chavous, 1998).

It has been said that "computer-mediated communication (CMC) and the Internet provide new opportunities for using Discourse and text to discursively construct and enact achieved identities in online environments" (Black, 2006, p.171). Conversing via CMC provides a distinct experience from what would be permitted during face-to-face interaction. Therefore, online conversations provide a unique opportunity to examine how the African American community uses language to express its position as subjects in Jena 6 discourse.

CMC offers a number of different affordances that make the study of ethnic identity and language in online communication interesting. However, the relationships among ethnic identity, language, and CMC are not always straightforward. On the one hand, ethnic identity is often deemed to be more performative and discursive on the Web due to the anonymity, freedoms of time and space, and reduced physical and social cues afforded by this communication channel. These characteristics of online conversations may provide a level of comfort to the participant as it makes the interaction non-threatening and non-intrusive (Boase & Wellman, 2006); "Given the physical and psychological distance created by lack of visual and perhaps aural information, the initiator is somewhat insulated from the potentially negative reactions of the receiver that may be conveyed through the receiver's facial expression and intonation" (Byrne & Findlay, 2004, p.51). Therefore, the discussant is more likely to be open, honest, and true to self during his/her expression. On the other hand, group communication in asynchronous online environments is often aligned to real world topics and tends to maintain traditional, hegemonic identities, roles, and other ties to physical embodiment (Herring & Martinson 2004). In addition, contributors to online discussions have been said to conform and behave in a fashion that is in support of hegemonic group norms due to the anonymity CMC affords. In other words, these individuals may become less aware of their individual identify and instead imitate the behavior and beliefs of the group (Pauley & Emmers-Sommer, 2007). To make sense of how identity is expressed in online settings, empirical studies of particular online communities are needed.

The Blackosphere

Black-oriented online communities are playing an increasingly important role in the construction of black identity and the advancement of black interests. According to Poster (1995), mass media like radio "are interpreted by individuals who are interpellated by them, but these readers and viewers are not addressed directly, only as a generalized audience and, of course, they respond in fully articulated linguistic acts". However, on the Internet, "individuals read and interpret communications to themselves and to others and also respond by shaping sentences and transmitting them…The magic of the Internet is that it is a technology that puts cultural acts, symbolizations in all forms, in the hands of all participants; it radically decentralizes the positions of speech, publishing, filmmaking, radio and television broadcasting, in short the apparatuses of cultural production".

The "Blackosphere", an informal group of black cultural producers, is described by Francis Holland (2007) as follows:

These blogs are by and principally for Black people, focusing not only upon Black people but upon people and issues deemed relevant to the Black people who write these blogs and post comments. At Black blogs, we comment on the issues of the day raised in white newspapers and blogs, but we also highlight issues that whites mostly ignore, such as the unfair criminal prosecution of individual humble and unknown Blacks. Our commentary and the relative importance that we give news are informed by our unique historical perspective on and position in America. From our vantage point, we share with each other a distinct perspective and critique that white people, including white progressives, cannot have and generally do not want.

The Blackosphere represents the collective efforts of individuals creating small public spaces to circulate information, create and rearticulate oppositional frameworks for expressing black identity without censorship from non-blacks, and provides opportunities for community interaction that fosters social activism. *The Chicago Tribune* reports that the Blackosphere has developed into a formidable grassroots organization that "within a matter of a few weeks collected 220,000 petition signatures—and more than $130,000 in donations for legal fees—in support of six black Jena teenagers who are being prosecuted on felony battery charges for beating a white student" (Witt, 2007). This "viral civil rights movement" was literally conjured out of the ether of cyberspace and spread via blogs, email, message boards and talk radio.

Internet Activism

Early efforts of the civil rights movement have centered on key institutions: the black church and the black media. According to Jeffries (2005, p. 338), "At the height of the Civil Rights Movement, radio, more so than television or print media, served as African Americans' main source of news and entertainment. Scholars, however, have generally overlooked this essential element of African-American life". Though centralized in the positions of speech and highly reliant on "deejays" who embodied the roles of political activist, community informant and entertainer,

benevolent broadcasters used radio to support and report on southern black activism. Such activism empowered the collective among the Southern Christian Leadership Conference, Black Panther Party, the National Association for the Advancement of Colored People and the Student Nonviolent Coordinating Committee. By the 1950s and 1960s, the binding ties of these and other black social activism groups were characterized by coded, though shared, sociolinguistics on relevant topics. These topics ranged from social activism regarding the Vietnam War, civil and economic rights, educational equity and racial identity.

Unlike these examples of early social activism in the black community, which were often guided by central figures and spearheaded by national organizations, today's social activists are piloted by Internet interactions based on grass-root causes. Because the community interactions are logged in their entirety, the data are complete and unmediated by interview, participant observation or survey methodologies. Researchers assume the role of lurkers who unobtrusively observe community engagement, which preserves the purity of the data.

According to Denning (2001), activism refers to normal, nondisruptive use of the Internet in support of an agenda or cause. This use typically includes browsing the web for information, constructing web sites and posting materials on them, transmitting electronic publications and letters through email, and using the Net to discuss issues, form coalitions, and coordinate activities. Denning provides a conceptual framework that includes five modes of online activism: collection, publication, dialogue, coordination of action, and lobbying decision makers.

In *collection* mode, the Internet is viewed as a vast digital library that houses factual information, as well as guides for effective Internet use for activities such as outreach, membership and fundraising, organizing, and advocacy. Search tools are often included on websites to improve users' ability to locate and extract useful information.

The Internet can also be used for *publication* to advance the authors' mission and policy objectives. Advocacy groups and individuals send information through email listservs, post to newsgroups or message boards, create posts on webblog or create entire websites, which can serve as a gathering place and source of information for supporters, potential supporters, and other audiences. Publication on the Internet is typically less costly than radio, newspaper, telephone, fax, television or other media distribution channels. By publishing their own content, authors retain control of the message, which can be presented and distributed to a global audience.

In addition, the Internet serves as a social space for public or private *dialogue* on issues of concern. Dialogue can be used to debate or comment on the latest issues, to influence the actions of others, or to answer questions. Discussion can be open to the public or can be limited to subscribers to an email list or weblog, or editors of a wiki. The dialogue taking place on interactive forums may help to shape policy decision and influence public opinion.

Coordination of action is another way in which groups use the Internet. The Internet aids in the decision making process by enabling individuals to post or distribute plans for mobilizing the actions of the group, coordinate schedules, and vote amongst alternative courses of action. Advocacy groups can coordinate action without regard to the constraints of time and geography.

Finally, the Internet is used for *lobbying decision makers* by asking individuals to write, phone, email, or fax their concerns to influence change by institutions of authority. Online petitions are used to protest against the actions of more powerful groups, while online reporting of local stories can garner the attention of mainstream media. According to Denning (2001, p. 62), "The most successful advocacy groups are likely to be those that use the Internet to augment traditional lobbying methods, including personal visits to decision makers and use of broadcast media to reach the public. These operations can be time consuming and expensive, favoring groups that are well-funded".

INTERNET ACTIVISM AND THE JENA 6 CASE

To frame our textual analysis of how and why the Blackosphere led in the call for collective action in response to the Jena 6 case, we use Denning's (2001) five modes of Internet activism.

Collection

Color of Change is an Internet-based civil rights organization whose goal is "to empower our members – Black Americans and their allies - to make government more responsive to the concerns of Black Americans and to bring about positive political and social change for everyone". The organization was created in the wake of Hurricane Katrina to harness the organizing power of the Internet to give Black Americans a strengthened political voice. Color of Change and its 400,000 members advocated on behalf of the Jena 6 and served as the primary website for factual information, fundraising, organizing, and advocacy for the Jena 6. The online petition received 320,860 signatures, which is 106% of the goal for 300,000 signatures.

Publication

Color of Change was the primary advocacy group promoting social justice for the Jena 6. At this website, visitors could sign petitions, purchase tee shirts, send correspondences to Louisiana Governor, Bobby Jindal, and District Attorney, Reed Walters, as well as access links to news reports from blogs and newspapers from around the world.

The NAACP[3], a venerable civil rights organization, posted "The Message" which outlines a series of actions that should be taken to redress the racial injustices enacted by the legal system in Jena.

- As Chairman Julian Bond stated, *"This is an American outrage that demonstrates the continuing shame of racial division in our country. Join us in making it one of the last."*
- In light of the circumstances surrounding Mychal Bell's case, we urge all concerned citizens to support the call for a new trial.
- It is unacceptable to selectively enforce the law based on race. Prosecutorial discretion should be used in a fair and equitable manner.
- The Jena Six should be tried by juries that reflect the racial and ethnic demographics of Jena, Louisiana.
- The hanging of nooses is not a "youthful stunt" or "prank." It is a hate crime. Such hate crimes should not be tolerated at any school. Jena High School must establish a curriculum which promotes cultural sensitivity and understanding.
- The NAACP calls on Louisiana Governor, Kathleen B. Blanco and Louisiana Attorney General, Charles C. Foti to thoroughly investigate and monitor the trials of Mychal Bell, Robert Bailey, Jr., Theo Shaw, Carwin Jones, Bryant Purvis and John Doe. The Governor and State Attorney General should do everything in their power to ensure that these young men's constitutional rights are protected.

Dialogue

Dialogue is the most commonly used vehicle for social activism. We provide two examples that are representative of the dialogue that took place in the Blackosphere shortly after the Jena 6 rally. Blogger Oliver Willis published a concise post on the Jena 6 rally that garnered much discussion: *"The thousands of people in Jena today show to me that the anti-war movement has lots to learn and that nobody is as organized on the left as civil rights organizations. Period."* Some individuals who participate in Willis' blog community critiqued this comparison of the Jena 6 rally with the civil rights movement. For instance, Joe wrote:

It kills me that people are actually comparing this to Selma. 6 kids beat the shit out of one kid and yet somehow there's an injustice going on because the perps were black and the victim was white. What kind of crazy freaking world do we live in?"

Spider J concurs when he wrote,

"I gotta agree with Jay on this one. I doubt King would be proud to defend the Jena 6, who did exactly what King refused to do when confronted with ugly racism–reacted with violence, and on somebody possibly innocent of any wrongdoing. How are the actions of the Jena 6 a victory for civil rights and a blow against racism? I'll bet you double or nothing that this just confirmed, in the minds of some people, that blacks are dangerous and violent and would kill all the whiteys if given the chance.

From the subsequent discussion that took place, we infer that Jay and Spider J are white males who regularly read and comment at the website. A black commenter responded in a way that seeks to help Jay and Spider J to understand the significance of the Jena 6 case for African Americans:

Jay: Now that you've heard, understood and been insulted by (: Tom:), I repeat: Attempted murder for a school brawl when there was no punishment for threatening the Black students with a shotgun, or beating up the Black student who showed up at an all-white party. THAT is what is being protested. The Constitution guarantees equal protection under the law, and against cruel and unusual punishment. THAT is what is being demanded. No one says there weren't issues to be addressed. And I said you have an incomplete picture because I've seen the CNN's coverage and Fox hasn't covered it at all, so you likely just heard of it yesterday. You and Spider J assumed the worst motivations, right off the top. And it's good you both heard the comments here...but it's bad that you had to.

While much of the dialogue in the Blackosphere declared that the Jena 6 serves as an example of how the US legal system allows prosecutors to over-charge black male juveniles, many black bloggers rejected the "free the Jena 6" message. At Bossip.com, a popular black entertainment and gossip blog, a commenter notes:

Jena 6 repulses me. Dumb ass people were marching to "Free Jena 6" when they committed a serious crime. It should have been "Justice for Jena 6", and that would entail punishment for the crime they committed. These kids have been involved with numerous criminal activities, and need to be held responsible, not made into heroes. And this doesn't excuse the noose at the tree, they should be dealt with as well, but WE need to stop making excuses for black kids acting like violent idiots, and try raising them to know what is right and acceptable and what is just plain wrong. But I have a feeling they will be back in the criminal justice system again REAL soon.

In a second example, just weeks after some thousands of demonstrators protested what they decried as unequal justice aimed at six black teenagers in Jena, controversy arouse over the accounting and disbursing of at least $500,000 donated to pay for the teenagers' legal defense. In one instance, Marcus Jones, the father of Jena 6 defendant Mychal Bell, called the fundraising efforts of Color of Change into question. While on Michael Baisden's syndicated radio show, Mr.

Jones and Mr. Baisden made misleading statements about Color of Change and the management of contributions to the Jena 6 funds. An account of the facts related to these false statements was posted on the Color of Change website[4]. After much public debate and disclosure of financial records, Mr. Baisden issued an apology to Color of Change[5].

Bloggers, who had closely followed the Jena 6 case, came to the defense of Color of Change. What About Our Daughters, for instance, published the following:

Before Baisden ever knew who they were, black bloggers were working the Jena 6. The families have now decided to cling to Bad Boy Baisden, I say LET 'Em! Let them cling to a man whose claim to fame is that he writes smutty books. Maybe he can get them on a few more red carpets or help them produce some more myspace videos. Sometimes, you really do need to pack up your toys and head back to the crib. Especially when folks start kicking sand in your face. You have done what you could for these families. The kids aren't facing attempted murder charges. There is no coalition to be shattered or broken. You did the work you set out to do. Eventually, the old media will get a clue and realize that the internet can magnify their power and is not a threat to it. They'll figure out that there are SOME activists that actually use donations for the intended purpose instead of buying houses, furs, cars, and, paying off paramours, and paying child support. YEAH I SAID IT! The folks at Color of Change have given me no indication that they are anything other than what they are: decent honorable people trying to do the right thing.[6]

Bossip was also a leading website for discussion about the misuse of Jena 6 defense funds. One post centered on a controversial YouTube video in which a Jena 6 defendant is shown laying on a bed covered in money.

This is why the smart folks over here at Bossip don't support Negro causes "just because" we are told to. Here is a picture of Robert Bailey Jr., a member of the Jena 6. According to a video on Youtube, he was braggin' about thuggin' on his Myspace and was caught showing off what looks to be Jena 6 Defense Fund stacks. SMH.

The dialogue about this incident was overwhelmingly one of disapproval, *"First those two fools go to the BET [Black Entertainment TV] awards now this one is on YouTube basically making every single black person who supported the Jena 6 look like fucking fools"*. Some responses used sarcasm to express their outrage, *"I guess it pays to be a Black criminal in America. And to think that we have not made any progress....I'm in the wrong line of work. I'm fixing to go beat up some White people so I can get stacks of cash and diamond chains. It worked for them so why not for me?"* A few community members noted that the irresponsible actions of the youths should not cloud the central issue – racial injustice in the legal system, *"Come on ppl! Just becuz these kids are acting a fool doesn't mean we agree they should go to jail. As I recall we were fighting against the unfair bargain these kids were getting from the justice system, a fact which still remains true!!!!!"*

At the Concrete Loop, a Black music and entertainment blog, community members also expressed outrage at the damaging YouTube video.

The Jena 6 deserve to be punished for jumping on that 1 person, but I don't think they need to be charged with attempted murder and sent to prison. Some jail time should do it. Why'd it take 6 of them to whoop on 1 person anyway? That's cowardly! And the way they paraded around flaunting donations and acting like they were superstars was ridiculous. They basically made a mockery of all the things black leaders and the community were trying to do for them. It's sad really!

Coordination of Action

Since the 1950s, planning and participating in protest marches have been an important black rite of passage into American political life. However, those who organized and marched in Jena were among the first to mobilize an Internet driven black youth protest in American history.

The NAACP included the following actions:

- Support the Jena 6: Continue to monitor the NAACP's website for announcements.
- Sign the "Justice for Jena" petition: Join over 175,000 other individuals who have expressed their concern. The petition will be presented to Louisiana Gov. Kathleen B. Blanco by the NAACP on September 19.
- Make a contribution: Contribute to support the NAACP's advocacy efforts and initiatives.
- Donate online to the: Jena 6 Defense Fund or mail donations to. Jena 6 Defense Committee, P. O. Box 2798, Jena, LA 71342
- Advocate in your community: Mobilize your community and local government to have a voice and unite on equality within the United States criminal justice system.
- Send a letter to the Louisiana Governor and the Louisiana Attorney General: Urge your local officials to investigate this matter to ensure that these young men's constitutional rights are safeguarded.
- Register to vote: Make your vote count.
- Join the NAACP: Become a member of the nation's oldest and largest civil rights organization and help make a difference.

While people are asked "to take action and come together to achieve racial healing and unbiased justice for the Jena 6", some actions make direct appeals to support the NAACP. It should also be noted that donations to the Jena 6 fund are directed to the Color of Change organization. There is, however, an online document that informs website visitors how the Jena 6 funds were obtained and spent.[7]

Lobbying Decision Makers

While the Jena 6 demonstration benefited from well known civil rights leaders, including the Reverends Jesse Jackson and Al Sharpton and the mainstream media, the viral civil rights movement did not depend on them due, in part, to its organic character and speedy momentum. Instead, the mainstream media and prominent black leaders had to scramble to catch up to the Blackosphere movement. The Jena 6 demonstration showed that a new generation of civil rights activists learned about the Jena case from black political, entertainment, gossip, and hip-hop music blogs that featured the story, or popular black entertainers who have turned it into a crusade. The presence of Sharpton, Jackson and the mainstream media was contested in the Blackosphere. As the halfricanrevolution blogger notes:

The relationship between Sharpton, Jackson, and the media is as consensual as sex on a conjugal visit. As long as Sharpton and Jackson stayed away from the Jena Six controversy, the mainstream media ignored it almost entirely. The reason is that Sharpton and Jackson provide convenient targets for white resentment. The media has until now ignored the racist injustice in Louisiana, but the moment Sharpton or Jackson makes an appearance, all that will change. The issue will no longer be the preposterous charge of attempted murder against six black boys for a school fight, or DA Reed Walter's menacing words to a group of black students who dared to protest the violently enforced segregated conditions in their local school. No, as soon as one of them shows up, the media will change the subject, and the conversation will center around whether Sharpton and Jackson are "hustlers" or "hypocrites" who are

simply seeking attention. No, it is the media, who has shown little interest in uncovering the injustices in Jena, Louisiana, who will soon chase the ratings and attention coverage of Sharpton and Jackson will bring.[8]

The NAACP, the civil rights organization that has historically played a prominent role in leading social activism in support of disenfranchised African Americans, was also relegated to a supportive role in the Jena 6 case. The NAACP website hosted petitions and solicited contributions for the teens' legal defense, but it was the Color of Change, an Internet-based civil rights group with more than 280,000 subscribers, that led in the lobbying efforts to raise the public profile of the Jena 6 case.

Solutions and Recommendations

Based on our study of Internet activism in the Jena 6 case, we recommend that the success of online social activism not be judged solely on whether or not it generates obvious political effects. Rather, online social activism should be seen as expanding the notion of what the Internet is and how it can be used in everyday life to increase the realm of freedom, community and empowerment (Kahn & Kellner, 2004). In the Jena 6 case, the Web serves as a new narrative space for representing a uniquely African American identity where black selfhood is constituted through opposition to both "whiteness" and a totalizing "black" discourse. In the Blackosphere, there were diverse discourses. For instance, BlackPerspectives.net posts an article written by Hotep (2007) that critiques the effectiveness of protest demonstrations for social change in the modern movement:

The Jena March, like all one-day mobilizations including the "historic" March on Washington in 1963 and the Million Man March in 1995, is at best symbolic and at worst diversionary. We know that it takes constant, long-term pressure by those, like Blacks, who lack the organized wealth and high level influence to make even the smallest change in the American political system. We also know that nothing of lasting value can be achieved in American politics by a one-day protest regardless of the numbers involved, except that it dupes us into believing that we have accomplished something concrete and tangible. And that's the hidden danger of protest politics.

However, other posts at BlackPerspectives.net were supportive and asked readers to contact media outlets to increase coverage of the Jena 6 case.

Again, with this in mind, I hope YOU will step up to the challenge of contacting at least just five national media outlets. What is it for you to put some email addresses in a send box, type up or copy a few words, and hit send? Better yet though, if you have a printer it would be great to print those same letters off, sign your name, and drop them in the mail. I think it's easier for a large news company to ignore an in box full of emails, but not to ignore mail bends full of letters staring them in the face in their office. A flood of calls would be great too. Maybe you could do this every week until they get the message. Just take whatever little time you have to do your part. If we all just do a little, a whole lot will get accomplished.

In the Jena 6 case, the widespread use of the Internet for information sharing, organizing, fund-raising, communication, and many other activities suggests that African Americans have become increasingly savvy users. African Americans also have a rich history of social activism for civil rights. Denning provides a useful framework for examining how social activism is enacted online. While the Internet played a central role in the Jena 6 organizing, traditional communication channels such as radio, TV and newspapers, and black neighborhood institutions like churches, barbershops and hair salons were also involved. With only 64% of African Americans online (Pew Internet, 2008), these traditional communication channels remain salient.

FUTURE RESEARCH DIRECTIONS

Future research on online social activism should take two directions. First, there is a need for studies that examine non-traditional Internet users and groups. While much of the literature on online social activism tends to focus on well resourced and technically adept specialist groups, the Blackosphere's response to the Jena 6 demonstrates how social groups that have been historically afforded fewer resources can successfully organize on the Internet. Black blogging communities are important because they provide an alternative venue for information dissemination and social action to promote economic, social, judicial and educational equity. Although social activists are increasingly using the Internet as an information and communication medium, the principles guiding these efforts are rooted in the tradition of the civil rights movement.

Black blogging communities also perform identity online through a number of commonly used CMC techniques. For instance, Kvasny and Igwe (2008) observed how members of a black blogging community used signification, kinesics and side conversations to suggest playfulness and provide levity when discussing HIV/AIDS. Co-signing simulated turn-taking by citing previous exchanges and creating the appearance of dialogue that suggests temporal immediacy. This bolstered coherence, improved addressability among participants, and provided a mechanism for offering evaluative feedback. Community members created identifiable personalities through screen names and gravatars, small images used in blogs and chat forums that enable users to personalize their identity. Participants also created a sense of presence and intimacy through the use of language to express action, inner state or emotion, and place. Additional research on black blogs and bloggers is noticeably absent from the published literature, with the exception of Poole's (2005) study of African American political bloggers and Brock's (2007) study of African American bloggers' response to mainstream media reports on Hurricane Katrina. Intensive studies of identity performance in computer-mediated environments can provide additional insights into how and why African Americans organize online.

Second, there is a need for research that examines Web 2.0 tools and services, and how they are employed by organizations to support social activism. Blogs, wikis, podcasts, photo and video sharing, and social networking services hosted by new media companies such as Google, Flickr, BitTorrent, MySpace, Facebook, and YouTube provide a low cost, easy to use platform for the delivery of engaging services and experiences. The constellation of Web 2.0 tools and services emphasize user control and content creation, and architectures of participation. Organizations that historically lacked the technical, economic and human capital to effectively harness the Internet can now use these Web 2.0 tools and services as an information and communication platform for social activism. Useful studies could examine how Web 2.0 technologies are used by organizations collaborating to redress on a social issue.

CONCLUSION

In this chapter, Denning's model of Internet activism was used as a sensitizing framework to examine how the Blackosphere effectively used the Internet to raise funds, to increase awareness in the black community and in the mainstream media, and to coordinate activities to host a rally to protest the Jena 6 case. The online discussions taking place in the black blogging community provide authentic accounts of African American discursive practices, lived experiences and cultural perspectives.

REFERENCES

Black, R. W. (2006). Language, culture, and identity in online fanfiction. *E-learning*, *3*(2), 170–184. doi:10.2304/elea.2006.3.2.170

Boase, J., & Wellman, B. (2006). Personal relationships: On and off the Internet. In Vangelisti, A., & Perlman, R. (Eds.), *The Handbook of Personal Relations* (pp. 709–723). Cambridge, UK: Cambridge University Press.

Brock, A. (2007). *Race, the Internet, and the hurricane: A critical discourse analysis of black identity online during the aftermath of Hurricane Katrina.* Unpublished doctoral dissertation, Library and Information Studies, University of Illinois at Urbana-Champaign.

Byrne, R., & Findlay, B. (2004). Preference for SMS versus telephone calls in initiating romantic relationships. *Australian Journal of Emerging Technologies and Society*, *2*(1), 48–61.

Crawford, I., Allison, K., Zamboni, B., & Soto, T. (2002). The influence of dual-identity development on the psychosocial functioning of African American gay and bisexual men. *Journal of Sex Research*, *39*(3), 179–189. doi:10.1080/00224490209552140

Denning, D. (2001). Activism, hacktivism and cyberterrorism: the Internet as a tool for influencing foreign policy. In J. Arquilla & D. Ronfeldt (Eds,), Networks and netwars: The future of terror, crime and militancy (pp. 239-288). Arlington, VA: Rand Corporation.

Greenwald, A. G. (1988). A social-cognitive account of the self's development. In Lapsley, D., & Power, F. (Eds.), *Self, ego, identity: Integrative approaches* (pp. 30–42). New York: Springer-Verlag.

Herring, S., & Martinson, A. (2004). Assessing gender authenticity in computer mediate language use: Evidence from an identity game. *Journal of Language and Social Psychology*, *4*(4), 424–446. doi:10.1177/0261927X04269586

Holland, F. (2007). *An essay on AfroSpear nomenclature: What we call ourselves and why*, Francis Hollander blog. Retrieved July 13, 2007, from http://francislholland.blogspot.com/2007/06/essay-of-afrospear-nomenclature-what-is.html.

Hotep, U. (2007). Retreived January 26, 2009, from http://www.blackperspective.net/index.php/the-jena-march-and-the-debate-over-protest-politics-pt2/

Kahn, R., & Kellner, D. (2004). New media and internet activism: From the 'Battle of Seattle' to blogging. *New Media & Society*, *6*(1), 87–95. doi:10.1177/1461444804039908

Kvasny, L., & Igwe, F. (2008). An African American weblog community's reading of AIDS in Black America. *Journal of Computer-Mediated Communication*, *13*(3), 569–592. doi:10.1111/j.1083-6101.2008.00411.x

Newman, M. (2007, September 24). Jena, La, The New York Times Company (New York). Retrieved February 2, 2008, from http://topics.nytimes.com/top/news/national/usstatesterritoriesandpossessions/louisiana/jena/index.html

Pauley, P. M., & Emmers-Sommer, T. M. (2007). The impact of Internet technologies on primary and secondary romantic relationship development. *Communication Studies*, *58*(4), 411–427. doi:10.1080/10510970701648616

Pew Internet. (2009). *Demographics of Internet users*. Retrieved May 15, 2009, from http://pewinternet.org/Static-Pages/Data-Tools/Download-Data/~/media/Infographics/Trend Data/January 2009 updates/Demographics of Internet Users 1 6 09.jpg

Poole, A. (2005, December). *Black bloggers and the Blogosphere*. Paper presented at the Second International Conference on Technology, Knowledge and Society, Hyderabad, India.

Poster, M. (1995). *CyberDemocracy: Internet and the public sphere*. Retrieved July 13, 2007, from http://www.uoc.edu/in3/hermeneia/sala_de_lectura/mark_poster_cyberdemocracy.htm

Robinson, E. (2007, September 21). Drive time for the Jena 6, *Washington Post*, A19. Retrieved August 19, 2008, from http://www.washingtonpost.com/wp-dyn/content/article/2007/09/20/AR2007092001956.html

Sellers, R. M., Smith, M. A., Shelton, J. N., Rowley, S. A. J., & Chavous, T. M. (1998). Multidimensional model of racial identity: A reconceptualization of African American racial identity. *Personality and Social Psychology Review*, *2*, 18–39. doi:10.1207/s15327957pspr0201_2

Witt, H. (2007, September 17). Blogs help drive Jena protest, *Chicago Tribune (Chicago, IL)*. Retrieved January 26, 2009, from http://www.chicagotribune.com/news/nationworld/chi-jena_blog_web19,0,4309628.story

Younge, G. (2007, September, 20). Jena is America, *The Nation (New York)*. Retrieved August 25, 2008, from http://www.thenation.com/doc/20071008/younge

ADDITIONAL READING

Alonzo, M., & Aiken, M. (2004). Flaming in electronic communication. *Decision Support Systems*, *36*(3), 205–213. doi:10.1016/S0167-9236(02)00190-2

Benwell, B., & Stokoe, E. (2006). *Discourse and identity*. Edinburgh, UK: Edinburgh University Press.

Brock, A. (2005). A belief in humanity is a belief in colored men: Using culture to span the digital divide. *Journal of Computer-Mediated Communication, 11*(1), 17. doi:10.1111/j.1083-6101.2006.tb00317.x

Buechler, S. M. (1995). New social movement theories. *The Sociological Quarterly, 36*(3), 441–464. doi:10.1111/j.1533-8525.1995.tb00447.x

Diani, M. (2001). Social movement networks: Virtual and real. In Webster, F. (Ed.), *Culture and Politics in the Information Age: A New Politics?* (pp. 117–128). London: Routledge.

Fernback, J. (1999). There is a there there: Notes toward a definition of cybercommunity. In Jones, S. (Ed.), *Doing Internet research: Critical issues and methods for examining the net* (pp. 203–220). Thousand Oaks, CA: Sage Publishing.

Herring, S., Kouper, I., Paolillo, J. C., Scheidt, L. A., Tyworth, M., Welsch, P., et al. (2005, January). *Conversations in the blogosphere: An analysis From the bottom up.* Paper presented at the 38th Annual Hawaii International Conference on System Sciences. Big Island, HI.

Herring, S., Scheidt, L., Bonus, S., & Wright, E. (2004, January). Bridging the gap: A genre analysis of weblogs. Paper presented at the 37th Annual HICSS Conference. Big Island, Hawaii.

Herring, S., Scheidt, L., Wright, E., & Bonus, S. (2005). Weblogs as a bridging genre. *Information Technology & People, 18*(2), 141–171. doi:10.1108/09593840510601513

Jeffries, H. K. (2005). Radio and the struggle for civil rights in the south (Book Review). *The Arkansas Historical Quarterly, 64*(3), 338–340.

Jena Six Navigator. (n.d.). *New York Times.* Retrieved January 26, 2008, from http://topics.nytimes.com/top/news/national/usstatesterritoriesandpossessions/louisiana/jena/index.html

Justice for the Jena 6 (n.d.). *colorofchange.org.* Retrieved January 26, 2008, from http://www.colorofchange.org/jena/

Justice for the People of Jena. (n.d.). *National Association for the Advancement of Colored People (NAACP).* Retrieved January 26, 2008, from http://www.naacp.org/getinvolved/activism/alerts/110aa-2007-7-20/index.htm

Kumar, R., Novak, J., Raghavan, P., & Tomkins, A. (2004). Structure and evolution of blogspace. *Communications of the ACM, 47*(12), 35–39. doi:10.1145/1035134.1035162

Moor, A., & Efimova, L. (2004, May). *An Argumentation Analysis of Weblog Conversations.* Paper presented at the 9th International Working Conference on the Language-Action Perspective on Communication Modeling, New Brunswick, NJ.

Nardi, B., Schiano, D., & Gumbrecht, M. (2004). Blogging as social activity, or, would you let 900 million people read your diary? In *Proceedings of the Conference on Computer-Supported Cooperative Work,* (pp.222-231), New York, ACM Press.

Nardi, B., Schiano, D., Gumbrecht, M., & Swartz, L. (2004). Why we blog. *Communications of the ACM, 47*(12), 41–46. doi:10.1145/1035134.1035163

O'Reilly, T. (2005). *What is Web 2.0.* Retrieved January 26, 2008, from http://oreilly.com/pub/a/oreilly/tim/news/2005/09/30/what-is-web-20.html

Omi, M., & Winant, H. (1986). *Racial formation in the U.S. from the 1960's to the 1980's.* New York: Routledge and Kegan Paul.

Papacharissi, Z. (2002). The virtual sphere: The Internet as a public sphere. *New Media & Society, 4*(1), 9–27. doi:10.1177/14614440222226244

Schmidt, J. (2007). Blogging practices: An analytical framework. *Journal of Computer-Mediated Communication, 12*(4), 1409–1427. doi:10.1111/j.1083-6101.2007.00379.x

Sunstein, C. (2004). Democracy and filtering. *Communications of the ACM, 47*(12), 57–59. doi:10.1145/1035134.1035166

KEY TERMS AND DEFINITIONS

Civil Rights: the rights belonging to an individual by virtue of citizenship. The 13th and 14th Amendments to the US Constitution provide Americans with fundamental freedoms and privileges such as due process, freedom from discrimination, and equal protection of the law. The Jena 6 case is sometimes compared to the civil rights movement during the 1950s and 1960s devoted to securing equal opportunity and treatment for African Americans.

Computer mediated communication (CMC): The process by which people create, exchange, and perceive informational messages using information and communication technologies. To be mediated by computers, the communication must be done by participants fully aware of their interaction with the computer technology in the process of creating and delivering messages.

Ethnic identity: Ethnicity is a cultural phenomenon that is shared among people who originate from the same geographic area and share language, food, ways of dress, customs and other cultural markers of group identity. Identity is the set of personal characteristics by which an individual is recognizable as a member of a group. Ethnic identity is the significance (how important is ethnicity) and qualitative meaning (what does it mean to be a member of this ethnic group) that individuals attribute to their membership within the group.

Internet activism: use of Internet communications technologies by citizen-led movements to enable rapid and widespread communications, disseminate information, raise funds, and/or mobilize and coordinate support for causes.

Weblog / blog: a website that displays in chronological order the postings by one or more individuals and usually has links to comments on specific postings. Blogs are valued by audiences who opt for news or information that is overlooked, interesting, unexpected, and important. Blogs can also serve as a virtual location for the author and audience to disseminate, interpret, provide additional facts, or alternative views on a subject matter. In this way, blogs are community-like in nature.

ENDNOTES

[1] http://www.blackperspective.net/index.php/the-jena-march-and-the-debate-over-protest-politics-pt1/

[2] In this article, we use "Black" and "African American" interchangeably to reflect people of African descent in the US.

[3] http://www.naacp.org/get-involved/activism/alerts/110aa-2007-7-20/index.htm

[4] http://www.colorofchange.org/jena/baisden/

[5] http://www.colorofchange.org/baisden/apology/member_email.html

[6] http://whataboutourdaughters.blogspot.com/2007/11/jena-6-families-to-black-blogospherewe.html

[7] http://www.naacp.org/news/press/2007-07-20b/THE.NAACP.ACCOUNTING.OF.FUNDS.COLLECTED.REGARDING.JENA.LOUISIANA.pdf

[8] http://halfricanrevolution.blogspot.com/2007/08/next-talking-head-to-talk-shit-about.html

Chapter 3
Textual Expectations, (Dis) Embodiment, and Social Presence in CMC

Deborah Leiter
Purdue University, USA

John Dowd
Purdue University, USA

ABSTRACT

This chapter adds depth to current theoretical approaches to the idea of social presence in computer-mediated communication by integrating ideas from deconstructionism, subaltern studies, phenomenological/dialogic approaches, and media ecology with current CMC perspectives on the (dis)embodied nature of CMC communication. The relation of the physical to online social environments naturally raises the question of the ways these environments inherit heteroglossic social expectations from other communication/media genres, especially from written media and from face-to-face conversational interactions. Ultimately, these inheritances, together with their ethical considerations, show that a variety of perspectives, even those that seem to be conflicting, simply serve to illuminate various aspects of the CMC environment and the ethical ramifications thereof.

INTRODUCTION

Many social scientific researchers studying computer-mediated communication (CMC) become quickly aware that the idea of bodily absence, or that of the connection of CMC to the *lived-body*, becomes a particularly important topic to unpack, yet few have deeply addressed this subject. Much social scientific thought regarding online interaction in computer-mediated communication approaches

this question from one of two seemingly competing theoretical perspectives. The first school of thought moves under the assumptions of social presence theory (Mehrabian, 1969; Short, Williams, and Christie, 1976), specifically theorizing that communication through disembodied media will produce less intimacy between those communicating due to a lack of nonverbal cues. The second school most generally approaches it using Walther's hyperpersonal perspective, which states that the primarily text based environment of the internet and its concomitant lack of non verbal

DOI: 10.4018/978-1-61520-827-2.ch003

cues increases both the speed and opportunities for people to foster interpersonal relationships. (Walther, 1996).[1]

Many social scientific researchers have approached these and related concepts empirically using quantitative methods (Birnie & Horvath, 2002; Cho, Trier, & E. Kim, 2005; Hian, Chuan, Trevor, & Detenber, 2004; Hu, Wood, Smith, & Westbrook, 2004; Kavanaugh, Carroll, Rosson, Zin, & Reese, 2005; H. Kim, G. J. Kim, Park, & Rice, 2007; Lombard & Ditton, 1997; Min, 2007; Nowak, Watt, & Walther, 2005; Sohn & Lee, 2005; Watts, 2007). We do not seek to challenge or replicate that or related work, but rather to draw on critical, philosophical, and media ecology theories to deepen the understanding of various aspects of both of these approaches, particularly their axiological dimensions. The purpose of this chapter is not to take sides among the two approaches just listed, but rather to show their complementarity. This complementarity, we argue, makes sense in light of CMC's cultural/social status at the intersection of (face-to-face) conversation and textual/written communication, whose cultural expectations clash depending on how people approach this hybrid space. In approaching this hybrid media space, we propose to present a deeper approach by way of explicating the way the *lived-body* is reconfigured through the online environment, which in turn inherits a variety of expectations from the way the *lived-body* interacts within/through both written media and face-to-face social environments. As explicitly articulated first by Merleau-Ponty (1962, 1969), the term *lived-body* refers to the ways in which as bodies we are always more than objectively or subjectively given. Rather, through our sensory capacities we make room for more than the here and now. In this way, our bodies are temporal and spatial clearings through which world (in the Heideggerian sense), objects, and others come into being (Anton, 2001). In other words, in our view of the body subjects and objects are not separate entities but rather are mutually arising correlates of one another.

The seeming conflict between the two perspectives noted above raises questions of whether the disembodied nature of CMC creates a space of exclusion, allowing for miscommunication and lack of depth, or a positive space, inviting engagement and feelings of intimacy. Dreyfus (2001) serves as an exemplar of the first approach as he argues that a lack of both psychological and physical presence contributes to depression and loneliness, saying that

This surprising discovery shows that the Internet user's disembodiment has profound and unexpected effects. Presumably, it affects people in ways that are different from the way most tools do because it can become the main way its users relate to the rest of the world. (2001, pp. 3-4)

This idea resonates with McLuhan's quip that the *medium is the massage*, which means that we shape our mediums and they in turn work over and shape us (McLuhan & Fiore, 1967). Those espousing this perspective might point out the potential anxiety that arises from lack of bodily cues in the online environment and the feeling of vulnerability that might attend online social situations as a result. One example might be that of a blogger who releases regular blog postings and knows people are reading them by viewing the blog's stats, but, since it is not a face-to-face situation in which he or she could read visitors' non-verbal cues, rarely gets comments in response and wonders what people think. Facebook has recently responded to this phenomenon by not only allowing people to comment on nearly everything posted by their friends, but also to click a link to show that they "like" something one of their friends has posted.

In contrast, Wellman states that the space has its "affordances" that can be positive or negative, arguing that online environments can be used to form or maintain either weak or strong ties among individuals (Wellman, 2001). An example of this perspective would point out that while the "commenting anxiety" might exist as a negative side-effect of disembodiment in CMC environments, this same anonymity can also have positive effects: for instance, there might be positive attributes to the blogger not seeing the occasional anonymous naysayer's sneer as he or she happens upon the blog. And at the same time, a Facebook user might re-establish bonds with a high school buddy through their positive responses to their comments and posts, with or without embodiment. This sort of contact may or may not lead to face-to-face contact, and may maintain both weak acquaintanceships and stronger friendships or family ties, as in the blogger who may not receive textual comments on the blog itself but may receive phone comments from close family and friends.

These approaches raise a series of questions: How much control does the medium itself (and the design of the specific online environment) have over the way people perceive this space? What agency do people have within online social spaces for identity (re)construction? And, what happens if the metaphor is mistaken for the phenomena itself? This chapter seeks to address the above questions, highlighting that the polyvocality of this new medium is such that highly varied perspectives can help contribute to understanding different aspects and ethical considerations for online spaces.

This is not a paper on *media effects*; instead, it takes an open and critical theoretical approach to the impacts of the lived-body and textual/social expectations in online communicative spaces, bringing the theories of media ecology and of other philosophical positions to bear on the issue. Briefly, media ecology explores the way in which various technologies, as environments, impact individuals and societies through the biasing of one sensory capacity or experience over another. Neil Postman states that, "Media ecology looks into the matter of how media of communication affect human perception, understanding, feeling, and value; and how our interaction with media facilitates or

impedes our chances of survival…Media ecology is the study of media as environments." *(1970)* Media ecology, then, sees CMC as one factor that may positively or negatively affect our bodily quality of life, depending on what experiences it encourages and favors over others.

This chapter also problematizes questions of disembodiment within CMC using concepts from the phenomenological and critical traditions. Phenomenology offers insight into the nature of embodiment and human engagement. Deconstructionists such as Derrida and practitioners of subaltern studies bring in metaphors such as the palimpsest, and invitational rhetoric advocates and the French philosopher Alain Badiou address other portions of this debate. Bringing in these viewpoints allows for a deeper theoretical understanding of how the self (de)materializes in CMC environments and how various factors affect online agency.

Exploring how world is revealed through our bodily senses sheds light upon the impact of various communicative technologies on human interaction. An exploration of how those characteristics affect the electric word (e.g. email, IM, etc.) and the disembodiment it allows for[2] will highlight the social expectations CMC has inherited from both the visual/face-to-face realm and from the written/printed word. Smaller examples will be given throughout the discussion, but a fuller example of the status-commenting feature on the social networking site Facebook will serve as a more in-depth illustration of these inheritances and issues. We will also explore issues of embodiment via sensory installment (Jonas, 1966; Straus, 1966; Poulet, 1969; Leder, 1990), in addition to literature on the unique spatial and temporal powers of sound/voice and sight (Merleau-Ponty, 1962; Ong, 1967; Ihde, 1983, 1986; Anton, 2001, 2002).

Finally, this project argues for a critical interrogation of our assumptions about the nature of CMC and our potential inability to maintain critical distance from it. Given that many technology enthusiasts envision a time when the human and computer merge (see Kurzweil's *The Singularity is Near,* 2005), the critical distance required to study the impact of disembodied forms of communication on human interaction becomes increasingly difficult to maintain. Experience of the lived-body within CMC environments complicates these questions—if we become no more aware of our technological environments than a fish is of water, are we at risk of losing our distance from which to study the affordances of online communication spaces? A brief overview of some theoretical arguments on presence and absence will serve as a launching point for our discussion.

BACKGROUND: SOME THEORETICAL PERSPECTIVES ON PRESENCE AND ABSENCE

As was mentioned in the introduction, two primary schools within CMC research theorize opposing points of view about the disembodied nature of CMC. The first thinks of text-based CMC environments as engaging fewer senses of the lived-body (therefore providing a lesser impression of social presence and therefore of intimacy) (Mehrabian, 1969; Short, Williams, and Christie, 1976). This view, as noted above, privileges the idea of face-to-face communication and especially the non-verbal communication that comes with it, looking at CMC communication as lacking in cues of social presence as well as some of the key senses that are available face-to-face. This perspective frequently draws attention to absences of these things within CMC in a negative way and is often called the "reduced cues" approach. The second school, largely represented by Walther's hyperpersonal perspective, counterpoints this view, arguing that the very lack of these cues in a primarily text-based electronic medium provides a possibility for a greater feeling of intimacy (Walther, 1996). This perspective highlights the potentially positive side of the lack of negative

non-verbal cues, which may, in face-to-face situations, reduce vulnerability. It posits that these lacks actually may stimulate CMC interactants imaginations, creating a heightened sense of personal relationship—or a hyperpersonal relationship—earlier on than in a face-to-face relationship. It also argues that, while it may take longer, strong ties may be created from solely online contact. These perspectives see presences and absences in different ways, and can be illuminated by their comparisons to the way other theorists of various traditions view presences and absences of the lived-body itself and of communicational signs provided by that lived-body (which is included in what is known as the cultural body, or semiotic body) (Ihde, 1963).

Social presence theorists in CMC approach the lack of non-verbal characteristics in primarily textual online contexts as a problem to be overcome. CMC theorists that view social presence on the web negatively are reminiscent of other approaches viewing absences with a critical eye; as a result, it is useful to compare their view of this absence to the terms and metaphors other such theorists use. The first of these concepts is the deconstructionist approach to absence: which is, as Derrida puts it, that something "in the process of being formed always remains inadequate relative to what it ought to be, divided, disjointed between two forces…carry[ing] in itself an unknowable weight" (Derrida, 1995, p. 29). Social presence theorists approach words in CMC textual environments in a similar way, viewing the words as carrying the "unknowable weight" of the non-verbal signals that accompany face-to-face conversation. A good example of this might be a joking comment delivered through CMC, which without the tonality, appropriate pauses, and smile that would accompany it if delivered face-to-face may be misinterpreted as being a serious comment. Words, and words without the time and revision given to those delivered through more deliberative textual circumstances, may indeed carry more weight than they can handle. The second theory of absence is represented by subaltern studies' metaphor of the palimpsest (e.g., Spivak, 1988; Shetty and Bellamy, 2000), in which critical theorists focus on the violence that is done to the "original" content on a slate that is scratched off and re-used. This metaphor is closely connected to Derrida's identification of one of the meanings of the word "impression" with the metaphor of circumcision, in which something has been cut out to create an absence (Derrida, 1995). Social presence theorists approach web content, not as completely new content, but as content that has been written over the surface of a conversation that could have been different—perhaps richer— if it had taken place in a face-to-face context. Again, to use the example of humor, social presence theorists would compare the joke text not to the way it would be delivered textually, as in a much-revised academic article or a novel, but would see the CMC-delivered version as "written over" the face-to-face version, complete with non-verbals. As such, although they often come from a social psychological background, social presence theorists approach CMC from a position that is axiologically related to these critical theorists' positions. On that level, these metaphors can be productive in dialogue with this social position in drawing attention to the potential for exclusion and violence present in absences such as that of the body.

Those espousing Walther's hyperpersonal perspective, on the other hand, see the very absence of non-verbal signs as potentially productive of strong social presence (Walther, 1996). The hyperpersonal perspective could be seen as imbuing both parties within a CMC dyad with a certain amount of agency, giving weight to their axiological choices and seeing the affordances of the medium not as limitations, but as spaces for possibility. Sullivan (2008) nicely sums up this approach by stating, "The message dictates the medium. And each medium has its place— as long as one is not mistaken for the other." This perspective can be usefully compared with

other theoretical perspectives that view certain kinds of absences not as exclusionary spaces, but as spaces of possibility in which new kinds of connections can fruitfully grow under certain conditions. Feminist rhetoricians Foss and Griffin put forth such a perspective when they propose a more conversational form of rhetoric than the style they view as overly masculine (1995), in which "brevity…[and] ambiguity…leaves open options for the audience and does not confine the terms of the interaction they initiated" (Foss and Griffin, 1995, p. 14). This perspective values the sort of social presence in rhetors that is hospitable in trying not to push their ideas on others, leaving space in a rhetorical situation for the audience to make up their minds about how to respond to the rhetoric that has been presented. Similarly, Walther's hyperpersonal perspective views the absence of non-verbal signs and brevity as leaving space either for each participant to feel ready to disclose or at least a greater sense that disclosure has taken place, leaving room for a relationship to grow in each communicant's mind—a largely imaginary relationship, perhaps, but one that, like face-to-face relationships, may have the option of becoming a deeper relationship in time. One example of this may be someone who discovers, by becoming "Facebook friends" with an acquaintance, that they like the same book. The fact that the person's relative value for that book or their opinion of that book may not be immediately disclosed. In this case, the gap, or lack of information, leaves the other person free to imagine a mutuality that may perhaps not yet be there yet, but may provide room for more exchanges that may lead to a greater sense of "real" relationship. This perspective is easily compared with perspectives of those who love the written word over visual media—for instance, those who prefer the book version to a movie version of a story because they see the absence of visual representations as leaving more scope for imagination within the written form in contrast to the overwhelming nature of visual presentations.

A second theoretical approach that can usefully add to Walther's hyperpersonal perspective is that of French philosopher Alain Badiou, who sees the *evental space* as a place that can be productive of new categories that break out of what is currently seen as legitimate (Badiou, 2005). In Badiou's system of belief, the revolutionary believer may retroactively intervene in a past event, becoming a subject to its truth (a relational example is that of lovers who hold to the truth of the event of falling in love) (Badiou, 2005). Walther's hyperpersonal perspective potentially sees the parties in an online relationship as doing something similar—intervening in the online textually-driven space and holding fidelity to the truth of a relational event formed there, until one may actually exist (Walther, 1996). A similar perspective to this in the world of sociological CMC research is Wellman's perspective, in which he sees possibilities for both strong and weak ties to be maintained or created through new communicational media if individuals choose to do so. He sees possibilities for the affordances of CMC to have negative effects worth watching, but since he sees CMC as one medium within a whole web of relationships that are mediated in different ways, he also sees it as a space that people can choose to use to maintain both strong and weak ties (Wellman, 2001).

The phenomenological view, in its differentiation between the lived-body and the cultural body (Ihde, 1967), further complicates conceptions of social presence and computer-mediated communication. Phenomenologists such as Georges Poulet believe strong social presence can be gained within written environments, even to the point that the reader's mind is temporarily occupied with another's thoughts during the reading process (Poulet, 1969). Walter Ong, on the other hand, argues that voice radically presences the interior of a self to the exterior world, thereby registering the living-present (1967). In this way he could be registered on the side of those with a negative impression of social presence within online environments, where the aural senses are largely absent. As will be seen more fully in the next section, however, his notion is complicated by his view that traces of aural sound can be found within written documents as well as his notion that the intersection of oral traces in written forms can mimic the polyphony of voices in oral society.

This situation, which is certainly present in online environments where the written meets the conversational, dislocates or decenters the presence of a person experiencing such a polyphonic condition, which can cause an intersubjective interiority in which both subjects are caught up in an exterior world. And yet, as Anton (2005b) points out, Ong, who privileged the aural sense, saw a primarily visual approach (even through the visuality of text) to this intersubjective condition as a potential problem: "Sight registers surfaces, which means that of itself it encourages one to consider even persons not as interiors but from the outside [i.e. visually]. Thus persons, too, tend to be thought of somehow as objects" (1967, p. 228). Despite the fact that humans can experience each other in print dominated environments, even those with a sort of "secondary orality" to them can potentially dehumanize the other through a sort of objectification. An example of this point might be that of a new Facebook acquaintance who, glancing over that acquaintance's profile page, might fix the contents of that page in their mind as the unitary identity of that person.

While affirming the possibility of intersubjectivity (or strong social presence) through print environments, this understanding also supports a negative view of social presence in online environments by providing a reasonable explanation for the caveats found in Walther's hyperpersonal perspective (1996) and Wellman's approach to the ability to maintain strong or weak ties through mediated interpersonal networks (Wellman, 2001). These caveats include Walther's finding that while real relationships may develop through online-only contact, initial feelings of close relationship are exaggerated and *true* relationships take longer to develop than those developing primarily through face-to-face interaction (Walther, 1996). These caveats show that the primary theoretical approaches to the disembodiment aspects of CMC today stray far from the medial utopianism toward intersubjectivity found in early approaches to online community (see, for example, Rheingold, 1993).

The implications of Ong's view that more objectification can be found in primarily written environments raises axiological points that are echoed by Poulet's approach to the sort of intersubjectivity that is found in written contexts—the intersubjectivity of a potentially mind-occupying force. Both of these views are reminiscent of the sort of forceful rhetoric the feminists espousing invitational rhetoric were concerned about—a rhetoric that objectifies and occupies its audience, leaving little room for the audience's enactment of agency. All of these perspectives together show some axiological concerns CMC has inherited from both print and face-to-face communication spaces—axiological concerns of which both CMC scholars and users alike should become aware.

These axiological concerns also raise a tension for research CMC environments that ethnographers also regularly address, which concerns how we might create enough distance to engage in useful critique while coming close enough to understand the object of study. This question is particularly complex in qualitative and theoretical studies of the online environment since communicative technologies, like our bodies, recede from focal awareness as we engage in activities through them. And yet one could in fact argue that in order to experience a strong sense of social presence through CMC one must be fully immersed in the experience. This begs the question as to whether one could or should retain a critical distance in studying this medium. On one hand, critics in maintaining distance risks objectifying the Other of the online social groups left at risk by the exteriority of their intersubjectivity—on the other hand, their immersion in these groups leaves them at risk of losing the important sight

of the medium's influence on these groups. One approach that may be usefully employed is the sort of alternate shifting between the "who" and the "how" that Gubrium and Holstein (1997) recommend for ethnography's alternate bracketing of the "who" and the "how". By alternately toggling between an immersion in the intersubjectivity with the group and the place both the medium and social/textual expectations have in creating such intersubjectivity, a researcher may be able to develop a critical understanding of the CMC environment while reducing the possibility that he or she will objectify those who participate in such a medium.

SOCIAL PRESENCE, CONVERSATION, AND THE WRITTEN WORD: CMC'S INHERITANCES

The affordances of social spaces within CMC, particularly those in social networking applications such as Facebook, are created by a complex set of factors that contribute to the intertwining of the dialogic perspectives just discussed. Some of these affordances are provided by the medium themselves, whereas others are created by the particular environment surrounding the experiencing of content in that medium. Other factors are created by other communication genres (such as the conversation) and still others are inherited from user and developer expectations created by previous media, their applications, and their usages. In this section we will focus on the unique interbreeding (and often clashing) of expectations that occur in social networking sites because of their strong connections both to the interpersonal social world and its communicative genres—particularly the oral tradition and the conversational genre—and to the (primarily mass-mediated) world of the written media.

A consideration of media ecologists such as Walter Ong, who sees traces of oral culture in the written world, is helpful for theorizing the overlaps that happen when the oral meets the written. While on one hand Ong argues that the spoken word reveals presence like no other form of language can, he also argues that it was the development of writing and print that allowed for enough distance from oneself to begin contemplating the individual 'I' in the first place. Furthermore, Ong, much like McLuhan, states that the new orality that has formed within our electric mediums is radically reopening us to others on a global scale (Ong, 1971, p. 20). As with writing, there are residual traces of primary orality within the electronic word, and readers often experience a certain tonality when experiencing it. The existence of these traces, along with writing styles adapted to the absence of non-verbals that has always been present in written texts, complicates the question of social presence in electronic texts. These "intersection of traces" that are characteristic of text is similar to the "polyphony of voices" that ride throughout the oral word, which means that secondary orality is "divided between two forces" (Derrida, 2001), but is also a new category in its own right. This intertwining of orality with textuality makes for complexities to consider that are further complicated by John Peter's contention that all communication, whether face-to-face or through media, is more likely to follow a mass-mediated pattern, in which only a few seeds are likely to take root, than the ideal of unmediated dialogue championed by Socrates in Plato's *Phaedrus*. He argues that we should strive to have reflexive dialogue with ourselves and expect a dissemination pattern when it comes to others. (Peters, 1999)

McLuhan and Farrell both emphasize the participatory co-authorship the internet inherited from oral social life. McLuhan believed the spoken word, as aurally configured, is far more involving and participatory by nature; far more *hot* than its *cool* successor the written, and subsequently, the electric words. "A hot medium is one that extends one single sense in "high definition" (larger amounts of data). "Hot media

[written words, photographs, radio, etc.] are low in participation, and cold media [spoken word, television, internet, etc.] are high in participation or completion by the audience" (McLuhan, 1964). Farrell agreed with this point in his essay called "Narrative in Natural Discourse: On Conversation and Rhetoric," in which he argues that because it is not pre-planned, conversational forms are more co-authored than artistic or rhetorical types of communications (Farrell, 1985).

Farrell also argues that conversation is different from written text in that it is seen to be perishable. He also distinguishes the conversational style as one in which: 1.) the conversational outcome is not planned or known in advance, but is emergent in nature, unlike the written style in the extreme (he places the rhetorical style between the two, as partly planned but with leaving the audience to finish out the outcome by implementing what they've been persuaded to do); and 2.) unlike in mass-mediated narratives, there is an "informal expectation that communication is somehow additive in significance" within and between conversations, allowing and requiring disclosure to develop gradually and developmentally across conversational bits but can't be easily forced to pick up again exactly where the last conversation left off. (Farrell, 1985).

As was mentioned earlier, Ong and other media ecologists view text as promoting objectivity in a negative sense. This does not, however, mean that all inheritances of written culture are negative for him. The reflective distance text allows for provides "intensified perspective and the fixed point of view...Socially, the typographic extension of man brought in nationalism, industrialism, mass markets, and universal literacy and education" (1964, p. 157). Thus, the rise of wide-spread literacy, as he sees it, is both bane and boon. This space for reflection, as Walther and others point out, does not preclude space for social presence to develop—in fact, as advocates of online intersubjectivity point out, it may remove negative cues present in face-to-face dominant relationships, potentially democratizing the web's textual relationships by allowing space for the marginalized to speak up (Rheingold, 1993). The fact that this exteriorization of an interiority is not perishable, as with conversation, makes the author, as Ong points out, more vulnerable, which may either be exploited by the audience members or actually promote a feeling of protectiveness or closeness on the part of the audience, which view would promote the idea of social presence through textual forms. Either way, John Peters argues that the exteriorization of the self present in written forms has its analog in oral cultures, in which verbal exteriorization had the goal of "writing on the…soul" of one's hearers—a goal which carried a similar vulnerability, if not in the same way (Peters, 1999, p. 48).

Extending insights on the discursive and rhetorical constructions of online identities, Nakamura (2002; 2008) tracks the many ways that race is "cybertyped" within the textual and graphical confines of the Internet. For example, in chat rooms and in online gaming environments users often create characters (*avatars*) for use in these communities. When representing their embodied selves they are performing online versions that are both raced and gendered (2002). When users employ avatars that are raced other than their embodied self, a mode of "identity tourism" takes place whereby more stereotypical versions of race are performed, which inevitably play off of and perpetuate long standing racial myths (pp. 38-39). In highlighting both the medium and the content Nakamura (2008) directs us to the multifaceted processes of identity formation and interrogation online, particularly as they arise though gender, race, and class identities. She states,

[The Internet] is an intensely active, productive space of visual signification where these differences are intensified, modulated, reiterated, and challenged by former objects of interactivity, whose subjectivity is expressed by their negotiations of the shifting terrain of identity, whose

seismic adjustments are partly driven by their own participations within it, the result of several major cultural shifts and a digital technology industry that both compels and confounds vision. (Nakamura, 2008, p. 34)

In other words, without voice these captured electric words (via CMC) that interpolate our identities provide an easy reference, but could also potentially impress upon us a kind of objectivity of the other and reinforce or reproduce the stereotypes generated in the offline world.

The asynchronous nature of textual forms is another inheritance from the world of written forms that has been treated in a variety of ways (e.g., Wise, Hamman, & Thorson, 2006; Haythornthwaite, Kazmer, Robins, & Shoemaker, 2000). McLuhan writes that electric mediums such as the radio, television, cellular technology, and the Internet, offer the possibility of experiencing distant people and locations in "real-time," which highlights his belief that asynchronous technologies increase the possibility of homogenization of the "Other." The instantaneous speed of electric technology, as he saw it, created an enormous vacuum or implosion of our intentional powers. Consciousness was again situated within the *now* of time and space (McLuhan, 1969). McLuhan saw that this would have a tremendous impact on cultural relations, but also believed that this contraction of time and space came with a price. He was concerned that individuals, when brought into such close proximity, may have the potential for both individual and large-scale violence.

While managing one's face (Goffman, 1967) in face-to-face interaction is accomplished more through situational and embodied cues/contexts, one's online face is, in a sense, already and literally *spelled* out. For example, when one goes to a website to chat with others one enters a space where general parameters may be already somewhat defined by the information that has already been captured in text on that web page. To exist online is to be potentially *interpolated* by the discourse and URL of the webpage one communicates on/through (Althusser, 1971). McLuhan was particularly concerned about the homogenization this interpolation may bring about. He saw this homogenization as a direct result of electric mediums contracting social and cultural environments. Critics following this line of thinking argue that the resources people have at their disposal for crafting their online personas are largely funded by objectified and homogenized cultural standards.

Others argue that online environments may counteract this homogenization by providing a social interaction that allow for finely nuanced crafting of self and "spelled out" perceptions of others, as well as for allowing disclosure of individualized and/or culture-specific responses to global phenomena (e.g., Rheingold, 1993). Through the use of pseudonyms, avatars, and publication of a variety of details about themselves, members of online communities may craft their own narratives about who they are as never before (Preece, 2000). Even without the pseudonyms, online disclosure may provide contextual information about a person that their offline friends and family may have never thought to ask. These disclosures, while they may become objectified, may also act as a springboard to further conversations which may create new ties or deepen existing ties (Wellman, 2001). Others say that the space for these globalized conversations is to some as likely to diversify opinions as it is to homogenize them, as each subgroup of each culture adapts the global ideas in their own way (Hannerz, 2002; Appadurai, 2002; Gupta and Ferguson, 1997).

Whether this approximation is considered to be healthy or unhealthy or a mix of the two, the situation that results from the mixture of the interpersonal and social dimensions with the mass-mediated written style is very similar to the dialogic heteroglossia Bakhtin describes in the novel genre, resulting in a seemingly-paradoxical state: "alongside verbal-ideological centralization and unification, the uninterrupted processes of decentralization and disunification go forward" (Bakhtin, 1981, p. 272). These inheritances create a situation in which expectations of those who come to it are constantly shifting between those of the reader (a mass media consumer, primarily), those of the author/rhetorician (the mass media producer), and those of the conversation partner or creator of invitational rhetoric. CMC spaces, having inherited these expectations, are constrained by all of them, and yet it also allows for all of these roles at once. It may be, in fact, as we propose, this very choice among these roles that may in part promote the feelings of strong or weak social presence through CMC—if author/reader roles or conversant/conversant roles meet corresponding user's expectations, high social presence may be felt, corresponding to Bakhtin's description of "unification," whereas if these pairs are disjoined, low social presence may be felt, corresponding to Bakhtin's description of "disunification" (1981, p. 272).

THE FACEBOOK STATUS: "WHAT'S ON YOUR MIND?"

The Facebook status is an exemplar of a merging of the mass-mediated and the conversational. Similar to the increasingly popular Twitter platform, the Facebook status feature provides its users a finite number of characters to express some affect or make general statements. A typical status message might comment on one's mood, express excitement regarding one's accomplishments, show gratitude for various well wishes, describe one's current or future activities, or even make political statements. In short, it has and can potentially communicate *anything*. Once entered the sentence is published to that person's profile and often appears on their friends' homepages as a short piece of mass-mediated communication. This status may then become conversational fodder in an offline conversation; increasingly, however, the ability for friends to comment directly within Facebook in response to their friends' statuses, or even with one click to express approval of them by saying they "like" them, has turned the textual area immediately surrounding this mass-mediated piece of textual information into a conversational space as well. Quite often long conversational threads ensue based on reactions and responses to a user's status. What begins as a "To whom it may concern," transforms into an open-ended dialogue that can include anyone within your "friend" network. Combined with the speed and mobility of current digital technology the spontaneity and creativity involved in these conversations can be exceedingly fulfilling. In short, the orality of the informal responses is heightened not only by their responsive nature, but also by the relational nature of these responses, which induces a style that mimics the auditory style of face-to-face conversation.

The status is thus a poignant example of Ong's secondary orality, in which conversation and written textuality combine in fascinating ways. Ong's comment that traces of orality remain in textual matter is particularly relevant to the style of writing available in these responses, which as previously mentioned are often informal and conversational in tone. Interestingly, however, the semi-public nature of the responses, which are often available to friends of the Facebook user who may or may not know each other, means that the tonalities present in the responses (humorous, ironic, etc.) may be understood by the Facebook user better than by other readers of the responses.

Like text, the status and its associated conversational history are retained: even after a new status acts as a palimpsest for the previous status, the older status (unless deleted by its author) remains on the author's profile page for any of their friends to refer to. However, like conversation, however, the status is ultimately perishable—after enough other statuses and events have "pushed it down" the profile page far enough, Facebook eventually pushes it to a secondary page, then deletes it. This negotiation between the expectations of face-to-face conversations and the conventions of written text again creates interesting situations. The profile owner has the option to delete their own statuses or any responses to it at any time, but the respondents only have the authority to delete their own comments on others' statuses.

The asynchronous nature of this conversation inherited from standard written forms provides some interesting twists on this situation. While in face-to-face conversations some threads get picked up and others dropped, the nature of face-to-face conversations means that many conversational threads are likely to receive some sort of response from the other conversational partners. The fact that this conversation takes place in mass-mediated text, however, introduces a lesser expectation of response to these conversations. The hybrid created of this expectation along with those of face-to-face conversation may leave either the author of the status or of responses feeling as though they have disclosed but feeling particularly vulnerable without having received a response—or, on the other hand, could have received an instantaneous response that was either negative or made them feel crowded because they had expected more space.

FUTURE STUDIES OF RELATIONAL MANAGEMENT IN CMC

Throughout this chapter we have addressed notions of online identity formation and some of the difficulties inherent in studying such processes as a base for deepening two dialogic threads about (dis) embodiment and CMC, ultimately showing that both threads apply within this complex medium. While admittedly falling on slightly different sides of the issue, both authors recognize the complexities and subtleties of relational formation and management within an online environment. What appears evident is that given the unique interplay of the oral, textual, and graphic modes of representation, the study of online relationships requires its own manner of digital exegesis. For better or ill these media have so permeated our interpersonal environments that the study of CMC, whether approached from those who wish to analyze or apply its lessons, can no longer merely be seen as a scholarly point of curiosity but rather should be approached from an ethical perspective. The above points are meant to provide a starting point for such inquiries, showing that both perspectives are applicable when one considers that they are tied to expectations social CMC contexts inherit from both the textual and face-to-face worlds of social interactions.

Our experiences of each other, including our race, gender, and class, have inevitably been altered by the modes and means through which we communicate. And, as was illustrated through the Facebook status example, each new media used for communication inherits expectations from previous media and social situations. Thus, given the ubiquity and mobility of digital communicative technologies, future research must take into consideration the ways that our media environments uniquely reconfigure the process of relational formation and maintenance. While analysis of content has taken great strides in this direction, media ecology theory contributes to the conversation through its emphasis on the ways the medium itself reorganizes the human sensorium and subsequently, our modes of engaging others. Furthermore, insights from the phenomenological, critical-rhetorical, and philosophical traditions mixed with those help enrich existing empirical CMC theory, providing CMC scholars with a powerful theoretical model from which to explore the axiological issues caught up in the interplay of the body, relationship formation and maintenance, and communicative technologies.

CONCLUSION

This chapter was created through a heteroglossic context similar to the one found in CMC. We started this project through textual conversations using the messaging feature on Facebook and then met in person to discuss its ideas before once again using the critical distance text provides to write this chapter. This critical distance will then likely be disseminated in book format. After that, who knows? Perhaps the book will be scanned and appear in computer-mediated contexts, or its contents will be responded to in a conference presentation or discussed in a classroom. No matter what happens, the traces of the oral, the written, and computer-mediated contexts of its composition will remain in all the representations of this discussion, proving that our interactions with various communication media causes them to overlap with one another in new and intriguing ways. We find that it takes a complex mixture of theoretical understandings to understand the social presence implications of such heteroglossic conditions, and therefore we hope we have added useful bits to deepen the theoretical underpinnings of social presence theory as applied to computer-mediated communication contexts.

REFERENCES

Althusser, L. (1971). Ideology and ideological state apparatuses (B. Brewster, Trans.). Lenin and Philosophy, and other Essays. New York: Monthly Review Press.

Anton, C. (2001). *Selfhood and authenticity*. Albany, New York: State University of New York Press.

Anton, C. (2002). Discourse as Care: A Phenomenological Consideration of Spatiality and Temporality. *Human Studies*, *25*, 185–205. doi:10.1023/A:1015552526781

Anton, C. (2005). Early western writing, sensory modalities, and modern alphabetic literacy: On the origins of representational theorizing. *Explorations in Media Ecology: The Journal of the Media Ecology Association, 4*(2), 99–122.

Anton, C. (2005). Presence and interiority: Walter Ong's contributions to a diachronic phenomenology of voice. In Farrell, T. J., & Soukup, P. (Eds.), *Ong and media ecology: Essays in communication, composition, and literary studies*. Hampton Press.

Appadurai, A. (2002). Disjuncture and difference in the global cultural economy. In Xavier Inda, J., & Rosaldo, R. (Eds.), *The anthropology of globalization: A reader* (pp. 46–64). Malden, MA: Blackwell Publishers.

Badiou, A. (2005). *Being and event*. New York: Continuum.

Bakhtin, M. M. (1981). *The dialogic imagination* (pp. 259–300). (Emerson, C., & Holquist, M., Trans.). Austin, TX: University of Texas Press.

Birnie, S. A., & Horvath, P. (2002). Psychological Predictors of Internet Social Communication. *Journal of Computer-Mediated Communication, 7*(4). Retrieved May 14, 2009, from http://jcmc.indiana.edu/vol7/issue4/horvath.html

Buber, M. (1957). Elements of the interhuman. *Psychiatry, 120*, 105–113.

Carpenter, E. (1973). *Oh, what a blow that phantom gave me!* New York: Bantam Books.

Cho, H., Trier, M., & Kim, E. (2005). The Use of Instant Messaging in Working Relationship Development: A Case Study. *Journal of Computer-Mediated Communication, 10*(4), 17.

Dreyfus, H. L. (2001). *On the Internet*. New York: Routledge.

Foss, S. K., & Griffin, C. L. (1995). Beyond persuasion: A proposal for an invitational rhetoric. *Communication Monographs, 62*, 2–18. doi:10.1080/03637759509376345

Goffman, E. (1967). *Interaction ritual: Essays in face-to-face behavior*. Chicago: Aldine Pub. Co.

Gubrium, J. F., & Holstein, J. A. (1997). *The new language of qualitative method*. New York: Oxford University Press.

Gupta, A., & Ferguson, J. (1997). Beyond "culture": Space, identity, and the politics of difference. In Gupta, A., & Ferguson, J. (Eds.), *Culture, Power, Place: Explorations in Critical Anthropology* (pp. 33–51). Durham, NC: Duke University Press.

Hannerz, U. (2002). Notes on the global ecumene. In (J. X. Inda and R, Rosaldo, Eds.), The anthropology of globalization: A reader (pp. 37-45). Malden, MA: Blackwell Publishers.

Haythornthwaite, C., Kazmer, M., Robins, J., & Shoemaker, S. (2000). Community development among distance learners: Temporal and technological dimensions. *Journal of Computer-Mediated Communication, 6*(1).

Hian, L. B., Chuan, S. L., Trevor, T. M. K., & Detenber, B. H. (2004). Getting to Know You: Exploring the Development of Relational Intimacy in Computer-mediated Communication. *Journal of Computer-Mediated Communication, 9*(3). Retrieved May 14, 2009, from http://jcmc.indiana.edu/vol9/issue3/detenber.html

Hu, Y., Wood, J. F., Smith, V., & Westbrook, N. (2004). Friendships through IM: Examining the Relationship between Instant Messaging and Intimacy. *Journal of Computer-Mediated Communication, 10*(1), Article 6.

Ihde, D. (1983). *Existential technics*. Albany, NY: State University of New York Press.

Ihde, D. (1986). A phenomenology of voice. In *Consequences of phenomenology* (pp. 27–48). Albany, NY: State University of New York Press.

Jonas, H. (1966). *The phenomenon of life*. New York: Dell Publishing Co., Inc.

Kavanaugh, A., Carroll, J. M., Rosson, M. B., Zin, T. T., & Reese, D. D. (2005). Community Networks: Where Offline Communities Meet Online. *Journal of Computer-Mediated Communication, 10*(4), article 3.

Kim, H., Kim, G. J., Park, H. W., & Rice, R. E. (2007). Configurations of Relationships in Different Media: FtF, Email, Instant Messenger, Mobile Phone, and SMS. *Journal of Computer-Mediated Communication, 12*(4), article 3.

Kurzweil, R. (2005). *The singularity is near: When humans transcend biology*. New York: Viking.

Lakoff, G., & Johnson, M. (1980). *Metaphors we live by*. Chicago: The University of Chicago Press.

Leder, D. (1990). *The absent body*. Chicago: The University of Chicago Press.

Lombard, M., & Ditton, T. (1997). At the heart of it all: The concept of presence. *Journal of Computer-Mediated Communication, 3*(2). Retrieved May 14, 2009, from http://jcmc.indiana.edu/vol3/issue2/lombard.html

McKerrow, R. E. (1989, June). Critical rhetoric: Theory and praxis. *Communication Monographs*, 56.

McLuhan, M. (1964). *Understanding media: The extensions of man*. Cambridge, MA: The M.I.T. Press.

McLuhan, M., & Fiore, Q. (1967). *The medium is the massage: An inventory of effects*. New York: Bantam Books.

Merleau-Ponty, M. (1962). *Phenomenology of perception* (Smith, C., Trans.). London: Routledge & Paul.

Merleau-Ponty, M. (1969). *The visible and the invisible*. Evanston, IL: Northwestern University Press.

Min, S. (2007). Online vs. Face-to-Face Deliberation: Effects on Civic Engagement. *Journal of Computer-Mediated Communication, 12*(4), 11. doi:10.1111/j.1083-6101.2007.00377.x

Nakamura, L. (2002). *Cybertypes: race, ethnicity, and identity on the Internet*. New York: Routledge.

Nakamura, L. (2008). *Digitizing race: Visual cultures of the internet*. Minneapolis, MN: University of Minnesota Press.

Nordon, E. (1969). The Playboy Interview: Marshall McLuhan. *Playboy*. Retrieved December 14, 2005, from www.vcsun.org/~battias/class/454/txt/mclpb.html

Nowak, K. L., Watt, J., & Walther, J. B. (2005). The Influence of Synchrony and Sensory Modality on the Person Perception Process in Computer-Mediated Groups. *Journal of Computer-Mediated Communication, 10*(3), article 3.

Ong, W. J. (1967). *The presence of the word: Some prolegomena for cultural and religious history*. New Haven, CT: Yale University Press.

Ong, W. J. (2002). Orality and literacy: The technologizing of the word (2nd ed.). New York: Routledge.Peters, J. D. (1999). Speaking into the Air: A History of the Idea of Communication. Chicago: University of Chicago Press.

Poulet, G. (1969). Phenomenology of reading. *New Literary History, 1*(1), 53–68. doi:10.2307/468372

Preece, J. (2000). *Online communities: Designing usability and supporting sociability*. Hoboken, NJ: Wiley.

Rheingold, H. (1993). *The virtual community: homesteading on the electronic frontier*. New York: HarperPerennial.

Shetty, S., & Bellamy, E. J. (2000). Postcolonialism's archive fever. *Diacritics, 30*(1), 25–48.

Short, J. A., Williams, E., & Christie, B. (1976). *The social psychology of telecommunications*. Hoboken, NJ: Wiley.

Sohn, D., & Lee, B. (2005). Dimensions of Interactivity: Differential Effects of Social and Psychological Factors. *Journal of Computer-Mediated Communication, 10*(3), article 6.

Spivak, G. C. (1988). Can the subaltern speak? In C. Nelson and L. Grossman, (eds.) Marxism and the interpretation of culture (p. 271-313). Urbana, IL: University of Illinois Press.

Straus, E. W. (1966). *Phenomenological psychology* (Eng, E., Trans.). New York: Basic Books INC.

Sullivan, A. (2008). Why I blog. *The Atlantic*, (Nov. 2008). Retrieved Nov. 1, 2008, from http://www.theatlantic.com/doc/200811/andrew-sullivan-why-i-blog/4

Walther, J. B. (1996). Computer-mediated communication: Impersonal, interpersonal, and hyperpersonal interaction. *Communication Research, 23*(26).

Watts, S. A. (2007). Evaluative Feedback: Perspectives on Media Effects. *Journal of Computer-Mediated Communication, 12*(2), article 3.

Wellman, B. (2001). Physical place and cyber place: the rise of personalized networks. *International Journal of Urban and Regional Research, 25*(2), 227–252. doi:10.1111/1468-2427.00309

Wise, K., Hamman, B., & Thorson, K. (2006). Moderation, response rate, and message interactivity: Features of online communities and their effects on intent to participate. *Journal of Computer-Mediated Communication, 12*(1), article 2. Retrieved (n.d.), from http://jcmc.indiana.edu/vol12/issue1/wise.html

ADDITIONAL READING

Anton, C. (2005). Early Western Writing, Sensory Modalities, and Modern Alphabetic Literacy: On the origins of representational theorizing. *Explorations in Media Ecology: The Journal of the Media Ecology Association, 4*(2), 99–122.

Barnes, S. B. (2001). *Online Connections: Internet interpersonal relationships*. Cresskill, NJ: Hampton Press.

Barnes, S. B. (2003). *Computer-mediated communication: Human-to-human communicaton across the Internet*. Boston: Allyn & Bacon.

Bolter, J. D. (1999). *Remediation: Understanding new media*. Cambridge, MA: MIT Press.

Bolter, J. D. (2001). *Writing space: Computers, hypertext, and the remediation of print* (2nd ed.). Mahwah, NJ: Lawrence Erlbaum Associates.

Carey, J. W. (1989). *Communication as culture: Essays on media and society*. Boston: Unwin Hyman.

Carpenter, E. (1973). *Oh, what a blow that phantom gave me!* New York: Holt, Rinehart & Winston.

Cheseboro, J. W., & Bonsall, D. G. (1989). *Computer-mediated communication: Human relationships in a computerized world*. Tuscaloosa, AL: University of Alabama Press.

Crowley, D. J., & Heyer, P. (Eds.). (2003). *Communication in history: Technology, culture, society* (4th ed.). Boston: Allyn & Bacon.

Gergen, K. J. (1991). *The saturated self: Dilemmas of identity in contemporary life*. New York: BasicBooks.

Goffman, E. (1959). *The presentation of self in everyday life*. Garden City, NY: Anchor Books.

Goffman, E. (1967). *Interaction ritual: Essays on face-to-face behavior*. Garden City, NY: Anchor Books.

Heim, M. (1987). *Electric language: A philosophical study of word processing*. New Haven, CT: Yale University Press.

Kolko, B. E., Nakamura, L., & Rodman, G., B. (2000). Race in cyberspace. New York and London: Routledge.

Ong, W. J. (1967). *The presence of the word: Some prolegomena for cultural and religious history*. New Haven, CT: Yale University Press.

Ong, W. J. (2002). *Orality and literacy: The technologizing of the word* (2nd ed.). New York: Routledge.

Peters, J. D. (1999). *Speaking into the air: A history of the idea of communication*. Chicago: University of Chicago Press.

Preece, J. (2000). *Online communities: Designing usability and supporting sociability*. Hoboken, NJ: Wiley.

Turkle, S. (1997). *Life on the screen: Identity in the age of the internet*. New York: Simon & Schuster.

ENDNOTES

[1.] This debate, while it has been raised in connection with what we think of as "new media," is not a new one - its roots go back at least as far as Socrates' concerns about written media. John Peters, in his book Speaking into the Air (1999), eloquently lays out Socrates' position, which closely resembles that of the social presence theorists, against that of Jesus', which aligns better with that of the hyperpersonal perspective.

[2] When we refer to disembodiment, we do not mean that our bodies are actually absent during any communication practices—they are there, of course, no matter the medium. We primarily refer to the unawareness of both communication parties of the other communicants' non-verbals as they communicate through certain communication media. For example, touch is accessible to each person while two people are communicating electronically, but even their bodies are spatially near to one another at the time, they cannot use the physical sense of touch to communicate to each other via electronic media. Another sense of this term as we use it is in the phenomenological sense that the body recedes from focal awareness as it attends those things revealed by the senses.

Chapter 4
Disclosure Decisions in Existing Relationships Online:
Exploring Motivations for CMC Channel Choice

Kathryn Greene
Rutgers University, USA

Kate Magsamen-Conrad
Rutgers University, USA

ABSTRACT

Use of mediated channels of communication, such as email and instant messenger, is rapidly increasing, especially with adolescents and college-aged populations. This increase may alter interpersonal relationship maintenance strategies and communication patterns. The role of mediated channels of communication in some types of relationship initiation is well documented however, research investigating use within existing relationships is more limited. Self-disclosure is an important part of relationship maintenance, both in the initial stages of development as well as in existing relationships. This chapter explores motivations for disclosure through computer mediated communication (CMC) in pre-existing relationships and describes theoretical perspectives to advance examination of this area. Examples presented indicate four primary motivations for disclose through computer mediated communication: self, other, relationship, and situational/environmental. Further, we propose several codes within each primary reason, many of which diverged from traditional motivations for FtF disclosure. Implications and future directions for interpersonal CMC research are discussed.

DOI: 10.4018/978-1-61520-827-2.ch004

INTRODUCTION

Non face-to-face (FtF) channels of communication are rapidly increasing in use and popularity (Pew Internet.org). This increase in the use of technology requires changes in the way interpersonal discourse is realized in computer-mediated communication (CMC) and also requires shifts in conceptualizations of interpersonal communication more broadly (cf. Bargh & McKenna, 2004). Much initial interpersonal CMC research focused on the development of relationships through CMC (e.g., Ellison, Heino, & Gibbs, 2006; Gibbs, Ellison, & Heino, 2006; Hian, Chuan, Trevor, & Detenber, 2004; Parks & Floyd, 1996; Whitty & Gavin, 2001) or use of CMC in organizations/business relationships (e.g., Baltes, Dickson, Sherman, Bauer, & LaGanke, 2002; Soukup, 2000) rather than use of CMC in maintenance of existing personal relationships. Given the extent of changes in CMC, we need to analyze how people are utilizing CMC to manage personal relationships. This chapter adapts models and frameworks of interpersonal communication to a CMC context to investigate how people report using CMC to disclose in existing relationships. The chapter will explore why participants report choosing CMC to share private information. By scrutinizing how individuals manage personal and private information, the chapter provides insight into interpersonal communication practices online. We begin with the increase in CMC use before turning to definitions of disclosure and reasons for using CMC disclosure.

BACKGROUND

Even 20 years ago, CMC use was not widespread outside of industry, yet today CMC is an integral part of how many people maintain personal relationships. Pew Internet (2007) reported that 62% of US adults communicated with family and friends using the Internet everyday or multiple times a week, compared to 38% who communicated via Internet several times a month or less. Many people use their home internet connection predominantly for interpersonal communication (Kraut, Mukhopadhyay, Szczypula, Kiesler, & Scherlis, 2000). People are also using mediated communication channels to seek information about others, which may be related to relationship maintenance (Westerman, Der Heide, Klein, & Walther, 2008). Finally, people are using email to maintain relationships in ways similar to FtF communication (Johnson, Haigh, Becker, Craig, & Wigley, 2008). One crucial feature of this relational maintenance is disclosing information online, and we turn next to definitions and description of self-disclosure literature.

There are several conceptualizations of self-disclosure, but self-disclosure is most commonly defined and studied as a voluntary, deliberate, intentional, and honest process (see Derlega, Metts, Petronio, & Margulis, 1993). We define self-disclosure as an interpersonal interaction where one person deliberately shares private information (including thoughts, feelings, and experiences) of a personal nature with another person (Derlega et al., 1993). This definition not equivalent to some researchers who equate disclosure with "openness." Self-disclosure is often, but not always, related to positive outcomes such as health and social support. For example, researchers have found that verbally discussing or writing about traumatic or upsetting life experiences (compared to trivial events) is associated with lower illness rates (Pennebaker & O'Heeron, 1984), fewer physician visits (Pennebaker, Colder, & Sharp, 1990; Pennebaker, Kiecolt-Glaser, & Glaser, 1988), less immune dysfunction (Pennebaker et al., 1988), and decreased severity of physical symptoms (Kelley, Lumley, & Leisen, 1997). These findings have been supported in aggregate by meta-analyses (Smyth, 1999), although the effect sizes are small and there are many moderators (Frattaroli, 2006). Self-disclosure of distressing information is often linked to catharsis (Kelly, Klusas, von Weiss, &

Kenny, 2001; Pennebaker, 1983). Self-disclosure may also provide an opportunity for the discloser to receive social support from others.

Many studies investigate the function of self-disclosure in relationship development, maintenance, and deterioration (see Derlega et al., 1993; Greene, Derlega, & Mathews, 2006; Derlega, Winstead, & Greene, 2008), although these studies have generally not incorporated CMC. Self-disclosure is often used to accelerate relationship development and to foster intimacy (Gilbert, 1976). This research tends focuses on disclosure in FtF interactions, implicitly assuming FtF communication as the primary (or only) communication channel. New/emerging technologies challenge this assumption and require reconceptualization of channels of communication and the process of disclosure in ongoing relationship maintenance. Communication channel may serve an important function in both information management and impression management.

At one time, studies comparing telephone and FtF interactions found no difference in the amount of self-disclosure (Janofsky, 1970) or accuracy of social perception (Williams, 1977). In the early nineties, however, researchers began to recognize distinct differences between FtF communication and non-FtF communication. For example, Poole, Shannon, and DeSanctis (1992) claimed that FtF communication is the most natural medium of communication, whereas artificial media are slower, more taxing, and more likely to generate annoyance. Drotlet and Morris (2000) argued that FtF contact is a facilitator of mutual cooperation. They refer anecdotally to the propensity for diplomats and business negotiators to travel in order to communicate FtF, now often replaced by various forms of technology including video conferencing. Other studies indicated that managers used to prefer FtF communication (e.g., Johansen, Vallee, & Vian, 1979; Mintzberg, 1980). Research also reports better outcomes in experiments when negotiators communicate FtF rather than in writing (e.g., Sheffield, 1989; Valley, Moag, & Bazerman, 1998).

People may self-disclose more online than in other contexts (e.g., Parks & Floyd, 1996; Reingold, 1993; Tidwell & Walther, 2002; Wallace, 1999; Wilkins, 1991), yet the authenticity of this increased disclosure may be questioned as people present themselves strategically (e.g., Ellison et al., 2006; Walther, 1996). We also know little about the motivations for choosing CMC to disclose in relationships. Researchers generally attribute the popularity of online communication to two features, visual anonymity and text only (non-verbal) channel (Joinson, 2001). Some research suggests that, due to these two factors, CMC is considered task oriented, low in socio-emotional content, and therefore lacks the opulence of FtF communication (Kinney & Dennis, 1994; Rice & Love, 1987; Walther, 1995). The relative anonymity of some online interactions may reduce perceptions of the risks inherent in self-disclosure, and potential disclosers may be less fearful of potential condemnation or rejection (McKenna & Bargh, 1998, 2000). For example, medical patients tend to report more symptoms and undesirable behaviors in computer mediated interviews compared to FtF interviews (Greist, Klein, & VanCura, 1973; see also Ferriter, 1993; Robinson & West, 1992). However, evidence of higher levels of self-disclosure within CMC also extends to interpersonal relationships unaffected by visual anonymity, such as known partners communicating electronically (Joinson, 2001). We turn next to several theories of disclosure and privacy that can assist with exploring CMC disclosure choices.

Relevant Theories of Disclosure and Information Management

The following section will review three prominent theories in the disclosure literature and provide a brief overview of each theory or framework, paying special attention to how the theory incorporates CMC or could be used to theorize about CMC choices for disclosing in established relationships. The theories reviewed in this section are Communication Privacy Management theory (Petronio, 2002), Disclosure Decision-Making Model (Greene, 2009), and the Decision Making Model of Self-Disclosure (Greene et al., 2006).

Communication privacy management. Communication Privacy Management Theory (CPM; Petronio, 2002) is a dialectic theory that explains how people regulate and control private information in relationships through a rule-based management system. CPM views privacy and disclosure as tensions in a dialectic. According to Petronio (2002), people attempt to exert control over private information for two main reasons. First, they feel they have the right to "own" or control that information including information sent via email. Second, revealing information contributes to feelings of vulnerability, and by controlling that information individuals may feel less vulnerable. The CPM framework does argue that technology can affect privacy, mostly through violations (e.g., monitoring email or electronic medical records), but this conceptualization is less focused on voluntary disclosure decision-making.

CPM does not explicitly theorize about channel or channel choice in the theory except in terms of privacy violations (not disclosure decisions), but CPM has been applied to mediated communication. Metzger (2007) applied CPM to understand the tension between information disclosure and privacy within e-commerce relationships. Results extended CPM into the domain of CMC by demonstrating that "similar kinds of balancing dynamics appear to operate in the Web environment as they do in face-to-face situations" (Metzger, 2007, p. 354). Thus, CPM is a broad framework that has been applied primarily to FtF disclosure and emphasizes dialectical tensions of disclosure/privacy management or risks/rewards; to date, CPM has not been applied to or tested with use of CMC existing relationships.

Disclosure decision-making model. The Disclosure Decision-Making Model (DD-MM, Greene, 2009) explains the decision-making

process surrounding disclosure of information. Because disclosure involves risk and contributes to disclosers' feelings of vulnerability (T. Afifi, Olson, & Armstrong, 2005), individuals make deliberate choices about the persons with whom they choose to share their private/personal information. Both the DD-MM and the Model of disclosure decision making (Greene et al., 2006, see next section) explicate how many features are considered when a potential discloser assesses information and recipients for possible sharing, including sharing online.

The DD-MM (Greene, 2009) elucidates a process prior to the disclosure enactment including both direct and indirect effects. The first part of this process is to assess the information, followed by an evaluation of a potential receiver (including relational quality and anticipated response), and finally exploration of perceived disclosure efficacy in predicting willingness to disclose. The DD-MM argues that disclosures are encouraged or discouraged by the relative evaluation of these factors. The DD-MM (Greene, 2009) is particularly relevant to the process of making health disclosure decisions, especially disclosure of negatively valenced information.

Channel choice is especially important once decision to disclose has been reached. The DD-MM argues that message enactment includes the discloser planning the setting, timing, channel/mode, and the message features, which may also include practice or rehearsal. The choice of disclosure channel, for example email or IM rather than FtF, maybe be influenced by assessment of information, receiver, or perceived efficacy. The only test of the DD-MM to date indicates that the process and variables proposed do represent the disclosure decision process, with anticipated response holding a central role (Greene et al., 2009). Future research on channel choice would also be useful in understanding CMC disclosure decisions.

Decision making model of self-disclosure. Greene et al. (2006) propose a Decision making model of self-disclosure that explicates how background factors and self-, other-, and relationship-, and situation factors contribute to an individual's decision to disclose. The situational assessment may include (but is not limited to) consideration of the availability of the disclosure target, privacy for disclosure, flow of conversation, self-efficacy for disclosure, relationship quality, and the anticipated response (Greene et al., 2006, p. 414). During the process, the potential discloser reviews these factors as well to whom, how much, where, when, and by what channel to disclose the information. The explicit references to CMC for disclosure are anecdotal and have not been tested systematically via this perspective.

Derlega and colleagues identify several motivations for disclosure (and nondisclosure), which have been organized into self-, other-, relationship- and situational/environmental-focused categories (see Greene et al., 2006, 2003 or Derlega et al., 2008, 2004 for reviews). Self-focused reasons for disclosure are related to tangible and psychological benefits of disclosure including catharsis, seeking help, and self-clarification. Other-focused reasons emphasize the recipient and include a duty to inform, desire to educate, and test others' reactions. Relationship-focused reasons for disclosure include being in a close relationship, similarity, and a desire to increase closeness/intimacy. Situational-environmental reasons include the availability of the target, the target's involvement in the content of the disclosure, and the recipient "demands" disclosure or asks questions. Derlega also provides groupings of reasons by category for nondisclosure, but those are not the focus on the present chapter.

Considering the relatively underexplored relationship between CMC and self-disclosure motivations, we now turn to a review of conceptual fundamentals of disclosure. The next section probes why participants report choosing CMC to share information. Finally, we examine issues of self and identity in online communication by scrutinizing how individuals manage personal and private information disclosure.

Issues, Controversies, Problems in Disclosing Online

Motivations Regulating Revealing via CMC

At the core of the examination of CMC disclosure in existing relationships is a discussion of reasons or motivations for choosing to share information via CMC. For this chapter, we adopt the category system developed by Derlega and colleagues (Derlega et al., 2004, 2008; Greene et al., 2003, 2006) as a framework to organize reports of motivations to share information through CMC.

The reasons for revealing personal information via CMC vary widely, and we focus here on IM and email as common vehicles for disclosure in existing relationships. Some people have tendencies to tell others and have incorporated technology as an integral part of some or most relationships. Others find it difficult to disclose either generally or online specifically and consequently conceal. Hence, people are motivated to disclose or keep the information private because of different needs. There are a number of issues that provide insight into disclosure decisions that depend on people's motivations to reveal or conceal. We look at reasons for revealing private information via CMC based on self, other, interpersonal, and situational motivations.

As previously discussed, people's motivations for disclosure can be broadly categorized in four ways (see Derlega, Winstead, Folk-Barron, 2000; Derlega et al., 2004, 2008; Derlega & Winstead, 2001), and to date these have been examined exclusively in FtF disclosure. The following sections will discuss separately these disclosure decision motivations. The first section will discuss how people have personal needs to fulfill, labeled self motivations. The second, how people are motivated to disclose based on others' needs (Derlega, Winstead, Wong, & Greenspan, 1987). Third, how people disclose to fulfill interpersonal or relational needs, for the sake of the relationship they have or want to have with the other person. Finally, people also disclose due to situational or environmental needs.

Solutions and Recommendations

Reports of Disclosure Decision Motivations in CMC

To explore these issues, we utilized examples from a survey investigating how non-FtF disclosure is utilized by participants in ongoing relationships ($N = 410$). Participants were asked to report on two occasions, one time when they shared information that was personal or private with another person through a non-FtF channel, and one time when someone shared private information with them non-FtF. Variables included motivation for choosing channel, what was shared (content), and channel (the current emphasis is on CMC including instant messenger (IM) use and email use). Based on these reports, we provide examples of self, other, relationship, and situational motivations for CMC disclosure and compare how these examples represent theories of disclosure and CMC use more generally. We begin with examination of self-focused reasons for disclosing via CMC.

Decisions Leading to CMC Disclosure for Self-Gain

The first motivation for CMC disclosure is based on benefits for self or using disclosure to further their own goals and needs. Greene et al. (2006; Derlega et al., 2008) described at three main reasons people decide to disclose that are based on motivations for fulfilling personal needs: striving for catharsis, seeking help, and self-clarification. In our data, prior categories did not represent the data well, instead four categories were represented in CMC disclosure: immediacy, convenience/efficiency, constrain and organize message and feelings, and ease/comfort. These categories do not overall mirror reports for FtF disclosure, and we begin with discussion of immediacy.

Immediacy. The first self-focused reason for CMC disclosure was labeled immediacy. People express concerns about holding information in and need to share as soon as possible. Examination of self based reasons for CMC disclosure lead us to change this label from catharsis to immediacy, and this represents the data better than similar discussion of catharsis (specifically, this label includes an immediate time element where catharsis does not necessarily involve sharing immediately but can build over time). This is similar theoretically to media richness theory (Lengel & Daft, 1988), describing how channel choice can be motivated by potential for rapid feedback (cf. Timmerman, 2002).

Descriptions of motivations for disclosure via instant messenger included "it was urgent" and "I had to reach her as quickly as possible." Another person told a friend about his suicide attempt and described, "I needed to tell someone right then." Finally, one person used IM to share his parents' reaction to his suspension from University: "because I needed to talk with someone immediately." Each of these brief descriptions emphasizes the temporal relevance of CMC for information management, specifically disclosure choices. These descriptions emphasize the role of timing in disclosure decisions.

In addition to straightforward descriptions of immediacy, other participants chose to compare motivations for CMC disclosure explicitly with potential FtF disclosure. This makes evident an underlying assumption that current relationships are created/enacted using multiple channels or modes. The theme that runs through each of these examples is again the time feature, needing to share immediately. One woman shared her grades with her boyfriend via email: "I was excited by my straight As and couldn't wait for face-to-face communication." Another person used IM with a friend to share fears about having an STI: "It was the fastest was to get in contact with me without leaving home at the moment." Another person reported using IM because it was "quicker than waiting 'til I saw him again." Finally, a woman reported using IM to connect with a friend who was being abused by her boyfriend and stated, "I could not see her soon enough." In these instances, participants recognized the utility of CMC channels for contact without delay. With technological connectedness continuing to increase, there may be further expectations for immediate contact.

Although this research is complex (see Kelly, 2002), there is considerable evidence that not sharing or keeping secrets (be it immediately or over time) may take a considerable toll physically and psychologically on people who hold sensitive information (Lane & Wegner, 1995; Lepore & Smyth, 2002; Pennebaker, 1995). Telling someone else may relieve this burden and take some of the pressure off the person. Limandri (1989) suggested that HIV disclosure may be a form of "venting." People may experience relief in letting a secret out. Stiles' Fever Model (1987, 1995) explains how psychological distress functions to promote disclosure and relieve distress in the same way that a fever breaks physical infection. Stiles reported that disclosure is more common among people experiencing anxiety or other-arousal than among those not experiencing distress (Stiles, 1987, 1995; Stiles, Shuster, & Harrigan, 1992). Despite the practicality of the fever model, some scholars argue that the fever model may not apply in non therapeutic settings and claim that instrumental relational goals (such as impression management) may override the expressive functions of disclosure (e.g., Afifi & Caughlin, 2006). Keeping secrets (nondisclosure) can be more of a liability for people than telling (Lane & Wegner, 1995), because this constant monitoring is draining. Thus, there comes a point when individuals need to release the weight of the information to someone else (e.g., Lepore, Greenberg, Brunjo, & Smyth, 2002; Lepore, Ragan, & Jones, 2000; Pennebaker, 1995).

For immediacy, a number of examples were evident in the data. Participants recognize that, at times, CMC is one reliable way to quickly reach a recipient. Although the current data emphasize CMC disclosure, some participants reported that email or IM were even more immediate than phone, as phones were recently considered the "best" rapid alternate to FtF communication. This preference was apparent even for cell phones (or texting) where people complained that recipients have their phones off, do not answer calls, or are unavailable, and thus disclosers are at times unwilling to leave messages. In previous research, college-aged IM users reported that communication through IM was very useful for personalized communication. Email and IM offer communicative options that are often faster and more affordable than other channels (Huang & Yen, 2003). Immediate disclosers might be seeking instrumental or expressive support (Derlega et al. have a code for seeking support) but this goal was not articulated as such in these responses to why they chose CMC. Besides disclosing for immediacy reasons, another reason for disclosing via CMC was convenience and efficiency, and we turn to that next.

Convenience and efficiency. There were numerous reports of choosing CMC for disclosure because "it was fast, efficient" and "it was quick and more efficient" (both via email). Others reported using IM because "it was just more convenient" and "it was more available." The terms efficient and convenience were repeated in our data. What separates this code from immediacy is recognition of the function rather than simply speed. As with immediacy, participants recognized how CMC functioned in relationships and the role of these channel choices. Computer mediated channels of communication, such as email and IM, allow users to maintain relationships "anywhere, anytime, on almost any computing platform, at very low cost" (Huang & Yen, 2003, p. 64). Because it lacks nonverbal cues, especially when compared to other channels such as telephonic channels, CMC is usually considered low in social presence/media richness (e.g., Daft & Lengel, 1984; Rice, 1993; Short, Williams, & Christie, 1976), even labeled "impoverished." Conceptualizations generally consider this feature to be a limitation of CMC, however, it may be precisely this reduction in "richness" that facilitates the ease and convenience of CMC, or as Sproull and Kiesler (1985) noted, the decreased information available does not necessarily negatively affect the interaction. This reinforces the notion that people use CMC strategically and actively shape technology use (e.g., Bargh & McKenna, 2004; Hughes & Hans, 2001). Besides immediacy and convenience/efficiency, the next reported motivation for CMC disclosure was constrain/organize self.

Constrain and organize message and feelings. Besides disclosing immediately to relieve the burden of holding in sensitive information or convenience/efficiency, people reported using CMC to disclose in order to contain their own emotions and provide opportunity to organize and edit messages. The descriptions emphasize a greater of time—rather than the previously reported less time in immediacy—in motivating some CMC choices, and this category included reports of both email and IM. This emphasizes CMC self-presentation as "more malleable and subject to self-censorship" (Ellison et al., 2006, p. 418; see also Lengel & Daft, 1988; Walther, 1996).

First, using IM, one person reported why a friend would choose IM to disclose: "He talks more freely and openly when he can write things down and look and them and reword them. He gets his point across better without saying anything offensive." This person acknowledges the feature of editing and planning that can be crucial in choosing CMC. Similarly, another person described how a friend shared her relationship issues over IM: "I would assume it was to give her time to think things (the situation) through as she expressed them to me through instant messaging." This example emphasizes reflection or using time to refine a message (see Huang & Yen, 2003).

In terms of email, themes were similar. One person described, "Overall, I wrote her an email because I could word myself better and because I wanted to be short and clear about what I was feeling." Another participant echoed her decision to disclose via email was "to ensure that I was able to present my info completely and in an organized manner without being distracted."

Finally, a person described using email because "I am very closed when it comes to sharing my emotions—good or bad. It is hard to say things straight out—even when it is positive and showing how much you love a person. Writing it down so that I could look at it, choose the words and sending it through email helped me say it the way I wanted to." These examples all point to the strategic aspects of CMC where planning and editing is maximized, much like prior reports of rewriting letters or other technology (see Bargh & McKenna, 2004, for historical review). Walther (1996) indicated that the lack of spontaneous cues in CMC allows for strategic self-presentation and may support information management. Asynchronous forms of computer-mediated communication allow people to communicate more strategically than they might when communicating FtF (e.g., Bargh & McKenna, 2004; Walther & Parks, 2002).

One portion of this category was participants' awareness of a desire to deny nonverbal cues to recipients, emphasizing the visual anonymity aspects oft-referenced in CMC literature (e.g., Joinson, 2001). For example, one person used IM to share his sexual past, "because it's easier to deal with something of this magnitude without having to see the person's facial and nonverbal response." One woman used email "because I don't want her to see that I am crying." Another woman was disclosing concerns about her relationship to her boyfriend via IM: "I was upset and I didn't want him to read my face." One person emailed his friend about his breakup "because he was crying so it was easier to type than to talk." In each of these examples, participants recognize one benefit of CMC for disclosure is restricting available cues to the other. CMC is described as being low in social presence when compared to FtF communication and other telecommunication media (see social presence theory, Short et al., 1976). CMC is also considered much *leaner* than telephonic communication (media richness theory, see, Lengel & Daft, 1988), with reduction of available cues. Rather than this being a detriment in interaction, strategic users may be taking advantage of these features (e.g., Bargh & McKenna, 2004; Sproull & Kiesler, 1985).

Several participants explicitly compared their choices of CMC to FtF disclosure, emphasizing consideration of disclosure FtF before relying on CMC. We note that most participants did not report first considering FtF and many specifically chose (rather than defaulted to) CMC because of the inherent benefits noted previously. These reports echo discussions of disclosure efficacy seen in DD-MM (Greene, 2009) described previously, that people need to feel confident to share difficult messages and may feel unable to accomplish this FtF due to "loss of words" or being overwhelmed by emotions. One woman broke up with her boyfriend over email: "I was ashamed and did not think I would physically be able to tell him face to face." Another participant used IM to disclose: "I tried to do it face-to-face, but my mind would always go blank and I couldn't think of the words." Finally, a man was sharing relationship issues with his friend who described, "I think he could not find the right words in person and needed more time to compose his thoughts." Thus, CMC may serve an additional function within organizing/constraining of facilitating disclosure efficacy when people feel unable to share a message FtF. The time to edit/revise and word the message in the desired manner was central to these reports, and future research on disclosure efficacy would be useful (see Greene, 2009), for example to see if disclosing via CMC increases perceived efficacy.

The constrain and organize message and feelings category is related to the concept of online disinhibition. CMC may present weakened social restraints, resulting in online disinhibition, defined by Joinson (1998) as "an apparent reduction in concerns for self-presentation and the judgment of others" (p. 44). CMC provides some individuals with the social freedom needed to communicate interpersonally by reducing social inhibition, anxiety, and self-consciousness (McKenna, 1998). People may thus feel more "free" to share messages via CMC or have increased efficacy to disclose (see DD-MM, Greene 2009). Now that we have discussed the constrain/organize self motivation for sharing online, we turn to the last self-focused reason of ease and comfort.

Ease and comfort. The next category represented in the data for self-focused reasons was ease and comfort. Participants repeatedly used phrases "easier" and "more comfortable" in describing why they used CMC to disclose. For example, a participant used email "because it was easier than having to say it", while another chose IM to share her bulimia with a friend "because it is easier to disclose." Similarly, a woman described sharing a past abusive relationship over email "because it was more comfortable for me than talking about it face to face." Additionally, participants reported that it was "less painful," "less personal," and "felt more safe" to disclose via CMC. Each of these examples emphasizes some emotional benefit of disclosing via CMC.

As with other codes, some participants explicitly referenced rejection of FtF options when describing reasons for disclosing via CMC. For example, one person shared with a friend that she was dropping out of school because she could not afford it after her parents' divorce: "email felt most comfortable not telling him face to face." Another friend shared her past eating disorder: "I think it was easier for her to tell me online because it was hard for her to tell me in person. I think that it's easier to say things that are personal without seeing them face to face." Another participant described a friend's sharing his arrest for drug possession via IM: "he was more comfortable expressing his situation via instant message and not having to actually tell me." A woman shared her same-sex feelings with a friend using IM: "she has been holding this back from her close friends for a long time and therefore probably felt much more comfortable online as opposed to face-to-face confrontation." Finally, a woman told a friend about her sexual assault via IM because "sometimes it's easier to type things rather than speak them."

We have noted how decisions to disclose via CMC for self-related reasons are motivated by four factors (immediacy, convenience/efficiency, constrain and organize message and feelings, ease and comfort). These factors emphasize personal reasons for disclosure. However, people may also factor in others' needs and characteristics in CMC disclosure decisions. Thus, individuals take account of other-related issues, as they factor in the other through constraining the other's reaction.

Decisions Leading to CMC Disclosure for Other-Gain

The second overall motivation for disclosure online is based on perceived benefits for the other person. Although people are motivated to disclose so they can achieve positive outcomes for themselves, they also consider how their disclosure affects others and balance these considerations in disclosure decisions. Derlega et al. (2004, 2008) described three main reasons people disclose that are based on considering others: duty to inform, educate others, and test others' reactions (see also Greene et al., 2003, 2006). In our data, these categories did not represent the data well, thus constrain other's reaction is our single category for CMC other-gain.

Constrain other's reaction. This other-focused category included explicit references to choosing CMC disclosure to direct or limit the reaction of

the recipient. This is slightly different from prior research test other's reaction, as in our descriptions people were relatively certain about the type of response they were likely to receive and thus did not use CMC to "test" a reaction. For example, one woman contacted a boyfriend after breaking up to ensure that her message was not ignored: "I emailed because he had to listen to me or read what I wrote." Another woman used IM to disclose to a friend that she had "hooked up" (had sex with someone she was not dating) because "my friend might have got mad and yelled at me if we were face to face, and I didn't want to give her the chance to yell at me." Finally, one woman shared her decision to abort with a friend via IM because "she knows I oppose abortion, so I'm sure she was afraid I would respond negatively but AOL IM is so detached and impersonal that it made it easy, I suppose." In these cases, participants wanted to limit options available to the other, and the emphasis is on how the receiver handles the information. This category is similar theoretically to the DD-MM (Greene, 2009) assess receiver, where anticipated response is a central variable. In testing the DD-MM, Greene et al., (2009) reported a strong relationship between anticipated response with efficacy and willingness to disclose. Specifically, negative anticipated response (e.g., gossip or negative relational consequences) reduced disclosure efficacy and disclosure. For CMC disclosure decisions, other's reactions should receive attention.

Avoiding as a type of constrain other's reaction. One aspect of constraining other's response is avoiding and focuses on specifically not engaging with the disclosure recipient's reaction to the shared information. For avoid other's reaction, the emphasis is not on limiting the other in a specific way, but many use CMC to disengage from the other's reaction while still completing the goal of sharing the information. Withholding information may be related to protection of self-identity or impression management (Afifi & Guerrero, 2000; Vangelisti & Caughlin, 1997; cf. Walther, 1996). This is especially true when information presents a threat to identity (Leary & Kowalski, 1990; Ogilvie, 1987). People do not share without attempting to estimate reactions of others for their own protection and safety (e.g., Greene, 2000, 2009; Greene & Faulkner, 2002; Greene et al., 2003, 2006; Holt, Court, Vedhara, Not, Holmes, & Snow, 1998; Kalichman, 1995; Kelly, Otto-Salaj, Sikkema, Pinkerton, & Bloom, 1998).

This avoid theme was repeated several times by participants reporting choosing CMC for disclosure "to avoid the reaction" and "I did not want to see what she thought." One participant emailed her mother about getting another speeding ticket because "I figured I would not have to hear or see the disappointment in her voice or face." Another person IM'd a friend to share her first sexual experience and avoid possible negative feedback: "I actually didn't want to see her facial expression when I told her." Another person emailed a friend that she is dating a married man because she "didn't want to see my reaction. Maybe she thought I would be critical." A participant emailed her boyfriend that she was pregnant because "I was nervous about his reaction—I didn't know if he would be angry." Another person sent an email to a roommate (indicating that she was moving out) because "it was something I really wasn't proud of; it made it easier not to have to look her in the eyes." Finally, a participant used IM to share with a friend that he is homosexual: "I think he might have been afraid to see my reaction (nonverbal)." In all of these cases (and others), participants estimated that others would respond negatively and sought to avoid these reactions. These anticipated responses were all negative and lead to decisions to share but attempt to limit reaction. There are studies about nondisclosure based on anticipated response, but one theoretical advancement of this finding is how people balance CMC disclosure rather than nondisclosure when expecting negative responses.

This calls to mind the issue of topic avoidance. When both parties know the (potentially private)

information but actively choose not to discuss it (e.g., because communication results in conflict, discomfort, or some other negative outcome) it is topic avoidance (Afifi & Caughlin, 2006, Caughlin & Afifi, 2004). Although theoretically-based arguments suggest that some topic avoidance may be functional in relationships, empirical research, in general, indicates that topic avoidance in relationships is related to dissatisfaction. However, using CPM to ground their investigation Caughlin and Afifi (2004) discovered that dissatisfaction is moderated by individuals' motivations for avoidance as well as by the personal and relational characteristics linked to these motivations. Topic avoidance may be circumstantially benign or, in fact, helpful. Moving forward, research should consider how using CMC for disclosure may be perceived by the discloser and/or recipient as "avoiding" [FtF] and how this perception might affect relational outcomes.

Avoiding embarrassment as a type of constrain other's reaction. One specific negative emotion described by participants is a desire to avoid embarrassment. Some references to avoiding embarrassment were direct. For example, one person emailed a friend about an STI diagnosis "probably because she was embarrassed." Another person IM'd a friend that he had gotten drunk and was unfaithful "probably it was less embarrassing for him." AIM is much easier to share feelings, especially for guys." Finally, a person IM'd a friend that she was having an affair with a married man, "probably because she was embarrassed and felt more comfortable talking this way." Common in these examples is protecting self from embarrassment by restricting others' responses. The emphasis is on identity and self-presentation, similar to themes present throughout CMC literatures (e.g., Ellison et al., 2006; Walther, 1992; 1996; Walter & Parks, 2002) such as in Social Information Processing (SIP) theory.

Other references to avoiding embarrassment directly referenced a choice not to utilize FtF communication. For example, a woman shared with a friend her relational infidelity via IM because "I was too embarrassed to disclose it face to face." Another person used email to share her eating disorder "because she did not have to feel the discomfort of face to face—she was embarrassed." Someone shared abuse in her home via IM "because it was more embarrassing to say face to face. You let your guard down more on the phone or online." Finally, a man reported that his sister shared via email that she was adopting a baby because "it was probably too intense and intimate for her to lay out all of her fertility problems in person, right in front of me." For all of these examples, participants mentioned how CMC can decrease embarrassment of FtF disclosure, again emphasizing uses of strategic self-presentation in channel choices.

We have noted how decisions to disclose for others are motivated by one factor, constrain other's reactions. These factors emphasize other or recipient focused reasons for disclosure, specifically concerning how the other would react to the disclosure. There were fewer of these examples than motivations for self-gain, and this is a substantive difference from FtF findings. One difference from prior research on motivations is the absence of educating others or generally duty to inform (although there were isolated reports of using CMC to notify a partner if someone was pregnant or had an STI), with CMC disclosure for other-gain emphasizing specific recipient reactions. These other motivations may be more implicit in CMC or perhaps prior research emphasizing health disclosure (e.g., HIV) does not generalize across all types of disclosed information. Besides other-focused motivations, people may also factor in interpersonal or relational needs in disclosure decisions. Thus, individuals take the relationship into account and factor in the relationship. In our CMC data, one code was apparent for relational gain: normal mode of contact.

Decisions Leading to CMC Disclosure for Interpersonal/Relational-Gain

Although people are motivated to disclose via CMC so they can achieve positive outcomes for themselves and others, they also consider how their disclosure would affect the relationship. These motivations for interpersonal gain in prior research establishing emotionally supportive relationships, similarity, and increasing closeness. But in our data one code was more representative: normal mode of contact.

Normal mode of contact. The interpersonal reason reported for CMC disclosure described CMC as "normal mode of business" in many of these relationships. For example, one person described, "our schedules are completely backwards, I never get to see or actually talk to him, so we rely on email." Participants described why they chose IM to reveal as "just how we normally talk," "it was our common means of communication," and "we regularly converse in this manner." Another person utilized IM for similar reasons, "We never have time to call or see each other, so we just IM when we're online and that way we can keep in touch." These participants have incorporated CMC into everyday relationships and are accustomed to communicating online. This is consistent with previous research that demonstrates how people use the internet as another means of contacting friends and family when FtF or telephonic communication would otherwise be difficult (Bargh & McKenna, 2004; Hampton & Wellman, 2001).

For others, the notion of normal contact is more extreme, rather than being common practice CMC was utilized by some as a default method of communication. One woman contacted her boyfriend's ex-girlfriend to share the timing of when they started dating (implying infidelity): "she only had my email and no other way to contact me." Another ex-girlfriend tested positive for an STI and emailed her boyfriend "because I would not accept her phone calls and would not want to see her." Finally, one person described, "Internet was our usual mode of communication, as we were broken up and rarely saw each other." For these participants, CMC was not necessarily the first choice of one (or both) of the parties, but the channel choice was a reflection of the status of the relationship. This is something of an aberration from the norm as Wellman, Haase, Witte, and Hampton (2001) reported that Internet users use email to supplement rather than replace FtF and telephone contact, especially to maintain longer distance relationships.

Others reported using CMC after making attempts through other communication channels. One person shared her past abuse with a professor via email because "I was a busy person and always got his voicemail." Another person shared an illness diagnosis with a staff person via email because "it was required because of the bureaucracy of a large institution." For this group, CMC was not the preferred means of disclosure but rather they resorted to it. These participants accept the role of a less personal channel to disclose based on a particular situation. Implicitly, some of these reports demonstrate preference for a more rich medium than CMC for certain disclosures (e.g., Lengel & Daft, 1988), and this is in stark contrast to the organize and constrain own feelings code where participants sought out a leaner medium to serve their own goals. This is somewhat consistent with what Bargh and McKenna (2004) reported in their review of Internet communication; that for some interactions CMC is preferred and results in better outcomes.

We have described one category people report as a motivation for disclosing online for interpersonal or relational gain, normal mode of contact. These motivations emphasize the relational features for channel choice and are not equivalent to previously reported categories close relationship, similarity, or desire to increase intimacy. In these CMC reports, decisions to disclose were motivated more by function than to strategically increase relationship closeness. Next, we turn

to reasons people may disclose for situational/ environmental reasons.

Decisions Leading to CMC Disclosure for Situational/Environmental Reasons

The final motivational grouping for CMC disclosure is based situational or environmental reasons. In our data five codes emerged: availability, distance, contact multiple people, privacy, and came up in conversation. Previous research identified three codes that were somewhat consistent with our data, availability, other person asked or demanded information (similar to same up in conversation), and the other person was involved. We begin examining availability.

Availability. The first situational/environmental code for CMC disclosing is based on availability; people report disclosing via CMC because they see this as a way to ensure contact with the recipient. For example, one person described using IM because "he knew that I check my e-mail every day and that I am busy with schoolwork, so he emailed it to me with all the information, so it saved time." Another person IM'd because "it was too late at night," similar to using IM because "she just got home and it was late." Finally, one person sent an email because "I didn't want to wake her up with a phone call, it was too late." Timing is key in many of these descriptions, where people acted to share the information but did not consider the information significant enough to disrupt the other (e.g., wake someone up at 6 am). According to Derlega et al. (2008), at times a disclosure recipient is chosen mainly because of proximal or situational availability. In this case, we extend the argument that not just a particular receiver is chosen based on the availability, the availability additionally drives channel choice. We turn next to distance, a similar category but emphasizing geographic proximity rather than temporal or situational availability.

Distance. By far, the most common reported relationship motivation for disclosing via CMC was related to distance or physical location (see Wellman et al., 2001). These participants primarily had previously established relationships and were utilizing CMC as a way to remain connected, thus disclosure was a crucial part in remaining involved in the other's life. We separate these reports for permanent versus temporary distance.

Some participants reported that CMC had become the primary means of communication with friends and family because of a change in geographic location. For example, one person used IM "because he is a friend from home and is at a different school." Another person emailed a coworker regarding an experience with a customer: "because my co-worker actually works in [Midwest] not [east coast]." Most of these examples in the data were similar. Strikingly, the majority of people reporting geography as a reason for CMC disclosure were sharing with friends and only occasionally with family or other groups. The topics of these disclosures were wide-ranging, including: friend was pregnant, relationship troubles, considering abortion, friend was sexually assaulted, friend had sex with an acquaintance, friend fears failing a class, friend began dating someone, friend considers himself bisexual, friend broke up with boyfriend, friend had job offer, friend started having sex, and a friend was diagnosed with an illness. One person IM'd because "I live too far away to talk face to face." Another IM'd a friend that he broke up with his girlfriend because "he goes to school in Philly-we don't see each other than often but like to keep up on events in our lives." Finally, a friend emailed about having sex for the first time because "that's the only way for us to communicate because we're both away at college in different states." For these participants, using CMC is a normal and expected part of a relationship. There is a naturalness to these descriptions of CMC, emphasizing integration of CMC into everyday lives and relationships.

For some participants, there was recognition that distance may be temporary, and they sought to creatively employ CMC to remain connected.

One woman emailed a pregnancy scare to a friend: "I shared it via email because I was out of the country at the time." Another woman used IM to share that she was thinking of cheating on her boyfriend because her friend "was away for the weekend and I wanted her to know." Finally, a woman IM'd that she was raped, because her friend "doesn't go to this school so he wasn't around." For these participants, the distance was temporary on some level, but the information needed to be shared (recall immediacy) or they wanted some type of support. Thus, CMC disclosure provides a means to maintain relationship across geographical constraints.

Contact multiple people. Another category that may be unique to CMC disclosure emerged in these data using CMC, contact multiple people. Several people reported using email (but not IM) to disclose to multiple recipients simultaneously. For example, a friend shared difficulties adjusting to college: "it was sent in a bulk email, so just to save time repeating the information. He couldn't deal with sending a note to each person." Another person emailed her cancer diagnosis to a group of friends: "the information needed to be passed onto a mass number of people." Finally, a participant used email to share with friends that he was getting divorced: "he told several people at once. That way everyone knew at the same time." In each of these examples, there is recognition of others' right to know or expectation to know certain information in addition to reducing the level of effort of the discloser. Thus, these decisions are deliberate uses of email to facilitate disclosure to multiple recipients. This is a special case of disclosure that has not received a great deal of attention except in "public disclosure" literature that occurs often for "educating others." For example Wiener, Heilman, and Battles (1998) studied when children become "poster kids" for a particular disease (i.e., HIV). In this situation, the "receiver" is difficult to detect and not selected per se, much like posting information online on a social networking site is certainly self presentation and information management but not the same kind of self-disclosure discussed in this chapter because it lacks a particular recipient. In our data, however, the emphasis for contact multiple people was placed on saving time and energy for the discloser rather than emphasizing needs of the receiver.

Privacy. The next situational motivation was privacy, and this is another difference in findings for CMC. Specifically, in prior literature (e.g., Derlega et al., 2004, 2008; Greene et al., 2003, 2006), privacy was noted as a reason for non-disclosure. In this case, however, perceptions of privacy are driving decisions to choose a particular channel to share a message rather than choosing nondisclosure as reported in prior research. There is an implicit recognition of selectivity in sharing information and carefully choosing recipients that is foundational to theories of disclosure and privacy.

Descriptions of privacy as a motivation for channel choice were rare. For example, a friend shared that she had hooked up (had sex with someone she did not know) via IM because "conversations behind closed doors in our house are always suspect—by using IM, we avoided dealing with questions from other housemates who would have wondered what we were talking about." This woman wanted to restrict the information to the particular recipient. Another woman shared her pregnancy via IM "because we rarely have class together and if she told me during class others might hear and make fun of her." Another man described, "I get tired of people listening in to my phone calls, so I try to use email or IM for really personal business, like telling her that I'd bounced our rent check." Another participant described how his friend came out using IM: "He was at work, so it's not like we could talk on the phone, so IM works very well in this kind of situation." Finally, one woman described trying to support her younger sister who was trying to begin dating against family wishes: "the only times we are face-to-face is at home. At home, my parents or grandmother is ALWAYS around. They either can

hear us, sneak up on us, or suspect things based on our reactions and movements whenever we would talk about such things. Online, however, they know we're talking but never know what it is we're talking about or who we are talking with." For each of these descriptions, the theme of privacy included emphasizing sharing with a particular receiver and not others. This is similar to CPM (Petronio, 2002) boundary notion where people feel that they "own" or control information, and this is expanded in Venetis, Greene, Banerjee, and Bagdasarov (2008) description of implicit or explicit rules used in gossip. The DD-MM (Greene, 2009) also considered the receiver and gossip in disclosure decision-making, and these themes are evident in some descriptions of CMC disclosure choices.

Came up in conversation. The final category of situational motivations was came up in conversation, and this is somewhat similar to prior reports of other asked/demanded information. This category only emerged with IM and not with email. With new and expanding technology including mobile phones and text message packages, there may be even further increase in reports of topics "emerging" in online conversations. In the simplest terms, "as we were talking on IM it just came up," "it just happened to come up in conversation [IM]," and "I was already taking to her through AIM so it kinda just happened." Some of these topics that "just came up" could be considered stigmatized (or secret), indicating that the context can create openings for disclosure (e.g., Petronio et al, 2006). These topics included: depression, stealing, drug use, sexual past, relational fidelity, and STI. Another person similarly described, "because we were already discussing the topic, so I figured I would tell her my personal problems with it." Another person wrote, "the subject had somehow come up while we were talking online so while he probably could have told me face-to-face, we had already been talking on instant messenger. He made the blog entry to even out the details and tell his side of the story with no interruption-it was easier in that case than doing it face to face." Finally, a woman described sharing her abortion online because "it was relevant to our discussion on AIM, she brought it up." This is similar to DD-MM's description of how reciprocity can bypass normal disclosure decision processes; specifically if a topic is raised by the recipient, someone may choose to share--even if they had not planned to--if they perceive some level of similarity. People may share with others who have a common background (Derlega, Lovejoy, et al., 1998; Derlega & Winstead, 2001). Because they have common experiences, these people are generally expected to react better. This may be due to the perception that the other person is likely to be supportive or less likely to be rejecting.

Decisions Leading to CMC Disclosure for Multiple Reasons

Thus far, the discussion has emphasized participants' reports of one of four reasons or motivations for CMC disclosure. This perspective, however, does not take multiple goals into account (see Berger, 1997; Goldsmith, 2004; O'Keefe, 1988). That is, people at times have more than one motivation for channel choices, and these motivations can reinforce or contradict one another. Some people factor in situations where two categories of motivations might apply (for example both a self-gain and an situational gain to disclose apply). People much balance what may be competing or complementary motivations to utilize the channel that will maximize benefits (and minimize risks). For example, some participants balanced distance with immediacy and chose to share via IM: "We both attend different schools, and he wanted to talk asap," and "she was in college in a different state and wanted to tell me right away." Another person balanced distance with constrain/avoiding reaction in choosing to email: "there are two reasons. The first because she lives out of state and the second because it was an embarrassing subject." These examples illustrate tensions in

multiple goals, and CPM (Petronio, 2002) argues that information management involves a constant balancing of these dialectical tensions. The DD-MM is more specific in identifying assessments of information, relationship (quality and anticipated response) and efficacy as central to managing these disclosure decision tensions.

Other examples of balancing multiple goals are more complex, beyond juggling two motivations. One man shared via CMC how his parents' ugly divorce was affecting him because "email is the fastest way to send out a message, the easiest to communicate with (I think I would have broken down if I talked on the phone). At that time it was late at night, and I didn't want to deal with the emotions." Another woman described her sexual past via IM because "I am shy and would have been embarrassed talking about it face-to-face. Plus, the subject came up while talking online, so it was convenient." Finally, a woman shared her pregnancy with a friend via email because "she is so distraught right now and busy, we don't see each other much, and in addition doesn't want to hear my immediate reaction." For each of these people, using CMC to disclose was an outcome of balancing a variety of goals and needs to maximize the choice and relational outcome. The themes presented, both singly and multiply, emphasize the significance of examining motivations for interpersonal communication processes in CMC in existing relationships.

FUTURE RESEARCH DIRECTIONS

This chapter discussed four CMC disclosure decision– self, other, relationship, and situational/ environmental focused motivations—and explored how these motivations are consistent with or required changes in CMC and interpersonal theories.

Self-focused reasons for disclosure dominated reports of motivations for disclosing via CMC. Many participants identified motivations for disclosure online that were related to the absence of context clues inherent in CMC. Theories of social presence (Short et al., 1976) and media richness (Daft & Lengel, 1984) propose that FtF is held to be the ideal, standard, and/or goal for interpersonal communication. However, these data indicate that people are deliberately utilizing and benefiting in particular from these oft-lamented "disadvantages" of CMC, such as leanness. Theories of CMC and relationships should consider how the widespread adoption and acceptance of interpersonal relationship maintenance not only makes mediated channels of communication "par" with FtF communication, but possibly even superior in some cases as indicated in this chapter. In particular, theories of disinhibition and efficacy can be adapted to explain these findings.

The data revealed one other-focused reason for disclosure through CMC, constrain and avoid other's reaction (including embarrassment). These constrain and avoidance goals were overall very well accomplished in these reports, at least temporarily. People made strategic decisions using CMC to constrain and avoid others' reactions, but it remains to be seen if in the longer-term these disclosers still manage to avoid the dreaded expected reactions (one participant called her friend "cowardly" for sending an IM instead of calling or seeing her FtF). That is, with time, are negative reactions to disclosure more or less intense? These reasons were also related to utilizing the features of CMC (not available in FtF communication) for the specific purpose of interpersonal communication. It is possible, for example, to use CMC to allow the recipient time to adjust before reacting, and this chapter notes that perceived reaction is crucial in CMC disclosure decisions. This is consistent with the DD-MM (Greene, 2009) where anticipated response is central to disclosure decision-making, and Caughlin et al. (2005) reminds us that disclosure reactions are often less negative than anticipated, with some intense exceptions (see also Greene & Faulkner, 2002).

Relationship focused reasons for disclosure through CMC were inconsistent with research in FtF communication, for example increasing closeness and similarity. For this group, using CMC for disclosure was simply the normal mode of communication. This may be related to the younger sample, who, having grown up with this technology, find CMC disclosure integrally incorporated in their friendships and dating relationships, and perhaps family relations as well (see Bargh & McKenna, 2004). That is not to say that participants failed to recognize when they were strategically managing a relationship by choosing CMC. We need to explore overall patterns of when people choose FtF compared to CMC and general technology use patterns in the relationship to delve into this further (cf. Lea & Spears, 1995; O'Sullivan, 1996).

Finally, the data revealed five situational/environmental focused reasons for disclosure through CMC, more categories than prior research and widely reported. The first category was availability, somewhat unique to constantly changing technology. A new reason that would not be applicable in FtF communication is distance. It is not uncommon for today's romantic relationships to be initiated and/or maintained across great physical distances. In addition, social mobility also extends to family relations and friendships, when people move with greater ease than prior generations. The third category included a different use of the concept of privacy. CPM (Petronio, 2002) argues that individuals feel they have the right to "own" or control their personal/private information, yet executing this notion becomes more complicated when others become "co-owners" of information and can gossip (see Venetis et al., 2008). The idea of co-ownership of information is especially interesting when considering CMC and the information sharing capabilities it allows. For example, future research could test this respect for "ownership" phenomenon with blind CC and forwarding of emails. The fourth situational motivation was *came up in conversation*, similar to prior reports of other asked (see also DD-MM, Greene, 2009, for asking questions). The final situational motivation was to contact many people at once, and this is clearly grounded in the context and ease afforded by technological options. It may be argued that the motivations underlying all reasons explicated are to some extent environmental/situational focused. This data collection intentionally sought descriptions of disclosure events through mediated channels of communication. Future research may endeavor to collect data encompassing both FtF and non-FtF disclosure so that other situational reasons for disclosure may be compared.

Extending Disclosure Theories to CMC for Existing Relationships

We proposed three theoretical perspectives of disclosure that could be applied to sharing information via CMC. The decision making model of self-disclosure (Greene et al., 2006) provided groupings of reasons to disclose via CMC overall that in the broadest sense matched the framework, but subcategories differed a great deal. One conclusion would be that future research on disclosure goals via CMC should explore self, other, relationship and situational focused structure but adopt the subcategories of FtF with caution. There are apparent similarities at the abstract level but differences are also apparent. Additionally, for this model, future research could test these motivations in relation to decisions for timing and setting, as utilized via CMC.

Next, the DD-MM (Greene, 2009) showed promise for explaining CMC disclosure decisions. As noted previously, the components of efficacy (cf. disinhibition) and anticipated response should be included in future research, along with information assessment such as valence (recall discussion of avoiding embarrassment, which is rooted in information content). We should seek to explicate channel choice in DD-MM. It is easy to specu-

late how assessment of information, relationship (relational quality and anticipated response), and efficacy could predict channel choice. We have seen examples and categories in these data that would support developing hypotheses. The DD-MM is developed to date to explicate the decision to disclose and not message enactment per se (e.g., channel choice or setting), thus one logical extension would be to use the model to hypothesize about channel selection and test the relations.

Finally, CPM (Petronio, 2002) had been utilized once previously for CMC but not with personal relationships. In the present context, CPM was useful to highlight balancing dialectical tensions in reports of multiple goals. Additionally, CPM can be used to conceptualize reports of privacy for situational motivations to disclose via CMC, but a different conceptualization of privacy goals may be required. In the present context, privacy was not a motivation for nondisclosure, rather it explained channel choice to restrict the information to specific recipients. The concept of perceived information ownership and gossip (see Greene, 2009; Venetis et al., 2008) is worthy of exploration. We can use CPM to extend CMC disclosure and examine how people protect information when they utilize CMC.

CONCLUSION

Technology use is embedded in many existing relationships. This chapter includes reports of widespread CMC use for the critical function of self-disclosure, part of information management in relationships. We concur with prior conclusions that people actively shape their technological interactions (see Bargh & McKenna, 2004; Hughes & Hans, 2001). We are also not concluding CMC has unilateral negative effects for heavy users, rather there are additional positive effects and benefits of CMC for social interaction through disclosure (cf. Bargh & McKenna; Sproull & Kiesler, 1985).

Examinations such as this one help us move beyond study of business relationships, relationship initiation, or exclusively online relationships to include management of information via CMC for people using both FtF and CMC channels. This is an important area for continued research, as people continue to expand their use of CMC technologies to maintain relationships. We emphasized IM and email examples in this chapter, one step in exploring the overall process. Some findings are consistent with both interpersonal and CMC theories, but in places pointed to need to expand and reconceptualize certain features, reinforcing similar calls by others (e.g., Bargh & McKenna, 2004; Lea & Spears, 1995). People are taking advantage of CMC technologies strategically in their disclosure choices and should reexamine assumptions embedded in FtF theories. Over time, with greater experience and more diffusion, we would expect increased skill, adaption, and use of CMC to disclose in interpersonal relationships. This will continue to be a crucial area for research, how people use CMC to maintain close relationships, emphasized here through disclosure and information management.

REFERENCES

Afifi, T. D., Olson, L. N., & Armstrong, C. (2005). The chilling effect and family secrets: Examining the role of self protection, other protection, and communication efficacy. *Human Communication Research*, *31*, 564–598. doi:10.1093/hcr/31.4.564

Afifi, W. A., & Caughlin, J. P. (2006). A close look at revealing secrets and some consequences that follow. *Communication Research*, *33*, 467–488. doi:10.1177/0093650206293250

Afifi, W. A., & Guerrero, L. K. (2000). Motivations underlying topic avoidance in close relationships. In Petronio, S. (Ed.), *Balancing the secrets of private disclosures* (pp. 165–180). Mahwah, NJ: Lawrence Erlbaum Associates.

Baltes, B. B., Dickson, M. W., Sherman, M. P., Bauer, C. C., & LaGanke, J. S. (2002). Computer-mediated communication and group decision making: A meta-analysis. *Organizational Behavior and Human Decision Processes*, *87*, 156–179. doi:10.1006/obhd.2001.2961

Bargh, J. A., & McKenna, K. Y. A. (2004). The Internet and social life. *Annual Review of Psychology*, *55*, 573–590. doi:10.1146/annurev.psych.55.090902.141922

Berger, C. R. (1997). Producing messages under uncertainty. In Greene, J. (Ed.), *Message Production: Advances in Communication Theory* (pp. 221–244). Mahwah, NJ: Lawrence Erlbaum Associates.

Berger, C. R. (2005). Interpersonal communication: Theoretical perspectives, future prospects. *The Journal of Communication*, *55*, 415–447. doi:10.1111/j.1460-2466.2005.tb02680.x

Buunk, B. P., & Gibbons, F. X. (1997). *Health, coping and well-being*. Mahwah, NJ: Lawrence Erlbaum Associates.

Caughlin, J. P., & Afifi, T. D. (2004). When is topic avoidance unsatisfying? Examining moderators of the association between avoidance and dissatisfaction. *Human Communication Research*, *30*, 479–513. doi:10.1093/hcr/30.4.479

Caughlin, J. P., Afifi, W. A., Carpenter-Theune, K. E., & Miller, L. E. (2005). Reasons for, and consequences of, revealing personal secrets in close relationships: A longitudinal study. *Personal Relationships*, *12*, 43–59. doi:10.1111/j.1350-4126.2005.00101.x

Daft, R. L., & Lengel, R. H. (1984). Information richness: A new approach to managerial behavior and organization design. *Research in Organizational Behavior, 6*, 191–233.

Derlega, V. J., Lovejoy, D., & Winstead, B. A. (1998). Personal accounts of disclosing and concealing HIV-positive test results. In Derlega, V. J., & Barbee, A. P. (Eds.), *HIV and social interaction* (pp. 147–164). Newbury Park, CA: Sage.

Derlega, V. J., Metts, S., Petronio, S., & Margulis, S. T. (1993). *Self-disclosure.* Newbury Park, CA: Sage Publications.

Derlega, V. J., & Winstead, B. A. (2001). HIV infected persons' attributions for the disclosure and nondisclosure of the seropositive diagnosis to significant others. In Manusov, V., & Harvey, J. H. (Eds.), *Attribution, communication behavior, and close relationships* (pp. 266–284). New York: Cambridge University Press.

Derlega, V. J., Winstead, B. A., & Folk-Barron, L. (2000). Reasons for and against disclosing HIV-seropositive test results to an intimate partner: A functional perspective. In Petronio, S. (Ed.), *Balancing the secrets of private disclosures* (pp. 53–69). Hillsdale, NJ: Lawrence Erlbaum Associates.

Derlega, V. J., Winstead, B. A., & Greene, K. (2008). Self-disclosure and starting a close relationship. In Sprecher, S., Wenzel, A., & Harvey, J. (Eds.), *Handbook of relationship beginnings* (pp. 153–174). New York: Psychology Press.

Derlega, V. J., Winstead, B. A., Greene, K., Serovich, J., & Elwood, W. N. (2004). Reasons for HIV disclosure/nondisclosure in close relationships: Testing a model of HIV-disclosure decision making. *Journal of Social and Clinical Psychology, 23*, 747–767. doi:10.1521/jscp.23.6.747.54804

Derlega, V. J., Winstead, B. A., Mathews, A., & Braitman, A. L. (2008). Why does someone reveal highly personal information? Attributions for and against self-disclosure in close relationships. *Communication Research Reports, 25*, 115–130. doi:10.1080/08824090802021756

Derlega, V. J., Winstead, B. A., Wong, P. T. P., & Greenspan, M. (1987). Self-disclosure and relationship development: An attributional analysis. In Roloff, M., & Miller, G. (Eds.), *Interpersonal processes: New directions in communication research* (pp. 172–187). Newbury Park, CA: Sage.

Drotlet, A. L., & Morris, M. W. (2000). Rapport in conflict resolution: Accounting for how face-to-face contact fosters mutual cooperation in mixed-motive conflicts. *Journal of Experimental Social Psychology, 36*, 25–50.

Ellison, N., Heino, R., & Gibbs, J. (2006). Managing impressions online: Self-presentation processes in the online dating environment. *Journal of Computer-Mediated Communication, 11*, 415–441. doi:10.1111/j.1083-6101.2006.00020.x

Ferriter, M. (1993). Computer aided interviewing and the psychiatric social history. *Social Work & Social Sciences Review, 4*, 255–263.

Festinger, L. A. (1954). A theory of social comparison processes. *Human Relations, 7*, 117–140. doi:10.1177/001872675400700202

Frattaroli, J. (2006). Experimental disclosure and its moderators: A meta-analysis. *Psychological Bulletin, 132*, 823–865. doi:10.1037/0033-2909.132.6.823

Gibbs, J. L., Ellison, N. B., & Heino, R. D. (2006). Self-presentation in on-line personals: The role of anticipated future interaction, self disclosure, and perceived success in internet dating. *Communication Research, 33*, 152–177. doi:10.1177/0093650205285368

Gilbert, S. J. (1976). Self-disclosure, intimacy and communication in families. *The Family Coordinator, 25*, 221. doi:10.2307/582335

Goldsmith, D. J. (2004). *Communicating social support*. New York: Cambridge University Press.

Greene, K. (2000). Disclosure of chronic illness varies by topic and target: The role of stigma and boundaries in willingness to disclose. In Petronio, S. (Ed.), *Balancing the secrets of private disclosures* (pp. 123–135). Mahwah, NJ: Lawrence Erlbaum Associates.

Greene, K. (2009). An integrated model of health disclosure decision-making. In Afifi, T. D., & Afifi, W. A. (Eds.), *Uncertainty and information regulation in interpersonal contexts: Theories and applications* (pp. 226–253). New York: Routledge.

Greene, K., Checton, M. G., Banerjee, S. C., Magsamen-Conrad, K., Venetis, M. K., & Bagdasarov, Z. (November, 2009). *Assessing information and relationships in disclosure decisions: testing an integrated model of disclosure decision-making*. Paper presented at the Annual conference of the National Communication Association, Chicago, IL.

Greene, K., Derlega, V. J., & Mathews, A. (2006). Self-disclosure in personal relationships. In Vangelisti, A., & Perlman, D. (Eds.), *Cambridge handbook of personal relationships* (pp. 409–427). New York: Cambridge University Press.

Greene, K., Derlega, V. J., Yep, G. A., & Petronio, S. (2003). *Privacy and disclosure of HIV in interpersonal relationships: A sourcebook for researchers and practitioners*. Mahwah, NJ: Lawrence Erlbaum Associates.

Greene, K., & Faulkner, S. L. (2002). Self-disclosure in relationships of HIV-positive African American adolescent females. *Communication Studies, 54*, 297–317.

Greist, J. H., Klein, M. H., & VanCura, L. J. (1973). A computer interview by psychiatric patient target symptoms. *Archives of General Psychiatry, 29*, 247–253.

Hampton, K., & Wellman, B. (2001). Long distance community in the network society. *The American Behavioral Scientist, 45*, 476–495. doi:10.1177/00027640121957303

Helgeson, V. S., & Mickelson, K. D. (1995). Motives for social comparison. *Personality and Social Psychology Bulletin, 21*, 1200–1209. doi:10.1177/01461672952111008

Hian, L. B., Chuan, S. L., Trevor, T. M. K., & Detenber, B. H. (2004). Getting to know you: Exploring the development of relational intimacy in computer-mediated communication. *Journal of Computer-Mediated Communication, 9*. Retrieved February 13 2009, from http://www3.interscience. wiley.com.proxy.libraries.rutgers.edu/cgi-bin/fulltext/120837925/HTMLSTART

Hoffman, M. A. (1996). *Counseling clients with HIV disease: Assessment, intervention, and prevention*. New York: Guilford.

Holt, R., Court, P., Vedhara, K., Nott, K. H., Holmes, J., & Snow, M. H. (1998). The role of disclosure in coping with HIV infection. *AIDS Care, 10*, 49–60. doi:10.1080/09540129850124578

Huang, A. H., & Yen, D. C. (2003). Usefulness of instant messaging among young users: Social vs. work perspective. *Human Systems Management, 22*, 62–72.

Hughes, R. Jr, & Hans, J. D. (2001). Computers, the internet, and families: a review of the role new technology plays in family life. *Journal of Family Issues, 22*, 778–792. doi:10.1177/019251301022006006

Janofsky, A. I. (1970). Affective self-disclosure in telephone versus face-to-face interviews. *Journal of Humanistic Psychology, 10*, 93–103.

Johansen, R., Vallee, J., & Vian, K. (1979). *Electronic meetings*. Reading, MA: Addison–Wesley.

Johnson, A. J., Haigh, M. M., Becker, J. A. H., Craig, E. A., & Wigley, S. (2008). College students' use of relational management strategies in email in long-distance and geographically close relationships. *Journal of Computer-Mediated Communication, 13*, 381–404. doi:10.1111/j.1083-6101.2008.00401.x

Joinson, A. N. (1998). Causes and implications of disinhibition on the Internet. In Gackenbach, J. (Ed.), *The psychology of the internet* (pp. 43–60). New York, NY: Academic Press.

Joinson, A. N. (1999). Social desirability, anonymity, and internet-based questionnaires. *Behavior Research Methods, Instruments, & Computers, 31*, 433–438.

Joinson, A. N. (2001). Self-disclosure in computer-mediated communication: The role of self-awareness and visual anonymity. *European Journal of Social Psychology, 31*, 177–192. doi:10.1002/ejsp.36

Kalichman, S. C. (1995). *Understanding AIDS: A guide for mental health professionals*. Washington, DC: American Psychological Association. doi:10.1037/10497-000

Kelley, J. E., Lumley, M. A., & Leisen, J. C. C. (1997). Health effects of emotional disclosure in rheumatoid arthritic patients. *Health Psychology, 16*, 331–340. doi:10.1037/0278-6133.16.4.331

Kelly, A. E. (2002). *The psychology of secrets*. New York: Kluwer Academic/Plenum.

Kelly, A. E., Klusas, J. A., von Weiss, R. T., & Kenny, C. (2001). What is it about revealing secrets that is beneficial? *Personality and Social Psychology Bulletin, 27*, 651–665. doi:10.1177/0146167201276002

Kelly, A. E., & McKillop, K. J. (1996). Consequences of revealing personal secrets. *Psychological Bulletin, 120*, 450–465. doi:10.1037/0033-2909.120.3.450

Kelly, A. E., Otto-Salaj, L. L., Sikkema, K. J., Pinkerton, S. D., & Bloom, F. R. (1998). Implications of HIV treatment advances for behavioral research on AIDS: Protease inhibitors and new challenges in HIV secondary prevention. *Health Psychology, 17*, 310–319. doi:10.1037/0278-6133.17.4.310

Kinney, S., & Dennis, A. (1994, January). *Reevaluating media richness: Cues, feedback, and task*. Paper presented at the twenty-seventh annual Hawaii International Conference on System Sciences, Kihei, Maui, HI.

Kraut, R., Mukhopadhyay, T., Szczypula, J., Kiesler, S., & Scherlis, B. (2000). Information and communication: Alternative uses of the Internet in households. *Information Systems Research, 10*, 287–303. doi:10.1287/isre.10.4.287

Lane, J. D., & Wegner, D. M. (1995). The cognitive consequences of secrecy. *Journal of Personality and Social Psychology, 69*, 237–253. doi:10.1037/0022-3514.69.2.237

Larson, D. G., & Chastain, R. L. (1990). Self-concealment: Conceptualization, measurement, and health implications. *Journal of Social and Clinical Psychology, 9*, 439–455.

Lea, M., & Spears, R. (1995). Love at first byte? Building personal relationships over computer networks. In Wood, J. T., & Duck, S. (Eds.), *Understudied relationships: Off the beaten track* (pp. 197–233). Thousand Oaks, CA: Sage.

Leary, M. R., & Kowalski, R. M. (1990). Impression management: A literature review and two-component model. *Psychological Bulletin, 107*, 34–47. doi:10.1037/0033-2909.107.1.34

Lengel, R. H., & Daft, R. L. (1988). The selection of communication media as an executive skill. *The Academy of Management Executive, 2*, 225–232.

Lepore, S. J., Greenberg, M. A., Brunjo, M., & Smyth, J. M. (2002). Expressive writing and health: Self-regulation of emotion-related experiences, physiology, and behavior. In Lepore, S. J., & Smyth, J. M. (Eds.), *The writing cure: How expressive writing promotes health and emotional well-being* (pp. 99–117). Washington, D.C.: American Psychological Association. doi:10.1037/10451-005

Lepore, S. J., Ragan, J. D., & Jones, S. (2000). Talking facilitates cognitive-emotional processes of adaptation to an acute stressor. *Journal of Personality and Social Psychology, 78*, 499–508. doi:10.1037/0022-3514.78.3.499

Lepore, S. J., & Smyth, J. M. (Eds.). (2002). *The writing cure: How expressive writing promotes health and emotional well-being*. Washington, D.C.: American Psychological Association. doi:10.1037/10451-000

Limandri, B. J. (1989). Disclosure of stigmatizing conditions: The discloser's perspective. *Archives of Psychiatric Nursing, 3*, 69–78.

McKenna, K., & Bargh, J. (1998). Coming out in the age of the Internet: Identity 'demarginalization' through virtual group participation. *Journal of Personality and Social Psychology, 75*, 681–694. doi:10.1037/0022-3514.75.3.681

McKenna, K. Y. A., & Bargh, J. A. (2000). Plan 9 from cyberspace: the implications of the Internet for personality and social psychology. *Personality and Social Psychology Bulletin, 4*, 57–75. doi:10.1207/S15327957PSPR0401_6

Metzger, M. J. (2007). Communication privacy management in electronic commerce. *Journal of Computer-Mediated Communication, 12*, 335–361. doi:10.1111/j.1083-6101.2007.00328.x

Mintzberg, H. (1980). Managerial work: Analysis from observation. In Leavitt, H., Pondy, L., & Boje, D. (Eds.), *Reading in managerial psychology* (pp. 551–559). Chicago, IL: Univ. of Chicago Press.

Morahan-Martin, J., & Scumacher, P. (2003). Loneliness and social uses of the Internet. *Computers in Human Behavior, 19*, 659–671. doi:10.1016/S0747-5632(03)00040-2

O'Keefe, B. J. (1988). The logic of message design: Individual differences in reasoning about communication. *Communication Monographs, 55*, 80–103. doi:10.1080/03637758809376159

O'Sullivan, P. B. (1996, May). *A match made in cyberspace: interpersonal communication theory and interpersonal communication technology*. Paper presented at the Annual Meeting of the International Communication Association, Chicago, IL.

Ogilvie, D. M. (1987). The undesired self: A neglected variable in personality research. *Journal of Personality and Social Psychology, 52*, 379–385. doi:10.1037/0022-3514.52.2.379

Parks, M. R., & Floyd, K. (1996). Making friends in Cyberspace. *The Journal of Communication, 46*, 80–97. doi:10.1111/j.1460-2466.1996.tb01462.x

Pennebaker, J. W. (1989). Confession, inhibition, and disease. *Advances in Experimental Social Psychology, 22*, 211–244. doi:10.1016/S0065-2601(08)60309-3

Pennebaker, J. W., Colder, M., & Sharp, L. K. (1990). Accelerating the coping process. *Journal of Personality and Social Psychology, 58*, 528–537. doi:10.1037/0022-3514.58.3.528

Pennebaker, J. W., Kiecolt-Glaser, J. K., & Glaser, R. (1988). Disclosure of traumas and immune function: Health implications for psychotherapy. *Journal of Consulting and Clinical Psychology, 56*, 239–245. doi:10.1037/0022-006X.56.2.239

Pennebaker, J. W., & O'Heeron, R. C. (1984). Confiding in others and illness rate among spouses of suicide and accidental death victims. *Journal of Abnormal Psychology, 93,* 473–476. doi:10.1037/0021-843X.93.4.473

Petronio, S. (2000). The boundaries of privacy: Praxis in everyday life. In Petronio, S. (Ed.), *Balancing the secrets of private disclosures* (pp. 111–122). Hillsdale, NJ: Lawrence Erlbaum Associates.

Petronio, S. (2002). *The boundaries of privacy: Dialectics of disclosure.* Albany, NY: State University of New York Press.

Pew Internet & American Life. (2007, 3 March). Getting serious online: as Americans gain experience, they use the Web more at work, write e-mails with more significant content, perform more online transactions, and pursue more serious activities. Washington, DC: Pew Internet & American Life. Retrieved 4 March 2007, from http://www.pewinternet.org/

Poole, M. S., Shannon, D. L., & DeSanctis, G. (1992). Communication media and negotiation processes. In Putnam, L. L., & Roloff, M. E. (Eds.), *Communication and negotiation: Sage annual reviews of communication research* (pp. 46–66). Thousand Oaks, CA: Sage.

Reingold, H. (1993). *The virtual community.* New York: Addison-Wesley.

Rice, R. E. (1993). Media appropriateness: Using social presence theory to compare traditional and new organizational media. *Human Communication Research, 19,* 451–484. doi:10.1111/j.1468-2958.1993.tb00309.x

Rice, R. E., & Love, G. (1987). Electronic emotion: Socioemotional content in a computer-mediated network. *Communication Research, 14,* 85–108. doi:10.1177/009365087014001005

Robinson, R., & West, R. (1992). A comparison of computer and questionnaire methods of history taking in a genitourinary clinic. *Psychology & Health, 6,* 77–84. doi:10.1080/08870449208402024

Sheffield, J. (1989). The effects of bargaining orientation and communication medium on negotiations in the bilateral monopoly task: A comparison of decision room and computer conferencing communication media. In *CHI '89 Conference proceedings: Human factors in computing systems* (pp. 43–48). New York: McGraw–Hill.

Short, J. A., Williams, E., & Christie, B. (1976). *The social psychology of telecommunications.* London: Wiley International.

Smyth, J. M. (1999). Written disclosure: evidence, potential mechanism, and potential treatment. *Advances in Mind-Body Medicine, 15,* 179–184.

Soukup, C. (2000). Building a theory of multimedia CMC: An analysis, critique and integration of computer-mediated communication theory and research. *New Media & Society, 2,* 407–425.

Sproull, L., & Kiesler, S. (1985). Reducing social context cues: Electronic mail in organizational communication. *Managerial Science, 11,* 1492–1512.

Stanton, A. L., Danoff-Burg, S., Cameron, C. L., & Snider, P. R. (1999). Social comparison and adjustment to breast cancer: An experimental examination of upward affiliation and downward evaluation. *Health Psychology, 18,* 151–158. doi:10.1037/0278-6133.18.2.151

Stiles, W. B. (1987). "I have to talk to somebody." A fever model of disclosure. In Derlega, V. J., & Berg, J. H. (Eds.), *Self-disclosure: Theory, research, and therapy* (pp. 257–282). New York: Plenum.

Stiles, W. B. (1995). Disclosure as a speech act: Is it psychotherapeutic to disclose? In Pennebaker, J. W. (Ed.), *Emotion, disclosure, and health* (pp. 71–91). Washington, DC: American Psychological Association. doi:10.1037/10182-004

Stiles, W. B., Shuster, P. L., & Harrigan, J. A. (1992). Disclosure and anxiety: A test of the fever model. *Journal of Personality and Social Psychology*, *63*, 980–988. doi:10.1037/0022-3514.63.6.980

Taylor, S. F., & Lobel, M. (1989). Social comparison activity under threat: Downward evaluation and upward contacts. *Psychological Review*, *96*, 569–575. doi:10.1037/0033-295X.96.4.569

Tidwell, L. C., & Walther, J. B. (2002). Computer-mediated communication effects on disclosure, impressions, and interpersonal evaluations: Getting to know one another one bit at a time. *Human Communication Research*, *28*, 317–348. doi:10.1111/j.1468-2958.2002.tb00811.x

Timmerman, C. E. (2002). The moderating effect of mindlessness/mindfulness upon media richness and social influence explanations of organizational media use. *Communication Monographs*, *69*, 111–131. doi:10.1080/714041708

Valley, K. L., Moag, J., & Bazerman, M. H. (1998). A matter of trust: Effects of communication on the efficiency and distribution of outcomes. *Journal of Economic Behavior & Organization*, *34*, 211–238. doi:10.1016/S0167-2681(97)00054-1

Vangelisti, A. L., & Caughlin, J. P. (1997). Revealing family secrets: The influence of topic, function, and relationships. *Journal of Social and Personal Relationships*, *14*, 679–705. doi:10.1177/0265407597145006

Vangelisti, A. L., & Timmerman, L. (2001). Criteria for revealing family secrets. *Communication Monographs*, *68*, 1–28. doi:10.1080/03637750128052

Venetis, M. K., Greene, K., Banerjee, S. C., & Bagdasarov, Z. (2008, May). *Comparing private and secret information in disclosure decisions.* Paper presented at the annual meeting of the International Communication Association, Montreal, Canada.

Wallace, P. (1999). *The psychology of the internet.* Cambridge, MA: Cambridge University Press.

Walther, J. (1996). Computer-mediated communication: Impersonal, interpersonal, and hyperpersonal interaction. *Communication Research*, *23*, 3–43. doi:10.1177/009365096023001001

Walther, J. B. (1995). Relational aspects of CMC: experimental observations over time. *Organization Science*, *6*, 186–203. doi:10.1287/orsc.6.2.186

Walther, J. B. (1997). Group and interpersonal effects in international computer-mediated collaboration. *Human Communication Research*, *23*, 342–369. doi:10.1111/j.1468-2958.1997.tb00400.x

Walther, J. B., & Parks, M. R. (2002). Cues filtered out, cues filtered in: Computer-mediated communication and relationships. In Knapp, M. L., & Daly, J. A. (Eds.), *Handbook of Interpersonal Communication* (3rd ed., pp. 529–563). Thousand Oaks, CA: Sage.

Weisband, S., & Kiesler, S. (1996, April). *Self disclosure on computer forms: Meta-analysis and implications.* Paper presented at the meeting of the Conference on Human Factors in Computing Systems, Vancouver, BC.

Wellman, B., Haase, A. Q., Witte, J., & Hampton, K. (2001). Does the Internet increase, decrease, or supplement social capital? *The American Behavioral Scientist*, *45*, 436–455. doi:10.1177/00027640121957286

Westerman, D., Van Der Heide, B., Klein, K. A., & Walther, J. B. (2008). How so people really seek information about others?: Information seeking across internet and traditional communication channels. *Journal of Computer-Mediated Communication*, *13*, 751–767. doi:10.1111/j.1083-6101.2008.00418.x

Whitty, M., & Gavin, J. (2001). Age/sex/location: Uncovering the social cues in the development of online relationships. *Cyberpsychology & Behavior*, *4*, 623–639. doi:10.1089/109493101753235223

Wilkins, H. (1991). Computer talk: Long distance conversations by computer. *Written Communication*, *8*, 56–78. doi:10.1177/0741088391008001004

Williams, E. (1977). Experimental comparisons of face-to-face and mediated communication: A review. *Psychological Bulletin*, *84*, 963–976. doi:10.1037/0033-2909.84.5.963

ADDITIONAL READING

Afifi, T. D., Olson, L. N., & Armstrong, C. (2005). The chilling effect and family secrets: Examining the role of self protection, other protection, and communication efficacy. *Human Communication Research*, *31*, 564–598. doi:10.1093/hcr/31.4.564

Afifi, W. A., & Caughlin, J. P. (2006). A close look at revealing secrets and some consequences that follow. *Communication Research*, *33*, 467–488. doi:10.1177/0093650206293250

Afifi, W. A., & Weiner, J. L. (2004). Toward a theory of motivated information management. *Communication Theory*, *14*, 167–190. doi:10.1111/j.1468-2885.2004.tb00310.x

Agne, R. R., Thompson, T. L., & Cusella, L. P. (2000). Stigma in the line of face: Self-disclosure of patients' HIV status to health care providers. *Journal of Applied Communication Research*, *3*, 235–261. doi:10.1080/00909880009365573

Altman, I., & Taylor, D. A. (1973). *Social penetration: The development of interpersonal relationships*. NY: Holt, Reinhart and Winston.

Babrow, A. S. (2001). Introduction to the special issue on uncertainty, evaluation, and communication. *The Journal of Communication*, *51*, 453–455. doi:10.1111/j.1460-2466.2001.tb02890.x

Babrow, A. S. (2001). Uncertainty, value, communication, and problematic integration. *The Journal of Communication*, *51*, 553–573. doi:10.1111/j.1460-2466.2001.tb02896.x

Bargh, J. A., McKenna, K. Y. A., & Fitzsimons, G. M. (2002). Can you see the real me? Activation and expression of the "True self" on the internet. *The Journal of Social Issues*, *58*, 33–48. doi:10.1111/1540-4560.00247

Baxter, L. A., & Wilmot, W. W. (1985). Taboo topics in close relationships. *Journal of Social and Personal Relationships*, *2*, 253–269. doi:10.1177/0265407585023002

Caughlin, J. P., & Afifi, T. D. (2004). When is topic avoidance unsatisfying? Examining moderators of the association between avoidance and dissatisfaction. *Human Communication Research*, *30*, 479–513. doi:10.1093/hcr/30.4.479

Caughlin, J. P., & Golish, T. D. (2002). An analysis of the association between topic avoidance and dissatisfaction: Comparing perceptual and interpersonal explanations. *Communication Monographs*, *69*, 275–295. doi:10.1080/03637750216546

Collins, N. L., & Miller, L. C. (1994). Self-disclosure and liking: A meta-analytic review. *Psychological Bulletin*, *116*, 457–475. doi:10.1037/0033-2909.116.3.457

Derlega, V. J., & Grzelak, J. (1979). Appropriateness of self-disclosure. In Chelune, G. J. (Ed.), *Self-disclosure: Origins, patterns, and implications of openness in interpersonal relationships* (pp. 151–176). San Francisco: Jossey-Bass.

Derlega, V. J., Metts, S., Petronio, S., & Margulis, S. T. (1993). *Self-disclosure*. Newbury Park, CA: Sage.

Derlega, V. J., Winstead, B. A., & Folk-Barron, L. (2000). Reasons for and against disclosing HIV-seropositive test results to an intimate partner: A functional perspective. In Petronio, S. (Ed.), *Balancing the secrets of private disclosures* (pp. 53–69). Hillsdale, NJ: Lawrence Erlbaum Associates.

Derlega, V. J., Winstead, B. A., Wong, P. T. P., & Greenspan, M. (1987). Self-disclosure and relationship development: An attributional analysis. In Roloff, M., & Miller, G. (Eds.), *Interpersonal processes: New directions in communication research* (pp. 172–187). Newbury Park, CA: Sage.

Dindia, K., & Allen, M. (1992). Sex differences in self disclosure: A meta-analysis. *Psychological Bulletin, 112*, 106–124. doi:10.1037/0033-2909.112.1.106

Gibbs, J. L., Ellison, N. B., & Heino, R. D. (2006). Self-presentation in on-line personals: The role of anticipated future interaction, self-disclosure, and perceived success in internet dating. *Communication Research, 33*, 152–177. doi:10.1177/0093650205285368

Greene, K. (2009). An integrated model of health disclosure decision-making. In Afifi, T., & Afifi, W. (Eds.), *Uncertainty and information regulation in interpersonal contexts: Theories and applications*. NY: Routledge.

Greene, K., Derlega, V. J., & Mathews, A. (2006). Self-disclosure in personal relationships. In Vangelisti, A., & Perlman, D. (Eds.), *Cambridge handbook of personal relationships* (pp. 409–427). NY: Cambridge University Press.

Greene, K., Derlega, V. J., Yep, G. A., & Petronio, S. (2003). *Privacy and disclosure of HIV in interpersonal relationships: A sourcebook for researchers and practitioners*. Mahwah, NJ: Lawrence Erlbaum Associates.

Greene, K., & Faulkner, S. L. (2002). Self-disclosure in relationships of HIV-positive African-American adolescent females. *Communication Studies, 54*, 297–317.

Joinson, A. N. (2001). Self-disclosure in computer-mediated communication: The role of self-awareness and visual anonymity. *European Journal of Social Psychology, 31*, 177–192. doi:10.1002/ejsp.36

Joinson, A. N. (1998). Causes and implications of disinhibition on the Internet. In Gackenbach, J. (Ed.), *The psychology of the internet* (pp. 43–60). New York, NY: Academic Press.

Jourard, S. M. (1971). *Self-disclosure: An experimental analysis of the transparent self*. NY: Wiley-Interscience.

Kelly, A. E. (2002). *The psychology of secrets*. New York: Kluwer Academic/Plenum.

Kelly, A. E., & McKillop, K. J. (1996). Consequences of revealing personal secrets. *Psychological Bulletin, 120*, 450–465. doi:10.1037/0033-2909.120.3.450

McKenna, K., & Bargh, J. (1998). Coming out in the age of the Internet: Identity `demarginalization' through virtual group participation. *Journal of Personality and Social Psychology, 75*, 681–694. doi:10.1037/0022-3514.75.3.681

Parks, M. R., & Floyd, K. (1996). Making friends in Cyberspace. *The Journal of Communication*, *46*, 80–97. doi:10.1111/j.1460-2466.1996. tb01462.x

Pennebaker, J. W. (1989). Confession, inhibition, and disease. *Advances in Experimental Social Psychology*, *22*, 211–244. doi:10.1016/S0065-2601(08)60309-3

Petronio, S. (2002). *The boundaries of privacy: Dialectics of disclosure*. Albany, NY: State University of New York Press.

Petronio, S., Reeder, H. M., Hecht, H. L., & Ros-Mendoza, T. M. (1996). Disclosure of sexual abuse by children and adolescents. *Journal of Applied Communication Research*, *24*, 181–199. doi:10.1080/00909889609365450

Rosenfeld, L. B. (2000). Overview of the ways privacy, secrecy, and disclosure are balanced in today's society. In Petronio, S. (Ed.), *Balancing the secrets of private disclosures* (pp. 3–18). Hillsdale, NJ: Lawrence Erlbaum Associates.

Tidwell, L. C., & Walther, J. B. (2002). Computer-mediated communication effects on disclosure, impressions, and interpersonal evaluations. *Human Communication Research*, *28*, 317–348. doi:10.1111/j.1468-2958.2002.tb00811.x

Vangelisti, A. L. (1994). Family secrets: Forms, functions, and correlates. *Journal of Social and Personal Relationships*, *11*, 113–135. doi:10.1177/0265407594111007

Wallace, P. (1999). *The psychology of the internet*. Cambridge, MA: Cambridge University Press.

Walther, J. B. (1997). Group and interpersonal effects in international computer-mediated collaboration. *Human Communication Research*, *23*, 342–369. doi:10.1111/j.1468-2958.1997. tb00400.x

Walther, J. B. (1996). Computer-mediated communication: Impersonal, interpersonal, and hyperpersonal interaction. *Communication Research*, *23*, 3–43. doi:10.1177/009365096023001001

Section 2
Interpersonal Relationships and Gendered Communication

Chapter 5
Relationship Development and Maintenance in a Mediated World

Jessica L. Moore
North Carolina State University, USA

Elizabeth A. Craig
North Carolina State University, USA

ABSTRACT

This chapter presents a review of contemporary scholarship on relational communication, particularly as it relates to interpersonal relationship development and maintenance. Throughout the chapter, special attention is given to the role new technologies play in the communication process. This chapter draws together a wide array of communication research findings ranging from attraction and initial interactions to relational routines and social support. Consideration is also given to some of the methodological and conceptual issues that face contemporary communication researchers. Fundamentally, the function of this multifaceted chapter is to provide an accessible and informed introduction to relational communication and computer-mediated scholarship for both an academic and general audience. A list of recommended readings on communication scholarship concludes this chapter.

INTRODUCTION

New technologies profoundly influence the conditions under which interpersonal relationships are constructed and sustained. In fact, computer-mediated interaction is becoming a way of life for many people. Wood notes, "The increasingly technological character of our society powerfully affects individuals and personal relationships" (2000, p. 110). This movement toward implementing

new technologies into the communicative process suggests an ever-escalating need for researchers and practitioners to consider the patterns within, and implications of, mediated interactions. Hence, this chapter explores several areas of contemporary scholarship on interpersonal and relational communication, particularly as it relates to the processes of "relationship development" and "relationship maintenance." It has been suggested that one of the more remarkable developments in modern society is the diffusion of new communication technologies from the organization into the sphere of social

DOI: 10.4018/978-1-61520-827-2.ch005

and personal relationships (O'Sullivan, 2000). Accordingly, this chapter also confers special attention to the function new technologies play in the communication process. A wide array of research findings ranging from attraction and initial interactions to relational routines and social support are presented herein. Consideration is also given to some of the methodological and conceptual issues that face contemporary communication researchers. Ultimately, this chapter hopes to convey that establishing and preserving interpersonal relationships is central to the human experience and that new technologies are progressively mediating that practice.

BACKGROUND

Many scholars argue that the evolution of media has decreased the significance of physical presence in the process of human symbolic exchange (Lin & Atkin, 2007; Meyerowitz, 1985; Shneiderman, 2003). That is, an increase in the availability, variety, and sophistication of communication media has progressively provided the opportunity for people to mediate their day-to-day interactions. For many individuals, it may be daunting to imagine living in a world without the Internet because it is now the central mechanism through which they most often work, relate, and play. According to a 2004 study conducted by the Pew Internet and American Life Project, 85% of Internet users believe that online interaction is a good way to communicate and 64% claim that their daily routines would be significantly affected if they no longer had access to the Internet. As technology continues to evolve, however, so do the notions of what it means to *communicate* and engage in *computer-mediated communication* (CMC). Thus, we will first offer a definition of communication, then note the subtle distinctions between the terms interpersonal and relational communication, and finally provide a frame for the use of the dynamic term CMC.

Communication is often regarded as the primary influence on our experience of developing and maintaining relationships (Knapp & Daly, 2002; Wood, 2000). In fact, most of us spend our lives attempting to communicate in significant ways with others. From the primitive expressions we communicate as infants to the complex behaviors we use to communicate our innermost thoughts and feelings as adults, it is the process of communication that enables us to connect with other people and ultimately develop and maintain meaningful human relationships.

Similar to human relationships, the various definitions of communication share common features although it is rare to find any that are identical. A definition of communication offered by the National Communication Association (2002), a professional organization representing scholars and practitioners in the field, seems to include many of the commonly shared features by positing that "*communication is the process through which people use messages to generate meanings within and across contexts, cultures, channels, and media.*" This particular definition highlights several fundamental features of human communication upon which many communication scholars continue to focus their research efforts. First, framing communication as a process suggests that it is not a static event or notion, but instead something that involves a constantly changing set of cognitions and behaviors. Second, this definition infers that communication is fundamentally situated in interaction, or the notion that communication is rooted in the symbolic exchange of messages within a social system. Third, noting that communication is contextually situated leads one away from the notion that communication occurs in a vacuum and toward the view that it is encompassed by a broad set of idiosyncratic and socio-cultural circumstances. It is also clarified in this definition that communication takes place across a series of sensory dimensions (e.g., verbal and nonverbal cues), or channels. And lastly, this particular definition offers a broad scope of communication by noting that people utilize a broad range of media types to engage in the symbolic exchange process. It is these fundamental elements, among others, about which communication scholars continue to ask interesting and important questions.

We have presented a definition of communication as the process through which people use messages to generate meanings within and across contexts, cultures, channels, and media; however, this chapter has a particular focus on *interpersonal* and *relational communication*. For many, the distinction between the two is subtle while others see them as being quite distinct. Interpersonal communication is generally viewed more broadly than relational communication and represents communication that takes place between two or more people in which unique interaction patterns in some way influence one another's thoughts, emotions, behaviors, and relationships over time. Interpersonal communication is often used to describe symbolic exchange across all sorts of relationships ranging from casual to intimate. Relational communication, on the other hand, is narrower in scope and specifically focuses on communication in close relationships such as those we share with family members, friends, and partners. Although scholars in the field of communication do not always agree on the distinctions between the two, many agree that the indispensable component for both interpersonal and relational communication is that two people involved in the communicative process perceive some degree of behavioral interdependence (Berscheid & Peplau, 1983). Issues of both interpersonal and relational communication will be intermingled throughout this chapter as we present details of relational (co) creation across both time and space.

It is clear that technology is changing the ways people accomplish communicative tasks; it seems we are infrequently out of touch with anyone, anywhere, anymore (Bugeja, 2005). This high degree of connectivity is due in part to CMC, which can be understood as the practice of human communication through a wide range of electronic or digital media, including e-mail, instant messages, chat rooms, discussion groups, personal data assistants, websites, and social networks, among others. Given the continued evolution of definitions of CMC, this chapter includes an extensive array of media in its discussion of technology use in the development and maintenance of relationships. The rapid technological transformations in the ways people communicate have become an appealing area of exploration for researchers and practitioners alike. This chapter is no exception as it presents contemporary information on the way relationships are developed and maintained in a mediated world.

CURRENT LITERATURE

How do relationships begin? What do people do in order to maintain relationships? These seem like fairly simple questions, yet the answers to them vary greatly. Most reading this book have experienced relationship initiation through a multitude of circumstances; we bump into someone new at a party, are set up on a blind date, meet a new colleague at work, or even add a new friend by proxy of an existing friend via an online social network such as Facebook. Yet meeting a new person does not always result in the establishment of an interpersonal or close relationship. Relationships indisputably grow and change over time through a developmental process. Through the act of communication, people who were once simple acquaintances may become significant individuals with whom we attempt to maintain close relationships. In the following sections, we will explore four areas of research which interpersonal and relational scholars have concentrated significant and enduring effort: attraction, initial interactions, relational routines, and social support.

Attraction

There has been an enormous amount of research conducted on attraction, perhaps because it has been shown to play such an important role in the development of various types of relationships (Berscheid & Reis, 1998). From friendships to romantic encounters, the forces of social attraction are complex and often difficult for individuals to clearly articulate. Although attraction is multifaceted, there are several significant influences on interpersonal attraction. In particular, researchers have given generous attention to the role proximity and similarity play in drawing people together.

Proximity, conceptualized as nearness, has been shown to be a major influence on initial attraction (Gilbertson, Dindia, & Allen, 1998; Herek & Capitanio, 1996; Wood, 2000). One of the earliest investigations on the impact of proximity on attraction found that the location of college students' apartments had an influence on who became friends (Festinger, Schlachter, & Back, 1950). In this classic study, students who lived in the same building were much more likely to take up social relationships with other students that lived nearer rather than farther from them in the building. Studies have also revealed that people have a tendency to build close friendships as well as intimate relationships with coworkers (Bridge & Baxter, 1992; Dillard & Witteman, 1985; Pierce, Byrne & Aguinis, 1996). Quite simply, in order to develop an attraction for someone we must first be able to meet them, and proximity is often what determines whether we meet someone in the first place.

Though researchers have traditionally examined proximity in terms of a literal physical nearness, advances in technology have changed perceptions of what it means to be near by allowing individuals to blur social presence and place (Bugeja, 2005). Second Life, for example, is a richly detailed virtual world where many individuals dwell in self- or other-created environments (Fitzgerald, 2007). Not only do people

visit Second Life, in part, to make online purchases or to game, but many of the more than 15 million users meet, communicate, and develop relationships with others in this world due in part to virtual proximity. In January of 2008, 38,000 people on average were exploring Second Life at any given moment and 28,274,505 hours were logged in the virtual world during this same time frame (Second Life, 2008). Online chat rooms also enable individuals to engage in group CMC as well as private one-on-one CMC with others one might not otherwise have the opportunity to meet in their physical environments. According to Madden and Rainie (2003), an estimated 29 million people participated in online chat rooms in 2002 and 5 million of them frequented chat rooms as least once per day. Moreover, Rice and Love (1987) report that individuals across these environments share interpersonal information and convey messages rich in socio-emotional content. Communication scholars generally affirm that the words we use and the way we use them are a primary means through which others come to know us, form impressions of us, and routinely determine whether an interpersonal relationship is potentially viable (McKenna, 2008). And, Walther (1996) suggests in some instances, the levels of affection and emotion expressed through CMC can surpass physically proximal relationships. In sum, proximity- whether virtual or real- continues to have an impact on attraction and the process of developing interpersonal and sometimes close relationships.

The relationship between similarity and attraction has also been studied extensively. Researchers have worked for many years to determine whether we tend to be initially attracted to people who are different from us or those who are similar to us. A preference for similarity seems to traverse issues of personal attitude, education level, socioeconomic status, race, religion, physical attributes, wellness difficulty (i.e., having a similar affliction or health experience), personal characteristics, among many other variables (Bargh & McKenna, 2004;

Davidson, Pennebaker, & Dickerson, 2000; Hill, Rubin, & Peplau, 1976; Kandel, 1978). It should be noted dissimilarity does not always preclude attraction (Sunnafrank, 1991); however, similarity remains a considerable force in the practice of seeking and developing interpersonal relationships with others.

CMC clearly acts as a developmental conduit through which individuals can seek, discover, and connect with similar others. In fact, many would argue that it is common knowledge that a variety of relationship types can and do form online (Bugeja, 2005; McKenna, 2008; Shneiderman, 2003). Explanations of the similarity and attraction phenomena range from models of social reinforcement (Byrne, 1971) that suggest we are attracted to others because they reify our world views, to the matching hypothesis (Berscheid, Dion, Walster, & Walster, 1971) which points out our tendency to be attracted to people with similar physical characteristics. While individuals are undeniably able to meet others with similar attitudes or world views or comparable levels of physical attractiveness through traditional forms of social interaction, the Internet has proved to be a useful means for accomplishing similar relational goals (Holland & Harpin, 2008). For example, a study on bloggers conducted by the Pew Internet and American Life Project (2006) suggests that a growing number of people seek out blogs for the purpose of engaging with those interested in a particular topic, such as politics or political campaigns. In fact, 18% of those who sought out blogs for online news desired doing so only on sites that shared a similar political worldview. Additionally, Ridings and Gefen (2004) suggest that virtual communities are ideal places to engage in CMC given the ability to dialogue with relative strangers about a particular topic of interest. It has been shown that individuals within virtual communities are willing to express views, provide and request information, suggest solutions, and communicate feelings to one another (Herring, 1996). McKenna (2008) also notes that relation-

ships, in general, are more successfully initiated and developed through common interests or goal settings, and that the online world and its many opportunities for social interaction seem to be increasingly mirroring those of our offline world. There is also evidence that physical attractiveness is playing an ever-increasing function in computer-mediated environments. From still photos to webcams, many people are making efforts to include as much as their physical being as possible in virtual environments. This is particularly true for online dating sites (Ellison, Heino, & Gibbs, 2006), but also is the case for many general online spheres. In a social networking study conducted by Holland and Harpin (2008), it seems clear that people, teenagers in particular, carefully select and showcase evidence of their physical selves on the Internet. Additionally, viewing and commenting on another's physical attributes-whether they are misrepresented or not- is a common way of communicating attraction. For instance, a respondent in the aforementioned study by Holland and Harpin notes, "It feels good if someone comments saying you look hot, like if you are trying out a new style and you get a load of good comments" (p. 128). Another respondent in the same study commented on how they feel reassured by others in their social network when positive comments were left about their photographs. It may be that individuals seek out similar others on the Internet due to a perception of ready acceptance by those online. Whatever the case, it is clear that many individuals capitalize on the accessibility of the Internet to search out and communicate with others who have similar goals and that this continues to be a fundamental basis for initial attraction.

Attraction in mediated environments is undoubtedly nuanced in ways that are distinct from face-to-face encounters. As new technologies emerge, so do questions about how people relate in computer-mediated environments. As such, there remains much to be discovered about what lies at the intersection of attraction, new technologies, and CMC. Though attraction tends to be thought of as an all-or-nothing concept (i.e., we are attracted to someone or we are not), it actually changes over the course of time through the process of interaction. Thus, the following section of this chapter presents information on some of the processes that unfold during the course of early relational interactions.

Initial Interaction

Although attraction serves an integral function in the developmental process of relationships, people do not rely on attraction alone to determine whether they want to pursue a relationship with a given individual. So how is the decision to continue a relationship made? Many communication scholars would argue that it is through a process of uncertainty reduction and information seeking that move relationships from being impersonal to interpersonal. Sunnafrank's (1986; 1988; 1990) predicted outcome value theory poses that individuals gather information about one another during initial encounters and subsequently use that data to form an outcome value for the relational other. Outcome values are generally framed as tentative forecasts which individuals use to decide how and whether to continue a given interaction or relationship. Indeed, it is evident that individuals gather information about one another during dyadic exchanges (Berger & Calabrese, 1975; Sunnafrank, 1986; 1988; 1990) and that this information can be obtained in many ways. Furthermore, research suggests that information gathered during interaction is then used to make evaluative decisions regarding the immediate interaction as well as potential future encounters. Thus, the messages people send and receive during any given interaction may be used to determine *how* or *if* a relationship will continue.

Afifi and Lucas (2008) note that researchers have much to discover about the information seeking process across the various stages of relational development. Even so, there is information about the process of information seeking in

computer-mediated environments that merit the attention of this chapter. Broadly speaking, information seeking strategies can be passive, active, or interactive (Berger, 1979, 1987). People who rely on nonintrusive observation of individuals are using passive strategies. Traditional passive strategies include paying attention to how a person interacts with others or perhaps examining the clothes they are wearing. Active strategies, however, consist of the purposeful manipulation of a social environment for the purpose of observing how someone will respond or simply asking third parties for information. And lastly, interactive strategies involve direct contact between the information seeker and the person of interest. In online environments, all three types of information seeking are prolific. A study by Lampe, Ellison, & Steinfield (2006) reports that beyond keeping in touch with old friends, the three most often reported reasons for using the social networking sites (e.g., Facebook) were: "check[ing] out a profile of someone I met socially, get[ing] information about people that live in my dorm, fraternity, or sorority," and "get[ing] information about people in my classes." This suggests that individuals are using sites like Facebook to passively seek information constrained to face-to-face contexts (Afifi & Lucas, 2008; Ellison, Steinfield, & Lampe, 2007). Given half of Facebook's 175 million students are college students, more than 15 million users update their status each day, and more than 3.5 million users become fans of individual Facebook pages each day, people are clearly relying on social networking sites for information seeking purposes (Facebook, 2009). Passive strategies have also been identified in investigations of online impression management. In a study by Ellison, Heino, & Gibbs (2006), a respondent noted that if an email was received from someone that could not spell or put a full sentence together, he/she often questioned what other parts of this person's life suffered from the same lack of attentiveness. There is evidence of active and interactive information-seeking strategies in online environments as well. The Pew Internet and American Life Project (2006) reports that one-third of bloggers post material simply to engage readers and elicit a response and 82% of bloggers report making comments on the blogs of others. Also, nine out of ten bloggers activate commenting functions on their blogs in order to encourage CMC. These studies reveal that people are seeking and sharing information in mediated environments, but to what end remains unclear.

Implicit in most examinations of initial interactions is the notion that people generally desire to reduce uncertainty by gathering information about their partner. Moreover, communication plays an important role in the process of initial interaction. Through information seeking and sharing, individuals are able to (co)construct an interpersonal framework upon which close relationships can be built. And as research has shown, the use of the Internet as a mechanism to seek and share information is becoming more widespread. Studies on the actual information-seeking strategies enacted during initial interactions, nonetheless, are paltry at best. It remains clear that many avenues of research remain available for future inquiries in this area.

Just as most relationships start by operating with generalized information and move toward more idiosyncratic detail, the progression of this chapter is no different. Thus, we now move from a general discussion of research on attraction and initial interaction to a more detailed discussion of research in the area of relational routines and social support.

Patterns of Interaction and Relational Routines

Many individuals seek inclusion, control, and affection (Schutz, 1966), and are able to accomplish these goals through the use of communication. Communication is the essence of relational maintenance, and as Dindia (2003) argues, to maintain a relationship *is* to maintain communication. The

maintenance process is just that, a dynamic interplay between partners who routinely and strategically engage in communicative behaviors.

Computer mediated interpersonal communication is often perceived as being a disadvantaged channel of communication which allows for only superficial forms of maintenance-related communication (Stafford, Kline, & Dimmick, 1999). However, it is through these "trivial" conversations that individuals create a deep sense of connection and interdependence with relational partners. Computer-mediated communication allows individuals to engage in everyday talk, which is fundamental to relational maintenance (Duck, 1994). With the emergence of newer technologies, individuals have the opportunity to engage in everyday conversations with computer mediated relationships, including purely online relational partners, online relationships which migrate offline, and traditional offline relationships when CMC supplements other channels of communication (Stafford, 2005). As such, CMC connects family members, friends, and a number of personal relationships with varied relational histories and cultures. Duck (1994) contends that it is within the routine, day-to-day communication that relationships are strengthened and become even more interdependent. This chapter argues individuals have integrated the Internet into their daily lives, and are maintaining or enhancing personal relationships through a variety of new technologies. The following sections highlight research focused on *how* individuals use CMC, and *what* they may be saying within these mediated contexts.

Research indicates there are relationally purposeful reasons for using CMC. The use of CMC has been shown to enhance trust within long-distance romantic couples (Dainton & Aylor, 2002), increase relational quality (Holladay & Seipke, 2007), allow individuals to stay in touch with family and friends (Stafford et al., 1999), and provide assurances to relational partners of the importance of their relationship (Johnson, Haigh et al., 2008). Howard, Rainie, and Jones (2001) argue CMC actually builds and expands an individual's social network by facilitating conversations between relational partners. Fifty-nine percent of respondents who e-mail indicated it allowed them to communicate more with family members, and 60% indicated that e-mail allowed them to communicate more with friends. Also, 31% reported being able to communicate with family members they had little contact with before using e-mail. Howard et al. (2001) conclude individuals were not in danger of isolating themselves from the outside world by using CMC, but instead, used mediated interaction to enhance opportunities to enlarge and develop their social network. Computer mediated connections allow individuals to sustain friendship and family ties that might otherwise be difficult to maintain. Stafford and colleagues (1999) found e-mail was mainly used for keeping in touch with friends and family. Additionally, due to the convenient asynchronous nature of the medium, individuals were able to share ideas and opinions with others at leisure. From a practical standpoint, e-mail was less expensive, quicker, simpler, and more convenient (Stafford et al., 1999).

To better understand the relationship between CMC and relational maintenance within family relationships, Harwood (2000) examined how grandparents and their college-aged grandchildren reported using different media to maintain contact. Results suggest frequency of telephone and written communication predicted relational closeness. The author argues written forms of communication such as letters and e-mail, "offer more opportunity for reflection before communication, rephrasing or deletion, and for expressing emotions with minimal face risk or threat" (Harwood, 2000, p. 70). Holladay and Seipke (2007) focused intently on the use of phone, e-mail, and face-to-face contact between geographically distanced grandparents and grandchildren. Fifty-eight percent of grandparents indicated they e-mailed a few times each month or more. Although the use of the phone predicted the highest levels of

relational quality, e-mail was used significantly more than face-to-face communication. These examples imply that due to the relational history of this particular relationship, it is plausible that individuals have learned to use low-richness media (i.e., written communication, e-mail) as compared to high-richness media (i.e., face-to-face contact) to share more intimate communications (for additional information on media richness theory see Daft & Lengel, 1984). Additionally, e-mail may provide a safe forum for individuals to engage in highly interdependent talk utilized to redefine the relationship due to the growth and change among relational partners. Here, grandparents and grandchildren are choosing "leaner" forms of media to maintain their relationships; more importantly, these relationships are satisfying and valued despite the sometimes lack of face-to-face communication.

Whether it is with friends or family members this sample of research suggests individuals are taking advantage of the many benefits of using CMC as a way to sustain personal relationships. As quicker, less expensive, and more convenient forms of technology are incorporated into everyday life, it remains important for scholars to continue asking users how they are engaging personal relationships within these contexts. It is also important to identify *what* individuals are saying to relational partners through computer-mediated channels. The discussion now turns to highlighting research which has focused specifically on the actual content of CMC and relational maintenance. Initial research which identified the actual content of e-mail messages and the maintenance strategies employed within the content of these messages relied on an established typology, initially created for face-to-face interaction (Canary & Stafford, 1994; Canary, Stafford, Hause, & Wallace, 1993). The following studies have successfully utilized this typology with minor modifications to the existing typology; however, readers can consult Canary and Stafford (1994) for descriptions and examples of each inductively derived category.

Rabby (1997) examined actual e-mail content, and found couples in ongoing relationships expressed *openness* (e.g., self-disclosure, meta-relational communication, advice, and opinion expression) and *narratives* (e.g., sharing stories among partners, routine activities, and objective descriptions of everyday life) in a majority of the e-mail content analyzed. By adding *narratives* as a category not initially conceptualized by Canary et al. (1993), Rabby (1997) was able to code all of the messages exchanged. He concluded the content of e-mail messages for these couples focused on personal self-disclosures which highlight the exchange of intimate forms of talk, as well as, narratives or routine talk which highlight everyday conversations. Johnson, Haigh et al. (2008) also collected personal email messages which included personal messages from friends, family members, and romantic partners over the period of one week. Canary and Stafford's (1994) typology was utilized with slight modifications such as adding categories for emoticons and signing-off behaviors, and expanding the category of social networks to include news about other friends, family members, school and work networks. E-mail communication with family members contained three prominent maintenance behaviors, *openness* (e.g., self-disclosure, meta-relational communication, advice, and opinion expression), *social networks* (e.g., relying on friends and family), and *positivity* (e.g., attempts to make interactions pleasant). These three maintenance categories were also most prominent in the content of e-mails between friends. However, the e-mails of romantic partners contained *assurances* (e.g., covertly and overtly assuring each other, supportiveness, and comfort), *openness*, and *positivity*. A finding of significance was higher use of *assurances* within romantic relationships and family relationships, than in friendships. Johnson, Haigh et al. (2008) conclude romantic partners may be using e-mail as a way to "communicate and reinforce the message of relational importance" (p. 395), while friends are utilizing e-mail to engage in everyday conversations. Although the authors expected to find differences in the content between geographically close and long-distance friends, family, and romantic partners, they did not. The authors argue as more people adopt new mediated channels of communication, long-distance relationships which would have deteriorated might now have more opportunities to thrive.

The Internet allows individuals to exchange e-mail with relational partners, stay in touch with friends, renegotiate relationships with family members, and supplement communication among romantic partners. More importantly, the aforementioned research suggests individuals are exchanging open, supportive, assuring messages with their relational partners. The range of discussions, such as coordinating activities, sharing a funny story, or giving advice to a friend is again, indicative of everyday conversations *and* intimate forms of talk. In addition to this research, the following section will highlight the importance of examining online social support as it facilitates relational maintenance. Through participation in social support groups, many individuals are finding valuable relationships within online communities. Consequently, the dynamics of their offline relationships may be influenced by the conversational exchanges they share with each other in their online groups. Next, this chapter focuses on the research of online social support groups, and some possible implications of this research for relational communication scholars.

Social Support

Research has long since identified social support as promoting overall health and well-being (Berkman, 2000; Gottlieb, 1981; Wellman, 1999). Social support provides protection for individuals who may need encouragement, tangible assistance in times of need, and advice on a number of different topics. Burleson and MacGeorge (2002) define supportive communication, "as verbal and nonverbal behavior produced with the intention of providing assistance to others perceived as needing that aid" (p. 374). Social support is prevalent throughout multiple stages of life (Pecchioni, Wright, & Nussbaum, 2005), provides buffers from stressful life events (Cohen & Wills, 1985), and most importantly, is enacted through communication with others (Goldsmith, 2004).

Traditional conceptions of social supportive partners have mainly consisted of family, friends, and significant dating or marriage relationships (Albrecht & Goldsmith, 2003). While people rely on the ones they know and love to help them through difficult times, CMC provides forums where social supportive messages can be exchanged among individuals not typically considered as part of one's intimate social network (i.e., weak tie networks). Adelman, Parks, and Albrecht (1987) conclude, "the term w*eak ties* refer to an umbrella concept that covers a wide range of potential supporters who lie beyond the primary network of family and friends" (p. 126). Weak tie networks allow individuals to obtain support from those not within their intimate circle (Granovetter, 1973). In certain situations this may provide more effective social supportive exchanges than those with close family and friends, as online support groups allow for safely disclosing high-risk information and avoiding possible stigma associated with the issues being discussed (Wright & Bell, 2003).

A major benefit of using online support is the extension of access to information and the ability to compare oneself to others (Adelman et al., 1987). Research indicates online members report that similarity to others online, and similar experiences are major advantages of utilizing online support (Wang, Walther, Pingree, & Hawkins, 2008; Wright, 2002). Albrecht and Goldsmith (2003) claim online support groups simultaneously offer homogeneity (i.e., people confronted with a similar issue) and heterogeneity (i.e., greater diversity of opinions and perspectives). With the ability to contact many different individuals, all dealing with a similar issue, individuals may gain

multiple perspectives in how to confront personal issues, and more importantly maintain successful offline relationships. Extending weak ties and discussing issues with multiple people is beneficial, as Adelman et al. (1987) state, "Self-evaluation is facilitated by comparison to weak ties because they provide a greater variety of information and thus a better ability to judge how typical or normal our own behavior is" (p. 135). Another major benefit of utilizing online support is that it allows individuals to avoid possible stigma surrounding a personal issue. By avoiding this stigma, individuals may be able to bypass the actual thing or issue which was preventing them from seeking help from those within their strong tie network. Wright and Bell (2003) state, "Stigma refers to the sense of shame, disgrace or taboo associated with a particular illness/condition, usually stemming from fears and prejudices surrounding cultural conceptions of a health issue" (p. 42). Online support groups become a place where individuals are able to move beyond their immediate social network, form valuable relationships which may increase self-esteem, and gather a larger repertoire of coping strategies.

Some of the more recent research regarding online support groups has examined medically based issues such as physical disabilities (Braithwaite, Waldron, & Finn, 1999), caregivers of individuals with Alzheimer's disease (Brennan, Moore, & Smyth, 1992), recovering addicts (King, 1994), eating disorders (Eichhorn, 2008) and cancer (Rodgers & Chen, 2005; Sharf, 1997; Sullivan, 2003; Weinberg, Schmale, Uken, & Wessel, 1995; Wright, 2002). One new trend identified in the online social support literature is on the supportive messages exchanged among online group members where the focus of the group is based on personal issues, not medical issues. Dunham, Hurshman, Litwin, Gusella, Ellsworth, and Dodd (1998) provided unlimited access for six months to a computer mediated social support network for forty-two single mothers. Many of these single mothers had been isolated from their social network of friends due to the responsibilities of a new baby. Results indicate women who were the most socially isolated were the most likely to participate in the social support group. Additionally, as they accessed the group more, they experienced a stronger sense of belonging to this particular group of single mothers and reported decreases in parental stress. A content analysis of the messages posted indicated 77% of these messages were topics directly related to the mother, such as the mother's mental health (e.g., complaints about boredom, social isolation, and social alienation), and the mother's adult relationships (e.g., stress related to the mother's partner and/or parents). Here, CMC not only helped these women establish relationships they so desperately needed, but it became an opportunity for online group members to acknowledge the relational dynamics single mother's face with children, partners, and parents.

In a content analysis of an online blended family support group, Christian (2005) proposed the importance of utilizing online support groups as a way to express narratives for stepmothers feeling stigmatized by the "wicked stepmother" myth. She argues this forum allowed individuals to not only share their stories with others in similar situations, but by expressing things in an online narrative format stepmother's were able to contest the stigma they felt surrounding their role. Johnson, Wright, Craig, Gilchrist, Haigh, & Lane, (2008) suggest perceptions of lowered satisfaction with social support networks were associated with stepmother's reporting greater perceived stress, and lowered marital satisfaction. Results indicate as stepmothers have fewer outlets for supportive exchanges, stress increases and ultimately this has a negative impact on their relationship with their spouse. In a content analysis of discussion board postings within this same online support group for stepmothers, Craig (2008) found discussions concerning offline relationships were prevalent within the online support group. Stepmothers expressed having difficulty negotiating relation-

ships with their stepchildren, their spouse, and the biological mother. In response, practical advice and emotional support was given which explicitly served the relationships outside of the technology being used. For example, when stepmothers expressed needing ideas for how to spend more time with their stepchildren, many women responded with things such as taking them to the park, doing crafts, or making dinner together as a way to engage in their stepchildren's lives.

This sample of research indicates online support groups are providing safe forums where individuals are free to express how they feel about their current situation and the stigma associated with that situation (Christian, 2005; Wright & Bell, 2003). More importantly, online support groups appear to have greater diversity of opinion and information, yet individuals feel as if they are sharing with others in similar stressful situations. Ultimately, this research indicates an important trend in understanding how computer mediated support may influence significant personal relationships outside mediated contexts (Craig, 2008; Johnson, Wright et al., 2008). Group members are often times offered understanding and practical advice regarding close relationships such as children, romantic partners and parents (Christian, 2005), and stepchildren, spouses, and biological mothers (Craig, 2008).

Advances have been made toward understanding the communicative processes that unfold in relational development and maintenance, but this progress has not been made without challenges. Understanding communicative processes within computer-mediated contexts, in particular, gives way to both theoretical and methodological concerns for researchers in this area. Thus, several concerns are discussed in the following section.

DISCUSSION

Scholars and practitioners know more about personal relationships and CMC than ever before.

Yet, several conceptual and methodological issues still remain. Haythornthwaite (2001) advises scholars who focus on the use of the Internet in everyday life to acknowledge the false dichotomy of online vs. offline relationships. Instead, it may be productive to place more focus on CMC as an extension or *complement* to ongoing relationship development and maintenance activities (Stafford et al., 1999). Shneiderman (2003) suggests that the payoff of technological innovation is the *support* some human need (e.g., relational needs) while minimizing potential evolutionary risks (e.g., inability to develop or maintain relationships). Baym, Zhang, and Lin (2004) extend this argument and claim social interaction is not separated into two distinct realms, but rather "internet interactions are woven into the daily maintenance of relationships" (p. 302). In some long-distance relationships, for example, CMC offers individuals a way to renegotiate the patterns of valued personal relationships. As Harwood (2000) and Holladay and Seipke (2007) indicate, when grandparents and grandchildren use CMC to maintain long-distance relationships, it provides an opportunity for renegotiation of the relationship in lieu of potential stagnation. This research also indicates that a mediator (i.e., the grandparent's child or grandchild's parent) is no longer relied upon as the sole intermediary of information; but that the grandchild and the grandparent are free to (co)create a close relationship independent of a third party. Rabby and Walther (2003) claim, "users, not systems, are what make a medium rich or lean" (p. 157). If individuals want highly intimate and satisfying relationships which transcend space and time, they are surely capable of accomplishing this task despite the "lean" or "rich" nature of the medium. As individuals initiate new relationships, reconnect with old friends, stay in touch with romantic partners, and update family members, they have the opportunity to engage in strategic and routine types of communication, offline *and* online, which serve to enhance and sustain these close interpersonal ties.

This chapter provides evidence that CMC can act as an extension, complement, and/or supplement to other channels of communication. Importantly, CMC also provides many people with a relatively economical and convenient way to engage in relational development and maintenance (Boneva, Kraut, & Frohlich, 2001).

Conceptual and Methodological Considerations

A conceptual question raised often by relational communication scholars interested in CMC is whether it is beneficial for those doing work on relational development and maintenance in computer mediated contexts to rely on traditional theories of relational communication, which often assume face-to-face contact. Wright (2004) identified relational maintenance strategies used in exclusively Internet-based relationships (i.e., EIB) and primarily Internet-based relationships (i.e., PIB). In terms of relational maintenance strategies employed, results indicate no differences between PIB and EIB relationships. Walther's (1996) hyperpersonal theory suggests that the interpersonal constraints inherent to mediated interaction may be overcome and that mediated communication, over time, often resembles traditional forms of interaction. Parks and Floyd (1996) offer support for Walther's hyperpersonal communication theory; moreover, they urge scholars to consider that while many relationships may develop and remain online, most ongoing close relationships are simply utilizing computer mediated communication as a supplement. Thus, it seems that many traditional theories of communication continue to be relevant to relationships developed and maintained in exclusively mediated environments as well as those that merely use CMC as a relational supplement. Undoubtedly, many factors affect the development and maintenance of computer mediated relationships. Researchers should ultimately expect some of these factors to be isolated to online environments; however, researchers should also anticipate many commonalities between relationships across online and face-to-face environments. Theoretical frameworks assuming face-to-face interaction applied to the use of e-mail have shown some fortitude, but it appears they have done so due to the fact that individuals have had face-to-face interaction at some point in their relational history. Would current theoretical thinking hold true if computer mediated partners have never had face-to-face contact? It is by examining the similarities and differences across contexts that researchers will come to have a better understanding of the processes inherent to the various types of relationship structures that exist in the modern world. Thus, we pose the following questions for researchers to consider: While the processes through which people develop personal relationships may differ (i.e., some develop online while others developed face-to-face), does this affect the manner in which these relationships are maintained? If so, how might we expect relational maintenance and support patterns to differ as a function of relationship development? These are but a few questions that remain for scholars.

Communication scholars remain committed to framing message production and exchange as a dynamic process. Methodologically, however, few studies have examined the *actual* content of computer-mediated exchanges (Boneva et al., 2001; Johnson, Haigh et al., 2008; Rabby, 1997); most rely solely on self-report data. If scholars are to understand these communicative exchanges more deeply, a combination of multiple methods and perspectives are needed. Self-report data remains useful in examining how individuals use CMC, and their perceived satisfaction in using technologies to form and maintain personal relationships. But do perceptions of satisfaction align with message content? We must question whether perceived relational satisfaction is due to the content of the message, the medium used to convey the message, or both. This could be extremely relevant for understanding what individuals are saying to convey attraction, similarity,

commitment, satisfaction, and trust not only in proximal relationships, but within long-distance relationships as well (Dainton & Aylor, 2002; Johnson, Haigh et al., 2008).

One must also consider the implications associate with content based studies, as researchers identify the content of messages from partners who still remain in contact with one another. Canary and Stafford's (1994) typology of maintenance behaviors includes avoidance (e.g., evasion of partner or issue) and antisocial behaviors (e.g., behaviors which seem unfriendly). Rabby and Walther (2003), additionally, indicate that negative maintenance behaviors are being used, but are not explicitly identified within e-mail content. To avoid is essentially not to maintain contact or not to reply to an e-mail message. If scholars know these behaviors exist, can they be measured effectively via content based studies? Since the literature up to this point has downplayed the importance of these maintenance behaviors in computer mediated contexts, should scholars focus their efforts on accumulating self-report data with regards to how individuals are utilizing these more negative maintenance strategies? With the examination of interaction avoidance and antisocial maintenance behaviors, scholars focused on relational conflict and relational repair might offer some insight into the nature of these behaviors within mediated contexts.

FUTURE DIRECTIONS

There is great promise for researchers intrigued by CMC and processes of relationship development and maintenance. From investigators interested in attraction and initial interaction to those interested in relational routines, many possibilities for structured exploration remain. Due to the dynamic nature of technology use, indeed, many areas of study have yet to be realized. Nonetheless, there are several future avenues of study that seem immediately relevant to the research presented in this chapter.

First, researchers may want to consider fundamental challenges associated with developing and maintaining relationships in mediated environments. It is clear that technology is changing traditional beliefs about what it means to "build a relationship" or "maintain a community." We must consider, then, the implications of physical location becoming a less salient predictor of the people with whom we develop and maintain relationships. It may be that individuals challenged by face-to-face relationship development for one reason or another turn to an exclusively mediated social world, which could intensify existing psychological or social issues. That is, people that turn to developing relationships solely in mediated environments may, over time, find themselves socially isolated or potential sufferers of their own conscious or unconscious social regulation. Once relationships have developed online, we must also consider the disadvantages of utilizing online support groups or social network sites as a primary source of social support. Due to the often large quantity of support group members, many individuals may find it difficult to contact a specific person online, thus making it more difficult to form significant long-term relationships with individuals in these environments (Wright & Bell, 2003). Questions that arise from the above mentioned are: What features of relationship development are affected by mediated interaction?, What issues do people face when restricting social interaction and support to mediated environments?, or What factors impact the efficacy of online social support systems?

Secondly, scholars should continue to explore the cognitive and affective components of mediated interaction. Although computer mediated support groups provide an opportunity for individuals to develop and maintain relationships that result in "supportive message exchange," this does not ensure that individuals *perceive* those exchanges as actually being supportive (Goldsmith, 2004). Indeed, Bugeja (2005) notes that people in crisis or in transition often wonder what is real in their

lives. As one can imagine, the perception of authenticity and substance of relationships exclusively developed and maintained in mediated environments could then be called into question in times of amplified stress or strain. People may wonder: Do you know the real me? Are you really my friend? How can I trust that what you are saying is true? Why are you so adamant that I follow your advice? Would you still support me if we met in person? To that end, more research is needed to explore the relational perceptions and expectations of individuals within these computer mediated support groups. Namely, are there certain expectations about how to behave, care for one another, express emotions, and maintain successful interactions in these contexts? Regrettably, Burnett and Buerkle (2004) found evidence of hostile interactive behaviors (e.g., flaming, trolling, spamming, and cyber-rape) in two health-related Usenet newsgroups. Researchers must continue examining CMC to identify what is being said, how it is conveyed, and ultimately, how people think and feel about those exchanges.

Third, the specific outcomes associated with developing and maintaining mediated relationships merit continued examination. Examining the benefits of using online environments to initiate and develop meaningful relationships, for example, should be salient to researchers and healthcare practitioners alike. Specifically, researchers might consider the effects of belonging to an online social network or support group. Weinberg et al. (1995) claim that the ability to strategically craft messages and responses to others' messages allows individuals to gain perspective through thoughtful reflection. If individuals are processing issues about offline relational partners as they are crafting these online messages, might the critical thinking and writing process serve a therapeutic function? Pennebaker (1997) suggests that the act of constructing narrative is a natural human process that not only allows individuals to understand their experiences, but among other things, understand themselves. Furthermore, the formation of written narratives allows individuals to organize thoughts, process information, and manage what are often complex emotional experiences and events (Richards, Beal, Seagal, & Pennebaker, 2000). Constructing written narratives has also been shown to assist individuals in maintaining a sense of predictability and control over their lives (Pennebaker & Seagal, 1999). Thus, it would be useful to know whether computer mediated rumination (i.e., in the form of online narrative construction) has an impact on offline relationships and relational maintenance processes. These concerns, among others, warrant further exploration.

It is said that relationships need both continuity and change to remain viable and that too much of either can destroy a close relationship (Wood, 2000). Perhaps the same is true of research in the area of relational communication. As new technologies continue to emerge, scholars must continue to investigate traditional conceptualizations of relational development and maintenance while concomitantly offering novel theoretical frameworks that more effectively elucidate the evolving process of human communication.

CONCLUSION

This chapter has provided ample evidence that new technologies play a key role in the development and maintenance of interpersonal relationships. This movement toward implementing new technologies into the communicative process suggests an ever-escalating need for researchers and practitioners to consider the patterns within, and implications of, mediated interactions. This chapter explored several areas of contemporary scholarship on interpersonal and relational communication, particularly as it relates to the processes of "relationship development" and "relationship maintenance." Moreover, a variety of research findings ranging from attraction and initial interaction to relational routines and social support have been presented.

Finally, consideration was given to some of the methodological and conceptual issues facing contemporary communication researchers. The authors encourage continued examination of the issues raised, as they impact our research as scholars and our relationships as humans.

REFERENCES

Adelman, M. B., Parks, M. R., & Albrecht, T. L. (1987). Beyond close relationships: Support in weak ties. In Albrecht, T. L., & Adelman, M. B. (Eds.), *Communicating social support* (pp. 105–125). Beverly Hills, CA: Sage.

Afifi, W. A., & Lucas, A. A. (2008). Information seeking in the initial stages of relationship development. In Sprechter, S., Wenzel, A., & Harvey, J. (Eds.), *Handbook of Relationship Initiation* (pp. 135–152). New York: Psychology Press.

Albrecht, T. L., & Goldsmith, D. J. (2003). Social support, social networks, and health. In Thompson, T. L., Dorsey, A. M., Miller, K. I., & Parrott, R. (Eds.), *Handbook of health communication* (pp. 263–284). Mahwah, NJ: Lawrence Erlbaum Associates.

Bargh, J. A., & McKenna, K. Y. A. (2004). The Internet and social life. *Annual Review of Psychology, 55*, 573–590. doi:10.1146/annurev.psych.55.090902.141922

Baym, N. K., Zhang, Y. B., & Lin, M. (2004). Social interactions across media: Interpersonal communication on the internet, telephone, and face-to-face. *New Media & Society, 6*(3), 299–318. doi:10.1177/1461444804041438

Berger, C. R. (1979). Beyond initial interaction: Uncertainty, understanding, and the development of interpersonal relationships. In Giles, H., & St. Clair, R. N. (Eds.), *Language and social psychology* (pp. 122–144). Oxford, UK: Basil Blackwell.

Berger, C. R. (1987). Communicating under uncertainty. In Roloff, M. E., & Miller, G. R. (Eds.), *Interpersonal processes: New directions in communication research* (pp. 39–62). Newbury Park, CA: Sage.

Berger, C. R., & Calabrese, R. J. (1975). Some explorations in initial interaction and beyond: Toward a developmental theory of interpersonal communication. *Human Communication Research*, *1*, 99–122. doi:10.1111/j.1468-2958.1975.tb00258.x

Berkman, L. F. (2000). Social support, social networks, social cohesion and health. *Social Work in Health Care*, *31*(2), 3–14. doi:10.1300/J010v31n02_02

Berscheid, E., Dion, K., Walster, E., & Walster, G. W. (1971). Physical attractiveness and dating choice: A test of the matching hypothesis. *Journal of Experimental Social Psychology*, *7*, 173–189. doi:10.1016/0022-1031(71)90065-5

Berscheid, E., & Peplau, L. (1983). The emerging science of relationships. In Kelly, H. H., Huston, T. L., & Leaving, G. (Eds.), *Close Relationships* (pp. 1–19). New York: Freeman.

Bersheid, E., & Reis, H. T. (1998). Attraction and close relationships. In S. Fiske, D. Gilbert, & G. Lindsey (Eds.), Handbook of social psychology (4th ed., Vol. 2), pp. 93-281. New York: McGraw-Hill.

Boneva, B., Kraut, R., & Frohlich, D. (2001). Using e-mail for personal relationships. *The American Behavioral Scientist*, *45*(3), 530–549. doi:10.1177/00027640121957204

Braithwaite, D. O., Waldron, V. R., & Finn, J. (1999). Communication of social support in computer-mediated groups for people with disabilities. *Health Communication*, *11*(2), 123–151. doi:10.1207/s15327027hc1102_2

Brennan, P. F., Moore, S. M., & Smyth, K. A. (1992). Alzheimer's disease caregivers' uses of a computer network. *Western Journal of Nursing Research*, *14*(5), 662–673. doi:10.1177/019394599201400508

Bridge, K., & Baxter, L. (1992). Blended friendships: Friends as work associates. *Western Journal of Communication*, *56*, 200–225.

Bugeja, M. (2005). *Interpersonal divide: The search for community in a technological age.* New York: Oxford University Press.

Burleson, B. R., & MacGeorge, R. L. (2002). Supportive communication. In Knapp, M. L., & Daly, J. A. (Eds.), *Handbook of interpersonal communication* (pp. 374–424). Thousand Oaks, CA: Sage.

Burnett, G., & Buerkle, H. (2004). Information exchange in virtual communities: A comparative study. *Journal of Computer-Mediated Communication*, *9*(2).

Byrne, D. (1971). *The attraction paradigm.* New York: Academic Press.

Canary, D. J., & Stafford, L. (1994). Maintaining relationships through strategic and routine interaction. In D. J. Canary & L. Stafford's (Eds.), Communication and relational maintenance (pp. 3-22). San Diego, CA: Academic Press, Inc.

Canary, D. J., Stafford, L., Hause, K. S., & Wallace, L. A. (1993). An inductive analysis of relational maintenance strategies: Comparisons among lovers, relatives, friends, and others. *Communication Research Reports*, *10*, 5–14. doi:10.1080/08824099309359913

Christian, A. (2005). Contesting the myth of the 'wicked stepmother': Narrative analysis of an online stepfamily support group. *Western Journal of Communication*, *69*(1), 27–47. doi:10.1080/10570310500034030

Cohen, S., & Wills, T. A. (1985). Stress, social support, and the buffering hypothesis. *Psychological Bulletin, 98*(2), 310–357. doi:10.1037/0033-2909.98.2.310

Craig, E. A. (2008). *"New to site and needing advice!": A content analysis examining role strain and social support in an online support group for childless stepmothers.* Unpublished doctoral dissertation, The University of Oklahoma, Norman.

Daft, R., & Lengel, R. (1984). Information richness: A new approach to managerial behavior and organization design. *Research in Organizational Behavior, 6,* 191–233.

Dainton, M., & Aylor, B. (2002). Patterns of communication channel use in the maintenance of long-distance relationships. *Communication Research Reports, 19*(2), 118–129.

Davidson, K. P., Pennebaker, J. W., & Dickerson, S. S. (2000). Who talks? The social psychology of illness support groups. *The American Psychologist, 55,* 205–217. doi:10.1037/0003-066X.55.2.205

Dillard, J., & Witteman, H. (1985). Romantic relationships at work: Organizational and personal influences. *Human Communication Research, 12,* 99–116. doi:10.1111/j.1468-2958.1985.tb00068.x

Dindia, K. (2003). Definitions and perspectives on relational maintenance communication. In Canary, D. J., & Dainton, M. (Eds.), *Maintaining relationships through communication* (pp. 1–28). Mahwah, NJ: Lawrence Erlbaum Associates, Publishing.

Duck, S. (1994). Steady as (s)he goes: Relational maintenance as a shared meaning system. In Canary, D. J., & Stafford, L. (Eds.), *Communication and relational maintenance* (pp. 45–60). San Diego, CA: Academic Press, Inc.

Dunham, P. J., Hurshman, A., Litwin, E., Gusella, J., Ellsworth, C., & Dodd, P. W. D. (1998). Computer-mediated social support: Single young mothers as a model system. *American Journal of Community Psychology, 26*(2), 281–306. doi:10.1023/A:1022132720104

Eichhorn, K. C. (2008). Soliciting social support over the Internet: An investigation of online eating disorder support groups. *Journal of Computer-Mediated Communication, 14*(1), article 3.

Ellison, N., Heino, R., & Gibbs, J. (2006). Managing impressions online: Self-presentation processes in the online dating environment. *Journal of Computer-Mediated Communication, 11*(2), article 2.

Ellison, N. B., Steinfield, C., & Lampe, C. (2007). The benefits of Facebook "friends:" Social capital and college students' use of online social network sites. *Journal of Computer-Mediated Communication, 12*(4), article 1.

Facebook. (2009) *Press room: Statistics.* Retrieved February 15, 2009, from http://www.facebook.com/press/info.php?statistics

Festinger, L., Schachter, S., & Back, K. (1950). *Social pressures in informal groups: A study of human factors in housing.* New York: Harper.

Fitzgerald, M. (2007, February). Only the money is real. *Inc. Magazine,* 80-85.

Gilbertson, J., Dindia, K., & Allen, M. (1998). Relational continuity constructional units and the maintenance of relationships. *Journal of Social and Personal Relationships, 15,* 774–790. doi:10.1177/0265407598156004

Goldsmith, D. J. (2004). *Communicating social support.* New York: Cambridge University Press.

Gottlieb, B. H. (1981). *Social networks and social support.* Beverly Hills, CA: Sage.

Granovetter, M. S. (1973). The strength of weak ties. *American Journal of Sociology, 78*(6), 1360–1380. doi:10.1086/225469

Harwood, J. (2000). Communication media use in the grandparent-grandchild relationship. *The Journal of Communication, 50*(4), 56–78. doi:10.1111/j.1460-2466.2000.tb02863.x

Haythornthwaite, C. (2001). Introduction: The internet in everyday life. *The American Behavioral Scientist, 45*(3), 363–382. doi:10.1177/00027640121957240

Herek, G. M., & Capitanio, J. P. (1996). "Some of my best friends": Intergroup contact, concealable stigma, and heterosexuals' attitudes toward gay men and lesbians. *Personality and Social Psychology Bulletin, 22*, 412–424. doi:10.1177/0146167296224007

Herring, S. C. (Ed.). (1996). *Computer-mediated communication: Linguistic, social and cross-cultural perspectives*. Philadelphia: John Benjamins.

Hill, C. T., Rubin, Z., & Plepau, L. A. (1976). Breakups before marriage: The end of 103 affairs. *The Journal of Social Issues, 32*, 147–168.

Holladay, S. J., & Seipke, H. L. (2007). Communication between grandparents and grandchildren in geographically separated relationships. *Communication Studies, 58*(3), 281–297. doi:10.1080/10510970701518371

Holland, S., & Harpin, J. (2008). "It's only MySpace": Teenagers and social networking online. In Holland, S. (Ed.), *Remote relationships in a small world* (pp. 117–136). New York: Peter Lang.

Howard, P. E. N., Rainie, L., & Jones, S. (2001). Days and nights on the internet: The impact of a diffusing technology. *The American Behavioral Scientist, 45*(3), 383–404.

Johnson, A. J., Haigh, M. M., Becker, J. A. H., Craig, E. A., & Wigley, S. (2008). College students' use of relational management strategies in email in long-distance and geographically close relationships. *Journal of Computer-Mediated Communication, 13*(2), article 1.

Johnson, A. J., Wright, K. B., Craig, E. A., Gilchrist, E. S., Lane, L. T., & Haigh, M. M. (2008). A Model for Predicting Stress Levels and Marital Satisfaction for Stepmothers Utilizing a Stress and Coping Approach. *Journal of Social and Personal Relationships, 25*(1), 119–142. doi:10.1177/0265407507086809

Kandell, D. B. (1978). Similarity in real life adolescent friendship pairs. *Journal of Personality and Social Psychology, 36*, 306–312. doi:10.1037/0022-3514.36.3.306

King, S. (1994). Analysis of electronic support groups for recovering addicts. *Interpersonal Computing and Technology, 2*(3).

Knapp, M. L., & Daly, J. A. (2002). *Handbook of interpersonal communication*. Thousand Oaks, CA: Sage Publications.

Lampe, C., Ellison, N., & Steinfield, C. (2006). A Face(book) in the crowd: Social searching vs. social browsing. In [New York: ACM Press.]. *Proceedings, CSCW-2006*, 167–170.

Lin, C. A., & Atkin, D. J. (2007). *Communication technology and social change*. Mahwah, NJ: Lawrence Erlbaum Associates.

Madden, M., & Raine, L. (2003). *America's online pursuits: The changing picture of who's online and what they do*. Pew/Internet. Retrieved January 10, 2009, from http://www.pewinternet.org/PPF/r/106/report_display.asp

McKenna, K. Y. A. (2008). MySpace or your place: Relationship initiation and development in the wired and wireless world. In Sprechter, S., Wenzel, A., & Harvey, J. (Eds.), *Handbook of Relationship Initiation* (pp. 235–248). New York: Psychology Press.

Meyerowitz, J. (1985). *No sense of place: The impact of electronic media on social behavior.* New York: Oxford University Press.

National Communication Association. (2002). *Definitions of communication.* Retrieved February 1, 2008, from http://www.natcom.org/nca/Template2.asp?bid=344

O'Sullivan, P. B. (2000). What you don't know won't hurt me: Impression management functions of communication channels in relationships. *Human Communication Research, 26,* 403–431. doi:10.1093/hcr/26.3.403

Parks, M. R., & Floyd, K. (1996). Making friends in cyberspace. *The Journal of Communication, 46*(1), 80–97. doi:10.1111/j.1460-2466.1996.tb01462.x

Pecchioni, L. L., Wright, K. B., & Nussbaum, J. F. (2005). *Life-span communication.* Mahwah, NJ: Lawrence Erlbaum Associates.

Pennebaker, J. W. (1997). Writing about emotional experiences as a therapeutic process. *Psychological Science, 8,* 162–166. doi:10.1111/j.1467-9280.1997.tb00403.x

Pennebaker, J. W., & Seagal, J. D. (1999). Forming a story: The health benefits of narrative. *Journal of Clinical Psychology, 55,* 1243–1254. doi:10.1002/(SICI)1097-4679(199910)55:10<1243::AID-JCLP6>3.0.CO;2-N

Pew Internet & American Life Project. (2004). *The Internet and daily life: Many Americans use the Internet in everyday activities, but traditional offline habits still dominate.* Retrieved October 11, 2007, from http://www.pewinternet.org/

Pew Internet & American Life Project. (2006). *Bloggers: A portrait of the internet's new storytellers.* Retrieved January 15, 2009, from http://www.pewinternet.org/PPF/r/186/report_display.asp

Pierce, C. A., Byrne, D., & Aguinis, H. (1996). Attraction in organizations: A model of workplace romance. *Journal of Organizational Behavior, 17*(1), 5–32. doi:10.1002/(SICI)1099-1379(199601)17:1<5::AID-JOB734>3.0.CO;2-E

Rabby, M. K. (1997, November). *Maintaining relationships via electronic mail.* Paper presented at the annual meeting of the National Communication Association, Chicago, IL.

Rabby, M. K., & Walther, J. B. (2003). Computer-mediated communication effects on relationship formation and maintenance. In Canary, D. J., & Dainton, M. (Eds.), *Maintaining relationships through communication* (pp. 141–162). Mahwah, NJ: Lawrence Erlbaum Associates, Publishing.

Rice, R. E., & Love, G. (1987). Electronic emotion: Socioemotional content in a computer-mediated communication network. *Communication Research, 14,* 85–108. doi:10.1177/009365087014001005

Richards, J. M., Beal, W. E., Seagal, J. D., & Pennebaker, J. W. (2000). Effects of disclosure of traumatic events on illness behavior among psychiatric prison inmates. *Journal of Abnormal Psychology, 109,* 156–160. doi:10.1037/0021-843X.109.1.156

Ridings, C. M., & Gefen, D. (2004). Virtual community attraction: Why people hang out online. *Journal of Computer-Mediated Communication, 10*(1). Retrieved June 28, 2005, from http://jcmc.indiana.edu/vol10/issue1/ridings_gefen.html

Rodgers, S., & Chen, Q. (2005). Internet community group participation: Psychosocial benefits for women with breast cancer. *Journal of Computer-Mediated Communication, 10*(4), article 5.

Schutz, W. (1966). *The interpersonal underworld*. Palo Alto, CA: Science and Behavior Books, Inc.

Second Life. (2008). *Economic statistics: raw data files*. Retrieved on February 2, 2009, from http://secondlife.com/statistics/economy-data.php

Sharf, B. F. (1997). Communicating breast cancer on-line: Support and empowerment on the Internet. *Women & Health, 26*(1), 65–84. doi:10.1300/J013v26n01_05

Shneiderman, B. (2003). *Leonardo's laptop: Human needs and the new computing technologies*. Cambridge, MA: The MIT Press.

Stafford, L. (2005). *Maintaining long-distance and cross-residential relationships*. Mahwah, NJ: Lawrence Erlbaum Associates, Publishing.

Stafford, L., Kline, S. L., & Dimmick, J. (1999). Home e-mail: Relational maintenance and gratification opportunities. *Journal of Broadcasting & Electronic Media, 43*(4), 659–669.

Stefanone, M. A., & Jang, C. (2007). Writing for friends and family: The interpersonal nature of blogs. *Journal of Computer-Mediated Communication, 13*(1), article 7.

Sullivan, C. F. (2003). Gendered cybersupport: A thematic analysis of two online cancer support groups. *Journal of Health Psychology, 8*(1), 83–103. doi:10.1177/1359105303008001446

Sunnafrank, M. (1986). Predicted outcome value during initial interactions: A reformulation of uncertainty reduction theory. *Human Communication Research, 13*, 3–33. doi:10.1111/j.1468-2958.1986.tb00092.x

Sunnafrank, M. (1988). Predicted outcome value in initial conversations. *Communication Research Reports, 5*, 169–172. doi:10.1080/08824098809359819

Sunnafrank, M. (1990). Predicted outcome values and uncertainty reduction theories: A test of competing perspectives. *Human Communication Research, 17*, 76–103. doi:10.1111/j.1468-2958.1990.tb00227.x

Sunnafrank, M. (1991). Interpersonal attraction and attitude similarity: A communication-based assessment. In Anderson, J. A. (Ed.), *Communication yearbook 14* (pp. 451–483). Newbury Park, CA: Sage.

Walther, J. B. (1996). Computer-mediated communication: Impersonal, interpersonal, and hyperpersonal interaction. *Communication Research, 23*(1), 1–43. doi:10.1177/009365096023001001

Wang, Z., Walther, J. B., Pingree, S., & Hawkins, R. P. (2008). Health information, credibility, homophily, and influence via the Internet: Web sites versus discussion groups. *Health Communication, 23*, 358–368. doi:10.1080/10410230802229738

Weinberg, N., Schmale, J. D., Uken, J., & Wessel, K. (1995). Computer-mediated support groups. *Social Work with Groups, 17*(4), 43–54. doi:10.1300/J009v17n04_04

Wellman, B. (1999). *Networks in the global village: Life in contemporary communities*. Boulder, CO: Westview Press.

Wood, J. T. (2000). *Relational communication: Continuity and change in personal relationships*. Belmont, CA: Wadsworth.

Wright, K. B. (2002). Social support within an on-line cancer community: An assessment of emotional support, perceptions of advantages and disadvantages, and motives for using the community from a communication perspective. *Journal of Applied Communication Research, 30*(3), 195–209. doi:10.1080/00909880216586

Wright, K. B. (2004). On-line relational maintenance strategies and perceptions of partners within exclusively internet-based and primarily internet-based relationships. *Communication Studies, 55*(2), 239–253.

Wright, K. B., & Bell, S. B. (2003). Health-related support groups on the Internet: Linking empirical findings to social support and computer-mediated communication theory. *Journal of Health Psychology, 8*(1), 39–54. doi:10.1177/1359105303008001429

ADDITIONAL READING

Bambina, A. (2007). *Online social support: The interplay of social networks and computer-mediated communication.* Youngstown, NY: Cambria Press.

Barnes, S. (2003). *Computer-mediated communication: Human-to-human communication across the internet.* Boston: Allyn and Bacon.

Barnes, S. B. (2001). *Online connections: Internet interpersonal relationships.* Cresskill, NJ: Hampton Press, Inc.

Baym, N. K. (1995). The emergence of community in computer-mediated communication. In Jones, S. G. (Ed.), *Cybersociety: Computer-mediated communication and community* (pp. 138–163). Thousand Oaks, CA: Sage.

Boyd, D., & Ellison, N. (2007). Social network sites: Definition, history, and scholarship. *Journal of Computer-Mediated Communication, 13*(1), 11.

Brehm, S., Miller, R., Perlman, D., & Campbell, S. (2002). *Intimate relationships.* New York: McGraw-Hill.

Burgoon, J. K., Bonito, J. A., Ramirez, A., Dunbar, N. E., Kam, K., & Fischer, J. (2002). Testing the interactivity principle: Effects of mediation, propinquity, and verbal and nonverbal modalities in interpersonal interaction. *The Journal of Communication, 52,* 657–677. doi:10.1111/j.1460-2466.2002.tb02567.x

Caplan, S. E. (2003). Preference for online social interaction - A theory of problematic Internet use and psychosocial well-being. *Communication Research, 30*(6), 625–648. doi:10.1177/0093650203257842

Cohen, S., Underwood, L. G., & Gottlieb, B. H. (Eds.). (2000). *Social support measurement and intervention: A guide for health and social scientists.* New York: Oxford University Press.

Ellison, N., Lampe, C., & Steinfield, C. (2009). Social network sites and society: Current trends and future possibilities. *Interactions Magazine, 16,* 1-9. Retrieved February 20, 2009, from https://www.msu.edu/~nellison/EllisonLampeSteinfield2009.pdf

Flaherty, L. M., Pearce, K. J., & Rubin, R. B. (1998). Internet and face-to-face communication: Not functional alternatives. *Communication Quarterly, 46*(3), 250–268.

Garton, L., Haythonthwaite, C., & Wellman, B. (1997). Studying on-line social networks. *Journal of Computer-Mediated Communication, 3*(1), article 1.

Hartelius, E. J. (2005). A content-based taxonomy of blogs and the formation of a virtual community. *Kaleidoscope: A Graduate Journal of Qualitative Communication Research, 4,* 71-91.

Hendrick, C., & Hendrick, S. S. (Eds.). (2000). *Close relationships: A sourcebook.* Thousand Oaks, CA: Sage.

Holland, S. (Ed.). (2008). *Remote relationships in a small world.* New York: Peter Lang.

Huffaker, D. A., & Calvert, L. L. (2005). Gender, identity, and language use in teenage blogs. *Journal of Computer-Mediated Communication, 10*(1), article 1.

Kelleher, T., & Miller, B. M. (2006). Organizational blogs and the human voice: Relational strategies and relational outcomes. *Journal of Computer-Mediated Communication, 11*(2), article 1.

Kim, H., Kim, G. J., Park, H. W., & Rice, R. E. (2007). Configurations of relationships in different media: Ftf, email, instant messenger, mobile phone, and sms. *Journal of Computer-Mediated Communication, 12*(4), article 3.

Newhagen, J. E., & Rafaeli, S. (1996). Why communication researchers should study the Internet: A dialogue. *The Journal of Communication, 46*, 4–13. doi:10.1111/j.1460-2466.1996.tb01458.x

Qian, H., & Scott, C. R. (2007). Anonymity and self-disclosure on weblogs. *Journal of Computer-Mediated Communication, 12*(4), 14. doi:10.1111/j.1083-6101.2007.00380.x

Sprecher, S., Wenzel, A., & Harvey, J. (Eds.). (2008). *Handbook of relationship initiation.* New York: Psychology Press.

Tidwell, L. C., & Walther, J. B. (2002). Computer-mediated communication effects on disclosure, impressions, and interpersonal evaluations: Getting to know one another a bit at a time. *Human Communication Research, 28*, 317–348. doi:10.1111/j.1468-2958.2002.tb00811.x

Utz, S. (2007). Media use in long-distance friendships. *Information Communication and Society, 10*(5), 694–713. doi:10.1080/13691180701658046

Viegas, F. B. (2005). Bloggers' expectations of privacy and accountability: An initial survey. *Journal of Computer-Mediated Communication, 10*(3), 12.

Walther, J. B. (1993). Impression development in computer-mediated interaction. *Western Journal of Communication, 57*, 381–398.

Walther, J. B. (2007). Selective self-presentation in computer-mediated communication: Hyperpersonal dimensions of technology, language, and cognition. *Computers in Human Behavior, 23*, 2538–2557. doi:10.1016/j.chb.2006.05.002

Walther, J. B., & Burgoon, J. K. (1992). Relational communication in computer-mediated interaction. *Human Communication Research, 19*, 50–88. doi:10.1111/j.1468-2958.1992.tb00295.x

Wang, H., & Andersen, P. A. (2007, May). *Computer-mediated communication in relationship maintenance: An examination of self-disclosure in long-distance friendships.* Paper presented at the annual meeting of the International Communication Association, San Francisco, CA.

Wellman, B. (1997). An electronic group is virtually a social network. In Kiesler, S. (Ed.), *Culture of the Internet* (pp. 179–205). Mahwah, NJ: Lawrence Erlbaum.

Wellman, B., & Gulia, M. (1999). The network basis of social support: A network is more than the sum of its ties. In Wellman, B. (Ed.), *Networks in the global village: Life in contemporary communities* (pp. 83–118). Boulder, CO: Westview Press.

Westmyer, S. A., DiCioccio, R. L., & Rubin, R. B. (1998). Appropriateness and effectiveness of communication channels in competent interpersonal communication. *The Journal of Communication, 48*, 27–48. doi:10.1111/j.1460-2466.1998.tb02758.x

Whitty, M., & Carr, A. (2006). *Cyberspace romance: The psychology of online relationships.* New York: Palgrave Macmillan.

Whitty, M. T., Baker, A. J., & Inman, J. A. (2007). *Online matchmaking.* New York, NY: Palgrave Macmillan. doi:10.1057/9780230206182

Zywica, J., & Danowski, J. (2008). The faces of facebookers: Investigating social enhancement and social compensation hypotheses; Predicting facebook and offline popularity from sociability and self-esteem, and mapping the meaning of popularity with semantic networks. *Journal of Computer-Mediated Communication, 14*(1), article 1.

Chapter 6
"Is it a Boy or a Girl?"
Anonymity and Gender in Computer–Mediated Interactions

Katheryn C. Maguire
Wayne State University, USA

ABSTRACT

This chapter examines the research on sex differences and gender identification in computer-mediated interaction (CMI), and presents a pilot study of synchronous, anonymous, one-to-one interactions, to understand the extent to which a person's "real life" sex can be identified in CMIs as well as the stylistic and linguistic cues that "mark" someone as "male" or "female." Although previous research has reported sex differences in a number of different variables (e.g., number of words, disagreements), analysis of the transcripts in this study revealed only one significant difference, in that men corrected themselves more often than women. Furthermore, participants correctly guessed the sex of their partner 62.5% of the time, felt approximately 65% sure of their guess, and used gender stereotypes to make their assessments. Implications for anonymity and CMI research are discussed, focusing on the conditions under which sex differences and gender stereotypes become relevant in on-line interactions.

INTRODUCTION

Over the past two decades, computer-mediated interaction (CMI) has become an accepted part of our professional and personal lives. A survey of internet use revealed a nearly 130% growth of internet usage in North America between 2000 and 2007, totaling over 248 million users (Internetworldstats, 2007). Its rise in popularity and potential to challenge

commonly held beliefs about communication have spurred a large body of research on text-based CMI. Early scholarship celebrated its potential to screen out a user's identifying information, such as his/her age, race, physical appearance, or sex (Chesebro & Bonsall, 1989; del-Teso-Craviotto, 2008; McCormick & McCormick, 1992; Parks & Floyd, 1996) and has highlighted a number of benefits, including better decision-making, increased communication satisfaction among discussants, the ability to re-

DOI: 10.4018/978-1-61520-827-2.ch006

ceive online therapy/support, and general relief from fear of retribution (Bronco, 2004; Hayne & Rice, 1997; Valacich, George, Nunnamaker, Vogel, 1994; Wallace, 1999). There are undesirable results as well, such as libel, impersonation, online fraud, spam, and hate mail (Teich, Frankel, Kling, & Lee, 1999).

One way that computer users have taken advantage of anonymity in CMI is to impersonate a member of the opposite sex or to experiment with their gender identity in on-line interactions (Danet, 1996; Witmer & Katzman, 1997). Indeed, in a survey of 823 internet users, Samp, Wittenberg, and Gillett (2003) found that 28% of the respondents had pretended to be a member of the opposite sex. In these instances, users "manipulate" the communication context to conform to the identity they wish to assume (Myers, 1987), often by employing gender-stereotyped language to "mark" themselves as "male" or "female." Thus, gender in CMI can be seen as a performance that can be altered to suit communicative goals. As such, some CMI users might be left questioning the gender identity of their interaction partners.

According to Scott (1998), "because so much of our interaction with others involves identified sources, many communicators are uncomfortable with anonymous sources and their natural tendency is to attribute a source to all messages" (p. 398). This may be especially true with biological sex, as individuals have a need to classify people as male or female (Danet, 1996). As Herring and Martinson (2004) explain, "It is important to know an interlocutor's identity in order to understand and evaluate the interaction; this is especially true for gender, which is conventionally associated with different norms, roles, and communication styles in most human cultures" (p. 425). Despite the apparent anonymity of CMI, some scholars believe that CMI users leave gender "traces" during a text-based interaction that competent communicators could decode, with varying degrees of certainty, to determine the "real life" sex of anonymous users (Sierpe, 2005). In a study of

an on-line text-based game, for instance, Herring and Martinson (2004) found that players who were trying to portray themselves as a member of the opposite sex would use stereotypic content to convince others of the "truth." Yet, an analysis of the players' postings revealed stylistic cues at the word and sentence levels (e.g., message length), performed unconsciously, that revealed the players' sex. Two questions arise from this dilemma. First, to what extent does CMI mask the sex of its users? Second, what are the "real" and/or perceived cues that may reveal the sex of anonymous CMI users?

To answer these questions, a number of researchers have sought to identify differences between men and women's on-line communication (e.g., Baron 2004; Guiller & Durndell, 2006; 2007; Herring, 2004; Herring & Paolillo, 2006; Palomares, 2004; 2008; Postmes & Spears, 2002; Reid, Keerie, & Palomares, 2003; Selfe & Meyer, 1991; Sarch, 1996) as well as people's ability to correctly identify the sex of CMI users (e.g., Cornetto & Nowak, 2006; Herring & Martinson, 2004; Koch, Mueller, Kruse, & Sumbach, 2005; Nowak, 2003; Savicki, Kelley, & Oesterreich, 1999; Thomson & Murachver, 2001). The present chapter reviews these lines of research and presents a pilot study that examines the extent to which one's sex is masked during a synchronous, on-line interaction between two anonymous chat mates. For the purposes of this chapter, the term *sex* will be used when categorization is based on the self-identified biological characteristic of the CMI user (e.g., male vs. female), and *gender* will be used when categorization is based on other properties (e.g., language, communication style). To begin, a brief discussion of anonymity and CMI is presented. Next, research on gender and CMI is reviewed, starting with a discussion of cues that may be used in the identification process. After the pilot study's procedure, results, and discussion are presented, the paper ends with a re-examination of gender issues in CMIs.

BACKGROUND

Anonymity and the CMI Context

Although anonymity is not a new communication construct, the advent of new computer technologies has brought anonymity back into the scholarly forum (Scott, 1998). Scott (writing as Anonymous, 1998) proposed the Model of Anonymous Communication (MAC) to explain the relationship among anonymity, communication, and identity. According to Scott, there are three types of anonymity that vary according to the level of knowledge among interactants and source specificity (i.e., the extent to which a source can be differentiated from other potential sources). If there is low source specificity (e.g., the sender of a message could be anyone), and low source knowledge (e.g., there is little or no familiarity between the source and receiver), then the communication is fully anonymous (e.g., "spam" from an unknown source). At the other extreme, if there is high source specificity and source knowledge, then the interactants are fully identified (e.g., an instant message from one's sister). Between these two extremes is the partially anonymous interaction—an interaction during which "either a source cannot be individually specified or when there is not a high level of knowledge, but not both" (p. 391) (e.g., an email from a group mate in another state who you have never met face-to-face).

As an extension to the MAC, Rains and Scott (2007) proposed the Model of Receiver Responses to Anonymous Communication (MRRAC) to better understand when and how identification efforts occur. The model focuses on the methods by which a receiver of anonymous communication could identify an anonymous sender, the characteristics of the communication situation that may enable or constrain a receiver's ability to identify a sender, and the receiver's motivations for attempting to identify (or further anonymize) the message source. According to the model, a

message receiver's desire and ability to identify an anonymous sender depends on the context in which the CMI takes place (interpersonal vs. mass communication) and features of the communication medium that may reveal (or conceal) potentially identifying information (i.e., level of synchronicity, channel bandwidth, control over message construction). For example, some modes of CMI, such as email and bulletin boards, have a longer delay in reciprocal interactions, thereby allowing the user more time to craft a message to hide his/her identity. There are other, more synchronous and interpersonal modes of CMI, such as instant messaging or one-to-one chat, that may hinder anonymization efforts due to the interdependent nature of the interaction (i.e., the need to keep the conversation going) (Rains & Scott).

Following Rains and Scott (2007), the extent to which someone's sex can be identified in CMI will depend on a number of factors, including whether or not gender is made salient in the interaction (which may influence motivation to identify), the context of the interaction (including level of synchronicity and nature of the communication), and the sex composition of the communicators (a key characteristic of the interaction). Because text-based CMI provides little information in terms of visual cues, receivers must rely on textual information, such as names or signatures attached to the message, pronouns used in the interaction, or use of certain phrases or terms to identify the sex of the sender (Scott, 1998). There may also be trace information (i.e., nonverbal cues that make someone unique) left behind that may help a receiver identify a sender (Rains & Scott, 2007). The next sections address the cues that may reveal a CMI user's sex as well as CMI users' ability to guess the sex of other users.

Gender, Language, and Style

Through observation, systematic investigation, and meta-analytic procedures, scholars have tried to determine whether there are sex differences in men and women's language choices (see Bischoeping, 1993; Eagly, 1995; James & Clark, 1993; James & Drakich, 1993; McFadyen, 1996; Pruett, 1989; Smythe & Schlueter, 1989; Tannen, 1990 for further information). In one of the most comprehensive studies to date, Newman, Groom, Handelman, and Pennebaker (2008) examined 14,324 texts from a mix of written and spoken sources to determine sex differences in a large number of variables. Their analysis showed that women used language to discuss people and what they were doing, as well as to communicate internal processes to others (e.g., emotions, senses, negations). Men used language to discuss external events, objects, and processes (e.g., occupation, money, and sports; used numbers, articles, prepositions, long words). Men and women were indistinguishable in references to sexuality, anger, time, number of words, question marks, hedges, and insertion of qualifiers in the form of exclusion words. Whereas males and females did follow a pattern of "gendered" communication, the effect size was small.

Given the nature of CMI to potentially "shield" visual indicators of biological sex from interactions, a significant number of scholars have sought to determine whether these sex differences exist in a variety of CMI contexts. Much of this research assumes that differences do exist: females are socialized to communicate in expressive, sometimes tentative ways to emphasize other people and/or relationships, and males are socialized to communicate in terse, unembellished, and sometimes aggressive ways that emphasize tasks or assert control (e.g., Baron, 2004; Fox, Bukakto, Hallahan, & Crawford, 2007; Guiller & Durndell, 2007; van der Meij, 2007). Other scholars, guided by theories such as Communication Accommodation Theory (CAT) (Coupland, Coupland, & Giles, 1991), Social Identity model of Deindividuation Effects (SIDE) (Lea & Spears, 1991), and Self Categorization Theory (SCT) (Turner, Hogg, Oakes, Reicher, & Wetherell, 1987), are also interested in determining the conditions under

which sex differences emerge. In these instances, the researchers make gender more "salient" by either manipulating the sex composition of participant groups (e.g., same sex or opposite sex) or "priming" the participants to be in a gendered mindset.

Sex Differences

When examining the research on sex differences, many scholars believe that context, content, and channel matter, and a close examination of the literature shows consistency in the presence of gendered communication across these variables. In a review of studies in the educational context, for example, Yates (2001) concluded that there are clear variations in men's and women's approaches to and use of language, in that males in CMI engage in tactics of "exclusion and de-legitimation" (p. 32). Research of an on-line discussion board for a psychology class by Guiller and Durndell (2006, 2007) seems to support Yates' assessment, in that females tended to use attenuated language and positive socio-emotional content, whereas men used authoritative language and negative socio-emotional content. The researchers believed that CMI users may, in fact, emphasize gendered communication to overcome the lack of context cues so that participants will recognize other users as "male" or "female."

Examinations of CMI in more "personal" settings have revealed similar results. For instance, several studies have been conducted using postings to asynchronous, one-to-many contexts such as fantasy websites, discussion boards, news groups, and blogs. In a study of the ways women construct and negotiate gender in multi-user dungeons (MUDs), Sarch (1996) found that women tended to use tag questions, hedges, empty adjectives, hypercorrect grammar, and super-polite forms of speech, whereas men were more likely to be blunt and used more crude language. Shephard and Williamson's (1996) examination of internet relay chat (IRC) found that women softened their language, used more questions, and posted more responses than men, and Selfe and Meyer (1991) reported that women asked more questions than men during IRC, whereas men used more verbal assertiveness and topic initiation in the interaction than women. Based on their results, the authors concluded that computer conferencing may not be as egalitarian as originally hoped. Similarly, Jaffe, Lee, Huang, and Oshagan (1999) examined postings to a message board, finding that women displayed "social interdependence" in that they made more references to others, references to self, and supporting statements in their postings than men. Women also chose pseudonyms that hid their sex more often than men. The authors noted the irony in this: whereas women chose to mask their identity, they still wrote in ways that were gendered. Witmer and Katzman (1997), on the other hand, found that women not only used graphic accents in their postings to newsgroups more than men, they also flamed more, a result that runs counter to the prediction that men are more aggressive in CMI than women.

More recent research has focused on differences that occur in weblogs (i.e., blogs). Herring and Paolillo (2006) used a program called "gender genie" that can purportedly identify the gender of an author based on language use. Instead of finding gender differences, they found that the type of blog mattered more, in that female-preferential features (i.e., those that are interactional) were more prevalent in diary blogs whereas male-preferential features (i.e., those that are informational) were more prevalent in news blogs. Similarly, Huffaker and Calvert (2005) examined diary blogs authored by teenagers, finding that self disclosure was prevalent in both male and female authored blogs, with 70% of users revealing their first name to others. While there were no gender differences in use of emoticons or communal language (i.e., language of connection), male authors did demonstrate more sureness in their writing.

Another line of research has focused on sex differences in one-to-one CMI contexts, such as asynchronous email messages and synchronous instant messaging (IM). Colley and Todd (2002) asked participants to write an email to a friend about a favorite vacation. Although feminine features were more evident than masculine features overall, emails from women showed more interpersonal sensitivity, awareness of the recipient, excitability, initial inquiries, and affectionate signoffs than emails from men. Also, content seemed to fall along gendered lines, where females talked about shopping and night life and males talked about the local people and the location. Finally, the sex of the recipient seemed to matter, in that self disclosure and self references were higher in opposite sex exchanges, perhaps signaling a greater desire for intimacy between the friends. Colley et al. (2004) also found that communicators sent messages that follow gender stereotypes, in that women wrote longer messages, used more positive intensifiers, multiple exclamation marks, and mentioned family, shopping, and positive emotions more than men. Men, on the other hand, used more offensive language and talked more about sports than women. Baron's (2004) study of IM found that female writers used more emoticons and followed grammatical rules more often than male writers, whereas males used contractions more than females. Last, Fox et al. (2007) reported few differences overall; however, women's IMs were generally more expressive than men's IMs. Additionally, whereas IMs sent to men had more words and more turns than IMs sent to women, IMs sent to women had more references to emotion than IMs sent to men, regardless of the sender's sex. In this instance, as before, the sex of the recipient seemed to matter.

Gender Salience

Whereas the research in the previous section was more concerned about identifying sex differences in CMI, the research in this section focuses on when a user's sex matters most. One context in which a CMI user's sex matters a great deal is in the dating context. For instance, Groom and Pennebaker (2005) studied online personal ads, finding that gender stereotypes corresponded well to actual group differences: women were more likely to use pronouns, discuss emotions, and use present tense, whereas men used more articles and made more references to their jobs. Indeed, del-Teso Craviotto (2008) saw gender as a performance in her study of dating chatrooms, where users must show that they are authentic members of a given sex in order to interact and engage in internet desire. Similarly, context mattered in Gooden and Winefield's (2007) examination of two discussion boards: one assumed to be populated primarily by men (prostate cancer) and one primarily populated by women (breast cancer). Although men and women seemed to engage in both informational and emotional messages/support, males cited research and medical reports, offered advice, and used humor to cope, whereas women clearly expressed emotion, and offered expressions of affection and nurturing.

In addition to the context, the content of the interaction may increase gender salience. Postmes and Spears (2002) used the SIDE model to explain when sex differences are more likely to occur. From a SIDE perspective, a lack of individuating information, as in anonymous CMI, may make group membership more salient, given that the focus is no longer on the individual but on their group identity (in this case, gender). Thus, CMI users are more likely to self stereotype and use gendered communication. In support of the model, the authors found that participants acted in more gendered ways when gender was made salient under conditions of anonymity than when gender was less salient.

Along the same lines, Palomares and colleagues (2004, 2008; Reid, Keerie, & Palomares, 2003) used SCT to explain the conditions under which gender is more salient. According to Palomares (2004), "individuals categorize themselves relative to the situational context to make sense of the world" and as such, use "social similarities and

differences between individuals to define the self and others as a member of a certain social group" (p. 557). In situations where gender is made salient, then, CMI users should use gender-linked language that is consistent with gender stereotypes, so that males will use typical male-linked language and females will use typical female-linked language. In support of this assumption, Reid, Keerie, and Palomares (2003) found that women in face-to-face interactions used more tentative language than men in the high gender salience condition, but not the low gender salience condition, where both men and women used moderate levels of tentative language. Palomares (2004) extended this work into the CMI context with his examination of email messages and the inclusion of gender schematicity as another explanatory mechanism. He believed that gender schematic individuals (i.e., sex-typed) would use language that is "appropriate" to their sex. Whereas males and females did not differ in their language use overall, or in terms of gender schematicity, results indicated that gender schematic males and females used gendered language in gender salient conditions. Similarly, Palomares (2008) found that women referenced emotion in emails more than men when gender was made salient. This result was particularly strong in the female-to-male gender-salient condition, in that the female participants further emphasized their group membership through the use of gendered language.

Informed by CAT, Thomson (2006) questioned whether group membership, as predicted by SIDE, was a better predictor of gendered language than accommodation to the recipient or the nature of the topic. According to CAT, participants in CMI can either accentuate similarities through the use of similar language as their conversation partner (i.e., convergence), or emphasize differences though dissimilar communication styles (i.e., divergence). In an examination of email messages written about a "female" topic verses a "male" topic, Thomson found that participants used gendered language consistent with the topic being discussed, regardless of sex: female-preferential language was used when discussing a feminine topic, and male-preferential language was used when discussing a masculine topic. Thomson, Murachver, and Green (2001) also challenged the simplistic assumption that sex differences in language are a given, instead claiming that "participants in a conversation both change the situation and are changed by it" (p. 171). They examined email messages sent to either a female "netpal" who used female-style language or a male "netpal" who used male-style language. Results showed that participants, regardless of their own sex, accommodated to the communication style of their netpal. In a second study, Thomson et al. replicated their finding regarding accommodation, yet also found a main effect for sex of the participant. They concluded that accommodation might only occur when the language style and the author's sex match; otherwise, divergence will occur (i.e., CMI users will maintain their own gender-preferential style). This assertion is consistent with Palomares' (2008) finding that women communicated in a more gendered manner when interacting with a male than another female.

The previous section reviewed research regarding the extent to which sex differences exist in CMI. Overall, the research suggests that while men and women often do communicate in gender stereotypic ways, they do so more when gender is made salient through either the composition of the communicators (i.e., same sex vs. opposite sex), the topic of conversation, or the nature of the context in which the interaction occurs. Given that communicators do tend to use gender stereotypic language in their CMI, it is possible that CMI users could identify the sex of their anonymous interaction partners based on the language and stylistic variables. Indeed, Lee (2007) believes that stereotypes are useful cognitive tools to help CMI users deal with the complexities of everyday life, and that such stereotypes can help them make gender identifications in on-line environments. Also recall that CMI users may leave gender traces, in

the form of language stereotypes (i.e., widely held beliefs regarding characteristics of male or female language) that a competent communicator should be able to decode during a text-based interaction (Sierpe, 2005). The next section addresses the accuracy of gender assessments in CMI.

Gender Identification Efforts

Similar to research on gender identification of spoken communication (e.g., Ferber, 1995; Martin, 1997), much of the CMI research indicates that individuals are fairly accurate (i.e., better than chance) in their determinations of a user's sex. Participants in a study of IRC by Koch et al. (2005), for instance, were able to correctly guess the sex of chat partners 66.25% of the time, while participants in a study by Thomson and Murachver (2001) were correct 60% of the time. Then again, Savicki et al. (1999) found that participants were accurate 70% of the time when guessing the sex of an email written by a male in low communication (i.e., masculine) style, but only 43% accurate with messages written by a male in high communication (i.e., feminine style) style. Likewise, participants were 65% accurate with messages written by a female in low communication (i.e., contra-gender) style, but only 55% accurate with messages written by a female in low communication style. Participants in Herring and Martinson's (2004) study of postings on an on-line, text-based "To tell the truth" identity game were also not very accurate; although participants generally felt that the players' performances were unconvincing, they were accurate only 47% of the time. Finally, participants guessing sex based on user names were correct 74% of the time, with 22% of the user names clearly indicating the owner's sex (Cornetto & Nowak, 2006). Then again, participants were only 50% correct in a study of synchronous IRC with a confederate (Nowak, 2003). It is interesting to note that over one third of participants in these last two studies decided not to make gender identifications at all, suggesting that some users may not be interested in knowing the sex of other anonymous interactants. This conjecture is supported by Samp et al.'s (2003) finding that only 45% of surveyed CMI users were ever curious about the gender of other anonymous users.

In addition to accuracy measures, Sierpe (2005) also asserted that researchers interested in gender identification should look at certainty measures as well. Savicki et al. (1999) found that participants were somewhat certain about their judgments (approximately 59%), with a higher degree of certainty regarding messages authored by male than females. Certainty was not significantly associated with accuracy. Similarly, certainty was not significantly associated with accuracy in the study by Cornetto and Nowak (2006), where participants were approximately 60% certain about their guesses. Although Sierpe (2005) suggests that a low degree of certainty occurs when there is a discrepancy between the markers used for gender assessments and the cultural expectations of the guessers, the lack of association between accuracy and certainty fails to support this assumption.

Finally, studies of gender identification have also sought to determine which of the cues available to CMI users are the best predictors of accuracy. For instance, Savicki et al. (1999) found that participants making gender identification in email messages were more accurate when they relied on the use of coarse language by the message author, and were less accurate when they relied on whether the author mentioned talking to others in their CMIs. Spelling and grammar errors were also helpful for participants making gender assessments when messages were written in a masculine style. In their study of anonymous IRC, Koch et al. (2005) determined that participants who relied on content-related stereotypic traits (i.e., hints from content, such as interest in sports for males and an interest in becoming a nurse for females), which was used 15% of the time, were the least accurate

(50%), whereas certain syntactic (i.e., hints from language and grammar, such as use of strong language for males, politically correct language for females) and pragmatic (i.e., hints from conversational behavior and style, such as competitive language for males, supportive language for females) markers led to more accurate predictions. Overall, syntactic cues had the best predictive value (88%) but were the least used (14%), and then almost exclusively by females; pragmatic cues, used in 70% of the cases, were also associated with a fairly high degree of accuracy (63%). Finally, Thomson and Murachver (2001) examined email messages sent between two anonymous individuals of the same sex. A weighted combination of twelve of variables (i.e., intense adverbs, hedges, references to emotion, personal information, insults, apologies, self derogatory comments, opinions, compliments, questions, adjectives, subordinate conjunctions) was able to differentiate between males and females: discriminate analysis of the data correctly classified 91.4% of the authors (94.7% of female authors, and 87.5% of male authors).

In review, the literature presented seems to indicate that CMI users are fairly good judges of sex, and are fairly certain about their assessments. There was a surprising amount of consistency in the results across multiple channels, despite Rains and Scott's (2007) assertion that level of interactivity and a channel's degree of "interpersonalness" may influence user's identification efforts. Perhaps the most "interpersonal" of anonymous CMI contexts is synchronous, one-on-one IRC—the one context that was not present in the research. Following Rains and Scott (2007), communication in this context may lead to the most accuracy in gender assessments, as it has a high level of both interdependence and synchronicity. To test this assumption, a pilot study was conducted in which two anonymous individuals chatted with each other over IRC. The first set of questions pertained to gender identification in CMI:

RQ1a: How well do CMI users correctly identify the sex of their partner?

RQ1b: How certain are CMI users of their identification effort?

RQ2: What information do CMI users employ to determine the gender of their interaction partner?

Furthermore, the reviewed research also showed sex differences in several language variables within the CMI context, such as quantity of communication, question asking, tag questions, disagreements, correctness of language, empty adjectives, and emoticons. This study follows the example of other investigations (e.g., del-Teso-Craviotto, 2008; Fox et al., 2007) that used actual chat transcripts to discover gender differences in these textual properties. To determine whether sex differences exist in synchronous, one-on-one IRC, the following question is posed:

RQ3: What linguistic sex differences emerge, if any, in the on-line interactions of CMI users?

PILOT STUDY

Procedure

To control for CMI use, participation in the study was limited to "novice users" whose only exposure to CMI was email. Twenty-six male and 46 female participants, ranging from 18 to 40 years of age ($M = 20.79$, $SD = 3.05$), were assigned to one of 20 same sex dyads (five male and fifteen female) or 16 opposite sex dyads. In order to ensure that the participants never saw or heard each other, the participants were asked to report to separate locations at their assigned times and then were seated in different rooms. Computers were networked together through a program that divides the screen into separate sections, where the participants could simultaneously see what they type as well as what their partner typed.

Participants were asked not to reveal their name to each other, nor to talk aloud during the session, to maintain confidentiality. This restriction was also used to insure that their guesses were based on the CMI interaction alone.

Once the participants were situated into their rooms, they were provided the topics to discuss. Given that gender salience may influence sex differences in CMI, a separate group of undergraduate students were asked to generate a list of topics they considered to be gender neutral, and then to evaluate the top five topics in terms of gender neutrality (5 = gender neutral; 1 = gender specific). Results indicated that campus issues were perceived as generally non-gender specific ($M = 4.23$, $SD = 1.22$), followed by the environment ($M = 3.33$, SD = 1.08), technology ($M = 3.12$, $SD = 1.36$), race relations ($M = 2.62$, $SD = 1.14$), and affirmative action ($M = 2.59$, $SD = 1.21$). Therefore, two topics pertaining to campus issues were chosen as the stimulus for the CMI interactions: (a) parking on campus and (b) reopening the observation deck of a campus landmark. The participants were given five minutes to discuss each issue. The order of the topics was alternated for each session to minimize the chance of order effects.

After the interaction, the researcher printed three copies of the interaction, providing both interactants with a transcript to help them recall the interaction, and retaining the third copy to analyze sex differences in several linguistic variables. At that time, the participants were also given a short form to complete in order to provide (a) their age, sex, and major; (b) whether they believed their interaction partner was male or female; (c) a rating of how sure they were sure about their guess about their partner's sex on a 1 to 10 scale (1 = completely unsure; 10 = completely sure); and (d) the type of information used to make their guess. After the participants completed the survey, they were debriefed as to the purpose of the study and the sex of their partner.

Responses to the open-ended survey question asking participants to provide the cues they used to determine the sex of their partner were inductively coded using the constant comparison method of analysis (Lindlof, 1995). After a preliminary reading of the responses, initial categories were identified based on perceived similarities and differences within and among the responses. Five themes emerged during this stage: topic of conversation, word choice, conversational tone, typing style, and intuition. All of the responses were then coded according to these five themes to verify that the categories were exhaustive and mutually exclusive. During this phase, several cues identified by the participants could not be categorized according to these labels, thus three new categories were formed: use of punctuation, use of emoticons, and brevity. The responses were once again reviewed to ensure the coding system accounted for all cues identified by the participants.

Data Analysis of Transcripts

Transcripts were coded for the occurrence of several linguistic variables identified previously as possible cues that may discriminate between male and female interactants: quantity of communication, correctness, use of emoticons, disagreements, expressive language, tag questions, and questions (see James & Drakich, 1993; McFadyen, 1996; Pruett, 1989; Sarch, 1996; Selfe & Meyer, 1991; Shephard & Williamson, 1996; Witmer & Katzman, 1997). *Quantity of communication* was assessed by two methods: (a) the total number of complete words per participant, and (b) total number of complete thought units per person. *Correctness* was measured in two ways: self corrections and syntax mistakes. First, self corrections were identified by square boxes used by the computer program to indicate the number of times the participants hit the "delete" key during the computer interaction, (e.g., "wen□b page"). Syntax mistakes were defined as uncorrected punc-

tuation, grammar, or spelling errors. Use of empty adjectives, punctuation (e.g., exclamation marks, ellipses), excessive descriptions, and emphatic language were grouped together under the code *expressive statements*. Interrogative statements that elicited responses from the other interactant were coded as *questions*. Remarks that had interrogative statements or question marks added to the end of the utterance were coded as *tag questions* (Aries, 1996). Finally, a *disagreement* was coded when interactants differed in their point of view about a topic.

Aries (1996) criticized studies that have reported differences without accounting for amount of speech produced by men and women as a baseline. To avoid this problem, the proportion of the number of occurrences of each of the linguistic features to the number of thought units per person was used to account for differences in amount of talk across participants. The total number of occurrences of each of these linguistic features was tallied for both the male and female participants. In addition, the transcripts were divided into complete units of interaction according to the start and completion of one thought unit. To ensure coding reliability, 25% of the surveys were provided to another researcher unconnected to the study. Percent agreement was 82.61% for the open-ended data, 85.71% for the thought units, and 73.14% for the coding of the chat transcripts.

Results and Discussion

Research question one sought to assess the participant's accuracy in gender identification efforts, and to determine their level of certainty in their identification efforts. To address RQ1a regarding accuracy, a series of chi-square analyses was conducted to determine if participants were accurate at a rate greater than chance, and to discover if level of accuracy differed depending on the participant's sex, the composition of the dyad (i.e., same sex vs. opposite sex), or the sex of the CMI partner. Results indicate that 45 out

Table 1. Cross-tabulation of accuracy by participant sex and gender composition of the dyad

| | | | Accuracy of Guess | | Total |
			Correct	Incorrect	
Sex of Participant	**Male**	Interacted with a Male	4 (40%)	6 (60%)	10
		Interacted with a Female	13 (81.2%)	3 (18.8%)	16
	Female	Interacted with a Male	11 (68.8%)	5 (31.2%)	16
		Interacted with a Female	17 (56.7%)	13 (43.3%)	30
Total		Count	45	27	72
		% of Total	62.5%	37.5%	100%

of 72 participants (62.50%) were able to correctly guess their partner's sex, doing so more often than would be expected by chance, x^2 (1, $N = 72$) = 4.50, $p = .034$. When examined according to the participant's sex, 28 out of 46 (60.87%) females were correct, compared to 17 out of 26 males (65.38%); the chi-square was not significant for either males, x^2 (1, $n = 26$) = 2.46, $p = .12$ or females, x^2 (1, $n = 46$) = 2.17, $p = .14$, likely due to the decreased cell size. Additionally, although it appears that males were more accurate than females, a cross-tabulation analysis revealed that level of accuracy was not dependent on sex of the participant, x^2 (1, $N = 72$) = .14, $p = .70$.

In terms of the composition of the dyad, whereas participants in same sex male dyads were accurate 40% of the time, participants is same sex female dyads were accurate 56.67% of the time, and those in opposite sex dyads were accurate 75% of the time. Although the chi-square was not significant in either the same sex male dyads, x^2 (1, $n = 10$) = .40, $p = .53$, or same sex female dyads, x^2 (1, $n = 30$) = .53, $p = .46$, it was significant in opposite sex dyads, x^2 (1, $n = 32$) = 8.0, $p = .005$, suggesting that participants interacting with a member of the opposite were correct in their gender identification efforts at a level greater than chance. Yet, a cross-tabulation analysis of sex composition in the dyad with accuracy was not significant, x^2 (2, $N = 72$) = 4.73 $p = .09$, indicating that accuracy level is not significantly related to the composition of the dyad.

Furthermore, participants interacting with a male were accurate 57.69% of the time, and participants interacting with a female were accurate 65.22% of the time. Whereas the chi-square for accuracy in terms of CMI partner sex was not significant for males, x^2 (1, $n = 26$) = .61, $p = .43$, it was for females, x^2 (1, $n = 46$) = 4.26, $p = .039$. As before, however, the results of a cross-tabulation of CMI partner sex with accuracy was not significant, x^2 (1, $N = 72$) = .40 $p = .52$.

At this point, although it appears that accuracy increased when one's CMI partner was female, interaction partner sex and accuracy were not significantly related to each other. Given that there was at least some indication that dyad composition and CMI partner sex could be related to accuracy, a final cross-tabulation was conducted that examined the association between accuracy and the sex of the CMI partner according to participant sex. As can be seen in the Table 1, males in opposite sex interactions were by far the most accurate, whereas males in same sex interactions were the least accurate. Indeed, the chi-square for males indicated that sex of the interaction partner and accuracy were related, in that males were more accurate with their gender identification efforts when interacting with a female than when interacting with a male, x^2 (1, $n = 26$) = 4.62, $p = .031$. The same did not hold true for females.

Taken together, then, the results of the analyses for RQ1a indicate that there is a complex relationship among participant sex, their CMI partner's sex, the composition of the dyad, and accuracy. In general, participants were fairly accurate in gender identification, with rates similar to those reported by other investigations of CMI contexts in which participants exchanged messages with each other either in small groups through IRC (Koch et al., 2005) or via email (Thomson & Murachver, 2001). According to Scott (1998), "knowledge communicators have of one another may provide hints and insights" that can be used to identify an anonymous interactant (pp.391-392). The current research does provide some support for this statement: using their knowledge of how males and females behave in on-line conversations, participants were able to correctly guess their interaction partner's sex at a rate greater than chance. Similar to Savicki et al. (1999), accuracy seemed to depend, in part, on the sex of the message author, where participants were more accurate in their gender identification efforts when interacting with a female than with a male. This finding was magnified for males, particularly in opposite sex interactions. One reason for this result may be because there were more females than males in the study; yet, the fact that accuracy went down in the same sex female dyads casts some doubt on this conclusion.

Given that the context in this study was the most "interpersonal" (i.e., a synchronous, one-on-one private chat) of those studied in the gender identification literature, a more likely reason for the result is the context itself. Indeed, a follow-up cross-tabulation of participant sex by guess reveals that the two are significantly related to one another, x^2 (1, $N = 72$) = 4.32, $p = .04$. Whereas males guessed female at a rate greater than chance (73.1% of the time, x^2 [1, $n = 26$] = 5.54, $p = .02$), the same did not hold true for females (47.82%, x^2 [1, $n = 46$] = .09, $p = .77$). Although care was taken to choose a gender-neutral topic, the fact that many of the students were recruited from an undergraduate interpersonal communication course with a focus on relationships might have led male participants to over-attribute the

conversations to females, for whatever reason (e.g., wishful thinking, the perception that there were more females in the class than males). And, given that females outnumbered males in the pilot study, accuracy level was higher when participants guessed female. Perhaps if participants were told that this study was investigating sex differences in CMI, they might have acted more stereotypically than they would otherwise to help their fellow participants identify themselves more accuately. Based on previous research, accuracy rates might also have been higher if participants were allowed to choose a user name (Cornetto & Nowak, 2006) or if gender was made salient by priming the participants to think about their own sex prior to the interaction (Thomson, 2006) or during the interaction through the use of gender-matched topic (Savicki et al., 1999). Future research is needed to confirm these conjectures.

In regards to RQ1b, results of the pilot study revealed that across the board, participants reported an average certainty rating of 6.53/10 (*SD* = 2.24). Accuracy was not significantly associated with certainty [$m_{correct}$ = 6.58, $sd = 2.14$, $m_{incorrect}$ = 6.46, $sd = 2.43$, $f(1,70) = .04$, $p = .85$, $\eta = -.025$]. Similarly, accuracy level was not significantly related to sex of the CMI partner [m_{males} = 6.07, $sd = 2.13$, $m_{females}$ = 6.79, $sd = 2.28$, $f(1,70) =$ 1.71, $p = .19$, $\eta = .15$], guess [$m_{guessed\,male}$ = 6.11, $sd = 2.21$, $m_{guessed\,female}$ = 6.85, $sd = 2.15$, $f(1,70) =$ 1.96, $p = .16$, $\eta = .16$], or composition of the dyad [$m_{male/male}$ = 6.10, $sd = 2.51$, $m_{male/females}$ = 6.40, sd = 2.38, $m_{female/female}$ = 6.81, $sd = 2.03$ $f(2,69) = .47$, $p = .63$, $\eta = .11$]. These results replicate those found by Cornetto and Nowak (2006) and Savicki et al. (1999), suggesting that accuracy level and certainly level are separate issues. While they were somewhat effective in their gender identification, they did not feel very certain about their guess. In fact, a great many of the participants openly expressed doubt about their guesses, and a few could not give any reason for their choice other than "it was just a hunch." It is likely that certainty ratings would have increase if participants were instructed at the start of the interaction to try to determine their partner's sex. What would make this interaction even more interesting is if participants were instructed to conceal their own sex at the same time that they tried to discover the sex of their other partner—an avenue for future research.

Next, RQ2 addressed the cues participants used to make their gender identification. Analysis of the open-ended data revealed a total of eight themes that represented participants' perceptions of male and female CMI users, which generally fall along gender stereotypes. Five of the themes pertained to both males and females, including topic of conversation, word choice, tone of conversation, typing style, and intuition. Yet, the content of the themes differed according to gender. For example, seven topics were generally associated with conversations with females: (a) health and safety issues, (b) concern or caring for others, (c) demographic information (e.g., living arrangements), (d) open expression of opinion, (e) family, (f) opinions of sporting events, and (g) knowledge of current events. Four topics were generally associated with conversations with males: (a) ignorance of issues, (b) reference to liking sports, (c) owning a car, and (d) problem behavior, such as getting drunk and getting traffic tickets. Whereas some of the topics attributed to females have been identified in previous research as female-linked topics (e.g., concern for others, family; Colley et al., 2004; Jaffee & Lee, 1999), open expressions of opinions and knowledge of current events could be indicators of sureness or authoritativeness, which have been identified as representing masculine communication style (Herring & Paolillo, 2006; Sarch, 1996). The lack of clear overlap between the topics participants used in this study and that of previous research may further support of Koch et al.'s (2005) finding that topic of conversation is not a good cue to use when guessing the sex of CMI users.

In addition to topic, several participants listed specific words they commonly associated with males or females. Similar to previous research (Colley et al., 2004; Fox et al., 2007), use of adjectives and modifiers such as "so," "totally," "omigod," "insane," and "really" led people to guess they were talking to females. Certain expressive phrases such as "super convenient," and "I completely agree," also were indicative of females for these participants. Participants frequently stated that words such as "suck" and "stuff," and phrases such as "no kidding" and "gonna happen" were more typical of men. Although syntactic cues like language choice were found to be helpful in the Koch et al. (2005) study, generalizations about what words or phrases males and females should use (e.g., "suck" and "barf" for males, "beauty" and "love" for females) proved to be confusing for several participants, particularly when other cues were present that would indicate the opposite gender.

Third, similar to pragmatic cues (e.g., conversation style) identified by Koch et al. (2005), several participants mentioned that the tone of the conversation seemed more "feminine" or more "masculine." For instance, one participant mentioned that females are "very talkative" and "ask a lot of questions," while another participant said simply that it "was the way she spoke." Along the same lines, a few participants mentioned that the way their interaction partner typed was the main cue. In their opinion, females typed faster and were more correct, while males typed slower and were sloppier. Participants also indicated that females tend to use more punctuation, were perceived to be more grammatically correct, and used emoticons, whereas men were perceived as being vague in their interactions (e.g., "he didn't have much to say... with men, you have to force their feelings") or simply more brief as a result of being "honest," "direct," or "seeming certain." Additionally, some participants stated that their partner's interaction "seemed like a guy's way of talking," or just "the way he worded stuff" made him think he was conversing with a male. And as previously stated, some participants mentioned that they were unsure of their guess and had to rely on intuition for their assessment, saying they guessed based on a "feeling," "an idea" they got, or an "impression." Whereas the observations about hypercorrectness, attention to grammar rules, use of emoticons, and use of punctuation have been cited in previous research (Baron, 2004; Sarch, 1996; Savicki et al., 1999; Witmer & Katzman, 1997), the observation about typing style has not, most likely as a result of the IRC program used in this study that allowed participants to see how their partner typed in real time.

It is noteworthy that participants made no overt efforts during the interaction to identify the sex of their interaction partner (e.g., asking them their sex). On the surface, this observation seems to go against beliefs that CMI users are motivated to know the sex of their anonymous interaction partner (Herring & Martinson, 2004), particularly in an interpersonal context like IRC (Rains & Scott, 2007). Yet, Scott (1998) proposed that receivers of messages will attempt to make identification efforts when their status is threatened, when the message is salient but disagreeable, or when the channel provides relative ease in the effort. In this study, the senders and receivers of messages were involved in an anonymous interaction about campus issues—a non-threatening, gender neutral topic. As such, they might not have been motivated to attempt identification efforts, thereby lending support to Scott's propositions about when a receiver attempts identification of an anonymous message.

In summary, results of the analysis for RQ2 suggest that participants rely on their gender stereotypes of how men and women typically behave in interactions, either directly or indirectly, as indicated by comments such as "boys would generally seem more opinionated," "the use word choice was very elementary and crude, which I think is very typical of the male gender," or "the other person types fairly slow-usually a male trait." When left with little information, CMI users may rely on the only knowledge they have—gender stereotypes—which can sometimes lead to accurate gender identification (Sierpe, 2005), but not all the time, particularly if relying on content cues to make the assessment (Koch et al., 2005). Instead, there may be certain generalizations about the on-line communication of men and women that may be more effective at discriminating between genders, such as syntactic or pragmatic cues (Koch et al., 2005). Future research should continue to investigate whether following stereotypes is an effective way to identity someone's sex, or if there are other ways to make this determination, such as making references to information only certain people would know (del Tesso-Craviotto, 2008; Scott, 1988).

The third RQ focused on whether the male and female participants differed in their use of a number of linguistic variables (i.e., number of words, number of thought units, self-corrections, grammatical mistakes-uncorrected, expressive statements, questions, tag questions, emoticons, disagreements). The t-tests revealed no significant differences in the total number of words used or in the number of thought units. In addition, the test of difference between the proportion of the other variables revealed a single difference: that men tended to correct themselves more often than women ($z = 2.49$, p < .05). On the surface, this result seems to contradict research by Sarch (1996), Baron (2004), and Savicki et al. (1999) which found that women tend to follow the rules of grammar and language more than men in their CMI. At the same time, although the difference was not statistically significant, men made more uncorrected mistakes than women. It is possible, then, that men may indeed make more errors, in general, in their on-line communication. What is left unknown, though, is why. One reason may be that, as indicated by the participants, men have more difficulty typing than do women. On the other hand, perhaps women are more concerned with correctness and as a result, do not make as many errors that need correcting in the first place (Baron, 2004). Given that most CMI channels do not show when users correct themselves, this particular cue may be irrelevant. The extent to which males and females follow grammatical rules, however, may remain a discriminating factor.

The lack of differences in the language variables examined in this study suggests that for this group of respondents, sex was not a differentiating factor. There are a number of reasons why this result emerged. Based on SIDE and SCT, it makes sense that sex differences failed to emerge, given that gender salience was low (i.e., they were discussing a gender-neutral topic and were not aware of the purpose of the study). If anything, it is likely that they were in a "student" frame of mind, resulting in more correct grammar and similar styles of communication (Palomares, 2004; 2008). Similarly, based on CAT, it is also feasible that the participants were "converging" in their communication styles, thereby diminishing differences (Thomson et al., 2001) and leading participants to correct their grammatical mistakes to be more in-line with the correctness of their interaction partner. It is not certain, however, whether ten minutes was enough time to allow for convergence or divergence to occur. Finally, power issues have been offered as an alternative explanation for differences between males' and females' use of language (Vangelisti, 1997). Less talk, more question asking, empty adjectives, and correctness of language have often been cited as examples of language used by the less powerful person (Eagly, 1995) and have been found in the CMI of female users (Baron, 2004; Colley & Todd, 2002; Sarch, 1996; Selfe & Meyer, 1991; Shephard & Williams, 1996). In this study, power was less of an issue, as the participants were all university students discussing non-threatening, gender-neutral topics; thus, differences failed to emerge.

Limitations and Future Research Directions

Although care was taken to conduct the pilot study, there were limitations that need to be considered when assessing this study. First, because only one mode of CMI was used in the investigation, generalizability is limited to the communication channel studied and not other modes of CMI. Work in the future should continue to determine how the results of the present investigation extend to other modes of CMI. Second, the instructions given to participants prevented a more naturalistic interaction from occurring. They were provided the topics, and instructed not to reveal their names during the interaction. As a result, self-disclosures typical of a first time interaction among strangers, that may reveal valuable information for gender identification, did not occur. Yet, previous researchers have found that many CMI users forego typical greeting rituals (e.g., Rintel & Pittam, 1997). Perhaps identifying information is exchanged later in the interaction. Third, a limited number of cues were used to code the transcripts for analysis. As was evident in the review, there are several other cues that could reveal sex differences that were not examined in this pilot study. As a result, future research should continue exploring the multiple language and style cues that may reveal sex differences in CMI. Finally, the participants were limited to a ten-minute interaction. Walther (1992) claims that over time, people develop impressions of others through the accumulation of multiple messages. Perhaps in extended interactions, CMI users make a better assessment of other people's sex than with an isolated interaction episode. Future researchers should conduct multiple sessions with the same pair of participants in order to see if judgments change over time, and what new information, if any, is revealed in the course of the extended interactions.

CONCLUSION

The purpose of this chapter was twofold: (a) to explore CMI users' ability to identify the sex of their anonymous partner, as well as the cues they can use in the process, and (b) to determine if there are textual "markers" CMI users leave that may reveal their sex. Based on a review of literature, as well as the pilot study of synchronous CMI, several conclusions can be offered. First, sex differences are likely to emerge when gender is made salient to the users; they may not emerge when CMI users are of equivalent status and/or gender salience is low. Although SIDE, SCT, and CAT offer competing explanations for why differences may occur in some situations and not in others, all three theories suggest that under certain conditions, CMI users will consciously or subconsciously communicate in ways that either coincide with their own gender identity (when gender is made salient and/or there is a desire to communicate one's sex to others) (Guiller & Durndell, 2006; 2007; Postmes & Spears, 2002; Palomares, 2004; 2008) or that of their communication partner (when some other issue is salient) (Thomson, 2006). Other times, CMI users may feel the need to diverge from communicating in a style associated with their own gender, such as when trying to convince others that they are a member of the opposite sex (Herring & Martinson, 2004).

Second, CMI users may attempt gender identification of other anonymous users, but only when motivated to do so (e.g., there is a romantic interest in the other user, they are told to make gender identifications by a researcher, they feel that the other person is hiding their sex for some reason). Indeed, motivation is a critical determinant of whether or not identification efforts will be made in the first place (Rains & Scott, 2007). For instance, in interpersonal settings, such as synchronous one-on-one interactions, users may feel an increased need to know more about their interaction partner if they anticipate future interaction with him/her (Rains & Scott,

2007; Scott, 1998; Walther, 1994). Then again, in asynchronous, one-to-many CMI situations, users may believe that they are fully anonymous and as such, may not think about their own or other users' sex. Furthermore, users may specifically choose CMI because they perceive that CMI "frees" them from the bonds of identifying traits such as race, age, and sex (Chesebro & Bonsall, 1989; del-Teso-Craviotto, 2008; McCormick & McCormick, 1992; Parks & Floyd, 1996). As a result, they may avoid identification efforts to respect the privacy of other CMI users desiring the anonymity afforded by the technology. In short, although researchers may be interested in looking for gender markers of CMI users, CMI users themselves may have little motivation to know the sex of other users and as such, do not make efforts at gender identification (Nowak, 2003).

Third, when the desire to know the sex of an anonymous CMI user is present, receivers will rely on a number of strategies and gender stereotypes to make their gender assessments. From an uncertainty reduction perspective, CMI users in these situations may employ interactive (e.g., directly asking the other person about their sex), active (e.g., asking other CMI users about that person), passive (e.g., look for gender traces or markers that may indicate sex based on gender stereotypes), or extractive (e.g., googling the person) strategies (Ramirez, Walther, Burgoon, & Sunnafrank, 2002) to make their assessments. It is interesting to note that a vast majority of the literature focuses on passive strategies explicitly by asking participants to reflect on their interactions to make retrospective guesses (e.g., Koch et al., 2005) or implicitly by looking for sex differences in CMI interactions. Only a handful of studies have looked at interactive strategies (e.g., Samp et al., 2003), and despite advances in CMI that make audio and visual communication more feasible (Herring, 2004), few researchers, if any, have studied extractive strategies. Although this chapter focused on text-based interaction, CMI users could also use avatars, photographs, or other types of information that reveal information about a user's identity (cf. Kane, Maguire, Neuendorf, & Skalski, 2009; Kang & Yang, 2006). In reference to text-based cues, however, CMI users have a better-than-average chance of correctly guessing the sex of other users, and feel somewhat certain of their guesses; some stereotypes, however, hold up better than others.

In closing, the present chapter is another step towards understanding how anonymity functions in the CMI context. It appears that CMI users can guess the sex of their partner slightly more often than not. Also, while only one difference emerged among the linguistic cues investigated in this research, some of the gender stereotypes, such as the use of certain words or phrases, may prove to be predictors of accuracy. Eagly (1995) warns that research which upholds matches between gendered stereotypes and actual sex differences may act to reinforce stereotypes. It is interesting to note, however, that when participants in the present study were informed whether or not they correctly guessed the sex of their partner, the ones who were incorrect were very surprised, even admitting that their stereotypes may not work in on-line settings. Instead of reinforcing existing stereotypes, perhaps CMI may begin to challenge individuals to question their stereotypes of male-female communication behavior.

REFERENCES

Aries, E. (1996). *Men and women in interaction: Reconsidering the differences*. New York: Oxford University Press.

Baron, N. S. (2004). See you online: Gender issues in college student use of instant messaging. *Journal of Language and Social Psychology, 23*, 397–423. doi:10.1177/0261927X04269585

Bischoping, K. (1993). Gender differences in conversation topics, 1922-1990. *Sex Roles, 28*, 1–18. doi:10.1007/BF00289744

"Bronco" a.k.a. Scott, C. R. (2004). Benefits and drawbacks of anonymous online communication: Legal challenges and communicative recommendations. In S. Drucker (Ed.), *Free speech yearbook (vol. 41,* pp. 127-141). Washington, DC: National Communication Association.

Chesebro, J. W., & Bonsall, D. G. (1989). *Computer mediated communication: Human relationships in a computerized world*. Tuscaloosa, AL: University of Alabama Press.

Colley, A., & Todd, Z. (2002). Gender-linked differences in the style and content of e-mails to friends. *Journal of Language and Social Psychology, 21*, 380–392. doi:10.1177/026192702237955

Colley, A., Todd, Z., Bland, M., Holmes, M., Khanom, N., & Pike, H. (2004). Style and content in e-mails and letters to male and female friends. *Journal of Language and Social Psychology, 23*, 369–378. doi:10.1177/0261927X04266812

Cornetto, K. M., & Nowak, K. L. (2006). Utilizing usernames for sex categorization in computer-mediated communication: Examining perceptions and accuracy. *Cyberpsychology & Behavior, 9*, 377–387. doi:10.1089/cpb.2006.9.377

Coupland, N., Coupland, J., & Giles, H. (1991). *Language, Society, and the Elderly: Discourse, Identity, and Ageing*. New York: Wiley Blackwell.

Danet, B. (1996, February). *Text as mask: Gender and identity on the Internet*. Paper presented at the conference, Masquerade and gendered identity; Venice, Italy. Retrieved (n.d.), from ttp://atar.mscc. huji.ac.il/~msdanet/mask.html

del-Teso-Craviotto, M. (2008). Gender and sexual identity authentication in language use: The case of chat rooms. *Discourse Studies, 10*, 251–270. doi:10.1177/1461445607087011

Eagly, A. H. (1995). The science and politics of comparing women and men. *The American Psychologist, 50,* 145–158. doi:10.1037/0003-066X.50.3.145

Ferber, R. (1995). Is speakers' gender discernible in transcribed speech? *Sex Roles, 32,* 209–223. doi:10.1007/BF01544789

Fox, A. B., Bukatko, D., Hallahan, M., & Crawford, M. (2007). The medium makes a difference: Gender similarities and differences in instant messaging. *Journal of Language and Social Psychology, 26,* 389–397. doi:10.1177/0261927X07306982

Gooden, R. J., & Winefield, H. R. (2006). Breast and prostate cancer online discussion boards: A thematic analysis of gender differences and similarities. *Journal of Health Psychology, 12,* 103–114. doi:10.1177/1359105307071744

Groom, C. J., & Pennebaker, J. W. (2005). The language of love: Sex, sexual orientation, and language use in online personal advertisements. *Sex Roles, 52,* 447–461. doi:10.1007/s11199-005-3711-0

Guiller, J., & Durndell, A. (2006). 'I totally agree with you': Gender interactions in educational online discussion groups. *Journal of Computer Assisted Learning, 22,* 368–381. doi:10.1111/j.1365-2729.2006.00184.x

Guiller, J., & Durndell, A. (2007). Students' linguistic behavior in online discussion groups: Does gender matter? *Computers in Human Behavior, 23,* 2240–2255. doi:10.1016/j.chb.2006.03.004

Hayne, S. C., & Rice, R. E. (1997). Attribution accuracy when using anonymity in group support systems. *International Journal of Human-Computer Studies, 47,* 429–450. doi:10.1006/ijhc.1997.0134

Herring, S. C. (2004). Slouching toward the ordinary: Current trends in computer-mediated communication. *New Media & Society, 6,* 26–36. doi:10.1177/1461444804039906

Herring, S. C., & Martinson, A. (2004). Assessing gender authenticity in computer-mediated language use: Evidence from an identity game. *Journal of Language and Social Psychology, 23,* 424–446. doi:10.1177/0261927X04269586

Herring, S. C., & Paolillo, J. C. (2006). Gender and genre variation in weblogs. *Journal of Sociolinguistics, 10,* 439–459. doi:10.1111/j.1467-9841.2006.00287.x

Huffaker, D. A., & Calvert, S. L. (2005). Gender, identity, and language use in teenage blogs. *Journal of Computer-Mediated Communication, 10*(2).

Internet World Stats. (n.d.). *Internet World Stats.* Retrieved October 9, 2008 from http://www.internetworldstats.com/stats.htm

Jaffe, J. M., Lee, Y.-E., Huang, L.-N., & Oshagan, H. (1999). Gender identification, interdependence, and pseudonyms in CMC: Language patterns in an electronic conference. *The Information Society, 15,* 221–234. doi:10.1080/019722499128385

James, D., & Clarke, S. (1993). Women, men, and interruptions: A critical review. In Tannen, D. (Ed.), *Gender and conversational interaction* (pp. 231–280). New York: Oxford University Press.

James, D., & Drakich, J. (1993). Understanding gender differences in amount of talk: A critical review of research. In Tannen, D. (Ed.), *Gender and conversational interaction* (pp. 281–312). New York: Oxford University Press.

Kane, C. M., Maguire, K., Neuendorf, K., & Skalski, P. (2009). *Nonverbal displays of self presentation and sex differences in profile photographs in Myspace.com.* Unpublished manuscript.

Kang, H.-S., & Yang, H.-D. (2006). The visual characteristics of avatars in computer-mediated communication: Comparison of internet relay chat and instant messenger as of 2003. *International Journal of Human-Computer Studies, 62,* 1173–1183. doi:10.1016/j.ijhcs.2006.07.003

Koch, S. C., Mueller, B., Kruse, L., & Zumbach, J. (2005). Constructing gender in chat groups. *Sex Roles, 53,* 29–41. doi:10.1007/s11199-005-4276-7

Lea, M., & Spears, R. (1991). Computer-mediated communication, de-individuation and group decision-making. *International Journal of Man-Machine Studies, 34,* 283–301. doi:10.1016/0020-7373(91)90045-9

Lee, E.-J. (2004). Effects of gendered character representation on person perception and informational social influence in computer mediated communication. *Computers in Human Behavior, 20,* 779–799. doi:10.1016/j.chb.2003.11.005

Lindlof, T. R. (1995). *Qualitative communication research methods.* Thousand Oaks, CA: Sage.

Martin, R. (1997). "Girls don't talk about garages!" Perceptions of conversation in same- and cross-sex friendships. *Personal Relationships, 4,* 115–130. doi:10.1111/j.1475-6811.1997.tb00134.x

McCormick, N. B., & McCormick, J. W. (1992). Computer friends and foes: Content of undergraduate's e-mail. *Computers in Human Behavior, 8,* 379–405. doi:10.1016/0747-5632(92)90031-9

McFadyen, R. G. (1996). Gender, status, and 'powerless' speech: Interactions of students and lecturers. *The British Journal of Social Psychology, 35,* 353–367.

Myers, D. (1987). "Anonymity is part of the magic": Individual manipulation of computer mediated contexts. *Qualitative Sociology, 10,* 251–266. doi:10.1007/BF00988989

Newman, M. L., Groom, C. J., Handelman, L. D., & Pennebaker, J. W. (2008). Gender differences in language use: An analysis of 14,000 text samples. *Discourse Processes, 45,* 211–236. doi:10.1080/01638530802073712

Nowak, K. L. (2003). Sex categorization in computer mediated communication (CMC): Exploring the utopian promise. *Media Psychology, 5,* 83–103. doi:10.1207/S1532785XMEP0501_4

Palomares, N. A. (2004). Gender schematicity, gender identity salience, and gender-linked language use. *Human Communication Research, 30,* 556–588. doi:10.1111/j.1468-2958.2004.tb00745.x

Palomares, N. A. (2008). Explaining gender-based language use: Effects of gender identity salience on references to emotion and tentative language in intra- and intergroup contexts. *Human Communication Research, 34,* 263–286. doi:10.1111/j.1468-2958.2008.00321.x

Parks, M. R., & Floyd, K. (1996). Friends in cyberspace: Exploring personal relationships formed through the Internet. *The Journal of Communication, 46,* 80–97. doi:10.1111/j.1460-2466.1996.tb01462.x

Postmes, T., & Spears, R. (2002). Behavior online: Does anonymous computer communication reduce gender inequality? *Personality and Social Psychology Bulletin, 28,* 1073–1083. doi:10.1177/01461672022811006

Pruett, B. M. (1989). Male and female communication style differences: A meta-analysis. In Lont, C., & Friedley, S. (Eds.), *Beyond boundaries: Sex and gender diversity in communication* (pp. 107–120). Fairfax, VA: George Mason University.

Rains, S. A., & Scott, C. R. (2007). To identify or not to identify: A theoretical model of receiver responses to anonymous communication. *Communication Theory, 17,* 61–91. doi:10.1111/j.1468-2885.2007.00288.x

Ramirez, A., Walther, J., Burgoon, J., & Sunnafrank, M. (2002). Information-seeking strategies, uncertainty, and computer-mediated communication: Toward a conceptual model. *Human Communication Research, 26,* 213–228.

Reid, S. A., Keerie, N., & Palomares, N. A. (2003). Language, gender salience, and social influence. *Journal of Language and Social Psychology, 22,* 210–234. doi:10.1177/0261927X03022002004

Rintel, E. S., & Pittam, J. (1997). "Strangers in a strange land": Interaction management on Internet relay chat. *Human Communication Research, 23,* 507–534. doi:10.1111/j.1468-2958.1997.tb00408.x

Samp, J. A., Wittenberg, E. M., & Gillett, D. L. (2003). Presenting and monitoring a gender-defined self on the internet. *Communication Research Reports, 20,* 1–12.

Sarch, A. (1996, November). *Keyboard encounters: Virtual sex and gendered identities.* Paper presented at the annual meeting of the Speech Communication Association, San Diego, CA.

Savicki, V., Kelley, M., & Oesterreich, E. (1999). Judgments of gender in computer-mediated communication. *Computers in Human Behavior, 15,* 185–194. doi:10.1016/S0747-5632(99)00017-5

Scott, C. R. (1998). To reveal or not to reveal: A theoretical model of anonymous communication. *Communication Theory, 8,* 381–407. doi:10.1111/j.1468-2885.1998.tb00226.x

Selfe, C. C., & Meyer, P. D. (1991). Testing claims for on-line conferences. *Written Communication, 8,* 163–192. doi:10.1177/0741088391008002002

Shephard, E. R., & Williamson, L. K. (1996, November) *The niceties of netiquette: Gender patterns in computer-mediated communication.* Paper presented at the annual meeting of the Speech Communication Association, San Diego, CA.

Sierpe, E. (2005). Gender distinctiveness, communication competence, and the problem of gender judgments in computer-mediated communication. *Computers in Human Behavior, 21,* 127–145. doi:10.1016/j.chb.2003.11.009

Smythe, M. J., & Schlueter, D. W. (1989). "Can we talk?" A Meta-analytic review of the sex differences. In Lont, C., & Friedley, S. (Eds.), *Beyond boundaries: Sex and gender diversity in communication* (pp. 31–48). Fairfax, VA: George Mason University.

Tannen, D. (1990). *You just don't understand: Women and men in conversation.* New York: Ballantine Books.

Teich, A., Frankel, M. S., Kling, R., & Lee, Y.-C. (1999). Anonymous communication policies for the internet: Results and recommendations of the AAAS conference. *The Information Society, 15,* 71–77. doi:10.1080/019722499128538

Thomson, R. (2006). The effect of topic of discussion on gendered language in computer-mediated communication discussion. *Journal of Language and Social Psychology, 25,* 167–178. doi:10.1177/0261927X06286452

Thomson, R., & Murachver, T. (2001). Predicting gender from electronic discourse. *The British Journal of Social Psychology, 40,* 193–208. doi:10.1348/014466601164812

Thomson, R., Murachver, T., & Green, J. (2001). Where is the gender in gendered language? *Psychological Science, 12,* 171–175. doi:10.1111/1467-9280.00329

Turner, J. C., Hogg, M. A., Oakes, P. J., Reicher, S. D., & Wetherell, M. (1987). *Rediscovering the social group: A self-categorization theory.* Oxford: Blackwell.

Valacich, J. S., George, J. F., Nunamaker, J. F. Jr, & Vogel, D. R. (1994). Physical proximity effects on computer-mediated idea generation. *Small Group Research*, *25*, 83–104. doi:10.1177/1046496494251006

van der Meij, H. (2007). What research has to say about gender-linked differences in CMC and does elementary school children's e-mail use fit this picture? *Sex Roles*, *57*, 341–354. doi:10.1007/s11199-007-9270-9

Vangelisti, A. L. (1997). Gender differences, similarities, and interdependencies: Some problems with the different cultures perspective. *Personal Relationships*, *4*, 243–253. doi:10.1111/j.1475-6811.1997.tb00143.x

Wallace, P. (1999). The psychology of the Internet. New York: Cambridge.

Walther, J. B. (1992). Interpersonal effects in computer mediated interactions: A relational perspective. *Communication Research*, *19*, 52–90. doi:10.1177/009365092019001003

Walther, J. B. (1994). Anticipated ongoing interaction versus channel effects on relational communication in computer mediated interaction. *Human Communication Research*, *20*, 473–501. doi:10.1111/j.1468-2958.1994.tb00332.x

Witmer, D. F., & Katzman, S. L. (1997). On-line smiles: Does gender make a difference in the use of graphic accents? *Journal of Computer Mediated Communication [on-line], 2(4).* Retrieved (n.d.), from http://ascusc.org/jCMI/vol2/issue4/witmer1.html

Yates, S. J. (2001). Gender, language, and CMC for education. *Learning and Instruction*, *11*, 21–34. doi:10.1016/S0959-4752(00)00012-8

Chapter 7
Gender Style Differences in Mediated Communication

Nancy A. Burrell
University of Wisconsin, USA

Edward A. Mabry
University of Wisconsin, USA

Mike Allen
University of Wisconsin, USA

ABSTRACT

This study investigates gender differences in linguistic features of communication styles in the context of mixed public discussion groups in asynchronous, text-based CMC. The study evaluates gendered communication and language styles in situational contexts of CMC. A sample of 3000 messages from 30 Internet discussion groups was content analyzed. Results revealed gender differences in stylistic features used by discussion group participants and partially support the expectation that women's online communication style is gendered. The data did not reveal an online communication style that significantly discriminated men's communication. Findings point to the important role of gender enacted through language in the construction of social identity in the context of public discussion groups in CMC. Implications of this investigation and directions for the development of future research on gender in CMC are discussed.

INTRODUCTION

Early research on computer-mediated communication (CMC) optimistically predicted democratizing effects of CMC in fostering equal participation and gender-free social equality. Anecdotal evidence of men posing as women, of women assuming pseudonymous identities, and of gender-switching in online social interaction appeared to support the potential liberating effects of anonymity in CMC. Gendered identity was thought of as either invisible or easily fungible in text-based CMC. The lack of physical (and visual) cues in text messages due to the isolation and anonymity of message senders can mask information on identity a message sender was unwilling to share (Barnes, 2003).

Herring (2000) argued that research on social interaction in CMC does not support this anonymity expectation. Her review of empirical research on gender in text-based CMC indicated that most

DOI: 10.4018/978-1-61520-827-2.ch007

social interactants do not attempt disguising or masking gender, when it would be advantageous. Much of the research pointed to a tendency for online participants to display culturally-learned gender styles in their text messages (Herring, 2000). Gendered attributes of language styles in CMC are nearly the same as face-to-face (FTF) communication. This suggests that rather than biological differences culturally learned patterns of gendered communication behavior, and to some extent power and status hierarchies, are carried over to online social interaction (Mabry, 1998; Postmes et al, 1998; Rafaeli & Sudweeks, 1998). This explanation, however, does not address the appearance and persistence of binary gender. An important justification for gender research in CMC is to search for new explanations for positive social uses and functions binary gender might serve. This investigation examines gender differences in the linguistic styles of Internet discussion group members in an effort to support Herring's explanation.

BACKGROUND

The social egalitarianism initially ascribed to the appropriation of computer-mediated communication has proved to be illusive. This expectation of social leveling was predicated on the theory that a loss of information in CMC, through a filtering out of social cues, would constrain the presence and impact of communicators (Short, Williams, & Christie, 1976; Culnan & Markus, 1987). Walther and Parks (2002) noted the theory tacitly assumed that attenuating communication channel cues limits communication functions, whereas research indicates that communicators in mediated communication contexts are able to successfully extrapolate levels of intensity, affect, or social cohesion and identity using restricted social information.

A similar conclusion premises social identity/ deindividuation [SIDE] theory (Lea & Spears,

1995; Spears & Lea, 1992, 1994; Postmes, Spears, & Lea, 1998, 2000). The SIDE model recognizes that social contexts facilitated by the use of CMC provide social information. Research indicates participants use either their contextual sensitization or individual identity as anchors in drawing inferences about message intent and the implications of interaction in a mediated social space depending on the perceived strength of social norms attached to their behavior.

Social contexts constructed through CMC are quite diverse either because of the range of goals motivating the need for communicating or the type of communication constraints associated with the communication technology that is used. Therefore, it is not surprising that while research typically reveals gendered expressiveness in CMC contextual analyses of mediated communication seldom generate specific reproducible results of particular behavioral markers.

Low interaction contexts like web logs (blogs) have not produced marked differences in female and male writers except for differences in the affective tone of messages (Herring & Paolillo, 2006; Huffaker & Calvert, 2005). Similar results have been observed in mediated contexts with higher interactive potential. Fox, et al. (2007) found that women's instant messaging [IM] messages were more expressive but otherwise were quite similar to messages sent by men. Results of studies using online discussion groups and forums have painted a similar picture. Guiller and Durndell (2007) studied online discussion groups and found men were more likely to use authoritative and negative language, whereas women's interaction employed a more positive style through the higher use of agreement, supportiveness, and a positive emotional tone. Women also appear more likely to employ graphical displays during online discussions. Witmer and Katzman (1997) observed that women in mediated discussion groups were more likely to use stylized graphical displays like emoticons and articons. Waseleski (2006) also found that women were more likely to use exclamation marks in online discourse, but the use of exclamations in general seemed motivated less by positive or negative emotionality and more for the grammatical function of thematic emphasis or salience. However, not all online discussion group contexts produce gender differences in participation behavior. Owen, et al.'s (2003) study of online cancer support group members showed that while the emotional content of discussions increased over time it did not differ for female or male participants.

The recent work of Palomares (2004, 2008) on gendered self-categorization and contextual salience reinforces the role of context. Palomares' work demonstrated that gendered self-categorizations were related to increased use of gendered language when gender was perceived as contextually salient through experimental manipulation. Conversely, Koch, et al. (2005) did not find that manipulating gender salience in anonymous online chat groups affected gender attribution. Gender itself can be a context defining factor. Savicki, et al.'s (1996a, 1996b) work demonstrated that the gender composition of online discussion groups influences observed behavior. Homogeneous women's groups were more likely to use personal pronouns, self-disclosure and opinionation compared to mixed groups. Women in homogeneous groups were also more satisfied with group interaction. And, Savicki et al. (1996c) observed that in mixed composition groups with a majority of men there was a greater use of factual claims and requests for action compared to groups where women were in the majority gender that produced more self-disclosures and attempts at tension reduction.

The initial currency of the cues filtered out model (Culnan & Markus, 1987), coupled with the egalitarian deliverables anticipated for mediated communication networks, was also a stimulus for assessing the transparency of gender in CMC that can be and often is intentionally rendered anonymous by communicator choice. Communication technologies are fungible enough that the uses and consequences of anonymous interaction may be addressed in a variety of contexts ranging from group decision making (Scott, 1999) to the current range of CMC contexts discussed in this paper (Anonymous, 1998; McKenna & Green, 2002; Rains & Scott, 2007).

The implications of anonymous interaction for understanding gendered communication are most visible in research aimed at discerning the extent to which gender can be accurately inferred from message cues without the benefit of knowing the sender of a message. However, just as the forgoing review of mediated communication contexts failed to present a singular view of CMC effects, an assessment of gender concealment or transparency under conditions of intentional or incidental anonymity are also characterized by an apparent overall trend that seems to mask a more diverse constellation of findings.

Somewhat surprisingly, studies indicate that gender can be accurately estimated beyond levels signifying random chance outcomes (see, for instance, Herring & Martinson, 2004; Koch, et al., 2005; Savicki, Kelley, & Oesterreich, 1999; Thomson & Murachver, 2001; Thomson, Murachver, & Green, 2002). A study by Cornetto and Nowak (2006) even revealed that raters did moderately well in correctly classifying the gender of electronic message senders when only supplied with message system user names. Most studies of this ilk require an important caveat: research procedures employed in these studies almost always include design variables that, in effect, meta-communicate about the gender of the message sender. This is most frequently accomplished by either manipulating the gender stereotypicality of message cue stimuli or gender salience of discussion topics. Therefore, a dispassionate case can be advanced that knowledge claims from this research risk being the products of methodological artifacts.

The potential risk of extending methodological artifacts is one potential drawback in focusing on anonymity. There are three other reasons to deemphasize the salience of anonymity. First, the efficacy of the cues filtered out model for undertaking a heuristically rigorous assessment of CMC is questionable because compelling alternative conceptual frameworks have emerged since the model's initial formulation (see, Walther & Parks, 2002). Second, gendered communication is a marker of institutionalized power in society. (Clerc, 1996; Gal, 1995). Cultural definitions of men's and women's speech that differentiate gender in communication behavior and style are linked to social role-positions and are therefore important sources of information about social power. The indexicality of situated contexts in which gender is enacted reflects the cultural value placed on linguistic forms that distinguish gendered communication styles of men and women (Henley & Kramerae, 1991; O'Barr & Atkins, 1998). Herring has even claimed that gender differences in CMC can disadvantage women. Asynchronous text-based CMC demonstrated greater inequity of participation between men and women. Synchronous text-based CMC showed greater sexual objectification of women (Herring, 2000, 2001). Therefore, research disambiguating gender cues in CMC is more parsimonious when cues are not masked by anonymity. Finally, articulated in a recent critique by Kennedy (2006) is the concern that Internet anonymity no longer profitably reflects the identity implications of participating in mediated communication. Whereas anonymity has been a tool for online identity manipulation, a more culturally sensitive reading of trends towards embracing, if not celebrating, personal validation through self-identification online attenuates the importance of anonymity as an intellectual point of entry for understanding the experience of mediated communication.

Research Hypotheses and Question

Aries' (1998) review of gender differences in interaction found women to be more expressive, supportive, facilitative, egalitarian and cooperative;

men were found to be more dominant, directive, hierarchical, and problem-solving oriented (p.65). Herring (1994) noted that men are more likely to indicate hierarchical status using signatures at the end of messages, post longer messages, are more challenging, and more likely than women to indicate their status in messages. Herring (1994) also characterized male online communication style as adversarial: put-downs, contentious assertions, lengthy postings, self-promoting and sarcastic. Mabry (2002) has reported that male CMC tends to be more formal than that observed for women.

The distinctive communication styles of men and women in CMC differ in gendered linguistic features which provide cues to or reveal their gender identity and reflect their differentiated power and status. Therefore, the following hypothesis regarding a male style of online communication is proposed:

Hypothesis One: Men argue, assert facts and opinions, use slang, flame, indicate status, initiate new topics, post longer messages, and are more challenging, directive and persuasive than women in online discussion groups.

The results of Dindia and Allen's (1992) meta-analysis on sex-differences in self-disclosure indicated that females disclose more in same-sex interactions than in opposite-sex interactions. According to Aries (1998), women are more expressive, focus more on relationships, and share more personally with others across a wide variety of research on gender differences in face-to-face [FTF] interaction. Recent studies of CMC bear this out as well. Boneva, Kraut, and Frohlich (2001), and Rumbough (2001), have found that women were more likely than men to report using Internet resources like email in the maintenance of their personal relationships. Women are also more likely than men to report providing personal information online, although they are also more likely to engage in self defensive lying and gender-switching.

O'Barr's and Atkin's (1998) research on features of Lakoff's "women's language" included politeness forms including linguistic gender markers like apology; hypercorrect grammar, and use of quotation marks. Women were found to use these less powerful language features slightly more than men. Moreover, Henley and Kramarae (1991) provide a perspective of observe that men and women have different conversational rules and styles. Men use strategies to ignore and to delay responses to women's messages as a male exercise of power. Mulac (1998) reported gender-linked language effects identifying aesthetic quality (beautiful/ugly, nice/awful, etc.) as a dimension of women's language style. In several studies, women were rated higher in aesthetic quality than men which suggests that women may use more articons than men in CMC.

Herring (1994) characterizes female online communication style as supportive (expressing appreciation, thanks and community-building activities) and attenuated (hedging, apologizing, asking questions, expressing doubt and suggesting ideas). Mabry (2002) has noted that women are more likely to engage in openness in CMC across a wider range of potentially self-revealing situations. Therefore, the following hypothesis regarding female style of on-line communication is proposed:

Hypothesis Two: Women self-disclose, address others by name, refer to others as "we," ask questions, agree, attempt to relieve tension, refer and relate to others' messages and use textual signs, quotes, apology and correct format including appropriate subject lines more than men in mixed discussion groups.

Thomson and Murachver (2001) attempted to identify differentiating language behavior of men and women sending online correspondence to a hypothetical acquaintance. They began by parsing a lengthy list of possible linguistic tags to an ultimately significant subset of discriminating items. Their research however did not focus on uniquely male or female online behaviors as a starting point for identifying potential discriminating behaviors as is preforced by the research

hypotheses advanced in this study. Therefore, to the extent these hypotheses are confirmed, answering the following research question could produce important insights about gendered online communication:

Research Question One: Can language behaviors posited as gendered significantly differentiate online discussion styles attributable to men and women?

METHODOLOGY

Data used in this study was obtained as part of an international, computer-mediated collaborative research project. It was the outgrowth of mediated group discussion on organizational communication supported within the structure of the Communication Institute for Online Scholarship. The principle goal of the project, labeled ProjectH, was to facilitate the investigation of actual computer-mediated messaging activities in Internet discussion groups. Over a period of months, basic research objectives and methodological practices were chosen, subsequently a trained group of coders analyzed samples of messages obtained from a sample of electronic discussion groups. A thorough explanation of the project is contained in Rafaeli, et. al. (1998).

Message Sampling

A complete discussion of sampling is available elsewhere (see, Rafaeli, et. al., 1998) and will be abbreviated here. Various computer bulletin boards, lists, and newsgroups were canvassed for a period of approximately one month prior to deciding on automating strategies to be implemented as part of a quota sampling design. Groups were thematically diverse ranging from wireless radio hobbyists to Irish literature buffs. Messages were randomly sampled across days and times. Sampling of a given group terminated when a target of 100 messages was reached. Messages were sampled, beginning with a randomly chosen entry point, and took, in some cases, up to six months before the target number of messages was reached. Only groups interacting in English were retained for the message pool. Approximately N = 3000 messages, from N = 30 different online discussion groups, comprised the project's complete database.

Message Coding

A standardized message content analysis coding protocol was collaboratively developed by participating project members during the first year of their work together (see, Rafaeli, et. al., 1998). The content analysis scheme measured 46 message variables; 40 variables were hand-coded and six were machine coded from automated sampling information.

The coding protocol required trained coders to read the literal text of a message and apply all code variables to each message (wherever possible). Each message was evaluated on whether it contained content descriptive of facts, opinions, humor, challenges, meta-communications, presence of graphic art, formality of composition, quoted material, emotional tone (or flames), sender characteristics (e.g., gender, status), and stylistic factors (e.g., appropriate subject line attribution, presence of personalized signature lines). Table 1 contains a summary of the defined variables used in this study.

Over 40 people participated as coders. Coders were furnished with a codebook (distributed electronically) and provided on-line training activities, tests, and guidance. Training involved coding a set of sample messages chosen to cover the range of code variables. Coders rated the messages and returned their results via electronic mail. Low concordance on the training sample of messages led to additional coaching and more training messages being sent for test coding.

High agreement with the pre-normed responses to training messages qualified the person as coder for the purpose of receiving messages to be included in the main study. Coders were sent sets of 100 messages. In addition to the set of messages, coders were supplied with various reporting style formats for submitting their work and, a post-task questionnaire requesting impressions of the list coded and information about their coding and reporting practices. Completed sets of formatted codes were returned to a host computer system. Work was automatically screened using custom software to debug technical errors (e.g., off line formats, typographical errors); rejected codes were returned to the coder for correction and reinforcement training.

To examine intercoder reliability, 37 sets of 100 messages were distributed to pairs of coders of which 20 were single coded, 12 were double coded and 5 remained uncoded. Four of the message sets were not finished. A detailed description of the message sampling and coding was provided in the project's technical report (Rafaeli, et. al, 1998). The codebook was constructed for a variety of research purposes and projects. Gender was determined either directly (through signatures or introductions/self-descriptions) or indirectly (though self-revealing narratives, e.g., "I'm a single mother and…."). Male authors generated 2,162 (72.1%) of the 3000 messages and female authors 427 (14.2%) of the messages.

The statistical procedures for this study included: (a) reliability tests, Cohen's *kappa* or Cronbach's *Alpha* coefficient; (b) t-tests (unequal n's and variances) for scaled variables to determine gender differences in style variables; (c) Chi-square tests of binary variables to determine gender differences in style variables; and (d) discriminant function analyses to predict the gendered and mixed communication styles of the discussion groups.

Table 1. Definition, measurement, and reliability analyses of variables

Variable	Definition and Measurement
Gender	Cannot Tell, Female, Male. K = .76.
Flame1	Argumentative Tone (1 = neutral to 7 = hostile). A = .69.
Flame2	Coarse or Abusive Language (1 none to 5 mixed use). K = .96.
Flame3	Message to relieve or prevent tension from flame (no, yes to prevent, yes to relieve). K = .95.
Opinion	Indicate author's opinion in first person (no, yes-main content, yes-not main content). A = .64.
Fact	Message as statement of fact (no, yes). K = n.s.
Style	Message contained colloquial spelling (no, yes). K = .71.
Status	Explicit indication of personal status in message (no, yes). K = .81.
Depend1	Reference to previous message (none, yes-one message, yes-more than one). K = .56.
Depend3	Relates to previous message content (no, yes). K = .76.
Depend4	Introduction of new topic (no, yes-no reference to prior discussion, yes reference to prior discussion). K = .66.
Message Lines	Number of lines in message (1-10, 11-25, 26-100, 100+). K = .77
Noise	Message not intended for list (misdirected, regular message, intended for list but not regular). K = .83.
Challenge	Message containing challenge, dare, bet (no, yes). K = .95.
Action	Message containing call to action, directive (no, yes-not main content, yes-main content). K = .83.
Nature	Nature of the message (provide information, request information, persuasive, opinionated, mixed). K/A = n.s.
First Person	Verbal self-disclosure including first person (no, yes). A = .50.
Coalition1	Measured degree of agreement in message (strong, mild, neutral). A = 80.
Coalition2	Used we to address others or refer to group (no, yes). K = .79.
Coalition3	Addressed others by name (no, yes). K = .71.
External	Degree of agreement with persons, organizations, opinions, ideologies outside Coalition group (strong, mild, neutral). A = .51
Question	Message as question or request (no, yes). K = .67.
Emoticon	Message used icons to express emotion (no, one, two or more). K = .87.
Emodevice	Message containing capitals, punctuation, etc., (no, one, two or more). K = .80.
Articon	Message contained artistic icons (no, one, two or more). K = .97.
Signature1	Message has signature characteristics (no, yes-simple, yes-complex). K = .66.
Signature2	Message with signature with ending quote (no, yes). K = .80.
Quote1	Message quoted text from discussion (no, yes-1-10 lines, yes 11-25 lines, yes-26+ lines). K = .77.
Quote2	Message quoted text from online source (no, yes-1-10 lines, yes 11-25 lines, yes-26+ lines). K = .96.
Quote3	Message quoted text from offline source (no, yes-1-10 lines, yes 11-25 lines, yes-26+ lines). K = .91.
Apology	Implicit or explicit apology/regret (no, yes-implied, yes-explicit). K = .94.

continued on following page

Table 1. continued

Format	Use of appropriate formatting-paragraphs, tabs, spacing (unformatted, minimal, mostly, over-formatted). A = .51.
Subject	Appropriateness of subject line (no, yes, none). K = .78.
A = Cronbach's Alpha; K = Cohen's *kappa*; n.s. = no statistically reliable result.	

RESULTS

Coding Reliability

For the reliability analyses, Cohen's *kappa* and Cronbach's *Alpha* were computed for the 33 variables used in this investigation. Cohen's *kappa* reliability is used for categorical variables while Cronbach's *Alpha* is used for continuous variables. The results indicated acceptable *kappa* values of .5 or more for 25 variables and Alpha values of .5 or more for 22 variables. Fleiss (1981) characterizes *kappas* of .40 to .60 as fair, .60 to .75 as good, and over .75 as excellent (see p. 82). Cronbach *Alpha* levels of .50 to .70 are typical reliability for variable with a low number of items (2 or 3, as in this analysis, McCroskey & Richmond, 1989). Reliability values for all variables are listed in Table 1.

Hypothesis 1

The first hypothesis predicted that males would differ from females in stylistic features of messages in CMC. The statistical results of t-tests and chi-square tests in significant gender differences for 6 variables of the male on-line style are listed in Table 2. T-tests for scale variables referring to male online communication style resulted in significant gender differences for argument (Flame1) ($t(243.46) = 3.81$, $p < .05$), message length, with categories treated as relative ratio intervals, ($t(538.) = 3.93$. $p < .05$), and directives (Action) ($t(72.22) = 2.05$. $p < .05$) but in the opposite direction posited by Hypothesis 1.

Women in the message sample were more argumentative (Flame1), wrote longer messages (Message lines), and issued more directives (Action). A partial distributional analysis showed that 696 of 1083 argumentative messages scaled towards the positive (or, friendly in tone) side of the scale. The proportion of female messages was nearly equal to the proportion of male messages in this category of argumentativeness (26.2% to 27%). In the remaining n = 387 messages, ranging from diverging opinion to hostile argument, a greater proportion of female messages than male messages were progressively argumentative in tone. A partial distributional analysis for message length indicated a greater proportion of male messages (67.7%) than female messages (60.9%) of 1 to 10 lines; messages of 11 to 25 lines were similar, 23.2% to 22.5%, male versus female, respectively; for n = 214 messages of 26 to 100 lines, the female proportion of messages (11.7%) exceeded the proportion of male messages (7.6%); and, for n = 54 messages of more than 100 lines, women produced a higher percentage (4.9%) of messages than men (1.5%). The partial distribution analysis for directives showed a slightly greater proportion of female messages (7.3%) than male messages (7.1%) for n = 184 messages included directives that were not related to the main point of the message. Female messages were greater in proportion to male messages (4.9% to 2.4%) for n = 72 messages that included directives on the main point of the message.

Chi-square tests for 4 male style variables having 2 coded categories indicated significant gender differences for fact ($\chi^2(1) = 20.96$, *delta* = . 25, $p < .05$), challenge ($\chi^2(1) = 18.59$, *delta* = .91, $p < .05$), and status displays ($\chi^2(1) = 4.00$, *delta* = .23, $p < .05$). Men used more factual statements

Table 2. Statistical analyses of gender differences

T-Tests						
		Mean scores				
		Male	Female	t	df	p
Male Style Variables						
Flame1		1.60	2.03	3.81	243.46	<.05
Message lines		1.42	1.60	3.93	538.00	<.05
Action		1.25	1.40	2.05	72.22	<.05
Female style variables						
Emoticon		1.18	1.33	2.63	147.18	<.05
Quote1		1.23	1.50	4.20	151.19	<.05
Apology		1.18	1.37	2.32	75.61	<.05
Format		1.26	1.36	2.78	435.63	<.05
Chi-square tests						
	χ^2		df		p	
Male style variables						
Fact	20.96		1		<.05	
Challenge	18.59		1		<.05	
Status	4.00		1		<.05	
Female style variables						
First person	59.19		1		<.05	
Depend3	4.22		1		<.05	
Coalition2	13.04		1		<.05	
Coalition3	15.16		1		<.05	
Subject	110.06		2		<.05	

whereas women were more challenging and indicated their status more than men. A greater proportion of male messages (57.7%) than female messages (45.7%) included factual information in n = 1441 messages. Female messages were greater in proportion to male messages (7.3% to 3%) in n = 95 messages which contained challenges. The proportion of female messages (15%) was greater than the proportion of male messages (11.5%) in n = 313 messages indicating the sender's status. Hypothesis 1 was not supported by the finding of significant gender differences for 6 of the 11

male style variables. The results indicated 1 style variable in the hypothesized direction and 5 style variables in the opposite direction.

Hypothesis 2

The second hypothesis predicted that females would differ in online communication style from males. The statistical data for t-tests and chi-square tests in significant gender differences for 9 female style variables are listed in Table 2. T-tests for 13 scale variables for female online communication style resulted in significant gender differences for 4 variables: emoticon ($t(147.18) = 2.62$, $p < .05$), apology ($t(75.61) = 2.32$, $p < .05$), quotes from previous discussions (Quote1) ($t(151.19) = 4.20$, $p < .05$), and format ($t(435.63) = 2.78$, $p < .05$). Women used emoticons, apologies, quoted from previous messages/discussion and formatted their messages more than men.

A partial distributional analysis of emoticon use indicated there was a higher proportion of female messages than male messages (14.3% to 8%) for $n = 233$ messages with 1 emoticon and, similarly, for $n = 71$ messages with 2 or more emoticons (7.3% to 1.9%). The partial distributional analysis for messages containing apologies showed that women posted a greater proportion of messages of apology. The proportion of messages indicating an implied manner of apology was greater for women (7%) than for men (4%) as was the proportion of messages that were clearly apologetic (4.2% to .9%), women compared to men, respectively. Of the $n = 753$ messages which included quotes from the ongoing discussion, the proportion of male messages (23.5%) for quotes of 1 to 10 lines in length was higher than the proportion of female messages (17.1%). The proportion of female messages (8.9%) was greater than the proportion of male messages (4.5%) including quotes of 11 to 25 lines in length, and, similarly, for quotes of 26 or more lines in length women also used more longer quotes than men (2.8% to 1.2%, respectively). A partial distributional analysis of formatted messages indicated that male messages were more likely to evidence minimal formatting structure (use of paragraphs) than messages from women (64.1% to 58.8%, respectively) or regularly formatted message structure (including paragraphs, constant line spacing and tabs) (20.1% to 17.6%, males compared to females, respectively). However, women's use of overformatted messages was higher than those observed for men (6.3% to 1.4%, respectively).

Chi-square tests for 7 categorical variables of the female online communication style found significant gender differences in self-disclosure (First Person) ($\chi^2(1) = 59.19$, *delta* = .53, $p < .05$), use of "we" (Coalition2) ($\chi^2(1) = 13.04$, delta = .49, $p < .05$), address by name (Coalition3) ($\chi^2(1) = 15.16$, *delta* = .26, $p < .05$), message relation (Depend3) ($\chi^2(1) = 4.22$, *delta* = .25, $p < .05$), and subject line appropriateness ($\chi^2(2) = 110.06$, *delta* = .47, $p < .05$). Women self-disclosed, referred to others as "we," addressed others by name and related their messages to previous messages more than men. Men used appropriate subjects in message headers more than women. In $n = 934$ messages indicating self-disclosure, the proportion of female messages (52.5%) was greater than the proportion of male messages (32.9%). Women posted a greater proportion (13.6%) of messages ($n = 233$) referring to others as "we" (Coalition2) than men (8.1%), and also a greater proportion messages addressing others by name, Coalition3, (45.2% to 35.2%, women compared to men, respectively). A greater proportion of messages contributed by females (13.3%) than males (10%) related to previous discussion (Depend3). Conversely, men posted a greater proportion (83%) of messages with appropriate subject lines in headers than women (70%). The results show significant gender differences for 9 of 20 female style variables provided partial support for hypothesis 2. Women used 8 of 9 significant features of the female online style more than men in the message sample. Men used only one female stylistic feature more than women.

Research Question

The research question asks if language behaviors posited as gendered significantly differentiate online discussion styles attributable to men and women. While tests of hypotheses were not unequivocally conclusive, there appeared to be a critical mass of results trending towards discernable gendered behavioral patterns to warrant attempting to answer the research question. Three separate discriminant function analyses tested the

Table 3. Discriminant analysis of gender using male online style variables

Variable	F	Significance	Standardized Coefficient
Flame1	23.92	.00	.29
Fact	20.97	.00	-.50
Flame2	55.36	.00	.51
Status	3.97	.04	.03
Depend4	11.23	.00	.18
Message Lines	20.91	.00	.34
Challenge	18.66	.00	.16
Action	5.96	.01	.06
Canonical R = .206, Chi-square test of canonical R = .957, F (1, 2582) degrees of freedom.			

Classification			
	Predicted Group		
Actual Group	Female Group	Male Group	Total Cases
1-Female Group	185	242	427
	43.3%	56.7%	
2-Male Group	629	1528	2157
	29.2%	70.8%	
Classification Accuracy (%) = 66.2% N =			

male style variables, female style variables and all style variables to determine differences between the gendered behavioral styles in the online group discussions.

Male Online Style

The statistical data for F-ratio tests, the standardized canonical function coefficients and the classification results are listed in Table 3. In the analysis of the 11 male on-line style variables, the F-ratio test indicated 8 significant variables (p < .05): (a) message length, (b) directive, (c) new topic, (d) argument, (e) flame, (f) fact, (g) challenge and (h) status.

The standardized canonical discriminant function coefficients for 1 function (the variable scale) determined the amount each of the male style variables contributed to differentiation between the gender groups and found 4 variables contributing more to differences between groups: flame, fact, message length and argument. The classification results indicated 70.8% accuracy of prediction for the male group and 43.3% accuracy of prediction for the female group in the differentiation of online communication styles between the gender groups. The classification of

n = 2,584 cases was 66.2% accurate in the prediction of differentiation in on-line communication styles between the gender groups.

Female Online Style

The results of the F-ratio test in the discriminant analysis of the female style variables indicated that 13 of the 20 variables were significant features

Table 4. Discriminant Analysis of Gender Using Female Online Style Variables

Variable	F	Significance	Standardized coefficient
First person	10.36	.00	.35
Coalition2	5.42	.02	.20
Flame3	18.60	.00	.34
Depend1	3.63	.05	-.09
Emoticon	28.24	.00	.22
Emodevice	5.22	.02	-.02
Articon	35.74	.00	.12
Signature1	4.88	.02	-.04
Quote2	42.53	.00	.49
Quote3	28.01	.00	.18
Apology	14.59	.00	-.05
Format	9.55	.00	.09
Subject	9.42	.00	.00
Canonical R = .534, Chi-square test of Canonical R = .714, F (1, 260) degrees of freedom.			
Classification			
	Predicted Group		
Actual Group	Female Group	Male Group	Total Cases
Female Group	18 (66.7%)	9 (33.3%)	27
Male Group	18 (7.7%)	217 (92.3%)	235
Classification Accuracy (%) = 89.6% N = 2587			

of the female online style: self-disclosure, use of "we," tension reduction, emoticon, emodevice, articon, signature articon, quotes from other CMC sources, non-CMC quotes, signature quotes, apology, subject and format. The standardized canonical discriminant function coefficients for one function showed three variables contributing more to the differentiation between groups: self-disclosure, tension reduction and quotes from other CMC sources. The classification results indicated 66.7% accuracy of prediction for the female group and 92.3% accuracy of prediction for the male group in the differentiation of on-line communication styles between the gender groups. The classification of n = 262 cases in the predicted differentiation between gender groups in on-line styles was 89.6% accurate. Statistical

results of this discriminant analysis of the female on-line style are found in Table 4.

Mixed Online Style

Failure to completely support the hypotheses made it necessary to examine the larger set of potentially predictive variables, see Table 1, in order to assess their ability to response to the research question. The F-ratio test in the discriminant analysis of 31 mixed style variables resulted in 17 significant variables: message length, argument, flame, status, self-disclosure, use of "we," tension reduction, emoticon, emodevice, articon, signature articon, CMC quotes from other sources, non-CMC quotes, signature quotes, apology, format and subject. The standardized canonical discriminant function coef-

Table 5. Discriminant Analysis of Gender Using Mixed Style Variables

Variable	F	Significance	Standardized coefficient
Flame1	4.68	.03	.08
Flame2	16.62	.00	.19
Status	4.50	.03	-.01
Message Lines	13.33	.00	.19
First Person	10.36	.00	.34
Coalition2	5.42	.02	.18
Ext. Coalition	3.25	.00	-.25
Flame3	18.60	.00	.32
Depend1	3.63	.05	-.05
Emoticon	28.24	.00	.17
Emodevice	5.22	.02	.00
Articon	35.74	.00	.12
Signature1	4.88	.02	-.06
Quote2	42.53	.00	.41
Quote3	28.01	.00	.16
Signature2	10.04	.00	.05
Apology	14.59	.00	-.02
Format	9.55	.00	.09
Subject	9.42	.00	.02

Canonical $r = .57$, chi-square test of canonical $r = .674$, F (1, 260) degrees of freedom.

Classification			
		Predicted	
Actual Group	Female Group	Male Group	Cases
1- Female Group	20	7	27
	74.1%	25.9%	
2-Male Group	12	223	235
	5.1%	94.9%	
Classification Accuracy (%) = 92.7%			

ficients indicated 4 variables contributing more to stylistic differences between the gender groups: quotes from other CMC sources, self-disclosure, tension reduction and slang. The classification results showed 94.9% accuracy for the male group and 74.1% accuracy for the female group in predicting differences in the online styles of the gender groups. The classification of n = 262 cases was 92.7% accurate in the predicted difference between the gender groups in online communication styles. The results of this discriminant analysis of the mixed on-line style are listed in Table 5.

Discussion

This study investigated gender differences in the communication styles of gender-identified participants in public discussion groups in text-based CMC. Results of the analysis did not support the presence of a unique men's online communication style (hypothesis 1) and partially support women's online communication style (hypothesis 2). The high level of accuracy in prediction of the mixed style for gender groups in the message sample demonstrated the social influence of gender membership and the importance of gendered communication behavior to the construction of social identity in the ProjectH sample groups.

Significant gender differences were found for 15 of the 31 style variables in this study, six variables of men's online style and nine variables of the women's online style. For the male on-line style in hypothesis 1, men used more factual information/statements. Women were more argumentative, challenging, issued more directives, wrote longer messages and indicated status more than men. An explanation for the divergence of women from the female online style may be attributed to the situational context with respect to the topics or tenor of group discussions. Women may have felt less powerful and generated messages using higher levels of power to compensate for a perception of social weakness.

This pattern of women using higher levels of power than men has been observed in mediation interactions (Burrell, Donohue, & Allen, 1989). In this case, untrained female mediators reacted with more intense and controlling language to gain control over the interaction when compared to untrained male mediators. However, it is also possible women were more comfortable resisting influence attempts in the online groups. This would be consistent with Gaudagno and Cialdini's (2002, 2007) findings on communication modality differences for male and female persuasibility. They found men were more likely than women to engage in rational evaluation of persuasive messages conveyed by email. Moreover, women's attitudes towards a same-sex sender of a persuasive message were positive only when the message was received FTF.

Findings for hypothesis 2 indicated significant gender differences for nine variables associated with the women's style, conceptualized by Herring as attenuated, supportive or less powerful than the men's style. Women self-disclosed, referred to others as "we," addressed others by name, related messages to and quoted from previous discussion, used emoticons, apologies and overformatted messages more than men. The felt need to build solidarity and identify as a member of the group is consistent with research showing that women are more likely to engage in relational maintenance online than are men (Boneva, Kraut, and Frohlich, 2001; Rumbough, 2001). Women may have exhibited some male characteristics but did not abandon women's style characteristics. This may indicate accommodation to an elevated level of gender salience in many of the groups (Palomares, 2004, 2008).

To summarize, the predominance of male participation in group discussions may have forced women's adaptation to features of the male online style. However, the finding of eight significant features of the women's on-line style demonstrated that women maintained a language pattern which distinguished a communication style partly consistent with Herring's description. This female gender pattern suggested the existence of gendered language styles in CMC.

The discriminant function analyses framed by the research question were intended to predict the extent to which the hypothesized gendered and mixed-attribute styles fit the styles used in the discussion groups. The discriminant analysis of the male online message style found eight significant features which differentiated the gender in the groups. Significant differences were found for six features. Women used five of these significant features more than men. The higher percentage of accuracy in characterizing the style indicated that male style was better defined than female style.

In the discriminant analysis of the women's online style, 13 message attribute variables were significant in differentiating the female discourse style in groups. Women used five of these significant features more than men. The greater accuracy for women in this discriminant analysis than in the analysis of the male style more clearly identified the female group with their gendered communication style. The greater accuracy for the males compared to females could be interpreted as women being more affected by contextual factors and thereby displaying behaviors that were more varied but also more contextually appropriate or comfortable.

Results of the discriminant analysis of the women's online style did not clearly demonstrate an emotional dimension of women's online style. Why women used more emoticons than men is unclear, especially in reference to the finding of no difference in the use of emotext devices. However, this finding is generally supportive of women's use of graphical expressions noted by Witmer and Katzman (1997) and Waseleski (2006). Whether women's use of emoticons was graphically emphatic (blatant) or attenuated and whether their use of emoticons was perceived as the stereotypic emotional expression of women is also unclear. A direct comparison between iconic and verbal emotional expression in the online styles of men and women would therefore be an appropriate follow-up investigation with respect to this issue.

A discriminant analysis of the mixed attribute style determined 17 variables to significantly differentiate the groups in the use of the mixed gender message style, four male style variables and 13 female style variables. Differences were found for nine of these significant features, and women used eight of the features more than men. The percentage of accuracy for both genders in this discriminant analysis was the highest of the three discriminant analyses and suggested the gendered construction of group identity within discussion groups according to the groups' culturally-sanctioned norms. The higher level of accuracy in characterization of the mixed-attribute style for both gender groups and the finding of significant differences for 9 of the 17 message attributes pointed to the important social role played by gender (enacted through language use) in the construction of social identity in the context of public discussion groups in CMC. This was somewhat less efficient outcome than the effort reported by Thomson and Murachver (2001), although their initial pool of linguistic behaviors was not as strongly empirically differentiated by gender prior to the group classification analysis.

Data supported significant gender differences in the use of six attributes: factual information/statements, arguments, self-disclosure, addressing others by name, quotes from previous discussion, and appropriate subject lines. Results did not consistently support a finding of distinct gendered communication styles in the message sample. The discriminant analyses involving the male online style defined the characteristic features of the male style with a fairly high degree of accuracy, but men used only factual statements more than women. These analyses showed that men in the message sample relied on an essential language style. Results of the discriminant analyses of the female online style provided moderate support for a women's online style consisting of five features: self-disclosure, use of "we," emoticons, apologies and over-formatted messages. Women, undoubtedly the minority gender group in the message sample, combined their gendered style with significant elements of the male style. This finding was supported by similar evidence found in Savicki et al. (1996c), in which the minority gender (male or female) in discussion groups moved in the direction of or adapted to elements of the online style of the majority gender group.

FUTURE RESEARCH DIRECTIONS

The results of this study are limited in respect to generalization beyond the communication context of online discussion groups using CMC. It would be necessary to examine or to generalize the style variables (and styles) in this study to quantitative studies in both similar and different online contexts to determine which gendered styles can be reproduced. In the sample, 407 messages were not gender-identified but appeared similar to the 417 messages authored by women. How the messages of unidentified discussion participants affected the gendered behavior of other discussion participants is also a question worthy of investigation. Evidence in support of a women's online language style was limited in this study to verifying a more general emotional dimension to women's style of behavior in online discussions. More research is needed, including more recently compiled computer-mediated databases, to verify gender differences in the use of textual signs (emoticons and emotext devices), to better differentiate contextual versus topical relevance for both men and women participating in online discussions, and to more precisely determine the complexity and layering of emotional expression in mediated contexts. The potential effect of cultural contexts also was not addressed in this study and it is evident from the literature that cross-cultural validation of gender and group participation is a necessary future research direction.

CONCLUSION

This chapter reports systematic research identifying gendered communication styles of men and women participating in online group discussions. A number of language attributes were found to mark differences in online message behaviors between men and women. However, when these markers were subsequently applied to empirically differentiate male and female online communication style profiles many did not significantly contribute to clearly identifying a unique style profile for each gender. Instead, a subset of attributes converged to form a mixed-attribute profile that differentiated male and female message behavior.

Henley and Kramarae (1991) presented a rationale for the study of gender which is ideal for research on gender in CMC. They recognize that "cultural differences are real," but gender differences may reflect "race, ethnicity, class, age, sexual preferences, etc." and power relations which are forces that interact with gender and vary in importance and meaning in different situational contexts (pp. 40-41). Theoretical research on gender in CMC should provide an informed understanding of the cultural, social and political impact of gender on online social interaction.

An understanding of gendered styles is important for people who choose to interact with others in CMC. People have expectations for gendered communication behavior and rules for conversation/social interaction with others of their own gender, the other gender, or in mixed groups in varied situations. Social interaction with others of different cultures in global settings is as accessible to personal computer users as social interaction with others locally. An informed understanding of gendered styles may afford social participants in CMC a richer interpretation of communicative interaction with others. An informed understanding of gender in CMC may allow people to look beyond gender stereotypes to find and compare the cultural and social meaning of gendered styles in mediated communication contexts.

REFERENCES

Anonymous,. (1998). To reveal or not to reveal: A theoretical model of anonymous communication. *Communication Theory*, *8*, 381–407. doi:10.1111/j.1468-2885.1998.tb00226.x

Aries, E. (1998). Gender differences in interaction: A reexamination. In Canary, D., & Dindia, K. (Eds.), *Sex differences and similarities in communication: Critical essays and empirical investigations of sex and gender in interaction* (pp. 65–82). Mahwah, NJ: Lawrence Erlbaum Associates.

Barnes, S. (2003). Cyberspace: Creating paradoxes for the ecology of self. In L. Strate, R. L. Jacobson, & S. Gibson (Eds.), Communication and cyberspace: Social interaction in an electronic environment (2nd. ed., pp. 229-253). Cresskill, NJ: Hampton Press.

Boneva, B., Kraut, R., & Frohlich, D. (2001). Using e-mail for personal relationships: The difference gender makes. *The American Behavioral Scientist, 45,* 530–549. doi:10.1177/00027640121957204

Burrell, N., Donohue, W., & Allen, M. (1988). Gender-based perceptual biases in mediation. *Communication Research, 15,* 447–469. doi:10.1177/009365088015004006

Clerc, S. (1996). Estrogen brigades and "Big Tits" threads: Media fandom online and off. In Cherny, L., & Weise, E. (Eds.), *Wired women* (pp. 73–97). Seattle, WA: Seal Press.

Cornetto, K. M., & Nowak, K. L. (2006). Utilizing usernames for sex categorization in computer-mediated communication: Examining perceptions and accuracy. *Cyberpsychology & Behavior, 9,* 377–387. doi:10.1089/cpb.2006.9.377

Culnan, M. J., & Markus, M. L. (1987). Information technologies. In Jablin, F. M., Putnam, L. L., Roberts, K. H., & Porter, L. W. (Eds.), *Handbook of organizational communication: An interdisciplinary perspective* (pp. 420–443). Newbury Park, CA: Sage.

Dindia, K., & Allen, M. (1992). Sex-differences in self-disclosure: A meta-analysis. *Psychological Bulletin, 112,* 106–124. doi:10.1037/0033-2909.112.1.106

Fleiss, J. L. (1981). *Statistical methods for rates and proportions.* New York: John Wiley.

Fox, A., B., Bukatko, D., Hallahan, M., & Crawford, M. (2007). The medium makes a difference: Gender similarities and differences in instant messaging. *Journal of Language and Social Psychology, 26,* 389–397. doi:10.1177/0261927X07306982

Gal, S. (1995). Language, gender, and power: An anthropological review. In Hall, K., & Bucholtz, M. (Eds.), *Gender articulated* (pp. 169–182). New York, NY: Routledge.

Guadagno, R. E., & Cialdini, R. B. (2002). Online persuasion: An examination of gender differences in computer-mediated interpersonal influence. *Group Dynamics, 6,* 38–51. doi:10.1037/1089-2699.6.1.38

Guadagno, R. E., & Cialdini, R. B. (2007). Persuade him by email, but see her in person: Online persuasion revisited. *Computers in Human Behavior, 23,* 999–1015. doi:10.1016/j.chb.2005.08.006

Guiller, J., & Durndell, A. (2007). Students' linguistic behaviour in online discussion groups: Does gender matter? *Computers in Human Behavior, 23,* 2240–2255. doi:10.1016/j.chb.2006.03.004

Henley, S., & Kramarae, C. (1991). Gender, power and miscommunication. In Coupland, N., Giles, H., & Wiemann, J. (Eds.), *Miscommunication and problematic talk* (pp. 18–43). Newbury Park, CA: Sage Publications.

Herring, S. (1994, June). *Gender differences in computer-mediated communication: Bringing familiar baggage to the new frontier.* Keynote talk at the American Library Association Annual Convention. Miami, FL. Retrieved May 2, 2000 from http://www.cpsr.org/cpsr/gender/herring.txt

Herring, S. (2000). Gender differences in CMC: Findings and implications. *Computer Professionals for Social Responsibility Newsletter, 18*(1). Retrieved (n.d.), from http://www.cpsr.org/publications/newsletters/issues/2000/winter2000/herring/htm

Herring, S. (2001). Computer-mediated discourse. In Schiffrin, D., Tannen, D., & Hamiliton, H. (Eds.), *Handbook of discourse analysis* (pp. 612–634). Oxford, UK: Blackwell.

Herring, S., Johnson, D., & DiBenedetto, T. (1995). This discussion is going too far! In Hall, K., & Bucholtz, M. (Eds.), *Gender articulated* (pp. 67–96). New York: Routledge.

Herring, S. C., & Martinson, A. (2004). Assessing gender authenticity in computer-mediated language use. *Journal of Language and Social Psychology, 23*, 424–446. doi:10.1177/0261927X04269586

Herring, S. C., & Paolillo, J. C. (2006). Gender and genre variation in weblogs. *Journal of Sociolinguistics, 10*, 439–459. doi:10.1111/j.1467-9841.2006.00287.x

Huffaker, D. A. & Calvert, S. L. (2005). Gender, identity, and language use in teenage blogs.

Journal of Computer-Mediated Communication. *10 (2)*. Retrieved March 23, 2009, from http://www3.interscience.wiley.com/cgi-bin/fulltext/120837938/HTMLSTART

Kennedy, H. (2006). Beyond anonymity, or future directions for Internet identity research. *New Media & Society, 8*, 859–876. doi:10.1177/1461444806069641

Koch, S. C., Mueller, B., Kruse, L., & Zumbach, J. (2005). Constructing gender in chat groups. *Sex Roles, 53*, 29–41. doi:10.1007/s11199-005-4276-7

Lea, M., & Spears, R. (1995). Love at first byte? Building personal relationships over computer networks. In Wood, J., & Duck, S. (Eds.), *Understudied relationships: Off the beaten track* (pp. 197–233). Thousand Oaks, CA: Sage.

Mabry, E. A. (1998). Frames and flames: The structure of argumentative messages on the Net. In Sudweeks, F., McLaughlin, M., & Sheizaf, R. (Eds.), *Network & Netplay: Virtual groups on the Internet* (pp. 13–26). Menlo Park, CA: AAAI Press.

Mabry, E. A. (2002). Ambiguous self-identification and sincere communication in CMC. In L. Anolli, R. Ciceri, & G. Riva (Eds.), Say not to say: New perspectives on miscommunication (pp. 247-264). Amsterdam, NL: IOS Press.

McCroskey, J. C., & Richmond, V. P. (1989). Bipolar scales. In Emmert, P., & Barker, L. (Eds.), *Measurement of communication behavior* (pp. 154–167). New York: Longman.

McKenna, K. Y. A., & Green, A. S. (2002). Virtual group dynamics. *Group Dynamics*, 116–127. doi:10.1037/1089-2699.6.1.116

Mulac, A. (1998). The gender-linked language effect: Do language differences really make a difference? In Canary, D., & Dindia, K. (Eds.), *Sex differences and similarities in communication: Critical essays and empirical investigations of sex and gender in interaction* (pp. 127–156). Mahwah, NJ: Lawrence Erlbaum Associates.

O'Barr, W., & Atkins, B. (1998). 'Women's Language' or 'Powerless Language. In Coates, J. (Ed.), *Language and gender* (pp. 377–387). Oxford, UK: Blackwell Publishers.

Owen, J. E., Yarbrough, E. J., Vaga, A., & Tucker, D. C. (2003). Investigation of the effects of gender and preparation on quality of communication in Internet support groups. *Computers in Human Behavior, 19*, 259–275. doi:10.1016/S0747-5632(02)00068-7

Palomares, N. A. (2004). Gender schmaticity, gender identity salience, and gender-linked language use. *Human Communication Research*, *30*, 556–588. doi:10.1111/j.1468-2958.2004. tb00745.x

Palomares, N. A. (2008). Explaining gender-based language use: Effects of gender identity salience on references to emotion and tentative language in intra- and intergroup contexts. *Human Communication Research*, *34*, 263–286. doi:10.1111/j.1468-2958.2008.00321.x

Postmes, T., Spears, R., & Lea, M. (1998). Breaching or building social boundaries? Side-effects of computer-mediated communication. *Communication Research*, *25*, 689–715. doi:10.1177/009365098025006006

Rafaeli, S., & Sudweeks, F. (1998). Interactivity on the Nets. In Sudweeks, F., McLaughlin, M., & Rafaeli, S. (Eds.), *Network & Netplay: Virtual groups on the Internet* (pp. 173–190). Menlo Park, CA: AAAI Press.

Rafaeli, S., Sudweeks, F., Konstan, J., & Mabry, E. (1998). ProjectH oveview: A collaborative quantitative study of computer-mediated communication. In Sudweeks, F., McLaughlin, M., & Rafaeli, S. (Eds.), *Network & Netplay: Virtual groups on the Internet* (pp. 265–281). Menlo Park, CA: AAAI Press.

Rains, S. A., & Scott, C. R. (2007). To identify or not to identify: A theoretical model of receiver responses to anonymous communication. *Communication Theory*, *17*, 61–91. doi:10.1111/j.1468-2885.2007.00288.x

Rodino, M. (1997). Breaking out of binaries: Reconceptualizing gender and its relationship to language in computer-mediated communication. *Journal of Computer-Mediated Communication, 3*(3). Retrieved August 22, 1999, from, http://www.ascusc.org/jcmc/vol3/issue3/rodino.html

Rumbaugh, T. (2001). The development and maintenance of interpersonal relationships through computer-mediated communication. *Communication Research Reports*, *18*, 223–229.

Savicki, V., Kelley, M., & Lingenfelter, D. (1996a). Gender and small task group activity using computer-mediated communication. *Computers in Human Behavior*, *12*, 209–224. doi:10.1016/0747-5632(96)00003-9

Savicki, V., Kelley, M., & Lingenfelter, D. (1996b). Gender, group composition and task type in small task groups using computer-mediated communication. *Computers in Human Behavior*, *12*, 549–565. doi:10.1016/S0747-5632(96)00024-6

Savicki, V., Kelley, M., & Oesterreich, E. (1999). Judgments of gender in computer-mediated communication. *Computers in Human Behavior*, *15*, 185–194. doi:10.1016/S0747-5632(99)00017-5

Savicki, V., Lingenfelter, D., & Kelley, M. (1996c). Gender, language style and group composition in Internet discussion groups. *Journal of Computer-Mediated Communication, 2*(3). Retrieved August 22, 1999, from http://www.ascusc.org/jcmc/vol2/issue3/savicki.html

Scott, C. R. (1999). Communication technology and group communication. In L. R. Frey (Ed.), D. S. Gouran, & M. S. Poole (Eds.), The handbook of group communication theory & research (pp. 313-334). Thousand Oaks, CA: Sage.

Short, J., Willims, E., & Christie, B. (1976). *The social psychology of telecommunications*. London: John Wiley.

Spears, R., & Lea, M. (1992). Social influence and the influence of the 'social' in computer-mediated communication. In Lea, M. (Ed.), *Contexts of Computer-Mediated Communication* (pp. 30–65). New York, NY: Harvester Wheatsheaf.

Spears, R., & Lea, M. (1994). Panacea or panopticon? The hidden power in computer-mediated communication. *Communication Research*, *21*(4), 427–459. doi:10.1177/009365094021004001

Thomson, R., & Murachver, T. (2001). Predicting gender from electronic discourse. *The British Journal of Social Psychology*, *40*, 193–208. doi:10.1348/014466601164812

Thomson, R., Murachver, T., & Green, J. (2002). Where is the gender in gendered language? *Psychological Science*, *12*, 171–175. doi:10.1111/1467-9280.00329

Walther, J. B., & Parks, M. R. (2002). Cues filtered out, cues filtered in: Computer-mediated communication and relationships. In M. L. Knapp & J. A. Daly (Eds.), Handbook of interpersonal communication (3rd. ed., pp. 529-563). Thousand Oaks, CA: Sage.

Waseleski, C. (2006). Gender and the use of exclamation points in computer-mediated communication: An analysis of exclamations posted to two electronic discussion lists. *Journal of Computer-Mediated Communication*, *11*, 1012–1024. doi:10.1111/j.1083-6101.2006.00305.x

Witmer, D., & Katzman, S. (1997). On-line smiles: Does gender make a difference in the use of graphic accents? *Journal of Computer-Mediated Communication, 2*(4). Retrieved August 23, 1999, from http://www.ascusc.org/jcmc/vol2/issue4/witmer1.html

KEY TERMS AND DEFINITIONS

Communication Style: A pattern or profile of language use in message behavior that constructs a unique identity of person, group, or social situation.

Computer-Mediated Communication: The sending and receiving of messages in any form requiring the use of computer technology.

Gendered Communication Style: Socially or culturally sanctioned, gendered communication behavior corresponding to the presentation of the gendered aspect of social/personal identity made salient in the situational context of the group.

Female Communication Style: A pattern or profile of language use by women in their message behavior that uniquely identifies them compared to men.

Male Communication Style: A pattern or profile of language use by men in their message behavior that uniquely identifies them compared to women.

Online Communication Style: A pattern or profile of language use in computer-mediated communication message behavior that constructs a unique identity of person, group, or social situation.

SIDE Model: The social identification/deindividuation (SIDE) model proposes participants in online social interactions are more likely to rely on social cues about the context and categorical information about other participants, inferred from computer-mediated messages, in helping themselves to establish their online identity (deindividuation) than use more personally identifying information unless the rewards (and risks) for doing so are highly favorable.

Section 3
Language Action and Discourse Features in CMC

Chapter 8
The Role of Metaphors in the Interpersonal Discourse of Online Forums

Agnès Vayreda
Open University of Catalonia (UOC), Spain

Francesc Núñez
Open University of Catalonia (UOC), Spain

ABSTRACT

This chapter focuses on the role that metaphors play in the social relationships of people who use CMC. We analyze the metaphors used by contributors to three different electronic fora when they refer to the process of interaction. One of our main objectives is to show that the study of metaphors allows us to understand how CMC users reach agreement as to the nature of the social space that they inhabit and what behavior is considered to be appropriate or inappropriate in such a space. This chapter will show that metaphors facilitate the construction of social life and allow CMC users to propose norms of behaviour; they also facilitate the process of identification, generate confidence in a group, and orient users to the cultural contexts in which social action takes place.

INTRODUCTION

A great deal of what we think, experience and do in our everyday lives is very much a matter of metaphors (Lakoff & Johnson, 1980, p. 3). Metaphors play an important role in the interpretation processes of experience, especially when this is a novel experience, as is the case with CMC. Thanks to this recourse, the novel becomes familiar.

From the origins of CMC, designers and the first users of these technologies (which, as we know, on many occasions are the same) have employed metaphors in order to make their experiences comprehensible as well as to divulge their projects as socio-technical projects rather than as merely technological ones. Thus, for instance, in the mid- seventies, Lee Felsestein, a hacker who had dropped out of Berkley University, worked on the *Community Memory* project, whose aim was to build an I.T. system designed for communities. This

DOI: 10.4018/978-1-61520-827-2.ch008

was referred to as a "hybrid of library", "cafe", "municipal park" and "post office" (Roszak, 1994). Similarly, in Hiltz and Turrof's (1993) book regarding computer-assisted teleconferences, it is said that these: "can constitute public spaces, bringing to mind an Italian villa on a Sunday afternoon" (p. 429). Rheingold (1993), one of the major pioneers of CMC and who coined the concept of "virtual community", referred to this type of 'social aggregate' by means of recurring to images which are well-known to all such as a "living encyclopedia" (p.56) or, also, as "a combination of intellectual marketplace and mind-game parlor" (p.56), in the same way as *The Well* was understood as the biggest world conversation. The Whole Earth 'Lectronic Link, normally shortened to The WELL, and located in the San Francisco Bay, is considered to be one of the first virtual communities. It is best known for its Internet forums.

Historians and sociologists of the Internet have been interested in these metaphors with the aim of analysing them as part of the social imaginary, as utopias and as a component of the analysis of culture (Stefik, 1997, Flichy, 2001). According to Flichy, for example, the Internet imaginary is organised on the basis of three grand metaphors: cyberspace as a frontier, in which this image signifies new space to be discovered and populated, the possibility of creating a new society; the community, one of the elements by which it is rooted at a local level, for the creation of common values and a basic cell of democracy; finally, the individual initiative to create one's own business (Flichy, 2001, p. 256). These metaphors have also been interpreted as one of the ways in which societies manage their tensions and uncertainties. On this basis, the study of CMC metaphors has become a good social indicator and a mirror of our times (Dubey, 2001, p. 18).

It would be a mistake to think that with the years, as CMC becomes more popular and an ever more common and universal type of communication (in the context of our Western societies),

these metaphors will no longer be necessary. However, Stefik (1997) warned a few years ago that the metaphors that people use to represent CMC will continue to be necessary for the future development of CMC, in the same way as they were in the past. Likewise, and according to Jones (1998), these metaphors are relevant "as they allow us to contemplate the history of the Internet as a project rather than only technology [...]" (p. 2). Indeed, the attraction that CMC has exercised over its own designers and many of its diverse users (individuals and collectives) resides, to some extent, in the always open opportunity to construct and inhabit (new) social spaces on the basis of their needs and desires without further limits than those imposed by their own capacity to imagine. This is what Serfaty (2005) has metaphorically called "discourse's territorialisation of the immaterial" (p.91).

In this chapter we will focus on the analysis of CMC metaphors in their most popular and everyday usage. And, to be more precise, we will only pay attention to those cases in which a group of people utilise CMC in order to create a given social space. We consider the metaphorisation of these social spaces – the fact that they are endowed with a figurative sense to be a constitutive part of any process of appropriation of group CMC.

Our first aim will be to show that the analysis of metaphors allows us to access and to understand how CMC users (users of an electronic forum, for example) manage to reach an agreement with regard to what this place is as a social space and, therefore, to what is an appropriate or inappropriate way of participating in it. Our second aim will be to show that the analysis of metaphors connects the three fundamental aspects of CMC: language, social interaction and technology. To make that argument, we shall examine two specific cases.

Our project would be of special interest to those researchers who are interested in studying the processes of constitution of online social spaces that emerge as a result of CMC.

BACKGROUND

Metaphors in the Context of CMC Analysis

The analysis of metaphors we are introducing here is framed within the context of CMC studies which focus on: (a) analysis of CMC language as social practice and (b) discourses that accompany and provide meaning to the use of CMC. This double perspective has proved to be especially pertinent for the study of the construction of online sociability. Let us indicate the three approaches to the analysis of CMC in which the study of metaphors has been relevant. The first one is the Computer-Mediated Discourse Analysis (CMDA) and Computer-Mediated Conversational Analysis (CMCA); the second one is the analysis of computer-mediated symbolic interactions; and the third one, coming from sociology of science and technology, is the analysis of the symbolic dimension which exists in all relations between technology and users. In this necessarily brief review of the extensive literature on these three main lines of CMC research, we will only highlight some of the approaches which could support an analysis of metaphors such as the one presented here.

First approach. The consideration of the importance of language in the construction and understanding of computer-mediated interaction represents a point of departure for all the approaches of CMDA and CMCA. The language of CMC [and also computer-mediated discourse, online discourse or electronic discourse, computer mediated conversation] has been studied from many perspectives in relation to the interests of different researchers (Baym, 1995; Bretag, 2006; Crystal, 2001; Hubler & Bell, 2003; McLaughlin, Osborne & Smith, 1995; Nastri, Peña, & Hancock, 2006; Reid, 1999). In the initial studies on this subject, and with the intention of characterising and classifying the language of CMC, the question arose as to whether this language constituted

an oral or written variation of language (Etzioni & Etzioni, 1999; Maynor, 1994), or whether it constituted an intermediate type between written and oral forms (Ferrara, Brunner & Whittemore, 1991). These ways of considering the language of CMC have determined the two main lines of CMDA and CMCA. On the one hand, the models used in conversation analysis (CA) have been adapted (Garcia & Jacobs, 1999; Simpson, 2005; ten Have, 2000; Vayreda & Antaki, in press). In this way, what "CA brings to these communicative environments is a perspective on people's use of the interactional expectations of turn-taking, the sequential placement of messages, and their internal design. These have been identified by Conversation Analysis as the basic tools with which people construct their actions"(Antaki, Núñez, Ardevol & Vayreda, 2005). For example, in this article, we presented an analysis of "accountable action", which is to say "(...) how people make their messages achieve recognizable social and personal objectives while attending to the discursive perils attendant on any contribution to the social scene." (Antaki et al., 2005).

The same logic has followed the constitution of CMDA. In this case, models of discourse and content analysis have been imported. One of the researchers who has published most extensively on this subject is Susan Herring (2001; 2002; 2004; 2007). According to this author, CMDA "applies methods adapted from language-focused disciplines such as linguistics, communication, and rhetoric to the analysis of computer-mediated communication" (Herring, 2001, p. 2) and "it may be supplemented by surveys, interviews, ethnographic observation, or other methods (...) but what defines CMDA at its core is the analysis of logs of verbal interaction (characters, words, utterances, messages, exchanges, threads, archives, etc.)" (Herring, 2004, p 2). The importance of language when studying social practices, and the utility of discourse-analytic methods, have been features of CMC research since its very beginning, both in its synchronous as well as in its asynchronous modalities (Antaki et al., 2005; Baym, 1995; Bretag, 2006; Duthler, 2006; Hubler & Bell, 2003; McLaughtin, Osborne & Smith, 1995; Nastri et al., 2006; Reid, 1999).

Second approach. In the early stages it was thought that computer-mediated interaction could be understood as one more type of social interaction (Baker, 1998; Danet, 1995; Jones, 1995; Kolko, 1995; Kollock, 1999; Paccagnella, 1997; Stone 1995; Walther, 1992). In this context, some authors have held the view that computer-mediated interaction, following Blumer's perspective (1969), is always mediated by the symbols and the interpretation of the others' actions. For example, according to Jones (1995), the "non-traditional social formations" that have emerged as a result of CMC have been constructed by symbolic processes initiated and maintained by individuals and groups (...). In a different study, Jones (1998) added that "it would be far easier to understand the physical, or hardwired, connections than to understand the symbolic connections that emerge from interaction" (p. 5). In this sense, the study of computer-mediated interaction is no longer understood as if it were merely the result of a mechanical mediation with CMC technologies (forums, distribution lists, etc.), and instead comes to be understood and studied as a product of a symbolic and intersubjective mediation. Since some years ago now, certain studies have predominated which follow this understanding: studies related to the social construction of identity (Ellison, Heino & Gibbs, 2006; Bortree, 2005; Huffaker & Kalvert, 2005), gender (Herring 1999; Herring, 2003; Danet, 1998; Donath, 1999; O'Brien, 1999; Waseleski, 2006) and race (Burkhaler, 1999; Poster, 1998;), the constitution of virtual communities (Baym, 1998; Smith, 1999), the creation of rules, conflicts and social order (Connery, 1997; Honeycutt, 2005; Kolko et al, 1998; Reid, 1999; Maltz, 1996), social and emotional bonds (Bar-Lev, 2008; Kollock, 1999), etc. In different ways, all these studies show the symbolic processes by means of which these realities are constructed.

Third approach. Finally, and consonant with the previous approach, our project explores the tradition in which a whole universe of significations is intercalated between CMC and its use and appropriation. This universe is more than a filter through which technology is grasped (Akrich, 1987). Some studies on the social construction of technologies have argued that, all throughout this process, different interpretations are given with regard to what technology is and what its usefulness is, always on the basis of the negotiations that take place between different interest groups (Pinch, 1996; Bijker et al., 1987). What is being suggested here is that, in this process, technologies have certain 'interpretative flexibility' (Pinch & Bijker, 1987) with regard to their meaning and use. When Hine (2000) applies this concept to the case of the social construction of the Internet, he concludes that its sense is at the same time closed and open to new interpretations. To some extent, a common agreement has been reached with regard to what CMC is and what its usefulness is, even though this agreement must be negotiated every time. For example, in the specific case of news groups, and even though these are considered to be social and collaborative instances, it is necessary to negotiate a type and style of communication and participation for every single project, to the extent that the same technology may end up having very different meanings and utilities on the basis of the interest group which appropriates it.

The analysis we suggest in this chapter complements the three approaches mentioned above and allows us to focus on the figurative and symbolic dimensions of CMC as well as on its performative dimension.

Metaphors

From a rhetorical perspective, a metaphor is a *trópos* (from the Latin *tropus*), which means direction, thus alluding to the change of direction of an expression that 'deviates' from its original content in order to host another content (Mortara,

1988, p.163). According to Aristotle, who was the first to delve into the nature of metaphors, "a metaphor consists in giving the thing a name that belongs to something else" (*On Poetics*, 21, 1457b). From our perspective, the essence of metaphor is to understand and experience something in the terms of something other (Lakoff & Johnson, 1980). All metaphors conceive something in the terms of something other, thus implying a mechanism of the following type: "it is as if ..." (Lizcano, 2006).

In terms borrowed from U. Eco (as cited in Mortana, 1988) we can say that a determinate nuance, belonging to the meaning of the meta-phorising term ('*conversation*'), is attributed to the 'metaphorised' term (*The Well* in the example cited above). *The Well* "is as if it was" *a conversation*. The persuasive strength of the metaphor resides, above all, in understanding the relationship established between the metaphorised term and the metaphorising term and the result this relationship produces: "it is as if ...". The relationship established between the two terms is dynamic by nature and produces a form of fusion between both (Bertinetto, 1979, p. 160).

Lakoff and Johnson (1980) have emphasised that metaphors are a mechanism that operates in everyday language. Metaphors create and manifest our way of seeing reality. Black (1966) argues that rather than expressing similarities, metaphors appear to create them: "some metaphors allow us to see aspects of reality that the creation of metaphors helps to construct" (p. 132). They should not be taken to be mere ornaments, because metaphors can create new social realities and become scripts for future actions (Lakoff & Johnson, 1980, p.145). We can read one of the most often quoted classic maxims of sociology as a confirmation of the importance of this mechanism: "If men define things as real, they are real in their consequences" (Thomas, 1923).

Nevertheless, three conditions are necessary for a metaphorical expression to give rise to a change. The first is that it must be probable for

its audience and possible speakers; the second is that it must find an appropriate medium in which to grow and become consolidated; the third is that if this metaphor finds other metaphors which contradict its project, it must oust them and take their place. "The struggle for power is, to a great extent, a struggle to impose one's own metaphors" (Lizcano, 2006, p. 69).

The rhetorical perspective we are defending here is close to the classical conception of the rhetoric of persuasion, the aim of which is to win an audience over. As rhetorical tools, metaphors are aimed at the *pathos* of an audience, modifying the feelings of the audience and predisposing them to act in one way or another, as Aristotle explains in his *Rhetoric*.

WHAT WE DO WITH METAPHORS. AN ANALYSIS OF TWO CASES.

In this section we will introduce two examples of analyses of metaphors that appear in two electronic fora, the meanings and usefulness of which are, however, rather different for the users in each of these two cases. This exercise will allow us to introduce the most relevant issues that our perspective permit us to deal with, helping us thus to complete the approaches to CMC to which we have previously referred.

In particular, our suggestion implies having to recognise the mediating role of metaphors in four fundamental CMC dimensions:

1. Construction of reality. Metaphors play a prominent role in the construction of social reality. Metaphors are an excellent tool to shape and fix the meanings of the social spaces that emerge from using communication technologies. Moreover, in converting the unknown into something familiar, they orient the participants' experience of CMC.

2. Normativisation. Metaphors are endowed with normativising force. Metaphors are a source of social norms in CMC, they orient the users's actions showing what should be said and done, and what is not, and make social consensus possible. In this sense, metaphors can also legitimise sanctions.

3. Confidence and identity. Metaphors generate confidence and identity (at an individual and group level). In emerging social spaces in CMC, metaphors facilitate the cohesion of identities, consolidate social links and reinforce the confidence of individuals and groups by confirming their actions. Metaphors generate social emotions.

4. Contextualisation. Metaphors contextualise, both historically and culturally, the reality constructed by CMC. Metaphors do not arise by chance and in an arbitrary manner, but they tend to have "elective affinities" with the social and cultural contexts in which they are suggested and adopted. Metaphors anchor social life.

Example (1): The Bipolarweb and Bipolarneuro Fora

In the first place, we will analyse the similar metaphors used in both fora, the objectives of which were always clearly explicated by their creators: They attempted to create a space of online social support for people suffering from bipolar disorder (BD), as well as for their relatives. From this space, the creators encouraged respect for a certain biomedical view of this disorder and encouraged sufferers to cooperate fully with their doctors (Estrada & Vayreda, 2007). This was a project with strong implications of a personal nature: The *Bipolarweb* page forum was created by a woman diagnosed with BD. The *Bipolarneuro* page forum was created by the wife of someone who suffers from this disorder. In both cases, their fora presented a very high level of activity during the period studied, in which an average of

100 messages was published every day[1] (Estrada & Vayreda, 2007).

For our purposes, we have selected two wide families of metaphors: in the first place we will pay attention to the images of the forum as social space and, secondly, to the images used to refer to the disorder and to how to relate to it.

First Family of Metaphors

In order to understand the uniqueness of this electronic forum as social space, something other than the general expectations of how to use it and how to take part in it was needed. What was necessary was a representation of the kind of support that one could expect. Thus, the metaphor "the forum is a family", which many active participants used to refer to these fora as, helped define and construct this space.

-*"Hi everyone, it's a pleasure to be part of this forum. You are like my family. Kisses and hugs.*

-*I am the little sister, ...hey, hey, hey*

-*And I am the big sister:))* "

We could say that this figurative sense exercised the function of a guiding image. In our culture, 'family' signifies an imaginary of affection, commitment and strong links that generates a feeling of interpersonal connection, care and trust (Berger & Berger, 1983; Bott, 1971; Kellerhals, Troutot & Lazega, 1984). In earlier analyses regarding the social support offered in these spaces, we concluded that the most common and usual kind of social support was the emotional support; namely, the exchange of affection, friendship and advice (Vayreda & Antaki, in press). In this sense, the fora encouraged a kind of interaction as the one we reproduce below:

- "Hello. Today I have had a bad day. I did not fulfil my daily tasks due to this depression that won't leave me."

- "Don't feel bad. If you couldn't do it yesterday ....you'll make an effort today to achieve your aims gradually, step by step, without huge efforts but without pauses. Come on ... [pseudonym deleted], you have a full day in front of you. Euthymising [poetic word, and italics, in original] kisses."

The image of family is also the image of the traditional community which, in our imaginary, is opposed to a kind of association based on the lack of strong links, to a kind of cold organisation without feelings (Tönnies, 2001). Thus, it is not a matter of an innocent symbolic recourse, especially if we take into account popular (and academic) conceptions and preconceptions which have circulated around CMC in general with regard to its capacity or incapacity to generate strong social links.

The second image frequently associated with the forum and which alternates with the image of family was the metaphor "the forum as a home":

- "I join the welcoming committee ... this is your home.... kiss. "

The metaphorising term "home" offers new clues to understand the perception the users had of these social spaces and the kind of online behaviour that was required. The home as image is not only a closed space, sheltered with walls, windows and doors. It is also a space that demarcates material and symbolic limits between the private and the public space (Musso, 2002, p.14). It signals the border between the domesticated (*domos*) and the gentle as opposed to the wild and the undisciplined. In a figurative sense, the dilemma between participating or not participating in these fora was considered in the same way as the other dilemma

between domesticating or not domesticating the illness or the discomfort.

The metaphor "the forum as a home" also implies an idea of property. For example, see below our transcription of how the creator of *Bipolarweb* reported a recent conflict with a group of participants who, according to her, complained about her taking over the forum:

"...the element that wanted to attack us, overthrow us, but this talk of overthrowing is absurd because you can't overthrow someone who has invited you to their home, is going to come to your place and tell you to leave your own home - no? - well you go yourself then. (...) You can destroy the page, but you can't overthrow the one who leads it."

As this shows, the figurative sense of 'home' also adds a kind of materiality to the way the virtual space is being imagined and managed by its owner. She interprets a disagreement with some participants as a matter of invasion of intimacy rather than, for example, as a matter of ideology or opinion, linked to the possibility of promoting treatments alternative to the biomedical ones that she favours.

Second Family of Metaphors

This second group of metaphors refers directly to BD and to 'being bipolar', and consequently, how to approach the relationship with this illness. We will also analyse a metaphor employed to indicate what the forum should *not* become. All these were suggested by the owner-users and commonly appropriated by the most active users in both spaces.

Due to the problem affecting all the participants, it was perfectly understandable that BD be at the centre of all their postings. It was normal to observe, in this sense, that BD was referred to in ways which were likely to attract potential users. In the case of *Bipolarweb*, BD was repeatedly referred to as the 'enemy' which had to be "known, fought, tamed" and also it was seen as important "to comprehend, to ascertain its mechanisms, how it works, what is needed to be able to survive, to adapt, to give it a helping hand". In a figurative sense, BD was being endowed with quasi-human features, at the same time that it was also granted some sort of identity; it was being constructed as a being separate from the identity of the ill person.

To admit these images would open a whole world of possibilities for how to confront BD, while closing down others. Or in other words, this family of metaphors guided BD sufferers down a given path towards finding the solution to their problem. 'The solution', however, implied that the person suffering from the disorder would have to be more proactive in their relationship with BD. Thanks to these images, the person suffering from the disorder was turned into the active agent of a whole series of tasks: "to know, to fight, to domesticate, to comprehend, to adapt and to give it a helping hand". Consonant with this, throughout the period during which we observed the forum, informative support was one the most common kinds of social support, together with the emotional support we have referred to above. This datum is consistent with the type of activity required to deal with the illness: information and knowledge regarding BD was an essential tool in order to understand and handle it (Vayreda et alt., 2007).

In *Bipolarneuro* we find the second example belonging to this family of metaphors. The following could be read before entering their fora:

The Bipolar Battlefield

(...) To be bipolar is to be a soldier in many battles in which you do not ask to take part and do not even understand. To be bipolar is to be 'cannon fodder' for the occurrences in life in a throat-cutting struggle fought with toy weapons. (...). If you are alone and have already lost many battles get in touch with pacifist groups such as the Associations of Bipolar Patients. You will find them all over our world like Red Cross camps, always close to fighters and battlefields.

In this introduction, the owner of the web chose the metaphor -"to be Bipolar is to be a soldier"- thus implying an externalization of the illness from the ill person's body. In this particular 'battlefield' that signified living with bipolar disorder, the people suffering from the disorder were exposed to failure ("are cannon fodder") in an inconsiderate manner. In this way, an imaginary populated with impotent figures ("toy weapons"), innocent or victims ("who have not asked to take part"), abandoned to their own destiny, was being designed in a fashion which was counter-productive to what the forum actually wanted to become: a space like a "Red Cross camp". Its particular "pacifist group" was being presented as a place of shelter. It is in this way that the imagination of the potential participants in the forum was being guided; expectations of care, assistance and rest were being created for potential users as opposed to the images of a battlefield associated with suffering the disorder in solitude.

The image of the forum as a Red Cross camp also expressed an idea of a rather unsettled place. A camp is a temporary settlement, a stop-off. This image was meant to indicate what the forum was not meant to become. Both fora showed strong concerns and paid close attention to ensure that people suffering from the disorder did not become 'addicted to the forum', as one of the participants we interviewed observed. The forum 'creates addiction' in the sense that some could not stop themselves constantly entering the forum. It was like an addiction and this didn't allow them to lead a 'normal' life outside the Internet. For these users, the forum had stopped being a temporary settlement.

The two families of metaphors we have just shown complemented each other when constructing a stage that was easily comprehensible and attractive for their participants: in this sense, the forum as a place for domesticating the illness and the suffering of those affected by the disorder was being counterposed to a non-domesticated outdoor space inhabited by their common 'enemy'. This play of oppositions was being deployed to persuade the potential audience of people suffering from BD about their need to participate in a determinate way in these online fora.

Unlike in the example we will see below, in these two fora no resistance was allowed with regard to what sharing these metaphors meant in relation to the norms and identity that were being generated.

Example (2): The Case of the Humanities Forum

As a second example we will analyse the metaphors that appeared in the Humanities Forum (HF), one of the many spaces of group CMC belonging to the virtual campus of the Universitat Oberta de Catalunya (OUC), the Open University of Catalonia, during its first years of existence in the mid-nineties. This was a social relations online space for Humanities students (although it could be accessed by the whole of the academic community) aimed to facilitate informal meetings amongst students. Although the virtual campus had many fora for each of its faculties, this was the only one that enjoyed relative success with regards to participation, with an average of more than 4 messages a day and more than 70 readers per message (the UOC campus has a device that gives access to the number of individuals who have opened a message).[2]

Unlike in the previous case, the creators of the virtual campus did not give any specific indications regarding how to use this space or concerning what the dynamics or the content of the messages should be, beyond general recommendations with regards to the code of behaviour of the campus. In order to show the interesting aspects regarding the analysis of metaphors which the participant invented in order to create this social space, we must also

bear in mind that the majority of participants in the HF were not habitual users of CMC prior to registering at university. Such participation thus signified a new, and up to then, fairly unknown way of communication.

In the following section we will analyse the metaphors that appeared during the interaction, as well as the metaphors suggested by three key participants in this forum during one of the face to face interviews that we conducted with them later.

Metaphors Suggested from the HF

In the first place we will focus on the metaphors that appeared in the messages sent to the forum. These metaphors were generally suggested during moments in which the participating activity was high and the debates were heated, or during periods of silence or absence of some of the more charismatic and active members. We can see below examples of each of these moments.

In moments of low participation, the students sent messages to the forum describing what was happening and why, all of a sudden, their fellow participants had stopped writing:

- *"It was so lively, and now the forum has stopped. What's going on?"*

-*Nothing to worry about. It's just the hibernation period".*

- *"Don't panic. Our forum, like the Phoenix, is always reborn again [from its ashes]... It has had worse times than this"*

- *The forum is like a fire; it's always live, although for the fire to start again we need to add more fuel".*

These metaphors burst in at times when the "routine" was being interrupted. This way, when stating "the forum is…" what was being proposed was an explanation of what was causing disquietness, for the lack of participation was jeopardising the continuity of the forum.

In the first two examples, the metaphorising term is a living being, the features of which allowed for an understanding of the situation of silence (the forum hibernates) and also allowed for a cherishing of the hope that the forum, like the mythological animal, would be reborn at any time. The metaphor of fire also explains the oscillating character of the forum. Furthermore, there was an appeal to the responsibility of all the participants to make an effort to revive the messages. The image of fire and the need to keep it lit became associated with a proposal for action.

This first group of metaphors, which we can qualify as ontological (Lakoff & Johnson, 1980), endowed the forum with a foundation and an entity beyond the different styles of participation that were taking place in it. Namely, what was really necessary was for the forum to maintain a good level of participation, regardless of the different types of messages that could be sent. These ontological metaphors worked to maintain that participation.

On another occasion, and now in a moment of participative euphoria, a student sent the following message:

"We should not be surprised if, at some point, this small, critical and, some times, freethinking collectivity of the most advanced University in Catalonia became a tumour that, in the long run, and should it begin to create problems, would have to be extirpated. It's a fiction, of course, although I don't think we are utterly innocuous."

On the other hand, one of the most active and charismatic female participants reassured one of her colleagues who had sent the HF a poem and feared for the quality of her verses and the attention they could attract:

"Anna!!! Please, no false modesty… Here every message is one piece more of this profound and intellectual Lego which indeed should be awarded the Nobel Prize as a collectivity. We are better than the Bloomsbury set – is that how you spell it? - and than all those belonging to the Institución Libre de Enseñanza [Free Institute of Education], and that… Well, my participative self-esteem is going sky-high."

In these two examples, the metaphors used also endow the forum with an identity – "it is a critical collectivity", "it is a profound and intellectual Lego", however, and unlike the metaphors shown earlier, these ones situate it in a more determinate social and cultural context. In the first case, the forum can become the critical core of the University, capable of spreading through all its organisational bodies. In the second case, the level of its contents, the intellectual fit of that Lego, is situated at the level of the Bloomsbury Group and is considered to be worthy of the Nobel Prize. These kinds of metaphors also created a sense of group and a collective identity.

Metaphors Suggested in the Interviews

In order to complement our analysis of the HF, we carried out interviews with three members of the forum who, during our study, we had identified as having a leading role in creating a very characteristic style of participation. Throughout the interviews, these members suggested a variety of metaphors in order to describe their experience of the HF.

The meaning of their metaphors fitted with the kind of messages they had produced throughout the period analysed as well as with the type of action they had carried out and had tried to generate in their colleagues. A great deal of the messages sent and the conversational threads that were being created could be classified within one of these three ways of understanding what the forum was, what it was for and how one should participate in it.

The first interviewee, who had been pro-claimed "king of the forum" due to his high level of participation (with regard to the number of messages and their length), stated that, for him, the forum was a "*tertulia*" [an informal intel-lectual round-table discussion] in the old sense of the term, like those that used to take place in the Café Gijón and the like …". Café Gijón was an old cafe in Madrid where many writers, politi-cians and intellectuals belonging to the spheres of the arts and sciences used to meet during the last third of the 19C and the first third of the 20C. These *tertulias* generated a mindset that filtered into the Spanish press and the political life of the country. The *tertulias* that took place in the Café Gijón became well-known in Spain until they were interrupted by the Spanish Civil War (1936-1939)[3] .This student's participation fitted perfectly with this image. The messages he sent to the HF were rather long (20, 30 or even more lines), they were well structured and, sometimes, had been prepared previously, as he admitted. The topics treated in those messages tended to be scholarly and of an academic nature. The HF, both in its conception and action, was a *tertulia* of a high intellectual level. To participate in a *tertulia* in the Café Gijón required a great com-mand of the spoken language as well as belonging to the social and intellectual elite.

Not all the students who participated in the forum shared this sense or use of the HF. For the second interviewee, who would represent another interest group, the forum was a space of relationship, for relaxation, and it was something much more informal:

"It could be the corridors [of the University], couldn't it? I think of the forum as if it were the corridors of university, as those moments when you feel more relaxed and talk about stuff that has nothing to do with what you are studying, but that has a lot to do with what you see, you know what I mean?"

In this case, and in accordance with his own metaphors, the messages sent by this student were short and were about trivial topics with which he tried to amuse the other participants. These messages inserted themselves in conversational threads that were much more fluent and covered different topics. In his interview, the student made it clear that he participated in the forum to have fun, to have a good time and to find a moment of "pleasure and satisfaction" amongst his academic tasks and everyday work. Another of the metaphors employed by this student was "the forum is the faculty bar": "you can be there in the same way as you would be in a *tertulia* in a bar, having a beer with some friends…". The student bar is very different from the Café Gijón and, in this sense, it would be closer to being the *backstage* of intellectual and physical relaxation in contradistinction to the more formal and academic atmosphere of the lecture rooms.

The third and last interviewee said that she used the forum as therapy, as she had already stated in some of her messages. For her, "the forum is a therapy".

Once again, we find a clear concordance be-tween participation in the HF and the metaphor suggested. She would send many messages to the forum, generally in parallel to the conversational threads that were being produced, full of personal reflections and private details. The messages were well received and many readers empathised with her. Following her example, some participants sent messages with specific details regarding their concerns, their personal problems or their existential anxieties. That created a new style of participation, totally different from the other two mentioned above. Nevertheless, the different styles of participation coexisted in parallel, and the stu-dents were able to move from one conversational thread to the other without being perceived as traitors by the rest of the participants.

In this second case, and in contradistinction to the BD forums, a variety of metaphors was being offered. Although these made evident the internal tensions of the forum, the different styles survived without crashing against each other. Students could go from one conversational thread to another [from one metaphor to another] without this resulting in a loss of confidence on the part of the other participants and without the 'change in register' being interpreted as a betrayal or disloyalty. The different metaphors which had been proposed and accepted legitimated changes in style. Nevertheless, it can also be argued that what was at stake behind each of these metaphors was a certain description of reality. The struggle to impose one metaphor over others revealed the desire to attract the maximum number of readers possible and convincing the maximum number of participants of the fact that that was the right way of participating.

FUTURE RESEARCH DIRECTIONS

We would like to indicate four possible lines of research in which the analysis of the metaphors appearing in CMC, or being employed in order to refer to this type of communication, can contribute both to understanding the particularities of the space of social relationship that CMC provides and to tackle some of the problems posed by it.

In the first place, we have seen how the users, assisted by metaphors, manage to particularise what are usually referred to as communities of support, of practice, of e-learning, etc., in other words, different uses of CMC. Nonetheless, if we take as an example the studies carried out on health-related support groups on the Internet, we will see how these tend to highlight the essential characteristics of online social support (Braithwaite, Waldron & Finn, 1999; Coulson; 2005; Robinson & Turner, 2003). Our project, which aims to complement these studies, focusses on the way in which the users appropriate these spaces, particularising them according to their own interests, and how this conditions the type of online social support. In this sense, the comparative analyses of metaphors

suggested by the users themselves to define these spaces of social interaction provide us with new data that will allow us to understand the nature of these types of communities.

In second place, the analysis of metaphors understood as contextual factors associated with the situation of CMC usage (Baym, 1998) allows us to recognise the creative role of the users in the processes of domestication of technologies (Lie & Sorenson, 1996). This way, the researcher will be more aware of the difficulties of specifying –and foreseeing– *a priori* which elements must be taken into account as contextual factors in the use of CMC.

Thirdly, and as Herring (2004) indicated some years ago, CMDA promises "to identify and adapt appropriate methods of graphical, video and audio analysis to computer-mediated communication, on the assumption that these modalities communicate discourse meanings" (p.25). Metaphors provide us with a bridge for the analysis of images, ever more present and persistent in CMC. As is the case with images, metaphors, in their flexible strength, directly appeal and engage the user's imagination.

In fourth place, we would like to note that the explosion of the so-called Web 2.0 and the hegemony of the Social Network Sites (SNS) introduce some modifications in the analysis of metaphors. In these kinds of CMC, the main source of metaphors resides in the way these spaces are talked about by the media, by their owners or by social researchers themselves (boyd, 2007). Today, the carriers of metaphors are mainly the discourses on SNS. Accordingly, the possibility for negotiation for users of SNS such as Facebook, Flickr or Youtube with regard to the meaning of these spaces or the type of action to which they are predisposed has been reduced. Studies on metaphors must take into account this shift and be more critical when elucidating not only the kind of space that is being constructed by metaphors, but also the limits that are being imposed in this very same way (Vayreda & Estalella, 2007).

CONCLUSION

As mentioned earlier, the analysis of metaphors complements some of the approaches to the study of CMC. The two cases analysed above show that the metaphorical expressions created by CMC users are not a mere ornament. The relevance of the analysis suggested here is that it allows us to see, paraphrasing J.L. Austin, what we do and undo with metaphors.

Accordingly, then, we have approached some of the concerns that have been, and continue to be, central to CMC analysis: what kind of social relationships and spaces are being generated by electronic communication technologies in which language plays a central role? What objectives do people have when they use CMC? How is trust built up? How are feelings of community and identity generated? How do users of electronic forums, for instance, reach an agreement on what their social space means?

Our approach makes manifest the creative role of users in the definition of social spaces emerging from CMC. The strength that metaphors possess to transform the novel or not well known into something comprehensible and familiar (a forum in a home; a forum in a university bar, etc.) reveals the resources employed by users to produce a new reality between the online and the offline, between the local and the global.

We have seen how metaphors are recourses employed for the construction of electronic forums as social spaces, the meaning and utility of which are the result of a task of negotiation and interpretation carried out by different interest groups. In this sense, and as we have shown, the different conflicts taking place in these spaces can be understood as disagreements between different suggestions regarding what the forum is as social space rather than as evidence of miscommunication. On the contrary, once an agreement has been reached by the participants, the conflict between metaphors and the imposition of one or the other, actually produces social cohesion and confidence in the participants insofar as this generates a framework of action and interpretation (of the action) which is taken as a given.

Ultimately, it must be emphasised that from our rhetorical perspective, the metaphor is an instrument of persuasion that is not directed toward reason but to imagination, and that it is used with the aim of imposing certain versions of social reality. This plasticity and 'irrationality' of metaphors must also warn us of its limitations as well as putting us on guard when confronted with the necessity of methodological strategies that differ from the usual ones in CMDA but which are closer to an interdisciplinary analysis of the image (visual anthropology, marketing, etc.).

REFERENCES

Akrich, M. (1987). Comment décrire les objets techniques? *Technology and Culture, 9*, 49–64.

Antaki, C., Ardévol, E., Núñez, F., & Vayreda, A. (2005). 'For she who knows who she is': Managing accountability in online forum messages. *Journal of Computer-Mediated Communication, 11*(1), article 6. Retrieved February, 2009, from http://jcmc.indiana.edu/vol11/issue1/antaki.html

Aristotle,. (1981). *On Poetics*. Pennsylvania: The Franklin Library. [translated by Ingram Bywater]

Baker, A. (1998). Cyberspace couples finding romance online then meeting for the first time in real life. *CMC Magazine*, July 1998. Retrieved May 2009, from http://www.december.com/cmc/mag/1998/jul/baker.html

Bar-Lev, S. (2008). "We are here to give you emotional support": Performing emotions in an online HIV/AIDS support group. *Qualitative Health Research, 18*(4), 509–521. doi:10.1177/1049732307311680

Baym, N. K. (1995). From practice to culture on Usenet. In Star, S. L. (Ed.), *The cultures of computing* (pp. 29–52). Oxford, UK: Blackwell.

Baym, N. K. (1998). The emergente of Online Community. In Jones, S. G. (Ed.), *Cibersociety 2.0. Revising Computer-Mediated Communication and Technology* (pp. 35–68). Thousand Oaks, CA: Sage.

Berger, B., & Berger, P. (1983). *The War over the Family*. London: Hutchinson.

Bertinetto, P. M. (1979). 'Come vi pare'. La ambiguetà di 'come' e I rapporti tra paragone e metafora. In Leoni, A., & Piglliasco, M. (Eds.), *Retorica e scienze dil linguaggio* (pp. 131–170). Roma: Bulzoni.

Bijker, W. E., Hugues, T., & Pinch, T. (1987). *The social construction of technological Systems. New Directions in the Sociology and History of Technology*. Cambridge, MA: MIT Press.

Black, M. (1966). *Modelos y metáforas*. Madrid, Spain: Editorial Tecnos.

Blumer, H. (1969). *Symbolic Interactionism: Perspective and Method*. Berkeley, CA: University of California Press.

Bortree, D. S. (2005). Presentation of self on the Web: An ethnographic study of teenage girls' weblogs. *Education, Communication, and Information Journal*, *5*(1), 25–40.

Bott, E. (1971). *Family and social network*. New York: Free Press.

Boyd, D. (2006, October 2). The Significance of Social Software. *BlogTalks Reloaded*. Vienna, Austria.

Braithwaite, D. O., Waldron, V. R., & Finn, J. (1999). Communication of social support in computermediated groups for people with disabilities. *Health Communication*, *11*, 123–151. doi:10.1207/s15327027hc1102_2

Bretag, T. (2006). Developping 'Third Space' interculturality Using Computer-Mediated Comunication. *Journal of computer-Mediated Communication, 11*(4), 981-1011, article 5. Retrieved February, 2009, from http://jcmc.indiana.edu/vol11/issue4/bretag.html

Burkhaler, B. (1999). Reading race online. In Smith, M. A., & Kollock, P. (Eds.), *Communities in Cyberspace* (pp. 60–75). London: Routledge.

Connery, B. A. (1997). IMHO: Authority and egalitarian rhetoric in the virtual coffeehouse. In Porter, D. (Ed.), *Internet Culture* (pp. 161–180). New York: Routledge.

Coulson, N. S. (2005). Receiving Social Support Online: An Analysis of a Computer-Mediated Support Group for Individuals Living with Irritable Bowel Syndrome. *Cyberpsychology & Behavior*, *6*(8), 580–585. doi:10.1089/cpb.2005.8.580

Crystal, D. (2001). *Language and the Internet*. Cambridge, UK: Cambridge University Press.

Danet, B. (1995). Playful expressivity and artfulness in computer-mediated communication. *Journal of Computer-Mediated Communication*, *1*(2). Retrieved February, 2009, from http://jcmc. indiana.edu/vol1/issue2/genintro.html

Danet, B. (1998). Text as Mask: Gender, Play, and Performance on the Internet. In Jones, S. G. (Ed.), *Cybersociety 2.0 revising Computer-Mediated Communication and Community* (pp. 129–158). Thousand Oaks, CA: Sage.

Donath, J. S. (1999). Identity and deception in the virtual community. In Smith, M. A., & Kollock, P. (Eds.), *Communities in Cyberspace* (pp. 29–59). London: Routledge.

Dubey, G. (2001). *Le lien social à l'ère du virtuel*. Paris: Presses Universitaires de France.

Duthler, K. W. (2006). The politeness of requests made via email and voicemail: Support for the hyperpersonal model. *Journal of Computer-Mediated Communication, 11*(2), article 6. Retrieved May, 2009, from http://jcmc.indiana.edu/vol11/issue2/duthler.html

Ellison, N., Heino, R., & Gibbs, J. (2006). Managing impressions online: Self-presentation processes in the online dating environment. *Journal of Computer-Mediated Communication, 11*(2), article 2. Retrieved May, 2009, from http://jcmc.indiana.edu/vol11/issue2/ellison.html

Estrada, M., & Vayreda, A. (2007). Support online? Computer-mediated social support and solidarity for people with bipolarweb disorder. In *Proceedings of the IADIS Press Publishes Conference.*

Etzioni, A., & Etzioni, O. (1999). Face-to-face and computer-mediated communities: A comparative analysis. *The Information Society, 15*(4), 241–248. doi:10.1080/019722499128402

Ferrara, K., Brunner, H., & Whittemore, G. (1991). Interactive written discourse as an emergent register. *Written Communication, 8*(1), 8–34. doi:10.1177/0741088391008001002

Flichy, P. (2001). *L'imaginaire d'Internet.* Paris: Édition la Découverte.

Garcia, A. C., & Jacobs, J. B. (1999). The eyes of the beholder: Understanding the turn-taking system in quasi-synchronous computer-mediated communication. *Research on Language and Social Interaction, 32*(4), 337–367. doi:10.1207/S15327973rls3204_2

Herring, S. (1999). The rethorical dynamics of gender harassment on-line. *The Information Society, 15*(3), 151–167. doi:10.1080/019722499128466

Herring, S. (2001). Computer-Mediated Discourse. In Schiffrin, D., Tannen, D., & Hamilton, H. E. (Eds.), *The handbook of discourse Analysis* (pp. 612–634). Nalden, MA: Blackwell Publishers.

Herring, S. C. (2002). Computer-mediated communication on the Internet. *Annual Review of Information Science & Technology, 36*, 109–168. doi:10.1002/aris.1440360104

Herring, S. C. (2003). Gender and power in online communication. In Holmes, J., & Meyerhoff, M. (Eds.), *The Handbook of language and gender* (pp. 202–228). Oxford, UK: Blackwell. doi:10.1002/9780470756942.ch9

Herring, S. C. (2004). Computer-mediated discourse analysis: An approach to researching online behaviour. In S. A. Barab, R. Kling, & J. H. Gray, (Eds.), Designing for Virtual Communities in the Service of Learning (pp. 338-376). New York: Cambridge University Press. Retrieved (n.d.), from http://ella.slis.indiana.edu/~herring/cmda.pdf

Herring, S. C. (2007). A faceted classification scheme for computer-mediated discourse. *Language@Internet, 4*(1). Retrieved February, 2009, from http://www.languageatinternet.de/articles/2007/761

Hiltz, S. R., & Turoff, M. (1993). *The Network Nation* (Revised Edition). Cambridge, MA: MIT Press.

Hine, C. (2000). *Virtual ethnography.* Thousand Oaks, California: Sage.

Honeycutt, C. (2005). Hazing as a process of boundary maintenance in an online community. *Journal of Computer-Mediated Communication, 10*(2), article 3. Retrieved May, 2009, from http://jcmc.indiana.edu/vol10/issue2/honeycutt.html

Hubbler, M. T., & Bell, D. C. (2003). Computer-mediated humor and ethos: Exploring threads of constitutive laughter in online communities. *Computer and composition, 20*(3), 277-294.

Huffaker, D. A., & Calvert, S. L. (2005). Gender, identity, and language use in teenage blogs. *Journal of Computer-Mediated Communication, 10*(2), article 1. Retrieved May, 2009, from http://jcmc.indiana.edu/vol10/issue2/huffaker.html

Jones, S. G. (1995). Understanding community in the information Age. In Jones, S. G. (Ed.), *Cibersociety: Computer-Mediated Communication and Community* (pp. 10–35). Thousand Oaks, CA: Sage.

Jones, S. G. (1998). *Cibersociety 2.0. Revising Computer-Mediated Communication and Technology*. Thousand Oaks, California: Sage.

Kellerhals, J., Troutot, P. Y., &, Lazega, E. (1984). *Microsociologie de la famille*. Paris: Presses Universitaires de France.

Kolko, B. E. (1995). Building a World With Words: The Narrative Reality of Virtual Communities. *Works and Days, 13*(1-2), 105–126.

Kolko, B. E., & Reid, E. (1998). Dissolution and fragmentation: problems in On-line Communities. In Jones, S. G. (Ed.), *Cybersociety 2.0 revising Computer-Mediated Communication and Community* (pp. 212–230). Thousand Oaks, CA: Sage.

Kollock, P. (1999). The economics of online co-operation: gifts and public goods in cyberespace. In Smith, M. Ä., & Kollock, P. (Eds.), *Communities in Cyberespace* (pp. 220–239). London: Routletge.

Lakoff, G., & Johnson, M. (1980). *Metaphors We Live By*. Chicago: Chicago University Press.

Lie, M., & Sorenson, K. H. (1996). *Making technology our own? Domesticating technologies into every day life*. Oslo, Norway: Scandinavian University Press.

Lizcano, E. (2006). *Metáforas que nos piensan. Sobre ciencia, democracia y otras poderosas ficciones*. Madrid, Spain: Ediciones Bajo Cero.

Maltz, T. (1996). Customary law and power in internet communities. *Journal of Computer-Mediated Communication, 2*(1). Retrieved May, 2009, from http://jcmc.indiana.edu/vol2/issue1/custom.html

Maynor, N. (1994). The language of electronic mail: Written speech? In Montgomery, M., & Little, G. D. (Eds.), *Centennial usage studies* (pp. 48–54). Tuscaloosa, AL: Alabama UP.

McLaughtin, M. L., Osborne, K. K., & Smith, C. B. (1995). Standards of conduct on Usenet. In Jones, S. G. (Ed.), *Cybersociety: Computer-Mediated Communication and Community* (pp. 90–111). Thousand Oaks, CA: Sage.

Mortara, B. (1988). *Manual de retórica*. Madrid: Alianza Editorial.

Nastri, J., Peña, J., & Hancock, J. T. (2006). The construction of Away Messages: a speech Act Analysis. *Journal of computer-Mediated Communication, 11*(4), 1025-1045. Retrieved May, 2009, from http://jcmc.indiana.edu/vol11/issue4/nastri.html

O'Brien, J. (1999). Writing in the body: gender (re) production in online interaction. In M. A. Smith, M., P. Kollock (Eds.), Communities in Cyberspace (pp.76-104). London: Routledge.

Paccagnella, L. (1997). Getting the seats of your pants dirty: strategies for ethnographic research. *Journal of Computer mediated Communication, 3*(1). Retrieved February, 2009, from http://jcmc.indiana.edu/vol3/issue1/paccagnella.html

Pinch, T. (1996). The Social Construction of Technology: A review. In Fox, R. (Ed.), *Technological Change. Methods and Themes in the History of Technology* (pp. 17–36). Oxford, UK: Oxford University Press.

Pinch, T., & Bijker, W. E. (1987). The social construction of facts and artifacts: or how the sociology of science and the sociology of technology might benefit each other. In Bijker, W. E., Hugues, T. P., & Pinch, T. (Eds.), *The social construction of technology Systems* (pp. 17–50). Cambridge, MA: MIT Press.

Poster, M. (1998). Virtual ethnicity: Tribal Identity in an Age of Global Communications. In S. G. Jones (Ed.) Cybersociety 2.0 revising Computer-Mediated Communication and Community (pp. (184-211). Thousand Oaks, CA: Sage.

Reid, E. (1999). Hierarchy and power: social control in Cyberespace. In Smith, M. A., & Kollock, P. (Eds.), *Communities in Cyberespace* (pp. 107–133). London: Routledge.

Rheingold, H. (1993). *Virtual Community. Homesteading on the Electronic Frontier.* Reading, MA: Addison-Wesley Publishing Company.

Robinson, J. D., & Turner, J. (2003). Impersonal, Interpersonal, and Hyperpersonal Social Support: Cancer and Older Adults. *Health Communication, 15*(2), 227–234. doi:10.1207/S15327027HC1502_10

Roszak, T. (1994). *Cult of Information.* Berkeley, CA: University of California Press.

Serfaty, V. (2005). Cartographie d'Internet: Du virtuel à la reterritorialization. *Cercles, 13,* 83–96.

Simpson, J. (2005). Conversational floors in synchronous text-based CMC discourse. *Discourse Studies, 7,* 337–361. doi:10.1177/1461445605052190

Stefik, M. (Ed.). (1997). *Internet Dreams. Archetypes, Myths, and Metaphors.* Cambridge, MA: MIT Press.

Stone, A. R. (1995). Sex and death among the disembodied: VR, Cyberespace, and the nature of academic discourse. In Star, S. L. (Ed.), *The culture of computing* (pp. 243–255). Oxford, UK: Blackwell.

Ten Have, P. (2000). Computer-Mediated Chat: Ways of Finding Chat Partners. *M/C: A journal of Media Culture, 3*(4). Retrieved May, 2009, from http://journal.media-culture.org.au/0008/partners.php

Thomas, W. I. (1923). *The Unadjusted Girl.* Boston: Little, Brown, and Co.

Tönnies, F. (2001). *Community and Civil Society.* Cambridge, MA: Cambridge University Press.

Vayreda, A., & Antaki, Ch. (in press). Unsolicited Advice in an Online Bipolar Disorder Forum: a Conversation Analysis of the "Matching Hypothesis". *Qualitative Health Research.*

Vayreda, A., & Estalella, A. (2007). Software social: ¿teoría social? In F. Tirado & and M. Doménech (Eds.), Lo Social y lo virtual. Nuevas formas de control y transformación social (p. 78-92). Barcelona, Spain: Editorial UOC.

Vayreda, A., Estrada, M., Balasch, B., & Tomàs, S. (2007). Redes virtuales de apoyo social y de autoayuda: análisis de un caso. In C. Guillen, & R. Guil (Eds.). *X Congreso Nacional de Psicología social. Psicología Social: un encuentro de perspectivas.* Cádiz, Spain: Asociación de profesionales de la Psicología Social.

Walther, J. B. (1992). Interpersonal effects in computer-mediated interaction: A relational perspective. *Communication Research, 19*(1), 52–90. doi:10.1177/009365092019001003

Waseleski, C. (2006). Gender and the use of exclamation points in computer-mediated communication: An analysis of exclamations posted to two electronic discussion lists. *Journal of Computer-Mediated Communication, 11*(4), article 6. Retrieved May, 2009, from http://jcmc.indiana.edu/vol11/issue4/waseleski.html

ADDITIONAL READING

Akrick, M. (1988). Les utilisateurs, acteurs de l'innovation. *Education permanente, 134*, 79-89.

Akrick, M. (1992). The de-Scription of technical Objects. In Bijker, W., & Law, J. (Eds.), *Shaping Technology/Building Society: Studies in Sociotechnical Change* (pp. 205–224). Cambridge, MA: MIT Press.

Barnes, B., & Edge, D. (1982). *Science in context. Readings in the sociology of science.* London: Open University Press.

Boyd, D., & Ellison, N. (2007). Social Network Sites: Definition, History, and Scholarship. *Journal of Computer-Mediated Communication, 13*(1), 11.

Callon, M. (1998). El proceso de construcción de la sociedad. El estudio de la tecnología como herramienta para el análisis sociológico. In Doménech, M., & Tirado, F. (Eds.), *Sociología simétrica. Ensayos sobre ciencia, tecnología y socieda* (pp. 143–170). Barcelona, Spain: Gedisa.

Dupont, O. (1998). Métaphores des réseaux: Appropriation par des réseaux de métaphores. In N. Guéguen, & L. Tobin (Eds.), Communication, société et Internet (pp. 315-328). Paris: L'Harmattan.

Fauconnier, G., & Turner, M. (2002). *The Way We Think: Conceptual Blending and the Mind's Hidden Complexities.* New York: Basic Books.

Goatly, A. (1997). *The Language of Metaphors.* New York: Routledge.

Jacobs, J. Q. (1999). Cyberespace is a Parallel World. A Metaphor Analysis. Retrieved February, 2009, from http://www.jqjacobs.net/anthro/metaphor.html

Kövecses, Z. (2002). *Metaphor: A Practical Introduction.* Oxford, UK: Oxford University Press.

Kövecses, Z. (2003). *Metaphors and Emotion: Language, Culture, and Body in Human Feeling.* Cambridge, UK: Cambridge University Press.

Kövecses, Z. (2005). *Metaphor in Culture: Universality and Variation.* Cambridge, UK: Cambridge University Press.

Lakoff, G. (1987). *Women, Fire, and Dangerous Things: What Categories Reveal about the Mind.* Chicago: The University of Chicago Press.

Lakoff, G., & Johnson, M. (1999). *Philosophy in the Flesh: The Embodied Mind and its Challenge to Western Thought.* New York: Basic Books.

Lévy, P. (1997). *Cyberculture.* Paris: Editions Jacob.

Musso, P. (2000). Le cyberespace, figure de l'utopie technologique réticulaire. *Sociologie et Sociétés, 32*(2), 31–56.

Proulx, S. (2000). *La construction des objects informationnels: matériaux pour une ethnographie des usages.* Retrieved February, 2009, from http://barthes.ens.fr/atelier/articles/proulx.2000.html

Ratzan, L. (2000). Making sense of the Web: a metaphorical approach. *Information Research, 6*(1), 1-22. Retrieved February, 2009, from http://informationr.net/ir/6-1/paper85.html

Rommes, E. (2002). *Gender Scripts and the Internet: The Design and Use of Amsterdam's Digital City.* Enschede, Spain: Twente University Press.

Ruiz de Mendoza, F. J. (1996). Understanding through metonymy: the role of metonymy in communication and cognition. In Penas, B. (Ed.), *The Pragmatics of Understanding and Misunderstanding* (pp. 197–208). Zaragoza, Spain: University of Zaragoza, Servicio de Publicaciones.

Sacks, S. (1979). *On Metaphor.* Chicago: The University of Chicago Press.

Schroeder, J. E. (2002). *Visual Consumption*. New York: Routledge.

White, M. (2006). *The Body and the Screen. Theories of Internet Spectatorsphip*. Cambridge, MA: The MIT Press.

KEY TERMS AND DEFINITIONS

Construction of Reality: The social process whereby social reality is in no way independent of the forms by which its participants define it. For example, in this process the social imagination and metaphors play an important role.

Electronic forum [virtual forum; Internet forum: Social space for the exchange of written messages by computer. There are different ways of technically configuring virtual forums and also different ways of inhabiting them.

Family of Metaphors: A group of metaphors used to refer to a specific social space and which are proposed by the users of that space with the aim of investing it with meaning and delimiting a field of action.

Figurative sense: The language of CMC, and also the way of referring to CMC, may transmit a meaning which does not belong to it; which is to say that it involves the use of metaphor or another figure of speech.

Metaphor: Discursive function which allows one to refer to something using a different word, to put something in the place of another. For example, we refer to a virtual forum as "a cafe" or as "the university corridors". Thanks to this function, that which is new or unknown becomes familiar.

Metaphorization: The process whereby a figurative meaning is brought to a specific social space, social relation, identity, etc. This involves a constitutive process with regards to any appropriation of CMC.

Normativisation: The process by which social action becomes fixed, produces social norms, directs the action (of users) and indicates what should

be said and what should not be said or done. In this way social consensus is favoured and sanctioning within the *online* groups is legitimised.

Performative Dimension: If, from a non-representationalist conception of language, we can state that to say is equal to doing, then, in the context of CMC, writing is a social action like any other.

ENDNOTES

[1] The data introduced in this section concerning Bipolarweb (http://www.bipolarweb.com/) are the result of a non-participating observation of the virtual forum of this page. This research was carried out alongside Mariona Estrada, Santi Tomàs and Marcel Balasch during a period of 9 months. During this period, open personal interviews and telephone interviews were conducted with the founder of this website as well with active participants in the forum. With regard to Bipolarneuro (http://www.bipolarneuro.com/), the data presented here are the result of a non- participating observation of the highest participation forum during a period of 3 months and 2 weeks. In this case, no interviews have been conducted to date.

[2] Our knowledge of the HF is based on a research project within which a direct observation on the HF was carried out between the months of August and January belonging to the academia year 1998-1999. Within the context of this research project, five face to face interviews with 5 different participants in the HF were carried out.

[3] Café Gijón's webpage: http://www.cafegijon.com/

Chapter 9
Self and Identity in Personal Blogs:
A Cross-Linguistic and Cross-Cultural Perspective

Wengao Gong
National University of Singapore, Singapore

ABSTRACT

This chapter describes how American bloggers and Chinese bloggers from similar age and gender groups represent themselves and their identities linguistically in their blogs and explores whether and to what extent the differences in terms of the blogging language and culture affect these representations. The author adopts a corpus-based approach and focuses on the description and the comparison of the orthographic features and semantic domain preference as revealed in the blog entries. By conducting a cross-linguistic and cross-cultural comparison between American bloggers and Chinese bloggers, the author finds that bloggers' linguistic practice is closely related to their developmental stage of life, their gender, and the cultural environment they are immersed in. Meanwhile, bloggers' linguistic practice is also constrained by the internal system of the language they use for blogging.

INTRODUCTION

Blogs are often defined as "frequently modified web pages in which dated entries are listed in reverse chronological sequence" (Herring, Scheidt, Wright, & Bonus, 2005, p. 142). Being a publishing and social communication platform simultaneously, blogging has rapidly gained great popularity among young people worldwide over the past few years.

Herring and colleagues (2005) classify blogs into three types: personal journals, filters, and k-logs (i.e., knowledge logs). Among them, personal journals are the most common. In fact, many bloggers take blogging as "a form of social communication in which blogger and audience are intimately related through the writing and reading of blogs" (Nardi, Schiano, & Gumbrecht, p. 224). Blogs have distinctive technological features that set them apart from other forms of internet-based communication.

DOI: 10.4018/978-1-61520-827-2.ch009

According to Karlsson (2006, p. 6), blogs are "a loose baggy monster, content-wise, tool-wise, feature-wise, author-wise, reader-wise," though their basic format is rather stable. Kendall (2007) offers a good summary of the hybrid nature of personal blogs as represented by LiveJournal, a well-known blogging website. As a *diary*, the blog provides a place for bloggers to record their feelings, opinions, daily events, and reflections. As a *communication tool*, it provides a forum for connection with others and public expression. As a *performance venue*, it provides a stage for self-presentation and artistic production. Theoretically speaking, anyone with internet access can publish blogs, and blogs are written about anything bloggers like and in whatever style they wish, typically with no editorial control (Argamon, Koppel, Pennebaker, & Schler, 2007). In other words, bloggers enjoy next-to-absolute autonomy in their writing. The hybrid nature and the high-level autonomy have made personal blogs a good medium for self expression and identity representation. As personal blogs are mainly textual stories and reflections about the bloggers themselves, they have also provided a special window for researchers to observe how self and identity are linguistically represented.

This chapter describes how American bloggers and Chinese bloggers from similar age and gender groups represent themselves and their identities linguistically in their blogs and explores whether and to what extent the differences in terms of the blogging language and culture affect these representations. The author adopts a corpus-based approach and focuses on the description and the comparison of the orthographic features and semantic domain preference as revealed in the blog entries. By conducting a cross-linguistic and cross-cultural comparison between American bloggers and Chinese bloggers, the author hopes to obtain some insights about the representation of self and identity in internet-based communication.

BACKGROUND

Defining Identity

Identity has never been an easy term to define ever since its very first appearance in academic works. As Lawler (2008, p. 1) rightly points out, "identity is a difficult term: more or less everyone knows more or less what it means, and yet its precise definition proves slippery." It is simply not possible to give a single, overarching definition which can fit in all the contexts where the notion of identity is being used, because the same term is used to mean quite different things in different disciplines.

Identity is, first and foremost, a psychological concept. According to Erikson (1969), a person's ego identity is shaped by that person's physiological characteristics, psychological needs, and the social and cultural milieus. Identity development is actually a person's pursuit of proper social roles and niches within a society which can accommodate his or her biological and psychological capacities and interests. This pursuit is normally believed to start during the mid- to late adolescence and will continue and reformulate throughout the life span as one's biological, psychological, and societal circumstances change (Kroger, 2007). Following Erikson, Kroger and Adair (2008, p. 8) define identity as "a configuration, an integration of biological givens, psychological needs, interests and wishes, significant identifications, and meaningful and consistent social roles." Identity in its psychological sense bears the following features: First, it is a multi-faceted concept which covers biological, psychological, and social aspects. Second, it develops with age and is subject to change. Third, it is a hybrid of intrapersonal sameness (i.e., self-sameness) and partial interpersonal sameness (i.e., partial identification with others in the society).

Aside from being a key concept in developmental psychology, identity has also made its way into the field of sociology. As Cerulo (1997) points out, the study of identity forms a critical cornerstone within modern sociological thought. In fact, nobody knows when the precise term "identity" was first adopted by sociologists. The original term Cooley and Mead used was "self." Early sociologists primarily focused on exploring the formation of the "me" and the ways in which interpersonal interactions mold an individual's sense of self (Cerulo, 1997). Sociologists emphasize the decisive roles that society plays in shaping people's identities. In Cooley's own words, "self and society are twin-born, we know one as immediately as we know the other, and the notion of a separate and independent ego is an illusion" (1909, p.5). Mead (1934) expresses a similar view, saying that the self is not innate but something "arises in the process of social experience and activity, that is, develops in the given individual as a result of his relations to that process as a whole and to other individuals within that process" (p. 135). According to Kroger (2007, p. 20), many different theoretical approaches to identity in the sociological line of thought share a common view that "an individual's identity is the product of the surrounding social context." As Côté (1996) remarks, "for many sociologists there is no identity without society, and society steers identity formation while individuals attempt to navigate the passage" (p. 133 cited in Kroger, 2007, p. 20). Lawler (2008) also contends that "identity, far from being personal and individual, is a deeply social category." According to him, "identities are lived out relationally and collectively. They do not simply belong to the individual; rather, they must be negotiated collectively, and they must conform to social rules" (p. 143). There are different lines of thought in identity-related social studies. Researchers taking an essentialist stance believe that the attributes and behavior of socially defined groups can be determined and explained by reference to cultural and/or biological characteristics which are believed to be inherent to the group (Bucholtz, 2003). Sociologists taking a social constructionist stance, on the

other hand, argue that identity is negotiated and constructed via social interactions. Scholars adopting a postmodernist approach take the variation within identity categories and that across identity categories as equally important. They advocate a shift in analytic focus, deemphasizing observation and deduction and elevating concerns with public discourse (Cerulo, 1997). The defining features of identity in sociology include: first, it is socially produced; second, it is plural in nature; and third, identity construction implies an agentive role of the individual.

Identity is also an important concept in linguistic inquiries, and sociolinguistics in particular. According to Edwards (1985, p. 3), "sociolinguistics is essentially about identity, its formation, presentation and maintenance." The term "identity" is generally used to mean "social identity" in sociolinguistic studies. According to Ochs (1993, p. 288), social identity is a cover term for "a range of social personae, including social statuses, roles, positions, relationships, and institutional and other relevant community identities one may attempt to claim or assign in the course of social life." Kroskrity (1999, p. 111) defines identity as "the linguistic construction of membership in one or more social groups or categories." According to him, identities may be linguistically constructed "both through the use of particular languages and linguistic forms and through the use of indexical communicative practices." Although language is not the only means for identity construction, it is generally believed to be the most important one for that purpose. As Ochs (1993, p. 288) points out, "linguistic constructions at all levels of grammar and discourse are crucial indicators of social identity" and "social identity is a crucial dimension of the social meaning of particular linguistic constructions", though the latter is rarely grammaticized or explicitly encoded in human languages. Tabouret-Keller (1997, 2000) holds that our individual identity and social identity are both mediated by language. Language features are the link which binds them together. Such features

cover a whole range of language use, "from phonetic features to lexical units, syntactic structures,
and personal names" (p. 317). Social identity in
linguistic studies has long been associated with
linguistic variation. For instance, Eckert (2000)
views identity as "one's meaning in the world,"
which finds its expression in one's place in relation to other people, one's perspective on the rest
of the world, and one's understanding of his or
her value to others (p. 41). She further points out
that the individual's engagement in the world is
a constant process of identity construction and
the study of meaning in sociolinguistic variation
is a study of the relation between variation and
identity. Chambers (2003) gives a more direct
explanation of the relationship between linguistic
variation and identity, saying that "the underlying cause of sociolinguistic differences, largely
beneath consciousness, is the human instinct to
establish and maintain social identity. Linguistic
variation shows the profound need for people
to show they belong somewhere, and to define
themselves, sometimes narrowly and sometimes
generally" (p. 274).

In fact, all linguistic variation studies involve
the issue of identity to a certain extent. Linguistic
differences may arise out of age, gender, sexuality, ethnicity, political stance, religion, and many
others, all of which could be manifestations of
identity.

Blogs-Related Studies

The rapid popularity of blogging as a new type
of internet-based communication has attracted
the attention of scholars from various disciplines.
Quite a number of studies devote themselves to
describing the origin of blogs, their technological
features, their categories, their functions, and their
similarities to and differences from conventional
diaries or journals (e.g., Blood, 2002; Herring et
al., 2005; Karlsson, 2006; Kendall, 2007; Nardi,
Schiano, Gumbrecht, & Swartz, 2004; Schiano,
Nardi, Gumbrecht, & Swartz, 2004; van Dijck,

2004). There are also studies about why people
keep blogs (e.g., Kumar, Novak, Raghavan, &
Tomkins, 2004; Nardi, Schiano, Gumbrecht et
al., 2004; Schiano et al., 2004). Some researchers
are interested in exploring how bloggers' age and
gender are related to their blogging topics and
writing styles. For instance, Kumar et al. (2004)
find high correlation between bloggers' age and
their topics of interest. Huffaker and Calvert (2005)
find that blogs written by males and females are
more *alike* than different. Nowson, et al. (2006)
report that blogs written by female bloggers are
more contextualized than those written by male
bloggers. Argamon and colleagues (2007) find
that older bloggers tend to write about externally-
focused topics, while younger bloggers tend to
write about more personally-focused topics. They
also find that with the increase of age, bloggers'
writing styles become more masculine. Some
researchers find that bloggers tend to use blogs
for real life identity construction. According to
Huffaker and Calvert (2005), teenage bloggers
tend to take blogs as an extension of their real
life identities rather than a place to pretend. Van
Doorn et al. (2007) also find that blog authors
tend to present themselves in almost exclusively
'real life' categories such as hobbies, family, work
and place of residence, thus "leaving no room for
the construction of gender identities that bear no
relationship to their offline lives" (p. 156). The
easy availability of blogging data has also made
blogs very useful to computational linguists in
author gender identification, emotion identification, and automatic text classification.

Blogging in Chinese as a novel practice has
also attracted the attention of researchers in
China. Xiao and Wang (2008), for instance, have
approached bloggers' word-formation strategies
from a subculture perspective and found that
Chinese bloggers tend to adopt the strategies
of "bricolage" and "homology" in creating new
words and expressions in blog writing. They hold
that this practice is actually a reflection of young
people's desire to distant themselves from adults

and seek their own identities. Long and Wang (2008) hold that Chinese blog writing is quite different from conventional literary writing in terms of style, content, and discourse organization, and they attribute these differences to the nature of blogs as a private diary for public reading, their unique technological affordances, the freedom enjoyed by bloggers due to anonymity, and bloggers' desire to express their individuality. Xiao (2008) discusses the influence of post-modernism on the writing style of blogs from an aesthetics perspective. He views the unconventional writing style displayed in blogs as a reflection of post-modernity features in societal development. Chen (2008a, 2008b) discusses the "grassroots" nature of blogs and attributes it to the easy-to-operate feature of blogging technology. Blogging as a free publishing platform for almost everyone will inevitably lead to the diversity in styles and differences in quality. Lou (2008) focuses on the prevalence of daily language (i.e., non-literary language) in blogs and shows her concern about the colloquialization tendency which she believes will undercut the beauty of literary language.

Methodology-wise, existing studies concerning blogging discourse have demonstrated the possibility of adopting different analysis approaches. Herring (2004, 2008) proposes what she calls an expanded pluralistic paradigm of Web Content Analysis which can be used to analyze almost any information included in the new media (blogs inclusive), linguistic or otherwise. Nevertheless, no existing studies adopting this approach could be found. In fact, content analysis on blogs can be conducted in other ways as well. For instance, Huffaker and Calvert (2005) have applied DICTION, a content analysis software package, to analyzing the front page of 70 adolescent weblogs for identifying gender differences. Some researchers adopt the approach of ethnography in blog analysis, which typically involves participant observation and interviews with small number of informants (e.g., Kendall, 2007; Nardi, Schiano, & Gumbrecht, 2004). This kind of analysis is mainly qualitative

and non-linguistic. There are also approaches which are corpus-based and more linguistically oriented. For instance, Nowson, Oberlander, and Gill (2005) have experimented with calculating the F Score of a blog corpus based on the frequency counts of parts of speech to measure the linguistic formality of blogging. Herring and Paolillo (2006) have conducted a quantitative analysis using a blog corpus to identify gender differences based on their observation of bloggers' use of personal pronouns and some predefined words preferred by males and females. A more recent and more insightful approach which focuses on the association between linguistic features and online identity (or culture) representation is the Wmatrix Approach proposed by Ooi, Tan, and Chiang (2007). Wmatrix is an integrated corpus linguistic tool developed by Paul Rayson (2003, 2008) from Lancaster University. This system is able to afford word frequency profiles, lexico-grammatical patterning, part-of-speech annotation, and semantic content analysis. By exploiting both the advantages and the limitations of the Wmatrix system, Ooi and colleagues have demonstrated the power of the system in investigating identity representation in unconventional written data such as personal blogs written in Singaporean English.

Due to limited space, the author can only present a very simple and rather selective review of existing literature pertaining to the notion of self and identity and a short introduction about studies concerning the blogging discourse. It is true that our self and identity can find their expression in almost every aspect of our life. As an indispensable part of our daily life, our daily language use is actually an important carrier of our sense of self and identity. Existing linguistic studies concerning self and identity are mainly based on spoken language and spoken data. There are very few studies about linguistic representation of self and identity in writing. Cross-linguistic studies in this regard are even fewer. Though there are studies about identity construction in blogging discourse, very few of them have discussed the linguistic strategies that bloggers employ to represent self and identity. By linguistic strategies, the author refers to the orthographic, lexical, syntactical, semantic, and pragmatic strategies. Qualitative analysis of discourse as an important means for identity-related studies has the strength of being able to reveal more in-depth information but its weakness is also obvious: it can only be used to deal with very small sample. Identity is actually the relationship between self and the norm. It involves intra-personal and inter-personal commonalities and differences, thus the analysis of identity will inevitably involve comparison. When this comparison involves different groups of people, a corpus-linguistic approach would be a more reasonable choice. With the help of natural language processing tools, a corpus-linguistic approach to self and identity representation can offer insights which cannot be easily obtained by qualitative analysis alone. In addition, by examining the strategies and the contents of bloggers from different linguistic and cultural backgrounds, we can explore whether there are any universal features about the notion of self and identity and how language and culture are shaping their representations.

THE DATA

Two small corpora have been constructed for this research: one is an English blog corpus consisting of 1,200 blog entries written by 240 American bloggers aged between 15 and 40, and the other is a Chinese blog corpus consisting of 400 blog entries written by 80 Mainland Chinese bloggers covering the same age range. The bloggers can be classified into six age groups: mid teens (15 to 17), late teens (18 to19), young adults (20 to 24), adults (25 to 29), mature adults (30 to 34) and older adults (35 to 40). Each of these group categories roughly corresponds to a developmental stage from secondary school, high school, college, after college or work starters, career

development period, and a period for assuming family responsibility. The English blog corpus is the primary corpus whereas the Chinese corpus is complementary.

This seemingly strange design is actually the result of considering many practical constraints. English and Chinese differ greatly in some important aspects. They have different orthographic systems, different repertoire of parts of speech, and different syntactical features, among other things. These differences have led to the differences between English processing software and Chinese processing software in terms of tagsets (e.g., part-of-speech tagging and semantic tagging). To cite just one simple example, as English adopts an alphabetic spelling system and a tradition of inserting a blank space between two orthographic words, it is relatively easier for language processing software to capture the word forms. As a consequence, any innovative or unconventional word form can be easily captured. For Mandarin Chinese, it is totally a different story. The ideographic nature of the writing system has made the recognition and segmentation of Chinese characters more difficult as there are no inserted blanks between characters. Although the problem of character recognition has already been solved since a long time ago and segmenting individual characters is no longer an issue, it is still very difficult even for the latest Chinese processing system to identify the innovative lexical items in online Chinese discourse. This makes the simple task of identifying "new" word forms an intensive manual job when it comes to processing a Chinese corpus. Not to mention the problems arising out of the differences between English and Chinese in parts of speech and the unavailability of tools for semantic annotation of the Chinese data. Such practical constraints have greatly reduced the feasibility of conducting a systematic, comprehensive cross-linguistic comparison. A more workable plan would be to use the English corpus as the primary data for identifying major strategies that English bloggers use in representing their identities in personal blogs first and then check whether these strategies could be found in the Chinese blogs and what other strategies Chinese bloggers tend to use, if any.

The author adopts Teubert's (2005) understanding of corpus linguistics as a guiding principle for data collection. According to him, the essence of a corpus-linguistic approach to language study is actually "an insistence on working only with *real language data* taken from the discourse *in a principled way* and compiled into a *corpus*" (2005, p. 4, my italics). All the data for this research are from two blogging websites: the LiveJournal.com[1] and the Blogcn.com[2]. The former is a very popular blogging site worldwide whereas the latter is a very popular Chinese blogging website in China. What is more important, both sites allow users to search for bloggers by location (countries or cities), age, interest, friends or any combination of these options. This has made the data collection slightly easier. The Blogcn.com also allows for searching by gender, so identifying blogger gender is not a big problem for the Chinese data. As LiveJournal does not offer searching by blogger gender, the job of differentiating male and female bloggers for the English data can only be done manually via reading through the blog entries. For each blogger, five blog entries are selected just to allow for a minimum amount of representativeness in terms of content, style, and length while at the same time makes the data collection more manageable. In fact, according to the pilot studies that the author has conducted, five entries from each blogger can produce an average of around 1500-1800 words of data for linguistic analysis. This is close to the word-limit of 2000 adopted by the constructors of British National Corpus (BNC) for each author. Only the main text of the blog entry has been collected and the topics have been limited to daily life experiences, reflections, and emotional expressions. As far as the regional varieties of the two languages (English and Chinese) are concerned, choosing the United States for English and Mainland China for Mandarin

Chinese is purely a matter of convenience and familiarity.

DATA ANALYSIS

The data analysis for this research has relied heavily on language processing tools. The software tools employed in this research include: WordSmith Tools (Scott, 2009), Concordance (Watt, 2004), Wmatrix (Rayson, 2003, 2008), Segmenter, and 3GWS (for processing Chinese data). Wmatrix provides a web interface to the CLAWS (Constituent Likelihood Automatic Word-tagging System) and USAS (UCREL Semantic Analysis System) corpus annotation tools. CLAWS is a system for part-of-speech tagging which can achieved 96-97% accuracy based on conventional written English. The USAS is a framework for undertaking the automatic semantic analysis of text with a success rate of about 92%. The default setting of Wmatrix (the one meant for processing conventional data) is very useful for spotting new features from the user's corpus data, especially when it comes to online discourse data such as personal blogs. One function of the system is that it assigns a label of Z99 to unknown word forms and pools them together as a single file for downloading. This feature is very useful for identifying creative linguistic forms which might be important markers of group or individual identities. Another important function of this software is that it allows the user to conduct intergroup comparisons at the word, part-of-speech, and semantic levels. This is, again, very useful for the current research because comparison is an important means for identifying linguistic similarities and differences between bloggers from different age and gender groups.

Of course, not all linguistic variables lend themselves to quantitative analysis. Some linguistic variables require what the author calls quanti-qualitative analysis. The first step of this kind of analysis is to manually annotate or label the data and then do quantitative analysis. The analysis of the Chinese data has not followed very closely what has been done to the English data. Rather, it has been analyzed in a more qualitative manner and the analysis is more like a verification of the findings and results obtained from the English data. Existing findings concerning Internet Chinese, inspirations from the wordlists generated from the Chinese blog data, and native-speaker intuition are used as the major means for analyzing the linguistic strategies that Chinese bloggers have employed to represent their identities in personal blogs.

FINDINGS

Due to the constraints of space, the author will only report the findings concerning bloggers' practice in two linguistic aspects: orthographic representation and semantic domain preference. Both aspects can reveal certain aspects of bloggers' conceptions of self and identity.

Orthographic Representations

The English Data

An English word can be orthographically engineered in a number of ways, for instance, abbreviating, lengthening, replacing letters or morphemes, blending two words together, shifting between upper and lower cases, or adding other orthographic symbols, and so on. After submitting the English corpus data to Wmatrix for part-of-speech and semantic annotation, the author gets an "unknown word" list generated by the system. Following that, the author has adopted a six-category scheme for classifying those orthographically engineered word-forms. They are: 1) unconventional contracted forms, 2) abbreviations, 3) letter repetition, 4) e-paralinguistic words, 5) misspellings, and 6) phonetic spellings.

The first category refers to word forms resulted from the omission of the apostrophe from normally contracted forms, for instance *dont* for *don't*, *im* for *I'm*. Omitting the apostrophe speeds up the typing and will not cause too much comprehension difficulty for the readers. Nevertheless, it makes the resultant discourse more speech-like and informal. Using contracted forms in writing is already a marker of informality. Omitting the apostrophe seems to be able to make the resultant word-form even more informal.

The second category refers to word forms resulted from deliberate removal of linguistic materials. According to Plag (2003), abbreviation is a word-formation strategy which involves the amalgamations of parts of different words. Abbreviations are most commonly formed by taking initial letters of multi-word sequences, though there are also cases where abbreviations incorporate non-initial letters. They can be further classified into initialism and acronymy (word-forms created by combining the first letter of each constituting words, for instance, *lol* for *laughing out loud* and *idk* for *I don't know*), clipping (or truncation) (word-forms created by taking away either the initial or ending part of a word, for example, *pic* for *picture*, and *toon* for *cartoon*), and omission of vowels (word-forms created by removing all the vowel letters from a word, e.g., *gd* for *good*, and *lvl* for *level*). Initials and acronyms can be used as in-group markers and used for screening target audience. As Plag (2003) has rightly pointed out, "within certain groups of speakers, the use of an abbreviation can be taken as a marker of social identity: speaker and listener(s), but not outsiders, know what the speaker is talking about" (p. 129).

The third category refers to word forms involving the repetition of one or more letters, for instance *soooo* for *so* and *reeeaaalllyyy* for *really*. Spelling a word with repeated letters is actually reminding the reader that the word-form so produced should be emphasized. Letter repetition words can not only work as a marker of informal discourse but also add a playful tone to the text.

The fourth category refers to word forms resulted from bloggers' efforts in trying to represent laughter or the act of laughing in orthographic forms, for instance *haha* and *hehe*. Similar to letter repetition, word-forms representing different kinds of laughter are mainly used to mimic paralinguistic behaviors. Laughter is something which typically accompanies face-to-face communication. Deliberately introducing typical oral discourse features into written texts is again a deviation from the conventional writing norm, which not only makes the resultant texts more informal but also adds a flavor of performance to the whole practice of blogging.

The fifth category refers to word forms resulted from slips of the keyboard or intentional erroneous spelling. Spelling a word wrongly either unconsciously or deliberately will produce a new word-form, for instance, *becuase* for *because*, *teh* for *the*, *definately* for *definitely*, *somethign* for *something*, and *dwunk* for *drunk*. The function of misspellings has a great deal to do with the nature of the misspellings. For unintentional misspellings such as slips of the keyboard or spelling errors resulted from bloggers' incomplete command of the word-forms, they can also be taken as a marker of informal style or even a marker of online discourse genres. The reason is not how ridiculously some bloggers are spelling the English words but rather their tolerance of the presence of such forms in a piece of writing. Again, this is a direct violation against the spelling conventions, revealing a rebellion against a collective identity.

The sixth category refers to word forms resulted from bloggers' attempts of mimicking how certain words are actually pronounced in speech by themselves or other people, for instance, *watever* for *whatever*, *foto* for *photo*, *alot* for *a lot*, *sorta* for *sort of*, and for *apsind-minded* for *absent-minded*. Phonetic spellings force the readers to read out the message or at least to pronounce them in their

mind. This will also give readers an impression of listening to people reading out their stories.

Regardless of the specific strategies involved, orthographic variation is a result of deviating from the established norm represented by conventional writing regulations. The employment and tolerance of deviated forms in blogging has actually become a means for bloggers to represent their own identities. On the one hand, orthographic variation as a whole has already become an identity marker which can mark off bloggers from non-bloggers and bloggers' online identity and their real life identity. On the other hand, orthographic variation could be associated with other aspects of bloggers' identities. In order to obtain information about the link between orthographic variation and blogger identity we can calculate the distribution of orthographically engineered forms or OEFs (that is, the total number of non-conventional contracted forms, abbreviations, letter repetition words, e-paralinguistic words, misspellings, and phonetic spellings) bloggers have used. By observing the distributions of the total number of OEFs across bloggers from different age and gender (or even regional) groups, we can get some insights about whether and to what extent orthographic variation is associated with identity aspects of age and gender. Table 1 shows the distributions of OEFs across all the age and gender groups for English bloggers.

If we compare blogger groups (ranked according to the relative frequency of OEFs per 10000 words) at the top with the four groups at the bottom, we will observe a great difference. Regardless of gender, teenage bloggers tend to use a great more orthographically engineered word forms than adult bloggers aged 30 to 40. Within the teenage groups, female bloggers tend to use more OEFs than their male counterparts. This pattern also holds for the 30-34 and 35-40 groups. For the age groups in the middle (the 20-24 and 25-29 age groups), male bloggers tend to use more OEFs than their female counterparts. In other words, age and gender seem to play an important

Table 1. Distributions of OEFs across groups (English bloggers)

Blogger Group	Raw Frequency	Text Size	Relative Frequency	Rank
15-17(female)	461	24,665	186.9	1
18-19 (female)	417	22,547	184.9	2
15-17(male)	339	21,761	155.8	3
18-19 (male)	324	23,967	135.2	4
20-24 (male)	325	34,208	95.0	5
20-24 (female)	261	37,719	69.2	6
25-29 (male)	195	29,074	67.1	7
25-29 (female)	225	35,495	63.4	8
30-34 (female)	160	31,365	51.0	9
35-40 (female)	175	37,050	47.2	10
30-34 (male)	112	30,998	36.1	11
35-40 (male)	80	27,289	29.3	12

role in bloggers' employment of orthographically engineered forms.

One more thing which is related to orthographic representation but not orthographic representations of words per se is bloggers' use of a special symbol – the asterisk (*). There are four basic uses of the asterisk (*) in personal blogs: 1) as an emphasis marker, 2) as wildcards, 3) as a marker for comments and whole chunks of text, and 4) as a separator marking off blogger behaviors from the main text (or action marker). The first two belong to lexical features whereas the last two belong to discoursal features. In terms of occurrence frequencies, asterisks as emphasis markers and action or behavior markers are much more common than the other two. The first use of the asterisk, the one as emphasis marker, can be taken as an innovative way of expressing prosodic features in written form. The function of the asterisks is to emphasize the words or expressions enclosed. By putting the asterisks on a word form, the blogger is actually making it more prominent orthographically and thus achieving the effect of emphasizing it. It is very similar to other strategies like spelling the whole word in upper case letters or lengthening a word by letter repetition. This function is more often used by older blog-

gers. Among the 52 instances of this use, 36 are from bloggers aged 25 to 40, accounting for 69%. There is only one instance from the mid teens. Gender-wise, 65% of the occurrences are from female bloggers. The following concordance lines (Figure 1) give a flavor of how asterisks are used by bloggers.

The second use of the asterisk, the one as the wildcard, is not very common in the corpus. Only six cases were found in the whole corpus and they exclusively appeared in different forms of the word *fuck*. The function of this use is to reduce the impact of using vulgar terms. In other words, this use is of euphemistic nature. The third use of the asterisk, the one as a device for bloggers to mark off important chunks of text or add comments to their own statements, is more frequently observed in the corpus than that of the second use. This use falls into the category of discoursal features, as it is mainly for highlighting or reminding purposes. The fourth use of the asterisk, which is also the most interesting one among the four, is to mark off blogger actions (or behaviors) from the main text of the entry. There are 115 cases of such use in the English blog corpus, a sample of which is shown in the following concordance lines (see Figure 2).

A number of observations can be made from

Figure 1. Concordance lines for asterisks as emphasis markers

N	Concordance
1	d 60 pounds since the beginning of the year. *35* of those pounds have been packed on in
2	head stopped shouting "THE ▨ HAS **ABANDONED** YOU" I did what any desper
3	us feel safe in situations where we will never *be* safe. And then once we feel safe, life ca
4	seconded the opinion. The doc also said that *currently* he's not concerned about her bon
5	la bliss from Sonic. And no, I don't drink them *every* day, but I do drink them a lot as well
6	running over the weekend because they take *FOREVER*). Had to cut through some pre-
7	oneself rather than on the cheater... le: Can *I* trust that this person will not ever cheat on
8	to be mounted on the wall. Sometimes rather *intelligent* students manage to get their deg
9	t I can take it the second week of July. So we *might* be going down there then. I still don't
10	we hung out with Hannah! Anyway, I'll give a *much* more detailed description of my week
11	es of the Caribbean: At World's End. She had *no* idea she was coming early to watch the
12	e on MONDAY for JB. ugh. i have to find the *perfect* outfit i guess. so...major diet time.
13	about it, then he said the one thing that is the *real* source of the problem at hand. "It's lik
14	really cool and definetely makes my costume *so* much more complete! I'm so glad FIRES
15	r since 1. we're a college and 2. we're even a *teaching* school. But I guess it's good they
16	a la "Fatal Attraction." As if. So who needed *that* ▨?? Not I. Off I ran, only this time
17	do that from time to time, again, as a special *treat*. I need to get back into the habit of

Figure 2. First, a great majority of the words and phrases enclosed by asterisks are verbs. Other categories include noun phrases and interjections, but they are not many in number. Second, most of the verbs or verb phrases are in the third person singular form, which is quite unusual. Since the logical subject of each of these verbs is exclusively *I* (the blogger), the verb should be in its first person present tense form as in line 15. To a great extent, the asterisks are signals which

Figure 2. Concordance lines for asterisks as action markers

N	Concordance
1	ho then also dropped off a pair of handcuffs in my LJ *beams* And to add to that, the wonderful shipperfe
2	what? XD Also, YAY! Sparkly, pink Nextel Cup hat! *bounces* And I don't have to spend 20 bucks for it,
3	younger sister of the girl played by Keira Knightley). *cries* It looks so sadd!! And I'm sorry, but I read th
4	tarts... Feb. 16th, 2008 | 06:16 pm mood: artistic *dances* YAY!!! We have a week-long break from s
5	rsday? 08 October 2007 Jiggity Jig! I'm home! *drops bags on the bed to unpack later* I never wa
6	e 6 or 7 hours. Bed now. *collapses* 3rd-Apr-2008 *dusts off LJ* So, time for a change. I'm in the proc
7	ow why I'm freaking out right now unnecessarily??!! *jumps up and down* Well, do ya? Do ya?..Well too
8	walk away. but i've already said that multiple times.. *looks down and thinks* i don't feel like wishing for a
9	riving the Impala = bouncy happy fangirl. Oh, Dean. *pats fondly* ETA (again): Who couldn't love excha
10	it's the worst pain i've ever felt. :'(goodnight all... *rolls eyes* come on sam... like your a lost confus
11	ys! What all have you been up to since the 28th? *runs off to see what kind of trouble y'all have been g
12	y roommate. She's been gone not even four days. *shakes head at herself* I only have 45 minutes left
13	...ughhh...and I had to read nine chapters for English *shoots Ms.Matthews*. Buttt I'm all done now so all
14	... Which will be the end of this chapter in my life.... *Sighs heavily* "Lilo" Aug. 18th, 2007 New Tinker
15	n trying to go to sleep the last 2 hours and I can't ... *sniffle* Ow... no fair 25 Jan 2007 mood: sore
16	days I did go I ended up swallowing my lunch twice. *sticks tongue out in gagging gesture* We're in high
17	ore. 14 September 2007 good god mood: calm *takes a deep breath* Ok...so for anyone who's inte
18	my friends, singing and drinking. 31 October 2007 *Turns on the Porch Light* Happy Halloween Gan
19	pie...u no what im talking bout megan..lol...**vomitz* *...ugh nasty!!!!! yea so we got outta work at about
20	y adress will follow for those of you who don't have it. (*waves at melly*) Current Mood: sleepy Friday,
21	Vorkosigan 21/05/2008 mood: chipper Mmmm *yawns* I am so tired everyone! So incredibly tired!

mark the beginning and ending of the time when the blogger exits from the narration and does something here and now. This is quite similar to play scripts where actors' actions are marked off from their lines by bracketed instructions which are featured by the use of simple present tense. The third person singular form is almost the default, as the actions of a particular character are put in brackets following his or her lines. As the logical subject is always the character name and the action is always a real-time one, it is quite natural to see verbs in their third person singular forms. By adopting a discourse structure which is characteristic of play scripts, the blogger is actually turning his or her autobiographical recording into a sort of narrating plus performing. Consequently, the reading of blogs has also been turned into a sort of watching. By inserting actions, the blogger is also making the entries more appealing to the readers. These actions and interjections help visualize the blogger in the reader's mind and give a sense of communication via webcam. Third, a great majority of the asterisked words or phrases are related to bloggers' emotional statuses while blogging. The top asterisked words and phrases include: *sigh* (35), *lol* (5), *bounce* (4), *cough* (4), *shrug* (4), *blink* (3), *cry* (3), *hug* (3), *shudder* (2), and *sniffle* (2). From this list we can see that many of these words are verbs or expressions which are related to body language or paralinguistic features. Through these words and expressions the bloggers are actually trying to create a sense of presence thus shortening the social distance between the blogger and the intended readers. If we take a further look at the distribution of this use among bloggers from different groups, we can also obtain certain insights about the identities of the bloggers who prefer this use. Among the 115 total occurrences of this use in the corpus, 83 are from female bloggers, accounting for 72%. Only 32 instances are from the male bloggers, taking up 28%. Age-wise, 74% of the occurrences are from bloggers aged 25 and above. Only 14 occurrences are from the teenage groups, accounting for around

12%. In other words, the use of asterisks as action markers can be taken as an identity marker of older age and female gender.

The Chinese Data

The Chinese blog data have also displayed certain features resulted from linguistic manipulation of forms. Nevertheless, both the types and tokens of such forms are rather limited. The most commonly observed category of orthographic representation is misspelling. In fact, misspelling is not a very accurate term. Chinese words are not spelled, so to speak. In handwriting it is quite normal for people to write a certain Chinese character wrongly by omitting or adding one or more strokes. In electronic writing this is almost impossible. The mainstream Chinese input systems are mainly Pinyin-based (a Romanized auxiliary writing system). They will offer a whole range of Chinese characters for the user to choose as long as the combination of the Pinyin letters is existent in the Chinese lexicon. That is to say, even when the user keys in a wrong combination, the system will still display correct Chinese characters which match that combination. This is also the case for those stroke-based Chinese inputting systems. As a result, some of the orthographic engineering strategies which are found in the English data may not be present in the Chinese data.

There are cases of misspelled words in the Chinese blog corpus, for instance, 在(*zai*, a progressive aspect marker in Chinese) for 再 (*zai*, meaning *again*); 进 (*jin*, meaning *come into* or *go in*) for 近 (*jin*, meaning *near* or *close*); 把 (ba, meaning *grasp* or *hold*) for 吧 (*ba*, a sentence final particle); 调 (*tiao*, meaning *adjust*) for 挑 (*tiao*, meaning *choose*); 不行(*buxing*, meaning *no/no way*) for 不幸 (*buxing*, meaning *unfortunate*); 一凡(*yifan*, meaningless in Chinese unless as personal name) for 一番(*yifan*, meaning *for some time*). All these "misspelled" characters (the first one in each pair) are correct characters but they are not the intended ones. The fact that Chinese notoriously abounds in homophones together with the keyboard- and Pinyin-mediated inputting systems has contributed greatly to the presence of "misspelled" characters in Chinese blogs. Like the misspellings in English blogs, these "misspelled" Chinese characters will usually not affect the readers' comprehension as they can get a hint about the intended character from the pronunciation of the "misspelled" one. The presence of "misspelled" characters is also a stylistic marker. The author's browsing of the Chinese blog data shows that "misspelled" characters of this kind seem to be more frequently observed in entries written by teenage bloggers. Since there is no way to identify the so-called misspelled Chinese characters automatically so far, this can only be accomplished through human judgment. Thus, this finding may sound rather impressionistic. Another possible reason for fewer misspelled characters in entries from older bloggers could be that adults care more about their face than teenagers. In China, blogging is taken more often as a platform for displaying bloggers' writing talents than for social interaction and personal emotion expression. A blog entry full of typos is often taken as either an indication of the sloppiness of the blogger's language or disrespect for the readers. Unless there is evidence to show that the blogger is trying to be playful or humorous. This is also why we can find cases where bloggers are exploiting the homophones for achieving special effects, just like what the English bloggers do with phonetic spellings. For instance, some bloggers use 鸟 (*niao*, meaning *bird*) to replace 了 (*le* or *liao*, a marker for perfect aspect in Chinese) or 滴 (*di*, meaning a drop of liquid) for 地 (*di* or *de*, an adverb marker) intentionally to add a flavor of playfulness or to represent a dialectal way of saying things. This practice is much more commonly observed in entries written by adult bloggers.

Another phenomenon which is also frequently observed in the Chinese data is the use of abbreviated terms. For instance, 小资 (*xiaozi, petit bourgeoisie*) is the abbreviation of 小资产阶级 (*xiao zichanjieji*), which refers to the lifestyle of people in the lower middle class. This is a revitalization of the previously politically-loaded term during the Cultural Revolution days. Now, this word is being used without any negative connotation in online Chinese discourses and informal daily speech. Other examples include: 高复 (*gaofu*) for 高考复习 (*gaokao fuxi*), meaning revision for preparing for the entrance examination for higher education (a high-stake examination in China), and 哈7 (*haqi*) for 哈里波特7 (*halibote qi*), meaning "Harry Potter (7)." This practice can be observed in all age groups of Chinese bloggers.

There are no real letter repetition cases in the Chinese blog data. Again, this is determined by the nature of the Chinese orthographic system: Chinese does not exist in Romanized letters unless it is written in Pinyin. As a consequence, there are only cases of word repetition in Chinese. A few cases of word repetition in the Chinese data has been identified, for instance, 无聊无聊无聊 (*wuliao wuliao wuliao*, meaning *bored, bored, and bored*), 啊啊啊啊啊啊啊啊啊 (*a a a a a a a a*, interjection *argh*), and 累累累累 (*lei lei lei lei*, meaning *tired, tired, tired, and tired*). Like the letter repetition in the English data, word repetitions in the Chinese blogs are also meant to amplify the meaning of the conventional spelling.

Like English bloggers, Chinese bloggers also tend to mimic paralinguistic features in written form. Three words or phrases have been used to imitate three different kinds of laughter in the Chinese blogs: 呵呵 (hehe), 哈哈 (haha), and 嘿嘿 (heihei). Altogether there are 118 tokens of these e-paralinguistic words: 64 tokens for 呵呵 (hehe), 34 tokens for 哈哈 (haha), and 20 tokens for 嘿嘿 (heihei). Among the 64 instances of 呵呵 (hehe), 34 are from teenage bloggers, accounting for 53%. For 哈哈 (haha), 56% of the occurrences are from teenage bloggers. No significant gender difference could be found in the use of 呵呵 (hehe) and 哈哈 (haha). The phrase 嘿嘿 (heihei) seems to be preferred by older bloggers: only 30% of the total occurrences are from the teens. 嘿嘿

(heihei) is preferred by male bloggers as 65% of the occurrence are from male bloggers.

Using the asterisk for special purposes is rare in the Chinese data. No other uses except three instances of asterisks used as emphasis marker have been found. Bracketed actions similar to those in the English data are also extremely rare: only one instance has been found. This may have a great deal to do with the Chinese orthographic system where the asterisk has almost no role to play at all.

From the strategies American bloggers and Chinese bloggers employed in realizing orthographic variations we can observe both similarities and differences. Both American and Chinese teenage bloggers tend to embrace unconventional orthographic representations more than bloggers from other age groups. This may well be a reflection of the universal nature of adolescents which tends to show less respect for established norms (conventional writing norms in this case) and their desire to seek independent identity. The much greater presence of unconventional orthographic forms in the American blog corpus can be attributed to three factors. First, the spelling system of the English language and its compatibility with the keyboard has made the orthographic manipulation of word forms almost effortless. Second, it may have something to do with the American cultural tradition of valuing individualism. The respect for individualism may have contributed to bloggers' innovative ways of using the language. The Chinese culture, on the other hand, values collective identity more, which might have contributed to bloggers' tendency of being less deviant in language use. Moreover, Chinese people tend to take their writing as an important aspect of their face. Substantial presence of "misspelled" characters will be taken as absolutely face-threatening if they are not for achieving special effects. This is especially the case for adult bloggers. That may help explain why unconventional orthographic representations appear less often in the Chinese

blog corpus. Third, the different sample size of the American blog corpus and the Chinese one may also be a contributing factor. Another possible factor would be that American bloggers take blogging more as a venue for emotional expression and social communication with other people whereas Chinese bloggers take blogging more as a place for displaying their writing talents, though they also use it for emotional expression and social communication.

Semantic Domain Preference

From what has been presented so far, we have obtained some interesting insights about how American and Chinese bloggers are trying to represent themselves linguistically by deviating from the orthographic norms. In fact, we can also observe how bloggers are representing themselves from what they talk about in their blog entries. If we say that we are how we talk, we can also say that we are what we talk about. As one of the major functions of blogging is to record bloggers' daily life experiences, different bloggers may choose to disclose different details. Even if people happen to share similar experiences, they may not necessarily feel the same about these experiences. It is sensible to believe that there is a link between what the bloggers write about in their blogs and certain aspects of their identities.

The English Data

If we can find a way to compare the contents of bloggers from different groups, we may be able to identify that link. This is where Wmatrix comes to play an important role. As mentioned earlier, the Wmatrix system is able to generate a report which contains lists of semantic tags (for details about the tags and their meaning, please refer to the Appendix) overused by one dataset against the dataset the client designated as reference dataset (or reference corpus). From this list of overused semantic tags, we can get a rough idea about what content has been more frequently mentioned in a particular dataset and from there we expect to obtain some insights about certain aspects of bloggers' identities. As a matter of fact, this kind of comparison is quite experimental as two problems may render the whole comparison meaningless. One problem is that semantic tagging itself is difficult due to the fact that words are used in specific contexts and no computer software is intelligent enough to be able to tell exactly which semantic domain a particular word should fall into. To make things more complicated English words are notoriously polysemous. The other is that online discourse is also notoriously unconventional, which will inevitably affect the accuracy rate of the semantic tagging results. The less pessimistic side of the story is that the semantic tagger of Wmatrix tends to be rather consistent in making judgments (wrong judgments inclusive). As for the unconventionality issue, we should not exaggerate its negative effects, either. Compared with other online discourse data, blogging texts are closer to conventional written texts. The number of the so-called unknown words only accounts for less than 2.5% of the total word tokens in the whole corpus. As the Wmatrix system generates lists of words which are found to be overused or underused as against the reference corpus (data) designated by the client, the author can always check the lists for tagging errors and decide whether the errors are likely to lead to distorted interpretations. In other words, despite the potential uncertainties, it is still worth trying. As there are six age groups altogether, for each age group there will be five sets of overused semantic domains relative to respective age groups. By pooling all the overused semantic domains of one particular group together, the author can see how many times each overused category has appeared. According to the number of times, the author is able to assign a degree of prominence value to each of these domains. The minimum value would be one and the maximum

five. The greater the value is, the more prominent the category. If a domain's degree of prominence is greater than two, it will be taken as one of the preferred semantic domain of that age group.

Before reporting the semantic domain preferences of different blogger groups, the author will give a brief account about the overall gender difference as revealed by the comparison based on the semantically annotated components of the English blog corpus. Table 2 lists the top ten preferred semantic domains identified by the Wmatrix system for male and female bloggers respectively. From this table we can see some interesting differences between male bloggers and female ones. Female bloggers seem to talk more about themselves and the people around them (revealed by Z8, S4, and S2.1), their bodies (revealed by B1), sickness (revealed by B3), clothes and personal belongings (B5), emotions (revealed by E1). They also seem to be involved more in oral communication with other people, as can be seen from the overuse of Q2.2. They also talk more about vehicles and land transportation (revealed by M3). The male bloggers, on the other hand, seem to talk more about general objects (O2), sports (K5.1), computers and the internet (Y2), and music (K2 and K3). They are more involved in written communication with friends and colleagues as revealed by the overuse of Q1.2. They seem to be less assertive about their statements (as revealed by the overuse of the category A8), probably for the purpose of creating a sense of vagueness so as to shorten the social distance between them and the intended readers. They appear to be more aware of the change of weather conditions as revealed by the overuse of category W4. In addition, their language seems to involve more grammatical words such as articles and prepositions (Z5).

The overall difference between male and female bloggers as revealed by the top semantic domains seems to match the stereotypical images of men and women, which means looking at this

Table 2. Top 10 preferred semantic domains across gender

Female			Male	
Semtag	LL	Semtag	LL	
Z8	85.71	O2	40.47	
S4	53.88	K5.1	27.78	
B3	43.26	Y2	24.25	
Z6	38.05	Q1.2	24.05	
S2.1	30.02	T1.1.3	23.6	
B5	24.83	Z5	23.14	
Q2.2	21.98	K2	21.22	
M3	21.93	K3	18.73	
B1	19.48	A8	17.81	
E1	18.97	W4	16.63	

linguistic aspect does have the potential to reveal certain link between the blogging content and the blogger's conception of self and identity.

If we compare the semantic domains used by bloggers from different age groups, we can obtain some insights about the potential influence of age on what bloggers tend to write about. Due to the constraints of space, the author will only present the semantic domain preferences of two groups: the mid-teens group and the older adult group. By putting these two groups side by side we can see more clearly whether and to what extent is the age variable is playing a role in determining what they write about. Table 3 lists the most prominent semantic domains of the mid-teens group as against the other five age groups.

Compared with the lists generated from the datasets of other blogger groups, the mid-teens list is the longest, suggesting that this group is more different from the rest age groups. The mid-teens seem to talk a lot about their education (P1) as school life is an important part of young people at this age period. They also talk a lot about people (Z1) (most probably their friends). Music (K2), sports (K5.1), and games (K5.2) are important part of their daily life as well. Feelings and emotions (revealed by E1 and E4.1+) are also important

Table 3. Preferred semantic domains for the 15-17 group

Semtag	Degree of Prominence	Semtag	Degree of Prominence
A5.1-	5	A14	3
K5.1	5	E4.1+	3
Z4	5	K2	3
Z99	5	N1	3
E1	4	Q1.3	3
K5.2	4	S9	3
P1	4	T1.1.2	3
Q2.1	4	Z1	3

Table 4. Preferred semantic domains for the 35-40 group

Semtag	Degree of Prominence	Semtag	Degree of Prominence
H5	5	A1.5.1	3
M3	5	A6.2+	3
B3	4	A9+	3
F2+	4	B4	3
F4	4	M6	3
I2.2	4	N3.8	3
L3	4	O1.2	3
N3.7	4	O3	3
W4	4	Q1.3	3
Z5	4	S1.1.1	3

topics for them. They seem to be frequently involved in face-to-face communication (Q2.1) and telecommunication with friends (Q1.3). They tend to use plenty of interjections or colloquial discourse markers in their blog writing (Z4) and their language tends to be more unconventional (Z99). The list for the oldest group of bloggers included in this research (the 35-40 group), on the other hand, is quite different, as Table 4 shows.

From Table 4 we can see that bloggers from the 35-40 group mention more about furniture and household fittings (H5), their possessions (A9+), their electronic gadgets (O3), health-related topics (B3 and B4), trees, plants, and flowers (L3 and F4), what usually or normally happens in bloggers' life (A6.2+), social interactions realized via phone (Q1.3) and visiting (S1.1.1), and activities related to shopping and selling (I2.2). They seem to be more aware of the weather conditions (W4). They also mention a lot about drinking water (O1.2) and excessive drinking of alcoholic drinks (F2+). They are very dynamic as they tend to move around in vehicles (M3, M6, and N3.8). If we take a closer look at some of the words which have been included in some of the semantic domains, we can find some extra information about this blogger group. For instance, the category B3 has included quite a few occurrences of the word *doctor* which is not used to refer to any real medical

doctor in real life but rather a TV serial entitled *Doctor Who*.

Limited space does not allow for more detailed discussion about the gender differences within each age group. From the very brief description presented above we can already see some link between the age of bloggers and the content of their blogging. The information bloggers put in their blog entries reveals a lot about their age, their gender, and their lifestyles, among other things.

The Chinese Data

As Wmatrix cannot process Chinese data, there is no way to conduct that kind of comparison described above. The author has to turn to other software tools such as WordSmith Tools for obtaining analysis results which may reveal what bloggers write about. One option is to compare the wordlist generated from the blog entries of one age group with the list of another group to identify the keywords. These keywords actually reveal a lot about the contents of the blog entries. As a matter of fact, the semantic comparison facilitated by Wmatrix is a comparison of wordlists in disguise. Table 5 shows the key words of the mid teens group as against the 35-40 group.

This table reveals a lot about the blogging content of mid-teens Chinese bloggers. The core

Table 5. Key words for the mid-teens group (Chinese)

Chinese Item	FRQ	English Translation	LL	Chinese Item	FRQ	English Translation	LL
啊	113	Interjection	95.0	开学	13	term starts	10.6
考试	21	exam	29.8	作业	13	exercises	10.6
高三	14	senior 3	24.6	成绩	6	score	10.5
讨厌	15	hate	19.9	补课	6	tuition	10.5
化学	11	chemistry	19.3	物理	9	physics	10.4
无聊	25	boring/bored	17.8	时间	43	time	9.6
写	20	write	17.8	明天	18	tomorrow	9.5
加油	10	work hard	17.6	日志	5	blog	8.8
学习	17	study	16.2	教官	5	military training officer	8.8
初三	9	junior 3	15.8	女生	5	girls	8.8
高考	9	entrance exam	15.8	实验	5	experiments	8.8
上课	11	having class	13.5	期中	5	mid-term	8.8
你们	20	you (plural)	13.5	骂	5	scold	8.8
你	94	you	12.5	军训	5	military training	8.8
考	16	exam, test	12.4	英语	9	English	7.5
友情	10	friendship	11.9	暑假	7	summer holidays	7.3
努力	12	work hard	11.7	害怕	7	fear	7.3
数学	12	mathematics	11.7	童年	4	childhood	7.0
我	566	I, me	11.4	朋友们	4	friends	7.0
班	22	class	11.0	学业	4	studies	7.0
题	13	exercise or test items	10.6	体育	4	PE	7.0

themes include: schooling (24 out of the 44 word types are about school life), people (I, me, you, friends, and girls: these words take up the greatest number of token – 689 tokens), and feelings and emotions (hate, bored, fear). Their blog entries contain a great number of the interjection 啊 (argh), indicating a more informal style of writing and a more frequent disclosure of emotions. From the semantic domains revealed by the key words, we can see that schooling is a very important part of their daily life. The high presence of the first person singular pronoun also reflects the egocentric nature of adolescents' life.

The keyword list for the 35-40 Chinese group, on the other hand, reveals something quite different (see Table 6).

None of the key words are related to studying any more. Bloggers from this age group are not as egocentric as the mid-teens. Instead, they talk a lot more about other people (most probably someone who has a special relationship with the blogger). This can be told from the overuse of the third person singular pronoun 他 (he or him). This list also reflects the living situations of the middle-aged bloggers as the so-called "sandwich generation." Apart from taking care of themselves,

Table 6. Key words for the 35-40 group (Chinese)

Chinese Item	FRQ	English Translation	LL
他	211	he, him	103.7
着	85	progressive particle	29.3
和	135	and	16.2
与	66	and	15.3
妈妈	38	mother	14.2
花	24	flowers	12.2
工作	22	work, employment	10.6
说	135	say, speak	9.7
孩子	32	child	8.4
俺	21	I, me (northern dialect)	7.6
人生	18	life	7.4
生命	17	life	6.6

they will have to take care of their own parents and support their children. One piece of evidence is the overuse of words like 妈妈 (mother) and 孩子 (child). This is also a reflection of the Chinese culture which highly values family ties. Bloggers at this age is also quite concerned about their work and employment. This is also an age when people start to think seriously about the meaning of life as revealed by the overuse of 人生 (life) and 生命 (life in the sense of a living being). Just like the English bloggers from the 35-40 age group, the Chinese bloggers also enjoy horticulture such as keeping flowers. They are also involved in plenty of verbal communication. Again, we can see a link between what bloggers write about and their conceptions of themselves and their identities.

From the preference for semantic domains of American bloggers and Chinese bloggers can observe similarities and differences again. Both American and Chinese mid-teens bloggers talk a lot about general education (i.e. schooling) as that is their major business at this age period. They also tend to be more egocentric and they talk a lot about the people around them, especially friends. This has plenty to do with their psychological development. The difference between American mid-teens bloggers and their Chinese counterparts is that the former's life seems to be richer than that of the latter. Apart from school life, American mid-teens talk more about music, games, and sports whereas the Chinese mid-teens appear to focus more on school life. This again has something to do with the cultural difference between the United States and China in terms of understanding about education. China's education (especially the secondary education) is notorious for being exam-oriented and unhealthily competitive, as a result of which the world of teenagers at this age period is almost nothing but studies and exams. As far as the older bloggers are concerned, American bloggers and Chinese bloggers display quite a big difference. The American bloggers have displayed a tendency of being materialistic in lifestyles whereas their Chinese counterparts have demonstrated a family-centred lifestyle and a greater concern about the meaning of life.

CONCLUSION

From what has been presented in this chapter we can see that personal blogs are a good place for individuals to represent themselves and their identities. As there are no imposed censorship and editing pressure, bloggers are more willing to employ more innovative ways to express themselves. This can be seen from the various strategies they have employed to realize orthographic variations. Both English bloggers and Chinese bloggers have displayed a tendency for manipulating the linguistic system for achieving special communicative and pragmatic purposes, though due to the constraints of the linguistic systems they may not be able to employ exactly the same strategies. From the orthographic representations bloggers have adopted and their preference for different semantic domains we can see a link between bloggers' linguistic practice and certain aspects of their identities, for instance, age, gender, and cultural background. The small sample size of the corpora used for this research may restrict the generalizability of the findings reported here. More detailed research involving greater number of bloggers and covering more linguistic aspects should be carried out before we can obtain a clearer picture about the linguistic representation of self and identity in personal blogs.

REFERENCES

Argamon, S., Koppel, M., Pennebaker, J. W., & Schler, J. (2007). Mining the Blogosphere: Age, gender and the varieties of self-expression. *First Monday, 12*. Retrieved April 7, 2008, from http://outreach.lib.uic.edu/www/issues/issue12_9/argamon/

Blood, R. (2002). *The weblog handbook: Practical advice on creating and maintaining your blog.* Cambridge, MA: Perseus Publishing.

Bucholtz, M. (2003). Sociolinguistic nostalgia and the authentication of identity. *Journal of Sociolinguistics, 7*(3), 398–416. doi:10.1111/1467-9481.00232

Cerulo, K. A. (1997). Identity construction: New issues, new directions. *Annual Review of Sociology, 23*, 385–409. doi:10.1146/annurev.soc.23.1.385

Chambers, J. K. (2003). *Sociolinguistic theory: Linguistic variation and its social significance.* Oxford, UK: Blackwell.

Chen, D. (2008a). Boke xiezuo tezheng jiqi shuangchongxiaoying yanjiu (The writing style of blogging and its dual effects). *Journal of Henan Normal University, 35*(4), 197–199.

Chen, D. (2008b). Boke: yizhong xinxingde wanluo xiezuo xingshi (Blogging: a newly emerged online writing). *Lilun chuangxin tanqiu (Theoretical Innovation Inquiry)*, 178-180.

Eckert, P. (2000). *Linguistic variation as social practice: The linguistic construction of identity in Belten High.* Oxford, UK: Blackwell.

Edwards, J. (1985). *Language, society and identity.* Oxford, UK: Basil Blackwell.

Herring, S. C. (2004). Content analysis for new media: Rethinking the paradigm. In *New research for new media: Innovative research methodologies symposium working papers and readings* (pp. 47–66). Minneapolis, MN: University of Minnesota School of Journalism and Mass Communication.

Herring, S. C. (2008). Web content analysis: Expanding the paradigm. In Hunsinger, J., Allen, M., & Klastrup, L. (Eds.), *The international handbook of internet research.* Berlin: Springer Verlag.

Herring, S. C., & Paolillo, J. C. (2006). Gender and genre variation in weblogs. *Journal of Sociolinguistics, 10*(4), 439–459. doi:10.1111/j.1467-9841.2006.00287.x

Herring, S. C., Scheidt, L. A., Wright, E., & Bonus, S. (2005). Weblogs as a bridging genre. *Information Technology & People, 18*, 142–171. doi:10.1108/09593840510601513

Huffaker, D. A., & Calvert, S. L. (2005). Gender, identity, and language use in teenage blogs. *Journal of Computer-Mediated Communication, 10.* Retrieved September 29, 2008, from http://jcmc. indiana.edu/vol10/issue2/huffaker.html

Karlsson, L. (2006). Acts of reading diary weblogs. *Human IT, 8*(2), 1–59.

Kendall, L. (2007). Shout into the wind, and it shouts back. In *Identity and interactional tensions on LiveJournal. First Monday, 12. Retrieved April 7, 2008, Kroger, J. (2007). Identity development: Adolescence through adulthood* (2nd ed.). Thousand Oaks, California: Sage Publications.

Kroger, J., & Adair, V. (2008). Symbolic meanings of valued personal objects in identity transitions of late adulthood. *Identity: An International Journal of Theory and Research, 8*(1), 5–24.

Kroskrity, P. V. (1999). Identity. *Journal of Linguistic Anthropology, 9*(1-2), 111–114. doi:10.1525/jlin.1999.9.1-2.111

Kumar, R., Novak, J., Raghavan, P., & Tomkins, A. (2004). Structure and evolution of blogspace. *Communications of the ACM, 47*(12), 35–39. doi:10.1145/1035134.1035162

Lawler, S. (2008). *Identity: Sociological perspectives.* Cambridge, UK: Polity.

Long, Y., & Wang, X. (2008). Shilun boke yuyande tedian ji chenyin (Characteristics of blog language and their contributing factors). *Yuwen xuekan (Journal of Chinese Language)*(1), 163-165.

Lou, C. (2008). Shilun wangluoxiezuozhong yuyanyunyongde tedian (Features of language use in online writing). *Yuwen xuekan (Journal of Chinese Language)*(2), 87-88.

Mead, G. H. (1934). Mind, Self and Society from the Standpoint of a Social Behaviorist. Chicago: The University of Chicago press.

Nardi, B. A., Schiano, D. J., & Gumbrecht, M. (2004). *Blogging as social activity, or, would you let 900 million people read your diary?* Paper presented at the 2004 ACM conference on computer supported cooperative work.

Nardi, B. A., Schiano, D. J., Gumbrecht, M., & Swartz, L. (2004). Why we blog. *Communications of the ACM, 47*(12), 41–46. doi:10.1145/1035134.1035163

Nowson, S., Oberlander, J., & Gill, A. J. (2005). *Weblogs, genres, and Individual differences.* Paper presented at the 27th Annual Conference of the Cognitive Science Society. Retrieved September 13, 2007, from http://www.ics.mq.edu.au/~snowson/papers/nowson-cogsci.pdf

Ochs, E. (1993). Constructing social identity: A language socialization perspective. *Research on Language and Social Interaction, 26*(3), 287–306. doi:10.1207/s15327973rlsi2603_3

Ooi, V. B. Y., Tan, P. K. W., & Chiang, A. K. L. (2007). Analyzing personal weblogs in Singapore English: the Wmatrix approach. *eVariEng (Journal of the Research Unit for Variation, Contacts, and Change in English), 2,* from http://www.helsinki. fi/varieng/journal/volumes/02/ooi_et_al/

Plag, I. (2003). *Word-formation in English.* Cambridge, UK: Cambridge University Press.

Rayson, P. (2003). Matrix: A statistical method and software tool for linguistic analysis through corpus comparison. Unpublished PhD thesis. Lancaster University.

Rayson, P. (2008). *Wmatrix: a web-based corpus processing environment: Computing Department.* Lancaster University.

Schiano, D. J., Nardi, B. A., Gumbrecht, M., & Swartz, L. (2004). *Blogging by the rest of us.* Paper presented at the Conference on Human Factors in Computing Systems (CHI 2004).

Scott, M. (2009). *WordSmith Tools 5.0* (Version 5.0.0.140).

Tabouret-Keller, A. (1997, 2000). Language and identity. In F. Coulmas (Ed.), The handbook of sociolinguistics (pp. 315-326). Oxford, UK: Blackwell Publishers.

Teubert, W. (2005). My version of corpus linguistics. *International Journal of Corpus Linguistics*, *10*(1), 1–13. doi:10.1075/ijcl.10.1.01teu

van Dijck, J. (2004). Composing the self: Of diaries and lifelogs. *Fibreculture, 3*. Retrieved May 11, 2008, from www.journal.fibreculture. org /issue3/issue3_vandijck.html van Doorn, N., van Zoonen, L., & Wyatt, S. (2007). Writing from experience: Presentations of gender identity on weblogs. *European Journal of Women's Studies, 14*(2), 143-158.

Watt, R. J. C. (2004). Concordance (Version 3.2.0.212).

Xiao, S. (2008). Lun boke wentide yuyan xing-shi shenmei tese (The aesthetic features of the linguistic styles in blogging). *Kaoshi zhoukan (Examination Weekly)14*, 204-205.

Xiao, W., & Wang, S. (2008). Lun wangluoyuy-ande qingnian yanwenhua tezheng (The youth subculture nature of internet Chinese). *Qingnian yanjiu (Youth Study)6*, 21-26.

ADDITIONAL READING

Barbieri, F. (2008). Patterns of age-based linguistic variation in American English. *Journal of Sociolinguistics*, *12*(1), 58–88. doi:10.1111/j.1467-9841.2008.00353.x

Blood, R. (2004). How blogging software reshapes the online community. *Communications of the ACM*, *47*(12), 53–55. doi:10.1145/1035134.1035165

Bucholtz, M. (2000). Language and youth culture. *American Speech, 75*(3), 280–283. doi:10.1215/00031283-75-3-280

Coates, J. (1993, 2004). Women, men, and language: A sociolinguistic account of gender differences in language. Harlow, UK: Pearson Longman.

Coupland, N. (2001). Language, situation, and the relational self: Theorizing dialect-style in socio-linguistics. In Eckert, P., & Rickford, J. R. (Eds.), *Style and sociolinguistic variation* (pp. 185–210). Cambridge, UK: Cambridge University Press.

Coupland, N. (2007). *Style: Language variation and identity*. Cambridge, UK: Cambridge University Press.

Crystal, D. (2006). *Language and the internet* (2nd ed.). Cambridge, UK: Cambridge University Press. doi:10.1017/CBO9780511487002

Erickson, T. (1999). Persistent conversation: An Introduction. *Journal of Computer-mediated Communication, 4*. Retrieved July 18, 2007, from http://jcmc.indiana.edu/vol4/issue4/erick-sonintro.html

Erikson, E. (1956, 2008). The problem of ego identity. In D. L. Browning (Ed.), Adolescent identities: A collection of readings (pp. 223-240). New York: The Analytic Press.

Fitzpatrick, L. (2008, August 12). Making an arguement for misspelling. *Time*, Retrieved (n.d.), from http://www.time.com/time/world/article/0,8599,1832104,00.html

Gong, W., & Ooi, V. B. Y. (2008). Innovations and motivations in online chat. In Kelsey, S., & St.Amant, K. (Eds.), *Research handbook on computer mediated communication* (*Vol. 1*, pp. 917–933). Hershey, PA: Information Science Reference.

Gumbrecht, M. (2004). *Blogs as "protected space"*. Paper presented at the Workshop on the Weblogging Ecosystem: Aggregation, Analysis, and Dynamics: WWW 2004.

Hogan, R. (1991). Engendered autobiographies: The diary as a feminine form. *Prose Studies: History, Theory. Criticism, 14*(2), 95–107.

Le Page, R. B., & Tabouret-Keller, A. (1985). *Acts of identity: Creole-based approaches to language and ethnicity*. Cambridge, UK: Cambridge University Press.

McGann, R. (2004). The blogosphere by the numbers. *The ClickZ Network*. Retrieved September 29, 2008, from http://www.clickz.com/ showPage.html?page=3438891

Mendoza-Denton, N. (2002). Language and identity. In Chambers, J. K., Trudgill, P., & Schilling-Estes, N. (Eds.), *The handbook of language variation and change* (pp. 475–499). Malden, MA: Blackwell Publishers.

Mondorf, B. (2002). Gender differences in English syntax. *Journal of English Linguistics, 30*(2), 158–180. doi:10.1177/007242030002005

Ooi, V. B. Y. (2002). Aspects of computer-mediated communication for research in Corpus Linguistics. In Peters, P., Collins, P., & Smith, A. (Eds.), *New frontiers of corpus research: Papers from the twenty first international conference on English language research on computerized corpora, Sydney 2000* (pp. 91–104). Amsterdam, New York: Rodopi.

Orlowski, A. (2003). Most bloggers "are teenage girls"- survey [Electronic Version]. *The Register*. Retrieved September 29, 2008, from http://www.theregister.co.uk/ 2003/05/30/most_bloggers_are_teenage_girls/

Pedersen, S., & Macafee, C. (2007). Gender differences in British blogging. *Journal of Computer-Mediated Communication, 12*(4). doi:10.1111/j.1083-6101.2007.00382.x

Riley, P. (2007). *Language, culture and identity: An ethnolinguistic perspective*. London: Continuum.

Romaine, S. (2003). Variation in language and gender. In Holmes, J., & Meyerhoff, M. (Eds.), *The handbook of language and gender* (pp. 98–118). Malden, MA: Blackwell. doi:10.1002/9780470756942.ch4

Stenström, A.-B., Anderson, G., & Hasund, I. K. (2002). *Trends in teenage talk: Corpus compilation, analysis and findings*. Philadelphia: Benjamins.

Thompson, N. (2003). *Communication and language: A handbook of theory and practice*. Basingstoke. Hampshire, UK: Palgrave MacMillan.

Thomson, R., & Murachver, T. (2001). Predicting gender from electronic discourse. *The British Journal of Social Psychology, 40*(2), 193–208. doi:10.1348/014466601164812

Vaughan, G. M., & Hogg, M. A. (2005). Introduction to social psychology (4th ed.). Frenchs Forest, Upper Saddle River, NJ: Prentice Hall.

Weber, S., & Mitchell, C. (2008). Imaging, keyboarding, and posting identities: Young people and new media technologies. In Buckingham, D. (Ed.), *Youth, identity, and digital media* (pp. 25–47). Cambridge, MA: The MIT Press.

ENDNOTES

[1] http://www.livejournal.com/

[2] http://www.blogcn.com/

APPENDIX: UCREL SEMANTIC TAGSET

Table 7.

A1.5.1	Using	N3.7	Measurement: Length & height
A14	Exclusivizers/particularizers	N3.8	Measurement: Speed
A5.1-	Evaluation: Bad	O1.2	Substances and materials: Liquid
A6.2+	Comparing: Usual/unusual	O2	Objects generally
A8	Seem	O3	Electricity and electrical equipment
A9+	Getting and possession	P1	Education in general
B1	Anatomy and physiology	Q1.2	Paper documents and writing
B3	Medicines and medical treatment	Q1.3	Telecommunications
B4	Cleaning and personal care	Q2.1	Speech: Communicative
B5	Clothes and personal belongings	Q2.2	Speech acts
E1	Emotional Actions, States And Processes General	S1.1.1	Social Actions, States And Processes
E4.1+	Happy	S2.1	People: Female
F2+	Excessive drinking	S4	Kin
F4	Farming & Horticulture	S9	Religion and the supernatural
H5	Furniture and household fittings	T1.1.2	Time: Present; simultaneous
I2.2	Business: Selling	T1.1.3	Time: Future
K2	Music and related activities	W4	Weather
K3	Recorded sound	Y2	Information technology and computing
K5.1	Sports	Z1	Personal names
K5.2	Games	Z4	Discourse Bin
L3	Plants	Z5	Grammatical bin
M3	Vehicles and transport on land	Z6	Negative
M6	Location and direction	Z8	Pronouns
N1	Numbers	Z99	Unmatched

Chapter 10
Discourse Features in Nigerian Online Discussion Forums

Rotimi Taiwo
Obafemi Awolowo University, Nigeria/University of Freiburg, Germany

ABSTRACT

This chapter investigates discourse features in asynchronous Nigerian discussion forums, which is now becoming a popular medium for discussing issues of interest to many Nigerians. The sample was based on extracts from CONCOMED, a corpus of Nigerian Computer-mediated English Discourse compiled by this researcher between 2006 and 2009. Four threads, one for each year were subjected to analysis based on Herring's (2004) Computer Mediated Discourse Analysis (CMDA) framework. Analysis focused on interaction features of turn-taking, topic focus and coherence. Turn-taking process in the threads was a complex phenomenon characterized by non-sequential turns and adjacency disruptions. Interactants typically self-selected and used Quoting as turn tracking device. Global topics often split into sub-topics to address details. Despite the limitations of messaging systems on sequential turn-taking and referencing, interactional and topical coherence was established in the threads, as participants were able to logically connect their ideas in this complex virtual conversational context through Quoting, Addressivity and topic focus.

INTRODUCTION

Connecting people across distance and time has always been the goal of communication. In contemporary times the emergence of social interactive technologies like the Internet, which serve as mediators between people has greatly increased the number of people that can be reached as fast as possible at a time. Since the Internet is a forum for disseminating various kinds of information, several discursive activities, such as electronic mailing, chats, discussions, blogging, social networking, and so on are its regular features. Chayko (2002: 40) describes the cyberspace as a socio-mental space where almost all we do in face-to-face contact, such as meeting, dating, chatting, counseling, teaching and so forth

DOI: 10.4018/978-1-61520-827-2.ch010

can be done. Emerging activities on the Internet and communicative forms in computer-mediated communication in recent times have been major focus of scholars in linguistics, communication studies, sociology, computer science, psychology and other related disciplines.

This chapter focuses on one of such activities, which is one of the most popular on the Internet – discussion forum. Discussion forum is sometimes referred to as message board, Internet forum, Web forums, newsgroups, discussion boards, (electronic) discussion groups and bulletin boards. In this chapter, discussion forum will be used interchangeably with Internet forum. Internet forums emerged to meet the need of humans to share their views with a wider audience within the cyberspace. An Internet forum is a website developed for people to share ideas or opinions about various topics. Internet forums have become very popular online media for individuals, corporate bodies and interest groups. It developed from the Bulletin Board Systems (BBSs), which were the first type of online discussion groups developed from the 1970s. The BBS is a system used in the early years of computing. A user with a personal computer could dial up to a computer that hosted a BBS and leave a message for any other users. Later in the 1980s, the Usenet, a network of newsgroup emerged in which each newsgroup functions like an Internet message board covering different topics. According to Edwards (2005), the format is similar to e-mail, but rather than a message being transmitted from a single user to another user, such a message is posted to many users. In the 1990s, the Usenet and bulletin board system merged to give us the Internet forums we have today.

An Internet forum is an asynchronous online medium usually created for specific community of online users and managed by an administrator who is responsible for the technical details and maintenance of the forum. The administrator also defines the kinds of topics that users can post and the appropriate conduct of users on the forum. Topics in Internet forums are posted in what is generally described as 'threads.' Each thread contains an original message and responses to that message. In some forums, users need to register before they can participate in discussion, while in many others, users do not require any prior registration to participate.

The concern of this chapter is to examine some discourse features in two selected Nigerian Internet forums – *Nairaland* and *Nigerian Village Square*. These forums are considered Nigerian because the topics discussed are Nigerian issues. They were chosen because of their relative popularity among internet users in Nigeria and Nigerians in the Diaspora. Topics discussed include the economic, political, religious and social situations in the country. Other specific topics include investment, information technology, automobiles, tourism, and so forth.

DIGITAL COMMUNICATION IN NIGERIA

Unlike in advanced economies, Nigerians did not start getting actively involved in digital communication until the late 1990s. The government of Nigeria, having recognized the crucial role Information and Communication Technologies could play in the socio-economic development of the nation in a rapidly changing global environment approved a National Policy for Information Technology for the nation in March 2001. In addition, later in the year, the government deregulated the telecommunication sector and introduced the Global System for Mobile Communications (GSM). Prior to this time there were only a few dial-up e-mail and Internet service providers in the country and digital communication was characterized by slow internet links, poor services and high cost due to the federal government owned Nigerian Telecommunications Limited's (NITEL) monopoly. The regulatory efforts of the Nigerian Communications Commission from the late 1990s led to the availability of a wide range of voice, data and internet applications and services. This boom in digital technology has led to increased communication through mobile phone and the Internet. Electronic mailing still remains the most popular form of Internet communication used in Nigeria and next to it is discussion forum.

Discussion forums started becoming popular when Nigerians were presented with the opportunity to have direct access to Internet facilities in their homes on their WAP-enabled mobile phones, smart phones and PCs using their phones as a modem. This enables many Nigerians, especially the young people to spend more time on the Internet in the comfort of their homes. It also saves them from the stress of patronizing internet cafes otherwise known in Nigeria as cybercafés where they sometimes have to take turns to use Internet facilities. As a result of the increased participation of young Nigerians in online communication, several Internet forums have emerged, whose major concern is mainly to discuss daily happenings in the nation and other issues that are of interest to people. Some of the general interest forums are, *Nairaland, Naijadiscussion, Nigerian Village Square, Motherland Nigeria, NaijaDotcom*. The range of issues discussed on these forums includes, entertainment, news, politics, economy, religion, culture, and so on. While many of the forums discuss general interest issues, several others are hosted by companies, celebrities and interest groups and therefore discuss more focused issues. The ones with more specific focus are: *Naijand* (a social discussion network), *MPACUK: Muslim Discussion Forum* (http://forum.mpacuk.org/), *The PC Guide Discussion Forum* (http://www.pcguide.com/vb/), *Dandali: Northern Nigerian Discussion Forum* (http://groups.yahoo.com/phrase/dandali), *Nigerian Christian Singles* (http://nigerianxtiansingles.forumotion.com/), and so forth.

PERSPECTIVES ON ONLINE DISCUSSION FORUMS

The rapid increase in communication through the Internet in the last two decades has attracted considerable interest from language researchers. One of the major issues scholars discuss is identity construction and the significant role language plays in the expression of identity in online forums (Warschuer, 2000; Warschuer and De Florio-Hansen, 2003). According to Donath (1998: 29), language patterns evolve within the community as the participants develop idiosyncratic styles of interaction - especially phrases and abbreviations, such as BTW, IMHO (By The Way, In My Humble Opinion). Despite that most online forums are organized in such a way that participants are able to appreciate quickly the overall structure of a conversation in the sense of specifically knowing who is replying to whom, since the writer's name is automatically included, identity cues are still sparse.

Several other scholars, mostly behavioral and educational psychologists have concentrated on how text-based learner online discussion forums or virtual learning forums can facilitate learning. Such forums are seen as socially constructive learning tool which can motivate positive and collaborative learning for students (Markel, 2001; Larkin-Hein, 2001; Althaus, 1997; and O'Reilly & Newton, 2001). Hwang (2008) conducted an experiment and examined the effectiveness of synchronous CMC (SCMC: text chatting) and asynchronous CMC (ASCMC: postings on bulletin boards) modes in Korean EFL instruction. The author discovered that asynchronous CMC may be more effective in promoting a richer lexicon and syntactically more complex output because learners had more time for choice of appropriate words. Fitze (2006) also supported this view as he observes that during written electronic conferences, learners were better able to use and practise a wide range of vocabulary related to the topics. The Internet also provides opportunities for cross-cultural contacts and some scholars view this as an opportunity for foreign language learners to interact with native speakers thereby connecting with the target culture. Hanna and de Nooy (2003) described how four Anglo-phone students based in Britain and USA explored a primarily Franco-phone forum to improve their French. In spite of the widespread agreement on the educational potential of CMC conferencing, Hewitt (2001) identify one apparent limitation of the medium – despite the fact that online environment supports electronic conversations that expand and branch, they are typically filled with reply-based interaction and participants rarely engage in convergent processes.

Apart from its use for expanding the frontiers of knowledge and motivating learning, internet forums serve to link many people interactively across great distances especially diasporic ethnic groups wishing to sustain identity in an 'alien' land and maintain constant touch with their 'home' (Bastian, 1999; Parham, 2004; Ojo, 2005). Bastian (1999), a pioneering study on the activities of Nigerians in the Diaspora on the Internet, discusses Nigerian immigrants' discourses on nationalism in what she called "a virtual nationalist community": *Naijanet*. She observes that despite that the discourse was in English, when the interactants wanted to make humorous statements, "they used Nigerian forms of English and/or interspersed proverbs in Nigerian languages (usually with English translations) in their stories." The use of domesticated Nigerian English, Pidgin and other Nigerian linguistic markers signify a measure of cultural identity of participants. Bastian just like Ojo (2005) noted how the Internet provided a forum for Nigerians residing in Europe and USA to participate in discussions on national issues and even mount political pressure on dictatorial governments and corrupt leaders (Ojo, 2005: 168, Taiwo, 2007)

Research work by language scholars on language use by Nigerians in digital discourse are very few and far between. Most of the work done so far focused on how language is used to construct the Nigerian identity in SMS. Some of the issues discussed include text multilingualism (Awonusi, 2004); the use of indigenous languages (Ofulue, 2004); text messaging in religious contexts (Chiluwa, 2008); and linguistic forms and functions of Nigerian SMS (Taiwo, 2008). Another study on language use in the digital media by Nigerians is Ifukor (2008). It is a pragmatic study on face claims by diasporic as well as home-based Nigerians in weblogs. The author investigates the socio-political influences, communal concerns and democratic aspirations that shaped the use of language in some selected weblogs and he concludes that virtual face claims by Nigerians are predicated on citizen activism whose goal is the collective well-being of the polity.

Some specific studies on CMC focus on discourse organization. While some scholars argue from the discourse organization and structural coherence approach that discourse is principally oriented around structural coherence and sequential coordination (Schiffrin, 1987; Bruce, 1996), others approach discourse organization from the interpersonally/interactionally oriented approach, which identifies how verbal elements in discourse implicitly anchor utterances "vis-à-vis the communicative restraints of a culture and society, the demands of aspects of politeness, and the prevalent norms of affect and involvement." (Ostman, 1995; Cook, 2001 quoted in Jung-ran Park, 2007). Such studies suggest that CMC employs a high degree of interpersonally oriented language (Jung-ran Park, 2007). In a study of real time synchronous chats of a math help chat group for K-12 students, Jung-ran Park (2007) submits that the students employed a variety of dynamic creative linguistic and paralinguistic devices to handle the flow of affective and interpersonal stances that are absent in CMC discourse. She identifies such devices as contractions of linguistic forms, prosodic features, and typographical conventions such as capital letters and emoticons to simulate gesture and facial expressions.

Related to the last approach discussed above is the work of a group of scholars (Harrison, 1998, 2004; Herring, 1999; Panyametheekul & Herring, 2003) who indicates that despite that CMC is different significantly from face-to-face interaction, some features whose occurrences have been copiously discussed in face-to-face interactions by scholars have also been found to be present. These interactional features include turn taking, turn allocation, and coherence. However, as noted by Herring (1999), participants in online discussion face certain challenges, such as lack of non-verbal cues and disrupted turn adjacency, a condition in which logically-related turns are separated by unrelated turns, often from other conversations. The latter is caused by technical properties of CMC systems such as delays in message transmission (e.g., system "lag") and the linear display of messages in the order received by the system, without regard for the senders' intentions to respond to a particular message (Panyametheekul & Herring, 2003). Herring (1999) also notes that topics decay quickly in asynchronous discussions because off-topic digressions and tangential observations often move the discussion away from its original focus. In a related work, Herring and Nix (1997) found in their study of a social chat channel that nearly half of all the turns were "off-topics" in relation to the turn to which they were responding. In order to track turns in asynchronous group discussion, strategies such as Linking (referring explicitly to the content of a previous message) and Quoting (copying portions of a previous message in the response) are used. Panyametheekul & Herring, (2003) in their investigation of Thai language chat room submit that turn allocation in the chat room is generally similar to that in face-to-face conversation, in the sense that participants address one another, rather than self-selecting to speak. This strategy promotes coherence by creating linkage between turns. Harrison (2004) also agrees that participants in electronic discussions engage in recognizable discussion and speaker change

also occurs as in face-to-face interactions. She corroborates Herring's (1999) submission that participants in asynchronous discussions indicate the topic they are contributing or responding to by using subject lines in the message header, quoting previous message, paraphrasing, and naming the writer of a previous message. It is obvious from the review of past work on synchronous and asynchronous online discourses that they focused on advanced and well developed online cultures. Despite that online culture is relatively new in Nigeria, it is the fastest growing and most vibrant in Africa. Building on the previous studies, the present study explored the extent to which some of the identified discourse features can be found in Nigerian online discourse.

METHODOLOGY

The research reported in this chapter is based on an investigation carried out on features of discourse in two popular Nigerian online discussion forums: *Nairaland* and *Nigerian Village Square*. The sample is based on extracts from CONCOMED, a corpus of Nigerian Computer-mediated English Discourse compiled by this researcher between 2006 and 2009. The corpus consists of 750,000 words postings to the two discussion forums, which are devoted to discussions organized around various issue on Nigerian socio-economic and political situations, such as, politics, religion, culture, romance, education, jobs/vacancies, career, properties, health, travel, food, business, family, entertainment, technology and so forth. A preliminary analysis of overall language structure showed that threads in the forums share similar patterns in terms of the discourse features examined. For easy referencing, each of the threads used was coded as follows:

F1: Speaking out against bride price practice
F2: Ekiti to immortalize Abacha

F3: Oyedepo curses robbers who raided his church

F4: New helmet rule in Lagos

Also, postings were numbered using the hash (#) symbol. For instance, an example with the numbering F2 #63 will mean the second thread above (Ekiti to immortalize Abacha) and the 63rd posting on the thread.

The samples were selected in such a way that the threads were also chosen to reflect the four broad dimensions of the Nigerian life that typically dominate online forums – cultural, political, religious and social issues.

The data from the forums were subjected to extensive discussion based on Herring's (2004) Computer Mediated Discourse Analysis (CMDA) framework. CMDA is a set of methods grounded in linguistic discourse analysis with focus on patterns of structure and meaning in CMC. CMDA typically focuses on four domains of language – structure, meaning, interaction and social behavior. This chapter is focused on the interactional aspect of online communication and my discussion is based on the observed patterns of turn taking, coherence and topic focus in the selected forums.

Turn taking is a basic feature of conversation first discussed in Sacks et al. (1974). According to Oreström (1983), it is a phenomenon deeply rooted in human communication founded on a mutual awareness of sharing something. According to Sacks et al. (1974), at one time in the conversation, one participant holds the floor and to avoid simultaneous talking or awkward pauses, speaker-change recurs, or at least occurs (p.706). Speakers also use different turn allocation techniques. For instance, current speaker may select a next speaker (as when he addresses a question to another speaker); or speakers may self-select (p. 716). For turn-taking, I focused on turn allocation techniques and the extent to which the three turn-allocation techniques identified by Sacks et al. (1974), i.e, current speaker selecting next speaker; next speaker self-selecting and current speaker continues) were used in the forums. I added another turn-allocation technique in which the current speaker simply throw an issue open to participants. I also looked at the turn-tracking devices identified by Herring (1999), i.e, Addressivity (the act of prefacing turn with user name of the intended addressee); Linking (referring explicitly to the content of a previous message in a posting); and Quoting (copying portions of a previous message in a posting).

In interpreting the data, I also examined the overall logical connectedness of the interactions in the threads (coherence). Coherence is an important textual feature which shows how the entire text sticks together to form a meaningful whole. In the data, I examined how the different postings in the threads unified to give the reader a meaningful discourse.

Another discourse feature examined is topic focus. In any meaningful interaction, participants always keep the topic in mind as they participate. One of Grice's (1975) conversational maxims of-

Table 1. Overview of the data selection

SN	Forum	Topic	Date	Type	No of Postings
F1	Nairaland	Speaking out against the bride price practice	March 18 2006	Culture	63
F2	Nigerian Village Square	Ekiti to immortalise Abacha	September 28, 2007	Politics	87
F3	Nigerian Village Square	Oyedepo curses robbers who raided his church	February 5 2008	Religion	58
F4	Nairaland	New helmet rule in Lagos	January 3 2009	Social	100
Total					308

ten tagged the 'supermaxim' because it is central to the orderliness of conversation – the maxim of relevance stresses the importance of participants in any discourse ensuring that the information being provided is relevant to the topic under discussion. Adherence to this topic limits random topic shifts in discourse. Since this work deals with threads in online discourse, I examined the extent to which participants focus on the topics that generated discussions in threads. These three discourse features examined (turn –taking, coherence and topic focus) are interwoven and core aspects of interactional discourse. It is expected that conversational turns should be relevant to the topic. It is also the case that the logical connection of all the turns produces a coherent conversation.

BACKGROUND INFORMATION ON THE DATA

The first thread (F1) posted on *Nairaland* on March 18, 2006 was a discussion based on a cultural practice in Nigeria during marriages, which is called 'bride price.' Since marriage is a family affair in the Nigerian culture, family members have to give their consent to the union of a couple. Before this consent is given, the groom's family is expected to pay a certain amount of money to the bride's family In addition to some gift items. The amount of money paid varies from one culture to another. This practice has been subject to abuse in some parts of Nigeria as some families sometimes demand exceptionally high 'bride price.' The thread started by asking for opinions of members on this practice. The poster felt the payment of bride price amounted to 'selling' women. The thread generated a lot of interesting arguments for and against the practice

The second thread (F2) was generated by a political news item published in *This Day Online*, a Nigerian newspaper on 28th September, 2007 and posted the same day on *Nigerian Village Square*. The news was about the plan of Ekiti State (one

of the states in southern Nigeria created in 1996) to honor General Sani Abacha, a former military ruler who created the state. General Sani Abacha was an unpopular military ruler who took over power from the quasi-civilian interim government that followed General Ibrahim Babangida after the latter annulled the June 12 1993 elections won by M.K.O. Abiola, a Yoruba businessman. His regime suffered stiff opposition both internally and externally from pro-democracy activists. He also remained resistant to both internal and international insistence on human rights reforms until he was reported to have died of cardiac arrest after six years of taking over power. The Yoruba people were the greatest opposition to Abacha's government, because of his opposition to their access to power. The posting generated heated discussions and series of flaming statements reflecting ethnic sentiments of members.

The third thread (F3), also a news item titled 'Oyedepo curses robbers who raided his church', was published in *Sun News Online* on February 4, 2008 and posted on *Nigerian Village Square* on February 5, 2008. David Oyedepo is the founder and presiding bishop of the Living Faith Church, reputed to have the largest church auditorium in the world by *Guiness Book of World Records 2008*. On January 31st 2008, armed robbers attacked three banks located within the premises of the Church, made away with an undisclosed amount of money and killed two policemen. Oyedepo was alleged to have directed his members to pray and invite the wrath of God on the criminals. Participants in the thread were divided along the lines of their opinions. While some agreed with the action of the preacher, others felt it was against the scriptures to curse one's enemies. Participants from the two sides made analogies from bible passages to support their positions.

The last thread (F4) was an opinion-seeking thread posted on *Nairaland* on January 3, 2009 titled 'New Helmet Rule in Lagos'. The use of motorcycles as commercial vehicles which has become very popular in Nigeria was the subject

Table 2. Turn allocation strategies in the data

SN	Turn allocation strategies	No	Percentage
1	Current speaker selects next speaker	21	6.82%
2	Next speaker self-selects	268	87.01%
3	Current speaker continues	08	2.60%
4	Current speaker throws an issue open to all	11	3.57%
Total		308	100%

of this thread. The Federal Road Safety Corps (FRSC) started enforcing a law that made it an offence to ride a motorcycle without putting on a crash helmet with effect from January 1st 2009. The poster who started the thread asked members to express their 'opinions and fears' on this new law. Various postings were made on the thread, stressing the socio-cultural implications of the law on those who daily use commercial motorcycles, popularly referred to in Nigeria as 'okada.'

DISCOURSE FEATURES OF NIGERIAN ONLINE FORUMS

The results of the analysis of turn allocation strategies for the threads as presented in Table 2 reveal that majority of the speakers (268: 87.01%) self-selected. This is different from what obtains in Thai online chats as presented in Panyametheekul & Herring (2003), where current speaker selects the next speaker was used the most. There were only 21 instances of current speaker explicitly selecting the next speaker in the data.

Findings also reveal that current speakers select next speakers mostly through the use of interrogative expressions directed to one of the participants, usually naming them, for instance:

Ex. 1 A, wetin be dis? Why your parapo dey embarrass man pikin like dis? (A, what is this? Why are your people embarrassing people?) (F2: #3)

Ex. 2 G, wetin dey puzzle you? (G, what surprised you?) (F2: #45)

Ex. 3 what did you do that he decided to dash you away? (F1: #58)

In most instances where the current speaker selects next speaker, the names of such next speakers were mentioned (Ex 1 and 2), and when they were not named, there would be enough contextual clues to indicate who the current speaker wanted to speak next. In Ex 3, where the next speaker was not named, a portion of one of the previous messages copied by the current speaker preceded the question, which showed clearly that the question was meant for the person who posted that message. There were also instances of current speaker throwing an issue open to all participants or an identified group of participants.

Ex 4 I would like to hear what more ladies think about this though (F1: #23)

Ex 5 Someone should please define bride price? Then define dowry… I am still …i am still waiting. (F1: #31)

In Ex 4, the topic of the forum is 'Speaking out against bride price. The poster had just expressed her idea in support of bride price and she wanted opinions of the female members of the forum. There were very few instances of the current speaker continuing (8: 2.60%). This is not likely to happen frequently in busy forums with heavy traffics like the ones used in this study. Some of the instances in the data may be cases of participants fragmenting their postings, thereby leading to multiple posting as response to previous ones in the thread. An example in the data is a case of one participant who made three consecutive postings in a thread within six minutes (7.18 – 7.26 pm) on January 4, 2009.

Participants post their contributions to threads in response to earlier posts. One post therefore naturally generates another in online threads and this gives a typical thread the structure of initiations and responses. It is however not always a smooth transition from initiations to responses. Sometimes, adjacency was broken with postings not directly related to the previous comment. This is illustrated in the sequence below from F2.

#25 Sept. 28, 2007, 5.58 pm (OS makes general comments)

#26 Sept. 28, 2007, 6.37 pm (FL quotes AU and responds to the issue)

#27 Sept. 28, 2007, 6.52 pm (AU addresses AB)

#28 Sept. 28, 2007, 6.56 pm (FL quotes AB's posting #15 and responds to the issue)

#29 Sept. 28, 2007, 7.14 pm (OM quotes FL's posting #28 and responds to the issue)

#30 Sept. 28, 2007, 7.21 pm (FL quotes OM's posting #29 and responds to the issue)

#31 Sept. 28, 2007, 7.21 pm (TS makes general comment)

#32 Sept. 28, 2007, 7.34 pm (AU addresses AB; cc: all)

#33 Sept. 28, 2007, 10.14 pm (DW quotes AB's posting #15 and responds to the issue)

#34 Sept. 28, 2007, 10.35 pm VO (addresses AU)

#35 Sept. 28, 2007, 10.39 pm (AU responds to VO's posting #34)

#36 Sept. 28, 2007, 10. 42 (AF makes general comment)

#37 Sept. 28, 2007, 11.00 pm (AU responds to AF's posting #36)

#38 Sept. 28, 2007, 11.14 pm (AM makes general comments)

#39 Sept. 28, 2007, 11.32 pm (AU makes general comments)

#40 Sept. 28, 2007, 11.43 pm (AB addresses AM)

#41 Sept. 28, 2007, (11.54 pm (GT quotes OS's posting #25 and responds to the issue)

In the sequences above, posting #30 came as a direct response to its adjacent post #29. Other responses adjacent to their initiations are postings #35 and 37. However, posting #41 did not come as a response to posting #25 until after several other postings have occurred, breaking the adjacency. This shows how complex turn taking can be in asynchronous online forums. There were also instances of initiations that were not responded to. Two peculiar instances were questions on identity of the poster of the issue that started F1, the thread on bride price.

Ex. 6 BG: BB by the way, are you a female? You sound like you are but am not sure (F1 #25)

EX. 9 TS: @BB, are you a Nigerian?

These two questions seeking to know the gender and nationality of BB were not answered by the addressee despite that he/she was a very active participant all through the thread. The masking of explicit identity reduces participants' accountability. It also allows people to be other than 'themselves,' or more of themselves than they normally express (Danet & Ruedenberg, 1994)

Two of the selected threads were started off with posting of news from Nigerian newspapers. These news items were the kinds that would naturally generate discussion in offline situations as in the context of newspaper vendor's stands in Nigeria, where readers who cannot afford to buy newspapers gather to read and discuss important national issues published in the newspapers. The

Table 3. Turn-tracking devices in the data

SN	Turn-tracking devices	No	Percentage
1	Addressivity	87	34.66%
2	Linking	15	5.98%
3	Quoting	149	59.36%
Total		251	100%

two others started off with opinions that later generated threads of arguments.

The turn-tracking devices used in the data as presented in Table 3 show that the most common turn-tracking device was Quoting, which accounts for almost 60% of the turn-tracking devices used.

Quoting is a very effective turn-tracking device in online forums because it helps participants and visitors to easily follow the trend of discussions without having to go back to previous postings or ask questions about issues that had already been addressed earlier in the thread. According to Herring (1999), "Quoting creates the illusion of adjacency in that it incorporates and juxtaposes (portions of) two turns - an initiation and a response within a single message". It therefore allows interactants to maintain and track patterns of turn-taking despite overlapping exchanges and delayed responses. The paucity of use of Linking may be due to the fact that Quoting, according to Herring (1999) functions as a subtype of Linking, and whichever is used is just a matter of choice for interactants. It may also be that it was more convenient for interactants to quote earlier posts than to link. Quoting is just a matter of clicking on a button to copy the relevant portions of the previous message, so it saves time. Linking on the other hand makes explicit reference to contents of previous messages, so it requires some form of construction.

Addresivity is also fairly used as a turn-tracking device, next to Quoting. The regular way of signaling addressivity in the threads was the use of the aspersand, the typographic character '@'

to preface the posting, eg, @ Amy. This is the regular convention in most asynchronous discussion forums. However, many of the interactants prefaced their turn with the addressee's user name, nickname or abbreviation of name of the intended addressee. This in some instances was done with a note of familiarity. Some of the names were not reproduced as given by the intended addressee, but written in the poster's own style to reflect familiarity. Some instances are given below

Online name of intended addressee Poster's version

Auspicious Auspy, Auspiro
Mikky Jaga Mikky Baba
UncleTisha UT
Osibinaebi Osinabros

Another interesting aspect of addressivity is that sometimes, instead of prefacing the post with the intended addressee's name, other endearing socio-cultural address terms, such as *Nne* (an Igbo name for 'mother', which is also used as an endearing address form for ladies); *my broda* (my brother); *Sista* (a Nigerian Pidgin phonemic spelling of sister) were used. Sometimes, participants explicitly addressed the entire community by prefacing their post with greetings, such as *'Hi folks', 'Dear all'*.

Despite that there were turn exchanges in the data they were not sequential in the sense of relevant responses occurring temporally to initiating turns as observed by Sacks et al. (1974) in face-to-face interaction, there were high incidences of disrupted exchanges. Sometimes, postings of related news were injected into a thread to redirect the flow of topic. For instance, in F2, three different postings were injected into the thread at different times. The first one was a quotation credited to late Dr Beko Ransom-Kuti, a social critic on General Obasanjo which was earlier posted in another thread.

EX. 10 I think the military government was a disaster for this country...General Obasanjo was a year below me at Abeokuta. People who joined the army at that time were either people who could not read or were so poor that they could not get on on their own. With that group of people ruling the country, they tended to develop a complex and they really didn't understand what they were doing, and they made a mess of the whole thing. (F2 #64)

This posting was meant to support some of the arguments made earlier about the atrocities committed by the military in government and also strengthen the argument that Obasanjo (a two-time ruler of Nigeria) was not different from Abacha. One of the other two postings was a press release by the campaign office of the opponent of the governor of Ekiti State during the 2007 elections. The posting succeeded in sustaining the argument of those who opposed the decision of the Ekiti State government to immortalize Abacha. The last of the injected, related postings came at a time when the thread was witnessing series of flaming utterances. The participants had started becoming aggressive and using overly provocative, rude and insulting language on one another. One of the participants described the situation as a 'brewing civil war' and another member as 'an internet militant'. The news item published in *Daily Independent*, announced the reversal of the decision to immortalize Abacha by the Ekiti State government. This posting doused the tension in the thread as it changed the direction of discourse tilting the topic away from its focus on

the situation in Ekiti State to the general political situation in the country for a while. Emotional outbursts in this discussion forum, leading to verbal abuse of other members was sparked off by perceived ethnic sentiments. Carnegie-Mellon researchers in an experiment comparing decision-making through face-to-face discourse with that conducted electronically, noted that electronic communications convey none of the nonverbal cues of personal conversation - the eye contact, facial expressions and voice inflections that provide social feedback and may inhibit extreme behavior therefore ''talking'' by computer took longer to agree (Eckholm, 1984). This is especially true in context of Nigeria's linguistic and ethnic heterogeneity, which usually makes discussions on political issues to generate heated debate and sometimes flaming utterances even in face-to-face interactions. Flaming and other impolite behavior directed at other participants in discussion forums are common in political threads by Nigerians because of intolerance of opinions on political figures by participants. It is also common for participants to direct their flaming at political leaders for their failure to move the country forward (Taiwo, 2009).

There were attempts by some interactants on the thread to post off-topic issues thereby leading to digressions, but this did not have any significant impact on the overall coherence of the threads. For instance the injection of a lengthy cover story of *The News*, a weekly magazine on another church leader in F3 had very little impact on the flow of topic in the thread. Interactants kept track on the original topic, quoting copiously from earlier postings and responding to them. Although there were cases of movement from global topics to more specific and detailed issues in the threads, there was never any time the threads went completely off the topics that started them off. The practice was to tie the specific issues to the broad topic that started the threads. For instance F4 started off asking for opinions and fears of members of the community on the new crash helmet rule. The first set of postings just commented generally on the policy. Much later, specific issues like the cost of helmets, hygienic aspect of the rule if riders have to share helmet, superstitions about the possibility of people being used for rituals, the social convenience of the practice for women and the possibility of individuals who patronize commercial motorcyclists having personal helmets came up. Discussions in a thread would normally continue until when members thought there was nothing else to discuss and they simply took their exit one by one usually without announcing it. It is unusual for a participant to announce his or her exit as done by one of the participants in F4

EX. 11 WW: I THINK I'VE HAD ENOUGH WITH THIS THREAD. BYE EVERYONE

The use of all capital letters here is significant. The expression is beyond just announcing WW's exit. It may be interpreted to mean WW was deliberately announcing his exit to make other participants know that one of the most active members was tired of the winding nature of the discussions in the thread. The use of all capitals in English CMC is usually interpreted to mean an expression of strong emotions or appearance of 'shouting' (Nishimura, 2007).

The posting reveal two major patterns of responding to initiations in the thread: single response to many initiating messages and multiple responses to a single message. Since it is not possible to reproduce a discussion list sequence due to its typically length, I present two sequences to show the representations of the two patterns identified in the threads.

F2: AB (posting #15)
Quote 1: DW (posting #3 and response)
Quote 2: GA (posting #4 and response)
Quote 3: UT (posting #5 and response)
Quote 4: MJ (posting #6 and response)

In the sequence above, AB in posting #15 responded to 4 different messages by quoting the original posters and then giving the response to the quoted message.

F4: SLB (posting #22)
Quote: EG (posting #12)
Response 1 (to the first argument in the first 3 sentences)
Response 2 (to the second argument in the fourth sentence)
Response 3 (to the third argument in the fifth sentence)
Response 4 (to the fourth argument in the fifth Sentence)

In the second sequence above, SLB responded to the different issues raised in a single message.

This complex pattern of interaction is constrained by the time lag between when messages were sent and when they were responded to and the amount of time spent by a participant online. For instance, a participant who logged on and noticed several posts he or she needed to respond to might decide to respond to all the posts in a single turn resulting to what we have in the first sequence. On the other hand issues discussed in a single post may interest a participant so much that he or she decided to take up each move in the message one after the other as shown in the second sequence. With these patterns of turn exchanges the threads generally presented sequentially incoherent discourse but topically coherent since the majority of the turns did not deviate from the global topics in spite of occasional narrowing of topics to discuss details.

ONLINE FORUM AND THE FUTURE OF DIGITAL DISCOURSE IN NIGERIA

With the widespread in the use of computer and the Internet, Nigerians' involvement in online activities has greatly increased. Electronic mail still remains the most popular online activity due to the potential power it has to replace letter writing. Online forum is fast becoming a popular medium for discussing issues of general interest to Nigerians. The use of forums for discussing Nigerian issues was started by Nigerians in the Diaspora interested in national political issues. Now, Nigerians living in Nigeria have adopted it not only as a medium for discussing national politics, but any issue at all. Many discussion forums in the country have been adapted to discuss things that would naturally interest many Nigerians, especially the youth. Such issues include job/vacancies, musicals and home videos, religion, football, business and investment, culture, technology market, entertainment, love and romance, and so forth. For instance, due to the high unemployment rate among graduates of Nigerian tertiary institutions, some forums have been dedicated to discussing job and career focusing on issues like how to write curriculum vitae and resume, improving employability skills, attending employment interviews, and so on. Now as most Nigerian newspapers have gone online, some of them provide forums for discussing the news they publish as a feedback measure. The potentials discussion forums have in connecting people of similar interest and enabling them to share their views and solve their problem is very great and many Nigerians are daily tapping into these potentials.

In the years to come, as many more Nigerians continue to have access to the Internet, the use of discussion forum will not just be limited to being the rallying point for leisurely discussion of national, social, economic and political issues. Discussions forums may also become virtual new space and public sphere for the young people for influencing political action in the country. In one of the threads on *Nairaland,* it was already being suggested by participants who felt their membership was strong enough to initiate a change in the Nigerian politics. Online forums may also grow to become a veritable medium in the hands of civil societies for mounting pressure on political leaders

and fighting all forms of injustices in the nation. The *Nigerian Village Square* parades an endless list of leftist Nigerian writers like Reuben Abati, the chairman of editorial board of *The Guardian* (one of Nigeria's most popular newspapers), Pat Utomi (a professor of Entreprenuership), Bolaji Aluko (a pro-democracy activist and Howard University professot), Okey Ndibe (a novelist, poet and political activist also based in the United States), Wale Adebanwi (a journalist, academic and Bill and Melinda Gates scholar at the University of Cambridge), Chinweizu (an author, historian and cultural critic), and so forth.. These people who are proponents of democratic and social reforms in Nigeria will have their views more popularized online and this provision of diverse forums may help to advance democratic norms in the nation.

CONCLUSION

In this chapter, I have examined the discourse features of interactions in asynchronous discussion forums by Nigerians. The chapter presents evidence of the complex patterns of online interaction by Nigerians. Turn taking process is a complex phenomenon in which participants typically self-select, because they consider forums as public spaces where they are free to speak whenever they desired without waiting for any other participant's consent. This is different from what obtains in real time synchronous chats, where current speaker typically selects the next speaker (Panyametheekul & Herring, 2003). A socio-political dimension to this is the fact that Nigerians see online forums as a new social space for them to exhibit their freedom of speech. In another study, Taiwo (2009) traces the high incidence of impoliteness and flaming behavior on political threads to the democratic nature of online discourse, which helps Nigerians to freely express themselves and agitate for social reforms.

Despite the frequent disruption of adjacency by unrelated turns, participants were still able to promote discourse coherence through the use of Quoting and Addressivity. Quoting is used as turn tracking device and it presents the picture of adjacency because participants were able to track patterns of turn taking despite the non-sequencing of such turns. Likewise, Addressivity through the use addressee's user name, nickname, abbreviation of name and endearing socio-cultural names, was also used to signal turns.

Topic flow in the threads developed around global topics with sub-topics, but there was never any abrupt topic change. There were often attempts by some participants to change topic, but there was not any instance in which threads went completely off the major topics. I conclude that interaction in asynchronous online discourse by Nigerians, though written is discursively organized like spoken communication and participants employ some linguistic strategies to signal both topical and interactional coherence.

ACKNOWLEDGMENT

My appreciation goes to Alexander von Humboldt Foundation for the post-doctoral fellowship award given me to study the discursive behavior of Nigerians on the digital media in the Department of English, University of Freiburg, Germany between September, 2008 and August, 2009).

REFERENCES

Althaus, S. (1997, July). Computer-mediated communication in the university classroom: an experiment with on-line discussions. *Communication Education, 46,* 158–174. doi:10.1080/03634529709379088

Awonusi, S. (2004). "Little Englishes" and the law of energetics: A sociolinguistic study of SMS text messages as register and discourse. In Awonusi, S., & Babalola, E. A. (Eds.), *The domestication of English in Nigeria* (pp. 45–62). Lagos, Nigeria: University of Lagos Press.

Bastian, M. L. (1999). Nationalism in the Virtual Space, Immigrant Nigerians on the Internet. *West African Review 1.* Retrieved November 13, 2008, from http://www.westafricareview.com/vol1.1/bastian.html

Chayko, M. (2002). *Connecting, how we form social bonds and communities in the Internet age.* Albany, NY: State University of New York Press.

Chiluwa, I. (2008). SMS Text-Messaging and the Nigerian Christian Context: Constructing Values and Sentiments. *The International Journal of Language Society and Culture, 24,* 11-20. Retrieved August 30, 2008, from http://www.educ.utas.edu.au/users/tle/JOURNAL/issues/2008/24-2.pdf

Cook, H. M. (2001). Particles. In Duranti, A. (Ed.), *Key terms in language and culture.* Malden, MA: Backwell.

Danet, B., Ruedenberg, L., & Rosebaum-Tamari, Y. (1994). "Smoking dope" at a virtual party: Writing, play, and performance on Internet Relay Chat. In Rafaeli, S., Sudweeks, F., & McLaughlin, M. (Eds.), *Network and Netplay: Virtual Groups on the Internet.* Cambridge, MA: MIT Press.

Donath, J. S. (1998). Identity and deception in the virtual community. In Kollock, P., & Smith, M. (Eds.), *Communities in Cyberspace* (pp. 29–59). London: Routledge.

Eckholm, E. (1984). Emotional outbursts punctuate conversation by computer. Retrieved January 22, 2009, from http://query.nytimes.com/gst/fullpage.html?res=9B0CEFDD123BF931A35753C1A962948260

Edwards, J. (2005). A short history of online discussion groups. Retrieved January 2, 2009, from http://www.lib.jmu.edu/edge/archives/Spring2005(1)/Article3.asp

Fitze, M. (2006). Discourse and participation in ESL face-to-face and written electronic conferences. *Language Learning and Technology, 10*(1), 67-86. Retrieved January 3, 2009, from http://llt.msu.edu/vol10num1/fitze/

Fraser, B. (1996). Pragmatic markers. *Pragmatics*, *6*(2), 167–190.

Grice, H. P. (1975). Logic and conversation. In Cole, P., & Morgan, J. (Eds.), *Syntax and semantics* (*Vol. 3*, pp. 41–58). New York: Academic Press.

Hanna, B. E., & de Nooy, J. (2003). A funny thing happened on the way to the forum: Electronic discussion and foreign language learning. *Language Learning & Technology*, *7*(1), 71–85.

Harrison, S. (1998). Email discussions as conversation: moves and acts in a sample from a listserv discussion. *Linguistik Online*, 1/98. Retrieved July 30, 2008, from http://www.linguistik-online.de/harrison.htm

Harrison, S. (2004, June) *Turn Taking in Electronic Environment*, Paper presented at *Inter*-Varietal Applied Corpus Studies Conference, Belfast, UK.

Herring, S. C. (1999). Interactional coherence in CMC. *Journal of Computer Mediated Communication, 4* (4). Retrieved December 23, 2008, from http://jcmc.indiana.edu/vol4/issue4/herring.html

Herring, S. C. (2004). Computer-mediated discourse analysis: An approach to researching online behavior. In Barab, S. A., Kling, R., & Gray, J. (Eds.), *Designing for virtual communities in the service of learning* (pp. 338–376). Cambridge, UK: Cambridge University Press.

Herring, S. C., & Nix, C. (1997). *Is "serious chat" an oxymoron?* Academic vs. social uses of Internet Relay Chat. Paper presented at the American Association of Applied Linguistics, Orlando, FL.

Hewitt, J. (2001). Beyond threaded discourse. *International Journal of Educational Telecommunications*, *7*(3), 207–221.

Hwang, P. (2008). Linguistic characteristics in synchronous and asynchronous CMC. *English Language & Literature Teaching*, *14*(2), 47–66.

Ifukor, P. (2008, October). *Face Claims on Weblogs*. Paper presented at First Conference of the International Society for the Linguistics of English, Freiburg, Germany.

Larkin-H., T. (2001, October). *On-line discussions: a key to enhancing student motivation and understanding?* Paper presented at the 31st Frontiers in Education Conference, Reno, NV.

Markel, S. L. (2001). Technology and Education Online Discussion Forums: It's in the Response. *Online Journal of Distance Learning Administration, 4*(2). Retrieved January 5, 2009, from http://www.westga.edu/~distance/ojdla/summer42/markel42.html

Matthew, S. (2007). Assessing Online Discussion Forum Participation. *International Journal of Information and Communication Technology Education, 3*(3), 39–46.

O'Reilly, M., & Newton, D. (2002). Interaction online: Above and beyond requirements of assessment. *Australian Journal of Educational Technology, 18*(1), 57-70. Retrieved January 5, 2009, from http://www.ascilite.org.au/ajet/ajet18/oreilly.html

Ofulue, C. I. Interconnectivity in "other tongues": A sociolinguistic study of SMS text messages in Yoruba. *Issues in Intercultural Communication, 2*(1), 1-12.

Ojo, T. (2005). ICTs and the Construction of "Imagined African Communities" Online. In Brigitte, Hipfl & Theo Hug (Eds.) Media Communities. 167-188. Münster, Germany: Waxmann Verlag.

Orestrom, B. (1983). *Turn-taking in English conversation*. Lund, Sweden: Gleerup.

Ostman, J. (1995). Pragmatic particles twenty years after. In Brita Warvick, Kaisa Tanskanen, and Risto Hiltunen (Eds.) Organization in discourse. 95-108. Turku, Finland: University of Turku.

Pahran, A. A. (2004). Diaspora, Community and Communication: Internet Use in Transnational Haiti. *Global Networks, 4*(2), 199-217. Retrieved January 6, 2009, from http://jcmc.indiana.edu/vol9/issue1/panya_herring.html

Panyametheekul, S., & Herring, S. C. (2003). Gender and turn allocation in Thai chat room. *Journal of Computer Mediated Communication, 9*(1). Retrieved December 23, 2008, from http://jcmc.indiana.edu/vol9/issue1/panya_herring.html

Park, Jung-ran (2007). Interpersonal and affective communication in synchronous online discourse. *Library Quarterly, 77*(2), (Special issue on Discourse Approaches to Information Seeking in Context), 133-155.

Sacks, H. A., Schegloff, E., & Jefferson, G. (1974). A simplest systematics for the organization of turn taking for conversation. *Language, 50*, 696–735. doi:10.2307/412243

Taiwo, R. (2008). Linguistic forms and functions of SMS Text Messages in Nigeria. In Kelsey, S., & St. Armant, K. (Eds.), *Handbook of research on computer mediated communication* (*Vol. 1*, pp. 969–982). Hershey, PA: Information Science Publishing.

Taiwo, R. (2009, July). *Discursive forms and functions of flaming in Nigerian online forums*. Paper presented at The International Conference on Linguistic Politeness and Rudeness, Lancaster, UK.

Thomas, M. J. W. (2002). Learning within incoherent structures: the space of online discussion forums. *Journal of Computer Assisted Learning, 18*, 351–366. doi:10.1046/j.0266-4909.2002.03800.x

Warschauer, M. (2000) Language, identity, and the Internet. B. Kolko, L. Nakamura, & G. Rodman (Eds.), Race in Cyberspace, (pp. 151-170) New York: Routledge.

Warschuer, M., & De Florio-Hansen, I. (2003). Multilingualism, identity, and theInternet. In Hu, A., & De Florio-Hansen, I. (Eds.), *Multiple identity and multilingualism* (pp. 155–179). Tübingen, Germany: Stauffenburg.

KEY TERMS AND DEFINITIONS

Discussion Forum: A web-based forum which is used for holding discussions. It allows people to post messages to a website where these messages can be read and commented on by other members of the community.

Turn-taking: A basic feature of conversation rooted in mutual awareness of speakers in a conversation about the rules of participation. It operates in such a way that only one speaker holds the floor at one time in a conversation and other speakers are aware of their turns when the current speaker finishes. Turn-taking makes conversation orderly.

Thread: A thread is a list of messages posted on a discussion forum. A thread contains an original message and responses to that message.

Coherence: Coherence is the logical connection of a written or spoken text. Coherence is seen in a text that can be read as a unified whole and not unrelated ideas.

Quoting: Quoting is a system of tracking turns in online discussion forums, which makes it possible for the participant to refer to previous posts by copying them and responding to them.

Addressivity: Addressivity is the act of prefacing a turn in an online discussion forum with user name or nickname of the intended addressee in order to signal that the turn is a response to the person's post.

Flaming: Flaming is the deliberate act of posting overly provocative and insulting language in a discussion forum. A flame is often filled with coarse and provocative language.

Discourse: Discourse is a contiguous stretch of language comprising more than one sentence or utterance in spoken, written and signed language and multimodal/multimedia forms of communication. It also includes fictional and non-verbal language.

Posting: Posting is any piece of message imputed in a discussion forum either as an original message or a response to another message earlier imputed by another participant.

Asynchronous: Asynchronous is a two-way transmission technique of messages that occurs with a time delay, allowing participants to respond at their own convenience. An internet discussion forum is an example of asynchronous communication.

Chapter 11

Complicating Communication in Computer Mediate Environments:
A Textual Analysis of Blogs in the First-Year Writing Classroom

Brittany Cottrill
Bowling Green State University, USA

ABSTRACT

Building on the research produced by early and current computers and writing scholars, this chapter will look at the results of an analysis of both virtual- and classroom-based texts produced by nine first-year writers, five from composition I and four from composition II courses at a mid-sized, Midwestern, public university. The research included in this chapter explores the results of how blogging affected student writing in the first-year writing classroom. Specifically, this chapter focuses on the results of this study in relation to the explicit and implicit textual signals and how these textual signals complicate communication in computer mediated environments.

INTRODUCTION

In the spring of 2005, while teaching an introductory writing course, I realized that certain terms were occurring repeatedly in the papers that students were submitting. For the first time in my experience, students began submitting essays that, with some consistency, had lexical errors often associated with communication in online environments. Even after commenting on the appearance of words such as "cuz" and "u" (for "because" and "you"), I found

that some students still turned in formal papers with these errors. That semester I incorporated blogs into my writing classes for the first time. Although their blogs were not graded on grammar or spelling but rather on content, I couldn't help but wonder if the Internet language markers that were appearing in student essays weren't somehow related to their use of blogs in the class.

The experiences I noted in my reflections about the semester became not only a point of interest, but also became the basis of a research study the following fall. That semester I set out to explore if blogging affected student writing in the composi-

DOI: 10.4018/978-1-61520-827-2.ch011

tion classroom. My goal was to have students write traditional academic essays in addition to their blog posts like I had in the spring. This time, however, I wanted to take my observations further and perform textual analysis. As I introduced my students to the blogging component of the class, I also explained to them that I would be asking for permission to analyze their blog posts and their essays at various drafting stages.

I hoped to explore how computer mediated environments, especially when introduced into the classroom, may complicate communication for students. I knew students entered an English class with certain expectations. For example, repeatedly students comment on how they are surprised that their required college English classes focus primarily on writing, whereas their high school required English courses were a mixture of literature and English. At the same time, I expected students to enter certain writing spaces with preconceived notions about what is appropriate. Students feel confident in the split between the personal and the academic writing they do – and in truth, often do not see their personal writing, which may very well occur in online spaces, as writing. While the research did demonstrate that few students blogged prior to entering the class, all had experience interacting in online spaces. In interacting in these spaces then, students were likely aware of the possibilities of creating text – and even if they were unsure of how to produce texts and products, they were aware of the possibilities. In asking students to blog, often seen as a very personal form of writing, as a class assignment, I wondered how the blogs would be approached. Would students take advantage of the images, links, text alterations, and the many other possibilities the web provides for writers, or would students default to traditional, academic prose? The complication in communication then rests in student expectations. Would there be a struggle between academic and personal writing with the blog, and if so, how would it play out? Additionally, would asking students to blog complicate their

understanding of more traditional essays? While getting students to write more is a good thing in a writing class, how would students demonstrate their ability to write in many, varied spaces to very different audiences and with very different expectations? The goal of my research was to create a sound beginning for further examination of the affect blogging and other web-based writing has on student writing and students' abilities to maneuver between various writing spaces.

While I had seen what I hypothesized as crossover of Internet dialects into the classroom, my suspicions were not new. For years educators and scholars have been concerned that the new, evil technology would ruin the pristine, established method of communication. Even though there is this fear, one that goes even back to the invention and introduction of writing, technology has been a guiding force behind the evolution of education as well as communication. Dennis Baron (1999) points out that composition instructors and writers in general have been the first to accept and embrace the technology advances in general. Baron says "the computer is simply the latest step in a long line of writing technologies. In many ways its development parallels that of the pencil" and he continues by saying "[a]lthough I'm not aware that anyone actually opposed the use of pencils when they began to be used for writing, other literacy technologies, including writing itself, were initially met with suspicion as well as enthusiasm" (1999, p. 17). Technology advances are and have been important to writing and the development of teaching writing. Were it not for items that we take for granted such as pencils and cheaply made paper or even writing, the teaching of writing would not be what it is today.

In the chapter that follows I will look at the results of a semester-long analysis of both virtual- and classroom-based texts produced by nine first-year writers, five from composition I and four from composition II courses at a mid-sized, Midwestern, public university. The research included in this chapter will explore the results of the study that aimed to better understand how blogging affected student writing in the first-year writing classroom. Specifically, this chapter will focus on the results of this study in relation to the explicit and implicit textual signals and how these textual signals complicate communication in computer mediated environments. Initially undertaken as a means to explore the changes that computer mediated communications had on both high-stakes and low-stakes writing assignments, this research ultimately focuses on issues of student understanding of technology and communication through technology, and their ability to transition between different communication situations.

BACKGROUND

In recent years the term "blog" has become much more familiar. Everyone from political candidates to fictional television characters are blogging, from academics to grade-school students. Used both inside and outside the academy, by the famous and unknown, it's difficult to listen to a news program or read and article in a magazine without a casual mention of blogs. While blogs function in many different ways for many different people, the one thing they have in common is that blogs have made it possible for anyone with access to the Internet and basic computer literacies to become a published writer.

"Blogging," or the act of posting to a blog, has only grown in popularity since its start in the mid 90's and in 2001 Blogger (one of the largest free blog services) hosted 117,970 blogs (Gurak, Smiljana, Laurie, Ratliff, & Reyman, 2004). In 2007 the estimated number of bloggers was closer to one-hundred million, and surely the number will continue to increase (McCullagh and Broache, 2007). What cannot be denied, and what the increased statistics in the last eight years show, is that technology is changing where we write, what we write, and how we interact.

Before moving forward with the discussion at hand, it is important to understand how the teaching of writing has evolved in recent years in order to truly understand how and why blogs are being used in writing classes. Aside from the fact that clearly blogs require writing, blogs are a way to bring together many long-held beliefs about writing and the teaching of writing. Beginning in the 1970s, writing teachers began to realize the importance of teaching writing as a process. The process movement sees writing as "a complex extended set of (teachable) activities in which a wide variety of invention procedures may be valuable, and an equal variety of drafting and revision activities" (Fulkerson, 2004, p. 671). Flower and Hayes (1981) said that "The process of writing is best understood as a set of distinctive thinking processes which writers orchestrate or organize during the act of composing" (p. 366). While the particularities of process and how process is understood varies depending on pedagogical beliefs, as Faigley (1986) points out, the process movement valued the steps the writer took in composing. In other words, in order to reach a final product or text, the student writer must go through various steps. All of the steps, not just the product, were and are beginning to be valued. Prewriting, writing, and rewriting became equally valued and the recursive nature of writing became the focus of the writing classroom.

At the same time that the process movement was beginning to gain momentum and attention, the writing field went through a time where journaling was stressed and valued. Peter Elbow (2002) wrote that "serious writers have long used private journaling for early explorations of feelings, thinking, or language. But many writing teachers seem to think that students can get along without the private writing serious writers find so crucial – or even that students will benefit from keeping their audience in mind for the whole time" (p. 200). With this in mind then, it is important to understand that "journal writing has become an intrinsic part of many English classes" (Glenn, Goldthwaite, & Connors, 2003, p. 215). While journals have been used over the years in very different ways, they are often used "as a repository of materials and concepts that can lead to more formal essays" and are used to meet varied pedagogical purposes (Glenn, Goldthwaite, & Connors, 2003, p. 215). What can be easily understood though is that journal writing or daily writing activities make sense in a writing class.

Because of the longstanding use of writing journals, when blogs began to gain more widespread attention, many saw them as a technological step up from the spiral bound notebook. Blogs created free spaces for students to write and publish. Because of pre-set formatting standards, students could also interact and comment on their classmates' blogs, and teachers no longer had to carry heavy piles of writing journals across campus to grade. Aside from that, blogs also created a space for students to write where they were already interacting online. As computers and the Internet reach more students before they enter the university, it becomes less likely that entering students have not spent some time in online spaces.

As evidenced by the discussion to this point, technology has long had a place in the writing classroom. Research to support such a claim is widely available as well, but the fear of language corruption is important still. David Craig (2004) addressed the fear "that the current generation of grade school students will graduate with a level of literacy that is lower than that of any preceding modern generation" because of the "attack" on the English language from the language of instant messaging (p. 117). The idea of emoticons and other Internet language markers infecting student writing has been a fear of the academy for years. However, this has not stopped technology from entering the classroom and becoming more accepted. The belief that technology will or is corrupting literacy and language has been a long-standing fear and also the source of much research. Be it the use of slang, the end to spell-

ing or reading, the inclusion of nonverbal cues or emoticons, in recent years the research behind the changing standards with express fear on the end or the distortion of acceptable communication has continued to grow.

In his study *A generational approach to using emoticons as nonverbal communication*, Franklin B. Krohn (2004) looked at the role emoticons play in communication today, with emphasis on business communication (p. 321). Krohn defined emoticons as "punctuation marks that viewed sideways resemble facial expressions" (p. 322), and found that "Millennial" (those born between 1980 and 2000) were far more accepting of emoticons and concluded by saying that emoticons will only become more common in formal communication (p. 326). Similarly, Reid Goldsborough (2005) found that "despite the fact that e-mail has been firmly entrenched in offices and homes for some time, [the] debate still rages online about e-mail usage and style" (p. 39). Before Krohn's study and Goldsborough's address of the need for e-mail etiquette, Alecia Woolf (2000) looked at the gender difference in emoticon use and found that use of emoticons is higher among females in single-gendered environments, but is more equal in mixed gender online environments.

No universal conclusion has been made about the use of emoticons in e-mail, and as these emoticons become more accepted in certain communications, it is likely they will slip in to areas where they are not accepted or expected (for example, in the composition classroom). There is, however, a thin line between where emoticons are accepted and not accepted since emoticons and Internet dialects emerged with the grandparents of the blog (various instant messaging programs and message boards) and are accepted in this new type of online publishing. This thin line, however, is what complicates the discussion at hand.

Blogs have continued to receive more scholarly attention including at regional and national conferences, in scholarly publications, and more. Though blogs have been around for well over ten years, scholarship on blogs is still relatively new and continuing to grow. Barrios (2005) says "very little critical literature exists on blogging," but he also addresses the often lengthy publication process as an obstacle for the lack of scholarship on the topic. Even though blogs have become a "buzz" word in both popular culture and the academic world, little has been published regarding the effect they have in the writing classroom. Because of this, I set out to undertake this research. I was interested in finding how often Internet slang showed up in graded assignments and if, and then where, these terms were left out or included in the writing process.

DISCUSSION

Although blogs are still a relatively new technology to many, they have been used for over ten years and harken back to the writing done by diarists and journalers for many hundreds of years. Even so, blogs have become increasingly popular in the classrooms across the country – particularly in writing classrooms. Huffaker (2005) looked at the use of blogs in promoting literacy in his study *The educated blogger: Using weblogs to promote literacy in the classroom*. In this study he concluded that blogs "create an excellent computer-mediated communication context for individual expressions and collaborative interactions in the form of storytelling and dialogue" which "are the foundation of language development, and more so, the foundation of learning" (Huffaker, 2005, p. 96). Alireza Doostadar (2004) referred to blogging as "an emergent speech genre and identif[ied] the structural features and social interactions that make this genre seem 'vulgar'" (p. 651). Renata Suzuki (2004) has suggested blogs be used as research diaries, while in a more recently published study, Chretien, Goldman, and Faselis explore the reflective spaces the blogs create as a way to promote professional development. In 2008, Boling, Castek, Zawilinski, Barton, and Nierlich looked

at how new technology, such as blogs, are being used in literacy education, while other scholars are looking at how bogs are being used in higher education (Shoffner, 2007; Shultz Colby, Colby, Felix, Murphy, Thomas, & Blair, 2005; and Bloch and Crosby, 2008), secondary education (Huffaker and Calvert 2005; Bortree, 2005), and even in the workplace (Lee, Hwang, & Lee, 2006). However, because research on blogging is still relatively new, few, if any, research studies have looked at students' abilities to acknowledge and transition between writing spaces.

With this in mind then, I approached this research study with a desire to look at how blogs function inside the classroom. For a semester, both my Composition I and Composition II courses blogged as way to engage in readings, classroom discussion, and community-building activities. Students were asked to complete four posts a week while also writing traditional academic essays. Texts produced during eight weeks of writing by a select group of students has become the basis for this discussion and creates a case study of how blogging effected student writing. The conclusion of this chapter aims to explore the results of this study based on compiled textual coding of blogs, rough drafts of essays, and revisions of essays.

Research Questions

I came to my research with one overarching question; I wanted to know whether blogging would have an effect on student writing. I saw this question significant at the time, and continue to see its significance, because of the increased interest in academic blogging and also the incorporation of technology in the classroom. This question not only guided me towards the research and through the research process, but also led me to the three secondary research questions for this project.

Initially undertaken as a means to explore the changes that computer mediated communication had on both high-stakes and low-stakes writing assignments, this research also addressed issues of student understanding of technology and communication through technology, and their ability to transition between different communication situations. In order to judge the effect of blogging on student writing I had three secondary research questions which included looking at whether the language choices made in blogging, a low-stakes writing assignment, crossed over into high-stakes assignments such as the first two academic essays of the semester. Additionally, I wanted to see whether students would see blogging as a low-stakes writing assignment; in other words, I wondered if students' blogs would demonstrate more formal writing than what might have been expected for in-class writing or a traditional blog. Finally, I wanted to see if the blogs demonstrated a difference in language, "correctness," tone, audience, and more depending on whether the blog was a pre-assigned topic or a "free post." At the heart of the study and behind each of the questions posed was trying to better understand the complications to communication discussed earlier.

Through these research questions I hoped to develop a better understanding of students' understandings of writing in various spaces and for various purposes. While the goals of the project were to explore the explicit and implicit textual signals found in traditional and non-tradition student texts, the results show that the textual signals may complicate communication in computer mediate environments and may be cause for further exploration both inside and outside the classroom.

Participant Selection

In order to find out how blogging affects student writing, students from the composition I and II courses that I was teaching were asked to participate. Because both classes were required to blog for a grade, students were not required to do any additional work, and they were also reassured that their participation in the research was completely voluntary and that their grades would

not be affected based on their participation or lack of participation in the research. In addition to signing informed consent forms, students were also told that they could withdraw their consent at any point throughout the semester and were told that if they chose to participate they would remain anonymous.

Of the thirty-two registered students, eighteen students submitted consent forms (eleven from composition I and seven from composition II). Out of the eighteen students who submitted consent forms, only nine students were selected for the final study (five composition I students and four composition II students). These nine students were picked because of their consistency early on in the blogging project and because they submitted their first two papers on time. Students who stopped blogging, even though a grade was being assigned, or who submitted late essays were removed from the study based on time restraints of the research.

In an attempt to better understand the group of students being studied, I administered two surveys early in the semester. The surveys asked students to answer questions based on their level of experience with computers and the Internet as well as their previous knowledge of Internet dialectical terms. The results from these surveys provided a more descriptive picture of where the students were coming from when entering the blog project as well as their insight into their believed expertise, or lack of expertise, in the use of computers.

The survey revealed that of the nine students, only one student had ever blogged before, but six had heard the term "blog." The one student who had blogged said she had done so in a previous writing course. All of the nine students owned a computer and had easy access to the Internet either at home or on campus. The survey also showed that all of the students had been online in some capacity for at least 3 years. Below is the breakdown of how long students had been online:

Table 1. Student response to experience online

Years online	3-5 years	6-9 years	10+ years
Comp I and II	2	6	1

In discovering that all of the students had some experience functioning in online environments and that all had access to the Internet, I was reassured as a researcher that problems such as access would be less of an issue. While there were times when servers were down, and I had no guarantee that students had continued, reliable access, I felt that this initial survey spoke to the fact that students were entering the project on the most equal terms possible. After collecting the initial survey data to better understand the students, I felt confident to move forward with answering my research questions.

Methods and Methodology

In order to answer the research questions set out at the start of this project, I used a combination of context-sensitive textual analysis and inductive discourse analysis to analyze the various texts that were collected. These two types of analysis worked well together to provide a broad understanding of the texts produced by students and also allowed for the data to drive the results. Methodologically, choosing context-sensitive textual analysis was important because it took into consideration the role that context and familiarity played with student writing. In addition to writing in a potentially new virtual environment with the blogs, students were also writing in a new or newer writing environment because they were all composition I and II students. It was likely students would "borrow ideas, language, genre conventions, and other aspects of prior texts" (Huckin, 1992, p. 84) in their blog and their academic essays, and taking this into consideration would be an important step in the analysis of data. In order to create context

I asked students to participate in surveys, to blog about their experiences with technology, and to reflect on their writing experience in the specific classes they were in and also on past writing experiences.

According to textual analysis scholars, the intended message of a text is important, but so too are the situations or contexts in understanding meaning. Context analysis then is a type of data analysis that "tries to account for as much of the context of situation as possible" which "relies...on plausible interpretations rather than on any kind of proof" (Huckin, 1992, p. 89). This then becomes a way to understand how life-experiences influence writing and products. Using Thomas Huckin's explanation of context-sensitive textual analysis, this research focused on finding salient patterns in the text while "looking for general patterns rather than detailed ones" (Schneider, 2002, p. 193) as a means to discuss students understanding of audience and context in writing, and to highlight possible issues of transfer between writing contexts. Student blogs were read holistically initially. After reading through the blogs, various patterns began to emerge. Based on these patterns then three types of dialectic markers were discovered. During this process, the first two graded essays were also coded to see how often issues of word choices, emoticons, and forms of emphasis appeared in their writing.

Traditionally, a dialect has been understood as a variation on language which reflects changes made to the language by people from similar areas (Hazen, 2001). Dialects can initially seem easy to distinguish by sound, but the dialect that became relevant to this discussion was one that is seldom, if ever, heard, but instead is read. People in online spaces are inhabiting a common area which in turn is reflected in their language usage. These dialects become clear markers or indicators of belonging in online spaces. These include issues of abbreviations, capitalization, exclamation, emoticons, and numerous forms of emphasis. Because people are spending more time online it is likely that these nuanced markers, which present themselves as Internet dialect, are showing up in not only virtual spaces but also possibly in non-virtual spaces. For the sake of this discussion then, Internet dialects should be understood as the language uses that are common among a community of people who inhabit a common space, be they spoken or written.

While the students who participated in the research project were each unique individuals with unique histories, they also possessed important similarities. All were from the Midwest, all were attending the same University, and all had spent some time in online environments. Because of this, many were familiar with the Internet dialect. To better understand their familiarity with writing and communicating in online spaces, at the beginning of the semester after students were introduced to the research project, they were asked to complete a survey that asked them to define various dialectic markers. The results from this portion of the study indicated that though students had different levels of familiarity with common markers, there were markers that possessed unanimous or near unanimous familiarity.

In investigating levels of familiarity and creating context, the survey could broadly be broken down into three types of dialect markers. Though participants were not aware of these three groups, these three types of markers helped guide the presentation of much of the rest of the data. The first group of Internet dialect markers were language markers. These included abbreviations, acronyms, and written words and phrases that were typically associated with chatting online, message boards, or emails. The second markers were nonverbal cues. These were most closely associated with stage directions one might read in a play. Examples of nonverbal markers might include typing out an action such as "sigh" or "shrug" and often were used to indicate direction for the reader or an explanation of visual or auditory response to a situation. The final set of markers were emoticons, or visual images created using letters, punctuation, or a combination of the two. The most common of these include the sideways smiley face:). In conjunction with Huckin and Barton's explanations of various textual-analysis then, texts that were collected were analyzed with these three markers in mind.

Following the initial surveys, students were introduced to the blog project and given instructions on creating their own blogs. Students were required to make four weekly entries in their blogs: two posts reflecting on readings for class or class discussion (one post per class each week), one reflective post on the students' writing process and progress, and one post considered a "free post" on anything the student wished to write about. In addition to the blogs, student essays were also collected and coded. Student papers were submitted for both peer review and instructor comments at least once throughout the semester. Once students received their grades and comments, they were given the opportunity to submit revisions as many times as they wanted for additional comments. However, among the nine students who participated in this project, most only submitted one additional revision, if they submitted any.

After students began their blog project, their posts were collected and analyzed for eight weeks. Again, context-sensitive textual analysis relies on the "'identification of salient patterns' through a textual scanning [Huckin] describes as 'holistic,' a 'looking for general patterns rather than detailed ones'" (Schneider, 2002, p.193). After discovering patters I reexamined the blogs for the dialectical markers that the initial analysis revealed, which included various word choices, nonverbal markers, and emoticons. In order to categorize and simplify the coding process I relied on David

Craig's (2004) method of categorization of slang in instant messaging as I worked with the salient patterns that emerged from the data, specifically as Craig's patterns applied to the word choice markers.

While the goal of Craig's study was discover an IM (instant messenger) vernacular among 12-17 year olds, my goal with this research was different. Rather than focusing on whether the vernacular existed, I hoped to look at how the language choices of young writers would play out. In other words, I hoped to see whether the language markers appeared in classroom blogs. During my study though, I considered Craig's four types of slang including phonetic replacements, acronyms, abbreviations, and inanities (2003, p. 120). Craig's four categories then, along with patterns present in the data, helped inform the development of the word choice category in the process of data analysis.

In addition to using Craig's (2004) method, I also built off of Shao-Kang Lo's (2008) discussion regarding meaning making. Lo points out that while there is a belief that computer mediated communication "lacks nonverbal communication cues and prevents the conveyance of emotions and attitudes to receivers" (2008, p. 596), the truth of the matter is that "channel expansion theory considers that. ... the communicator accumulates specific knowledge and skills" and that in fact various nonverbal cues, such as emoticons, do affect meaning-making (2008, p. 595). Using both Craig's and Lo's discussion then, I explored how and whether it appeared that students were making rhetorical choices as they were interacting in computer mediated spaces, and whether those choices differed in a more traditional academic setting.

Finally, along with Huckin's context-sensitive textual analysis, Craig's method of categorization, and Lo's stance on the significance of emoticons in meaning, I turned to Ellen Barton's inductive discourse analysis which became a supplemental means of dealing with data. This type of analysis

looks for what Barton calls "rich features" in a text. These rich features are "linguistic features which point to the relation between a text and its context" (Schneider, 2002, pp. 192). The data then was analyzed through identifying patters as Huckin proposes, categorizing the patters building off of Craig's (2004) methodology, and connecting the patterns between text and context as Barton suggests. These three steps were used in analyzing blog posts and student essays to see if, when, and how often the predetermined markets appeared in student writing.

RESULTS

Through careful analysis of text and coding for the three types of Internet dialectic markers, the results from this study indicate that Internet slang and casualness did not appear to infect academic writing. In what follows is a discussion of some of the findings from this research. In an attempt to represents each type of dialect markers, the included results are broken up in to three sections. The first section looks at two examples of language markers that were significant in the data. The second section looks at the use of nonverbal cues presented in texts. The final section is a discussion of the emoticons as they appeared in blogs and in academic essays.

Word Choice Markers

In the process of writing or compositing a text, the writer makes choices in the words he/she will use. These choices are at times unintentional but more often are intentional. The rhetorical choices of the writer include not only the selecting of the type of word, the way one might expect a poet to do, but also choices that the writer chooses not to make. The data suggested that writers made more conscious choices to abstain from what may be considered expected writing protocol, such as proofreading or spell checking. This is significant in understanding how students view writing in various spaces and in better understanding how to address the changes to communication in virtual spaces.

One of the most significant finding to fall under the language makers in this research was the capitalization and lack of capitalization of the word "I" throughout the blogs. Of the nine students, only three consistently capitalized the word "I" in all eight weeks, but all students capitalized "I" at least once throughout their blogs. However, in their papers, only one student used the lower case "i" to reference the personal pronoun and all other students consistently capitalized "I" in their submitted papers.

Although the blogging program used for this project did offer a spell check system which did consider the lowercase personal pronoun "i" a typo, this system differed from typical word processing programs in one significant way. In order for this error to be addressed students much elect to spell check. The option is not automatic, nor did a red or green squiggle mark highlight words that may be spelled wrong[1]. In Microsoft Word, the most commonly used word processing program used by students in this study, a lower case "i" for the personal pronoun is automatically converted to the "I" through auto-formatting. Similarly, students who use programs such as Microsoft Works, which comes standard on most PCs, also have auto-formatting to automatically capitalize the personal pronoun.

Because of auto-formatting, students no longer need to capitalize "I" or even the first word in a sentence because Word, Works, and many similar programs do it for the writer without the student even asking for the help as long as auto-formatting is still enabled on the computer, which is a default setting for most programs and must physically be shut off to be deactivated. If, however, students do turn off the auto-formatting, both Word and Works pick up on the lower case "i" in the spell checking process. The fact that the lowercase "i" shows up so consistently in the blogs suggests

that students have become accustomed to the auto-formatting that word processing programs offer. However, because no student consistently didn't capitalize the personal pronoun "I," the research suggests that students are aware of the rules of capitalization.

As with the capitalization of the proper pronoun "I," students were more likely to use creative spelling in their blogs, which ultimately resulted in error. Although all spelling errors were not counted in either blogs or papers, and errors were not calculated in blog grades, a handful of creative spellings were considered including gotta (for "got to"), cause (for "because"), and juss (for "just"). One student had more consistent spelling errors. He used apon once for "upon" and atol twice for "at all". Although these spellings would have been detected by Blogger's spell check, the students had to make a conscious decision to spell check their entries before posting them. While I note that traditional errors were at times noted in the research, because of the scope of this research, further analysis was not conducted. The scope of the language choice markers were too great and so only prominent patterns were addressed.

As evidenced from this discussion of two of the most common word choice markers that appeared in the data, potential "errors" are most likely to occur in online spaces because word processing programs make accommodations for writers.

Emphasis

In speech emphasis can be created through the use of stress, tone, or even body language. Emphasis in speech and writing is one way meaning is created. Drawing attention to specific ideas, points, or words is often important to form complete understandings of a meaning. Writers, perhaps student writers more so, struggle to find ways of creating emphasis in similar ways. Whereas in speech one can verbally stress a word, finding a way to denote stress or emphasis in writing is a challenge. Perhaps the most expected form of emphasis in writing would come from more traditional choices the writer makes including word choice or sentence structure. These expected and traditional choices are often transparent in how they create emphasis and in fact were easy to overlook. In coding the academic essays nearly all the emphasis was created through the development of the text, choice of words, and structure of sentences. The coding process of student blogs, however, demonstrated a use of less regular or expected forms of emphasis such as repetition, capitalization, and bolding of words or phrases. These irregular forms were not as consistent as more traditional forms of emphasis and also visually suggested emphasis in a way that traditional emphasis might not.

Some common forms of irregular emphasis in the blogs were repetition, capitalization, and bolding of words or phrases. These irregular forms of emphasis may have been an attempt to help the reader(s) better understand the significance of a point, but they also likely correspond to speech emphasis patterns. The blogs suggest that students know they need to emphasize an idea in some way above and beyond the normal sentence to get their emotions across to their audience but are unsure of how to do so.

During the eighth week one student wrote in her blog about her upcoming summer trip to Las Vegas and said "it should be really really fun." Through repetition this student attempted to create emphasis. The idea of her trip being fun wasn't enough but instead it was going to be "really, really" fun. In conversation, repetition may be an expected way to stress the importance of the fun. In fact, when reading the earlier quote, it is easier to almost hear someone say that sentence with a sense of excited urgency about the fun.

In addition to the use of repetition, students also utilized capitalization to express emphasis. For example, in week five one student wrote about his third paper of the semester, a website analysis. His post revolved around how much he had disliked the assignment and said, "this is one

i dont wanna have to think about EVER AGAIN!" Capitalization in this case brings visual emphasis that might be expressed in speech through body language or facial expression. The fact that no other word or letter is capitalized in this example only further shows the use of capitalization for emphasis.

In week one another student said that he would finish his first paper "Friday ***AFTER*** noon" making reference to when the blogs needed to be posted by each week. By bolding the word "after," the student created a cue for his reader to place emphasis on the word to get his point across. The repetition, capitalization, and bolding all create cues for the readers on how to read the sentences and where to place emphasis. Like a play may include stage directions, these forms of emphasis create directions for the reader to better understand and almost "hear" the text that was being composed. It is interesting to note that only one student used multiple forms of emphasis on the same word or phrase. Oftentimes students picked one form of emphasis, but as shown above, during week one a student italicized, bolded, and capitalized the entire word. This appears to be an attempt to only strengthen the emphasis or perhaps even a way of emphasizing the emphasis.

After coding blogs and essays, it is clear that the students attempted to create emphasis through less regular forms more often in their blogs than in their academic essays. This seems to imply that those students see the two types of writing as different. Though emphasis is equally important in an academic argument, the fact that students used visual cues to indicate emphasis in their blogs may indicate that they related their content and message more closely to that of speech. It would not be uncommon for one person to say to their friend that their vacation will be really, really fun. At the same time, because speech is a complex form of communication that includes tone, pitch, body language, and context, in addition to content, emphasis can easily be placed on a specific word, phrase, or idea in a face-to-face situation. In a

Table 2. Emoticon survey results chart

	I / Correct	I / Incorrect	II / Correct	II / Incorrect
:) (happy smile)	5	0	4	0
:((sad smile)	5	0	4	0
:D (laugh/big smile)	3	0	3	1
:P (sticking tongue out)	4	1	2	2

written environment where the writer is removed from the reader completely, emphasis needs to be expressed in a different way. The student writers who used various visual forms of emphasis were aware of this, but they also were possibly unsure of how to accomplish their goal. However, it is an interesting point to note that emphasis in a blog was more visual and less expected than the use of emphasis in an academic essay.

Although all forms of emphasis in the students' blogs work in similar ways, students did tend to use the various types of emphasis differently. Repetition often suggested a sense of urgency or extreme – the student from above didn't think her trip to Las Vegas would just be really fun, but really really fun. One "really" just wouldn't adequately express how much fun her trip would be in her mind. The capitalization of entire words and bolding of words function in similar ways. In the world of online communication, words in capital letters often equate to yelling. Although usually considered yelling in an angry tone, this raising of one's voice can also be seen as a form of excitement. In bolding a word or words, students create a visual shift to show where the emphasis needs to be. Without even reading a text, words in bold jump out to the reader, and students have been taught that the bolded words in text books are important terms. In creating emphasis in their blogs, students are attempting to verbalize their writing. If we remember that classical rhetoric is spoken and "the rhetor/writer [is] a social actor within a public forum" (Flower, 2003, p. 745) then we can see the students' attempts at emphasis as an attempt at creating a written sentence that

expresses its meaning in the same way a spoken sentence, with inflections, might.

Emoticons

In approaching this research, one Internet dialect marker that I expected to find throughout the coding process were emoticons. Because emoticons have reached such a cultural status, especially the smiley face, and are an expected marker of writing and communicating on the Internet I expected a high use of them, especially in blog posts. In reflecting on the data, however, far fewer emoticons were used in blogs than I had initially expected, and not a single emoticon showed up in the academic essays.

In the introductory survey students were asked to identify ten common emoticons that represented various forms of smiley faces. This survey was a way to help establish student familiarity with various types of communication in online spaces. Overall, students were most familiar with the happy smiley face and the sad smiley face. Of the ten emoticons included in the initial survey, only four occurred in the blogs. Below is a chart that identifies the four types of emoticons that occurred in the blogs and students initial understanding of them. The chart is broken up between correct and incorrect answers and between the composition I and II classes.

In both classes 100% of the students knew the meaning behind the two most common emoticons,:) and:(. The other two emoticons used most often in the blogs were well known, but not universally.

Table 3. Emoticon use in blogs based on gender and course

Gender/Course/ID	M/I/1	M/I/5	F/II/7	F/II/8	F/II9
Number of Emoticons	7	1	4	2	1

The data showed that four of the nine students never used an emoticon or any form of facial expression in their blogs. The other five students used less than seven emoticons each over the eight weeks. Below is a chart that shows the use of various emoticons between male and female students and composition I and II students.

It is interesting to note that the student to use the most emoticons was a male in the composition I course. Scholars, such as Alecia Wolf (2000) who looked at issues of gender and the use of emoticons, have blurred the expectations of emotion, emoticon use, and gender. As the study at hand suggest, the expectations that females would use emoticons as a way to express emotion more often than males is complicated. While there has been research done on this phenomenon (Herring, 1994; Wolf, 2000), further examination could be beneficial to understanding the relationship between gender and the use of emoticons and visual depictions of emotion in purely text-driven communication. While the above results are interesting and seem to indicate that at least one male student seemed to use emoticons equal to three of his female counterparts combined, it is also clear that the data selection is small and the results of the number of emoticons in relation to gender would need further investigation.

While the use of emoticons was present in the blogs, overall the appearance and use of such icons were minimal and patterns were difficult to distinguish. If anything, the data suggested that, at least in the case of these specific classes, students did not feel the need to emote in their academic essays and, for the most part, left emotion to the reader to decipher or conveyed emotion through other means, such as emphasis as already discussed.

FUTURE RESEARCH

Continued research on this and similar topics is clearly needed. Aside from the fact that this research is limited in breadth and scope, from an educational standpoint, it is important to truly understand how our students respond to and understand the tasks we are assigning them. Professionals are expected to be able to communicate to various audiences and in doing so must consider their needs, expectations, values, and more. More so now than ever, however, professionals must also consider the mode of delivery. As we continue to move in to what James Bolter (2001) calls the late age of print, we must prepare future professionals to know how to interact in various spaces, including digital spaces. Gunther Kress and others remind us that literacy is changing. Kress points out that there has been a "move from the now centuries-long dominance of writing to the new dominance of the image and, on the other hand, the move from the dominance of the medium of the book to the dominance of the medium of the screen" (2003, p. 1). The way we communicate and ask students to communicate is changing, and because of this we also need to understand better how communication is taking place in computer mediated environments and also

Though this research can be seen as an important step towards better understanding the affect technological spaces are having on student writing and communication, it is clear that this is only a first step. As the results from this study indicate, this specific group of first-year writing students seemed to be able to understand differing audiences for various writing spaces. Students seemed to be able to switch between audiences, tones, and context for the most part which implies an awareness of audience needs and audience expectations. While this may be true from this study, further research on a larger sample population may be useful to understand the true scope and breadth of these results. Because this research focuses only on a small group of students with a common instructor and from somewhat common backgrounds, as earlier discussed, research with multiple instructors or with students with different backgrounds may demonstrate different results.

In addition to larger sample populations, future research about the way computer-mediate environments are complicating communication may benefit from reaching beyond the writing classroom. Students often understand in the first-year writing classroom that they are being assessed on certain criteria that they seem to not apply to other environments and classes where they may be asked to write. Because of this, studying students' abilities to transition between audiences and expectations in other courses in the humanities, social-sciences, or hard sciences may reveal insightful and useful research results.

While this research is a good start, additional research is still needed to fully understand how blogging affects writing and communication in general. Questions that remain include:

- What are the similarities and differences between speech and blogging? Because the results of this research suggest a strong connection to speech patterns, it may be useful to understand the possible connections between the two.
- Because scholars are using blogs, do their blogs suggest an audience awareness or understanding? If so, how? How do their blogs reflect publishing conventions of their field?
- Based on purpose, how does audience awareness and understanding differ in blogs from traditional print texts?

CONCLUSION

This research began as an attempt to further explore an experience in the classroom. In teaching first-year writing I became aware of various Internet language markers appearing in student texts and wondered how technology was and might influence student writing. In asking students to blog in their first-year writing class I asked them to interact in two distinct spaces where audience expectations differed greatly. Through the coding process where I looked for salient patterns and coded based on the patterns, it was evident that overall students were able to tailor their writing to the spaces they were writing. In previous instances which led up to the research conducted, I noted the appearance of Internet dialect and language markers in traditional essays. When I asked students to compose in the two different spaces, the traditional essay and the blog, a freer space where such language markers and dialectical terms were acceptable, it appears that students were able to rationalize the difference in space and appropriateness. Additionally, the research suggests that students see blogging as an extension of speech and composed their texts the way one might expect a discussion to be spoken. With this in mind then, this research suggests that students do understand the needs of a text, their audience, and of the writer. When asked to compose if various spaces, students realize and adjust to the expectations placed on the form of communication.

While this study is limited by size, the results do raise interesting points of departure from previous thought. From the difference in gendered emoticons to how writers create emphasis and the correspondence between emphasis in written communication versus verbal communications, this study brings light to points that deserve closer examination because of the possibility they provide for better understanding communication in computer mediated environments. Furthermore, the fact that this study was initiated because of an observation that was not replicated, this study may suggest that asking students to participate in various spaces in the classroom allows them to think about the needs of these spaces, but that drawing student's attention to the differences is equally important.

The research also demonstrates an important point to those who have long feared the evolution of technologies as the degeneration of language and writing. While there surely is evidence to suggest that perhaps students have a different usage of language, as can even be evidenced by the genesis of this project, it is also clear that standard expectations are not lost. Students understand the different between writing environments, though at times discussions and reminders of the differences may be relevant. Regardless of discipline or field, asking writers to consider who they are writing to and why they are writing and in turn what their reader will expect from them asks them to stop, reflect, and react in their writing. It may be appropriate to shorten words, include emoticons, or use acronyms in a blog post, but, when students are aware that they will be graded on correctness to some degree though, they are more likely to demonstrate knowledge of writing that is expected of them.

REFERENCES

Baron, D. (1999). From pencils to pixels: The stages of literacy technologies. In Hawishier, G., & Selfe, C. (Eds.), *Passions, pedagogies, and 21ˢᵗ century technologies* (pp. 15–33). Logan, UT: Utah State UP.

Barrios, B. (2005). Blogs: A primer: A guide to weblogs in the classroom and in research for compositionists, rhetoricians, educators, &c. *Computers and composition online*. Retrieved February 24, 2009, from http://www.bgsu.edu/departments/english/cconline/bap/

Bloch, J., & Crosby, C. (2008). Blogging and academic writing development. In Zhang, F., & Barber, B. (Eds.), *Handbook of research on computer-enhanced language acquisition and learning* (pp. 36–47). Hershey, PA: Information Science Reference.

Boling, E., Castek, J., Zawilinski, L., Barton, K., & Nierlich, T. (2008). Technology in literacy education collaborative literacy: Blogs and Internet projects. *The Reading Teacher*, *61*(6), 504–406. doi:10.1598/RT.61.6.10

Bolter, J. D. (2001). *Writing space: Computers, hypertext, and the remediation of print* (2nd ed.). Hillsdale, NJ: Erlbaum Associates.

Bortree, D. S. (2005). Presentation of self on the web: An ethnographic study of teenage girls' weblogs. *Education Communication and Information*, *5*(1), 25–39.

Chretien, K., Goldman, E., & Faselis, C. (2008). The reflective writing class blog: Using technology to promote reflection and professional development. *Journal of General Internal Medicine*, *23*(12), 2066–2070. doi:10.1007/s11606-008-0796-5

Craig, D. (2004). Instant messaging: The language of youth literacy. *Essays from the program in writing and rhetoric at Stanford University* (pp. 116-133). Retrieved January 1, 2009, from http://www.stanford.edu/group/pwr/publications/Boothe_0203/PWR%20Boothe-Craig.pdf

Doostadar, A. (2004). 'The vulgar spirit of blogging': On language, culture, and power in Persian weblogestan. *American Anthropologist*, *104*(4), 651–662. doi:10.1525/aa.2004.106.4.651

Elbow, P. (2002). Closing my eyes as I speak: An argument for ignoring audience. In Johnson, T. R., & Morahan, S. (Eds.), *Teaching composition: Background readings* (pp. 197–218). Boston: Bedford/St. Martin's.

Faigley, L. (1986). Competing theories of process: A critique and a proposal. *College English*, *48*(6), 527–442. doi:10.2307/376707

Flower, L. (2003). Cognition, context, and theory building. In Villanueva, V. (Ed.), *Cross-talk in comp theory: A reader* (2nd ed., pp. 739–771). Urbana, IL: National Council of Teachers of English.

Flower, L., & Hayes, J. (1981). A cognitive process theory of writing. *College Composition and Communication*, *32*(4), 365–387. doi:10.2307/356600

Fulkerson, R. (2004). Composition at the turn of the twenty-first century. *College Composition and Communication*, *56*(4), 654–687.

Glenn, C., Goldthwaite, M. A., & Connors, R. (2003). *The St. Martin's guide to teaching* (5th ed.). Boston: Bedford St. Martin's.

Goldsborough, R. (2005). Keeping e-mail in top form. *Black Issues in Higher Education*, *22*(3), 39.

Gurak, L. J., Antonijevic, S., Johnson, L., Ratliff, C., & Reyman, J. (2005). Introduction: Weblogs, rhetoric, community, and culture. In L. J. Gurak, S. Antonijevic, L. Johnson, C. Ratliff, & J. Reyman (Eds.), *Into the blogosphere: Rhetoric, community, and culture of weblogs*. Retrieved December 17, 2008, from http://blog.lib.umn.edu/blogosphere/introduction.html

Hazen, K. (2001). Teaching about dialects. *Eric clearinghouse on language and linguistics Washington DC*. Retrieved February 9, 2009, from http://permanent.access.gpo.gov/websites/eric.ed.gov/ERIC_Digests/ed456674.htm

Herring, S. (1994). Gender differences in computer-mediated communication: Bringing familiar baggage to the new frontier. *CPSR newsletter, 18*(1). Retrieved January 15, 2009, from http://cpsr.org/issues/womenintech/herring/

Huckin, T. (1992). Context-sensitive text analysis. In Kirsch, G., & Sullivan, P. A. (Eds.), *Methods and methodology in composition research* (pp. 84–104). Carbondale, IL: Southern Illinois UP.

Huffaker, D. A. (2005). The educated blogger: Using weblogs to promote literacy in the classroom. *Advancement of computing in education journal, 13*(2), 91-98.

Huffaker, D. A., & Calvert, S. L. (2005). Gender, identity, and language use in teenage blogs. *Journal of computer-mediated communication, 10*(2), retrieved February 20, 2009 from http://jcmc.indiana.edu/vol10/issue2/huffaker.html

Kress, G. (2003). *Literacy in the new media age*. London: Routledge. doi:10.4324/9780203164754

Krohn, F. B. (2004). A generational approach to using emoticons as nonverbal communication. *Journal of technical writing and communication, 34*(4), 321-328.

Lee, S., Hwang, T., & Lee, H. H. (2006). Corporate blogging strategies for the Fortune 400 companies. *Management Decision, 44*(3), 316–334. doi:10.1108/00251740610656232

Lo, S.-K. (2008). The nonverbal communication functions of emoticons in computer-mediated communication. *Cyberpsychology & Behavior, 11*(5), 595–587. doi:10.1089/cpb.2007.0132

McCullagh, D., & Broache, A. (2007). Blogs turn 10 -- Who's the father? *CNET news*. Retrieved February 9, 2009, from http://news.cnet.com/2100-1025_3-6168681.html

Schneider, B. (2002). Nonstandard quotes: Superimpositions and cultural maps. *College Composition and Communication, 54*(2), 188–207. doi:10.2307/1512145

Shoffner, M. (2007). Preservice English teachers and technology: A consideration of weblogs for the English classroom. *Contemporay issues in technology and teacher education, 7*(4). Retrieved February 1, 2009, from http://www.citejournal.org/vol7/iss4/languagearts/article1.cfm

Shultz Colbey, R., Colby, R., Felix, J., Murphy, R., Thomas, B., & Blair, K. (2005). A role for blogs in graduate education: Remediating the rhetorical tradition? *Computers and composition online,* retrieved February 13, 2009, from http://www. bgsu.edu/cconline/colbyetal/colbyetal.htm

Suzuki, R. (2004). Diaries as introspective research tools: From Ashton-Warner to blogs. *Teaching English as a second or foreign language, 8*(1). Retrieved December 13, 2008, from http://tesl-ej. org/ej29/int.html

Wolf, A. (2000). Emotional expression online: Gender differences in emoticon use. *Cyberpsychology & Behavior, 3*(5), 827–833. doi:10.1089/10949310050191809

ADDITIONAL READING

Akayoglu, S., & Altun, A. (2009). The functions of negotiation of meaning in text-based CMC. In R. de Cassia, Veiga Marriott & P. L. Torres (Eds.) Handbook of research on e-learning methodologies for language acquisition (pp. 291-306). Hershey: Information Science Reference.

Almjeld, J. (2006). Making blogs produce: Using modern academic storehouses and factories. *Computers and Composition Online,* Retrieved May 13, 2009, from http://www.bgsu.edu/cconline/almjeld/almjeld.htm

Barrie, G. (2009). Blogging – private become public and public becomes personalized. *Aslib Proceedings, 61*(2), 120–126. doi:10.1108/00012530910946875

Bouldin, A. S., Holmes, E. R., & Fortenberry, M. L. (2006). "Blogging" about course concepts: Using technology for reflective journaling in a communications class. *American Journal of pharmaceutical education, 70*(4). Retrieved 10 May 2009, from http://www.pubmedcentral.nih. gov/articlerender.fcgi?artid=1636988

Carrington, C. (2005). The uncanny, digital texts and literacy. *Language and Education, 19*(6), 467–482. doi:10.1080/09500780508668698

Derks, D., Arjan, E. R. B., & Von Grumbkow, J. (2008). Emoticons in computer-mediated communication: Social motives and social context. *Cyberpsychology & Behavior, 11*(1), 99–101. doi:10.1089/cpb.2007.9926

Herring, S., Scheidt, L. A., Wright, E., & Bonus, S. (2005). Weblogs as a bridging genre. *Information Technology & People, 18*(2), 142–171. doi:10.1108/09593840510601513

Herring, S. C. (2004). Slouching toward the ordinary Current trends in computer-mediated communications. *New Media & Society, 6*(2), 26–36. doi:10.1177/1461444804039906

Higdon, J., & Topaz, C. (2009). Blogs and wikis as instructional tools: A social adaption of just-in-time teaching. *College Teaching, 57*(2), 105–110. doi:10.3200/CTCH.57.2.105-110

Howard, R. G. (2008). The vernacular web of participatory media. *Critical Studies in Media Communication, 25*(4), 490–513. doi:10.1080/15295030802468065

Joinsen, A. N. (2001). Self-disclosure in computer-mediated communication: The role of self-awareness and visual anonymity. *European Journal of Social Psychology, 31*, 177–192. doi:10.1002/ejsp.36

Kelleher, T. (2009). Conversational voice, communicated commitment, and public relations outcomes in interactive online communication. *The Journal of Communication, 59*(1), 172–188. doi:10.1111/j.1460-2466.2008.01410.x

Kim, H. N. (2008). The phenomenon of blogs and theoretical model of blog use in educational contexts. *Computers & Education, 51*(3), 1342–1352. doi:10.1016/j.compedu.2007.12.005

Kress, G., & van Leeuqen, T. (2003). *New literacies*. London: Open University Press.

Marika, L. (2008). Conceptualizing personal media. *New Media & Society, 10*(5), 683–702. doi:10.1177/1461444808094352

Nardi, B. A., Schiano, D. J., Grumbrecht, M., & Swartz, L. (2004). Why we blog. *Communications of the ACM, 47*(12), 41–46. doi:10.1145/1035134.1035163

Nowson, S., Oberlander, J., & Gill, A. J. (2005). Weblogs, genres and individual differences. *In Proceedings of the 27th Annual Conference of the Cognitive Science Society*, 1666-1671.

Paulus, T. M., Payne, R. L., & Jahns, L. (2009). "Am I making sense her?" What blogging reveals about undergraduate student understanding. *Journal of interactive online learning, 8*(1), 2-22.

Penrod, D. (2007). *Using blogs to enhance literacy: The next powerful step in 21-st century learning*. Lanham, MD: Rowman & Littlefield Education.

Repman, J., Zinskie, C., & Carlson, R. D. (2005). Effective use of CMC in interactive learning. *Computers in the school, 22*(1 & 2), 57-69.

Schmidt, J. (2007). Blogging practices: An analytical framework. *Journal of Computer-Mediated Communication, 12*(4), Retrieved 10 May 2009, from http://jcmc.indiana.edu/vol12/issue4/schmidt.html

Shaw, P. (2008). Spelling, accent and identity in computer-mediated communication. *English Today, 24*, 42–49. doi:10.1017/S0266078408000199

Stefanone, M. A., & Jang, C. Y. (2007). Writing for friends and family: The interpersonal nature of blogs. *Journal of Computer-Mediated Communication, 13*(1), Retrieved May 1, 2009, from http://jcmc.indiana.edu/vol13/issue1/stefanone.html

Wang, S.-K., & Hsua, H.-Y. (2008). Reflections on using blogs to expand in-class discussion. *TechTrends, 52*(3), 81–85. doi:10.1007/s11528-008-0160-y

Wilde, E. (2008). Deconstructing blogs. *Online Information Review, 32*(3), 401–414. doi:10.1108/14684520810889691

ENDNOTE

[1] Newer versions of Internet browsers offer an automatic spell check function much like traditional word processing programs. However, at the time this research was conducted this was not the case.

Chapter 12

Learning to Work Virtually:
Conversational Repair as a Resource for Norm Development in Computer–Mediated Team Meetings

Kris M. Markman
University of Memphis, USA

ABSTRACT

This chapter presents an analysis of interaction in computer-mediated group meetings. Five undergraduate students used a quasi-synchronous chat interface to conduct four virtual team meetings. Using the framework of conversation analysis, I describe how self-initiated self repair of minor errors such as typos was used by team members as a vehicle for group norm development. The norms for typing style (punctuation, correcting typos and spelling mistakes) vary widely across computer-mediated communication (CMC) contexts. I show how the main function of the repair attempts was not to clarify meaning, but rather to help team members, particularly in their first meeting, work out an agreed-upon set of typing conventions for their subsequent interactions, thus contributing to the development of a norm of informality.

INTRODUCTION

Scholars in a variety of fields, including organizational communication, management, and educational technology, have sought to better understand the obstacles to computer-mediated collaboration and teamwork, and to explain how virtual groups can be used effectively in a variety of contexts. Often this scholarship focuses, directly or indirectly, on the communicative practices of computer-mediated

groups, and how these practices relate to factors such as trust, interaction style, conflict management, leadership, relationship building, etc. For example, research has found that computer-mediated communication (CMC) does not present a de facto obstacle to successful group problem solving, and that groups can and do compensate for any limitations imposed by the medium (Potter & Balthazard, 2002). The style of interaction that the group as a whole exhibits, as opposed to the personalities of the individual team members, can predict contextual outcomes in virtual teams (Balthazard, Potter,

DOI: 10.4018/978-1-61520-827-2.ch012

& Warren, 2004). Positive outcomes in virtual teamwork have also been linked to the presence or development of shared understanding among team members (Majchrzak, Rice, King, Malhotra, & Ba, 2000), as have listening and paying attention (Furst, Blackburn, & Rosen, 1999). Additional research has shown that effective virtual teams are able to fit their communication patterns to the task (Maznevski & Chudoba, 2000). As a whole, this scholarship points to the need for further examinations of specific communicative practices, particularly as they relate to the development of virtual groups and teams.

This chapter expands the research on computer-mediated group development by taking a different approach, focusing specifically on *how* conversation in virtual team meetings unfolds. I draw on the methodological tools of conversation analysis (CA) (e.g. Heritage, 1984; Silverman, 1998) to demonstrate empirically how conversational repair can be used as a tool for the development of group norms (Tuckman, 1965). In this context, repair refers to occasions when participants stop the ongoing trajectory of talk to fix troubles in their own or in another participant's prior turn. Within research on spoken interaction, repair has been shown to be evidence of how participants in conversation achieve intersubjective understanding (Schegloff, 1992, 2000). However, in this chapter I will show that repair can be used for more than fixing misunderstandings, and that, in the course of virtual meetings, it can serve as a resource for team members to test the boundaries of their interaction style.

I begin with a short discussion of norms and computer-mediated group development, followed by a brief review of research on repair in spoken and computer-mediated interaction. I will then present data drawn from a larger case study of conversational structures in virtual team meetings and show how repair is used as a tool during the norming process. I conclude with a discussion of the implications of this research for the study of virtual groups and suggestions for future research directions.

BACKGROUND

Norms and Virtual Groups

Group development has been the subject of much research over the last 50 years, with the result being a number of different models that attempt to describe, and sometimes prescribe, the ways that groups form over time (for a review, see Chidambaram & Bostrom, 1996). One of the most prominent models, Tuckman's (1965) foundational work on the stages of group development, distinguishes between the interpersonal stages of group development and the task behaviors exhibited in groups. During the initial stage, *forming*, groups members engage in testing behaviors as they attempt to identify boundaries in the newly-formed group. After a period of conflict (*storming*), groups engage in *norming*, where roles are adopted, standards evolve, and cohesiveness develops. Groups then enter the final phase, *performing*, where they settle into doing the work of the group. Tuckman and Jensen (1977) later added a fifth phase, *adjourning*, to accommodate those groups with a specific life-span. A different approach to group development is found in the punctuated equilibrium model put forth by Gersick (1988). Based on field studies of organizational groups, Gersick found that rather than moving through a linear series of stages, groups tended to establish working and communication patterns early on, usually in their first meetings, that remained stable until a change period at the midpoint of the group's life. Although these two models are indicative of how differently group development can be modeled, the research overall shows the initial interactions to be critical for how groups will learn to work and collaborate (Chidambaram & Bostrom, 1996).

Although most research on group development has been based on face-to-face groups, the rise in prominence of CMC for group interaction has led to an attendant focus on the development of computer-mediated groups, and specifically the development and expression of normative behavior in mediated groups. For example, messages within computer-mediated groups have been shown to become more prototypical over time, showing the development of norms for message content (although this pattern did not hold for message form (Postmes, Spears, & Lea, 2000). Birchmeier, Joinson, and Dietz-Uhler (2005) found that members of an online discussion forum did not follow the expected pattern of looking to higher status group members for the development of a normative response to deviant behavior in the group. Dietz-Uhler, Bishop-Clark, and Howard (2005) noted a positive, but weak, linear correlation between the formation of and adherence to a norm of self-disclosure and time in asynchronous discussion groups. They found that the norm, once formed, tended to be reinforced by normative behaviors, while non-normative behaviors were ignored. In computer-supported learning groups, familiarity among team members can contribute to members' perceptions of greater critical and exploratory group norms (Janssen, Erkens, Kirschner, & Kanselaar, 2009). In addition, research has found that the following of formally stated rules in computer-mediated teams can enhance both the material and affective dimensions of group work (Walther & Bunz, 2005).

Research has shown that the norming experience in computer-mediated groups varies with respect to traditional models of group development. In Graham's (2003) model of computer-mediated group norm development, groups were given instruction on the importance of forming group norms and expectations. His model diverges from the Tuckman (1965; Tuckman & Jensen, 1977) model of group development, in that Graham found that norm development could take place at any point in the group's lifecycle. Graham's model depicts norms as being developed through a cyclical process whereby norms are refined from generalized behaviors with fuzzy boundaries to operationalized norms with clear expectations and behaviors. However Johnson, Suriya, Yoon, Berrett, and La Fleur (2002) found closer support for

the Tuckman rather than Gersick (1988) model in their virtual learning teams. In their study, teams were not given formal guidance on norm development, but the groups' interactions included an initial discussion of group norms and expectations, generally skipping the storming stage proposed by Tuckman. What seems clear is that time and communication are as important to the development of computer-mediated groups as they are to traditional face-to-face groups.

Repair and Shared Understanding

As noted previously, scholarship on virtual teams has stressed the importance of communication to successful virtual collaboration (Hughes, O'Brien, Randall, Rouncefield, & Tolmie, 2001), and more specifically its role the development of group norms (Ahuja & Galvin, 2003). The development of group norms also rests upon the team's ability to understand each other. Shared understanding is not a given, however, but must be achieved by parties through interaction, and this achievement may be complicated by the structural properties of computer chat. Whereas face-to-face teams have additional resources, such as intonation, gesture, and gaze, to call upon to aid mutual understanding, in Ahuja and Galvin note that in virtual team meetings talk (in text form) is often the only mechanism members have for communication. One important property of talk is that it serves as a primary mechanism for parties in interaction to display their understanding, and at the same time functions as a tool for recognizing and repairing problems in conversations (Schegloff, 1992). Repair, as it is usually discussed within conversation analysis, involves instances when participants in an interaction stop the ongoing trajectory of talk in order to deal with possible trouble (Schegloff, 2000). There are two components to repair: the initiation, or location of some trouble source, and the repair proper. Repair can be initiated by the self (the speaker of the trouble source turn) or by any party other than the speaker of the trouble source, and there is a preference within repair for self-correction (Schegloff, Jefferson, & Sacks, 1977), i.e. the overwhelming majority of repair turns are performed by the speaker of the trouble source turn.

Schegloff, Jefferson and Sacks (1977) note that one reason for the predominance of self-correction is that opportunities for self-repair present themselves before opportunities for others to repair a trouble source. For example, the most common type of repair, self-initiated self-repair (SISR), occurs most frequently within the same turn as the trouble source, with the next most frequent opportunity being in the transition space after the trouble source turn. In spoken interaction, these locations are only available to the current speaker, thus leading to the preponderance of SISR. When others initiate repair, it is usually in the next turn, that is, the turn immediately following the trouble-source turn, although slots for other-initiation of repair beyond the next turn have also been identified (Schegloff, 1992, 2000).

The types of problems that constitute trouble sources in talk are varied, but can generally be grouped into a few categories: problematic words, problems with person reference, and problems with next speaker selection (Schegloff et al., 1977). The techniques used to initiate repair can also be grouped according to who is doing the initiating. Same turn self-initiations are generally accomplished by devices such as word cut-offs, sound stretches and similar perturbations, while other-initiations fall into several groups of turn constructional devices (Schegloff et al.). These include question words, partial repeats, and partial repeats with a question word. Schegloff (1992) noted that third-position SISR is generally initiated by the use of a particle such as "no," "no, no," or "oh." These repair moments allow participants to deal with a myriad of troubles, but they also provide a context for other interactional moves. For example, Schegloff (1997) noted that other-initiated repair can be used as an instrument for accomplishing other types of actions, such

as displaying doubt, disagreement, rejection, etc. Of particular relevance here are findings by Waring (2005) that other-initiated repair can be used as a vehicle for doing affiliation and disaffiliation in multi-party interaction and by Keating (1993), who found that in face-to-face groups, self-repair by group members was an important tool for fleshing out negotiation and inviting collaboration. Furthermore, Robinson (2006) found that apology-based other-initiated repair (i.e. I'm sorry? Sorry?) allows for the management of relationships via the management of trouble responsibility, i.e. it allows for face-saving by assigning responsibility for the trouble to the hearer, not the speaker.

Repair in Chat

Traditionally, conversation analysis has been focused on the study of spoken (oral) communication, either in face-to-face or telephone-mediated settings. However, with the increasingly widespread use of the Internet for recreational and institutional communication, language and social interaction scholars have begun to turn their attentions to the various types of CMC channels. Specifically, researchers adopting a CA perspective have noted that participants in so-called "synchronous" CMC environments, such as chat rooms, display an orientation towards the interactions as being fundamentally conversational (for example, Colomb & Simutis, 1996; Herring, 1999; Simpson, 2005; ten Have, 2000; Werry, 1996; Zitzen & Stein, 2004). This growing body of research has begun to document the properties of emerging forms of text-based conversation, particularly with respect to interactional coherence and turn organization (e.g. Garcia & Jacobs, 1998, 1999; Herring, 1999; Markman, 2005; O'Neill & Martin, 2003; Panyametheekul & Herring, 2003; Simpson, 2005). However, repair, another interactionally crucial conversational resource, has received only minimal attention from researchers of computer-mediated discourse.

Schonfeldt and Golato (2003) found that participants in German IRC channels adapted the same basic repair mechanisms used in oral conversation to this medium. Trouble sources, once identified, caused the ongoing sequence to be stopped while the trouble was addressed. Schonfeldt and Golato noted the preference for self-repair in oral interaction also holds for chat. The most frequent type of repair they found was other-initiated self-repair, followed by self-initiated self-repair, although the positions normally associated with repair (transition space, third turn) were not available because of the nature of the chat medium. They also identified a trouble source unique to the chat environment, the non-response (Rintel, Pittam, & Mulholland, 2003), finding that participants frequently initiated repair when a first-pair part was felt to be ignored. Markman's (2006) research also noted the preference for self-correction in chat, which suggests that this is a characteristic more fundamental to interaction than to a specific channel of communication.

In this chapter, I focus specifically on SISR. In particular, I examine instances where participants repair simple typos or spelling errors. I will show that these repair attempts have interactional significance beyond furthering basic understanding. I argue that they also function as a vehicle for the team to develop group norms.

SOCIAL REPAIR: ESTABLISHING CMC CONVENTIONS

The data for this chapter come from a case study of conversation in virtual team meetings. The team members are five undergraduate students from a large southwestern university who were enrolled in a summer semester independent study course. The researcher also participated in the team meetings. Their goal for the course was to work as a virtual team to research a project on innovative student uses of technology. They held four virtual meetings using the chat function in the Blackboard course management system. Computer software was used to make video recordings of each participant's computer screen during the meetings, and the chat conversations were also automatically logged by the Blackboard system. Both the video recordings and the chat logs were used as data for this analysis.

Using the framework of conversation analysis, I identified and extracted all instances of repair from the four meetings, for a total of 54 instances. In the textual medium of computer chat, turns do not unfold, but rather appear all at once, as self-contained units. Chat participants can, and do engage in a form of self-initiated, same-turn repair, but this type of repair is not visible to the other chat participants, and thus does not have immediate interactional significance. However, once a chat participant has posted a turn to the chat, there are other types of repair that occur in chat that are interactionally relevant. As with spoken conversation, repair in computer chat can be either self- or other-initiated, and likewise, the repair can be completed by oneself or another. The most common repair strategy used by the team members in this case study was self-initiated self-repair. In general, these attempts at repair came in the speaker's immediately next turn[1]. This means that participants posted a turn, and then quickly noticed a mistake or error, and acted immediately to correct the problem. Half of all SISR turns (n=30) in this dataset were done to correct typos or similar errors, and it is on these specific instances of repair (which I will call Type 1 SISR) that this chapter will focus.

Table 1 shows the distribution of Type 1 SISR over the course of the four meetings. I propose that the most common type of SISR turns found in these meetings, turns that fix typos or other minor mistakes, have a dual purpose. Nominally, these turns are undertaken to further the accomplishment of intersubjective understanding. More importantly, I contend that these turns also serve as a form of social repair.

Note that most of these repair turns occur during the team's first meeting on June 10th. In order to better understand how these turns are facilitating

Table 1. Frequency of Type 1 SISR by participant

Participant[a]	Meeting Date				
	6/10	6/16	6/22	6/29	Total
Evan	1	0	1	1	3
I-Fang	0	1	0	1	2
Rebeca	3	0	0	0	3
Sidney	1	0	0	0	1
Thadine	0	1	1	0	2
Researcher	3	0	1	1	5
Total	8	2	3	3	16

aNote. Names of all participants have been changed.

the process of norm formation, I will present a few examples from this meeting. In each of the examples, the trouble source and its repair have been highlighted in their respective turns. The left column indicates the time the turn was received by the chat server.

Examples 1 and 2 show two very simple types of errors, and two very straightforward ways of handling the repair. In example 1 the researcher has accidentally hit enter and posted a turn before completing her thought, a mistake which is marked in the immediate next turn by the word "oops." While it might not have been immediately clear to the other team members that the turn posted at 10:19:08 was a mistake, it is clearly marked as such by the next turn. Even more common are troubles such as we see in example 2, where the

researcher makes a simple typing error "giys," which gets repaired in the next turn by simply retyping the problem word.

Example 3 also comes from the first meeting. Here team member Evan makes a slightly more elaborate correction, by calling attention to his mistake with the repair turn "or fine" to correct the typo "fint."

Example 4 shows yet another device for correcting typos in chat, the use of an asterisk. Although of unknown origin, it is a commonly used convention in chat to retype the word with an asterisk either before or after the correction as a way of signaling repair. Here Sidney has left out one "o" in "good" in his post at 10:34: 26, which he corrects with "good*" at 10:34:29. These first four examples show how participants employ a variety of devices to repair minor errors in their posts. The simplest form of repair is simply to re-post the corrected trouble source in the next turn, but participants can also use conjunctions, symbols, or interjections to further mark these turns as repair attempts. What is also notable about these turns is how minor these mistakes generally

Example 1. Meeting 1

10:19:08	RESEARCHER: Sidney,
10:19:12	RESEARCHER: oops

Example 2. Meeting 1

10:23:02	RESEARCHER: I think you giys need to talk about your network trees,
10:23:05	RESEARCHER: guys

Example 3. Meeting 1

10:57:41	EVAN: That meeting time is fint
10:57:47	EVAN: or fine

Example 4. Meeting 1

10:34:26	SIDNEY: sounds god
10:34:29	REBECA: I feel like i have some kind of goal now!
10:34:29	SIDNEY: good*

are. Although in example 1 the accidental enter could prove confusing for other participants, the researcher's use of a simple "oops" to repair the trouble shows an orientation to the problem as a minor one not requiring further clarification. Similarly, all of the participants are engaged in the same activity, namely typing their turns at a computer keyboard, and thus they could reasonably be expected to figure out, from the context and/or from the layout of the keyboard, that "fint" was supposed to be "fine" or "giys" was meant to be "guys." It seems then, that in repairing these simple mistakes, participants are doing more than just promoting understanding of meaning. A look at a few more complex examples from the first meeting will further illustrate my claim.

In example 5, Rebeca mistakenly types the number 1 instead of an exclamation mark. She uses her next turn (which is displaced two positions by other actions) to not only re-type, but explain her mistake ("i meant hello all!"). Once again, anyone familiar with (or indeed looking at) a standard U.S. QWERTY computer keyboard will see that the numeral 1 shares the same key as the exclamation point; the "!" symbol is obtained by depressing the shift key along with the "1" key. It is a common mistake and one that would likely go unnoticed, and yet Rebeca not only repairs this turn, she calls attention to it by explicitly stating the obvious.

Finally, in example 6 shows an even more complex instance of Type 1 SISR, one that very clearly illustrates the function of these turns for the team. In this example, Rebeca posts a SISR turn at 10:19:33 in response to having typed "ge" instead of "he" at 10:19:20. Here Rebeca acknowledges and accounts for a problem without specifically fixing the trouble. That she does *not* fix it reflects her probable assumption that the rest of the team not only understood the trouble source to which she refers, but also her intended meaning; the letter 'g' is next to the letter 'h' on the QWERTY computer keyboard and the word in question is situated exactly where the personal pronoun "he" would be expected. In effect, what Rebeca offers for a repair is closer to an account. Her hyperbolic use of double exclamation points and using "spell" when she is really referring to typing convey an apologetic stance, reflecting the tentative nature of interaction in the team's first meeting. I-Fang's response at 10:20:10 that given the late time of the meeting, Rebeca's mistake was "justifyable" shows her acceptance of Rebeca's account, and her laugh token at 10:20:11 could be a response to her own misspelling, or it could also be a way of further diffusing any possible tension in the interaction (or possibly both). What we see in this example is the closest to an explicit development of a norm for interaction, i.e. that typos and spelling mistakes made in the chat will not have negative social consequences. When Rebeca responds to I-Fang at 10:20:33 that it makes her feel good, what she is really doing is displaying her comfort with the idea that the team will have a relaxed attitude towards typing style. In effect, the team has established a rule for their interactions, and it's notable that this is the last

Example 5. Meeting 1

10:10:28	REBECA: hello all1
10:10:29	RESEARCHER: so, depending on how big your movie files are, you might be able to send it to me that way.
10:10:33	[THADINE joined the session]
10:10:37	REBECA: i meant hello all!

Example 6. Meeting 1

10:19:20	REBECA: Evan is not online, i have in Windows messenger and ge is not active.
10:19:32	SIDNEY: works for me
10:19:33	REBECA: I cannot spell!!
10:19:50	RESEARCHER: I also just emailed him (evan)
10:19:57	REBECA: right on!
10:20:10	**I-FANG: hey it's 10pm...not being able to spell is justifyable**
10:20:11	**I-FANG: hehe**
10:20:21	RESEARCHER: So would Thursday after 5pm work for all of you?
10:20:31	SIDNEY: yes
10:20:33	**REBECA: thanks that makes me feel good!**
10:20:38	**REBECA: Ha Ha**

time that Rebeca will engage in this type of repair for the duration of the team's project.

In the next set of examples we move away from the first meeting, to see how well this new norm for correcting typos has held up.

Examples 7 and 8 are from team member Thadine. Thadine did not post any Type 1 SISR turns in the first meeting; in fact, examination of the chat logs revealed that out of her 34 posts in that meeting, she made only three typos. Further examination of her screen recordings reveals Thadine to be quite a skilled and conscientious typist, and she generally fixes her errors while she is composing her posts. Thus it is likely that those three errors from the first meeting simply escaped her notice. In example 7, from the team's second meeting, she makes a mistake approximately four minutes after entering the chat room, and it is in fact the first typo to appear in one of her posts during this meeting. As with previous examples, it is easily recognizable as "obviously" with a few transposed letters, but Thadine offers both an apology and retypes the trouble source in her

repair attempt at 5:25:08. Given that this is still the second meeting, and that Thadine may have a heightened sense of the importance of good typing skills, she may be testing out her own boundaries, as well as those of the group. Example 8 shows Thadine's only other Type 1 SISR attempt, from early on in the third meeting. This example is of the most simplified type, where only the trouble source word is retyped, in this case "problem," perhaps indicating that by this time Thadine has become more comfortable with the norm of not fixing typos, although again they remain rare in her posts.

Examples 9 and 10 represent the only two instances of Type 1 SISR from team member I-Fang in this dataset. In both cases, the problem I-Fang repairs is one unique to a textual medium such as chat--accidental use of uppercase letters. In example 9, she is greeting one of her fellow teammates, and in example 10 she is typing a response to someone's question, and both times the latter part of the turn was typed in all caps. Although the conventions for punctuation and capitalization in CMC are fairly fluid, one widely-

Example 7. Meeting 2

5:25:02	THADINE: but apparently he is pretty busy obvi-souly
5:25:08	THADINE: sorry obviously

Example 8. Meeting 3

5:10:12	THADINE: no proble,
5:10:17	THADINE: problem

Example 9. Meeting 2

5:21:15	I-FANG: hi rEBECA
5:21:18	[THADINE joined the session]
5:21:20	REBECA: hey
5:21:20	I-FANG: oops

held convention holds that using all capital letters is the textual equivalent of shouting, and it is generally frowned upon. Although I-Fang's use of all-capitals was clearly a mistake, she nonetheless is oriented to its social consequences. In example 9 she uses her next turn to acknowledge this accidental transgression with "oops." The use of this exclamation initiates repair by calling attention to her mistake, while simultaneously offering a weak apology. Although the literal meaning of her turn at 5:21:15 was not obscured by her use of all-capitals, I-Fang's use of SISR in her immediate next turn can be understood as a repair to the social meaning of her previous turn. She repeats this use of "oops" in the first part of her post at 5:06:22 in example 10, using ellipses to separate the repair attempt off from a continuation of her thought from her previous post. It is interesting to note that, in contrast to Thadine, who seems to take great care in her typing as a general rule, I-Fang's posts are rife with typos, although her screen recordings show that she does catch and correct some mistakes as she types (see Table 2 for a comparison of errors vs. turns for all participants). Based on my interactions with her, it's likely that I-Fang was not a native English speaker, and thus some of her difficulties may have been linguistic in nature. However, she does display, as we see in example 6, a sensitivity to the need

for team members to explore these boundaries with each other, even if she does not attempt to repair her own errors.

DISCUSSION

The phenomena that get repaired in these turns are somewhat analogous to mispronunciations and mistakes of this kind in spoken interaction. However, timing plays an important role in the function of this type of repair in chat and how it differs from spoken conversation. SISR attempts in spoken conversation are undertaken on the fly. Speakers fix problems as they are being produced, and listeners are following along with them in real time. Chat, as with all forms of CMC, separates the production of an utterance from its reception, making it possible to fix mistakes before the turn becomes interactionally relevant. Recall from Table 1 the number of Type 1 SISR turns is markedly larger in the team's first meeting on June 10. At this point, four of the five team members have met face to face (with their professor and the researcher) on one occasion, and the fifth has met only with the researcher. The team is still in the beginning phases of formation, and they are still learning about how to work with each other, as well as how to work virtually. I would argue that the team members are oriented to the fact that CMC conventions are fluid and evolving.

Research has shown that both novice and experienced CMC users can be sensitive to paralinguistic cues (including typographical marks and spelling/typing errors), and that the presence of these cues are "associated with the formation of impressions of the personal attributes of the mes-

Example 10. Meeting 4

5:06:12	I-FANG: yeH IT USUALLY HAVE THE SOUND THING
5:06:16	THADINE: Evan, that news clip file is 33MB. Maybe it would be best for me to give you it on CD?
5:06:22	I-FANG: oops...it's not ur imagination

Table 2. Frequency of Type 1 error by participant

Participant	Meeting Date # of errors (total turns)				Total
	6/10	6/16	6/22	6/29	
Evan	2 (7)	12 (17)	19 (43)	33 (71)	66
I-Fang	10 (60)	12 (88)	14 (54)	10 (55)	46
Rebeca	5 (76)	10 (121)	7 (82)	4 (63)	26
Sidney	4 (36)	6 (65)	0 (5)	0 (6)	10
Thadine	3 (34)	3 (99)	3 (100)	0 (67)	9
Researcher	21 (125)	5 (35)	4 (20)	6 (27)	36
Total	45	48	47	53	193

sage senders" (Lea & Spears, 1992, p. 335). For some people, typos in email, IM, chat, and other CMC channels can be interpreted as rude or inconsiderate. By initiating repairs on simple technical mistakes, the team members can test the waters, so to speak, to see how others react. In particular, those repair turns that do not explicitly correct the error by re-typing, but instead call attention to the error with the use of apologies (as in example 7), accounts or explanations (as in examples 5 and 6) or exclamations like "oops" (as in examples 1, 9 and 10) reinforce the argument that the primary function of these turns is not semantic, but rather relational. That is, they deal primarily with the existence of an error, rather than the substance of it. In effect, they are using these SISR turns to test and develop norms about the team's CMC; what kind of problems need to be fixed, and what kind do not. By spending time in the initial meeting fixing minor typing mistakes, they can determine if there will be any social consequences to ignoring these mistakes in the future. These SISR turns therefore helped establish a norm of informality, which can have a secondary benefit of increasing perceptions of immediacy (O'Sullivan, Hunt, & Lippert, 2004) and contribute to rapport building in the team (Park, 2007).

Two final examples reinforce this point by providing a contrast to the earlier examples.

Examples 11 and 12 are both from team member Evan, and both are from the latter stages in the team's interaction. Example 11, from the third meeting, occurs towards the end of the meeting, in contrast to most of the Type 1 SISR turns, which tend to be clustered early in the meetings. Here there are actually two typos in Evan's turn at 5:44:56, but only one of them, incorrectly typing "side" for the proper name "sid," gets repaired. The word spelled "bouat" is analyzable as "about," and indeed Evan's decision not to repair this error shows his orientation to its obviousness. However, in the case of side/ sid, this typo could cause possible confusion, as it turned the name of another team member into another word. Similarly, in example 12, Rebeca asks Evan for his phone number as the meeting is about to come to a close. At 5:40:03 he posts his number, but the final sequence is one digit too long. Although Rebeca could be expected to know that there were too many numbers, she could not know which number was incorrect, and thus at 5:40:06 Evan repairs only that portion of his number that needed correcting. I would like to argue that Evan's selective use of repair at this juncture in the team's development is further evidence that the team has generally accepted the norm of not correcting typos and similar mistakes during their chat sessions. Evan, as well as most of the other team members, makes numerous typing errors in this and the other meetings (see

Example 11. Meeting 3

5:44:56	EVAN: what bouat side
5:45:00	EVAN: sid

Example 12. Meeting 4

5:39:57	REBECA: if i have any questions evan, can i contact you by phone?
5:40:03	EVAN: 555-555-15456
5:40:06	EVAN: 1545

Table 2), yet he has chosen only to repair these specific mistakes because he recognizes that in these two instances there is the potential for misunderstanding of meaning. In example 11, the incorrectly typed word "about" does not get repaired, but the person reference does. Similarly, in example 12, the phone number is an important piece of information that cannot be inferred from the context, but in fact must be repaired by the speaker of the trouble source turn.

The use of conversational repair to develop a norm of informality highlights the differences between the face-to-face and computer-mediated environments. Spoken conversations in casual settings are usually seen as being informal, whereas, prior to the popularity of CMC, written forms were generally held to be more formal. However, many CMC conversations, including the ones in this study, take place in contexts that much more closely resemble casual conversations. Thus there is a tension, not fully resolved in society, between the perception of CMC as casual conversation and the perception of written text as a formal medium. Repair, then, can be a device employed for working out these tensions in specific situations.

CONCLUSION AND FUTURE DIRECTIONS

In this chapter I have used data from a case study of computer-mediated team meetings to demonstrate how conversational repair can be used to further group development. Specifically, I have shown how team members repair simple typing and spelling errors as an implicit way of working out group norms for computer-mediated interaction. While repair attempts are superficially employed to clarify meaning in the furtherance of intersubjective understanding, my analysis of what I identified as Type 1 errors demonstrates that repair attempts are used for social purposes as well.

In computer-mediated settings such as the chat room used in this study, participants have a more restricted set of communicative resources, and the medium is still relatively new. In addition, these data represent a team moving from formation to completion. Therefore we see that the team members are faced with two tasks--working out their interactional norms as a group, and working out the norms for this medium. Because conventions and stylistic preferences can vary, the team members must work out a set of agreed upon conventions. My analysis has shown that by repairing simple errors that would probably not otherwise be singled out as trouble sources, they can make visible their orientations to the possible transgressive nature of making mistakes that *could* be prevented. This orientation is particularly salient in the first meeting, when the team members have had very little prior interaction and the group is still in its formative stage. It is in this formative stage, however, that they can develop the patterns of interaction that will underlie the rest of the group's meetings (Gersick, 1988).

This research furthers our understanding of group CMC in several ways. Graham (2003) notes that our understanding of *how* group norms emerge is limited. By focusing on a specific conversational practice at the micro-level, this study offers empirical evidence for the formation of implicit group norms through communication.

As such, this work also points to the usefulness of the conversation analytic approach to the study of computer-mediated group interaction. Future research on other conversational practices, such as accounts, assessments, and side-sequences could help to further explicate the development and adherence to (or transgression of) norms in computer-mediated groups. In addition, this research further extends our understanding of how repair works in computer-chat interactions, a still largely understudied area. As a case study examination of a single student team over only four meetings, the findings of this study are limited in scope, and are not intended to generalize to computer-mediated groups as a whole. However, as Yin (2009) points out, case studies can be analytically generalizable to broader theories and concepts. The research presented here provides added support for Gersick's (1988) punctuated equilibrium model of group development, and for the argument made in previous research that text-based interactions can be studied as conversations. At the same time however, this research underscores the need to take into account the specific affordances and constraints of the channel being used. Conversational resources are said to be both context-free and context-sensitive; this analysis of repair in computer chat demonstrates the validity of this maxim. Repair is crucial to the development of intersubjectivity in chat, yet the way repair is deployed is necessarily shaped by the structure of the chat environment. As researchers we must therefore be sensitive to the ways that participants adapt conversational practices to new media, while at the same time also taking care to identify those practices which may be unique to a specific channel. Additional research could apply this approach to other computer-mediated interpersonal and group settings, such as instant messaging, asynchronous discussion boards, and email.

REFERENCES

Ahuja, M. K., & Galvin, J. E. (2003). Socialization in virtual groups. *Journal of Management, 29*(2), 161–185. doi:10.1177/014920630302900203

Balthazard, P. A., Potter, R. E., & Warren, J. (2004). Expertise, extraversion and group interaction styles as performance indicators in virtual teams. *The Data Base for Advances in Information Systems, 35*, 41–64.

Birchmeier, Z., Joinson, A. N., & Dietz-Uhler, B. (2005). Storming and forming a normative response to a deception revealed online. *Social Science Computer Review, 23*, 108–121. doi:10.1177/0894439304271542

Chidambaram, L., & Bostrom, R. P. (1996). Group development (I): A review and synthesis of development models. *Group Decision and Negotiation, 6*, 159–187. doi:10.1023/A:1008603328241

Colomb, G. G., & Simutis, J. A. (1996). Visible conversation and academic inquiry: CMC in a culturally diverse classroom. In Herring, S. C. (Ed.), *Computer-mediated communication: Linguistic, social and cross-cultural perspectives* (pp. 203–222). Philadelphia: John Benjamins.

Dietz-Uhler, B., Bishop-Clark, C., & Howard, E. (2005). Formation of and adherence to a self-disclosure norm in an online chat. *Cyberpsychology & Behavior, 8*, 114–120. doi:10.1089/cpb.2005.8.114

Furst, S., Blackburn, R., & Rosen, B. (1999). Virtual team effectiveness: a proposed research agenda. *Information Systems Journal, 9*, 249–269. doi:10.1046/j.1365-2575.1999.00064.x

Garcia, A. C., & Jacobs, J. B. (1998). The interactional organization of computer mediated communication in the college classroom. *Qualitative Sociology, 21*, 299–317. doi:10.1023/A:1022146620473

Garcia, A. C., & Jacobs, J. B. (1999). The eyes of the beholder: Understanding the turn-taking system in quasi-synchronous computer-mediated communication. *Research on Language and Social Interaction, 32*, 337–367. doi:10.1207/S15327973rls3204_2

Gersick, C. J. G. (1988). Time and transition in work teams: Toward a new model of group development. *Academy of Management Journal, 31*, 9–41. doi:10.2307/256496

Graham, C. R. (2003). A model of norm development for computer-mediated teamwork. *Small Group Research, 34*, 322–352. doi:10.1177/1046496403034003003

Heritage, J. (1984). *Garfinkel and ethnomethodology*. Cambridge, UK: Polity Press.

Herring, S. (1999). Interactional coherence in CMC. *Journal of Computer-Mediated Communication, 4*(4). Retrieved May 4, 2003, from http://www.ascusc.org/jcmc/vol4/issue4/herring.html

Hughes, J. A., O'Brien, J., Randall, D., Rouncefield, M., & Tolmie, P. (2001). Some 'real' problems of 'virtual' organisation. *New Technology, Work and Employment, 16*, 49–64. doi:10.1111/1468-005X.00076

Janssen, J., Erkens, G., Kirschner, P. A., & Kanselaar, G. (2009). Influence of group member familiarity on online collaborative learning. *Computers in Human Behavior, 25*, 161–170. doi:10.1016/j.chb.2008.08.010

Johnson, S. D., Suriya, C., Yoon, S. W., Berrett, J. V., & La Fleur, J. (2002). Team development and group processes of virtual learning teams. *Computers & Education, 39*, 379–393. doi:10.1016/S0360-1315(02)00074-X

Keating, E. (1993). Correction/repair as a resource for co-construction of group competence. *Pragmatics: Quarterly Publication of the International Pragmatics Association, 3*, 411–423.

Lea, M., & Spears, R. (1992). Paralanguage and social perception in computer-mediated communication. *Journal of Organizational Computing, 2*, 321–341. doi:10.1080/10919399209540190

Majchrzak, A., Rice, R. E., King, N., Malhotra, A., & Ba, S. L. (2000). Computer-mediated interorganizational knowledge-sharing: Insights from a virtual team innovating using a collaborative tool. *Information Resources Management Journal, 13*, 44–53.

Markman, K. M. (2005). To send or not to send: Turn construction in computer-mediated chat. In C. Sunakawa, T. Ikeda, S. Finch & M. Shetty (Eds.), *Proceedings of the twelfth annual Symposium About Language and Society-Austin* (Vol. 48, pp. 115-124). Austin, TX: Texas Linguistic Forum.

Markman, K. M. (2006). *Computer-mediated conversation: The organization of talk in chat-based virtual team meetings*. Unpublished doctoral dissertation, The University of Texas at Austin.

Maznevski, M. L., & Chudoba, K. M. (2000). Bridging space over time: Global virtual team dynamics and effectiveness. *Organization Science, 11*, 473–492. doi:10.1287/orsc.11.5.473.15200

O'Neill, J., & Martin, D. (2003). Text chat in action. In *Proceedings of the 2003 international ACM SIGGROUP conference on Supporting group work* (pp. 40-49). New York: ACM Press.

O'Sullivan, P. B., Hunt, S. K., & Lippert, L. R. (2004). Mediated immediacy: A language of affiliation in a technological Age. *Journal of Language and Social Psychology, 23*, 464–490. doi:10.1177/0261927X04269588

Panyametheekul, S., & Herring, S. C. (2003). Gender and turn allocation in a Thai chat room. *Journal of Computer-Mediated Communication, 9*(1). Retrieved April 3, 2004, from http://www.ascusc.org/jcmc/vol9/issue1/panya_herring.html

Park, J. (2007). Interpersonal and affective communication in synchronous online discourse. *The Library Quarterly, 77*, 133–155. doi:10.1086/517841

Postmes, T., Spears, R., & Lea, M. (2000). The formation of group norms in computer-mediated communication. *Human Communication Research, 26*, 341–371. doi:10.1111/j.1468-2958.2000.tb00761.x

Potter, R. E., & Balthazard, P. A. (2002). Virtual team interaction styles: Assessment and effects. *International Journal of Human-Computer Studies, 56*, 423–443. doi:10.1006/ijhc.2002.1001

Rintel, E. S., Pittam, J., & Mulholland, J. (2003). Time will tell: Ambiguous non-responses on Internet relay Chat. *Electronic Journal of Communication, 13*(1). Retrieved January 13, 2004, from http://80-www.cios.org.content.lib.utexas.edu:2048getfile%5CRINTEL_V13N1

Robinson, J. D. (2006). Managing trouble responsibility and relationships during conversational repair. *Communication Monographs, 73*, 137–161. doi:10.1080/03637750600581206

Schegloff, E. A. (1992). Repair after next turn: The last structurally provided defense of intersubjectivity in conversation. *American Journal of Sociology, 104*, 161–216.

Schegloff, E. A. (1997). Practices and actions: Boundary cases of other-initiated repair. *Discourse Processes, 23*, 499–545. doi:10.1080/01638539709545001

Schegloff, E. A. (2000). When 'others' initiate repair. *Applied Linguistics, 21*, 205–243. doi:10.1093/applin/21.2.205

Schegloff, E. A., Jefferson, G., & Sacks, H. (1977). The preference for self-correction in the organization of repair in conversation. *Language, 53*, 361–382. doi:10.2307/413107

Schonfeldt, J., & Golato, A. (2003). Repair in chats: A conversation analytic approach. *Research on Language and Social Interaction, 36*, 241–284. doi:10.1207/S15327973RLSI3603_02

Silverman, D. (1998). *Harvey Sacks: Social science and Conversation Analysis*. New York: Oxford University Press.

Simpson, J. (2005). Conversational floors in synchronous text-based CMC discourse. *Discourse Studies, 7*, 337–361. doi:10.1177/1461445605052190

ten Have, P. (2000). Computer-mediated chat: Ways of finding chat partners. *M/C: A Journal of Media and Culture, 3*(4). Retrieved May 5, 2003, from http://journal.media-culture.org.au/0008/partners.php

Tuckman, B. (1965). Developmental sequence in small groups. *Psychological Bulletin, 63*, 384–399. doi:10.1037/h0022100

Tuckman, B., & Jensen, M. C. (1977). Stages of small-group development revisited. *Group & Organizational Studies, 2*, 419–427. doi:10.1177/105960117700200404

Walther, J. B., & Bunz, U. (2005). The rules of virtual groups: Trust, liking, and performance in computer-mediated communication. *The Journal of Communication, 55*, 828–846. doi:10.1111/j.1460-2466.2005.tb03025.x

Waring, H. Z. (2005). The unofficial business of repair initiation: Vehicles for affiliation and disaffiliation. In Tyler, A., Takada, M., Kim, Y., & Marinova, D. (Eds.), *Language in use: Cognitive and discourse perspectives on language and language learning* (pp. 163–175). Washington, DC: Georgetown University Press.

Werry, C. C. (1996). Linguistic and interactional features of Internet Relay Chat. In S. C. Herring (Ed.), Computer-mediated communication: Linguistic, social and cross-cultural perspectives (pp. 47-63). Philadelphia: John Benjamins.

Yin, R. K. (2009). *Case study research: design and methods* (4th ed.). Thousand Oaks, CA: Sage.

Zitzen, M., & Stein, D. (2004). Chat and conversation: A case of transmedial stability? *Linguistics*, *42*, 983–1021. doi:10.1515/ling.2004.035

ADDITIONAL READING

Burnett, C. (2003). Learning to chat: Tutor participation in synchronous online chat. *Teaching in Higher Education*, *8*(2), 247. doi:10.1080/1356251032000052474

Chatman, J. A., & Flynn, F. J. (2001). The influence of demographic heterogeneity on the emergence and consequences of cooperative norms in work teams. *Academy of Management Journal*, *44*, 956–974. doi:10.2307/3069440

Chidambaram, L., & Bostrom, R. P. (1997). Group development (II): Implications for GSS research and practice. *Group Decision and Negotiation*, *6*, 231–254. doi:10.1023/A:1008655312311

Chou, S., & Min, H. (2009). The impact of media on collaborative learning in virtual settings: The perspective of social construction. *Computers & Education*, *52*, 417–431. doi:10.1016/j.compedu.2008.09.006

Cox, G., Carr, T., & Hall, M. (2004). Evaluating the use of synchronous communication in two blended courses. *Journal of Computer Assisted Learning*, *20*, 183–193. doi:10.1111/j.1365-2729.2004.00084.x

Danis, C., & Lee, A. (2005). Evolution of norms in a newly forming group. In Proceedings of Human-Computer Interaction - Interact 2005, (Vol. 3585, pp. 522-535).

Davidson-Shivers, G. V., Muilenburg, L. Y., & Tanner, E. J. (2001). How do students participate in synchronous and asynchronous online discussions? *Journal of Educational Computing Research*, *25*, 351–366. doi:10.2190/6DCH-BEN3-V7CF-QK47

Flanagin, A. J., Park, H. S., & Seibold, D. R. (2004). Group performance and collaborative technology: A longitudinal and multilevel analysis of information quality, contribution equity, and members' satisfaction in computer-mediated groups. *Communication Monographs*, *71*(3), 352–372. doi:10.1080/0363452042000299902

Graetz, K. A., Boyle, E. S., Kimble, C. E., Thompson, P., & Garloch, J. L. (1998). Information sharing, face-to-face teleconferencing, and electronic chat groups. *Small Group Research*, *29*, 714–743. doi:10.1177/1046496498296003

Ikpeze, C. (2007). Small group collaboration in peer-led electronic discourse: An analysis of group dynamics and interactions involving preservice and inservice teachers. *Journal of Technology and Teacher Education*, *15*, 383–407.

Li, S. S. (2007). Computer-mediated communication and group decision making. *Small Group Research*, *38*, 593–614. doi:10.1177/1046496407304335

Markman, K. M. (2009). "So what shall we talk about": Openings and closings in chat-based virtual meetings. *Journal of Business Communication*, *46*, 150–170. doi:10.1177/0021943608325751

Orvis, K. L., Wisher, R. A., Bonk, C. J., & Olson, T. M. (2002). Communication patterns during synchronous Web-based military training in problem solving. *Computers in Human Behavior*, *18*, 783–795. doi:10.1016/S0747-5632(02)00018-3

Rintel, E. S., & Pittam, J. (1997). Strangers in a strange land: Interaction management on Internet Relay Chat. *Human Communication Research*, *23*, 507–534. doi:10.1111/j.1468-2958.1997.tb00408.x

Scott, C. R. (1999). Communication technology and group communication. In Frey, L. R., Gouran, D. S., & Poole, M. S. (Eds.), *Group communication theory and research* (pp. 432–472). Thousand Oaks, CA: Sage.

Walther, J. B. (1995). Relational aspects of computer-mediated communication: Experimental observations over time. *Organization Science, 6*, 186–203. doi:10.1287/orsc.6.2.186

Walther, J. B. (1996). Computer-mediated communication: Impersonal, interpersonal, and hyperpersonal interaction. *Communication Research, 23*, 3–43. doi:10.1177/009365096023001001

Wang, Z., Walther, J. B., & Hancock, J. T. (2009). Social identification and interpersonal communication in computer-mediated communication: What you do versus who you are in virtual groups. *Human Communication Research, 35*, 59–85. doi:10.1111/j.1468-2958.2008.01338.x

Witt, P. L. (2004). An initial examination of observed verbal immediacy and participants' opinions of communication effectiveness in online group interaction. *Journal of Online Behavior, 2*(1). Retrieved February 9, 2009, from http://www.behavior.net/JOB/v2n1/witt.html

Zemel, A., & Cakir, M. P. (2007, November). *Reading's work: The mechanisms of online chat as social interaction.* Paper presented at the Ninety-third annual meeting of the National Communication Association, Chicago, IL.

KEY TERMS AND DEFINITIONS

Computer-Mediated Discourse: Human-human conversations that take place entirely through (usually text-based) computer channels.

Chat: A platform for conducting synchronous, multi-party, text-based conversations through networked computers.

Computer-Mediated Groups/Teams: Groups or teams composed of members who conduct their interaction through various computer-based channels.

Conversation Analysis: A method for the collection and analysis of naturally-occurring interaction that focuses on describing micro-level characteristics of conversation.

Repair: As used in conversation analysis, repair is the audible/visible correction of errors, misunderstandings, etc., in conversation.

Norms: Shared rules (implicit or explicit) that guide interaction in a given group.

ENDNOTE

[1] It is important to note that in chat, 'next' does not refer to what is sequentially next in the chat window, because those sequences are controlled by the chat server and not the individual participants. Here, I use next to refer to the sequentially next turn posted by a particular participant, relative to his or her previous turn.

Section 4
Online Learning and Collaboration

Chapter 13
In a Virtual Classroom, Who Has a "Voice":
A Discourse Analysis of Student–Instructor Interactions in Two *Second Life*-Based Courses

Sharon Stoerger
Indiana University, USA

ABSTRACT

Much of the literature argues that educational initiatives that take place in three-dimensional virtual worlds such as Second Life (SL) enable students to construct their knowledge and take ownership for their learning. The notion of a more student-centered learning environment is not new; in fact, similar claims were made about text-based MUD environments and to some extent, educational chat spaces. This study is an attempt to more rigorously examine some of the claims made about the democratic nature of communication in virtual worlds such as SL and the potential for these electronic spaces beyond social exchanges. The findings support the notion that deep learning is possible in virtual worlds using synchronous text chat. However, evidence to suggest that the structure of the educational activities is student-centered is lacking. Contrary to the claims, instructional activities used in the SL courses under investigation relied heavily on a teacher-centered model.

INTRODUCTION

Today's young people are thought to be prolific and proficient users of technology. A common stereotype of the tech-savvy student is of an individual who is adept at multi-tasking both offline and online and who is constantly connected – always in touch –

anytime, anyplace. When asked to describe their physical classroom experiences, Prenksy (2001) claims that these students often respond using words such as "boring" and "dry." According to Edwards, Watson, Nash, and Farrell (2005), the passive "shovelware" approach to instruction with its emphasis on quantity rather than quality is no longer tolerable to these students. Moreover, there are scholars who suggest that information technology is reshaping the

DOI: 10.4018/978-1-61520-827-2.ch013

mindset of students (e.g., Dede, 2005; Oblinger & Oblinger, 2005; Prensky, 2001). Some educators such as Cross (2007) also believe that alternatives to rote learning techniques, which are viewed as a form of punishment, are needed.

In an attempt to make teaching and learning activities more appealing to these students, educators are examining ways to integrate new technologies into the curriculum. Advocates of this approach suggest that there are benefits to the interactions that take place within visually rich, complex virtual worlds, like *Second Life* (SL); however, there is little research to support these assertions. In fact, decisions to move educational initiatives into these game-like environments appear to be made on the basis of "leaps of faith" rather than on empirical evidence (Hays, 2005, p. 9). Further, the data indicate that as of November 2008, just over 41% of the residents in SL were female, and approximately 59% were male (Linden Lab, 2008). Ondrejka (2008) interprets these numbers as suggesting that the gender balance in SL is approximately equal. Even though there are a number of females visiting SL, there are some scholars who question the female-friendliness of this space (e.g., Wajcman, 2007). And an unfriendly learning environment could impact the learning potential of the students.

Librarians are leading the way in conducting and promoting educational activities in virtual worlds, and currently, there are more than 400 in SL (Abram, 2007). Creating a library in SL and other virtual worlds is one way to reach out to and meet the needs of members of that community (Erdman, 2007). Further, Erdman argues that the avatar representation gives "a face to a virtual librarian who can gesture and walk the users to the resources found in-world" (p. 35). Because many of the librarians behind these virtual world programs are early adopters, their work often serves as a model for other educational groups within SL (Arreguin, 2007). Librarians also play a central role in the pedagogical uses of virtual environments for learning and are at the forefront of the information literacy movement (Alexander, 2008).

One example of librarian-led educational initiatives can be seen in a joint effort between a library system and a research university's continuing education program, both located in the Midwest region of the United States. Together they offer a series of non-credit courses about virtual worlds. The courses cover a broad range of topics such as Second Life 101, setting up an educational presence in virtual worlds, basic scripting skills, and machinima. These SL-based courses are designed for librarians, educators, and others interested in providing alternative forms of library services and educational programs. They are offered for a fee – between approximately $100 and $300 per course – and individuals from around the world enroll in and attend these sessions. Because the sessions are held in an open air auditorium, non-student "visitors" may inadvertently show up for class, as well.

Courses conducted by the educators and librarians in SL share certain characteristics. First, students and instructors sit at their own computers. It is in the virtual space where they bring together multiple experiences and diverse levels of expertise. SL residents create the content and navigate the environment through an avatar (i.e., a digital, graphic character) that is "known" by its SL name, which is a unique in-world identity. Communication is conducted through synchronous and asynchronous modes. In SL, text and audio chat are used for group discussions, whereas instant messaging (IM) is available for more private conversations. One advantage of using the text chat or IM modes of communication for student-instructor course interactions in SL is that the system records them for free. Transcripts of these sessions are available for students and instructors to review at a later time.

Graphical three-dimensional virtual worlds are relatively new. For example, SL was released to the public by Linden Lab in 2003 and is the largest three-dimensional virtual world (EDUCAUSE

Learning Initiative, 2008). Regardless, the concept of educational uses of virtual worlds is not a new one. This chapter will begin by examining the initiatives that took place in text-based environments such as MUDs. Because the SL courses included in this study were conducted via text chat, the literature on synchronous educational chat will be examined, as well. Following a discussion about the research design, the methods, and data analysis, the findings of this study will be presented. The chapter will conclude with an examination of what these results may mean for SL teachers and their students.

BACKGROUND

Education and Virtual Worlds

The current three-dimensional virtual worlds are visually rich spaces; however, the overall concept dates back to text-based virtual worlds (i.e., MUDs). MUDs were developed in the late 1970s. While the MUDs of the 1970s were set in fantasy worlds and were focused on role-playing activities, variations on the genre emerged starting in the late 1980s (Reid, 1994). In 1989, for example, James Aspnes, who at that time was a graduate student at Carnegie Mellon University, removed the battle components to create a modifiable space where participants could interact socially with each other. By the early 1990s, educators like Amy Bruckman, Cynthia Haynes, and Tari Fanderclai began to investigate the use of MUDs for teaching, learning, and scholarly collaboration. In fact, Bruckman's MediaMOO is one of the first examples of a MUD used for serious purposes.

A primary feature of MUDs was that while individuals were geographically dispersed, they were able to come together to collaborate in a common space. In these shared rooms people met, socialized, and created content entirely by text. In MUD environments, social interactions

were necessary; MUDding alone was pointless (Bruckman, 1998). Because the MUD content was created by its users, they were able to actively create artifacts that were meaningful to them through the use of creative expression. MUDs had the potential to be effective teaching and learning spaces for college students, as well. In contrast to the physical institution, the MUD university was not confined within the walls of a classroom, the boundaries of a university, or the even the borders of a country. In some cases, students and teachers in the virtual classroom never met each other face-to-face. Because this was a text-based environment where individuals communicated through writing, it was an ideal place to learn about writing. In addition, participants were able to multitask and have multichannel conversations. MUDs also disrupted the hierarchy of the physical classroom, which allowed students to take control of their own learning and become more independent. In the MUD, Fanderclai's (1995, 1996) composition students had to work out their own methods and schedules for meeting goals. In addition, the students were responsible to people outside their own on-site classes, which appeared to contribute to their willingness to work through difficulties.

While MUDs enabled educators to transgress the boundaries of traditional education, most virtual educational spaces simply replicated a physical classroom approach (Haynes, 1998). In fact, according to Bruckman (1998), the use of educational technologies has not resulted in dramatic changes to the teaching and learning process; rather, the opposite has occurred – these technologies tend to be used in very unoriginal and instructionist ways. Further, the move toward innovative educational practices has not been very effective, because "it is always easier to adopt a new gadget than to adopt a new philosophy" (Fanderclai, 1996, p. 239). MUDs were designed to be interactive spaces where the "sage on the stage" lecture model was counterproductive (Fanderclai, 1996). Yet, teachers in these virtual spaces often assigned a set of rote tasks for students to complete, rather than allowing students to design their own meaningful projects (Bruckman, 1998; Fanderclai, 1996).

As was stated earlier, the roots of the graphical, three-dimensional virtual worlds extend back to text-based MUD environments. Indeed, Kalay (2004) and Pearce (2004) refer to these visually rich worlds as graphical MUDs. One virtual world that has caught the attention of many individuals, including educators, is Second Life. Over the years, interest in the educational uses of such as SL has grown. For example, between April 15, 2007 and May 16, 2007, Jennings and Collins (2008) identified 170 educational institutions in SL. In August 2007, Sussman (2007) reported that more than 300 universities had incorporated SL into their teaching activities. These virtual world activities are not solely confined to the space of SL. There is also an active group of educators involved in the Second Life educators email discussion list (SLED) hosted by Linden Lab. Between 2006 and 2007, the membership increased from 500 to almost 3,900 members (Arreguin, 2007, p. 3). In a recent discussion list post, Pathfinder Linden (2009) announced that there are more than 5,000 SLED members.

In this persistent and diverse three-dimensional environment that is available 24 hours a day, 7 days a week, individuals can construct an identity, become an inhabitant of the space, and participate in SL life. Individuals in SL are referred to specifically as "residents," a label given to them by Linden Lab. All residents begin their SL as an adult. When individuals log in for the first time, they are asked to select an avatar name and create an appearance for their avatar. Many residents begin their in-world life on Orientation Island, which is the default starting location. In this space, residents can learn how to navigate the environment (e.g., walking, flying, picking up artifacts) through the manipulation of the computer's arrow keys and mouse, change their appearance, and meet others who are new to this virtual world. What

is surprising to many newcomers is that it takes time to become adept at performing these actions and learning the accepted SL norms.

Virtual worlds such as SL enable residents to be anyone they want to be. A GMI Poll (2007) indicates that 24% of respondents claim they go to SL to escape real life. In addition to escaping, some people use SL as a way to alter their appearance. This poll found that 64% present themselves differently; 45% give themselves a more attractive body, whereas 37% make themselves younger. As is the case with other online environments, including email, discussion lists, and MUDs, race is not discussed in SL. In her ethnographic study of the MUD Blue Sky, Kendall (2002) found that characters were assumed to be White males unless proven otherwise. Au (2008) tells a similar story about Bel Muse and her virtual world experiences. In the physical world, Bel Muse is an African American woman, but in SL, she is a Caucasian female avatar with blonde hair. No one ever asks if her in-world persona matches the image she presents in the physical world.

Overall, there is evidence that educational uses of virtual worlds such as MUDs were successful at encouraging students to take responsibility for their learning and to engage in collaborative activities, at least in some cases. However, MUDs had a limited life span. This was true even of popular spaces such as MediaMOO. Moreover, educational MUDs tended to replicate traditional teaching models rather than moving beyond them. At present, educators and students are investigating the educational potential of three-dimensional virtual worlds. Not only are these worlds textually rich, like MUDs, but they are visually engaging spaces, as well. While audio chat is an option in worlds such as SL, many residents, including educators, communicate using text chat.

Synchronous Educational Chat

The effectiveness of chat tools to facilitate deep learning has been much debated in the literature.

However, many of these studies have not been rigorous or in-depth in their investigations. Regardless, there is research to suggest that there are benefits associated with these tools. For example, chat tools are thought to invite more informal, more interactive, and more social types of conversations (Herring & Nix, 1997; Paulus, 2007). Some educators believe that chat enables the virtual classroom to be more student-centered because no one has to wait to be called on by the teacher – the lines of communication are open to anyone at anytime. In other words, no single voice can dominate the conversation; this includes the instructor (e.g., Jenkins, 2004). Students can also ask questions and receive feedback instantaneously, which makes communication more immediate and dynamic.

Despite the possible benefits, there are limitations to chat that educators should be aware of. While the environment enables geographically dispersed individuals to come together, the different time zones may make it difficult for them to participate in synchronous chat discussions. Also, the Second Life courses are conducted in SL Time (SLT), which is Pacific Time. For some, translating SLT into their own time can be a tricky mathematical calculation. When students are coming together from geographically dispersed locations, language proficiency may be an issue, as well, and non-native English speakers may have difficulty contributing due to the rapid pace of the discussions. Further, not everyone is an accomplished typist. With chat, fast typists are privileged and may dominate class discussions. Technological issues may also complicate chat discussions. For example, in SL, it is not uncommon for the system to "crash." This can cause portions of the conversation to be lost and may block course participants out of the discussion. Lag time may also result in the delay of the appearance of messages.

The current iteration of visually and textually rich computer-based simulated environments enables individuals to communicate through synchronous and asynchronous modes. In the case of the SL virtual world librarianship courses included in this study, text chat and instant messaging were forms of communication available to the students and their instructors. For the most part, text chat was the prevailing form of communication during the courses, and IM was used in case of an "emergency" (e.g., getting lost and/or needing a teleport to class). At the beginning of the sessions, the instructor asked the students not to use IM unless necessary. While audio chat became an option in 2007, the instructors of these sessions made a conscious decision not to use this mode of communication. When asked about this in a class session, Instructor IE (a pseudonym) noted that she prefers text chat over audio chat for a number of reasons, including that it makes communication more democratic and egalitarian.

A DISCOURSE ANALYSIS OF VIRTUAL EDUCATIONAL ACTIVITIES

Educators, students, and software developers are exploring virtual worlds for teaching and learning purposes. Librarians initiated and continue to guide these efforts, which serve, in turn, as models for other educators. However, there remain a number of concerns regarding the use of virtual worlds for educational purposes. One common theme throughout the literature is that more empirical research is needed to better understand and fully utilize these spaces.

While research efforts are underway, a plethora of questions about the educational possibilities and potential remain unanswered. In a pilot study conducted by this author involving ethnographic methods – participant observation and informal interviews – the work was guided by the following question: "How and why are the teaching and learning activities in the three-dimensional virtual world Second Life different from those that take place in physical classrooms?" Contrary to many of the claims about education in virtual worlds, the ethnographic findings did not suggest that SL will radically alter the educational process. In fact, characteristics such the classroom location (i.e., a large auditorium), the seating arrangement (i.e., students seated facing the front), and the pedagogical practices (e.g., lectures and PowerPoint-like slides) were similar to the physical classroom. To further investigate these educational activities in SL, the synchronous text chat that was collected during the class sessions was analyzed.

Research Questions

The purpose of the study described in this chapter was to examine the educational discussions that take place in virtual worlds. In hopes of supporting or refuting some of the findings revealed in the earlier ethnographic work, a discourse analysis approach was used to examine the student-instructor interactions that took place during the SL courses. Thus, the research questions guiding this study are as follows:

RQ1: To what extent is participation in the educational chat balanced between the students and the instructors?

RQ2: To what extent do the participation levels in the educational chat differ by gender?

RQ3: To what extent are these educational chat messages exchanged during the *Second Life* course cognitive in nature, as opposed to more social or other types of functions?

RQ4: To what extent do the types of functional moves exchanged via chat differ by role?

RQ5: To what extent do the types of functional moves exchanged by student differ by gender?

The Research Methods

The first set of synchronous text chat data was collected in the summer of 2007. At that time, audio chat was not a viable option, so the course was conducted through text chat. One of the affordances of the text chat in SL is that it is automatically logged. This resulted in a corpus of data from six, two-hour class sessions that took place between July 20, 2007 and September 7, 2007. Participant observation notes, informal interviews, and a set of chat data from a comparable SL course in Spring 2008 were collected. This one was also offered by the same group of librarians and many of the April instructors taught in the 2007 course. Even though the course topics were identical, the number of sessions differed. In the end, the data collected from the Spring course included four sessions that were each two-hours in length.

The computer-mediated communication that takes place as a result of educational initiatives in SL is relatively undescribed at this time; thus, a framework designed to investigate this specific type of environment has not been developed. But due to the fact that there are many similarities between text-based and graphical virtual worlds, the expectation was that guidance would be readily obtained from the work conducted on educational MUDs. However, much of that research was not replicable. More specifically, details regarding the coding schemes used to analyze text-based spaces were scarce if not completely absent from that literature. Therefore, the focus was shifted to the work of scholars, such as Herring (e.g., 2004), who have documented the steps needed to replicate their evaluation processes.

First, Herring's (2004) computer-mediated discourse analysis (CMDA) approach was used to assess the structural characteristics of the data and the levels of participation among the participants. This procedure was carried out by analyzing the number of messages that qualified for inclusion and the length of those messages. These figures were also calculated by role in the class (instructor, guest, student) and by gender (male, female, unknown gender group).

Chat transcripts from all 10 class sessions were collected for analysis. Using the work of Paulus (2007), as well as Osman and Herring (2007) on educational chat as a guide, functional moves were investigated. Paulus (2007) defines a functional move as the "purpose served by a particular part of a message, similar to speech acts" (p. 1328). Each move was classified as one of the following: cognitive, social, technical, logistical (Osman & Herring, 2007; Paulus, 2007). An "other" category was added to the scheme to classify those messages that did not fall into the pre-established ones. Following the message coding process, the number of functional moves exchanged in each session was calculated by type of participant (instructor, guest, student) and by gender. Because the numbers for the "other" and "guest" categories were low and did not greatly contribute to the results of this study, they are not presented in the Research Findings and Discussion section.

The author was the primary coder for the discourse analysis data, but another individual was trained for the purposes of intercoder reliability testing. Using Holsti's coefficient of reliability formula, a coder agreement level of 87% was eventually achieved.

Structural Hypotheses

Based on earlier studies of educational chat and virtual world environments, two structural hypotheses were advanced:

H1: Osman and Herring (2007) claim that even when the status of the participants is not available, the participation in the chat discussions remains unequal overall. In fact, the results of that study found that the facilitators contributed more words and messages than the students. Thus, it is anticipated that the chat discussions in the SL courses will be relatively unbalanced

among the participants, with the instructors contributing more messages to the discussion.

H2: The literature is mixed as to whether females are disadvantaged when it comes to their participation in online educational settings. Bruckman (2006) found that females who were engaged in the MOOSE Crossing activities had a very successful experience. However, Graner Ray (2004) and Herring (1993, 2003) observed gender differences in terms of participation in online spaces. Even though there are a large number of female residents in SL, there are scholars who note that the proliferation of pornography and sexual fetishes create an environment that may not be very female-friendly (e.g., Wajcman, 2007). Consequently, it is likely that the levels of participation in the virtual world courses will favor the males over the females.

Functional Moves Hypotheses

Studies that examined educational chat from a functional moves perspective were consulted, as was the literature about gendered discourse, to form the following hypotheses:

H3: Because the SL courses are designed to be educational, one would expect the chats to be cognitive in nature. In her case study of the communication modes used by students in a distance education course, Paulus (2007) examined the types of functional moves that were exchanged in chat. In this mode, she found that logistical moves were commonly exchanged; cognitive moves were the most frequent after the logistical moves. And, as the analysis conducted by Osman and Herring (2007) revealed, the messages in their analysis contained more cognitive functional moves than any other functional move type. So, the third hypothesis put forth for this study is that the SL course chat will include a high percentage of cognitive functional moves in comparison to the other functional move types.

H4: Osman and Herring (2007) found that the types of functional moves exchanged during chat varied by role. In that study, the students contributed more social moves, whereas the facilitators posted more logistical and cognitive moves. Based on this, it is expected that students and instructors in the SL courses will follow a similar pattern.

H5: Researchers have found that gender may be revealed though an individual's language characteristics even in cases where pseudonyms are used. For example, Herring (1994) notes that individuals who interact online give off cues as to their true gender through their discourse styles. Therefore, the types of functional moves used by the students in the SL courses will follow gender patterns.

Research Findings and Discussion

The first question to be addressed is whether the student-instructor interactions that took place in the class sessions under investigation were balanced. While scholars argue that text chat makes participation in discussions more democratic in that no one voice can dominate the discussions (e.g., Fanderclai, 1995; Jenkins, 2004; Ruhleder, 2004), the findings of this study suggest the opposite. In fact, the instructors posted the highest percentage of messages in four of the six sessions conducted in Summer 2007 (Figure 1). In the July 27, 2007 session, for example, the instructors posted approximately 70 percentage points more than the students. In addition to posting more messages, the Summer 2007 instructors used more words and characters per message. Starting with the words per message, the instructors posted 3.5% more than

the students. They also used 16.25 characters per message more than the students.

However, this is not to imply that the students were passive participants. On the contrary. In fact, there were two class sessions – August 10 and August 31 – when the participation levels of the students, particularly the females, slightly exceeded those of the instructors. It is worth mentioning that in both sessions the number of female students was approximately five times greater than the number of male students and instructors combined.

In the Spring 2008 course, the instructors posted more messages than the students; this was the case in all four class sessions (Figure 2). However, the student participation levels did approach those of the instructors in the April 4 session – 47.25% and 50.92% respectively. Not only did the instructors post a greater number of messages in comparison to the students, the number of words per message and characters per message for the instructors was higher, as well. On average, the Spring 2008 instructors used eight words per message and 34 characters per message more than the students who participated in these sessions. This indicates that the instructors took longer turns, which can make the discussion feel less interactive (Cherny, 1999). Overall, as Osman and Herring (2007) found in their analysis of educational chat, the participation in the SL discussions for the Summer 2007 and Spring 2008 courses was unequal (H1).

The second hypothesis that was put forth suggested that the levels of participation would favor the males over the females. With the exception of an incident that occurred in the August 17 session where a male "visitor" told the instructor, "fack you" and was consequently evicted from the auditorium, there were no overt acts or statements made against the female students and instructors. On the whole, the female students who participated in the Summer 2007 courses contributed a higher percentage of posts to the discussion than their male peers.

In contrast, the male students in the Spring 2008 sessions on average posted approximately

Figure 1. Summer 2007 structural analysis comparison by role

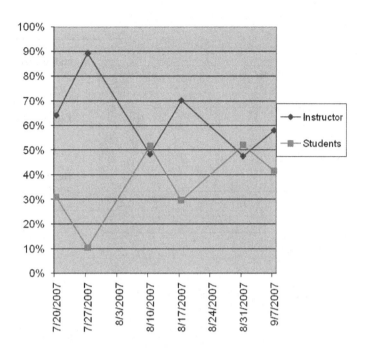

Figure 2. Spring 2008 structural analysis comparison by role

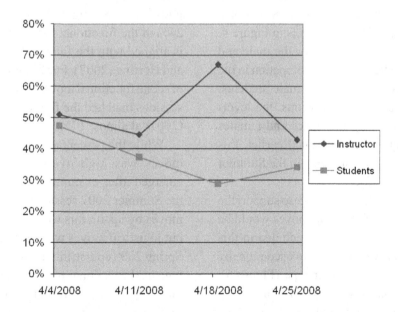

Figure 3. Summer 2007 average student comparison by gender

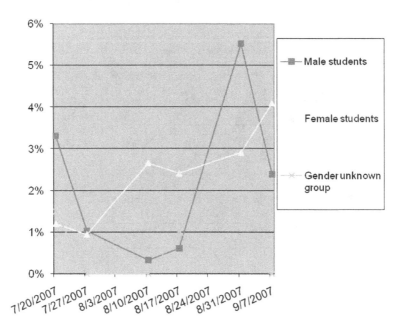

three percentage points more messages than the females in the course as a whole. In examining the individual sessions, however, the males contributed a higher number of posts during the April 4 and April 25 sessions; females contributed more during the April 11 and April 18 sessions. In reviewing the participation levels in Figure 4, an interesting pattern emerged for the male and female students. The levels of participation in the first session heavily favored the male students. But, over the course of the sessions, the levels of participation between the males and females became more equal. As was noted earlier, this was not the outcome for students in the Summer 2007 course (Figure 3).

As expected, there was evidence to support the notion that cognitive functional moves would be heavily used in the SL courses included in this study (H3). Cognitive moves were used more by the participants than any other type (Figure 5). In the Summer 2007 sessions, social functional moves, followed by logistical moves were the next most commonly used. Social functional moves were also the second most commonly used

category in the Spring 2008 courses, but technical functional moves outranked the logistical moves. The analysis conducted by Osman and Herring (2007) found that 25% of the moves were social in nature, compared to 17% in Paulus' study. Interestingly, in the Spring 2008 course, approximately 24% of the functional moves were social, which is aligned with the findings put forth by Osman and Herring (2007). Furthermore, the percentage of social functional moves from the Summer 2007 sessions matched the figure presented by Paulus (2007) at almost 17%.

While the percentage of cognitive functional moves was high overall, a different picture emerged after examining the moves by role. In the Summer 2007 sessions, cognitive functional moves by instructors were used most frequently, but logistical moves were in a close second. The Spring 2008 course instructors favored the use of logistical functional moves over those that were more cognitive in nature (Figure 6). The students in these sessions did not exercise the same types of functional moves as their instructors. Like Osman and Herring (2007), this study found that

Figure 4. Spring 2008 average student comparison by gender

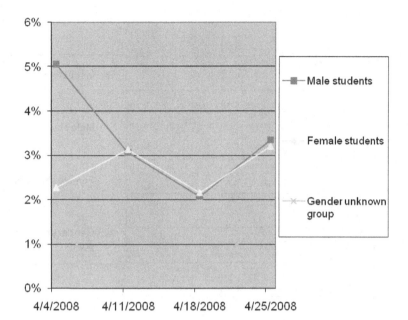

the students contributed more social moves to the discussion than the instructors (H4). The fact that a large percentage of the functional moves were cognitive in nature and that they would be heavily favored by the SL instructors was anticipated (H3); however, the sizable increase in the use of logistical messages in the Spring 2008 course was not.

And finally, female students in both course offerings privileged cognitive and logistical

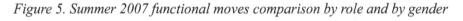

Figure 5. Summer 2007 functional moves comparison by role and by gender

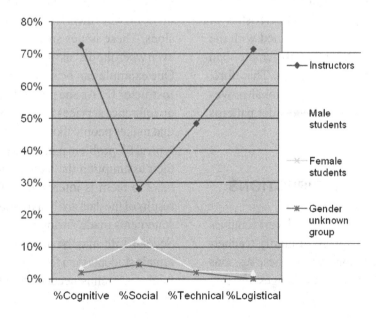

Figure 6. Spring 2008 functional moves comparison by role and by gender

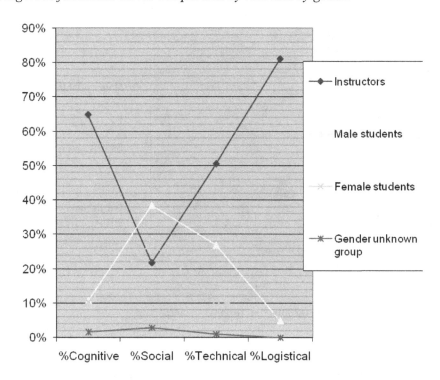

functional moves, which were aligned with the discourse patterns exhibited by the instructors. In contrast, their male peers relied more heavily upon social functional moves. While it is true that the analysis of functional moves carried out in the SL courses differed depending on the individual's role in the course, the overall characteristics of the female students were more aligned with the instructors, who were predominantly female, than with the male students in the group. Therefore, the assumption (H5) that the functional moves used by the students will follow gender patterns is supported.

FUTURE RESEARCH DIRECTIONS

The findings suggest that the virtual world courses examined for this study were primarily teacher-centered experiences. Nonetheless, these sessions were more than simply social exchanges; instead,

the cognitive interactions were the norm. What are less clear are the differences between the male and female students. While the females were active participants in the sessions, there were times when the males dominated the discussion. Also, situations and problems females may encounter in-world were mentioned during several class sessions. These issues surfaced during the sessions even when the discussion was not related to gender. One example can be seen in a statement made by Instructor IE. As she pointed out during a session on reference services in virtual worlds, "The thing that makes people like Random – an example of a typical SL problem patron – a potential problem is their assumption that any attractive woman who talks to them is interested in them." The mixed results of the data analysis combined with assorted statements made during the sessions suggest that Second Life may be a less egalitarian space for female students than for their male peers; however, more research is needed to better understand the implications gender differences in virtual worlds may have on the learning process.

This discourse analysis study was exploratory. The research was conducted on a small scale as a way to test the appropriateness of this method to explore educational activities in virtual worlds. Only one type of course was examined: a for-fee, non-credit, continuing education course. There are other models that could be investigated. For example, the San Jose State University School of Library and Information Science program offers for-credit courses that take place in SL. In addition, there are free courses in SL such as the ones offered by New Citizens Incorporated. Further, the librarians who conducted the Summer 2007 and Spring 2008 virtual world librarianship sessions included in this study continue to develop and teach similar in-world courses. Thus, a larger data set could be collected and analyzed utilizing the same research methods.

In addition, the courses included in this study were introductory in nature. As Salt, Atkins, and Blackall (2008) suggest, a more teacher-centered approach may be needed to assist students who are new to SL. For students who have not acquired a core set of competencies, a student-centered approach alone may undermine the educational potential of virtual worlds. Therefore, it is possible that the pedagogical practices will be more teacher-centered in the beginner level courses. In contrast, students enrolled in more intermediate and advanced level courses are expected to know the basics about SL and to be comfortable navigating SL. For these courses, more student-centered practices may be employed by the instructors. Consequently, research that investigates upper level courses may reveal different types of student-instructor interactions.

CONCLUSION

The findings of this study provide empirical support to research that suggests that synchronous discussions have the potential to support deep learning. A large percentage of the messages that was posted during the Summer 2007 and Spring 2008 sessions were cognitive in nature. Many of these messages were posted by the instructors. In general, the instructors posted a considerably higher percentage of messages to the discussion when compared to the student activity levels. Not only did the instructors post a large number of cognitive messages, but they also relied heavily on the use of logistical moves, particularly in the Spring 2008 sessions. Because learning in virtual environments often appears to be chaotic (Fanderclai, 1995, 1996; Jenkins, 2004), the reliance on logistical messages may be an indication that the instructors were trying to manage the class sessions. Further, the instructors more actively contributed to the discussions than the students, and they took longer turns. Individuals interested in creating a more student-centered and egalitarian learning space may want to reflect upon their method of instruction and how that approach may translate in-world.

While the female students did post messages, there were sessions where the males had more active levels of participation. This was found in three sessions conducted in the Summer 2007 course and one conducted in the Spring 2008. In the Spring 2008 sessions, specifically, the participation patterns of the average male and female student became more similar after the first session. Because most of the instructors and students were female, it is possible that the males adjusted their behavior to match the majority gender group. Regardless of the behavioral patterns in these courses, gender differences in virtual worlds is still a relatively unexamined area (Williams, Consalvo, Caplan, & Yee, 2009), even in environments such as SL where the participation levels of females is approaching that of the males. This is also an important point to keep in mind when attempting to create a more student-centered and democratic learning environment. In the end, it is to be hoped that research directed toward answering the types of questions examined in this chapter will enable librarians and other educators to meet more effectively the educational and informational needs of learners in their first life, as well as in their Second Life.

REFERENCES

Abram, S. (2007, April). At Second Life, info pros will find much to see, do, learn, play with, try out. *Information Outlook, 11*(4), 34-26. Retrieved June 5, 2008, from http://findarticles.com/p/articles/mi_m0FWE/is_4_11/ai_n19311182

Alexander, B. (2008, July/August). Games for education: 2008. *EDUCAUSE* Review, *43*(4), 64-65. Retrieved July 10, 2008, from http://www.educause.edu/ir/library/pdf/ERM0849.pdf

Arreguin, C. (2007). Reports from the field: Second Life community convention 2007 education track summary. *Global Kids Series on Virtual Worlds Report*. Retrieved March 23, 2008, from http://www.holymeatballs.org/pdfs/Virtual-WorldsforLearningRoadmap_012008.pdf

Au, W. J. (2008). *The making of Second Life: Notes from the new world*. New York: Collins.

Bruckman, A. (1998). Community support for constructionist learning. *Computer Supported Cooperative Work: The Journal of Collaborative Computing, 7,* 47–86. doi:10.1023/A:1008684120893

Bruckman, A. (2006). Analysis of log file data to understand behavior and learning in an online community. In Weiss, J. (Eds.), *The international handbook of virtual learning environments* (pp. 1449–1465). New York: Springer. doi:10.1007/978-1-4020-3803-7_58

Cherny, L. (1999). *Conversation and community: Chat in a virtual world*. Stanford, CA: CSLI Publications.

Cross, J. (2007). *Informal learning: Rediscovering the natural pathways that inspire innovation and performance*. San Francisco: Pfeiffer.

de Freitas, S. (2008). Emerging trends in serious games and virtual worlds. *Becta: Emerging Technologies for Learning, 3*, 57-72. Retrieved April 10, 2008, from http://partners.becta.org.uk/upload-dir/downloads/page_documents/research/emerging_technologies08_chapter4.pdf

Dede, C. (2005). Planning for neomillennial learning styles. *EDUCAUSE Quarterly, 28*(1), 7-12. Retrieved October 31, 2008, from http://www.educause.edu/ir/library/pdf/eqm0511.pdf

EDUCAUSE Learning Initiative. (2008, June 11). 7 things you should know about Second Life. *EDUCAUSE*. Retrieved June 13, 2008, from http://www.educause.edu/ir/library/pdf/ELI7038.pdf

Edwards, S. L., Watson, J., Nash, R., & Farrell, A. (2005). Supporting explorative learning by providing collaborative online problem solving (COPS) environments. *Proceedings of the OLT-2005 Conference: Beyond delivery* (pp. 81-89). Brisbane, Australia, Retrieved January 15, 2008, from http://eprints.qut.edu.au/archive/00002146/

Erdman, J. (2007). Reference in a 3-D virtual world: Preliminary observations on library outreach in "Second Life.". *The Reference Librarian, 47*(2), 29–39. doi:10.1300/J120v47n98_04

Fanderclai, T. L. (1996). Like magic, only real. In Cherny, L., & Weise, E. (Eds.), *Wired women: Gender and new realities in cyberspace* (pp. 224–241). Seattle, WA: Seal Press.

Fanderclai, T. L. (1995, January 1). MUDs in education: New environments, new pedagogies. *Computer-mediated Communication Magazine, 2*(1). Retrieved Spring 23, 2008, from http://www.ibiblio.org/cmc/mag/1995/jan/fanderclai.html

Graner Ray, S. (2004). *Gender inclusive game design: Expanding the market.* Hingham, MA: Charles River Media.

Haynes, C. (1998). Help! There's a MOO in this class! In Haynes, C., & Holmevik, J. R. (Eds.), *High wired: On the design, use, and theory of educational MOOs* (pp. 161–176). Ann Arbor, MI: University of Michigan Press.

Hays, R. T. (2005, November). *The effectiveness of instructional games: A literature review and discussion.* Technical Report. Naval Air Warfare Center Training Systems Division. Orlando, Florida. Retrieved April 11, 2008, from http://adlcommunity.net/file.php/23/GrooveFiles/Instr_Game_Review_Tr_2005.pdf

Herring, S. C. (1993). Gender and democracy in computer-mediated communication. *Electronic Journal of Communication, 3*(2). Retrieved April 16, 2008, from http://ella.slis.indiana.edu/~herring/ejc.txt

Herring, S. C. (1994). Politeness in computer culture: Why women thank and men flame. In M. Bucholtz, A. Liang, L. Sutton, & C. Hines (Eds.), *Cultural Performances: Proceedings of the Third Berkeley Women and Language Conference* (pp. 278-94). Berkeley, CA: Berkeley Women and Language Group.

Herring, S. C. (2003). Gender and power in online communication. In J. Holmes and M. Meyerhoff (Eds.), *The handbook of language and gender* (pp. 202-228). Oxford: Blackwell Publishers. Retrieved April 16, 2008, from http://ella.slis.indiana.edu/~herring/gender.power.pdf

Herring, S. C. (2004). Computer-mediated discourse analysis: An approach to researching online behavior. In Barab, S. A., Kling, R., & Gray, J. H. (Eds.), *Designing for virtual communities in the service of learning* (pp. 338–376). Cambridge, UK: Cambridge University Press.

Herring, S. C., & Nix, C. G. (1997, March). Is "serious chat" an oxymoron? Pedagogical vs. social uses of Internet Relay Chat. *Paper presented at the American Association of Applied Linguistics Annual Conference,* Orlando, FL.

Jenkins, C. A. (2004). The virtual classroom as ludic space. In Haythornthwaite, C. A., & Kazmer, M. M. (Eds.), *Learning, culture and community in online education* (pp. 163–176). New York: Peter Lang.

Kendall, L. (2002). *Hanging out in the virtual pub: Masculinities and relationships online.* Berkeley, CA: University of California Press.

Latest GMI poll reveals Second Life's potential for virtual consumer marketing and branding. (2007, April 23). *GMI.* Retrieved March 20, 2008, from http://www.gmi-mr.com/gmipoll/release.php?p=20070423

Linden, P. (2009, January 1). Looking to the New Year. Message posted to SLED electronic mailing list. Retrieved (n.d.), from https://lists.secondlife.com/pipermail/educators/2009-January/028481.html

Linden Lab. (2008, November). *Second Life virtual economy demographic summary information through November 2008.* San Francisco: Linden Research, Inc. Retrieved January 14, 2009, from http://static.secondlife.com/economy/stats_200811.xls

Oblinger, D. G., & Oblinger, J. L. (2005). Is it age or IT: First steps toward understanding the Net Generation. In D. G. Oblinger & J. L. Oblinger (Eds.), *Educating the net generation* (pp. 2.1-2.20). Retrieved March 1, 2008, from http://www.educause.edu/ir/library/pdf/pub7101c.pdf

Ondrejka, C. (2008). Education unleashed: Participatory culture, education, and innovation in Second Life. In K. Salen (Ed.), *The ecology of games: Connecting youth, games, and learning* (pp. 229-252). The John D. and Catherine T. MacArthur Foundation Series on Digital Media and Learning. Cambridge, MA: MIT Press. Retrieved April 3, 2008, from http://www.mitpressjournals.org/doi/pdfplus/10.1162/dmal.9780262693646.229

Osman, G., & Herring, S. C. (2007). Interaction, facilitation, and deep-learning in cross-cultural chat: A case study. *The Internet and Higher Education, 10*, 125–141. doi:10.1016/j.iheduc.2007.03.004

Paulus, T. M. (2007). CMC modes for learning tasks at a distance. *Journal of Computer-Mediated Communication, 12*, 1322–1345. doi:10.1111/j.1083-6101.2007.00375.x

Pearce, C. (2004). Towards a game theory of game. In N. Wardrip-Fruin & P. Harrigan (Eds.), *First person: New media as story, performance and game.* Cambridge, MA: MIT Press. Retrieved June 2, 2008, from http://www.electronicbookreview.com/thread/firstperson/tamagotchi

Prensky, M. (2001). *Digital game-based learning.* New York: McGraw-Hill.

Reid, E. M. (1994). *Cultural formations in text-based virtual realities.* Unpublished master's thesis, University of Melbourne, Melbourne, Australia.

Ruhleder, K. (2004). Changing patterns of participation: Interactions in a synchronous audio+chat classroom. In Haythornthwaite, C. A., & Kazmer, M. M. (Eds.), *Learning, culture and community in online education* (pp. 229–242). New York: Peter Lang.

Salt, B., Atkins, C., & Blackall, L. (2008, October). *Engaging with Second Life: Real education in a virtual world.* Retrieved February 8, 2009, from http://slenz.files.wordpress.com/2008/12/slliteraturereviewa1.pdf

Sussman, B. (2007, August 1). Teachers, college students lead a Second Life. *USA Today.* Retrieved January 20, 2008, from http://www.usatoday.com/news/education/2007-08-01-second-life_N.htm

Wajcman, J. (2007). From women and technology to gendered technoscience. *Information Communication and Society, 10*(3), 287–298. doi:10.1080/13691180701409770

Williams, D., Consalvo, M., Caplan, S., & Yee, N. (2009). Looking for gender (LFG): Gender roles and behaviors among online gamers. [from http://dmitriwilliams.com/LFGpaperfinal.pdf]. *The Journal of Communication, 59*(4), 700–725. Retrieved January 29, 2009. doi:10.1111/j.1460-2466.2009.01453.x

ADDITIONAL READING

Armitt, G., Slack, F., Green, S., & Beer, M. (2002). *The development of deep learning during a synchronous collaborative online course.* Paper presented at the CSCL 2002 conference, Boulder, CO. Retrieved April 9, 2009, from http://citeseerx.ist.psu.edu/viewdoc/summary?doi=10.1.1.16.8256

Barnett, R. (2007). *A will to learn: Being a student in an age of uncertainty.* New York: Open University Press.

Bayne, S. (2005). Deceit, desire and control: The identities of learners and teachers in cyberspace. In Land, R., & Bayne, S. (Eds.), *Education in cyberspace* (pp. 26–41). New York: Routledge/Falmer.

Bayne, S. (2008a, August). Higher education as a visual practice: Seeing though the virtual learning environment. *Teaching in Higher Education, 13*(4), 395–410. doi:10.1080/13562510802169665

Bayne, S. (2008b, September). Uncanny spaces for higher education: Teaching and learning in virtual worlds. *ALT-T, 16*(3), 197-205. Preprint retrieved February 16, 2009, from http://www.malts.ed.ac.uk/staff/sian/bayne_virtual_worlds.pdf

Bober, M. J., & Dennen, V. P. (2001). Intersubjectivity: Facilitating knowledge construction in online environments. *Educational Media International, 38*(4), 241–250. doi:10.1080/09523980110105150

Boellstorff, T. (2008). *Coming of age in Second Life: An anthropologist explores the virtually human.* Princeton, NJ: Princeton University Press.

Boostrom, R. (2008, November). The social construction of virtual reality and the stigmatized identity of the newbie. *Journal of Virtual Worlds Research, 1*(2). Retrieved May 4, 2009, from http://journals.tdl.org/jvwr/article/viewPDFInterstitial/302/269

Boulos, M. N. K., Hetherington, L., & Wheeler, S. (2007). Second Life: An overview of the potential of 3-D virtual worlds in medical and health education. *Health Information and Libraries Journal, 24*, 233–245. doi:10.1111/j.1471-1842.2007.00733.x

Branon, R. F., & Essex, C. (2001). Synchronous and asynchronous communication tools in distance education: A survey of instructors. *TechTrends, 45*(1), 36, 42.

Bronack, S., Riedl, R., & Tashner, J. (2006). Learning in the zone: A social constructivist framework for distance education in the 3-dimensional world. *Interactive Learning Environments, 14*(3), 219–232. doi:10.1080/10494820600909157

Carr, D., & Oliver, M. (2009). Second Life, immersion and learning. In P. Zaphiris & C. S. Ang (Eds.), *Social computing and virtual communities.* London: Taylor and Francis. Preprint retrieved April 4, 2009, from http://learningfromsocialworlds.wordpress.com/immersion-and-sl/

Carr, D., Oliver, M., & Burn, A. (2008). Learning, teaching, and ambiguity in virtual worlds. *Paper presented at ReLive08 at the Open University, Milton Keynes, UK, November 2008.* Retrieved April 4, 2009, from http://learningfromsocialworlds.wordpress.com/paper-for-relive-08-at-the-ou/

Collis, B., & Moonen, J. (2008). Web 2.0 tools and processes in higher education: Quality perspectives. *Educational Media International, 45*(2), 93–106. doi:10.1080/09523980802107179

Conole, G. (2002). *Review of JTAP projects: Perspectives on teaching and learning.* University of Southampton, Research and Graduate School of Education. Retrieved February 28, 2009, from http://www.jiscinfonet.ac.uk/InfoKits/infokit-related-files/jtap-review

Cousin, G. (2005). Learning from cyberspace. In Land, R., & Bayne, S. (Eds.), *Education in cyberspace* (pp. 117–129). New York: Routledge/Falmer.

Davidson-Shivers, G. V., Muilenburg, L. Y., & Tanner, E. J. (2001). How do students participate in synchronous and asynchronous online discussions? *Journal of Educational Computing Research, 25*(4), 351–366. doi:10.2190/6DCH-BEN3-V7CF-QK47

de Freitas, S. (2007). Learning in immersive worlds: A review of game-based learning. Retrieved October 8, 2007, from http://www.jisc.ac.uk/media/documents/programmes/elearning_innovation/gaming%20report_v3.3.pdf

de Freitas, S., & Griffiths, M. (2008). The convergence of gaming practices with other media forms: What potential for learning? A literature review. *Learning, Media and Technology, 33*(1), 11–20. doi:10.1080/17439880701868796

Dumbleton, T. (2007). Games to entertain or games to teach? *Becta: Emerging Technologies for Learning, 2*, 55-63. Retrieved April 10, 2008, from http://partners.becta.org.uk/page_documents/research/emerging_technologies07_chapter5.pdf

Guest, T. (2007). *Second lives: A journey through virtual worlds*. New York: Random House.

Haynes, C., & Holmevik, J. R. (Eds.). (1998). *High wired: On the design, use, and theory of educational MOOs*. Ann Arbor, MI: University of Michigan Press.

Hemmi, A., Bayne, S., & Land, R. (2009). The appropriation and repurposing of social technologies in higher education. [from http://www.malts. ed.ac.uk/staff/sian/JCALpaper_final.pdf]. *Journal of Computer Assisted Learning, 25*(1), 19–30. Retrieved February 17, 2009. doi:10.1111/j.1365-2729.2008.00306.x

Herring, S. C., & Nix, C. G. (1997, March). Is "serious chat" an oxymoron? Pedagogical vs. social uses of Internet Relay Chat. *Paper presented at the American Association of Applied Linguistics Annual Conference,* Orlando, FL.

Im, Y., & Lee, O. (2003-2004). Pedagogical implications of online discussion for preservice teacher training. *Journal of Research on Technology in Education, 36*(2), 155–170.

Jenkins, H., Purushotma, R., Clinton, K., Weigel, M., & Robison, A. J. (2008). *Confronting the challenges of participatory culture: Media education for the 21st century*. Chicago: The John D. and Catherine T. MacArthur Foundation. http://digitallearning.macfound.org/atf/cf/%7B7E45C7E0-A3E0-4B89-AC9C-E807E1B0AE4E%7D/JEN-KINS_WHITE_PAPER.PDF

Levin, B. B., He, Y., & Robbins, H. H. (2006). Comparative analysis of preservice teachers' reflective thinking in synchronous versus asynchronous online case discussions. *Journal of Technology and Teacher Education, 14*(3), 439–460.

Lobel, M., Neubauer, M., & Swedburg, R. (2006). Comparing how students collaborate to learn about the self and relationships in a real-time non-turn-taking online and turn-taking face-to-face environment. *Journal of Computer-mediated Communication, 10*(4). Retrieved April 9, 2009, from http://jcmc.indiana.edu/vol10/issue4/lobel.html

Natriello, G. (2005). Modest changes, revolutionary possibilities: Distance learning and the future of education. [from http://www.tcrecord.org]. *Teachers College Record, 107*(8), 1885–1904. Retrieved February 5, 2008. doi:10.1111/j.1467-9620.2005.00545.x

Nesson, R., & Nesson, C. (2008). The case for education in virtual worlds. *Space and Culture, 11*(3), 273-284. Retrieved March 4, 2009, from http://www.eecs.harvard.edu/~nesson/ed-vw-1.3.pdf

Orvis, K. L., Wisher, R. A., Bonk, C. J., & Olson, T. M. (2002). Communication patterns during synchronous Web-based military training in problem solving. *Computers in Human Behavior, 18*(6), 783–795. doi:10.1016/S0747-5632(02)00018-3

Park, Y. J., & Bonk, C. J. (2007a, September). Is online life a Breeze? Promoting a synchronous peer critique in a blended graduate course. *Journal of Online Learning and Teaching, 3*(3). Retrieved April 13, 2009, from http://jolt.merlot.org/vol3no3/park.htm

Park, Y. J., & Bonk, C. J. (2007b, Winter). Synchronous learning experiences: Distance and residential learners' perspectives in a blended graduate course. *Journal of Interactive Online Learning, 6*(3), 245–264.

Poole, D. M. (2000). Student participation in a discussion-oriented online course: A case study. *Journal of Research on Computing in Education, 33*(2), 162–177.

Pope, K., Galik, B., & Bell, L. (2007). Alliance Second Life Library: End of the year report 2007. East Peoria, IL: Alliance Library System. Retrieved April 2, 2008, from http://www.alliancelibraries.info/slendofyearreport2007.pdf

Reeves, B., Malone, T. W., & O'Driscoll, T. (2008, May). Leadership's online labs. *Harvard Business Review*, 59–66.

Squire, K. (2008). Open-ended video games: A model for developing learning for the interactive age. In K. Salen (Ed.), *The ecology of games: Connecting youth, games, and learning* (pp. 167-196). The John D. and Catherine T. MacArthur Foundation Series on Digital Media and Learning. Cambridge, MA: MIT Press. Retrieved April 3, 2008, from http://www.mitpressjournals.org/doi/pdf/10.1162/dmal.9780262693646.167

Steinkuehler, C. A. (2006, January). Massively multiplayer online video gaming as participation in a discourse. *Mind, Culture, and Activity, 13*(1), 38–52. doi:10.1207/s15327884mca1301_4

Taylor, T. L. (2006). *Play between worlds: Exploring online game culture.* Cambridge, MA: MIT Press.

Thomas, D., & Brown, J. S. (2007). The play of imagination: Extending the literary mind. *Games and Culture, 2*(2), 149–172. doi:10.1177/1555412007299458

Wesch, M. (2008, Spring). Anti-teaching: Confronting the crisis of significance. *Education Canada, 48*(2), 4-7. Retrieved May 7, 2008, from http://www.cea-ace.ca/media/en/AntiTeaching_Spring08.pdf

Wesch, M. (2009, January 7). From knowledge-able to knowledge-able: Learning in new media environments. *Academic Commons*. Retrieved March 15, 2009, from http://www.academic-commons.org/commons/essay/knowledgable-knowledge-able

KEY TERMS AND DEFINITIONS

Electronic Learning (E-learning): Pedagogical practices supported through the use of technology.

MUDs (Multi-User Dungeons): Virtual worlds where the environment and the content are created entirely by text. The early MUDs of the 1970s were primarily role playing games set in a fantasy universe. By the late 1980s, MUDs had evolved to focus on social interactions.

Pedagogy: A particular style of instruction.

Student-Centered Learning: An instructional method that focuses on the educational needs of the student where the student takes a more active role in their learning process. This approach is typically contrasted with teacher-centered learning where students adopt a more passive educational role.

Synchronous Communication: Direct communication between individuals who are present at the same time.

Virtual Learning: Technologies that are integrated into the instructional process to support a student's educational experience.

Virtual Teaching: The digital transmission of instructional materials to students who participate in an online or in a blended course that includes a face-to-face component.

Chapter 14
Blended Learning Communities:
Relational and Identity Networks

S. Annese
University of Bari, Italy

M. Traetta
University of Bari, Italy

P. F. Spadaro
University of Bari, Italy

ABSTRACT

Blended learning communities are defined by specific learning and psychosocial processes based on the multilayered sense of belonging of the group's members, related to the merging of both virtual and real interactive contexts. This chapter focuses on the psychosocial dynamics of blended communities, in order to identify some specific participation strategies and identity dynamics, which both vary with the double interactive context. We used a qualitative variant of Social Network Analysis to analyse the interactions of two blended student communities, identifying various participation trajectories and identity positionings of the group members. The results revealed that the blending of two communication contexts generates different psychosocial dynamics from those activated by the same community in a wholly on- or offline context. The combination of interactive environments results in participation strategies in which members can choose distinctive trajectories, shaping their original identity positionings.

INTRODUCTION

The integration of computer mediated and face to face communication has been recently implemented in numerous educational and professional contexts to create blended learning communities (Bonk & Graham, 2006; Ligorio, Cacciamani & Cesareni, 2006; Ligorio & Sansone, 2009) that improve learning processes through participation, sustaining

a sense of belonging and the subsequent identity construction process (Lave, 1991; Zucchermaglio, 2002).

This chapter focuses on these psychosocial dynamics, particularly on the idea that learning as a social process (Annese, 2005) accentuates the interweaving between psychosocial and psycho-educational conceptual frameworks.

From a sociocultural perspective, learning is an intersubjective process among individuals who co-participate in a meaningful, goal-directed interaction

DOI: 10.4018/978-1-61520-827-2.ch014

(Lave, 1993; Matusov, 2001; Wells, 1993). From this perspective, the identity construction process bridges social and individual aspects of learning, as it emerges from the development of a sense of belonging to the learning community (Wenger, 1998). Moreover, in blended learning activities, students' self-perception is affected differently by the online and offline contexts (Spadaro & Ligorio, 2007).

A psychosocial approach to group dynamics helps in understanding the social norms, communicative networks, language structure and setting characteristics that make blended communities suitable for implementing effective learning processes.

BACKGROUND

Cultural Perspective: Learning as Participation

The reformulation of learning as participation, from a psychosocial perspective, and as acculturation, from a cultural perspective (Bruner, 1966, Wenger, 1998), establishes the relevance of the social context in which people negotiate their meanings. The sociocultural approach is based on the assumption that during social activities individuals interact through cultural representations, so modifying their psychological processes (Cole, 2004).

In group research, cultural psychology provides a conceptual framework able to rethink psychological processes such as learning, participation, sense of belonging and identity through the construction of Communities of Practice (CoP) (Wenger, 1998). Learning is a central concept in CoP theory, with sense of belonging and identity being two of the possible objectives of learning in both formal and informal contexts.

According to Reckwitz (2002), a practice is a routinised behaviour consisting of bodily and mental activities, artefacts and their use, shared

knowledge, emotions and motivations. According to Wenger (1998) these processes involve individuals in interaction, and collective learning is accomplished through common practices. Thus conceptualised, practices can both achieve a current goal that is meaningful for practitioners and embody the historical memory of community. Through practices, meanings are negotiated and reified in material or cultural products.

Communities of Practice (CoP) are based on three dimensions: a) *shared repertoire* (Wenger, 1998) is the collection of reified objects socially negotiated and belonging to the community's history, aimed at allowing new members to learn the community's practices; b) *mutual engagement* implies that each participant is responsible for the expected goals of the practice and accepts his/her own and others' individuality during involvement in common practices; c) *joint enterprise* requires that the community members perceive the same meaning in participating in the same activity; in other words, each practice should be continuously negotiated among participants.

CoP are an arena where even identity is negotiated; in fact they enable a multi-step identity project (Wenger, 1998). Firstly, each member can define "who he/she is" through his/her experience of ways of participating in practices and his/her relationships with others. Secondly, members identify themselves by distinguishing between what is familiar and what is unfamiliar in their world. Thirdly, they delineate their identity in a trajectory starting from one position and moving towards another; the variety of positions of different memberships are coherently integrated in a unique identity. Finally, they differentiate themselves by negotiating a local sense of belonging in a larger constellation of communities.

Lave and Wenger (1991) explain the identity trajectory through "Legitimate Peripheral Participation": newcomers can participate in practices with different degrees of engagement depending on the level of the appropriation of community's culture. Usually they move in a participation trajectory from the periphery to the centre, while following an identity trajectory that exchanges individuality for membership. Participation in the construction of the community's cultural models is a learning process realised reciprocally by individuals and community, supplying both with identity resources.

So community and individuals shape each other through the sense of belonging that comes from engaging in common goals, being able to envision practice and community and alignment and coordination with others (Lave & Wenger, 1991). The experience of active involvement in social interactions leads to a strong sense of belonging to the community, characterised by the sharing of common experiences, the perception of similarity with other participants and assimilation into a stable whole (Saranson, 1974). Physical co-presence is not enough to perceive oneself as part of a whole: only the feeling of being psychologically and socially integrated in a community develops the sense of belonging to it.

The awareness of belonging influences our perception of ourselves and of others. A "sense of community" (McMillan & Chavis, 1986) allows each group member to consider him/herself as part of a unit where he/she can negotiate individual and collective identity. It also allows the construction of an intersubjective field where group members can recognise each other as practitioners in the same group unit.

Sense of community engages the individual in an identification process, in which he/she employs his/her membership as an essential resource for constructing self-concept. As the individual goes through multiple memberships, his/her identity becomes an effective organisation of them. According to Lifton (1993), a thus-constituted identity is not pathologically split; on the contrary, its inner coherence derives from the ability to relate the parts in a flexible network. Bachtin (1973) suggests that identity is a storytelling where the author plays multiple voices, a polyphony of selves involved in a dialogic plot. Similarly, Smith (1988) maintains

that specific *positionings* of the self emerge during social practices; while Davies and Harré (1990) explain that each positioning represents the way an individual "is" in the specific situation and context. So to participate in social practices means to interiorise new ways of thinking of themselves, new positionings to engage in dialogic interplays (Harré & Van Langenhove, 1991).

The Dialogical Self Theory (Hermans, 1996) provides an explanation of this shifting identity through a dynamic overview of the movement of positionings in the self's organisation. This theory proposes a spatialised self whose various aspects are settled in specific positions. Positionings may be both internal and external to the individual: decisive positionings are internal (e.g. "I, daughter", "I, student"), while contextual positionings are external (e.g. "my parents", "my teachers").

Internal and external positionings are engaged in networked dialogues that give specific configurations to the self. Each configuration depends on the specific situation and moment the individual is living. Furthermore, during social interactions the internal dialogues (between internal and external positionings) interweave with the interpersonal dialogues (with other social actors' positionings), producing a network of individual and social levels of the dialogical self.

Finally, a community of individuals builds a new collective identity, which is different from the sum of the individuals' identities. A gathering of individuals becomes a community when their collective identities build an intersubjective identity in which each member is considered as a positioning of the collectivity (Ligorio & Spadaro, 2005). Individual and social levels thus intermesh with a collective level of the networked self.

According to this conceptual framework the community needs not so much a shared physical space as an engagement in meaningful social activities enabling a collective identity to emerge. If the group is built around social engagement, the community can easily interact in virtual settings: "people construct community symbolically, making it a resource and repository of meaning, and a referent of their identity" (Cohen 1985, p. 118). In a network of social belongings digital communities become complementary to physical ones (Wellman, 2001).

This conceptual framework can help in investigating group dynamics in online or offline teams, but also in teams operating in the mixed context of blended communities.

From Blended Learning to Blended Community

The meaning of Blended Learning (BL) varies (Ligorio, Cacciamani & Cesareni, 2006) with the chosen focus. It could mean the multiplicity of communication environments (face to face and computer mediated); the combination of learning modalities (collaborative and individual); the involvement of multiple cognitive processes (acquisition of factual information and knowledge building); or the flexible arrangement of the learning time (synchronous and asynchronous) (Driscoll, 2002; Garrison & Kanuka, 2004; Graham, 2006). Generally it means a mixture of offline and online lessons.

The efficacy of BL is visible in various learning variables, such as reduced student dropout, improvement in academic achievements (Dziuban & Moskal, 2001) and the teachers' opportunity to design flexible courses for complex pedagogical models (Voos, 2003).

Studying BL involves investigating educational practices and effects, but also exploring social dimensions connected with learning processes and group dynamics in blended learning communities. Compared with fully online and with traditional face to face learning, BL has positive effects on the development of a sense of connectivity with others (Rovai & Jordan, 2004) and the building of the community, with identity-related consequences for its members.

Great attention should be paid to the specific psychosocial dynamics produced by BL, since the communities that adopt it differ from communities interacting exclusively in online or offline settings. In fact blended learning communities have specific features produced by the mix of the two interactive contexts. Their study might be interesting for psychosocial and psychoeducational researchers, teachers and designers of educational environments.

The study presented here is a first attempt to propose a psychosocial analysis of blended learning communities, in order to understand their specific social interaction patterns and discourse practices, under a multiple conceptual framework.

BLENDED LEARNING COMMUNITIES BETWEEN PARTICIPATION AND IDENTITY

Two Blended University Courses

To identify specific participation strategies and the subsequent identity dynamics in the double interactive context of blended communities, we analysed the interactions of two groups of students (Group 1 and Group 2) attending a blended course on E-learning Psychology at the University of Bari (IT) in two different academic years. Students were asked to attend offline classroom lessons and to participate in online activities hosted by the platform Synergeia (http://bscl.gmd.de/; Ligorio & Veermans, 2005), designed to support collaborative learning processes and based on the Progressive Inquiry Model (PMI) (Muukkonen, Hakkarainen & Lakkala, 1999).

The courses were strongly structured, as the professor planned them according to the above mentioned educational model. They consisted of:

- weekly offline lessons, during which the professor assigned a topic and explained it through key concepts, finally setting a relevant research question for student discussions in the online forum;

- A set of online activities, including group discussions in online forums under the PMI. During the online activities there was a systematic distribution of roles, such as e-tutor, weekly discussion summariser and critical friend (the evaluator of the trajectory followed by the group and the products created by the students during the week). Playing these roles helps to gain study and group work skills together with professional profiles typical of e-learning.

At the end of the course students participated in a face to face focus group discussion during which they reflected upon the experience of the blended course they had taken and discussed their learning process.

Methodology

The two courses were analysed with the following aims:

1. describe individual participation trajectories and the ensuing relational structure of the community;
2. analyse identity construction in terms of positionings;
3. observe the differential inquiry of online and offline contexts in participation strategies and identity dynamics.

Specifically, we analysed:

a) group 1: an online discussion of a web forum (forum 1), and an offline discussion of a focus group (focus 1).
b) group 2, divided into two subgroups (A and B): three online discussions (forum A and forum B - where students of each subgroup interact within their subgroup, and forum 2 - where the students of both subgroups

interact), and an offline discussion of a focus group (focus 2).

In both offline and online environments, participation strategies and positioning dynamics were analysed by Social Network Analysis (SNA) (Scott, 1997; Wasserman & Faust, 1994; Mazzoni, 2006) in a qualitative way suitable for the general exploration of social interactions.

The qualitative use of SNA produces an original methodological device able to analyse both general participation dynamics and specific identity positionings.

Analysis of Participation Strategies

Our first step in building the participation networks was to identify the recipients of each message through qualitative content analysis, in an attempt to reconstruct the networks of social relations in the different contexts.

Two independent analyses were performed on the whole data corpus for both participation strategies and identity dynamics, and were found to have a high inter-reliability.

In online asynchronous discussions, messages are seldom directed to an explicit addressee so identification of the recipient/s is often complex. To solve this problem we adopted a qualitative content analysis procedure following two identification criteria: a) explicit or implicit reference to a specific recipient within the text, b) identification of multiple recipients through three indicators: absence of reference to a specific recipient, an explicit reference to multiple recipients or an explicit reference to the whole community.

The results of the content analysis were arranged in adjacency matrices and imported in NetMiner 3, a Social Network Analysis software. By cross-linking senders and recipients we obtained cells showing the communicative exchanges between the participants.

We then performed Social Network Analysis through three indices:

a) the density index investigates the level of cohesion among community participants in a range from 0 to 1, where 1 represents a complete sociogram in which every node is linked with all nodes of the network;

b) the degree centrality index examines each actor's centrality and his/her social power; actors having more links than others are in a central position (each community is also analysed through a centralisation index to verify if the relational structure as a whole is based on central nodes, identified through the centrality index);

c) cohesion analysis identifies "sub-structures" in the network, known as "cliques": actors can participate in the whole social structure through groups and sub-groups. Every clique is composed of at least three completely inter-connected nodes.

Analysis of Identity Dynamics

In order to build identity networks we performed three complementary stages of analysis:

1. qualitative content analysis
2. Social Network Analysis
3. three levels of inquiry

The first step included the construction of a category grid where a range of data and theory driven positionings (Hermans 1996; Spadaro, 2008) was produced.

The grid consists of 15 categories, clustered in 5 core categories:

- *individual positionings*: emotions, ideas, experiences, interior and exterior aspects related to personal identity;

- *collective positionings*: participants speak as members of the community and define themselves as belonging to a 'we' representing the entire community or one of its subgroups;

- *interpersonal positionings*: community members explicitly address one or more group participants, for example through use of "you" or by indirectly quoting the person concerned;

- *intergroup positionings*: by directly or indirectly interacting with other subgroups, the speaker defines him/herself as a member of a subgroup;

- *boundary positioning*: linguistic expressions marking the member's temporary estrangement from the community.

The results of the content analysis were arranged in adjacency matrices representing the links between eliciting and elicited positionings, in order to perform SNA.

An innovative form of SNA called Positioning Network Analysis (PNA) (Ligorio, Annese, Spadaro & Traetta, 2008), which represents network nodes as positionings, was used to build identity networks. In the second step of the analysis process, PNA was performed through two indices: density and degree centrality. The density index investigates the level of cohesion among nodes/positionings by representing the complete repertoire of positionings of each participant and of the whole community. The degree centrality index examines each positioning's centrality and lets us identify positionings that are crucial for the Self as they are tied to most of other positionings.

In the third step, the positioning trajectories were analysed according to three levels of inquiry: individual, interpersonal and community levels, marking the dialogical interplay of identity. The individual level examines the dialogue between positionings within a single individual; the interpersonal level reveals the dialogue between positionings of different social actors; the community level connects all the individual and interpersonal positionings of the community members.

Figure 1.

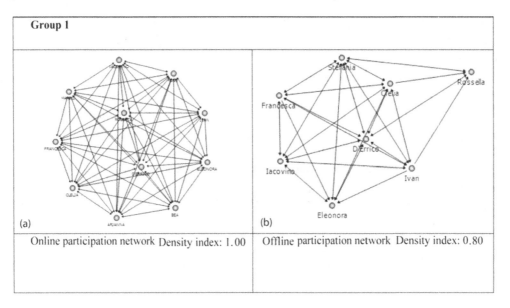

Group 1	
(a)	(b)
Online participation network Density index: 1.00	Offline participation network Density index: 0.80

Participation Dynamics and Building Community Networks

Some studies show that participation strategies in online communities depend on a mixture of dimensions such as personal identity, collective identity and kind of practices performed (Ligorio, Annese, Spadaro & Traetta, 2008). This mix determines both the participants' sense of belonging and the sense of constructing a community, both also influenced by the specific features of the interactional objectives and context.

According to this assumption, the results show the essential role of the communication environment in influencing community participation dynamics and consequently in defining its relational network. In both groups we identified different community relational structures in the double interactive environment: the online discussion showed higher density index values than the offline discussion (see Figure 1a, 1b, 2a, 2b), thus underlining a more consistent and solid community network in the online context.

The online context seems to allow more compact, homogeneous participation strategies; it harmonises and stabilises the community structure through a more democratic distribution of communicative resources and social power.

The peculiarities of online environments, and especially of asynchronous discussions, let each participant personalise their rhythms and ways of interaction, as they can take part in the discussion in different ways and at different times, by reading and re-reading the written messages when they like and so expanding the community's participation network; each member can activate a personal thinking process to organise his/her participation in the discussion, unrestricted by the turn-taking distribution of conventional offline discussions with their rigid ways and times of participation.

According to Zembylas and Vrasidas (2006), in asynchronous communication partners in a interaction focus their attention on the content of other participants' messages rather than on the complementary aspects of communication (e.g. non verbal, physical aspects, etc.). In online discussions the possibility to read notes has an important role in keeping the discussion alive: the notes act as a "partner" to which the writer has to refer during the discussion. They thus represent a

Figure 2.

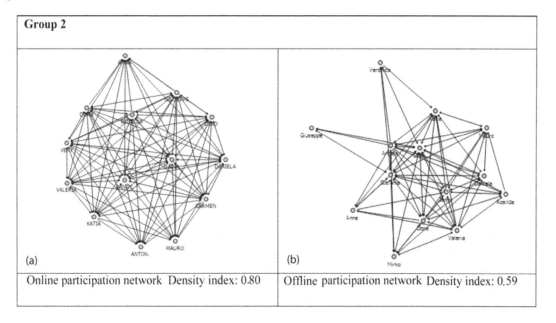

Group 2	
(a)	(b)
Online participation network Density index: 0.80	Offline participation network Density index: 0.59

visible artefact that supports reflection on other participants' notes.

In the following example, we report two notes written in forum 1: the former guides the latter, even through they are not consecutive but are separated by five other notes. Specifically, the topic of note 1 is recalled by that of note 7, keeping the discussion alive. Roberta, the author of note 7, responds directly to the content of note 1, which is therefore acting as her partner of communication:

"[...] The subject is easy: let talk about digital identity!!! How and why do we build it? What are the advantages and the dangers of a nickname? How useful are emoticons in CmC?" (Ivan, note 1, forum 1)

"The idea of a contextual construction of identity supports some researchers' statements about social presence in CmC. In other words, the absence of "social cues" wouldn't generate a condition of social isolation or de-individuation, but it would *strengthen social identity (Spears and Lea). The construction of a virtual identity is strongly grounded in the context and its actors, and it allows the creation of "a coherent but not unique self" (Giuliano)". (Roberta, note 7, forum 1)*

Even if the note written by Roberta doesn't contain an explicit reference to Ivan, her answer makes it clear how Ivan's previous questions caused reflection even some time later. Therefore notes are an artefact that works as a mediator between the task and the cognitive performance of the group, according to Hutchins' distributed cognition conceptualisation (1995). Of course, this guiding role of artefacts is absent in offline discussion, where the conversational turn-taking is invisible. This could explain the low cohesion and some lateral spread of discussion contents in the offline environment, where participation strategies are more fragmented. As a consequence, in the online context, notes as artefacts allow a more democratic distribution of participation with a strong involvement in the community and an ensuing sense of belonging.

Figure 3.

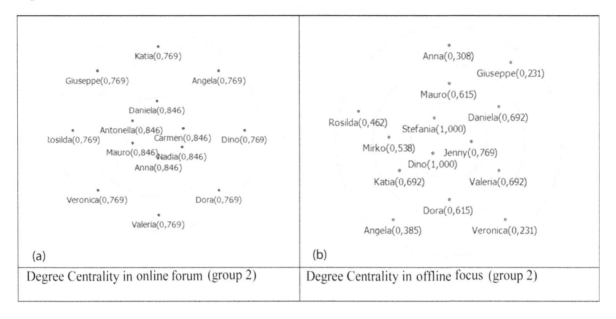

| Degree Centrality in online forum (group 2) | Degree Centrality in offline focus (group 2) |

Another interesting result concerns the variety of individual participation trajectories in the same group. Observation of the two blended communities shows different trajectories not always consisting in a linear participation: they are both stable and unstable, depending on the individual and the situation. Some members follow stable participation trajectories by activating the same strategies in both interactive contexts. For example, some students maintain the same popularity in both online and offline discussions; they are always crucial reference points for the whole community. These include Daniela from Group 2, whose trajectory is stable in both forum and focus discussions. Daniela's degree centrality index is high in both online (0.85) and offline (0.69) contexts, identifying her as a central actor (see Figure 3a and 3b):

Other students change their participation style according to the interactive environment, generating specific trajectories. For example, students like Anna (see Figure 3a and 3b), who are peripheral in face to face discussion (0.31), become central members in online discussion (0.85), being per-

fectly integrated in the community's participation network. In contrast, other students show opposite trajectories, such as Dino, who plays a central role (1.00) in face to face discussion (see Figure 3b) but becomes less essential (0.77) in virtual discussion (see Figure 3a).

These different trajectories influence the community structure: students who maintain a stable centrality throughout the course represent a reference point for communicative exchanges within the community. In return, the community structure affects individual participation strategies: when the community is well distributed, its even structure determines the absence of central and peripheral participants; conversely, when the community is not compact, its uneven structure lets some members implement more active participation strategies, becoming the functional leaders or counter-leaders in community life. Within the observed blended communities, leaders - charismatic and popular figures enjoying the consensus of all members - live side by side with counter-leaders, who try to channel dissent even if the community does not legitimise them.

Table 1. Degree centrality indexes of communication (forum subgroup A, group 2)

Members	Incoming	Outgoing
Daniela	1.00	1.00
Dino	0.33	1.00
Katia	0.50	0.17
Mauro	0.50	0.17
Antonella	0.50	0.17
Angela	0.50	1.00
Nadia	0.50	0.33

Counter-leaders are active participants in message production only, not in receipt of messages from other members. The interactional profile of Dino gives an example of the difference between incoming (0.33) and outgoing communication (1.00) of a counter-leader (see table 1):

In other words, counter-leaders are generally not respected by other participants, who prefer to give their approval to members recognised as leaders. In contrast, leaders present a balanced interaction profile, like Daniela, who combines a high centrality index (1.00) for notes posted in forum discussions and self-selection in offline conversations with a high centrality index (1.00) for receipt of communications in both digital and real interactions (see table 1). In this sense the community structure is based on a positional logic that defines the individuals in terms of social power and popularity.

Furthermore, by analysing research data from the second group, we found two different leadership styles in the online discussions of the two subgroups: a directive style with a high centralisation index (52.8%), producing fragmentary participation strategies (see Figure 4a); and a distributed style with a low centralisation index (8.33%), allowing more balanced strategies in a compact group structure (see Figure 4b).

Of course, the leaders' positioning makes sense according to the other participants' positionings and all members' positionings contribute to define the community as a whole. In this way, participation strategies of individual members take on a meaning as the essential part of a collective participation network defining group dynamics and the very structure of the community.

Finally, in the online setting, we observed the impact of a different sense of belonging on the community participation network. When students interact in group discussions, their sense of belonging to the subgroup decreases while their belonging to the whole community increases, influencing the community network construction. In group discussion, the interaction between subgroups creates a more inclusive sense of community and thorough participation network, also affecting identity positionings.

By studying participation dynamics we are able to understand the mediation of technological artefacts in both interaction patterns and identity dynamics.

Positioning Trajectories and Building Identity Networks

According to our results, the communication environment does not seem to play a central role in differentiating positioning trajectories; in fact the two groups produced different identity networks.

In group 1, identity positionings changed according to the communication context, being based on the individual dimension in the online environment and on the collective dimension in the offline one.

Figure 4.

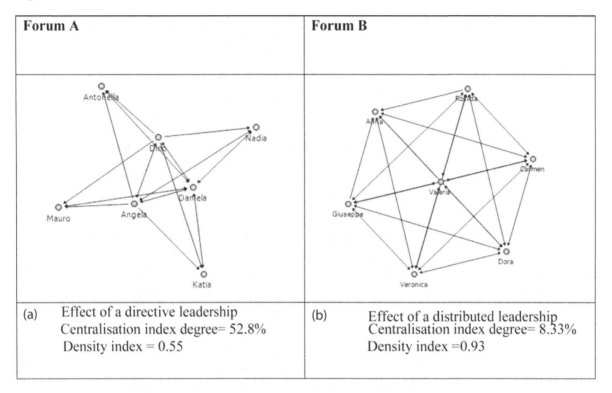

Forum A	Forum B
(a) Effect of a directive leadership Centralisation index degree= 52.8% Density index = 0.55	(b) Effect of a distributed leadership Centralisation index degree= 8.33% Density index =0.93

The individual dimension is marked by the use of the internal individual positioning referring to linguistic expressions in which the speaker reveals private characteristics, emotions or ideas marking his/her personal identity (see Figure 5a). The collective dimension emerges through use of the internal collective positioning that refers to expressions in which the participant talks as a community member, defining him/herself as belonging to a 'we', and marking his social identity through his/her sense of belonging (see Figure 5b).

In the online context (see Figure 5a) the internal individual positioning is central (0.87): several discursive markers reveal students' private ideas or feelings that emphasise the subjectivity of each single actor:

"My curiosity is awakened by reflection on these differences..." (Clelia, note 50, forum 1).

In this example, Clelia shows her own specific inclination to curiosity, thus sharing part of her personal identity with her colleagues.

In contrast, in the offline context (see Figure 5b), the internal collective positioning is central (1.00): students show many discursive markers of their belonging to the community, such as the use of collective pronouns, especially "we":

"Now sometimes we meet in chat too, and we use our Skype..." (Francesca, conversational turn 123, focus 1)

In this example, Francesca speaks as a community member by taking a collective perspective and explaining that the common experience of the blended course has increased the shared repertoire of communicative tools and social interaction by empowering the sense of community.

Figure 5.

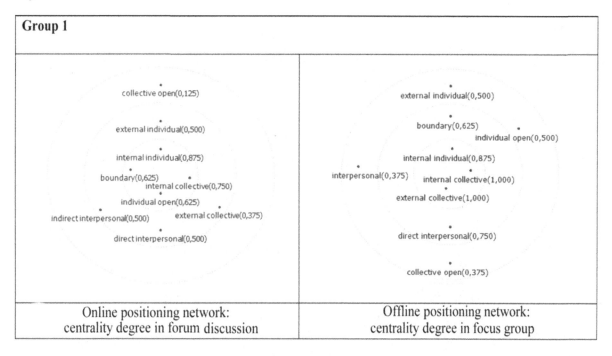

Group 1	
Online positioning network: centrality degree in forum discussion	Offline positioning network: centrality degree in focus group

In contrast with group 1, group 2 shows a similar network both on and offline, both based on an individual dimension closely related to alterity (see Figure 6a e 6b).

In the online environment the individual dimension (internal individual positioning) is central (0.71) and is related to alterity through the internal collective (0.71) and the direct interpersonal positionings (0.71) activated by participants to explicitly refer to one or more community members (see Figure 6a). For instance, direct interpersonal positioning represents alterity through use of collective pronouns or the pronoun 'you' employed in a particular way:

"Anto, what kind of needs do you think might convince people to interact on line?" (Daniela, note 10, forum 2)

This question shows the important role that others play in the definition of individual identity: Daniela needs to integrate her peer's perspective in her own conceptual framework in order to assimilate it as an aspect of her own thought and personal identity.

In the offline environment (see Figure 6b) too, the individual dimension (internal individual positioning) is central (0.571) and is related to alterity, represented by the internal collective positioning (0.571) and indirect (0.571) and direct (0.5) interpersonal positioning.

Indirect interpersonal positioning recalls other participants through a third person reference to one or more participants, as in the following example:

"As Dino said, all students have contributed in a similar way". (Dora, note 150, focus 2).

In this note Dora mentions Dino's position to support her idea about group work. The indirect interpersonal positioning shows that the construction of individual attitudes is centred on other participants' contributions just as the construc-

Figure 6.

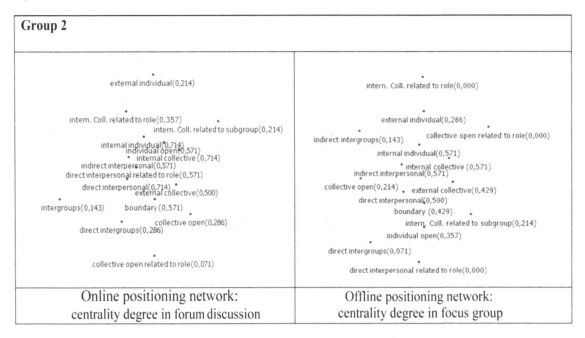

Group 2	
external individual(0,214) intern. Coll. related to role(0,357) intern. Coll. related to subgroup(0,214) internal individual(0,714) individual open(0,571) internal collective (0,714) indirect interpersonal(0,571) direct interpersonal related to role(0,571) direct interpersonal(0,714) external collective(0,500) intergroups(0,143) boundary (0,571) collective open(0,286) direct intergroups(0,286) collective open related to role(0,071)	intern. Coll. related to role(0,000) external individual(0,286) indirect intergroups(0,143) collective open related to role(0,000) internal individual(0,571) internal collective (0,571) indirect interpersonal(0,571) collective open(0,214) external collective(0,429) direct interpersonal(0,500) boundary (0,429) intern. Coll. related to subgroup(0,214) individual open(0,357) direct intergroups(0,071) direct interpersonal related to role(0,000)
Online positioning network: centrality degree in forum discussion	Offline positioning network: centrality degree in focus group

tion of social identity is based upon a continuous reference to interaction with others.

The results for forums A and B (the online discussions of the two subgroups of group 2) are consistent with the general outcomes of group 2. The internal individual positioning is central for the identity network; but there is a link with alterity represented by the internal collective positioning, which is activated in a different way than in the full group 2. In these subgroups, the internal collective positioning represents the belonging to the sub-structure rather than reference to the entire community, which is given by the same positioning in the full group 2.

For example, Daniela marks her belonging to a subgroup, of which she is the tutor, by giving information on the discussion procedure exclusive to that subgroup:

"We can create a hundred other questions, but we need to start from this one now..." (Daniela, note 1, forum A, group 2)

In the same note, Daniela marks her belonging to the full group 2 when she explains that the procedural decision was taken together with the other subgroup members:

"After discussion with some members of the other group, we have finally decided the question of the week..." (Daniela, note 1, forum A, group 2).

This example clearly shows that each student is able to develop a sense of belonging to his/her subgroup and to the full group at the same time. In this double perspective, the use of the pronoun "we" may refer to the smaller or the larger group, depending on the discursive situation.

Dissimilar findings between the two groups confirm that positioning trajectories change according to the members' individuality. Moreover, the emerging possibility of personalising participation patterns in blended communities defines identity building as a process closely dependent on the group's history and specificity.

Both groups show a strong link between the subjective dimension, represented by 'individual' positionings, and the alterity, represented by 'social' positionings, in the identity networks. In fact, when describing their individual identity trajectory, participants often refer to collective experiences that reveal a very strong sense of belonging. This mediates between personal identity building processes and the involvement in the community; it can be particularly complex when the community is made up of various subgroups, thus creating different community stages and, consequently, several levels of belonging. In these cases group members adapt their positioning to the interactional context: when interacting in a subgroup discussion, the pronoun "we" identifies the more restricted substructure; while during discussions extended to the whole community, the pronoun "we" broadens its boundaries to the entire group. Identity therefore develops through integrating the different senses of belonging. The constant reference to the other as an essential element for identity building leads to an ongoing reconstruction of the individual's social identity, as well as the possibility of building a collective community identity, which is the outcome of the negotiation between the individual identities of its members. Participating in and belonging to a community involve the sharing of a common space inside which one's individual positioning can be made available to the other, in order to overcome the boundaries separating the individual from the group.

The findings of the PNA application become more interesting if we consider the three levels of inquiry - individual, interpersonal and community – marking the dialogical interplay of identity.

In both groups, the online environment shows a predominance of the individual level looking towards the alterity; whereas the offline environment marks the prevalence of the interpersonal level looking towards the individuality. In the virtual context, the social nature of the dialogical identity emerges through the multitude of voices intertwining in the weft of the self, in contrast, in real context the identity emphasises the dialogical interplay through reference to a shared repertoire of experiences at the interpersonal level. Mutual engagement and joint enterprise with others (Wenger, 1998) are the weft on which individuality can develop. In face to face contexts the community framework represents the cultural dimension of dialogical identity. Furthermore, in the blended communities we studied, the network of positionings seems to be enhanced as we move away from the individual towards the community level, passing through the interpersonal level.

Specifically, in the first group it was possible to identify a funnel-like trajectory, especially in the online discussion, where the network gradually opens up from the predominance of individual internal positioning, at the individual level, to the social dimension. The boundary positioning was integrated in the interpersonal level not merely through identification with others, but also through opposition to others and to the group. Lastly, the network becomes even more structured in the community level, where the identity space is dilated in the social context, making the internal collective positioning pertinent. The offline discussion context also produced a funnel network, but one going in the opposite direction. In fact, the offline discussion is oriented towards collective positioning on all levels. The predominance of the collective positioning inside the individual level is, therefore, attenuated by the relevance of the boundary positioning in the interpersonal level and further tempered in the community level with a greater frequency of individual internal positioning.

On the other hand, the second group presented far more similar online and offline settings. In both cases, the network of positionings appears to be oriented, on all levels, towards the individual internal positioning, with receptiveness towards the alterity. Such alterity is represented in online discussion by internal collective and direct interpersonal positioning and in offline discussion also by boundary positionings, which act as a mediating element between the individual and collective dimensions.

These levels of inquiry in the identity positionings show a trajectory constructed in a dialogical way. A "blended identity" develops in the close relationship between individual and community trajectories: individuals' positionings, practices, artefacts, and objectives of the interaction define the community structure. Individual identity is intermingled with community identity.

Group Dynamics in Blended Learning Communities

In order to study group dynamics in blended learning communities, it is necessary to understand how the different contexts play a role in changing the group's interaction patterns and the social aspects of learning. After all, artefacts play an important role in community practices: they are mediators between individuals and context and they make collective experience accessible to the individual, although they can also limit it. The use of artefacts is the product of a negotiation process; community members make sense of their use in specific practices of the interactional context. The introduction and use of new artefacts can thus produce organisational and psychological changes.

In particular, communication technologies can be conceptualised as artefacts able to change a community's thinking processes and social practices. Asynchronous communication environments, such as the ones observed in the blended communities of this study, particularly enhance the intersubjective processes of negotiation; they promote the members' active and reciprocal attention in constructing community practices. For this reason, it is useful to analyse the effects of the mediation of technological artefacts on group dynamics and interactional patterns.

Our study suggests that the mediation of technology affects psychosocial group dynamics, not only in online communication contexts but also in face to face interactions, in this way generating a blended community. Digital contexts help members create a strong "sense of community" (McMillan & Chavis, 1986) by supporting a more compact interactional network than do face to face contexts, whose interaction is in turn influenced by the sense of community developed online. This does not required a physical shared space but rather a symbolic and cultural space generated by a strong interdependence, "a feeling that members have of belonging, a feeling that members matter to one another and to the group, and a shared faith that members' needs will be met through their commitment to be together" (McMillan & Chavis, 1986; p. 4). It is an intersubjective architecture created by a virtual context and maintained in the real context, allowing members to overcome the perception of being single individuals and recognise themselves as interacting individuals, as part of a whole.

According to our results, the development of a sense of community is fostered by the virtual environment, which produces a balanced interactional network allowing more democratic participation strategies through an equal distribution of communicative resources. The outcomes of this participation support findings of the democratic nature of Computer Mediated Communication (Sproull & Kiesler, 1991), and confirm the influence of the communication environment on the quality of community interaction.

Furthermore, an intersubjective architecture is determined by balanced participation in virtual context. Intersubjectivity supports building of identity and construction of sense of community, in both offline and online interactions of the blended community, enabling a constant reference to the other. Alterity can be considered as a crucial aspect of two building processes: construction of the individual's social identity and negotiation of the community's collective identity. Blended communities seem to be more effective in promoting and supporting such processes because of the members' involvement in a double context, where the ability to personalise their way of participation increases the possibility of constructing a personal and collective identity.

The different participation strategies contribute to the formation of an intersubjective space that helps to construct the individuals' social identity through community experiences and the community's collective identity through the individuals' sense of belonging. The intertwining of individuality and collectivity is mediated by the sense of belonging to the community, in other words the blending of individuality and collectivity lies in the pivotal sense of belonging. Thanks to this, each member becomes "someone" and develops his/her identity inside the weave of experiences generated by the community.

In learning communities, the individual consolidates his/her sense of belonging when the community identifies a common goal, such as the construction of a collective product (Spadaro & Ligorio, 2005). The ensuing collaboration produces the sharing of ideas and the finding of solutions that develop new knowledge and expertise for both participants and the community, in a social learning process that increases the sense of belonging of its members. Collectively built knowledge contains the history of the community and its practitioners, and is a reification of the sense of community.

In contrast with a simple collection of individuals, communities are characterised by a continuous process of interpersonal exchanges and negotiation of meanings that contributes to create a shared culture and vision. The construction of a group culture and the individuals' involvement in that culture are woven into a weft of intersubjectively negotiated meanings.

In conclusion, the reciprocal influence between virtual and real contexts and individual and collective identity defines the community: contexts influence participation dynamics and the ensuing identity dynamics influence contexts, by mingling individual and collective dimensions of the community. Blending face to face and technologically mediated contexts is a way of rethinking community as characterised by personalised and diversified participation trajectories and a dialogical building of identity.

FUTURE PERSPECTIVES

As this study attempts to highlight the psychosocial features of learning contexts, it would be helpful to explore the social dimension of groups through their analysis of communicative strategies.

Future research should focus on the distribution of social power in the relational architecture of blended communities, by identifying leadership dynamics through discursive devices. The discursive analysis of leadership processes could reveal some interesting aspects, such as the influence of the different interactive environments on leadership dynamics or the modified role of the teacher in virtual and, above all, blended learning contexts. For instance, the greater cohesion produced in virtual environments could be justified by a distribution of the leadership – to be studied through discursive markers - as a sharing process among different members, possibly including the teaching role. According to Hutchins' "distributed cognition" (1995), distribution dynamics can involve all features of a community of practices, starting with the leadership process, that can be conceived as the outcome of the group negotiation. Different participants negotiate their positions and share the role of leader at different times and according to specific interactive situations.

The blended learning community, which supports the active participation of each member in order to foster collaborative knowledge building, could also perfectly complement the complex dynamics of the leadership process - performed not only by the teacher, as is traditional in an educational context, but also by the new roles found in the blended context, such as e-tutor, summariser or critical friend.

We also believe that future research should devote greater attention to the blended dimension. In order to understand how offline and online merge, it would be interesting to develop a research trend able to identify the specific psychosocial and psychoeducational markers of this merging. Some of these markers have emerged in our study, but they need to be investigated in more depth:

- If the number and the composition of cliques – the informal and spontaneous subgroups composing the larger community – is balanced in the two interactive contexts, they give cohesion and organisation to the whole blended structure;
- Long term consistency in the two different community environments improves the blended feature;
- Some formal roles assigned in an interactive context (online discussion) are kept central in the other (offline discussion), enhancing the blended trait of community through the common attribution of essential positions (such as leadership) in both contexts;
- The migration of status and skills from an interactive to another context fosters a blended mode of working;
- Similar group dynamics between and within interactive contexts can increase the blended quality of the community.

These further investigations could improve on this study's description of social interactions and the subsequent construction of communities and identities, but its aim is above all to propose blended communities as amplifiers of the efficacy of the learning context.

CONCLUSION

The general purpose of this study was to understand the psychosocial dynamics involved in learning trajectories. We focussed on learning communities that blend mediated and face to face communication. In this context, the learning process becomes more complex, involving cognitive, social and identitary changes.

Blended communities improve cognitive functioning thanks to collaborative learning, which involves an increasing distribution of cognitive processes among participants and through artefacts. The exchangeable reference to "you" and "I" or the common reference to "we" lets knowledge advance through reciprocal reflection in both online forums and offline discussions.

Distributed processes conceptualise community as a collective agent, a social actor engaged in the flexible movements of mutual adjustment between the context and the personal needs of its participants. According to our research these movements are framed in a general social process of intersubjective negotiation: communicative practices are co-constructed both by members and through their interaction with the artefacts.

Both in face to face and online discussions, members negotiate community culture and the identity of its participants. To make sense of community practices they choose a particular style of communication, with identitary consequences. Learning in blended communities involves numerous types of participation and self-perception, enabling a flexible self to try out a variety of positionings. In blended communities individuals have the chance to select their favourite context to engage in the negotiation of a distinctive sense of belonging. In particular, online settings such as asynchronous discussion forums confirm their role as tools for supporting democratic interaction and dialogical selves.

Finally, our research shows the emerging of blended communities as social places revealing unexpected psychological processes and unusual methodological procedures. With an approach that combines social and educational perspectives, this study has strived to launch a new research trend where an innovative use of Social Network Analysis determines an original method called Positioning Network Analysis.

REFERENCES

Annese, S. (2005). Processi di negoziazione e posizionamenti identitari in una comunità di pratiche. *Ricerche di Psicologia, 28*(3), 33–63.

Bakhtin, M. (1973). *Problems of Dostoevsky's Poetics* (Emerson, C. (Trans. Ed.)). Manchester, England: Manchester University Press.

Bonk, C. J., & Grahm, C. R. (2006). *Handbook of blended learning: global perspectives, local designs*. San Francisco: Pfeiffer.

Bruner, J. (1996). *The Culture of Education*. Cambridge, MA: Harvard University Press.

Cohen, A. P. (1985). *The Symbolic Construction of Community*. London: Tavistock. doi:10.4324/9780203323373

Cole, M. (1996). *Cultural Psychology*. Cambridge, MA: Harvard University Press.

Davies, B., & Harrè, R. (1990). Positioning: the discursive production of selves. *Journal for the Theory of Social Behaviour, 20*, 43–63. doi:10.1111/j.1468-5914.1990.tb00174.x

Driscoll, M. (2002). Blended Learning: Let's get beyond the hype. *E-learning, 54*.

Dziuban, C., & Moskal, P. (2001). Evaluating distributed learning in metropolitan universities. *Metropolitan Universities, 12*(1), 41–49.

Garrison, D. R., & Kanuka, K. (2004). Blended learning: uncovering its transformative potential in higher education. *The Internet and Higher Education, 7*(2), 95–105. doi:10.1016/j.iheduc.2004.02.001

Graham, C. R. (2006). Blended Learning Systems: Definition, Current Trends, and Future Directions. In Bonk, C. J., & Graham, C. R. (Eds.), *Handbook of blended learning: Global perspectives, local designs*. San Francisco: Pfeiffer Publishing.

Harrè, R., & Van Langenhove, L. (1991). Varieties of positioning. *Journal for the Theory of Social Behaviour, 21*, 393–408. doi:10.1111/j.1468-5914.1991.tb00203.x

Hermans, H. J. M. (1996). Voicing the self: From information processing to dialogical interchange. *Psychological Bulletin, 119*(1), 31–50. doi:10.1037/0033-2909.119.1.31

Hermans, H. J. M., & Kempen, H. J. G. (1993). *The dialogical self: meaning as movement*. San Diego, CA: Academic Press.

Hutchins, E. (1995). *Cognition in the Wild*. Cambridge, MA: MIT Press.

Lave, J. (1991). Situated Learning in Communities of Practice. In Resnick, L., Levine, J., & Teasley, S. (Eds.), *Perspectives on Socially Shared Cognition* (pp. 63–82). Washington, DC: American Psychological Association. doi:10.1037/10096-003

Lave, J. (1993). The practice of learning. In Chaiklin, S., & Lave, J. (Eds.), *Understanding Practice* (pp. 3–32). Cambridge, UK: Cambridge University Press. doi:10.1017/CBO9780511625510.002

Lave, J., & Wenger, E. (1991). *Situated learning. Legitimate Peripheral Participation*. Cambridge, UK: Cambridge University Press.

Lifton, R. J. (1993). *The Protean Self: Human Resilience in an Age of Fragmentation*. New York: Basic Books.

Ligorio, M. B., Annese, S., Spadaro, P. F., & Traetta, M. (2008). Building intersubjectivity and identity in online communities. In Varisco, B. M. (Ed.), *Psychological, pedagogical and sociological models for learning and assessment in virtual communities of practice* (pp. 57–91). Milan: Polimetrica.

Ligorio, M. B., Cacciamani, S., & Cesareni, D. (2006). *Blended Learning: dalla scuola dell'obbligo alla formazione adulta*. Rome: Carocci.

Ligorio, M. B., & Sansone, N. (2009). Structure of a Blended University Course: Applying Constructivist principles to blended teaching. In (Ed.), Carla R Payne. Information Technology and Constructivism in Higher Education: Progressive Learning Frameworks. Hershey, PA: IGI Global.

Ligorio, M. B., & Spadaro, P. F. (2005). Digital positioning and online communities. In Oles, P. K., & Hermans, H. J. M. (Eds.), *The Dialogical Self: Theory And Research*. Lublin, Poland: Wydawnictwo KUL.

Ligorio, M. B., & Veermans, M. (2005). Preface: Perspectives and patterns in developing and implementing international web-based Collaborative Learning Environments. *Computers & Education*, *45*(3), 271–275. doi:10.1016/j.compedu.2005.04.007

Mantovani, G. (1995). *Comunicazione e identità*. Bologna, Italy: Il Mulino.

Matusov, E. (2001). Intersubjectivity as a way of informing teaching design for a community of learners class. *Teaching and Teacher Education, 17*, 383–402. doi:10.1016/S0742-051X(01)00002-6

Mazzoni, E. (2006). La Social Network Analysis: analisi strutturale delle comunità virtuali. In Calvani, A. (Ed.), *Rete, Comunità e conoscenza* (pp. 193–215). Trento, Italy: Edizioni Erickson.

McMillan, D. V., & Chavis, D. M. (1986). Sense of Community: A Definition and Theory. *Journal of Community Psychology, 14*, 6–23. doi:10.1002/1520-6629(198601)14:1<6::AID-JCOP2290140103>3.0.CO;2-I

Muukkonen, H., Hakkarainen, K., & Lakkala, M. (1999). Collaborative Technology for Facilitating Progressive Inquiry: Future Learning Environment Tools. In C. Hoadley & J. Roschelle (Eds.), *Proceedings of the CSCL '99: The Third International Conference on Computer Support Collaborative Learning*, (pp. 406-415). Mahwah, NJ: Erlbaum.

Reckwitz, A. (2002). Toward a Theory of Social Practices. A development in culturalist theorizing. *European Journal of Social Theory, 5*(2), 245–265. doi:10.1177/13684310222225432

Rovai, A. P., & Jordan, H. M. (2004). Blended learning and sense of community: a comparative analysis with traditional and fully on line graduated courses. *International Review of Research in Open and Distance Learning, 27*.

Saranson, S. B. (1974). *The Psychological Sense of Community: Prospects for a Community Psychology*. San Francisco: Josses-Bass.

Scott, J. (1997). *Social Network Analysis. A Handbook*. London: Sage.

Smith, P. (1988). *Discerning the subject*. Minneapolis, MN: University of Minnesota Press.

Spadaro, P. F. (2008). Grid for activity analysis (GAct). In Varisco, B. M. (Ed.), *Psychological, pedagogical and sociological models for learning and assessment in virtual communities of practice*. Milano, Italy: Polimetrica.

Spadaro, P. F., & Ligorio, M. B. (2007, August). *Perception of the self on ftf and online learning contexts*. Paper presented at the meeting of the EARLI, Budapest, Hungry.

Sproull, L., & Kiesler, S. (1991). *Connections: New ways of working in the networked organizations*. Cambridge, MA: MIT Press.

Voos, R. (2003). Blended learning--What is it and where might it take us? *Sloan-C View, 2*(1), 2–5.

Vygotskij, L. S. (1972). Apprendimento e sviluppo intellettuale nell'età scolare. In Vygotskji, L. S., Luria, A., & Leont'ev, A. N. (Eds.), *Psicologia e Pedagogia*. Rome: Editori Riuniti.

Wasserman, S., & Faust, K. (1994). *Social Network Analysis. Methods and Applications*. Cambridge, UK: Cambridge University Press.

Wellman, B. (2001). *The Persistence and Transformation of Community: From Neighbourhood Groups to Social Networks.* Toronto, Canada: Report to the Law Commission of Canada.

Wells, G. (1993). Intersubjectivity and the Construction of Knowledge. In C. Pontecorvo (a cura di), La Condivisione della Conoscenza, (pp. 353-380). Rome: La Nuova Italia.

Wenger, E. (1998). *Communities of Practice: learning, Meaning, and Identity.* Cambridge, UK: Cambridge University Press.

Zucchermaglio, C. (2002). *Psicologia Culturale dei Gruppi.* Rome: Carocci.

ADDITIONAL READING

Aviv, R., Zippy, E., Ravid, G., & Geva, A. (2003). Network Analysis of Knowledge Construction in Asynchronous Learning Networks. *JALN, 7*(3), 1–23.

Berger, P., & Luckmann, T. (1966). *The social construction of reality.* Harmondswarth, UK: Penguin.

Bersin, J. (2004). *The blended Learning Book. Best Practices, Proven Methodologies, and Lessons Learned.* London: Wiley Publishers.

Dietz-Uhler, B., & Bishop-Clark, C. (2001). The Use of computer-mediated communication to enhance subsequent face to face discussion. *Computers in Human Behavior, 17,* 269–283. doi:10.1016/S0747-5632(01)00006-1

Gergen, K. J. (1985). The social constructionist movement in modern psychology. *The American Psychologist, 40,* 266–275. doi:10.1037/0003-066X.40.3.266

Gergen, K. J., & Shotter, J. (1989). *Texts of identity: Inquiries in social construction.* Newbury Park, CA: Sage.

Graham, C. R., Allen, S., & Ure, D. (2003). *Blended learning environments: A review of the research literature.* Unpublished manuscript, Provo, UT.

Grodin, D., & Lindlof, T. (1996). *Constructing the Self in a Mediated World.* Thousand Oaks, CA: Sage.

Grossen, M., & Apothéloz, D. (1999). Positions and position markers in conversational episodes containing sensitive topics. In J. Verschueren (Ed.), *Selected papers from the 6th International Pragmatics Conference* (pp. 181-188). Antwerp, Belgiium: International Pragmatics Association.

Hermans, H. J. M. (2001). The dialogical self: Toward a theory of personal and cultural positioning. *Culture and Psychology, 7,* 243–281. doi:10.1177/1354067X0173001

Hermans, H. J. M., Kempen, H. J. G., & Van Loon, R. J. P. (1992). The Dialogical Self: Beyond Individualism and Rationalism. *The American Psychologist, 47*(1), 23–33. doi:10.1037/0003-066X.47.1.23

Kelly, P., Gale, K., Wheeler, S., & Tucker, V. (2007). Taking a stance: promoting deliberate action through online postgraduate professional development. *Technology, Pedagogy and Education, 16*(2), 153–176. doi:10.1080/14759390701406760

Kirscner, P. A., & Lai, K.-W. (2007). Online communities of practice in education. Special issue in *Technology. Pedagogy and Education., 16*(2), 127–131. doi:10.1080/14759390701406737

Ligorio, M. B. (in press). Dialogical relationship between identity and learning. *Culture and Psychology.*

Linehan, C., & McCarthy, J. (2000). Positioning in practice: Understanding participation in the social world. *Journal for the Theory of Social Behaviour, 30,* 435–453. doi:10.1111/1468-5914.00139

Marková, I., Linell, P., Grossen, M., & Salazar Orvig, A. (2007). *Dialogue in focus groups: Exploring socially shared knowledge.* London: Equinox.

Martinez, A., Dimitriadis, Y., Gomez, E., Jorrin, I., Rubia, B., & Marcos, J. A. (2002). Studying participation networks in collaboration using mixed methods. *International Journal of Computer-Supported Collaborative Learning, 1*(3), 383–408. doi:10.1007/s11412-006-8705-6

Mazzoni, E. (2005). La Social Network Analysis a supporto delle interazioni nelle comunità virtuali per la costruzione di conoscenza. *TD. Tecnologie Didattiche, 35*(2), 54–63.

Mazzoni, E., & Bertolasi, S. (2005). Software per analizzare le interazioni di gruppo: Cyram NetMiner e Ucinet. *TD. Tecnologie Didattiche, 35*(2), 64–69.

Much, N. (1995). Cultural Psychology. In Smith, J. A., Harré, R., & Van Langhenove, L. (Eds.), *Rethinking Psychology.* London: Sage.

Preece, J. (2000). *Online Communities.* Chichester, UK: John Wiley & Sons.

Shotter, J., & Gergen, K. J. (1994). Social construction: knowledge, self, others, and continuing the conversation. In Deetz, S. A. (Ed.), *Communication yearbook* (pp. 3–33). Thousand Oaks: Sage.

Chapter 15
Blurring Boundaries with Computer–Mediated Communication:
Academic–Personal Palimpsest as a Means of New Knowledge Production

Kayla D. Hales
The Pennsylvania State University, USA

Stephanie Troutman
The Pennsylvania State University, USA

ABSTRACT

The authors survey the landscape of CMC and education by relating it to increasingly popular hybrid course structures. This chapter maps findings associated with academic learning and subjective knowledge in a graduate course assignment: the "electronic palimpsest". This became a vehicle for the exploration of embodiment, identity, and virtual learning. Within the electronic palimpsest these themes were sustained, complicated, and evaluated from multiple standpoints, as demonstrated through content analysis of postings. Ultimately, this case study contributes to and supports the belief that case-specific accounts of alternative CMC projects are highly valuable in providing future directions for the requisite evolution of technologies associated with hybrid learning. The electronic palimpsest challenges typical assumptions of learning communities, as well as assessments and outcomes of learning in virtual environments. This study promotes possibilities for different pedagogical approaches to the question: what is the relationship between knowledge production and the development of learning communities?

INTRODUCTION

Academic learning environments have been historically comprised of physical classrooms as the primary social space for interaction and learning.

With technology, namely the Internet, spaces of learning within traditional academic institutions have undergone significant transformation. While online learning and web-based classes gain momentum, an interesting and underexplored phenomenon remains: the "hybrid" learning environment. As

DOI: 10.4018/978-1-61520-827-2.ch015

educators continue to integrate online technologies, interpersonal relations in online learning and education have only just begun to receive the attention necessary for understanding how education plays a key role in individuals' larger socio-communal learning (Freedman, Striedieck & Shurin, 2007). In an age of institutional change, the use of technology in classrooms remains not only fluid, but also contested. The continuing evolution of methods for the inclusion of various types of eLearning remains a subject for pedagogical inquiry. We contend that purposeful classroom communication and new types of learning are enabled by the creative use of hybrid learning environments between the traditional classroom and Information and Communication Technologies (ICTs; see Ellsworth 2003).

The blurred boundary, or "in-between" space, produced by moving between online and offline environments serves as a conduit that allows academic expression and "out of school" identities to not only meet, but to negotiate their place in both a real and imagined social continuum. Where Boler (2002) is apprehensive about the ability of Computer-Mediated Communication (CMC) to foster the transformation of the individual's growth both as a learner and within the educational context, we would offer a case study as a vehicle for such an assessment. Hayles (2002) posits that "living in a technologically engineered and information-rich environment brings with it associated shifts... changes in the experiences that constitute the dynamic lifeworld we inhabit" (p.299). This "lifeworld" is the essence of culminating, blurred spaces. It is within these spaces that our personal and academic identities collide to create non-bordered spaces where learning and meaning can be produced. The "formation of identity is a spatialized process" (Drzewiecka & Nakayama, 1998) with outcomes that result in both academic learning and new interpersonal interactions across languages and cultures.

In this chapter, we explore a computer-mediated academic project executed in a "hybrid"

course at the graduate level (i.e. a course utilizing both offline and online learning environments). Through content analysis of the completed project "document", we will show how learning that is culminated in this new and transformative way can be used for new knowledge production. For this particular case, we build from the assertion of Mitra and Watts (2002); the Internet can be "read" as a text disclosing information that expresses the identity of the authors – it is a cultural conveyance. We also extend and complicate this assertion with the concept of a palimpsest - the idea of constructing, then dismantling and rebuilding something that changes from inception to outcome. We are invested in understanding such a project with regard to how the personal and the academic co-conspire to produce multicultural and diverse knowledge. We are also interested in how this merging of knowledge, which may only be achievable through computer mediation, is made possible and becomes valuable through the electronic palimpsest exercise.

If, as suggested by Emig (2001), "learning can take place only through transactions with literal others in authentic communities of inquiry" (p.272), then it seems relevant to not only illustrate examples in which computer-mediated academic projects lead to new types of academic learning communities, but also go further in suggesting future directions for learning through computer-mediated environments. While debates continue about whether students can best achieve academic learning in the physical classroom setting or in online environments, much of the emphasis remains entrenched at this comparative level (see Emig, 2001; Wingard, 2004; Conrad, 2002). However, some scholars continue turning their attention toward 'hybrid' cases of learning that integrate technology to produce alternative educational outcomes (Ahmed & Stacey, 2001; Springgay, 2005; Keifer-Boyd, 2007). These hybrid cases raise multiple questions. For the purposes of this chapter, we will explore the following research questions:

(1) What value can be added to learning through increased awareness of the 'personal' identity in virtual classroom spaces?

(2) How can alternative academic projects produce community engagement by blurring boundaries typically associated with embodied learning?

(3) What new knowledge emerges as a result of utilizing hybrid education environments?

In the following section, we provide background information on CMC and hybrid learning. We then present our case study and discuss our research methodology and the results and interpretations of our content analysis. The chapter concludes with suggestions for future research and a brief summary of the chapter's content, purpose, and relevance.

BACKGROUND

Computer-Mediated Communication and the Hybrid Learning Model

As indicated by Johnson (2004), the introduction of computers allows individuals to do things never before imaginable, but it also allows them to simply do old things in new ways. The same can be said for other technological advancements that have influenced not only human behavior but also learning. Prompted by a Wall Street Journal special report on eLearning (2001), Skill and Young (2002) developed a theoretical research study based on eLearning. The resulting work focused on teaching and learning via "mediated technologies". Focus on teaching and learning, or one of these subjects in isolation, has and continues to characterize much of the work being done on eLearning, online education, and hybrid models. However, in addition to embracing both real and virtual spaces, Skill and Young offer a caveat; learning environments must "embrace, empower, and sustain learners of differing capabilities and interests" (p.24). This issue around learners in the electronic space, communicating via these mediated channels (i.e. CMC), continues to be underdeveloped and assessed in simplistic ways.

Earlier views of CMC have indicated that CMC is most effectively used for information exchanges and is ineffective for social interactions. These theories that view CMC as a social disadvantage are situated within the cues-filtered-out (or reduced cues; Culnan & Markus, 1987) perspective. Scholars that apply this perspective are often viewed as "technological determinists" who believe that the CMC participants have little to no influence on the impact the technology has on their interaction. By this, we mean that scholars in this arena focus on the features afforded by the media and ignore the participants (both sender and receiver). Ultimately, supporters of this perspective believe that the 'limitations' of CMC prevent valuable social information from being transmitted. Scholars that support this perspective tend to conduct research that compares CMC to face-to-face (FtF) interactions. For these scholars CMC is an impersonal media that leads to an increase in ambiguity and uncertainty when used for any interactive purposes. Therefore, they feel it should not be used for learning purposes if the intent is to be effective.

On the other hand, there are some scholars who do not view the reduced social cues (i.e. aural, contextual, and visual cues) in CMC to be a shortcoming. These scholars oppose the technological deterministic view and follow more of a "social shaping of technology" perspective; they believe that although numerous people use the same media, the media is often used for multiple purposes, in various ways, and often influences its users in different manners (Williams and Edge, 1996). In other words, users of CMC are contributors and actively create information and meaning; they are not the passive receivers that the technological deterministic view proposes. Therefore, in this perspective CMC is not neutral and detached but is capable of affording an emotionally rich, personal interaction. Unlike the cues-filtered-out perspective, scholars within this realm see the reduction of social cues positively in that it adds other dimensions not afforded by FtF interactions.

When it comes to CMC and learning, much work exists regarding the development of hybrid courses (i.e. courses that combine traditional classroom learning and electronic learning). However, the trajectory of hybrid courses continues to rapidly evolve; the literature indicates that there are competing paradigms and models for instruction. This evolution relies heavily on information technologies to create new learning communities in which students can share expertise, understanding and common values (Parsons and Ross, 2002). This "sharing of expertise" is not limited to course content, but takes on different modes as the internet and its myriad resources make multi-modal learning and explanation possible. The electronic environments in which CMC takes place are very similar to physical environments. By this, we mean that some of the issues individuals grapple with in electronic environments parallel those experienced in physical environments.

Olapiriyakul and Scher (2006) note that "the internet as a supportive tool for the learning process, provides students with new learning experiences, aggregates learning resources, facilitates student's lifestyle… and provides more options for educational access" (p.288). Keeping student-centered learning in mind, Garnham and Kaleta (2002) define the goal of hybrid learning as improvements of the educational experience for students by joining together the best features of in-class teaching with the best features of online learning. In doing this, active and independent learning outside the physical classroom is promoted with the reduction of in-class seat time.

Incorporating CMC into classes reduces the restrictions of physical locations and physical proximity. It can, therefore, break down the geographic and social barriers imposed by society that might hinder the learning process. While distance learning, carried out predominantly through web-based and online courses, involves promoting educational access to students who are geographically too far from physical campus sites to attend class, hybrid learning occurs as an electronic (or online) component of a traditional class setting. Like distance learning, hybrid courses also provide a level of access to students. While this access feature of hybrid courses is appealing, an additional body of research specifies that this feature has substantial benefits, such as more efficient use of campus classroom space and alternatives for students whose learning styles are hindered by typical classroom instruction (Hinterberger et. al., 2004; McCray 2000). Of course, institutions could benefit as well since students may be partially "housed" in virtual spaces instead of classrooms; this could allow the enrollment of more students without creating more physical space (Olapiriyakul and Scher, 2006, p. 288).

While much of the literature recognizes eLearning and hybrid learning as not only beneficial but inextricably bound to the future of higher education, some scholars and researchers claim otherwise (see Lockard and Pegrum, 2007). Qiuyun (2008) notes that, while educational hybrids increase in popularity, the effect of this type of learning is limited because of "its recent debut in the landscape of educational technology" (p. 53). In other words, additional and more innovative research is needed in this area to determine learning support and student experiential effects. Aside from some of the more practical and logistical factors regarding hybrid courses, students' interpersonal relationships, their relationship to course material and projects, as well as the learning and knowledge outcomes produced by these relationships are of utmost importance; as courses (traditional, online, or hybrid) continue to incorporate technology there will be a growing need to examine the various modes and materials associated with eLearning as a process enhanced by CMC. Beyond looking at student evaluations and assessments used by instructors to measure learning and skills, individual attention should be paid to the value of individual electronic assignments. These assignments offer unique possibilities for learning that are made viable through the hybrid courses design.

The electronic palimpsest is one example where traditional learning and CMC culminate in a form of hybridized eLearning. This makes possible what Doering (2006) terms a transformative learning experience, or an experience in which students become "reflective practitioners within online collaboration spaces…" (p. 214). In her comparison of student perceptions on traditional, hybrid, and distance courses, Biggs (2006) found that graduate students assessed personal relevance, student interaction, and collaboration to occur with higher frequency and more efficaciously in hybrid environments (p. 48). In addition to recognizing eLearning possibilities for transformation, Joseph (2005) found the hybrid model's greatest strength in its ability to maintain some of the structure of meeting in person, while enabling students to approach course content based on their own learning objectives and interests. This in no way implies that 'standard' learning objectives differ significantly across traditional, online, and hybrid learning environments. However, it does show that students interact differently within the hybrid course context and often incorporate their own goals and objectives. Therefore, student-controlled learning communities are an essential component of hybrid courses (Skill and Young, 2002). Therefore, we posit that an electronic palimpsest is a way to rethink types of learning and knowledge production in hybrid learning communities.

PRINCIPLE INVESTIGATION

Learning Through an Electronic Palimpsest: An Empirical Example

As a mode of learning, the electronic palimpsest anticipates and represents the potential bridging of space between present and future learning. It resolves tensions in hybrid learning in two important ways. First it serves as a potential assignment that facilitates linkages between in-class and online environments by allowing a movement between the two. Second, it encourages a sense of praxis: continuous reflexivity, modification, freedom to expose (or not) the learning self. An additional benefit of this form is that it allows students freedom to seek and prioritize relations through learning without having to settle on specific, predictable, "finished" product- hence, a new paradigm for knowledge outcomes. The electronic palimpsest then, is a means for inscribing personal onto academic and vice-versa by way of computer mediation.

This process becomes a paradigm for unlearning some of the relational modes of knowledge ascribed to the scholarly process. It calls for rigor that exceeds the boundaries of read, write, talk, and test. The palimpsest acknowledges the interrelatedness and inter-disciplinarity that has been evolving and continues to reinvent itself along the shifting contours of learning in 21st century. This learning must be validated as going beyond the project to incorporate and promote different ways of seeing and being with ourselves, others. It goes beyond the efforts we expend in the name of building communities within and beyond the walls of the academy.

It is important that we clarify here how this document adheres to and varies from original palimpsest paradigms. While the origin of the palimpsest defines it as a physical tablet that is written, erased, and re-written (possibly multiple times, with traces of previous and new inscriptions both legible), in the context of this assignment the palimpsest did not engage in direct erasure. Instead, the collaborative element remained visible throughout, with emphasis on editing and changing the structure of the object toward ending up with a different product from start to finish. A palimpsest differs from other popular mediated forms (wikis, blogs, discussion boards), because a palimpsest is one morphing document generated to evolve toward individual outcomes for the involved participants. When comparing the electronic palimpsest to a jointly-authored wiki, for example, vital features specific to the electronic palimpsest can be ascertained as follows: (1) Anonymity - the inability to precisely track/record what changes were made, when, and by whom; (2) Accessibility - the fact that students are not able to see the document modifications in the palimpsest *as* they are being made, or make any other additions or modifications until they are tagged; (3) Distribution - the palimpsest flows on a person to person level (i.e. 1-to-1 and not 1-to-many); and (4) Version Control - one is unable to revert back to previous versions of the document once changes have been made in the palimpsest and forwarded on. Given the unique nature of the palimpsest, we decided that the best way to methodologically assess the document was with close attention paid to the content of postings, course contexts, and approaches to identification and identity.

Participants and Data Collection

The electronic palimpsest was used in place of two traditional classroom meetings at a northeastern university. The palimpsest circulated for a period of approximately two weeks. It was developed by a population of 13, primarily female, graduate students during the spring 2008 semester. While course meetings were primarily conducted in person, alternative web-based class assignments and meetings were occasionally used. Since a focal point of the course was "knowledge production in and through the body", the palimpsest project was intended to provide an 'electronically embodied' educational experience. The electronic palimpsest was disseminated by classmates 'tagging' one another through email when it was their turn to contribute. The 'tagging' was random, with one student keeping track of the document flow as well as any technical difficulties that arose. The

student who generated the original post created it in 'cyberspace', attached it to an email, and forwarded it to another student to modify the document. The document continued to be circulated in email attachment form from a single student to a single student. There was no moderator of the discussion, so students were free to introduce and discuss any topic. Students were also given the opportunity to contribute multiple times; all 13 students participated at varying levels. The diversity and multiculturalism of the group (e.g. Asian, Black, White, Hispanic, parents and non-parents, etc.) manifests itself both directly and indirectly through the content of the electronic palimpsest, though often it cannot be fully ascertained in predictable ways.

Methodology

Manual content analysis of the electronic palimpsest document was the method of data analysis used for our theoretical articulation. Nine of sixteen contributions to the electronic palimpsest document were included in our analysis. We excluded posts that were simply a point of technical clarification as students attempted to learn about the format of the document and purpose of the assignment.

It is worth noting here that, aside from the technological problems experienced by the participants, other issues emerged regarding assessment and distinction of posts. First, the nature of an electronic palimpsest makes it difficult to determine who actually said what; a number of additions to the document were anonymous because some students did not date or sign their name to their contributed post. Additionally, since this is an 'open' document, it is impossible to determine when and by whom alterations to previous content were made as the document was being forwarded from student to student. While this may lead to a reduction in the instructor's ability to account for mastery of course content and participation, this anonymity added an interesting variable to the overall product and opens a new space for reflexivity in the end goals for learning. In other words, the electronic palimpsest may be seen as an alternative to standardized measurements of learning; something unique that calls for new directions in knowledge production, class participation, and active learning.

In order to make sense of the student contributions to the electronic palimpsest relevant to learning and blurred boundaries, we used a five category schema (academic, academic-personal, personal, electronic resources, and embodiment). The first category, *academic*, refers to the direct referencing of educational materials (e.g. curriculum or content). *Personal* relates to interpretation(s) of lived experiences and memories that informs the student's point of view; this could be an opinion, feeling, action, etc. *Academic-Personal* is a combination of academic and personal. In other words, it is personal information that is shared through an academic context or academic information that is shared via a personal anecdote. *Electronic resources* incorporates any digital sources (e.g. web addresses, images) incorporated into the palimpsest. Finally, *embodiment* is composed of any references made in the palimpsest regarding the manifestation of the body. These coded categories of the palimpsest will be used in the upcoming section as exemplars to support our claim that the electronic palimpsest as a hybrid mode of learning mobilizes student engagement on levels that may exceed expected outcomes.

Summary and Interpretation of Palimpsest Content

This section will construct a narrative that illustrates the ways in which education may play a key role in socio-communal learning and vice-versa. This narrative will also be used to inform a discussion on how the transmission and subsequent transformation of the palimpsest, as a multi-authored electronic document, touches culture, home-life preoccupations, memories, and

artifacts deemed (sometimes paradoxically) both relevant and tangential by the group of students who engaged with it.

While the initial focus of the project was to reflect on (1) embodiment, (2) art-based learning, and (3) ways of knowing through the virtual environment, the content of the palimpsest demonstrates shifts between direct academic treatment of the subject matter to experiential applications of the scholarly materials and themes. The document begins with a student's (P1) account of her experience reading the assigned class article ("Body Interfaces in Curriculum" by Karen Keifer-Body) followed by her posing two questions: (1) "How are we touching each other through these digital environments?" and (2) "How can I transition these concepts into the classroom?".

Rather than focusing solely on the information provided by the instructor, the originating contributor took it a step further (as did most contributors) and examined new sources using Keifer-Boyd's viewpoints as a lens to examine this new information. The student describes her interaction with this new source and invites other students to do so by posting hyperlinks to the content. This exemplifies an extension of learning situated within the academic-personal realm. In describing her ability to "experience" the artist's work, the student positioned herself in what Keifer-Boyd (2007) calls "a negotiation of the real and the virtual" (p. 59). By calling attention to the course material, the broader relevance of it, and her personal relationship to it, the author of the first post makes an attempt to enrich the dialogue through a topical extension of the discussion. This original post notably exemplifies each of our categories (i.e. academic, personal, academic-personal, electronic resources, and embodiment) for analysis and displays how the personal and academic co-construct learning in this online space. The remaining posts, however, could have taken a turn in any direction as there was no moderator to guide the discussion. It is interesting to see which direction each of the posts took in response to the preceding posts. As is the case with the previous example, student contributions to the electronic palimpsest seem, more often than not, to incorporate the personal and the academic in tandem rather than in isolation. While this personal-academic connection is not new, the form it takes in the virtually embodied space of the electronic palimpsest requires attention.

Internet technologies allow participants to share and alter their personal and academic identities in relation to both the assignment and the class. This identity-play is enabled by the CMC aspect of the class and works to renegotiate and integrate new identities previously unexposed due to the confines of the classroom. This is further complicated by students' attempts to "locate" themselves in relation to others within this new branch of the learning community. An awareness of the difference between being physically present with others and trying to be with them in virtual time/space manifests itself in multiple ways. This complex desire to cultivate a "hybrid third space" (i.e. somehow being with others as experienced in class, but in an online space; Keifer-Boyd, p. 59) leads to an almost constant reflection on computer-mediated academic projects. Therefore, it is important to note the ways in which "touching" occurs, or does not occur, during computer-mediated interactions. This can be done through students' recount of their own participation in chat rooms, online communities, web-based courses, and so forth.

It was observed that there were mixed feelings regarding the inclusion of computer-mediated interactions into the academic learning process and being able to connect in a physically present atmosphere; some students were receptive while others were not. One of the most significant indications of this in the electronic palimpsest document was the outward discontent and reluctance expressed by some students about being physically "out of touch" during electronic interactions. One student (P2) discusses an academic situation through personal reflection by noting how she was

enrolled in a distance learning course electronically, but ultimately felt she had "*to make hour and a half bi-weekly trek(s) into the city so that [she] could sit amongst people -bodies- living and breathing, so that [she] could see their faces, engage in small talk, and perhaps even make a few friends*". While computer-mediation affords linkage between groups of individuals across distances and eliminates academic 'face-threats', some students maintain a preference for traditional classroom settings. As this embodiment example articulates, it is possible for even engaged and participatory students to feel a sense of absence even when 'present' online. In this case and others, the student's desire for a sense of community and perhaps friendship can only be sated in the meeting environment that a traditional classroom setting typically provides.

I did not want my body to come to KNOW other bodies through the medium of the internet. I wanted to use other technologies – the train system that brought me physically to the class, the power grid, that lit the dark path from the train station to the classroom – I wanted to use these technologies to interact with people because I felt as though the interaction that they allowed would be more beneficial not only to me but to the class as a whole. Sitting in front of a computer screen, staring at a live streaming video, I would have felt little commitment to that community. (P2)

A different student (P3) contends this in her statement that "*the internet may not allow for touch in the bodied sense of the word, but our emotions and identities are touched*". In her personal account, she discusses her desire to use Twitter when she is lonely because her "*technology class has established a community [that] has given [them] a window into each other's lives, a way to touch beyond the walls of the classroom*", which helps her to feel connected or a sense of embodiment. For this particular student "*It feels safe to reveal [her]self on the computer*" (P3), which may not be the case when she is physically present in the classroom. In addition to this, an international student from Asia (P4) emphasizes how online interactions enacted through instant messengers allow her to reveal her identity through her screen name. For this student, *"it shows that it is also possible for us to [have] an unspoken conversation or response online through our other identities on cyberspace"*. We draw your attention to the student's choice of the word 'other' as this supports the notion that identities are not lost through the shifting between online and offline spaces, but that they are simply swapped and sometimes transformed.

A number of students also chose to enhance the learning experience by providing graphical images and hyperlinks (i.e. electronic resources) to strengthen the content of their textual contributions. One student (P3) incorporated a screen shot depicting the Twitter conversation she was having with other members of the learning community established for her other class. The inclusion of this image pushes the blurring of boundaries even further by accessing and sharing one online community within another. Another student (P4) discusses her interactions with the instant messaging program she uses and provides two screen shots of the application which incorporates symbols from the Asian culture. This not only adds a cultural element to the learning exercise but opens the door further into her identity. Yet another student (P2), tangentially, mentions that while she is engaging with the document she is also brewing tea. She then inquires if anyone has heard of the Kombucha tea she is brewing and goes into an educational discussion regarding the history and benefits of the tea (which she later brought into the classroom to share with participants). She includes an image of the tea being fermented to support the information she provided. A final student (P5), provides a number of hyperlinks to information on Google that students can use to expand their knowledge of the topics being discussed; more specifically the initial posting of P1.

As demonstrated by the analysis of student postings to the electronic palimpsest, the online environment has the ability to enhance the dimensions of the classroom. In the traditional classroom setting students are afforded the opportunity to bring and utilize organic experiences and subjectivities. However, graphic capabilities and other virtual modes afforded by technologies enhance students' ability to incorporate the personal in unique ways. Dialogue in cyberspace promotes continuity amongst established group of learners. Using electronically mediated projects as a vehicle for knowledge production and expansion, their collaboration speaks to broader notions of embodied identity and the morphological possibilities within hybrid learning communities. However, these possibilities are not without their obstacles.

Issues, Controversies, and Problems

The utility of the internet in providing graphics, links, and additional information at the click of the mouse is unable to be disputed. However, one student (P2) goes on to assert in a later posting relevant to embodiment *"… maybe we don't always want our body knowledge, or habits of communication, to be influenced by internet technology. Or at least not our primary ones"*. This comment points to the complicated struggle to interface the human body with evolving technologies and their related demands (see Donna Haraway's "Cyborg Manifesto," 1991). In addition to complications of the body, and its connection to virtual environments and technologies, internal experiential developments with relation to prior eLearning experiences also find their way into the electronic palimpsest as an additional subjective element.

Another student (P6) also discusses negative memories in relation to an online learning experience in which she determined that *"some [members of the online class community] seemed to feel less accountable for group work…"* This same student discusses how technological proficiency impacted students' ability to be *"in the right place at the right time"* presumably in terms of online spaces. A third negative criticism this student makes regarding the online course was the anonymity that helped people find it *"easier to berate the views of others (even to the point of injury)…"*. Her full reflection, coded as academic-personal, reads:

I must say that I found certain tasks difficult to complete "on-line" but the communicative efforts seemed to work in both productive and counter-productive ways. Some seemed to feel less accountable for group work, while others checked in more frequently than they would have been able to in a once or twice weekly meeting format. Sometimes people were confused and "in the wrong place at the wrong time." Sometimes people found it easier to berate or criticize the views of others (even to the point of injury) because of a sense of anonymity…which may be expressed as 'unfamiliarity' and Otherness. (P6)

This particular example is notable because it speaks of harm done in the virtual realm, which runs counter to the establishment of community amongst classmates/peers. Keeping in mind that this refers to a totally online class and did not occur in the context of the course associated with the electronic palimpsest, this post indicates the importance of learning communities. It also illustrates one of the issues that plague pure online courses; student disengagement, which often stems from consistent dealings with technological malfunctions coupled with an overall lack of face-to-face, in-person contact. In contrast to online course, hybrid courses are helpful in establishing communal accountability because students also meet in person. This is not to say that "harm" cannot be done in the traditional classroom space, but to point out that certain aspects of online course interaction can be renegotiated through and within the hybrid model. Alleviating a sense of unfamiliarity amongst students - which many hybrid courses are able to achieve - can reduce the chances of

counter-productive exchanges between individuals utilizing online/virtual learning environments. What the student mentioned here also substantiates the electronic palimpsest as a transformative space that opens reflective dialogue on the personal for the benefit of the whole group.

While we can make no claims about the tensions, anxieties, or shortcomings of the electronic palimpsest in terms of feedback or summative evaluation, we do not seem to be able to detect within the document any signs of harmful or damaging communication, negativity, or questionable treatment of classmates or peers. Technical difficulties withstanding, the electronic communication does have other shortcomings. As articulated by one unidentified student, *"in touching each other digitally, some things get lost"*. Therefore, information that could lead to enriching discussion in a traditional classroom environment may get overlooked during online communication.

Our data analysis found the sentiment of "loss" as a result of not "being with" (i.e. in person or in the traditional classroom environment) to be prominent among the palimpsest posts. Specifically, not only were "identity issues" spoken about by students, but these issues seemed to assert themselves itself through the choices made available by the electronic media affordances at work in the palimpsest itself. Another finding that relates to student/learner identity uncovered during data analysis has to do with students simultaneously engaging with media (i.e. completing the assignment, resigning themselves to the lack of physical presence) while critiquing it's limitations as well as a way to make meaning of themselves within this "hybrid 3rd space" (Keifer-Boyd, 2007).

Having established the electronic palimpsest as an alternative mode of learning compatible with and amenable to hybrid learning contexts, we recognize that it comes replete with its own unique set of principles and limitations. Paradoxically, these very same issues and limitations are also its strengths; the fact that it allows for multiple levels of engagement, without face threats or fear of rejection, and the freedom to experiment across time and space are the elements that make it a purposeful tool in the classroom setting.

Solutions and Recommendations

During our analysis, we observed that the palimpsest assignment not only addressed course content and curriculum as proposed, but went further by fostering growth of student identity relationships and inter-personal dialogues. This manifested in the emergence of new spaces where the typical norms associated with learning and knowledge acquisition are both extended and challenged through a blurring of boundaries. If the palimpsest, and similar assignments, were more broadly incorporated into traditional classroom settings, some of the aforementioned challenges and concerns (e.g. assessment and technological difficulty) might be remedied - not by standardization, but by setting clear expectations and addressing individual's technological proficiency levels. Designating a discussion moderator could be another way to enhance the CMC 'learning' experience of participants in these hybrid classes. The moderator could be responsible for encouraging participation, maintaining dialogue, tracking conversation threads, and even providing topics for discussion.

It is important to note that, no matter what modifications are made to ease tensions and work out both technological and content issues in hybrid courses there will, of course, always be some students who crave the familiar physical connection of the traditional classroom structure. Some students will simply miss "*the bodily cues and the facial expressions and so on and so forth through which [they] feel [they] could work these issues out together*" (Unidentified Student). Even with this potential inconvenience, a transformative, teachable moment is created. As part of the eLearning pedagogy, instructors of hybrid courses could take opportunities like this to help students cultivate beyond conventions to push boundaries

further. In doing this, students may discover new ways of knowing and feeling comfortable with the unfamiliar. One of the ways to facilitate hybrid learning in creative and expeditious ways is not only to pedagogically rethink our perspectives as educators, but also to adjust our sensitivity to the interesting quandaries students encounter in relation to the tasks assigned in virtual spaces.

FUTURE RESEARCH DIRECTIONS

While many articles have been published with the intention of analyzing eLearning, hybrid models, distance education, and so forth, this chapter is unique in that it emphasizes the positioning and utility of an old concept (i.e. the palimpsest) within a new learning context (i.e. electronic spaces). We posit that existing research depicts teaching experience, teacher perspectives, ethics of online learning, course design and web-based platforms, and student feedback. However, there exists a need for research examining alternative computer-mediated projects within hybrid learning models. Therefore, the approach we have taken to hybrid learning by analyzing the contours of the electronic palimpsest serves as a single case study for the future research that will attempt to address community formation, hybrid learner identities, and the academic outcomes of eLearning (both hybrid and strictly online models).

Future scholars might explore the reasons students seem to feel the need to discuss personal information about themselves in these academic electronic spaces. Could this be their way of making up for the lack of physical embodiment or social presence? Another point of interest to dictate ongoing research agendas comes from the notion that student identities in the virtual and classroom space culminate to produce new knowledge systems, which offer ways to rethink hybrid learners as constituting a new style or unique modality. The elaboration and inclusion of this 'new personal knowledge' contributes significantly to community building - an essential feature in creating a sense of shared purpose amongst classmates in educational and learning environments, especially online. This type of individual intentionality is often regarded as tangential (due, in part, to limitations like time present in the traditional classroom). However, the electronic palimpsest demonstrates the contrary in most instances; students reveal themselves in relation to socio-personal dimensions that expose the ways in which they make sense of information and/or construct knowledge. This self-exposure acts as a sort of 'think-aloud' pedagogy that invites others to be with them on their learning journey.

Ultimately, the value of computer-mediated academic projects, like the electronic palimpsest, must be further tested by trials, modifications, and analysis of outcomes with other groups and other course content. It is our hope that this chapter demonstrates the importance of exploring the implementation and outcomes of such projects. These projects may be a way to promote and enhance interactive learning that resides in a multi-modal learning space where the academic and the personal can converge.

CONCLUSION

This chapter contributes to knowledge by: (1) providing an empirical example, through the analysis of an electronic palimpsest, of computer-mediated environments as a place that fosters academic and socio-communal learning, (2) discussing and explaining the importance of expanding the analysis of electronic projects, as a way to gain information about hybrid learners and reasons to incorporate alternative computer-mediated projects into offline classes and hybrid learning environments, and (3) adding to the, currently limited, literature that explores 'hybrid' learning environments, specifically the types of projects conceived of as bridging online and offline learning in classroom communities. However, it is

important to note the limitations of our study as well. Since the analysis in this chapter was done from a single palimpsest document developed in one course of a northeastern university over the course of two weeks, the findings cannot and should not be generalized to other populations, or even other classes within the same university. Instead, this information can and should be used as an introduction to this topic as well as encouragement for scholars to further pursue this area of study. In much the same way as Greg Ulmer's *Florida Rushmore* (Ulmer, 1994), we argue that computer-mediated projects, like palimpsest documents, constitute "electronic monuments" or artifacts. Palimpsests, and variations thereof, can function to extend the uses of mixed-media learning and online collaboration between academic knowledge and popular culture, while mapping new frontiers for the utility of CMC in education related projects.

Though limited to a single case study, this chapter has, ultimately, demonstrated that the computer-mediated academic projects can educate a group by becoming a collaborative cultural artifact that travels in and through 'spaces of identity'; simultaneously engaging and transcending the original goals that may have been established. Through this chapter, the affordances of electronic media and online spaces have also been shown to support these types of educational outcomes. These features present interesting possibilities for broadening traditional views of what constitutes learning as well as how and where these unexpected transformations can occur. Such unavoidable transitions expand the intersection where media, mind, body, and scholarship meet. Is this not the goal of learning and education?

REFERENCES

Ahmed, S., & Stacey, J. (2001). *Thinking through skin*. London, UK: Routledge.

Biggs, M. (2006). Comparison of student perceptions of classroom instruction: Traditional, hybrid, and distance education. *Turkish Online Journal of Distance Education*, 7(2), 46–58.

Boler, M. (2002). The new digital Cartesianism: Bodies and space in online education. In the Philosophy of Education Society (ed.), Philosophy of Education (pp.331-340). Urbana, IL: Studies in Philosophy and Education.

Conrad, D. L. (2002). Engagement, excitement, anxiety, and fear: Learners' experiences of starting an online course. *American Journal of Distance Education*, 16(4), 205–226. doi:10.1207/S15389286AJDE1604_2

Darrington, A. (2008). Six Lessons in e-Learning: Strategies and Support for Teachers New to Online Environments. *Teaching English in the Two-Year College*, 35(4), 416–421.

Doering, A. (2006). Adventure Learning: Transformative hybrid online education. *Distance Education*, 27(2), 197–215. doi:10.1080/01587910600789571

Drzewiecka, J., & Nakayama, T. (1998). City Sites: Postmodern Urban Space and the Communication of Identity. *The Southern Communication Journal*, 64(1).

Emig, J. (2001). Embodied learning. *English Education*, 33(4), 271–280.

Freedman, Debra, Striedieck, Iris, & Shurin, L. (2007). Not Without My Body: Embodied Learning With/In the Online Learning Environment. In S. Springgay & D. Freedman (Eds.), *Curriculum and the Cultural Body* (pp.39-49). New York: Peter Lang.

Garnham, C., & Kaleta, R. (2002). Introduction to hybrid courses. Teaching with Technology Today. 8(6).Retrieved (n.d.), from http://www.uwsa.edu/ttt/articles/garnham.htm

Garrison, D. R., & Kanuka, H. (2004). Blended learning: Uncovering its transformative potential in higher education. *The Internet and Higher Education*, 7(2), 95–105. doi:10.1016/j.iheduc.2004.02.001

Haraway, D. (1991). A Cyborg Manifesto: Science, Technology, and Socialist-Feminism in the Late Twentieth Century. In *Simians, Cyborgs and Women: The Reinvention of Nature* (pp. 149–181). New York: Routledge.

Hayles, N. K. (2002). Flesh and metal: Reconfiguring the mindbody in virtual environments. *Configurations*, 10(2), 297–320. doi:10.1353/con.2003.0015

Hinterberger., et al. (2004, September). From hybrid courses to belended learning: A case study. International Conference on New Educational Environments (ICNEE) Switzerland: University of Neuchatel.

Joseph, D. (2005). Hybrid Design Enables Individualized Learning Experience. *Distance Education Report*, 9(5), 6.

Keifer-Boyd, K. (2007). Body Interfaces in Curriculum. In Springgay, S., & Freedman, D. (Eds.), *Curriculum and the Cultural Body* (pp. 51–60). New York: Peter Lang.

Lockard, J. (2007). Manifesto for Democratic Education and the Internet. In Lockard, J., & Pegrum, M. (Eds.), *Brave New Classrooms: Democratic Education and the Internet* (pp. 285–310). New York: Peter Lang.

McCray, G. E. (2000). The hybrid course: Merging online instruction and the traditional classroom. *Information Technology and Management*, 1(4), 307–327. doi:10.1023/A:1019189412115

Mitra, A., & Watts, E. (2002). Theorizing cyberspace: the idea of voice applied to the internet discourse. *New Media & Society*, 4(4), 479–498. doi:10.1177/146144402321466778

Olapiriyakul, K., & Scher, J. M. (2006). A guide to establishing hybrid learning courses: Employing information technology to create a new learning experience, and a case study. *The Internet and Higher Education, 9,* 287–301. doi:10.1016/j.iheduc.2006.08.001

Parsons, P., & Ross, D. (2002). Planning a campus to support hybrid learning. *Maricopa Center for Learning and Instruction.* Retrieved January 10, 2009, from http://www.mcli.dist.maricopa.edu/ocotillo/tv/hybrid_planning.html

Qiuyun, L. (2008). Student Satisfactions in Four Mixed Courses in Elementary Teacher Education Program. *The Internet and Higher Education, 11*(1), 53–59. doi:10.1016/j.iheduc.2007.12.005

Rovai, A. P., & Jordan, H. M. (2004, August). Blended learning and sense of community: A comparative analysis with traditional and fully online graduate courses. *International Review of Research in Open and Distance Learning.* Retrieved February 12, 2009, from http://www.irrodl.org/content/V.S.2rovai-jordan.html

Skill, T., & Young, B. (2002). Embracing the Hybrid Model: Working at the Intersections of Virtual and Physical Learning Spaces. *New Directions for Teaching and Learning, 92,* 23–32. doi:10.1002/tl.76

Springgay, S. (2005). Thinking through bodies: Bodied encounters and the process of meaning making in an e-mail generated art-project. *Studies in Art Education, 47*(1), 34–50.

Wingard, R. G. (2004). Classroom teaching changes in web-enhanced courses: A multi-institutional study. *EDUCAUSE Quarterly, 1,* 26–35.

Young, J. (2002, March 22). Hybrid teaching seeks to end divide between traditional and online instruction [Electronic version]. *The Chronicle of Higher Education.* Retrieved January 10, 2009, from http://chronicle.com/free/v48/i28/28a03301.htm

ADDITIONAL READING

Colley, A., & Comber, C. (2003). Age and gender differences in computer use and attitudes among secondary school students: what has changed? *Educational Research, 45*(2), 155–165. doi:10.1080/0013188032000103235

Collis, B., & Moonen, J. (2001). *Flexible learning in a digital world.* London: Kogan Page.

Dede, C. (2005). Planning for neomillemial learning styles: implications for investments in technology and faculty. In D.L. Oblinger and J.D. Oblinger (Eds.), *Educating the Net Generation,* 15.1-15.2 Boulder, CO: Educause. http://www.educause.edu/content.asp?page_id=6069&bhcp=1

El Mansour, B., & Mupinga, D. (2007). Students' Positive and Negative Experiences in Hybrid and Online Classes. *College Student Journal, 41*(1), 242–248.

Hiltz, S. R. (1992). Constructing and evaluating a virtual classroom. In Lea, M. (Ed.), *Contexts of computer-mediated communication* (pp. 188–208). New York: Harvester Wheatsheaf.

Hiltz, S. R. (1995). Teaching in a virtual classroom. *International Journal of Educational Telecommunications, 1*(2/3), 185–198.

Hoadley, C., & Enyedy, N. (1999). Between information and collaboration: Middle spaces in computer media for learning. In Hoadley, C. M., & Roschelle, J. (Eds.), *CSCL '99: Proceedings of Computer Supported Collaborative Learning 1999* (pp. 242–250). Hillsdale, NJ: Lawrence Erlbaum Associates.

Hoven, D. L. (2007). The affordances of technology for student teachers to shape their teacher education experience. In Kassen, M. A., Lavine, R., Murphy-Judy, K. A., & Peters, M. (Eds.), *Preparing and Developing Technology-proficient L2 Teachers. Computer Assisted Language Instruction Consortium (CALICO), Texas State University, Texas. USA. Farrell, G. M. (1999). The development of virtual education: A global perspective.* Vancouver, Canada: The Commonwealth of Learning.

Jolliffe, A., Ritter, J., & Stevens, D. (2001). *The online learning handbook: Developing and using Web-based learning*. London: Kogan Page.

Jonassen, D., Howland, J., Moore, J., & Marra, R. (2003). *Learning to solve problems with technology*. Englewood Cliffs, NJ: Prentice Hall.

Kreijns, K., & Kirschner, P. (2001). The Social Affordances of Computer-Supported Collaborative Learning Environments. 31th ASEE/IEEE Frontiers in Education Conference, Reno, NV

Kwan, and F. L. Wang (Eds.): ICHL 2008, LNCS 5169, pp. 157–167.

Mishra, P., & Koehler, M. J. (2006). Technological pedagogical content knowledge: A new framework for teacher knowledge. *Teachers College Record, 8*(6), 1017–1054. doi:10.1111/j.1467-9620.2006.00684.x

Murphy, D., Walker, R., & Webb, G. (2001). *Online Learning and Teaching with Technology: Case Studies, Experience and Practice*. London: Kogan Page.

Palloff, R., & Pratt, K. (1999). *Building learning communities in cyberspace*. San Francisco: Jossey-Bass.

Palloff, R. M., & Pratt, K. (2001). *Lessons from the Cyberspace Classroom: The Realities of Online Teaching*. San Francisco: Jossey-Bass.

Peters, L. (2001). *Through the Looking Glass: Student Perceptions of Online Learning, Technology Source*, Retrieved February 1, 2009 from http://technologysource.org/article/through_the_looking_glass/

Salmon, G. (2000). *E-Moderating: The Key to Teaching and Learning Online*. London: Kogan Page.

Simpson, O. (2000). *Supporting Students in Open and Distance Learning*. London: Kogan Page.

Sloan Consortium. (2003). *Sizing the Opportunity: The quality and the extent of online education in the United States, 2002 and 2003*. Needham, MA: Sloan Consortium. http://www.sloan-c.org/publications/survey/pdf/sizing_opportunity.pdf

Tapscott, D. (1998). *Growing Up Digital*. New York: McGraw-Hill.

Tu, C. H. (2000). Critical examination of factors affecting interaction on CMC. *Journal of Network and Computer Applications, 23*, 39–58. doi:10.1006/jnca.1999.0100

Tu, C. H. (2002). The Impacts of Text-Based CMC on Online Social Presence. *The Journal of Interactive Online Learning, 1*(2).

Van de Meij, H. (2007). What Research Has to Say About Gender-Linked Differences in CMC and Does Elementary School Children's E-mail Use Fit This Picture? *Sex Roles, 57*, 341–354. doi:10.1007/s11199-007-9270-9

Webster, F. (2006). *Theories of the Information Society* (3rd ed.). New York: Routledge.

Xu, Z. (2008). Online Computer-Mediated Communication (CMC) Discourse and Classroom Face-to-Face (FTF) Discourse Analysis. In Fong, J. (Ed.), *R*. When Hybrid Learning Meets Blended Teaching.

Chapter 16
Mediated Group Development

John A. McArthur
Queens University of Charlotte, USA

ABSTRACT

This chapter focuses on an interpersonal approach to understanding small group development in mediated environments. Whereas much of the literature in this area has emerged in the study of workplace and organizational development, this chapter is grounded in small group development theory and folds in relevant studies of virtual communication in groups. This approach is designed to complement a larger work based in interpersonal communication by providing students of interpersonal communication with a basic introduction to small groups and the impact of communication technology on small group development.

INTRODUCTION

- Three marketing staffers engage in a conference call about ad copy for a product launch.
- A twenty-member interpersonal communication class gathers around a seminar table.
- Twelve avatars study together in a gray stone church in a virtual world.
- A family of five gathers for a mother's birthday dinner.
- A reporter chats with two news anchors via satellite hologram.

DOI: 10.4018/978-1-61520-827-2.ch016

These scenarios deviate from the scope of study in interpersonal communication, not because of their varied uses of technology, but rather because they include too many people.

A dyad of two people becomes something different when a third member is added. Their collective communication changes. Harris and Sherblom (2005) suggest that when members are added to a communication environment, the number of interactions increases exponentially. A dyad in communication shares two possible interactions, one from person A to person B; one from person B to person A. Three people communicating share nine possible interactions. When a group reaches eight people, a possible 1,016 interactions are available for study. This exponential growth of the possible number of interactions creates a complex environment in which communication can flourish.

The collective study of these interactions, small group and team communication, has been well defined over the last five decades, and its study has been compiled in various textbooks on the subject (e.g. Beebe, Beebe, & Ivy, 2009; Beebe & Masterson, 2006; Engleberg & Wynn, 2007; Harris & Sherblom, 2005; Rothwell, 2006). As part of a greater body of work in this text, this chapter's main objective is to provide a brief introduction to small group development for people studying interpersonal communication by synthesizing some of the key theories in the study of small group development and folding in a discussion of current technology which impacts this development.

BACKGROUND

Small Groups and Communication

Small groups generally contain at least three, and as many as 20, individuals who are united around a common goal or purpose. These members are involved in a complex set of communication transactions which are shaped by each member of the group. From a systems theory perspective, groups are sets of interrelated, interdependent parts that influence and are influenced by each other. These groups share a common ground, bond, or focus which drive them to achieve a purpose. For this reason, people standing in line at a grocery store would not be considered a group, whereas a group might be found meeting in an online discussion board.

Because groups share a common purpose, communication observed in small groups often consists of one of four types of group communication: task, pattern, process, and self-centered (Harris & Sherblom, 2005; Rothwell, 2006). Task

communication relates to the core aims of the group and the content of its work. Consider a study group. Task communication might sound like, "Let's review interpersonal communication," or, "Who knows what the Tuckman article was about?" These statements focus on the main content of the group's goals.

Pattern communication relates to the relationships between group members. In the same study group, pattern communication might sound like, "This is a fantastic group! I know we can knock this out," or, "Taylor, you make a great leader for our group." These statements relay information about the relationships between members.

Process communication clarifies procedural elements of the group. In our study group, process communication might include, "Our next meeting will be at six o'clock on Tuesday night," or, "Heidi, you take chapter three and I'll take chapter four." These statements reflect the "how" component of the group's actions.

Self-centered communication occurs when members of the group talk about things that are off-topic. For example, self-centered communication might occur when a group member says, "I'm really hungry," or tells a joke.

The four types of communication transactions considered here can be a useful guide for discussing the verbal and nonverbal exchanges that occur in groups, but they do not give the entire story of small group communication. Like communication in interpersonal dyads, small group communication combines a delicate balance of verbal and nonverbal cues with a sense of interdependence. Thus, each member of the group bears some responsibility for the effectiveness of the group's communication, and the overall communication exhibited occurs on a larger and more complex scale than that of the interpersonal dyad.

As this book has demonstrated, the study of interpersonal communication becomes more complex when communication is mediated by technology. Likewise, technology creates another level of complexity for the study of small group communication.

Considering Virtual Groups

Virtual groups existed before the advent of the personal computer. Groups worked together using written text, telephone, and television technologies to create gathering points. These types of virtual groups still exist and are frequently used by small groups for various needs. Letter writing allowed families to keep in touch, conference calls influenced business practice, and videoconferencing allowed people to be "beamed in" to remote locations for a more personal interaction. The computer and the Internet have made these three forms of virtual communication more synchronous and more widespread. In addition, computer-based applications provided shared online spaces in which groups can interact and collaborate with varying levels of possibilities related to timing, mode, and presence of non-verbal cues.

Gopal and Melkote (2007) suggest that virtuality in groups is defined by the degree to which communication occurs through electronic media. To this end, Gopal and Melkote point to the growing body of research in management and organizational development literature surrounding factors common to virtual groups: lack of physical or temporal proximity, interdependence with shared outcomes, and the use of electronic media for communication. For the purposes of this chapter, we will consider the communicative aspects of computer-mediated communication.

To understand communicative practice in virtual groups, one must consider three particular undercurrents of computer-mediated communication: synchronicity, media richness, and social presence (Harris & Sherblom, 2005). Synchronicity is related to the timeliness of message delivery. Synchronous interactions occur simultaneously. Face-to-face communication is the best example of this, because members of a group respond to each other immediately. The synchronicity of this communication can be replicated in an audio or video conference, or through any other medium in which group members are working together at the same time. Conversely, a discussion board and a letter-writing campaign would be considered asynchronous.

Media richness is the ability of a particular medium to provide a rich sensory experience for the user (Daft & Lengel, 1986). This ability is directly tied to the medium's propensity for providing simultaneous verbal and non-verbal communication. A medium with high media richness would closely approximate face-to-face communication (e.g. videoconferencing), whereas a medium with low media richness would provide fewer sensory cues (e.g. text-based interaction).

Social presence refers to the participant's feeling that other participants are involved in the group communication (Short, Williams, & Christie, 1976). Considering two text based examples, a textbook has lower social presence than an autobiography. A blog may be able to have a higher social presence than a static webpage. A videoconference would have higher social presence than a discussion board, but the impact of media richness on creating this higher social presence is hard to distinguish from the social presence itself. For this reason, the social presence available for small groups in a particular medium is often tied to the medium's synchronicity and media richness.

Much of this early research in to computer-mediated communication implies that high synchronicity, high media richness, and high social presence may create better, more effective communication. Current research suggests that these assumptions may not be true.

As computer-mediated communication has become more advanced and widespread, these three undercurrents have been re-examined by researchers. Walther's (1992) social information processing theory (SIP) lays the foundation for much of this study. Walther suggests that participants in mediated communication will adjust their communication to recreate non-verbal cues in some other form. This adaptation is an attempt to form relationships through the use of style, language, and other cues as determined by the medium of interaction. For example, participants in a tele-conference (audio only) might state their names before they begin speaking. SIP has established a foundation for much of the study of interpersonal communication in mediated environments, and it has implications for small groups as well.

Furthermore, SIP led to the theory of hyperpersonal interaction (Walther, 1996), which suggests that computer-mediated communication may produce relationships that surpass face-to-face interpersonal relationships. Nowak, Watt, and Walther (2005) examined this theory through a study of the effects of synchronicity and non-verbal cues on social attraction, involvement, conversational effectiveness, and credibility. Their findings suggest that the main effects of synchronicity, media richness, and social presence mentioned above may not be the most effective way to study computer-mediated communication. Rather, the conversational processes involved in computer-mediated communication may be more important to understanding how interpersonal interaction occurs.

Thus, the effectiveness of a medium may not be determined by its ability to provide non-verbal cues, as was previously suggested by the concepts of media richness and social presence. Even though Nowak, Watt, and Walther's work examined dyads in a task-oriented partnership, this work has compelling implications for small group development. To be effective, computer-mediated communication may not have to engage in media richness and social presence. Rather, it must adequately facilitate the group's conversational processes.

Virtual groups must also consider the tools they use to create a shared group space which will allow the conversational process to emerge. When we think about a small group, most of us would picture six or seven people huddled around a conference table talking to each other or a team of basketball players huddled on the court. Likewise, virtual groups must find virtual gathering spaces so that they can "huddle together" to communicate as teams. McArthur (2009) suggests that virtual spaces found online can re-create the sense of shared space among group members, and Hodgson (2009) offers that virtual spaces might also provide opportunities for enhanced communication patterns when effectively paired with physical spaces. Thus, chat rooms, multi-user applications, and social networking sites can function as platforms in which group members can gather to advance their group's development.

GROUP DEVELOPMENT

Small group development theory studies the process through which groups come together and learn how to perform as a unit. Through a review of literature on small group processes in 1965, Bruce Tuckman developed a model that has now become ubiquitous in small group communication. This model divides the group development process into four stages. The first stage, *forming*, details the process of coming together and initial uneasiness. *Storming*, the second stage, is a period of conflict related to task definition. The third stage, *norming*, occurs when groups develop rules and guidelines for behavior in the group. *Performing*, the fourth stage, is often characterized by cooperation, teamwork, and production.

Like face-to-face groups, virtual groups may move through these four stages as they develop. This section will address each of the stages and the means whereby virtuality impacts each stage. The discussion of each stage will address specific issues and opportunities present in the stage, as well as research-based findings and recommendations for group development.

Beyond Tuckman's original model, Tuckman and Jensen (1977) added a fifth stage, adjourning, to the group process. In addition, Gersick (1988) suggested that the Tuckman model was less necessary to a discussion of small groups than a discussion of each element of group communication. Furthermore, much of the previously mentioned research has demonstrated that mediation of small groups adds to the complexity of interaction that can occur within groups. Nevertheless, this model provides a worthwhile construction, in defined terms, for one interpretation of a process through which groups may form. Thus, for the purposes of this chapter, Tuckman's group development process can serve a simple framing device to begin a discussion of how groups develop with the intent of identifying some key claims about the ways whereby group process is mitigated by communication technology.

Forming

Before discussing the forming stage at the point of the group's first gathering, one must consider the reasons that groups come together. In other words, why do we join groups? Texts on small group development suggest that we join groups as a response to personal attraction; to contribute to group goals; and for reasons of necessity (Beebe & Masterson, 2006; Rothwell, 2007; Harris & Sherblom, 2005).

Personal attraction often relates to an interpersonal connection with members of a group or with attraction to the goals of the group. Beebe and Masterson (2006) defines four significant factors that influence interpersonal attraction: proximity, similarity, complementarity, and physical attractiveness. Proximity is related to physical closeness between individuals. Similarity corresponds to the tendency to connect with people who are like one's self. Complementarity occurs when people seek out others who differ from themselves to meet a particular need. Physical attractiveness relates to our desire to seek out individuals who appeal to our senses. These four factors of attraction suggest several means for group affiliation.

Often, we seek out groups which have goals with which we identify. These groups may be groups that perform certain activities, like a poker group or a hiking club. They may have a shared vision or mission, like a community service organization or a political action group. Or, they may be comprised of members who share certain characteristics, like a carpool group, a study group, or a support group.

Need satisfaction often relates to the need to affiliate with a particular group. Maslow's (1982) hierarchy of needs lists belonging as a fundamental need, and joining groups and teams help to satisfy this need. Sometimes, however, joining a group is a response to the need to complete a specific task. Often in these cases, affiliation is arbitrarily assigned by a supervisor, teacher, or other authority.

Once the group has come together for the first time, the forming stage officially begins. During this stage, group members begin to adjust to the group and its members and try to discover what their roles in the group might be. Group members are typically tentative and hesitant in preliminary meetings. This initial awkwardness is called primary tension (Harris & Sherblom, 2005). Common communication patterns that emerge in this stage include nonverbal cues, questions, pauses, and tentative discussion of the group task. Ahuja and Galvin (2003) suggest that these communicative behaviors occur in mediated groups, but relate more to information-seeking than socialization.

The group's goal is to develop a common sense of trust in the group and its members. Virtuality complicates this stage of group development along the issues of identity and trust. Satchell and Foth (2008) suggest that the re-creation of identity in virtual environments may allow organizations to target like-minded participants for the purpose of forming groups. By revealing one's self in a digital space, the user reveals information to many more people than is possible in physical space. Thereby, the digital identity becomes a representation of and an enhancement of identity in the real world.

Dube (2009) exposes the issues of false identities in online platforms. Identities in an online world can appear trustworthy, but may be false. However, these same issues of identity and trust may promote more open conversations. Coulson, Buchanan, and Aubeeluck (2007) assessed the communication in an online support group for people with Huntington's disease. One precept of their study is that the anonymity associated with online support groups may improve disclosure of sensitive information. The benefits of this anonymity relate to lessened fears of embarrassment or judgment.

The issue of trust, while widely studied in group and organizational dynamics in both face-to-face and mediated forms, hinges on this issue of identity through social presence in mediated platforms. Once we know the other members of our group, then we can begin to trust them. Bente, et. al. (2008) suggest that video-based modes (in which participants can see each other) and avatar-based modes (in which participants can see computer-generated representations of each other) share similar levels of interpersonal trust.

The interplay between trust and identity in avatar-based modes adds a whole new level of concern about identity in group dynamics. Can an elf and a wizard in an MMORPG (massively multiplayer online role playing game) create the same kind of interpersonal trust as two people in a virtual world? Both scenarios provide users with the opportunity to select their identities, genders, physical appearances, and actions. Can two people in a virtual world develop the same level of trust that might be found in videoconferencing or face-to-face communication? Trust and identity work together in the forming stage, and computer-mediated communication in its current form dramatically complicates their relationship to group process.

Storming

The storming stage is defined by conflict over the processes of task definition. Once group members have gotten to know each other enough to be comfortable, members begin to disagree about the group's next steps. Tuckman (1965) suggests that this stage is a phase of heightened expression of emotion for group members. Many researchers agree that this storming stage, if done effectively and civilly, is a healthy experience in the group process. It is a complex and crucial step for the group, and virtuality complicates it even more. If a group fails to storm or if it creates unhealthy communication patterns, the group creates secondary tensions based on unresolved issues that can threaten the health of the group.

The question posed by the rise of computer-mediated groups is whether storming is either enhanced or impeded by the use of technology. Redfern and Naughton (2002) suggest that online spaces of interaction, which help us to focus on and collaborate on the group task, may contribute to a lack of social presence. This social presencing, as aided by synchronicity and media richness, plays an important role in the storming phase, by creating possible spaces and opportunities for relationship building.

Turning to studies of self-disclosure and information processing might help us consider this question about storming. Conventional wisdom about self-disclosure, the willingness of a person to provide personal information to an other, suggests that people are less likely to give out personal information online than in a face-to-face setting. However, Tidwell and Walther (2002) report that participants in online groups ask more direct questions of one another, enabling them to reveal more personal information online than they might in face-to-face settings. This may or may not relate to their ability to storm and conflict, but it may indicate something about participants' willingness to speak and share ideas in mediated groups, which is a key component of the storming phase.

Norming

During Tuckman's (1965) norming stage of group development, members settle into standard communication patterns, group norms, and member roles. Graham (2003) has suggested that norming in virtual teams may be more complex than in face-to-face teams, and may be better described as an ongoing process than a stage. In either scenario, the group develops a set of shared behaviors, called norms. For example, a group might have an explicit, stated norm that everyone will arrive early to meetings so that the meetings can begin on time. If a group member violates this norm, he or she might be rebuked by the group. Groups also develop implicit, unwritten or understood, norms, such as each person speaks in turn or everyone dresses casually for meetings. These norms set the foundation for how the group will interact. Each group has distinct norms which guide group procedure and lead toward cohesion, the process of coming together.

Timing in virtual groups and teams plays a role in norming. This relates back to the ability of the media to facilitate a group's conversational processes. Bente, Ruggenberg, Kramer, and Eschenburg (2008) identify three functional levels of nonverbal communication present in face-to-face interactions that may be lacking in computer-mediated interactions: discourse functions, dialogue functions, and socioemotional or relational functions. The discourse functions of non-verbal communication contribute to meaning-making by reinforcing, negating, amplifying, and otherwise modifying their verbal counterparts. The dialogue functions regulate verbal communication by providing cues for participation. The socioemotional or relational functions create opportunities for perception and impression making. The absence of these three functions suggest that groups engaged in computer-mediated communication may encounter more misunderstandings and may require more time to establish group communication patterns, or norms. When combined with the results of Nowak, Watt, and Walther (2005), these findings may suggest that a even though a group takes more time to develop patterns of behavior, the group may develop better relationships overall. This speculation requires future research to assess the development of mediated norms.

Member roles also develop during the norming process. Categorized by Benne and Sheats (1948), member roles are generally divided up into three types: task roles, maintenance roles, and individual roles. Task roles involve behaviors related to the core mission and work of the group. These might include behaviors that initiate conversation, question the group, record the group history, or clarify and summarize group decisions. Maintenance roles include behaviors impacting the relationship of group members and the overall climate of the group. These roles include behaviors that relieve tension, encourage group members, resolve conflict, or follow group decisions. Individual roles are behaviors which are self-centered that detract from the group in favor of the individual. These might include behaviors like clowning, dominating, blocking, and personal agenda-setting. Wang, Walther, and Hancock (2009) suggest that the impact of member roles can be felt interpersonally in mediated groups and, thereby, can influence each member's identification with the group.

Hodgson (2009) gives an example of a study group establishing roles and creating cohesion in an online platform. Students in his example used a computer-mediated site to take collective notes on readings and lecture in class; correspond with each other; and process information. One member records information, one member organizes the information, one acts as the group spokesman and clarifies discrepancies, and one adds references and information from outside the group. These group members establish a pattern of set behaviors for their group to complete the task at hand. Interestingly, this group used two discussion areas in the site, one for the information processing and the other for personal interaction. Hodgson records that the personal interaction area was used for functions both on and off topic. This study illustrates the ability of a mediated group to perform task and maintenance functions simultaneously, even in a text-based online platform. Such performance is necessary for continued group cohesion.

Hodgson also points out in a footnote that even though other group members joined the group, the core dynamic of the group interaction remained the same. The other members of the group "lurked" in the room potentially contributing little, but with access to all group information. This dichotomy between participants and observers appears heightened in computer-mediated groups over face-to-face groups (Blaskovich, 2008). Ramirez, Zhang, McGrew, and Lin (2007) assessed the perspectives of participants and observers. The study's findings suggest that the difference in role impacts the understanding of relational messages (more than the use, or non-use, of technology). This finding contributes to the understanding of member roles as assumed, developed, and reinforced by group behaviors and norms in mediated communication.

Performing

When groups begin to function as groups by making group decisions and focusing on the group task, they have entered Tuckman's (1965) performing stage. This stage is characterized by the procedural functioning of the group toward group goals. Research on group performance in mediated settings has included studies of group success (Walther & Bunz, 2005), group decision making (McNamara, Dennis, & Carte, 2007); group efficacy (Hardin, Fuller, & Valacich, 2006); team member satisfaction (de Pillis & Furumo, 2007); social loafing (Blaskovich, 2008); overall group effectiveness (Dube & Robey, 2008); psycho-social development (Rodgers & Chen, 2005); and the impact of synchronicity (Markman, 2009).

Much of the previously mentioned research and writing about the performance stage has been completed with the aim of increasing the effectiveness of mediated groups (e.g. Rutowski, Vogel, van Genuchten, Bemelmans, & Favier, 2002; and de Pillis & Furumo, 2007). Even though improving group effectiveness is not the present aim of this chapter, research on effectiveness is valuable to the field and to the greater body of literature on this topic.

Moreover, the relationship between communicative patterns and group effectiveness has spawned new theories about mediated groups. Walther and Bunz (2005) proposed and researched six rules related to successful group performance in mediated settings: (1) begin immediately; (2) communicate frequently; (3) multitask; (4) read and acknowledge each others' messages; (5) explicitly state agreement or disagreement; and (6) set and uphold deadlines. The researchers tested these six hypothetical rules in computer-mediated task groups, finding that the implementation of these six rules increased the effectiveness of group performance.

These six rules for effective group performance draw on the various stages of group development theory and combine it with Walther's (1992) social information processing theory. This theoretical combination is a compelling step in understanding the specific communicative acts that lead to effective performance in mediated groups.

FUTURE RESEARCH DIRECTIONS

Much of the growing body of literature surrounding computer-mediated small groups deals with effectiveness in leading and managing teams and originates in business and organizational development theory. While it is a growing and extensive body of literature, this research will become even more important and complex as rapid changes in technology shape computer-mediated communication patterns.

Furthermore, the application of communication theories related to meaning-making (e.g. attribution-making, affinity seeking, agenda setting, symbolic convergence, uncertainty reduction etc.) continue to provide a richer and more complete picture of this field. In a growing body of work, Joseph Walther and colleagues have devised a viable framework for this type of study over the last decade. Textual analyses and critical studies of group-based media production and consumption could provide further insight into these issues of meaning-making. These studies will likely continue to involve issues of created, real, and shared online identities, and such research provides insight into the minds of media users.

Studies in information and user-experience design offer another lens through which this conversation can be researched. Scholars in this area examine each medium as both a route to communication content and as communication content itself. In addition, this research seeks to create, understand, and describe the experiences of the users of these technologies.

Finally, research into each of the growing number of computer-mediated platforms for group interaction will provide a comprehensive picture of group process using these technologies. This chapter has mentioned teleconferencing, video-conferencing, asynchronous discussion boards, chat rooms, social networking, virtual worlds, MMORPGs, satellite holograms, and other current tools for virtual collaboration. The list of virtual group spaces includes a variety of other technologies, each of which can be thoroughly studied and tested for usability, ability to encourage group member interaction, media richness, and other opportunities discussed herein. As technology changes, the dynamics of virtual groups will continue to shift and change alongside the technology and its system of rules.

In sum, all of these future research directions will complicate and improve our understanding of the issues and opportunities present in computer-mediated communication. Technology is changing at a dramatically rapid pace. Researchers in this and other information technology forums have

dynamic opportunities to continually update and revise theory alongside technological advancement.

CONCLUSION

This chapter on mediated small groups is meant to be a brief introduction to small group development theory among a series of chapters on interpersonal communication. Volumes of research have been written about small groups and teams, and this chapter synthesizes some of those works around the issue of development and the impact of virtuality. This chapter sought to add to the discussion of small group development by compiling works on computer-mediated communication and folding these works into a discussion of group development.

Thus, alongside the greater text, this chapter seeks to promote the study of computer-mediated group development from an interpersonal perspective. Such research is an exciting opportunity for scholars in interpersonal communication, group development, media studies, and mass communication. The discussion of virtuality complicates an already complex series of interactions present in group development, but the benefits and opportunities of virtuality and computer-based connectivity will continue to impact group development and those who advance its study.

REFERENCES

Ahuja, M. K., & Galvin, J. E. (2003). Socialization in virtual groups. *Journal of Management*, *29*(2), 161–185. doi:10.1177/014920630302900203

Beebe, S. A., Beebe, S. J., & Ivy, D. K. (2009). Communication Principles for a Lifetime: *Vol. 3. Communicating in groups and teams* (2nd ed.). Boston, MA: Pearson Education, Inc.

Beebe, S. A., & Masterson, J. T. (2006). *Communicating in Small Groups: Principles and practices* (8th ed.). Boston, MA: Pearson Education, Inc.

Benne, K. D., & Sheats, P. (1948). Functional roles of group members. *The Journal of Social Issues*, *4*, 41–49.

Bente, G., Ruggenberg, S., Kramer, N. C., & Eschenburg, F. (2008). Avatar-mediated networking: Increasing social presence and interpersonal trust in net-based collaborations. *Human Communication Research*, *34*, 287–318. doi:10.1111/j.1468-2958.2008.00322.x

Blaskovich, J. L. (2008). Exploring the effect of distance: An experimental investigation of virtual collaboration, social loafing, and group decisions. *Journal of Information Systems*, *22*(1), 27–46. doi:10.2308/jis.2008.22.1.27

Coulson, N. S., Buchanan, H., & Aubeeluck, A. (2007). Social support in cyberspace: A content analysis of communication within a Huntington's disease online support group. *Patient Education and Counseling*, *68*, 173–178. doi:10.1016/j.pec.2007.06.002

Daft, R., & Lengel, R. (1986). Organizational information requirements, media richness, and structural design. *Management Science*, *32*, 544–571. doi:10.1287/mnsc.32.5.554

de Pillis, E., & Furumo, K. (2007). Counting the cost of virtual teams: Studying the performance, satisfaction, and group dynamic of virtual and face-to-face teams. *Communications of the ACM*, *50*(12), 93–95.

Dube, L., & Robey, D. (2008). Surviving the paradoxes of virtual teamwork. *Information Systems Journal*, *19*, 3–30. doi:10.1111/j.1365-2575.2008.00313.x

Dube, S. (2009, January 14). Online verification: Who can you trust in the virtual world? *Business Week Online*, Retrieved January 31, 2009, from Business Source Premier Database.

Engleberg, I. N., & Wynn, D. R. (2007). *Working in Groups* (4th ed.). Boston, MA: Houghton-Mifflin Company.

Gopal, Y., & Melkote, S. (2007). New work paradigms: Implications for communication and coordination in cross cultural virtual teams. In Hinner, M. B. (Ed.), *The Role of Communication in Business Transactions and Relationships*. Frankfurt, Germany: Peter Lang.

Hardin, A. M., Fuller, M. A., & Valacich, J. S. (2006). Measuring group efficacy in virtual teams: New questions in an old debate. *Small Group Research*, *37*(1), 65–85. doi:10.1177/1046496405284219

Harris, T. E., & Sherblom, J. C. (2005). *Small Group and Team Communication* (3rd ed.). Boston, MA: Pearson Education, Inc.

Hodgson, J. (2009). New media scholars, old media students: A complicating of the guard. *Rocky Mountain Communication Review*, *6*(1), 66–70.

Markman, K. M. (2009). "So what shall we talk about?": Openings and closings in chat-based virtual meetings. *Journal of Business Communication*, *46*(1), 150–170. doi:10.1177/0021943608325751

Maslow, A. (1982). *Toward a Psychology of Being* (2nd ed.). Princeton, NJ: Van Nostrand.

McArthur, J. A. (2009). Digital subculture: A geek meaning of style. *The Journal of Communication Inquiry*, *33*(1), 58–70. doi:10.1177/0196859908325676

McNamara, K., Dennis, A. R., & Carte, T. A. (2007). It's the thought that counts: The mediating effects of information processing in virtual team decision making. *Information Systems Management*, *25*(1), 20–32. doi:10.1080/10580530701777123

Nowak, K. L., Watt, J., & Walther, J. B. (2005). The influence of synchrony and sensory modality on the person perception process in computer-mediated groups. *Journal of Computer-Mediated Communication, 10*(3), article 3. http://jcmc.indiana.edu/vol10/issue3/nowak.html

Ramirez, A. Jr, Zhang, S., McGrew, C., & Lin, S. (2007). Relational communication in computer-mediated interaction revisited: A comparison of participant-observer perspectives. *Communication Monographs, 74*(4), 492–516. doi:10.1080/03637750701716586

Redfern, S., & Naughton, N. (2002). Collaborative virtual environments to support communication and community in internet-based distance education. *Journal of Information Technology Education, 1*, 201–211.

Rodgers, S., & Chen, Q. (2005). Internet community group participation: Psychosocial benefits for women with breast cancer. *Journal of Computer-Mediated Communication, 10*(4), article 5. http://jcmc.indiana.edu/vol10/issue4/rodgers.html

Rothwell, J. D. (2006). *In Mixed Company: Communicating in small groups and teams* (6th ed.). Belmont, CA: Thompson Wadsworth.

Rutowski, A. F., Vogel, D. R., van Genuchten, M., Bemelmans, T. M. A., & Favier, M. (2002). E-collaboration: The reality of virtuality. *IEEE Transactions on Professional Communication, 45*(4), 219–230. doi:10.1109/TPC.2002.805147

Satchell, C., & Foth, M. (2008). The re-creation of identity in digital environments and the potential benefits for non-profits and community organizations. *3CMedia: Journal of community, citizens, and third sector media and communication, 16*-27.

Short, J., Williams, E., & Christie, B. (1976). *The social psychology of telecommunications*. London: Wiley.

Tidwell, L. C., & Walther, J. B. (2002). Computer-mediated communication effects on disclosure, impressions, and interpersonal evaluations. *Human Communication Research, 28*(3), 317–349. doi:10.1111/j.1468-2958.2002.tb00811.x

Tuckman, B. W. (1965). Developmental sequence in small groups. *Psychological Bulletin, 65*(6), 384–399. doi:10.1037/h0022100

Walther, J. B. (1992). Interpersonal effects in computer-mediated interaction: A relational perspective. *Communication Research, 19*, 52–90. doi:10.1177/009365092019001003

Walther, J. B. (1996). Computer-mediated communication: Impersonal, interpersonal, and hyperpersonal interaction. *Communication Research, 23*(1), 3–43. doi:10.1177/009365096023001001

Walther, J. B., & Bunz, U. (2005). The rules of virtual groups: Trust, liking, and performance in computer-mediated communication. *The Journal of Communication, 58*(4), 828–846. doi:10.1111/j.1460-2466.2005.tb03025.x

Wang, Z., Walther, J. B., & Hancock, J. T. (2009). Social identification and interpersonal communication in computer-mediated communication: What you do versus who you are in virtual groups. *Human Communication Research, 35*(1), 59–85. doi:10.1111/j.1468-2958.2008.01338.x

ADDITIONAL READING

Bolter, J. D., & Gromala, D. (2003). *Windows and Mirrors: Interaction design, digital art, and the myth of transparency*. Boston, MA: Massachusetts Institute of Technology.

Brandon, D., & Hollingshead, A. (1999). Collaborative learning and computer-supported groups. *Communication Education, 48*(2), 109–126. doi:10.1080/03634529909379159

Brown, M. K., Huettner, B., & James-Tanny, C. (2007). *Managing Virtual Teams: Getting the Most from Wikis, Blogs, and Other Collaborative Tools.* Plano, TX: Worldware Publishing, Inc.

Dennis, A. R., Valacich, J. S., Connolly, T., & Wynne, B. E. (1996). Process structuring in electronic brainstorming. *Information Systems Research, 7*(2), 268–277. doi:10.1287/isre.7.2.268

Hinner, M. B. (2007). *The Role of Communication in Business Transactions and Relationships.* Frankfurt, Germany: Peter Lang.

Kress, G., & van Leeuwen, T. (2001). *Multimodal Discourse: The modes and media of contemporary communication.* London: Hodder-Arnold.

Postmes, T., & Spears, R. (2002). Behavior online: Does anonymous computer communication reduce gender inequality? *Personality and Social Psychology Bulletin, 28,* 1073–1083. doi:10.1177/01461672022811006

Preece, J., & Maloney-Krichmar, D. (2005). Online communities: Design, theory, and practice. *Journal of Computer-Mediated Communication, 10*(4), article 1. http://jcmc.indiana.edu/vol10/issue4/preece.html

Prensky, M. (2001). Digital Natives, Digital Immigrants. *Horizon, 9*(5), 1–6. doi:10.1108/10748120110424816

Rheingold, H. (2000). *The virtual community: Homesteading on the electronic frontier* (Rev. ed.). Cambridge, MA: MIT Press.

Rubin, A. J. (Ed.). (1998). Media literacy (special edition). *The Journal of Communication, 48*(3/4).

Shedroff, N. (2001). *Experience Design 1.* Indianapolis, IN: New Riders Publishing.

Spears, R., Lea, M., & Lee, S. (1990). De-individuation and group polarization in computer-mediated communication. *The British Journal of Social Psychology, 29,* 121–134.

Venezky, R. L. (2004). Technology in the classroom: Steps toward a new vision. *Education Communication and Information, 4*(1), 4–21. doi:10.1080/1463631042000211024

Walther, J. B. (1997). Group and interpersonal effects in international computer-mediated collaboration. *Human Communication Research, 23,* 342–369. doi:10.1111/j.1468-2958.1997.tb00400.x

Walther, J. B., Anderson, J. F., & Parks, D. W. (1994). Interpersonal effects in computer-mediated interaction: A meta-analysis of social and antisocial communication. *Communication Research, 21,* 460–487. doi:10.1177/009365094021004002

Walther, J. B., & Bazarova, N. N. (2008). Validation and application of electronic propinquity theory to computer-mediated communication in groups. *Communication Research, 35*(5), 622–645. doi:10.1177/0093650208321783

Walther, J. B., & Burgoon, J. K. (1992). Relational communication in computer-mediated interaction. *Human Communication Research, 19,* 50–88. doi:10.1111/j.1468-2958.1992.tb00295.x

Walther, J. B., & D'Addario, K. P. (2001). The impact of emoticons on message interpretation in computer-mediated communication. *Social Science Computer Review, 19,* 324–347. doi:10.1177/089443930101900307

Walther, J. B., Loh, T., & Granka, L. (2005). Let me count the ways: The interchange of verbal and nonverbal cues in computer-mediated and face-to-face affinity. *Journal of Language and Social Psychology, 24*(1), 36–65. doi:10.1177/0261927X04273036

Walther, J. B., & Parks, M. R. (2002). Cues filtered out, cues filtered in: Computer-mediated communication and relationships. In Knapp, I. M. L., & Daly, J. A. (Eds.), *Handbook of interpersonal communication* (3rd ed., pp. 529–563). Thousand Oaks, CA: Sage.

Chapter 17

Collaborating with a (Non)Collaborator:
Interpersonal Dynamics and Constructions of Identity in Graduate Online Learning

Carolyn Kristjánsson
Trinity Western University, Canada

ABSTRACT

In a climate of increasing globalization with calls for the development of online learning communities that thrive on diversity, it is important to consider how diversity might influence the nature of interpersonal action and the dynamics of collaboration in computer-mediated education. This chapter considers the case of problematic collaboration in an online graduate program. Discourse analysis grounded in Systemic Functional Linguistics is applied to illustrate how various aspects of stakeholders' identities can be traced in the discourse related to online collaborative processes. A model of situated multidimensional identity is used to consider how localized constructions of identity may be linked to broader frames of reference. Findings suggest that when stakeholders from a range of backgrounds are drawn together, online collaboration becomes a complex social practice.

INTRODUCTION

Despite various definitions of collaborative learning, those who hold to a participatory view of education recognize human communication as fundamental to collaborative processes (McInnerney & Roberts, 2004; Sorenson, 2004, p. 244). In the case of computer-mediated learning communities, stakeholders are frequently drawn together from a wide range of contexts, including diverse geographical, sociocultural, and ideological backgrounds to name a few (e.g., Hudson, Hudson, & Steel, 2006; Reeder, Mcfadyen, & Chase, 2004; Tapanes, Smith, & White, 2009; Treleaven, 2004). How might this diversity influence the nature of interpersonal interaction and the dynamics of collaboration in the online learning environment? What happens when there is a clash between a participant's sense of self and the action needed to reach collaborative goals?

To investigate questions like these and ultimately enhance understandings of best practice in online education, it is necessary to expand conceptual

DOI: 10.4018/978-1-61520-827-2.ch017

frameworks presently applied to the evaluation of diversity in computer-mediated learning. One of the current challenges is for researchers to "conceptualize identity...to go beyond simplistic stereotyping, and use qualitative methods to understand how people define themselves" (Gunawardena, Wilson, & Nola, 2003, p. 771). This chapter takes a step in that direction by considering the case of problematic collaboration in an online graduate program. Discourse analysis grounded in Systemic Functional Linguistics (SFL) is applied to illustrate how various aspects of stakeholders´ identity can be traced in the discourse related to the online collaborative process, and a model of Situated Multidimensional Identity (Kristjánsson, 2006; 2008) is used to consider how localized constructions of identity may be linked to broader frames of reference.

BACKGROUND

Good teaching and learning practice deserve strong theoretical conceptualization (Treleaven, 2004, p. 174). The framework for this discussion is drawn from studies pertaining to the conceptualization of social interaction in online learning, work that views self and identity as inextricably intertwined with social situation, and a theory of language that understands linguistic choice as being constitutive of and constituted by features of social context.

Social Presence

There is wide recognition that social interaction is vital to rich learning in online environments (e.g., Belz, 2002; Dirkx & Smith, 2004; Garrison, 2000; McLoughlin & Luca, 2003; Rovai, 2007). Effective interpersonal communication is seen as a key factor in facilitating group involvement and collaboration (Park, 2007). To bring focus to an understanding of interpersonal interaction in online learning, it is helpful to consider the con-

struct of social presence, one of three overlapping "presences" that have been proposed to frame and account for meaningful online educational experience (the others being teaching and cognitive presence) (Arbaugh et al., 2008; Garrison, Anderson, & Archer, 2000; Garrison, Anderson & Archer, 2001). Social presence is defined as "The ability of participants to identify with the community (e.g., course of study), communicate purposefully in a trusting environment, and develop interpersonal relationships by way of projecting their individual personalities" (Garrison, cited in Arbaugh, et al., 2008, p. 134). Among a range of findings, studies conducted in recent years provide evidence to suggest that social presence is indicative of the feeling of community that a learner experiences in an online environment (Tu & McIsaac, 2002, p. 131), is essential to developing cohesion and facilitating collaboration (Na Ubon, 2005; Paloff & Pratt, 2005), is an integral component of shared knowledge construction (Goertzen & Kristjánsson, 2007), and correlates with perceptions of overall learning (Richardson & Swan, 2003). In a recently developed quantitative survey tool, social presence has been operationalized with reference to the overarching categories of open communication, group cohesion, and personal/affective projection (Arbaugh, et al., 2008).

Although research conducted to date indicates that the construct of social presence is a significant factor in online education, as far as can be determined, with rare exception (e.g., Yildiz, 2009), little has yet been done to study the interface of social presence and diversity. In an era of ever increasing internationalization in online education (Gunawardena et al., 2003; Mason, 2003; Reeder et al, 2004; Tapanes, 2009; Visser, 2003), it is important to understand how the diverse backgrounds, values, and assumptions of stakeholders come to bear on the nature of communication, group cohesion and projections of self. An exploration of such elements requires some understanding of identity.

Identity

In educational research and theory, considerations of identity have often focused on categories such as class, race/ethnicity, and sex/gender (Berard, 2005). The result has been a simplistic view of identity at best. As Berard notes, these categories "are not always relevant in particular educational contexts, and even when they are, their relevance cannot properly be understood without an appreciation for the *multiplicity* and *diversity* of identities which become relevant in particular contexts and courses of action" (p. 67) [italics in original]. Given such limitations, in recent years there has been a shift in some quarters from largely static uni-dimensional representations of identity to fundamentally relational views that conceptualize identity as multidimensional, changing, a site of tension, and negotiated through language and other forms of social interaction. (Beckerman, 2001; Berard, 2005; Johnston, 2003; Norton & Toohey, 2002; Varghese, Morgan, Johnston, & Johnson, 2005). Central to this perspective is an understanding that a person's sense of self is "historically and locally situated in social interactional events…largely created and recreated through social discourse" (Beckerman, 2001, p. 465).

Ishiyama's (1995a, 1995b) Validation Model represents *self* as a multidimensional construct that is comprised of interrelated physical, familial, sociocultural, transcultural-existential, and transpersonal components. The physical element relates self to the body and physical aspects of experience while the familial element has to do with family roles and relationships. The sociocultural component represents the experience of self as it relates to roles and memberships outside the family context, including but not limited to, vocational, academic, gendered, ethnic, and national groupings. The transcultural-existential aspect refers to the element of self that is capable of relating to others at a level beyond the restrictions of roles, fear of contravening social norms, or externally imposed values. The transpersonal element of self represents the spiritual, collective, or ego-transcending self. These various dimensions of self are not mutually exclusive categories, but are understood as fluid and holistic. Research conducted by Kristjánsson (2003) further suggests that the various dimensions of self can be experienced in multifaceted ways that may foreground mental, emotional, physical, or spiritual elements depending on circumstances. For example, an outworking of the sociocultural category of "student" typically means an emphasis on mental, or cognitive, development and understanding. However, there may be concurrent implications for physical experience (e.g., late nights, limited exercise), emotional experience (e.g., elation or frustration depending on perceptions of achievement) and spiritual experience (e.g., congruence or clashes of values when school policies, content, and/or practices (in)validate perspectives of faith or touch on matters considered (in)appropriate to spiritual sensibilities).

In this view then, identities are formed and validated or invalidated around the five basic dimensions of self and related experiences which exist in various relational contexts of human existence. These relational contexts can be represented by four overlapping domains: interpersonal relationships, activities, symbolic and practical objects or things, and places or landmarks (Ishiyama, 1989). Kristjánsson (2006, 2008) notes that the substance and construal of these domains do not spring up in a vacuum. They are historically and locally situated within a constellation of sociocultural structures such as educational institutions, organized religion, and government to name a few. These sociocultural structures are themselves embedded in broader orientations toward the world, including but not limited to cultural and ideological frames, here encompassed by the term worldviews. Worldviews have implications for how all aspects are understood and interpreted in constructing identities for self and positioning others. These combined layers of influence are depicted in the model of Situated

Figure 1. Situated multidimensional identity (adapted from Ishiyama 1995a, 1995b; Kristjánsson, 2006)

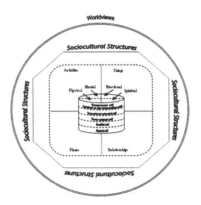

Multidimensional Identity (Kristjánsson, 2006, 2008) seen in Figure 1.

In considering the limitations of current research in computer-mediated education, Gibson (2003, p. 159) notes that North American educators and researchers typically "ignore the fact that the learner exists within a larger system of interrelating roles and responsibilities, mores and laws" which come to bear on the learning experience. While some work is being done to address such matters (e.g., Rovai, 2007; Tapanes et al., 2009), much has yet to be gained by considering the relationship between offline "situation," perceptions of self and others, and patterns of interpersonal interaction in online collaborative processes.

To facilitate this endeavor, it is helpful to consider the link between identity and language given the prominence of text-based interaction in online learning. Furthermore, to get beyond the broad essentialized identity categories of much research (e.g., socioeconomic position, gender, ethnicity), it is helpful to see identity as something performed through language rather than simply reflected in language (Pennycook, 2001, p. 162). This implies an understanding of human agency that enables the claiming and construction of identities through linguistic choice rather than assuming only a passive linguistic mirroring of externally assigned categories. The view of language developed in

Systemic Functional Linguistics (SFL) (Halliday, 1994) supports such an understanding.

Language

From an SFL perspective, the linguistic and social elements of experience are brought together through particular types of language use which contribute to the realization of different social contexts, including those of academic inquiry (Mohan, 2001; Schleppegrell, 2004; Unsworth, 2000). More specifically, social contexts are instantiated through linguistic choices that pertain to three contexts of situation, including subject matter (*Field*), the relationship between participants (*Tenor*), and expectations for how texts, including written and spoken, should be organized (*Mode*). Three kinds of meaning are correspondingly mapped on to every act of communication. This includes meaning pertaining to the subject matter (*ideational meaning*), the manner in which relationships between people are negotiated (*interpersonal meaning*), and the nature and structure of information flow (*textual meaning*) (Martin & White, 2005; Schleppegrell, 2004).

Of interest in the present discussion, is a consideration of interpersonal meaning, particularly elements of language use which indicate "the subjective presence of writers/speakers in texts as

Table 1. Coding for interpersonal attitudinal elements in computer-mediated interaction (adapted from Goertzen & Kristjánsson, 2007, p. 218)

Category	Description	Guiding Question
APPRAISAL: *Appreciation:*	Reaction to and evaluations of reality; along range of positive to negative	What does the person think of that?
APPRAISAL: *Affect*	Expression of emotional states; along range of positive to negative	How does the person feel about it?
APPRAISAL: *Judgement*	Evaluations of the ethics, morality, or social values of people's behavior; along range of positive to negative	How does the person judge that behaviour?
INVOLVEMENT: *Naming*	Use of naming (vocatives) to construct varying degrees of intimacy and interactional direction	Who addresses whom? How does the person address others?
Humor	Use of teasing, ironic remarks, jokes, and other devices considered humorous by participants.	What does the person do to be "funny"?
Paralanguage	Use of non-standard spelling, abbreviations, punctuation, and capitalization to express attitude and degrees of intimacy/informality.	What unconventional forms does the person use?
Emoticons	Use of symbols to convey emotional tone; along range of positive to negative	What symbols does the person use to convey non-verbal expressions?

they adopt stances towards both the material they present and those with whom they communicate" (Martin & White, 2005, p. 1). These are evaluative elements of language that can be associated with social presence (Goertzen & Kristjánsson, 2007). Linguistic resources for this purpose are available through the semantic systems of appraisal and involvement (Eggins & Slade, 1997; Martin & White, 2005). Attention to these systems along with humor, a related semantic resource often employed to facilitate the social work of appraisal and involvement, and typographical and symbolic indicators of interpersonal expression, allows for linguistic profiling of elements that signal social presence. This is seen in the coding scheme adapted from Goertzen & Kristjánsson (2007, p. 218) represented in Table 1.

Finally, to gain insight into the values and beliefs that come to bear on the outworking of online interaction, it is additionally helpful to consider the perspectives provided by both action discourse and reflection discourse, components of *social practice*. Rooted in the SFL paradigm, Mohan's model of social practice (Mohan, 1986; Luo, 2005) frames social activity as a combina-

tion of practice and theory which can be seen in action discourse, (the language of practice) and reflection discourse (knowledge or beliefs and assumptions about practice). Online interaction may be understood as a social practice (Mohan & Luo, 2005; Goertzen & Kristjánsson, 2007). As such, it is represented by the written discourse that enacts online collaborative processes along with reflection about online collaboration which provides perspectives on the knowledge and beliefs that shape the online action.

Coming Full Circle: Discourse Analysis, Social Presence, and Identity

A review of linguistic realizations of attitudinal aspects of interpersonal interaction is useful in getting at the nature of social presence in the collaborative process. Such an analysis provides linguistic snapshots indicative of characteristics of communication, the nature of group cohesion, and the manner in which participants represent themselves--categories identified above as operationalizing social presence (Arbaugh, et al.,

2008). When action discourse is complemented by an analysis of related reflection discourse, participant profiles are enhanced by a view of beliefs and assumptions that inform the interpersonal interaction. If identity is understood as something performed through language (Pennycook, 2001), then the interpersonal expressions in a particular online context may be seen as localized constructions of identity. Such understandings, while useful, are nevertheless incomplete if viewed in isolation from the broader contexts which inform the choices enacted in the particular online community. A consideration of language use with reference to categories of situation such as those represented in the model of Situated Multidimensional Identity facilitates a glimpse of how wider frames of reference and identity construction can come to bear on localized collaborative processes. These considerations lead to the following questions which guide a review of the case examined below:

1. How do projections of social presence construct participant identities in the discourse of collaborative learning?
2. How might such online expressions be linked to more complex constructions of identity?
3. What might this contribute to an understanding of online collaborative interaction?

A CASE OF (NON)COLLABORATION

This case is excerpted from the data of a larger study described elsewhere (Goertzen & Kristjánsson, 2007) which explored the interaction of pre-service and in-service teachers enrolled in two courses of a collaborative online master's program in Teaching English to Speakers of Other Languages (MA TESOL) at a private Canadian university. Twelve students, including native and non-native speakers of English, were in the cohort enrolled in this particular set of courses (Sociolinguistics and Materials Design, hereafter called Course 1

and Course 2). The collaborative structure of the program required that students work in groups to complete course assignments in each of the four three-week modules per course. In the context of the larger study, action discourse from assignment discussion pages and assignment comment pages was examined along with reflection discourse from reflective reports written by students at the conclusion of four three-week modules.

Overall, linguistic profiling provided evidence to suggest that students in the target cohort were positive about the each other and the collaborative learning process. However, following a group reconfiguration in Module 2 of both courses, the reflective reports from some members of two groups revealed that collaboration was not without challenge. These accounts were accompanied by expressions of negative attitudinal orientation regarding certain aspects of group interaction. At issue was a lack of participation by one person in the first group and a series of individualistic efforts by another person in the second group. Both groups included a speaker of English as an additional language from the same country of origin. By Module 4, the concerns of the second group had been successfully resolved and members ended the term with a heightened sense of appreciation for each other and what had been gained from the process of working through collaborative challenges. In contrast, the concerns of the first group were not resolved in the manner hoped for. At the end, the collaborative process failed and the final group assignment for Course 2 was left incomplete. Given this lack of success, it is worthwhile to purposefully select and examine the deviant case (Creswell, 2003, p. 185; Gall, Gall, & Borg, p. 180) to better understand what might have contributed to collaborative difficulties. The reporting approach taken in this chapter is that of data presentation, data analysis, and data summary (Huberman & Miles, 1994; Cresswell, 2003).

Phantom Partner

The group under consideration was comprised of four students (one male, and three female), from two countries of origin (Canada and Taiwan), residing in two countries (Canada and Korea) at the time of course enrollment. One of the students spoke Mandarin as a first language while the other three spoke English as their first language. Students ranged from mid-twenties to mid-forties in age. The Mandarin speaking student was the youngest in the group.

In Module 2, the "non-collaborator," Lucy (pseudonyms are used), was assigned a major role in Course 1 and a supporting role in Course 2. Although the group tried to draw her in, she contributed only two postings of the 31 generated during assignment discussion for Course 1 and only one posting of the 57 generated in Course 2. Her postings in the first course were interpersonally engaging (e.g., "Thurs after 9 p.m. is OK! I can also make it on Sat. ^^ !" Just post whatever you guys think is good under those headings! ^^ Have fun!"), but did not contribute anything of substance to the assignment. In Course 2, her contribution to the group effort consisted of a spreadsheet posted late--without date and time of posting and without comment--after similar contributions from others had been posted and incorporated into the assignment. The website activity record indicated that she had deleted the date and time of posting following the uploading of her spreadsheet. Lucy's reflective report for the Module 2 of Course 2 was positive in orientation; however, reflective reports submitted by the two most active group members indicated a mixture of frustration and concern.

The problematic engagement prompted intervention on the part of the course instructor who offered Lucy extra support. Although the course was an online course, Lucy lived within driving distance of the university. She was invited to meet with the instructor regularly to clarify and discuss coursework face to face, and was also

given the option of additional on-campus support. Lucy accepted all offers of assistance. At the same time, the instructor began to provide additional interpersonal support to other group members via email, simultaneously encouraging them to let Lucy take responsibility for her role in group assignments. In this way, the group managed to complete assignments for Module 3 and began the work in Module 4. Overall, when Lucy's contributions were insufficient, others in the group covered for her, although Greg, the oldest group member, and Cindy the second oldest, tended to do the most. Pat, living in another time zone, usually fulfilled her responsibilities, but was more peripherally engaged than Cindy and Greg and sometimes unavailable when the group needed her. The contributions Lucy made were most apparent in response to the scaffolding and requests of others, in particular Cindy.

In Module 4, Lucy rotated into a supporting role in Course 1 and a major role in Course 2 requiring that she coordinate the main section of the group assignment, including the implementation of ideas from others and the preparation of a final write-up. Although she made only two brief postings in Course 1, in Course 2 she was initially visible on the discussion board posting three messages in four days in an effort to coordinate a potential Instant Messaging discussion session. The discussion session did not materialize. The day before the group assignment was due, Lucy posted a fourth message stating that she had made a contribution and would be adding more the following day. That was her last posting. She did not respond to the instructor's attempt to contact her by email. Others in the group moved quickly in an effort to partially address the large gaps in the main section of the assignment. The instructor intervened and told the group to consider the assignment finished. Only Cindy and Greg submitted reflective reports for the final module in Course 2.

A quantitative profile of each group member's participation in discussion board interaction across both courses is seen in Table 2.

Table 2. Discussion board participation by postings (mean)

Participants	Course 1			Course 2			Combined Mean
	M2	M3	M4	M2	M3	M4	
Greg	29.0	13.3	12.5	26.8	6.9	17.2	17.6
Cindy	38.7	60.0	37.5	35.7	51.7	41.4	44.2
Pat	12.9	13.3	15.6	16.1	6.9	10.3	12.5
Lucy	6.5	6.7	3.1	1.7	3.4	13.8	5.9
Instructors	12.9	6.7	31.3	19.6	31.0	17.2	19.8

Review of Action Discourse

How do projections of social presence construct participant identities in the discourse of collaborative learning? An examination of all discussion board interaction indicates that communication is purposeful and pleasant; furthermore, there is no overt emotional expression of frustration or irritation evident in the postings by group members. Instead, the tone of the interaction suggests a collegial and supportive atmosphere even though there are questions about Lucy's whereabouts along with prompts and occasional direct requests for her participation. (See Appendix A for discussion board excerpts). Throughout the interaction there is clear evidence of participants projecting their individual personalities as they take stances with reference to the task at hand and each other.

A review of discussion board exchanges for Modules 2, 3, and 4 of Course 2 indicates that Greg projects the image of a cooperative, task-focused individual. He draws primarily on resources of APPRECIATION evidenced in expressions of task-focused attitudinal evaluation (e.g., "*Very concise and thorough. As a graphic arts person*, I would suggest some different formatting to make it *more readable*") accompanied by JUDGEMENT of the same (e.g., "*Well done* on the definition, Cindy"). There is no evidence of explicit expression of AFFECT although Greg does use paralanguage to express elation relative to task achievement (e.g., "*Whooee*. That was some bit of work.") and he

occasionally uses emoticons to index a particular affective overtone (e.g., "I'll be back after breakfast *;)*"; "I'm 'finished.'*:)*"). There is also no explicit evidence of attitudinal language used in comments relating to Lucy or her work. There is, however, some invoked, if not lexically inscribed, JUDGEMENT (e.g., "Lucy, where are you? We need your Reference check..."). Greg addresses Lucy by name to ask about her tasks in Module 2, but in the absence of any response from her, makes no further attempt to engage her directly in the discussion of Modules 3 and 4, in effect dismissing her from the interpersonal action of collaborative work. In contrast, he addresses both Cindy and Pat by name at various times throughout all modules, thereby positioning them as active partners. Greg is a team player, willing to do more than his share if others are willing to do the same as indicated by his use of linguistic resources of JUDGEMENT and an accompanying emoticon with reference to Cindy and Pat's anticipated behaviour (e.g., "If I get time I'll do Lucy's reference article... I expect when I'm in Cyprus *you guys will cut me some slack:-)*"). Overall, Greg projects himself as a personable, task-focused individual. He highlights his expertise relative to the task and constructs his relationship to others based on their contributions to and participation in the task creation process.

Cindy makes use of attitudinal language for social pleasantries as well as task-related purposes. Like Greg, she draws primarily on resources of APPRECIATION and JUDGEMENT. Her use of resources of APPRECIATION facilitates both social (e.g., "Have a *great weekend*, Lucy!" "Have a *good trip*, Greg!") and task-focused (e.g., "Your initial ideas *sound great*.") dimensions of interaction. Her use of JUDGEMENT is typically related to the accomplishment of task purposes (e.g., "… we're *a little behind*". "I *haven't been able to do much*…"). While Cindy makes limited use of the linguistic resources of AFFECT, usually when noting limited progress on the task ("I'm *concerned*…"), she frequently uses a smile emoticon to index a positive affective disposition in a range of contexts (e.g. "Talk to you all soon *:)*"; "what's new this week?? *:)*" "…no pun intended *:)*" "I'm not sure if you need it or not..if not, delete! *:)*"). She addresses the group as a whole (e.g., "Do what you can, *everyone*." "The tpov looks really good, *people*!") and also addresses individual members directly by name at various times, both to direct communication and to affirm individual group members. Cindy's use of names combined with positively loaded attitudinal language functions to invoke positive JUDGEMENT relative to the behaviour of group members (e.g., "It *looks great, Lucy*!"; "*Thanks* for answering those questions, *Pat*!" "The table *looks good, Greg*!"), thereby validating their membership in the group. In one instance Cindy adds a humorous overlay to her comments by substituting a playful vocative for Greg's name. (e.g., "Just let me know what direction you want me to take, oh *Grand Pooba*") Patterns of naming, along with Cindy's use of paralanguage (e.g., "I'm off to get some *zzz's* now. *ttyl*"), project a sense of social proximity and comfortable informality in the collaborative interaction. Like Greg, Cindy does not explicitly draw on negative attitudinal resources with reference to Lucy or her work; however, there is occasional implicit negative JUDGEMENT (e.g. "Lucy is *??*"). On the other hand, Cindy repeatedly attempts to scaffold Lucy's participation, drawing on linguistic resources of APPRECIATION to indicate sources of value pertinent to the group assignment and suggesting helpful courses of action (e.g., "Lucy,

your article sounds like it *could be useful*. Could you post the summary, please? Thanks." "Lucy, there are *some excellent points* in the Nelson article from our readings that could add to the stuff in the definition…"). When Lucy is assigned a major role, Cindy encourages her to take leadership in ways that imply favorable JUDGEMENT of her ability to manage the collaborative task (e.g., "Lucy, *we need your leadership here… :)*"). Overall, Cindy is personable, conscientious, and nurturing. She presents herself as a team player, available to do whatever is needed (e.g., "Lucy, *what can we do to help?*" "…let me know *what direction you want me to take*.") and constructs her relationship with group members in a manner that generally positions them and their task contributions--potential or real--in a positive light.

Pat does not participate in discussion board interaction as often as Greg and Cindy; however, her linguistic profile suggests that she too is positively oriented toward the group and the task at hand, although she notes her own challenges. She draws on resources of APPRECIATION (e.g. "I always think the TU section is *the hardest*.") along with limited use of resources of AFFECT (e.g., "I'm *happy* with how the TPOV looks…") as well as invoking, although not lexically inscribing, positive JUDGEMENT of the involvement of others (e.g. "Thanks for your editing, emails and suggestions."). She is not always available when the group needs her; however, she demonstrates an awareness of her responsibility as well as her commitment to the group, (e.g. "Lucy, *I missed any MSN chat* you had so please tell me where you're at with the problem so I know if *I can do more*.") and explicitly employs linguistic resources of JUDGEMENT when commenting on an oversight in her own contributions (e.g., "I *really dropped the ball*."). Pat addresses the group in general (e.g. "Thanks for your contributions, *everyone*.") and members individually (e.g., "Thanks for the table and task list, *Greg*." "It's looking good, *Cindy*" "That was probably me, *Lucy*. Sorry!"), positioning others in the group as valued collaborators. She uses positively oriented resources of APPRECIATION with reference to Lucy's work (e.g. "*Good ideas so far!*") and implies positive JUDGEMENT regarding her ability to contribute meaningfully (e.g., "Lucy, *do you have more ideas* about EFL settings and implications?"). Pat does not use emoticons nor does she engage in social pleasantries unrelated to the task, although there is a humorous overtone in one of her postings (e.g. "Not to put my nose in another person's section (usually a strategy for procrastinating)..."). Overall, Pat is amiable, but more reserved in her attitudinal expression and generally less engaged in the group and the collaborative process than Cindy and Greg.

For her part, Lucy makes no use of evaluative language in her limited postings to the discussion board interaction of the group in Modules 2 and 3 of Course 2. However, in Module 4, she is in a lead role in the group assignment activity and initially posts three messages in an effort to coordinate an online meeting. Each message makes use of positively oriented attitudinal language. She draws on resources of APPRECIATION to explain the late start (e.g., "It really has been a *busy* week.") and to express wishes of wellbeing (e.g., "Hope everyone has had *some good time* on Sun." "Hope you guys have *a great* reading time") and she cheerily offers holiday greetings ("Happy Thanksgiving"), mistakenly assuming that her Canadian group members celebrate the event according to the American holiday calendar. She draws on resources of JUDGEMENT to comment on the instructor's willingness to extend the assignment due date (e.g. "CK is *soooo gracious to postpone our due day!!* ") and intensifies the positive attitudinal orientation in three of the four messages by adding emoticons representative of a pleasant Asian facial expression (e.g., "...good time on Sun... ^^" "...gracious to postpone our due day!! ^^ "). Her use of paralanguage projects a sense of reduced social distance and comfortable interpersonal relations (e.g., "*CK is soooo* gracious..." "99~~ everyone!!") In her last posting she excuses an earlier lack of contribution indicat-

ing her desire not to negatively influence the work of another group member ("*...didn't want to mess up your work*"). When posting messages she directs her comments to the group, at no time addressing specific group members by name. Lucy's focus and use of linguistic resources when she is in a leadership role portray her as someone who is carefully attentive to establishing a positive interpersonal environment. Her choice of emoticon indexes her Asian identity. Overall, Lucy projects herself as a friendly and engaged partner, who constructs her relationships with others primarily on a social level. She comes across as cheery and personable, demonstrating a high level of social presence in socio-emotional terms, but is unreliable in the collaborative process. In terms of contributions to task content, Lucy is a near phantom partner who participates minimally at best.

Review of Reflection Discourse

How might online projections of social presence and identity be linked to more complex constructions of identity? A review of corresponding privately submitted reflection discourse suggests there is more attitudinal intensity and a wider set of influences coming to bear on group dynamics than meets the eye in the action discourse. In response to a question about group process in the Reflective Report for Module 2 of Course 2, group members include the following comments submitted directly to the instructor. The term "TPOV" as used by participants refers to the main group assignment.

Greg: I am finding I'm beginning to hate this question. I feel uncharitable, unChristian, and possibly unCanadian, if I answer it with honesty. Surely instructors can see who is doing what. Collaboration is difficult in our group. Pat is 16 hours out of phase and we can rarely MSN. Lucy once again was incommunicado (not on MSN, no postings, didn't reply to email) for a long period. Cindy and I did coordinate using MSN regularly. Mostly we worked directly on the TPOV and workspace; Pat, Cindy and I contributed a lot there. Hardly anything from Lucy. Please see our workspace. I understand there are language difficulties and that where us NS [native speakers] find material difficult, NNS [non-native speakers] must find it near impossible, but... What is the point of rehashing this type of stuff every cycle. Do the instructors have any constructive suggestions for handling these situations? If not, I won't be speaking of it again.

Cindy: Greg, Pat, and I seemed to work the most on the assignment; Lucy's work was not evident until the end. I'm not sure what happened, but she did not keep much in contact with the rest of us. For sociolinguistics, she had been extremely busy and did not let us know what was going on. Greg and I talked with her about that and asked her to keep in better contact with us, as we will all be unable to contribute as much as we should at times. We confronted her kindly, I thought, with no hard feelings intended. I don't know whether or not she felt bad about it, but she kept to herself mostly for this TPOV. I hope she doesn't have hard feelings towards us about it and that we will be able to work together better in future TPOVs. Already for sociolinguistics she has been great about communicating her time constraints. I hope and pray that the rest of us don't seem like we're overbearing, because honestly, I don't think we are. On the other hand, I hope that Lucy can be honest with us if she is feeling badly. I pray that things will go better and that our collaboration will grow from these difficulties. Most important, I pray that we will continue to work together as Christians should – honestly, and with sensitivity.

Pat: The lines of communication were down with one member of the group. I really appreciated how the other members contributed to all sections of the TPOV whether their responsibility or not. Although the collaborative work went smoothly enough I definitely prefer keeping in touch via MSN or email with all the group members. It helps me stay accountable for getting work done.

Lucy: We had great discussion time, and the manager was specific about each group member's job. Although I was a little bit behind in this module due to the big event of Taiwan's National Day, I could still manage to contribute to the group because of our group's support.

In contrast to discussion board postings, these reflective comments indicate considerable tension not to mention a mismatch in perceptions of the collaborative process, the greatest frustration and concern being expressed by Greg and Cindy, the two most active members. Pat and Lucy, less engaged, register an overall positive assessment.

In reflective comments for Module 2, for example, Greg, who did not use resources of AFFECT in discussion board interaction, begins his reflective response with an outburst of intense emotion ("I'm beginning to *hate* this question...") and further suggests that an honest assessment of the collaborative process from his perspective exposes feelings and dispositions inconsistent with cherished values and constructions of self (" I feel *uncharitable, unChristian,* and possibly *unCanadian* if I answer it with honesty"). He evaluates the process and Lucy's interaction negatively ("Collaboration is *difficult*" "Lucy was once again *incommunicado*..."), although trying to be understanding ("I understand there are language *difficulties*...where us NS [native speakers] find material *difficult,* NNS [non-native speakers] must find it *near impossible*"). The experience is so frustrating that Greg threatens to withdraw from any further related discussion unless instructors provide solutions.

Cindy's response is not as emotionally intense, but it corroborates Greg's representation of the difficulties. She documents additional communication between herself, Greg, and Lucy, drawing on evaluative language in ways that foreground her concern for the relationship with Lucy ("We *confronted her kindly*...." "I hope she *doesn't have hard feelings* towards us...that we will be able to *work together better*..."), She also makes a point of positioning Lucy favorably when describing subsequent interaction ("Already...*she has been great about communicating* her time constraints."). In the final portion of her comments, Cindy indexes the presence of a spiritual element in her quest for desirable interpersonal relationships ("I hope and *pray* that the rest of us *don't seem like we're overbearing*..." I *pray* that *things will go better* and that our *collaboration will grow* from these difficulties."). She concludes with a statement that explicitly frames the standard for desirable interpersonal interaction with reference to religious identity and values ("I *pray* that we will continue to *work together as Christians should--honestly, and with sensitivity*.").

In contrast to Greg and Cindy, Pat and Lucy see the collaborative experience in a favorable light in spite of a few difficulties. Pat draws on evaluative language to note the communication problem with Lucy in pragmatic terms, indexing reduced emotional engagement ("The *lines of communication were down* with one member"). She registers a generally positive impression of the collaborative process ("the collaborative work went *smoothly enough*"). Her comments do not explicitly touch on aspects of identity outside of the student role. For her part, Lucy expresses a very favorable view of the process ("We had *great discussion* time...") and positive view of the group ("*I could still manage to contribute* to the group *because of our group's support*."). She also notes that that her involvement in the collaborative process had been affected by a home

country celebration of significance ("I was *a little bit behind*...due to the big event of Taiwan's National Day."), indicating the importance of this aspect of her identity.

In spite of Lucy's positive assessment in the reflective report of Module 2, there was no visible improvement in her online participation. Neither she nor Pat submitted a reflective report for Module 4. Greg and Cindy expressed a mixture of resignation, regret, and relief.

Greg: Oh man! When this TPOV thing works, it can be very effective, when it doesn't it can be very draining. This round some of us decided we had to focus more on our own work that we needed to do to finish this semester well and are letting this TPOV's chips fall as they may. Some of us find it very difficult to leave things half done but there just isn't enough time to do it all. I wish the best to all but had hoped we had been able to resolve some issues.

Cindy: This was a tough one to say the least. We started it late for one thing, and never got a chance to have any msn discussions. We used the discussion board quite a bit to talk and contribute instead, and interaction there was alright. My email to you explained some of the frustrations we experienced with Lucy's lack of participation. We wanted to carefully set our boundaries this time and let Lucy take control of her role.

Unfortunately, this decision ended up causing our TPOV to be incomplete and it's difficult to leave it like that because the quality of our work is not up to the standards we would like it to be. It's quite disappointing to end our course in this way, as I would have liked to have gone out on a strong note. I guess it's all a learning experience. Although I do feel compassion for Lucy and whatever she is going through, I will also be glad to work in a new group. I don't feel as if I got to know her very well, which is sad because I've learned so much through getting to know everyone else I've worked with. Success depends on everyone working together, and sadly, our collaboration really fell on its face for this module.

Greg's struggle with issues pertaining to the final outcome is evident in his choice of appraising agent ("some of us" rather than "I" or "we") which indexes an attempt to distance himself from the situation and discuss it in general terms, a strategy further reinforced by no use of names. The tension between individual needs and group needs arising from Lucy's non-participation is not easy to resolve but ultimately leads to a decision to let the "chips fall as they may" with undesirable consequences for the final group assignment. In highlighting the tension ("Some of us find it *very difficult to leave things half done*") there is also an implicit laying of blame on those who apparently do find it acceptable to leave something incomplete in spite of undesirable consequences. While there is a final general expression of goodwill ("I wish *the best to all*") Greg's last comment expresses disappointment at the group's inability to resolve the issues of concern ("*hoped we had been able to resolve some issues*")

Cindy's final reflective comments in Module 4 indicate more emotional investment than Greg at this stage. The difficulties are expressed in a straightforward manner, even an understatement indicating the degree of challenge ("This was *a tough one to say the least.*") Lucy's actions were not without emotional consequence ("My email to you explained some of the *frustrations we experienced…*"). Setting and maintaining boundaries, rather than helping Lucy, intensified the situation due to the undesirable results ("*Unfortunately,* this decision ended up *causing our TPOV to be incomplete* and it's *difficult to leave it like that* because *the quality of our work is not up to the standards we would like* it to be"). While Cindy expresses care for Lucy, it is coupled with relief at the prospect of a change in group ("Although *I do feel compassion* for Lucy…*I will also be glad*

to work in a new group."). She frames her final comments with reference to feelings of sadness, both at what she perceives to be a failed interpersonal relationship with Lucy ("I don't feel as if I got to know her very well, *which is sad…*") and with the lack of success in collaborative efforts ("*…sadly, our collaboration really fell on its face* for this module.").

A few months later, in the context of ongoing efforts to help her work through problematic collaborative patterns, Lucy submitted a reflective report clarifying her perspective.

Lucy: The way the university designs this program is very different from the traditional way of completing an MA TESOL. This MA TESOL's collaborative process is a fabulous way for teachers and students to learn from each other and listen to each other's voices. Interactions, comments, and critiques are provided everywhere at anytime. However, this approach may not reach its greatest goal for certain students' personality, study habits, and study preference.

Personally, I find it very challenging for me to co-work an assignment with a group of other people. I feel very uncomfortable to tell other people what to do or listen to my ideas (although I have been learning to cope with it). I do not interrupt people and or tell them what I think how the work should be done in a group. I rather stay quiet and listen to other's way even when I have very different views from theirs. Unless I have read everything and understand everything, it is hard for me to express my point of view because I am very concerned about making mistakes. Interactions and discussion are great for me only when I feel confident of the task that I am doing.

Aggressiveness (in a positive way) seems to be beneficial in a program like this university's MA TESOL. From a psychological point of view, high performance anxiety and perfectionism can actually lead to bad performance result. Because of caring too much on making mistakes, I sometimes procrastinate in order to avoid anxiety. This causes frustration to a program that heavily relies on collaborative work.

With this submission, Lucy indicates tension between her understanding of the interactional characteristics of the online program in which she is enrolled and what she calls "traditional" academic programs. She notes the conflict between her sense of self and preferred ways of interaction and what she understands to be the desirable qualities for successful participation in the online program. While the design of the collaborative process has clear advantages ("*a fabulous way* for teachers and students to learn from each other and listen to each other's voices"), it may not be the best fit for all ("*this approach may not reach its greatest goal* for certain students' personality, study habits, and study preference"). Lucy identifies herself as one of those for whom it is not the best fit ("*I find it very challenging* for me to co-work an assignment with other people.") and notes the undesirable emotions that accompany this type of engagement for her ("*I feel very uncomfortable* to tell other people what to do or listen to my ideas") while also indicating her attempt to adjust ("I have been *learning to cope*…"). Lucy's own preferred patterns of interaction are contrary to what she perceives to be desired in the online program ("*I do not interrupt*…or *tell them what I think* how the work should be done…*I rather stay quiet and listen*…even when I have very different views…"). She is not unwilling to express her opinion, but finds it difficult unless she is confident in her understanding ("*I am very concerned about making mistakes*… Interactions and discussion are *great for me only when I feel confident*…"). She identifies her struggles in terms of high performance anxiety, perfectionism, and avoidance, and acknowledges the negative influence this can have on the collaborative process ("This causes *frustration* to a program that heavily relies on collaborative work"). She stops short of illustrating

the general observation with reference to specific collaborative interactions she has had.

When drawn together, the reflective comments submitted by members of this group create a picture that is far more complex than the perspective provided by any single report. There is also evidence of a wider set of influences on participant identity and related patterns of interaction than is apparent in the give and take of online action discourse alone. Apart from the reflective comments submitted by Pat, who keeps her responses within the parameters of student identity, there is explicit and implicit reference to ways in which multiple dimensions of identity come to bear on the student experience. These indicate links to sociocultural, transcultural, and transpersonal aspects of self and related identity construction, along with the taking up of different subject positions and the foregrounding of various elements of the student experience by different participants. For example, in Greg and Cindy's comments, along with mention of moral considerations, there is explicit invoking of religious and national identity. Whereas Greg does not ultimately withdraw from a discussion of the collaborative process as threatened in his first reflective report, he does subsequently withdraw from any direct engagement with Lucy or discussions about Lucy, arguably an attempt to avoid compromising his ability to enact deeply held values linked to his sense of identity. For her part, Cindy explicitly invokes spiritual practices and values in managing the collaborative challenges and appeals to religious identity to establish the standards for appropriate interpersonal interaction. It is these standards that have been guiding the group interaction in her opinion, and these standards may be understood as an invisible but formative influence in her contributions to the online interaction. As for Lucy, in her first reflective report, she clearly indicates the importance of national identity in the overall claim of priorities on her time. Her subsequent account of tensions in the outworking of collaborative activity, although framed as personal preference,

Table 3. Sampling identity construction in reflection discourse

Student	Appraising Items	Appraiser	Appraisal Category & Polarity	Appraised	Sense of Self (Subject Position)	Realization of Experience
Greg:	hate	I	Affect -	Question re group participation		Emotional
	uncharitable	I	Judgement - (Affect -)	Greg	Transcultural-existential Self ("human" position)	
	unchristian	I	Judgement - (Affect -)	Greg	Transpersonal Self (spiritual position)	
	unCanadian	I	Judgement - (Affect -)	Greg	Sociocultural Self (national position)	
	answer with honesty	I	Judgement + (-)	Greg		
Cindy:	confronted (Lucy) kindly	(Cindy)	Judgement + (-)	Cindy & Greg	Sociocultural Selves (academic collaborator position)	Mental
	no hard feelings intended	(Cindy)	Affect +	Cindy & Greg		Emotional
	hope and pray...don't seem overbearing	I	Judgement +	the rest of us	Sociocultural Selves (academic collaborator position)	Mental Spiritual
	honestly don't think we are (overbearing)	I	Judgement +	the rest of us		
	pray ... as Christians should	(Cindy)	Judgement +	continue work together	Transpersonal Selves (spiritual position)	Spiritual
	work together honestly and with sensitivity	(Cindy)	Judgement +	Christians		
Pat:	definitely prefer	I	Affect +	keeping in touch by MSN or email		Emotional
	stay accountable	(Pat)	Judgement +	me	Sociocultural Self (academic collaborator position)	Mental
Lucy	feel very uncomfortable	I	Affect -	tell other people what to do or listen to my ideas		Emotional
	learning to cope with it (telling others what to do)	I	Judgement +	Lucy	Sociocultural Self (academic collaborator position)	Mental
	do not interrupt people	I	Judgement + (-)	Lucy	Sociocultural Self	
	do not tell them how the work should be done in a group	I	Judgement + (-)	Lucy		
	stay quiet and listen even when have very different views	I	Judgement + (-)	Lucy		

may arguably be linked to preferences shared by many in her collectivist oriented cultural group. In addition, each participant foregrounds different elements of the student experience based on their particular interpretive lens. The convergence of these components is illustrated in Table 3, which provides an example of how comments in the reflective discourse link to categories of self and broader identity construction represented by the model of Situated Multidimensional Identity.

A Panoramic View

What might this contribute to an understanding of online collaborative interaction? As illustrated by the diagram in Figure 2, participants in the target group come together from a range of backgrounds. They are enrolled in a graduate online program designed within a Western philosophy of constructivist education. This framework is additionally influenced by a perspective that allows for the presence of religious values in the academic environment. The MA program is situated within the context of Canadian higher education in general and the field of applied linguistics in particular, and is additionally located within the context of a private liberal arts university. The language of instruction is English. Three of the four group members are Canadian and speak English as their first language. The fourth group member is from an Asian country and speaks English as

an additional language. They come together in a virtual place, the online community of the MA TESOL program, and are engaged in the activity of collaborative learning for the purpose of academic assignment construction, something that is part of the process and product of learning. Their relationships with each other and the instructors both shape and are shaped by the practices and perspectives associated with involvement in these domains. The action and reflection discourse generated by group members at the nexus of personal and shared frames of reference provide glimpses of the outworking of diversity in the context of online collaborative learning. Identity and sociocultural issues emerge most clearly in the process of reflection on collaborative interaction. In this case, the combined discourse data suggest that the activities of collaboration and non-collaboration are complex enactments of participants' sense of self. Difficulties in the collaborative process cannot simply be attributed to an unwillingness or inability to participate in the learning experience on the part of one group member. Nor can they be attributed to language proficiency in itself. A diverse range of beliefs and assumptions linked to broader frames of reference are brought to bear on the enactment and interpretation of interpersonal engagement and academic processes by all group members.

Figure 2. Multidimensional situated identities in online collaborative learning

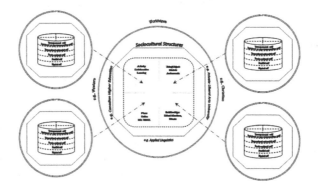

CONSIDERATIONS & RECOMMENDATIONS

Online presence is established through the posting of comments, an activity which has the dual function of communicating content and communicating presence. Social presence, a fundamental component of collaborative knowledge building, is threatened by lack of visible participation and interpersonal engagement (Sorensen, 2004, pp. 249, 259). Yet participation in the online academic environment is not necessarily straightforward. As demonstrated in the data reviewed in this case study, social presence not only infuses an interpersonal dimension into online exchanges, but embedded in these localized constructions of identity are standards for interpersonal interaction informed by a diverse range of guiding values and assumptions derived from broader memberships and frames of reference. These broader influences may or may not be immediately discernible in the online interaction--in this case, many of the most powerful guiding influences pertaining to sense of self, interpersonal interaction, and preferred academic process were not.

It is important to recognize that individuals belong to more than one culture, and that variations within cultures may account for as much or more variation than differences between the cultures of participants in any intercultural interaction (Gunawardena et al., 2003). Nevertheless, the use of technology for academic purposes and related standards for desirable interaction cannot be abstracted from educational culture and the broader frames in which that educational structure and its stakeholders are situated (e.g., Zhang, 2007). To return briefly to the case study above, what at first glance might be understood as a simple case of non-collaboration might also be viewed as a case where different standards for collaboration collide to the disadvantage of one participant. Lucy's "non-collaboration" might arguably be interpreted as collaboration guided by a different frame of reference, a frame of reference

where, to name a few parameters, harmonious communication and relationships are considered paramount and characterized by adaptation and avoidance of confrontation, where those who have less experience or are younger defer to those who are older, where diligence and quality of effort is demonstrated by content mastery, and where uncertainty is to be avoided in the presentation of knowledge (Gunawardena et al, 2003; Scollon, 1999; Tapanes et al., 2009; Zhang, 2007).

In this situation, the practices of online collaborative work were at odds with the values that guided Lucy's understanding of desirable interpersonal interaction and academic process, values that also informed her sense of self in related contexts. Although she had sufficient prior academic success and English competence to be admitted to the MA program, her preferred patterns of interaction were not supported by the program design, and by extension, her academic identity was not fully validated. Not unlike Lucy, the interaction patterns of the two most active group members, Greg and Cindy, were informed by frames of references that value interpersonal harmony. The way in which these participants viewed moral, religious, and national identities were brought to bear on, and challenged by, the outworking of the collaborative process. In the end, their own academic identities risked invalidation when an assignment was left undone.

The question as to what subject positions and identities and related frames of reference are accommodated in an educational community is not insignificant in understanding the dynamics of teaching and learning (e.g., Lee, 2008; Pennycook, 2001; Varghese, et al., 2005). The particular academic context in which this case was situated did not fully accommodate the academic identity Lucy claimed for herself (c.f., Remedios, Clarke, & Hawthorne, 2008), nor were other stakeholders initially aware of some of the frames of reference that informed her participation in the online community. It did allow for expressions of spiritual identity as seen in comments by Greg and Cindy, an identity construction of significant influence often not allowed a visible presence in academic contexts (e.g., Huerta & Flemmer, 2005; Johnston, 2003; Mayes, 2001; Vandrick, 1997).

In a climate of increasing globalization and internationalization of education (Hudson et al, 2006; Mason, 2003), with calls for the development of online learning communities that thrive on diversity (Mason, 2003; Visser, 2003), understandings of best practice will be significantly enriched by theories of learning that accommodate the complexity of that diversity. This includes theory building that facilitates an understanding of the cognitive, social, emotional, and spiritual dimensions of learning; of how constructions of identity are linked to interaction, priorities, and persistence; of ways in which competence is context dependent; and of how institutional structures and practices influence learning opportunities for stakeholders from diverse contexts--and vise versa (Lee, 2008, Osborn, 2006). In addition, principles of best practice will be significantly enriched by the intentional pursuit of self-awareness on the part of program providers for the purpose of increasing the visibility of assumptions pertaining to best practice and related guiding frames of reference. Such awareness, along with assessments of (in)compatibility with the frames of reference that inform the interaction of other stakeholders, will enable increased clarity in defining, representing, and evaluating expectations and options.

FUTURE RESEARCH DIRECTIONS

It has been noted that research is typically characterized by a type of intellectual apartheid where there is little dialogue or serious synthesis across paradigms such as cognitively oriented research of how people learn, studies that focus on culture and multiculturalism, and research in the world of human development (Lee, 2008). Research pertaining to computer mediated learning and diversity could arguably be added to this list

(Treleaven, 2004), although there are exceptions (e.g., Gunawardena, et al., 2003; Yildiz, 2009).

A valuable contribution to an understanding of online learning has been the conceptualization and development of the Community of Inquiry framework which proposes social presence, along with teaching and cognitive presence, to account for meaningful online educational experience (Arbaugh et al., 2008; Garrison et al., 2000; Garrison et al., 2001). How do the conceptualization, definition, and operationalization of these "presences" reflect Western frames of reference? How might understandings and interpretations be similar or different if explored through the lenses of diverse cultural and educational contexts with varying philosophical and ideological frames of reference? Collaborative research conceptualized, designed, and implemented by teams representing diverse perspectives or with access to diverse learner populations would provide a wealth of insight into questions such as these and further enhance the contributions of the Community of Inquiry framework.

In similar fashion, studies of technologically mediated education informed by frameworks that provide for multiple perspectives of diversity such as the model of Situated Multidimensional Identity described in this chapter would be beneficial. Specifically, studies that adapt, critique, refine, and expand that model along with investigations of online pedagogical applications of the same (c.f., Kristjánsson, 2008), could add to an understanding of how diversity is realized, facilitated, or constrained in various contexts of teaching and learning.

Among numerous additional possibilities, a significant direction for future research includes investigations that explore the connection between identity, diversity, online education, and matters of equity and social justice (Kristjánsson, 2007; Osborn, 2006). What value is attributed, explicitly or implicitly, to the social and cultural capital (Bourdieu & Wacquant, 1992; Coleman 1990; Field, 2003) brought to the online learning community by diverse stakeholders? What are the advantages or disadvantages for stakeholders from diverse backgrounds, and how might this be evident in the process and outcomes of teaching and learning? What might those who are perceived as, or perceive themselves as, disadvantaged in a particular context suggest to more effectively optimize their learning experience? These and other related questions have the potential to yield rich insights that can enhance an understanding of online education in the 21st century.

CONCLUSION

This case study has presented a snapshot of the outworking of diversity in the context of online collaboration. It is limited in various ways. Among other things, abbreviated justification is provided for the coding choices used to trace social presence in discourse (see Goertzen & Kristjánsson, 2007 for a fuller explanation), the gendered identity (Tannen, 2001) of participants is not discussed, an analysis of the instructor's social presence is not included, nor is the influence of teaching presence or cognitive presence (Garrison & Anderson, 2003) examined through the lens of diversity to understand what role these might have played in facilitating or hindering the collaborative process.

Nevertheless, the case study does illustrate that interaction in the online learning environment can be far more complex than an examination of online interaction alone might suggest. How collaboration or the lack thereof is understood and enacted, interpreted and evaluated, can be linked to perceptions of self, constructions of identity, and frames of reference that merge online and offline situations of context. When stakeholders from a range of backgrounds are drawn together in the context of computer mediated learning, online collaboration becomes a complex social practice that cannot be fully understood or assessed apart from a consideration of the dynamics of diversity.

ACKNOWLEDGMENT

The author wishes to thank the students who gave permission to cite their reflective reports in this study and Cynthia Caswell, Bill Acton, and Kay McAllister who provided helpful feedback on earlier drafts of the chapter.

REFERENCES

Arbaugh, J., Cleveland-Innes, M., Diaz, S., Garrison, R., Ice, P., Richardson, J., & Swan, K. (2008). Developing a community of inquiry instrument: Testing a measure of the community of inquiry framework using a multi-institutional sample. *The Internet and Higher Education, 11*(3-4), 133–136. doi:10.1016/j.iheduc.2008.06.003

Beckerman, Z. (2001). Constructivist perspectives on language, identity, and culture: Implications for Jewish identity and the education of Jews. *Religious Education (Chicago, Ill.), 96*(4), 462–473. doi:10.1080/003440801753442375

Belz, J. (2002). Social dimensions of telecollaborative foreign language study. *Language Learning & Technology, 6*(1), 60–81.

Berard, T. (2005). On multiple identities and educational contexts: Remarks on the study of inequalities and discrimination. *Journal of Language, Identity, and Education, 4*(1), 67–76. doi:10.1207/s15327701jlie0401_4

Bourdieu, P., & Wacquant, L. (1992). *An invitation to reflexive sociology*. Chicago: University of Chicago Press.

Coleman, J. (1990). *Foundations of social theory*. Cambridge, MA: Belknap Press of Harvard University Press.

Cresswell, J. (2003). *Research design: Qualitative, quantitative, and mixed methods approaches*. Thousand Oaks, CA: Sage.

Dirkx, J., & Smith, R. (2004). Thinking out of a bowl of spaghetti: Learning to learn in online collaborative groups. In Roberts, T. (Ed.), *Online collaborative learning: Theory and practice* (pp. 132–159). Hershey, PA: Information Science Publishing.

Eggins, S., & Slade, D. (1997). *Analyzing casual conversation*. New York: Continuum.

Field, J. (2003). *Social capital*. New York: Routledge.

Gall, M., Gall, J., & Borg, W. (2007). *Educational research: An introduction* (8th ed.). New York: Pearson.

Garrison, D. R. (2000). Theoretical challenges for distance education in the 21st century: A shift from structural to transactional issues. *International Review of Research in Open and Distance Learning, 1*(1), 1-17. Retrieved June 15, 2007 from http://www.irrodl.org/index.php/irrodl/article/viewFile/2/22

Garrison, D. R., Anderson, T., & Archer, W. (2000). Critical inquiry in a text-based environment: Computer conferencing in higher education. *The Internet and Higher Education, 2*(2-3), 87–105. doi:10.1016/S1096-7516(00)00016-6

Garrison, D. R., Anderson, T., & Archer, W. (2001). Critical thinking, cognitive presence, and computer conferencing in distance education. *American Journal of Distance Education, 15*(1), 7–23. doi:10.1080/08923640109527071

Garrison, D. R., & Anderston, T. (2003). *E-learning in the 21st century*. New York: RoutledgeFalmer. doi:10.4324/9780203166093

Gibson, C. (2003). Learners and learning: The need for theory. In M. Moore W. & Anderson (Eds.), Handbook of distance education (pp. 147-160). Mahwah, NJ: Lawrence Erlbaum.

Goertzen, P., & Kristjánsson, C. (2007). Interpersonal dimensions of community in graduate online learning: Exploring social presence through the lens of Systemic Functional Linguistics. *The Internet and Higher Education, 10*(4), 212–230. doi:10.1016/j.iheduc.2007.06.005

Gunawardena, C., Wilson, P., & Nolla, A. (2003). Culture and online education. In Moore, M., & Anderson, W. (Eds.), *Handbook of distance education* (pp. 753–775). Mahwah, NJ: Lawrence Erlbaum.

Halliday, M. (1994). *An introduction to functional grammar* (2nd ed.). London: Edward Arnold.

Huberman, A. M., & Miles, M. B. (1994). Data management and analysis methods. In Denzin, N. K., & Lincoln, Y. S. (Eds.), *Handbook of qualitative research* (pp. 428–444). Thousand Oaks, CA: Sage.

Hudson, B., Hudson, A., & Steel, J. (2006)... *British Journal of Educational Technology, 37*(5), 733–748. doi:10.1111/j.1467-8535.2006.00552.x

Huerta, G., & Flemmer, L. (2005). Identity, beliefs and community: LDS (Mormon) pre-service secondary teacher views about diversity. *Intercultural Education, 16*(1), 1–14. doi:10.1080/14636310500061615

Ishiyama, F. I. (1989). Understanding foreign adolescents' difficulties in cross-cultural adjustment. *Canadian Journal of School Psychology, 5*, 41–56.

Ishiyama, F. I. (1995a). Use of validationgram in counseling: Exploring sources of self-validation and impact of personal transition. *Canadian Journal of Counselling, 29*(2), 134–146.

Ishiyama, F. I. (1995b). Culturally dislocated clients: Self-validation and cultural conflict issues and counseling implications. *Canadian Journal of Counselling, 29*(3), 262–275.

Johnston, B. (2003). *Values in English language teaching*. Mahwah, NJ: Lawrence Erlbaum.

Kristjánsson, C. (2003). *Whole-person perspectives on learning in community: Meaning and relationships in teaching English as a second language*. Unpublished doctoral dissertation. University of British Columbia, Vancouver, Canada.

Kristjánsson, C. (2006, June 17-20). *Projections of presence and perceptions of identity: Dynamics and dilemmas in online MA TESOL*. Paper presented at the joint AAAL and ACLA/CAAL Conference, Montreal, Canada.

Kristjánsson, C. (2007). The word in the world: So to speak (a Freirean legacy). In Smith, D., & Osborn, T. (Eds.), *Spirituality, Social Justice and Language Learning* (pp. 133–153). Charlotte, NC: Information Age Publishing.

Kristjánsson, C. (2008, May 29-31). *Language, identity, and pedagogy for adult immigrants*. Workshop presented at the TESL Canada 2008 Conference, Moncton, Canada.

Lee, C. (2008). 2008 Wallace foundation distinguished lecture. The centrality of culture to the scientific study of learning and development: How an ecological framework in education research facilitates civic responsibility. *Educational Researcher, 37*(5), 267–279. doi:10.3102/0013189X08322683

Luo, L. (2005). *A systemic functional perspective on native and non-native English speaking students' online discussion in a mixed-mode graduate seminar*. Unpublished doctoral dissertation. University of British Columbia, Vancouver, Canada.

Martin, J. R., & White, P. R. R. (2005). *The language of evaluation: Appraisal in English*. New York: Palgrave Macmillan.

Mason, R. (2003) Global education: Out of the ivory tower. In M. Moore W. & Anderson (Eds.), Handbook of distance education (pp. 743-752). Mahwah, NJ: Lawrence Erlbaum.

Mayes, C. (2001). Cultivating spiritual reflectivity in teachers. *Teacher Education Quarterly, 28*(2), 5–22.

McInnerney, J., & Roberts, T. (2004). Collaborative or cooperative learning? In Roberts, T. (Ed.), *Online collaborative learning: Theory and practice* (pp. 203–214). Hershey, PA: Information Science Publishing.

McLoughlin, C., & Luca, J. (2003). Overcoming "process-blindness" in the design of an online environment: Balancing cognitive and psycho-social outcomes. In G. Crisp, D. Thiele, I. Scholten, S. Parker, and J. Baron, (Eds.), *Interact, integrate, impact: Proceedings of the 20th annual conference of the Australasian society for computers in learning in tertiary education*. Adelaide, 7-10 December 2003. Retrieved, March 20, 2006, from http://www.ascilite.org.au/conferences/adelaide03/docs/pdf/332.pdf

Mohan, B. (1986). *Language and content*. Reading, MA: Addison-Wesley Publishing Company.

Mohan, B. (2001). The second language as a medium of learning. In Mohan, B., Leung, C., & Davison, C. (Eds.), *English as a Second Language in the Mainstream: Teaching, Learning and Identity* (pp. 107–126). Harlow, UK: Pearson Education.

Mohan, B., & Luo, L. (2005). A systemic functional linguistics perspective on CALL. In Egbert, J. L., & Petrie, G. M. (Eds.), *CALL research perspectives* (pp. 87–96). Mahwah, NJ: Lawrence Erlbaum.

Na Ubon, A. (2005). *Social presence in asynchronous text-based online learning communities: A longitudinal study using content analysis*. Unpublished doctoral dissertation. The University of York, Heslington, York, UK. Retrieved, March 20, 2006, from http://www.cs.york.ac.uk/ftpdir/reports/YCST-2005-08.pdf

Norton, B., & Toohey, K. (2002). Identity and language learning. In Kaplan, R. B. (Ed.), *The Oxford Handbook of Applied Linguistics* (pp. 115–123). Oxford, UK: Oxford University Press.

Osborn, T. (2006). *Teaching world languages for social justice: A sourcebook of principles and practice*. Mahwah, NJ: Lawrence Erlbaum.

Palloff, R., & Pratt, K. (2005). *Online learning communities revisited*. Paper presented at The 21ˢᵗ Annual Conference on Distance Teaching and Learning. The University of Wisconsin. Retrieved, March 20, 2006, from http://www. uwex.edu/disted/conference/Resource_library/ proceedings/05_1801.pdf

Park, J. (2007). Interpersonal and affective communication in synchronous online discourse. *The Library Quarterly, 77*(2), 133–155. doi:10.1086/517841

Pennycook, A. (2001). *Critical applied linguistics: A critical introduction*. Mahwah, NJ: Lawrence Erlbaum Associates.

Reeder, K., Macfadyen, L., Roche, J., & Chase, M. (2004). Negotiating cultures in cyberspace: Participation, patterns and problematics. *Language Learning & Technology, 8*(2), 88–105.

Remedios, L., Clarke, D., & Hawthorne, L. (2008). The silent participant in small group collaborative learning contexts. *Active Learning in Higher Education, 9*(3), 201–216. doi:10.1177/1469787408095846

Richardson, J., & Swan, K. (2003). Examining social presence in online courses in relation to students' perceived learning and satisfaction. *JALN, 7*(1), 68–88.

Rovai, A. P. (2007). Facilitating online discussions effectively. *The Internet and Higher Education, 10*(1), 77–88. doi:10.1016/j.iheduc.2006.10.001

Schleppegrell, M. (2004). *The language of schooling: A functional linguistics perspective*. Mahwah, NJ: Erlbaum.

Scollon, S. (1999). Not to waste words or students: Confucian and socratic discourse in tertiary the classrom. In Hinkel, E. (Ed.), *Culture in second language teaching and learning*. New York: Cambridge University Press.

Sorensen, E. K. (2004). Reflection and intellectual amplification in online communities of collaborative learning. In Roberts, T. (Ed.), *Online collaborative learning: Theory and practice* (pp. 242–261). Hershey, PA: Information Science Publishing.

Tannen, D. (2001). *Talking from 9-5*. New York: Quill/Harper Collins.

Tapanes, M., Smith, G., & White, J. (2009). Cultural diversity in online learning: A study of the perceived effects of dissonance in levels of individualism/collectivism and tolerance of ambiguity. *The Internet and Higher Education, 12*(1), 26–34. doi:10.1016/j.iheduc.2008.12.001

Treleaven, L. (2004). A new taxonomy for evaluation studies of online collaborative learning. In Roberts, T. (Ed.), *Online collaborative learning: Theory and practice* (pp. 160–180). Hershey, PA: Information Science Publishing.

Tu, C., & McIsaac, M. (2002). The relationships of social presence and interaction in online classes. *American Journal of Distance Education, 16*(3), 131–150. doi:10.1207/S15389286AJDE1603_2

Unsworth, L. (2000). *Researching language in schools and communities: Functional linguistic perspectives*. Washington, DC: Cassell.

Vandrick, S. (1997). The role of hidden identities in the postsecondary ESL classroom. *TESOL Quarterly, 31*(1), 153–157. doi:10.2307/3587980

Varghese, M., Morgan, B., Johnston, B., & Johnson, K. (2005). Theorizing language teacher identity: Three perspectives and beyond. *Journal of Language, Identity, and Education, 4*(1), 21–44. doi:10.1207/s15327701jlie0401_2

Visser, J. (2003). Distance education in the perspective of global issues and concerns. In M. Moore W. & Anderson (Eds.), Handbook of distance education (pp. 793-810). Mahwah, NJ: Lawrence Erlbaum.

Yildiz, S. (2009). Social presence in the web-based classroom: Implications for intercultural communication. *Journal of Studies in International Education, 13*(1), 46–65. doi:10.1177/1028315308317654

Zhang, J. (2007). A cultural look at information and communication technologies in Eastern education. *Educational Technology Research and Development, 55*(3), 301–314. doi:10.1007/s11423-007-9040-y

KEY TERMS AND DEFINITIONS

Action Discourse: the linguistic communication that is generated as people participate in an activity; the language that constructs the doing of an activity.

Collaborative Learning: a process that involves two or more people learning with and from each other as they share expertise and responsibility while working together to jointly construct knowledge and complete a shared task.

Collaborative Process: the process engaged in by two or more people working together for the purpose of joint knowledge construction and shared task accomplishment.

Diversity: dissimilarities among people resulting from, but not limited to, differences in values, beliefs, characteristics and practices related to factors such as culture, ethnicity, gender, sexual orientation, language, economic status, education, political ideology, and religion.

Identity: the dynamic multidimensional positioning of self and others, negotiated through language and social interaction across time and space.

Reflection Discourse: the linguistic communication that is generated as people think about an activity; the language that communicates knowledge and beliefs about an activity.

Social Practice: a culturally situated social activity that involves both knowledge and action in a theory/practice, reflection/action relationship.

Social Presence: the perception and salience of interpersonal engagement, positioning, and presence demonstrated by participants in computer-mediated communication.

APPENDIX A

The sample below includes all of Lucy's postings in Modules 2 and 4 of Course 2 and covers the period when her contributions were urgently needed to complete the final group assignment (identified by participants as a *TPOV*).

Table 4.

Post	Course 2 - Module 2: Lucy in support role
1	*Posted at Oct 07 09:13 AM:* **Greg:** I've duplicated as a table and spreadsheet the Littlejohn task analysis checklist...
10	*Posted at Oct 11 08:55 AM:* **Cindy:** Thanks for the tip on working here and seeing our tpov at the same time. Pat's gone to bed. Lucy is ?? I'm going to email Phil and perhaps call her. I need some breakfast and then I'll be back on shortly.
13	*Posted at Oct 11 10:09 AM:* **Cindy:**....[message] PS - About our other tpov, Pat's going to do Lucy's ref check and add to the problem if need be. I can do some reorganizing. I'll let you know what Phil says.
17	*Posted at Oct 12 03:32 AM:* **Greg:** OK. New plan.... Lucy, if you download the spreadsheet and click on it, what happens? When would be a good time for MSNing later this week?
20	*Posted at Oct 13 01:41 PM:* **Greg:** Whooee. That was some bit of work. But our summary chart is posted.
21	*[Date and time of posting deleted]* **Lucy:**[POSTS SPREADSHEET WITH HER CONTRIBUTION TO ANALYSIS WITHOUT COMMENT.]
41	*Posted at Oct 16 03:49 PM:* **Cindy:** ...Lucy, how are the name checks going?
42	*Posted at Oct 16 04:39 PM:* **Greg:** ... Lucy, we need the name checks, how's that going?
46	*Posted at Oct 17 10:39 AM:* **Cindy:** I've begun editing by taking out our names and such. I'll post any comments here for you, Lucy, for your final editing.
49	*Posted at Oct 17 02:39 PM:* **Cindy:** Lucy, I've added some points in the analysis part.... Please look through and add anything more you feel we need.... Talk to you soon!:)
Post	**Course 2 - Module 4: Lucy in primary role**
1	*Posted at Nov 21 10:00 AM:* **Cindy:** Hello everyone. Here we go on this one as well. Today's Sunday, and so we're a little behind where we normally are - what's new this week??:)
2	*Posted at Nov 22 04:55 PM:* **Lucy:** Now is Monday evening. Will be on-line after 10pm I am also O.K for MSN on Tue, Wed night. It really has been a busy week... Hope everyone has had some good time on Sun... ^^ Good that C.K is soooo gracious to postpone our due day!! ^^ Let's work!
3	*Posted at Nov 25 09:29 AM:* **Lucy:** Hi, where is everybody? Hope you guys have a great reading time!! Happy Thanksgiving~~ ^^
4	*Posted at Nov 25 09:03 PM:* **Cindy:** Sorry, Lucy. I haven't been able to do much on this one yet, and missed your message on your msn times. We'll maybe try on the weekend? I'll email.
5	*Posted at Nov 26 06:22 AM:* **Pat:** In response to Cindy's email: Sorry, I can't make 8pm on Saturday to MSN. I'll be online at 4 pm BC time Sunday or 10:30 pm Sun....
7	*Posted at Nov 26 02:03 PM:* **Lucy:** Sun 10:30 pm is OK for me!

8	*Posted at Nov 27 03:05 PM:* **Cindy**: I'll be on Saturday night anyway, as well as 4pm and 10:30pm-11pm Sunday, BC time. Your initial ideas sound great, Pat. Let's keep posting our ideas on here or the tpov as they come, everyone. Take care until we talk.:)
18	*Posted at Nov 29 06:01 PM:* **Pat**: It's looking good, Cindy. Lucy, I missed any MSN chat you had so please tell me where you're at with the problem so I know if I can do more. I suppose you saw my ideas. Please post something here so I'm in on what's happening.
19	*Posted at Nov 30 09:39 PM:* **Cindy**: Thanks, Pat. There didn't turn out to be any chats, after all. I guess we'll just keep posting on the tpov and the problem. This has to be wrapped up by Thursday at the latest so that Friday and Saturday others can comment. Do what you can, everyone. Lucy, we need your leadership here…:) What do you want this to look like?
21	*Posted at Dec 01 01:38 AM:* **Lucy**: Couldn't post stuff this afternoon since that you guys were doing some other editing.... didn't want to mess up your work ^^. So, I just came again and posted some stuff .... take a look! and will keep posting tomorrow.... 99~~ everyone!!
22	*Posted at Dec 01 05:27 AM:* **Pat**: That was probably me, Lucy. Sorry! Good ideas so far!
23	*Posted at Dec 01 09:35 PM:* **CK**: [THURSDAY EVENING. TPOV TO BE FINISHED BEFORE FRIDAY. LITTLE DONE IN LUCY'S SECTION, MAIN SECTION OF THE TPOV.] Hi guys—looks like you've got some good things happening with this last TPOV! Just thought I'd remind you that people will start dropping by your page tomorrow to start posting their comments…so the clock is ticking. (Another way of looking at it is that you're almost at the end of another semester and Christmas is just around the corner!!:-)) I'd suggest you post whatever you've got for the remaining sections by early tomorrow afternoon and then make any other changes when you do the final tweaking. Sound okay?
24	*Posted at Dec 01 11:05 PM:* **Cindy**: Sounds good, Carolyn. Thanks for the ideas for the tu section, Pat. Lucy, what can we help with in the problem? I added stuff for the topics and themes, as you saw. Have you got anything for #3? It's a big part and there's nothing there. I'll check back tomorrow afternoon at about 3:30-4:30pm to see what else I can do.
25	*Posted at Dec 02 05:26 PM:* **CK**: [NO FURTHER WORK ON ASSIGNMENT PAGE BY LUCY] Me again. Lucy (and all)…I wonder if you're not trying to do WAY MORE than I intended for #3. Looks like another group was heading down this path. Please see my "green note" on the homepage. I'd say wrap this up as quickly and simply as possible so you can take a TPOV break! My guess is that every one of you deserves it.:-)
26	*Posted at Dec 03 08:17 PM:* **Cindy**: I hope you don't mind, Pat, but I posted your ideas (along with your name) for endpoint activities on the tpov as other examples of what might have been done in that section, for a "simple" wrap up as ck said.
27	*Posted at Dec 03 10:20 PM:* **CK**: Good idea, Cindy. A TPOV is, after all, a work in progress--and I think this work in progress has progressed far enough! Time for y'all to move on and let visitors to the TPOV use their imaginations to visualize what's there in spirit if not in print. You can simply leave it as is now or one of you can put a brief note at the top of the comment section saying that it's to be commented on as is--and then leave it. You decide. Either way, consider it "finished."
28	*Posted at Dec 04 04:35 PM:* **Greg**: I did a bit more this morning on problem section #3 because I thought we needed to take a stab at the actual sequencing. Feel free to modify or add, if you like, otherwise I think I'm "finished":).
29	*Posted at Dec 05 08:21 PM:* **Cindy**: Thanks, Greg. It helps a lot.
	Note on Comment section of group assignment: Please comment on our TPOV as is. It is finished as far as it's going to get, regrettably.

Section 5
Social Support and Networking and Social Technology

Chapter 18

A Cross–Cultural Comparison of American and Overseas Chinese Prenatal and Postnatal Women's Online Social Support Behavior in Two Online Message Boards

Yuping Mao
University of Alberta, Canada

Yuxia Qian
Albion College, USA

William Starosta
Howard University, USA

ABSTRACT

Taking a culture-centered approach within the uses and gratifications theoretical framework, a quantitative content analysis was conducted to analyze the support messages of two online message boards: the Dear Baby message board created and moderated mainly by overseas Chinese prenatal and postnatal women, and the BabyCenter message board created and moderated mainly by USAmerican prenatal and postnatal women. Both similarities and differences of the two message boards were identified in message type (seek or give support), content, support type and support behavior. Constructed narratives were produced to qualitatively analyze the voices within the context of both USAmerican and overseas Chinese online communities. The results can help researchers and practitioners to better understand how cultural characteristics of Chinese and USAmerican groups influence the patterns of women's online social support seeking/giving behaviors, enabling them to customize specific communication programs and services to meet the needs of members of those two cultural groups.

DOI: 10.4018/978-1-61520-827-2.ch018

INTRODUCTION

With the rapid growth of the Internet, an increasing number of people now seek health information, social support, and consult with health professionals (Cline & Haynes, 2001) through various online mediums, such as websites, listservs, message boards, chat rooms, and emails. Based on the data collected in 2008, 61% U.S. adults had the experience of seeking health information online, 41% of e-patients have read someone else's commentary or experience about health or medical issues on an online news group, website, or blog (Fox, 2009).

In this era of new technology, the Internet becomes a primary venue for social support groups to address their health concerns and reduce stress. Social support groups provide mutual aid and self-help for people facing chronic disease, life-threatening illness, and dependency issues (Cline, 1999). A few studies investigate computer-mediated support groups of people with disabilities, breast cancer, AIDS, and smoking addiction (Boberg et al., 1995; Braithwaite, Waldron, & Finn, 1999; Schneider & Tooley, 1986; Shaw, McTavish, Hawkins, Gustafson, & Pingree, 2000). However, little research examines online social support groups of prenatal and postnatal women who actively seek health information from various sources (Bernhardt & Felter, 2004) when undergoing one of their major life changes.

Because the transition to parenthood is often stressful and "people tend to seek affiliation under conditions of actual or anticipated stress" (Wandersman, Wandersman, & Kahn, 1980, p. 333), numerous online support groups appear for prenatal and postnatal women from diverse cultural groups to connect, share experiences, and provide mutual aid. Researchers and practitioners reach a consensus that it is important to understand the health communication preferences of minority groups who have been traditionally marginalized from mainstream health communication discourse (Johnson et al., 2004). However, to our knowledge, no research explores the cultural differences in online social support of prenatal and postnatal women. This study fills the literature gap by comparing support messages of two online support groups of maternal women—a mainstream USAmerican group (http://community.BabyCenter.com/post) and an overseas Chinese group (Dear Baby bulletin board on www.wenxuecity.com: http://web.wenxuecity.com/BBSList.php?SubID=kids).

In the process of cultural adaptation, overseas Chinese women might have assimilated some Western health beliefs and practices about pregnancy and parenting, but still maintain some Chinese beliefs and practices, which results in their unique health concerns and support needs. Therefore, Chinese women turn to online communities for their own health needs, as do a disproportionate number of American women (Warner & Procaccino, 2007, p. 788). Physically separated from their social networks in their home country, Chinese women join online support groups to connect with other Chinese women with similar experiences. As cultural minorities in their host country, many Chinese women have weak ties with their counterparts of other countries because of language and cultural barriers. Thus, social alienation also prompts Chinese women to resort to online support groups of Chinese women in similar situations.

Taking a culture-centered approach within the uses and gratifications theoretical framework (U & G), the authors conducted a content analysis to analyze the support messages of two online message boards, one created and moderated mainly by overseas Chinese prenatal and postnatal women, and the other created and moderated mainly by USAmerican prenatal and postnatal women. The researchers identified the communication patterns in the online support communities of overseas Chinese women and USAmerican women through a quantitative content analysis and then presented composite voices within the context of their own online communities, as quantitative methodologies can be used to effectively inform the qualitative methods in interpretive media research (Jensen & Jankowski, 1991). The combination of quantitative and qualitative analysis applied in this research answers the call that "communication researchers should be encouraged to employ U & G more frequently in conjunction with qualitative methodologies in a holistic approach" (Ruggiero, 2000, p. 24).

In response to Kreuter and McClure's (2004) critique that culture's role "in public health practice and research to date has been more rhetorical than applied" (p. 440), this study takes into account marginalized cultural voices in health communication and provides experience-close insights that health professionals may apply culture in their practices. Understanding the cultural differences in online social support between USAmerican and overseas Chinese prenatal and postnatal women helps both researchers and practitioners tailor health messages to cultural characteristics of the audience, and then to better serve the unique needs of cultural minorities in the prenatal and postnatal period.

THEORETICAL FRAMEWORK

Uses and Gratifications Theory

Within the uses and gratifications perspective, people actively use different mass media to gratify their various needs such as surveillance, information learning, entertainment, personal identity, parasocial interaction, companionship and escape (Blumler, 1979; Katz, Blumler, & Gurevitch, 1974). Uses and gratifications theory provides the theoretical framework for this study to understand what kind of support USAmerican women and overseas Chinese women seek to gratify their own needs or give to gratify others' needs using online discussion board at their pre- and post-natal stages.

There is an increasing interest by communication scholars to apply uses and gratifications theory

to investigate online communication because of the three important natures of the Internet: interactivity, demassification, and asynchroneity (Ruggiero, 2000). This study focuses on the interactivity nature of the USAmerican social support group and overseas Chinese social support group by investigating how the users actively give and retrieve information, and conduct other activities in the two bulletin boards to meet their cultural-specific needs. Interactivity is defined as "the degree to which participants in the communication process have control over, and can exchange roles in their mutual discourse" (Williams, Rice, & Rogers, 1988, p. 10). There are five dimensions of interactivity: playfulness, choice, connectedness, information collection, and reciprocal communication (Ha & James, 1998). In both USAmerican message board and the overseas Chinese message board, connectedness, information collection, and reciprocal communication are exemplified by the different types of social support provided and sought by members in the USAmerican and overseas Chinese communities.

Swanson (1987) emphasized that uses and gratifications research should make more linkage between media content to gratifications. In order to do so, Swanson (1987) suggested researchers focus on connections between audience motivations, attributes of message content, and the interpretation of content by audience members. This research analyzes the post type (seeking or giving support), which can help to understand people's motivation to use the two maternal online discussion boards. Different topics and social support types are also analyzed quantitatively followed by qualitative interpretations within the specific socio-cultural contexts. Through making the linkage between message content, message type, and women's needs, this research fulfill its task of understanding how women's different needs are met both in topical area and the type of social support through the online message boards.

Due to cultural differences between the U.S. and China, USAmerican women may use the online discussion board differently than overseas Chinese women to serve culture-specific needs. Therefore, culture, as a factor closely related to people's use of mass media and health behavior, is examined in this study. Findings of this study on how culture influences different cultural communities' use of the Internet to meet their own needs can make contributions to extend the uses and gratifications theory into mediated multicultural contexts.

Culture-Centered Approach in Health Communication

Researchers propose that the dominant approach to health communication has overlooked at the dimension of culture (Lupton, 1994). In response to this critique, recent studies examined the role of culture in health communication theories and practices (Dutta, 2007; Johnson et al., 2004). Geist-Martin, Ray, and Sharf (2003) emphasize the powerful roles played by the culture of communities and suggest that health practitioners should understand the cultural community before providing or seeking care. Dutta (2007) proposes a culture-centered approach that empowers cultural communities in developing health communication practices and creates a space for the marginalized voices. The culture-centered approach conceptualizes culture as "a complex and dynamic web of meanings that is continuously in flux," and culture is "articulated in the meanings constructed by the cultural participants, and these meanings are located within the local context of the culture" (Dutta, 2007, pp. 310-311).

The culture-centered approach as applied in this study analyzes the online messages created and monitored by the cultural participants themselves. Due to the apparent absence of direct influence by researchers in the sampled online discussions, overseas Chinese and USAmerican prenatal and postnatal women's own voices are expressed directly in the online message boards. By quantitatively and qualitatively comparing

the messages on the Chinese website and the USAmerican website, health practitioners can better understand how cultural characteristics of Chinese and USAmerican groups influence the patterns of women's social support seeking/giving behaviors, enabling them to customize specific communication programs and services to meet the needs of members of those two cultural groups.

LITERATURE REVIEW

Social Support and Maternity

A large amount of literature has documented the role of social support in dealing with stressful situations and events. Social support is defined as "verbal and nonverbal communication between recipients and providers that reduces uncertainty about the situation, the self, the other, or the relationship, and functions to enhance a perception of personal control in one's experience" (Albrecht &Adelman, 1987, p. 19).

Adaptation to parenthood has often been described as a stressful period, one that demands social support from various sources. New parents are faced with changing roles, demands, reward structures, and expectations (Wandersman et al., 1980). Therefore, prenatal and postnatal women, especially women with their first pregnancy, feel more stressful, due to the changes of their bodies, health conditions, roles, and responsibilities. Research has shown that social support could help reduce stress in the transition to parenthood. Admittedly, support from family and friends is important for pregnant women and new mothers. However, social support groups could be more beneficial to coping with stress of women at this stage. Hochschild (1973) argues that the fostering of a "we" feeling is the most comforting process of all. Social support groups could create a trusting and caring atmosphere in which group members with similar experiences could feel easily identified with each other. Social support groups have been found to be positively related to the well-being and marital interaction for new mothers (Wandersman et al., 1980). Support groups for mothers also serve the function of "cracking the code" of health institutional practices and of "bonding" group members through sharing stories and experiences (Tardy & Hale, 1998).

Online Social Support

With the rapid growth of the Internet, online support groups have proliferated as a venue for communicating with people who share similar health problems. They provide several advantages of online support groups over face-to-face groups. First, online support groups allow members to overcome geographic barriers in connecting with people who share similar experiences. This feature is especially relevant to overseas Chinese prenatal and postnatal women because they are often physically isolated from their extended family and social networks in China. Second, the asynchronous feature of online communication allows group members to deliberate more before responding to messages. It also allows members to communicate at their most convenient time. Third, people can choose to be anonymous in online communication, which could avoid the embarrassment when talking about "taboo" topics in face-to-face communication. Fourth, public online support messages benefit not only the group members but also those who choose to "lurk" in online forums. The "lurkers" can learn from the online messages even though they do not actively participate in the online discussion. Finally, the lack of "social context cues" in online communication can encourage more equalized participation. People are less concerned with and inhibited by the differences in social status.

In addition, joining online social support groups offers several benefits to patients: universality, personal social networks, and altruism (Shaw et al., 2000). Universality is the realization that others share similar health problems, allowing group members to feel less isolated. Furthermore, it might be difficult for patients with particular illnesses to find others with analogous problems in their personal social networks. Online communities provide an avenue for patients to connect with other patients. Finally, seeking support is not the only form of communication in the online communities, many people join online groups for altruistic reasons—to provide information and show support for other members. Shaw et al. (2000) found that "those who give support presumably derive some psychological rewards from fulfilling a caregiver role" (p. 148).

However, online support groups have many disadvantages. Online messages might be misinterpreted because of the absences of contextual cues. In addition, most of the online support group members are nonprofessionals. As a result, online messages might be inaccurate and inappropriate, and most of their information may be based on personal experiences. Therefore, online messages in support groups could be misleading. Culver, Gerr, and Frumkin (1997) found that one third of the medical information provided by online discussion groups was classified as unconventional.

Despite the disadvantages, there has been a rising trend of forming online social support groups for people with similar illnesses and experiences. However, few known studies focus on the online support messages of prenatal and postnatal women. Although online and face-to-face social support might share some similarities, online support might have its own unique features. For example, it is more difficult to render tangible aid through online social support groups than through face-to-face support groups.

Chinese Immigrants and Their Health Information Needs

There is an increasing number of overseas Chinese in different countries, especially in the U.S. Chinese immigrants have been the fastest growing ethnic minority population in the U.S.

over the past two decades. They constitute the second largest immigrant group in the U.S. after Mexicans (Camarota, 2007). It is reported that the number of Chinese students exceeded 60,000 in 2004, making the Chinese the largest international student group on campuses across the U.S. (Yin, 2007). Many of them secured a job and acquired permanent residency and American citizenship after completing their education.

Despite the continuing growth of the Chinese immigrant community, research shows that Chinese and South Asian ethnic groups in the U.S. are disadvantaged with respect to health-information access and "little is known about their experiences and perceptions about the effective means of promoting health information" (Ahmad et al., 2004, p. 23). The research also finds that loss of extended social networks and language barriers are the two primary reasons that Chinese and South Asian immigrants have difficulties in accessing health information. Those findings might also hold for overseas Chinese women in some other countries, because lack of social networks and language barrier are two common difficulties that most overseas Chinese experience. Women of ethnic groups wanted health information in their first language because many are unfamiliar with Western concepts and disease terminologies.

In addition, since the majority of the Chinese immigrants are raised in the Chinese culture, they still hold strongly to Chinese cultural values, beliefs, and health practices after migration. Furthermore, lack of understanding of the Western treatments and the time constraints of physicians prevent them from obtaining adequate health information from health care providers. Therefore, Chinese immigrants show a pattern of utilizing a mixture of Western and traditional Chinese health remedies and services (Ma, 1999).

Because the health information needs of Chinese immigrants can hardly be met solely by the Western health care providers, the Internet has provided a convenient platform to draw together their fellow migrants to exchange health infor-

mation, health care experiences, and to provide social support. Literature documents the various offline overseas Chinese communities and their roles in helping Chinese immigrants adapt to the host societies, however, very few studies have addressed the role of virtual communities in Chinese immigrants' adaptation to the host culture (Chan, 2006). Chan (2006) argues that the online communities help build a sense of solidarity and cohesion based on their common homeland and marginalized identities in the host country. More importantly, the online communities have emerged as a significant means to meet overseas Chinese immigrants' health needs and concerns. Yet, no research has studied the role of online communities in addressing the health concerns of overseas Chinese immigrants.

This study compares differences and commonalities between the Chinese prenatal and postnatal women and their USAmerican prenatal and postnatal counterparts in terms of the message content and social support types. Rather than imposing the cultural variables on the online social support groups, we take a culture-centered approach and intend to explore the unique patterns of social support from the group participants' own perspectives. The study considers the following research questions:

RQ1: What balance is struck between giving and receiving support on selected support websites for USAmerican and overseas Chinese women?

RQ2: What main topics are covered in the online boards for USAmerican and overseas Chinese support groups?

RQ3: What types of social support do the online group members commonly seek and give?

RQ4: What sample messages can be constructed to exemplify the comparative cultural content of the examined postings?

METHOD

The authors take method to be a means of certifying the accuracy of interpretations offered for data, rendering those meanings evident to a variety of potential users and stakeholders, and making correct action based upon those certifications more possible. While method usually reports central tendencies in data, our approach extends method in the direction of sense-making by those of the research community, the stakeholders, and practitioners. Method does not speak only to data; rather, it speaks to persons who vary in statistical sophistication and intent. We posit that an effective method should speak to multiple users; hence, an effective method should either systematize the unstructured, or it should render a statistically-secured finding more concrete and accessible. Our study does each of these in turn.

Our approach to evidence straddles the boundary between the positivist, the hermeneutic, and the critical, and works from the idea that the best method clearly points the way toward improved (and moral) (Alexander, 2008; Denzin & Lincoln, 2008) practice, and that the best practice should be turned into systematized and generalized theory. The authors propose that findings based on statistical inference, while vital to theorists, tend to mean less to those who would try to understand the conclusions at an experiential level or at the level of application. This dilemma is central to the formulation of applied theory (Starosta & Chen, forthcoming). By enhancing sense-making at all levels of the project, in a closer union between science and the humanities (Denzin & Lincoln, 2008), and with respect for praxis (Jones, 2008), our approach blurs methodological distinctions

that may have operated over the years (Denzin & Lincoln, 2008).

The implications of this "sixth moment" overview of procedures (Denzin & Lincoln, 2008, p. 27; Starosta & Chen, forthcoming) for the present study lead the authors to adopt a binary method: we first perform a statistical analysis of the initial conversational postings on a Chinese-language message board and an USAmerican message board about maternity in order to derive a sense, as quantitative researchers, what structural and thematic elements may best characterize the postings. A content analysis was conducted on the posts selected from the selected Chinese and USAmerican message boards to answer the first three research questions proposed in this study, because content analysis serves "to reduce the total content of a communication (e.g., all of the words or all of the visual imagery) to a set of categories that represent some characteristic of research interest" (Singleton, Jr. & Straits, 2005, p.371). This we do from a critical distance.

Then we produce illustrations of the sorts of postings that might be found for each of the derived categories, particularly for cases where the use of categories differs statistically between websites. These illustrations bring us more experience-close as researchers, since we read the pertinent postings that seem to us to best represent the disclosed categories, we pair some words from these postings with understandings of our own that have emerged during our coding, and we aim toward enhanced understanding, improved intervention, and manifest points of possible leverage for health officials.

Insofar as we succeed at the inferential and sense-making levels, both readers and practitioners should gain appropriate insights into the patterns found in the data, and about the embodiment of those patterns as "typical" messages. No single sample posting can be found completely in the data set; the postings are composites of actual website words quilted with the authors' experience-close summaries. That is to say, postings *like ours* typify the messages found on the website (Salander, 2002; Starosta & Hannon, 1997).

About the Websites

The authors conduct a cross-cultural analysis of two online maternal message boards. One board is created and moderated by the mainstream USAmerican culture group (http://community.BabyCenter.com/post), while the other board is created and moderated by an overseas Chinese cultural group (http://web.wenxuecity.com/BBSList.php?SubID=kids). In both message boards, although it is almost impossible to find out members' identities and backgrounds, there is little trace of outside researchers or experts imposing their opinions on the online discussion. Therefore, both message boards reflect prenatal and postnatal women's own voices.

BabyCenter.com is one of the most popular websites for new and expectant parents. It was launched in 1997 by BabyCenter, LLC, a San Francisco-based commercial company, which is a member of the Johnson & Johnson family of companies. The BabyCenter team includes a diverse group of experienced writers, editors, designers from the parenting field, web engineers, marketers, and a board of medical advisors. The BabyCenter message board offers a platform for new and expectant parents to connect with each other and provide social support ("company overview," n.d.; "about BabyCenter," n.d.). The BabyCenter online community includes a variety of interest groups such as birth clubs, parenting advice, baby names, pregnancy, and bargain hunters, etc. BabyCenter is a global interactive parenting network, which attracted users from all over the world, including Australia, Austria, Brazil, Canada, China, Germany, India, Malaysia, Mexico, the Middle East, Philippines, Singapore, Spain, Sweden, Switzerland, and the United Kingdom. The authors selected the bulletin board for USAmerican users in conducting the research.

The overseas Chinese message board named

Dear Baby is part of a popular and comprehensive community portal website for overseas Chinese called Wenxue City (www.wenxuecity.com). Wenxue City website is ranked the 29th in traffic among the top 100 Chinese websites. According to the information provided by the Wenxue City website, the majority of the users of Wenxue City website are at the age of 25-35, and most of them have a college degree or above ("about us," n.d.). There are Chinese users from all over the world visiting the Wenxue City website, including the U.S., Canada, Australia, Japan, Singapore, England, and many other countries. As the Wenxue City website is blocked by the Chinese government, very few mainland Chinese have access to this site through Internet proxies. Therefore, Wenxue City website is mainly an overseas Chinese online community.

Sample

Our sample includes 500 original posts on the Dear Baby message board in Wenxuecity website and another 500 original posts from BabyCenter message board. The posts responding to the original posts are not included in this sample, as the original posts are posted by people who actively seek/give social support on the bulletin board, and original posts initiate responding posts. Therefore, the original posts decide the communication tone and content of the bulletin board and lead the online discussions. Furthermore, this study focuses on the content and topical areas of the online discussion instead of the micro-level interpersonal interactions among group members. In most cases, replying posts are around the same topic that the original posts propose, therefore, replying posts are not included in this study. In addition, the replies to the same original posts might provide different types of social support, which makes it problematic to classify the social support types if we use thread as the unit of analysis. Analyzing the replies to the original posts belongs to a different study.

The structures of the two selected message boards are different, but those differences do not appear to have impacts on the content of the two message boards. In the BabyCenter message board, there are more than 4,500 groups formed by different members and all the registered members can form groups. Some of the groups are popular but many of them remain inactive. Individuals can go into particular groups to read or participate in the discussions, or choose to read all the posts across all the groups chronologically. As the groups in BabyCenter message board are formed and managed by the users, they are just part of the larger discussion in the bulletin board. Differently, the Dear Baby bulletin board does not have any groups, and posts are displayed chronologically. Some of the posts are highlighted by the webmaster and selected into a collection named "Posts of Essence." In order to avoid sampling bias that might be led by webmasters, the researchers decided to draw random samples from all the posts that could be retrieved from the message boards. When the researchers started the sampling procedure, posts from March 13, 2008 to January 13, 2009 could be retrieved from BabyCenter message board. In order to avoid sampling bias that might be caused by the significant social events happened in different time periods, the researchers decided to use the same time frame to draw sampling posts from both BabyCenter message board and Dear Baby bulletin board.

When the researchers started to retrieve the posts on January 13, 2009, there were 24,151 pages of posts with the earliest one posted on March 13, 2008 on BabyCenter message board. On each page, there were 13 posts without showing the replies. The researcher randomly generated 500 numbers ranging from 1 to 24,151 to be the page numbers to select posts from. Other 500 numbers were randomly generated ranging from 1 to 13 as the post number selected from each page. Each generated post number was assigned to a generated page number, therefore 500 posts were randomly selected from BabyCenter website for analysis.

The random numbers were generated using the Random Number Generation function of Excel 2003. Discrete distribution was chosen to generate the random numbers. Each number within the range was assigned an equal opportunity to be selected to ensure the random process.

To be identical with the time frame (from March 13, 2008 to January 13, 2009) within which posts were selected from BabyCenter message board, 500 posts were randomly selected from page 1 to page 241 of the Dear Baby message board in Wenxuecity website. On each page of Dear Baby message board, there were 100 posts without showing the replies. Following the same random sampling procedure as a way to select posts from BabyCenter website, 500 random numbers were generated from 1 to 241 as page number, and other 500 random numbers were generated from 1 to 100 as the post number on each selected page. Therefore, 500 posts were randomly selected from Dear Baby message board.

Coding System

Different categorical systems of social support behaviors have been identified. Among them, Cutrona and Suhr's (1992) five-type category system is widely acknowledged. This study applies Cutrona and Suhr's (1992) Social Support Behavior Codes (SSBC) to code types of social support expressed in the messages. Other items in the coding sheet are developed by the researchers of this study to code main topics in the posts and whether the post is to seek or give social support.

SSBC categorizes 23 social behaviors into five categories: information support, tangible assistance, esteem support, network support, and emotional support. Information support provides information about the stress itself or how to deal with it; tangible aid provides goods or services needed in the stressful situation; emotional support communicates love or caring; network support communicates belonging to a group of persons with similar interests and concerns; esteem support communicates respect and confidence in abilities. The SSBC was developed by Suhr (1990) to code frequency of support behaviors during ongoing interaction. Cutrona and Suhr (1992) use the SSBC to assess the frequency of occurrence of support-intended communication behavior. The SSBC was also applied to analyze social support in computer-mediated groups for people with disabilities (Braithwaite et al., 1999). Previous research uses the SSBC to code social support giving behavior, while the present study uses the SSBC to code both social support giving and receiving behaviors.

Braithwaite et al. (1999) report that individuals with disabilities have some unique support behaviors in online communication: humor, nonverbal cues, poetry, and signature lines. In this study, those four unique behaviors are added to the coding scheme.

Other than social support behavior types, this research also examines the content of the posts to display the main areas of concerns that US American and overseas Chinese women have during their prenatal and postnatal periods. Therefore, the researchers of this study developed a separate section to code the content of the posts, which include: medical issues, doctors and hospitals, nutrition and diet, parenting, maternal and baby products, insurance and cost, family relationship, balance of work and life, actively trying to conceive, news sharing, baby's picture(s) or video(s), community activities, issues on taking baby back to China, fitness and exercise, cooking, current social and political issues, poll, baby naming, pregnancy and delivery, and postpartum recovery. Message content that does not belong to any categories above is coded as others with a note including more details.

Intercoder Reliability

The SSBC was tested by different studies. Cutrona, Suhr, & MacFarlane's (1990) study reported the mean intraclass correlation across the five support categories between independent ratings was .77 (p< .001). Similarly, another study conducted by Cutrona and Suhr (1992) reported the mean intraclass correlation between independent ratings of support categories was .76 (p<.001). Braithwaite et al.'s (1999) research on online social support behavior of people with disabilities reported the simple agreement within all five categories of SSBC was 80%, and Scott's (1955) pi statistic was .76. Furthermore, simple agreement for all subcategories was above 70% except the understanding-empathy subcategory (55%).

In order to test the coding system for this study, two independent coders were trained to do the coding. Each coder was given a codebook containing operational definitions for each variable. The two coders independently coded 50 posts from the sample set drawn from BabyCenter message board and 50 posts from the sample set drawn from Dear Baby message board, which constitutes 10% of the whole sample. An intercoder reliability analysis using the Kappa statistic, which corrects for chance agreement, was performed to determine consistency between the two coders. The intercoder reliability of post type (seeking or giving support) exhibited excellent reliability (Kappa=.90, p< .001). The intercoder reliability of most variables of the content of the posts was high (Kappa ranges from .74 to 1, p< .001), except family relationship items showing moderate intercoder reliability (Kappa= .39, p< .001). The intercoder reliability of support type in SSBC was substantial (Kappa ranges from .56 to 1, p< .001). The intercoder reliability of support behaviors (humor, nonverbal cues, poetry, and signature lines) was excellent: Kappa ranges from .66 to 1, p<.001.

Table 1. Descriptive statistics for post type

Post type	Frequency (BabyCenter)	Percentage of the total (BabyCenter)	Frequency (Dear Baby)	Percentage of the total (Dear Baby)
Giving support	34	6.8%	62	12.4%
Seeking support	377	75.4%	309	61.8%
Giving and seeking support	6	1.2%	8	1.6%
Others	83	16.6%	121	24.2%
Total	500	100%	500	100%

$X^2=22.27$, df=3, p< .001

RESULTS

RQ1: Post Type—Giving Support or Seeking Support?

The first research question asks about the purposes for which women use the bulletin board: seeking support, giving support, or some other objectives. Sometimes, people seek support as well as give support in the same message. In both the American bulletin board and the overseas Chinese bulletin board, the majority of the posts were seeking support, while some of the posts were neither giving nor seeking support. However, the American message board and the overseas Chinese message board show different overall pattern of the type of the posts ($X^2=22.27$, df=3, p< .001). More USAmerican women went to the message board to seek support, while more overseas Chinese women used the bulletin board to give support. Table 1 shows the frequency of different types of the posts on both bulletin boards.

RQ2: Main Topics Discussed in the Online Support Groups

Research question 2 asks about the main topics discussed in the bulletin boards. Similar number of messages included personal narratives in BabyCenter message board (n=73, 14.6%) and Dear Baby message board (n=70, 14.0%). Popular topics emerged from both BabyCenter message board and Dear Baby message board included: parenting, pregnancy and delivery, medical issues, maternal and baby product, doctors and hospitals, baby's picture(s) or video(s), family relationship, nutrition and diet. Table 2 demonstrates the frequency of different topics discussed in the online support groups.

The BabyCenter message board and the Dear Baby message board shared a lot of commonalities in covering various topics, but there were a few significant differences too. The following topics were covered significantly more frequently in BabyCenter message board than the Dear Baby message board: pregnancy and delivery ($X^2=12.82$, df=1, p< .05), news sharing ($X^2=4.30$, df=1, p< .05), actively trying to conceive ($X^2=13.06$, df=1, p< .05), cooking ($X^2=3.95$, df=1, p< .05), and fitness and exercise ($X^2=9.08$, df=1, p< .05). In contrast, the Dear Baby message board covered the following topics more frequently than the BabyCenter bulletin board: maternal and baby product ($X^2=12.82$, df=1, p< .05), baby's picture(s) or video(s) ($X^2=36.39$, df=1, p< .05), and postpartum recovery ($X^2=5.48$, df=1, p< .05). Furthermore, some overseas Chinese women discussed issues related to taking baby back to china in the Dear Baby bulletin board, which is a unique topic that Chinese women share because of their status of stay as sojourners in their visiting countries.

Table 2. Descriptive statistics for topics discussed in the online support group

Topic	% of the total	Frequency (Dear Baby)	% of the total (Dear Baby)	Frequency (BabyCenter)	% of the total (BabyCenter)
Parenting	21.3%	119	23.8%	94	18.8%
Pregnancy and delivery*	16.0%	47	9.4%	113	22.6%
Medical Issues	13.8%	75	15.0%	63	12.6%
Maternal and baby product*	10.7%	71	14.2%	36	7.2%
Doctors and hospitals	9.7%	43	8.6%	54	10.8%
Baby's picture(s) or video(s)*	6.2%	54	10.8%	8	1.6%
Family relationship	6.1%	27	5.4%	34	6.8%
Nutrition and diet	4.6%	29	5.8%	17	3.4%
News sharing*	4.1%	14	2.8%	27	5.4%
Actively trying to conceive*	3.5%	7	1.4%	28	5.6%
Current social and political issues	3.1%	15	3.0%	16	3.2%
Community activities	2.9%	10	2.0%	19	3.8%
Cooking*	2.6%	8	1.6%	18	3.6%
Postpartum recovery*	1.5%	12	2.4%	3	.6%
Balance of work and life	1.3%	10	2.0%	3	.6%
Insurance and cost	1.3%	9	1.8%	4	.8%
Baby naming	1.2%	3	.6%	9	1.8%
Taking baby back to China*	1.0%	10	2.0%	0	0
Fitness and exercise*	.9%	0	0	9	1.8%
Poll	.7%	1	.2%	6	1.2%
Others	19.5%	103	20.6%	92	18.4%
Total	100%	500	100%	500	100%

Note. Topics with an asterisk are significantly different between groups (* p < .05).

RQ3: Types of Social Support

Five categories of social support and some unique support behaviors were coded in this study. The five categories of social support are information support, tangible assistance, esteem support, network support, and emotional support. The unique support behaviors include humor, nonverbal cues, and signature line. The content analysis show that information support was given or sought most frequently by members of both the BabyCenter message board and the Dear Baby message board. However, there were significantly more percentage of giving and seeking suggestions/advices in Dear Baby message board than that in BabyCenter message board (X^2=7.12, df=1, p< .05). In BabyCenter message board, significantly more posts provided the following types of support than Dear Baby message board: teaching (X^2=4.64, df=1, p< .05), listening (X^2=7.99, df=1, p< .05), and companions (X^2=56.17, df=1, p< .05). Table 3 shows the frequency of each type of support behavior as below.

Table 3. Descriptive statistics for social support type and behaviors in the online support group

Support type	% of the total	Frequency (Dear Baby)	% of the total (Dear Baby)	Frequency (BabyCenter)	% of the total (BabyCenter)
Information					
Suggestions/Advice*	54.6%	294	58.8%	252	50.4%
Teaching*	1.4%	3	.6%	11	2.2%
Referral	4.7%	30	6.0%	17	3.4%
Situational appraisal	.2%	1	.2%	1	.2%
Emotional support					
Relationship	0	0	0	0	0
Physical affection	.2%	2	.4%	0	0
Confidentiality	0	0	0	0	0
Sympathy	1.3%	4	.8%	9	1.8%
Understanding of empathy	2.2%	7	1.4%	15	3.0%
Listening*	2.9%	7	1.4%	22	4.4%
Encouragement	1.3%	7	1.4%	6	1.2%
Prayer/blessing	3.9%	15	3.0%	24	4.8%
Network support					
Access	.9%	3	.6%	6	1.2%
Presence	.7%	3	.6%	4	.8%
Companions*	15.6%	35	7.0%	121	24.2%
Esteem support					
Compliment	.2%	1	.2%	1	.2%
Validation	3.2%	13	2.6%	19	3.8%
Relief of blame	0	0	0	0	0
Tangible assistance					
Loan	.7%	5	1.0%	2	.4%
Perform direct task	.4%	3	.6%	1	.2%
Perform indirect task	0	0	0	0	0
Active participation	.7%	5	1.0%	2	.4%
Express willingness	0	0	0	0	0
Other support behavior					
Humor	1.2%	10	2.0%	2	.4%
Nonverbal cues*	9.1%	24	4.8%	67	13.4%
Signature lines*	1.7%	0	0%	17	3.4%
Poetry	.3%	3	.6%	0	0
Total	100%	500	100%	500	100%

Note. Social Support Type and Behaviors with an asterisk are significantly different between groups (* p < .05).

RQ4: Different Stories on the Two Message Boards

The quantitative content analysis yields solid results on the different themes, support types, and support behaviors emerged in the Dear Baby message board and the BabyCenter message board. In order to answer the research question of how the differences and similarities appear in the two selected websites, the researchers compiled the representative posts of each type and reconstructed the original messages to provide typical examples. Those examples support and interpret the quantitative data in a qualitative way, and can help readers to have a deeper understanding of the online discourses on both message boards. The discussion focuses on the major differences that the quantitative content analysis indicates.

Pregnancy and Delivery. Pregnancy and delivery emerged as a popular topic in both websites, but was a more popular topic in the BabyCenter message board than in the Dear Baby message board. Posts coded as pregnancy and delivery include questions, information or/and experience on issues during pregnancy or/and delivery. Although there were significantly more posts on pregnancy and delivery in BabyCenter website (n=113, 22.6%) than in Dear Baby bulletin board (n=47, 9.4%), posts on both websites covered similar issues such as sharing their feeling of baby kick, some special symptoms during pregnancy, narratives including a lot of details about the delivery process, questions on certain medical check during pregnancy, etc. In both websites, the following exemplary posts are typical:

Mary: "I feel my baby! I am 12 weeks today, and I just felt a thump and it is right where my bean is sitting in my tummy! I am so excited!"

Jenny: "When I played with my little son today, he knocked my stomach with his elbows. It was instant pain and now I am spotting. Will my baby

be OK? Shall I go to the emergency room? I am so worried……"

In the posts on BabyCenter message board, many women asked for experiences from their fellow pregnant women and also mentioned they would seek help from the doctors on that issue too. Sometimes, USAmerican women even tried to confirm the information that they received from the doctors with people online. In posts on BabyCenter message board, it was common to find sentences like "I will see my doctor tomorrow morning, but I really want to know how you dealt with it in similar situations" or "my doctor told me my baby was OK, but I am still worried about my weight loss in these 2 weeks. Any suggestions?" USAmerican women's use of the BabyCenter website for maternal health information echoes Warner and Procaccino's (2007) finding that individuals use the Internet to find health advice from near-experts, other users or affected populations, and the near experts' suggestions offer reassurance of the expert (medical professional)'s advice. Very differently, overseas Chinese women rarely mentioned whether they would see their doctor for that issue or not. Chinese women just tried to get help through the Internet on particular questions even sometimes answering those questions need some specialized medical knowledge and doctors might be the best person they should ask. Overseas Chinese women appear to rely more on other Chinese women's suggestions than USAmerican women rely on other USAmerican women as some overseas Chinese women may feel reluctant to see the doctor for the language barriers and their unfamiliarity of the medical system in their host countries.

News Sharing. After being a member of the message board for a while, both overseas Chinese women and USAmerican women show their connections with the group through sharing their life news with other members. Although news sharing was neither a popular topic in the Chinese Dear Baby bulletin board nor the USAmerican

BabyCenter website, more USAmerican women (n=27, 5.4%) tended to post their personal news on the message board than overseas Chinese women (n=14, 2.8%). Both overseas Chinese women and USAmerican women shared good news such as birth of baby and celebration of baby's birthday. Typical posts looked like the following examples:

Jenny: "My baby is two years old today! Happy birthday!"

Alice: "I had my baby yesterday! My baby is doing superb! He is healthy and beautiful!"

Interestingly, there was almost only good news shared in the Chinese message board, while the quantity of good news and bad news was much more balanced on the BabyCenter message board. This might be explained by the Chinese cultural tradition of "releasing good news, hiding bad news," which encourages people to share good news and the happiness with others but keep bad news and the sadness themselves. In contrast, some USAmerican women shared their sad life events in a very emotional way on BabyCenter message board, for example:

Jen: "Our doctor just confirmed that I lost my baby. This is my first pregnancy. I feel so lost and cannot focus on anything. It is difficult for me to hang out with my pregnant friend and to think about holding a baby. My family are so disappointed, but we are trying to work through it."

Actively Trying to Conceive. In our quantitative content analysis, actively trying to conceive emerged as a more popular topic in the BabyCenter message board (n=28, 5.6%) than the Dear Baby message board (n=7, 1.4%). The difference might be attributed to some social and cultural differences in China and the U.S. In the USAmerican

bulletin board, typical posts were similar to the following:

Anita: "I don't temp but the O calculator on BabyCenter says I could O starting around the 14th. We are trying the Shettles Method for a girl b/c I figure it can't hurt. I was ordered by my Gynecologist to have a D&C in September to have a proper clean out and get things back to a fresh start."

Sandy: "I started Clomid this month and although I wasn't able to do OPKs, I am almost positive I o'd. I observed several days of EWCM. Anyways, I guess I was just wondering if there is still hope for me this month. I'm starting to put PCOS in remission."

Six observations concern the discussion of attempts to conceive. First, every post recorded instance of someone trying to conceive appeared in the English-language site. On its face, this suggests an openness about what could be considered a private and taboo subject among some populations of women. Second, and by contrast, the Chinese women rarely spoke of conception on their site unless they need some information on some medical treatment associated with conception. It is conjectured that this is a taboo subject, on the one hand, and third, that by admitting their inability to conceive, Chinese women risk damage to own face by admitting a personal inadequacy. Fourth, the prevailing policy of having only one child in the Mainland China makes the inability to conceive a potentially even greater failure, and heightens the risk to face. Fifth, USAmerican women turn to technique and technology to influence what is, at its heart, a natural process. They have turned infertility into a problem, and have come up with technological or procedural solutions. Chinese women may be closer to not substituting technology for natural process. Sixth, the lexicon for aspects of conceiving, the host of abbreviations, names of techniques, and the degree of specificity suggest that USAmerican women consider their posts to be commonplace matters that are not in themselves a noteworthy occurrence.

Cooking. The number of posts on cooking on BabyCenter message board was more than twice that on Dear Baby message board. The majority of posts on Dear Baby message board focused on special recipe for babies and pregnant women. However, the BabyCenter message board included many posts asking for general cooking recipe or tips for the family. USAmerican women tended to also use BabyCenter to serve their other information needs than pregnancy and baby issues. The Dear Baby message board belongs to a major overseas Chinese website which has another bulletin board for cooking. Perhaps overseas Chinese women mostly used the bulletin board for cooking on the same Chinese website to meet their needs on cooking issues and kept the discussion on cooking related to pregnancy and little baby on the Dear Baby message board.

Exercise and Fitness. Exercise and Fitness was a unique topic only found in the selected posts on the BabyCenter message board. USAmerican women discussed ways to lose weight and keep fit during pregnancy and after delivery, including exercise, diet and some other ways on the BabyCenter message board. In the Dear Baby message board sample, no posts were found on this topic. This difference reflects the general social differences in China and the U.S. Obesity has been a persistent and serious health problem in American society, while it is not a big concern for the Chinese population. Exercise and fitness is a popular topic in American society, so it is not surprising to find that prenatal and postnatal women discuss it. For example, Kathy wrote:

"Before I got pregnant I vowed I would keep my shape and be a hot mom. Now, my baby is 10 months old and I have lost 10 lbs. I still need to lose 10 more lbs. Does anyone have any tips on losing pregnancy weight? I am struggling!"

Maternal and Baby Products. One of the most popular topics on both bulletin boards was maternal and baby products. However, the Chinese bulletin board, Dear Baby, had significantly higher number of posts (N=71, 14.2%) on this topic than the USAmerican message board, BabyCenter (N=36, 7.2%). Posts on both message boards included such similar issues as news about sales and discounts of the products and recommendations or comments on certain brands. Typical posts on this topic looked like the following:

Lucy's Mom: "Toddler's music table is on sale at Toys R Us, 20% off till Dec. 2nd, I bought one for my daughter and she loves it."

Amy: "Hi, I am a new mom. I feel like I have so much to learn about baby stuff. Anyone could recommend some good brands of diapers and pumps for me? There are a variety of brands at Walmart. Don't know which one to choose. Thanks."

Even though both message boards shared some similarities on this topic, differences between the two boards were easily discernable as well. First, besides maternal and baby products, the Chinese message board also included lots of posts on baby care services, such as daycare service and hiring nannies. Therefore, the authors decided to code baby care services into the category of maternal and baby products. The posts on baby care services typically sought advice on looking for a high-quality day care center or a good nanny. Such posts were quite common in the Chinese bulletin board:

Dear Baby's Mom: "I just moved to the Oaktree area. I have a two-year old son. For those of you who live in the area, could you please recommend some good day care centers that you've been used? Thanks for any suggestions."

The reason that the overseas Chinese women seek more information on day care services from online message board might be related to the lack of immediate Chinese interpersonal networks in their living area. Overseas Chinese women tend to look for social support from other overseas Chinese women as Harris and Dewdney's (1994) principle of information behavior suggests that individuals "frequently review their own experience first, then turn to people like themselves, including their friends and family" (p. 24). Furthermore, overseas Chinese women might tend to get health information in Chinese resources rather than in English resources. For instance, Chinese immigrant women in Canada identify linguistic difficulty as an important barrier of effectively seeking health information, thus want health information in Chinese through different channels such as newspapers, television, Internet, workshops, health workers, and pamphlets (Ahmad et al., 2004). The research finds that loss of extended social networks and language barriers are the two primary reasons that Chinese immigrants have difficulty in accessing health information. To compensate for the lack of Chinese social networks in their neighborhood, overseas Chinese women resort to the online message board to obtain the information from other overseas Chinese women that they perceive as people similar to themselves. The second difference is that the posts on the Chinese bulletin board were mostly concise and direct, with shorter narratives on recommendations about products. However, the USAmerican message board contained longer narratives, which not only covered product recommendations, but also problems with certain brands of products. For example, a post discussed a brand of diapers causing burn on baby's skin. Finally, the posts on the Chinese board talked mostly about baby products, whereas, BabyCenter had more posts on maternal products.

For health practitioners in the U.S., the differences revealed that overseas Chinese women need more information on maternal and baby products in general, as most of them are unfamiliar with brands and product names in the U.S. Moreover, physically separated from their Chinese counterparts, overseas Chinese women rely more on the online community for child care service information.

Baby Pictures or Videos. Both the Chinese and USAmerican message boards contained baby pictures or videos. The Chinese message board had a higher percentage of baby pictures or videos (N=54, 10.8%) than the USAmerican board (N=8, 1.6%). This type of posts typically begins with a few sentences on baby's recent progress or news sharing, followed by the pictures. For example,

Anna, "Today is my daughter's 2-year old birthday. She can already recognize the 26 letters two months ago! Today, she pointed at her book and spelled the word, "baby." How exciting! This is a picture of her eating the birthday cake!"

In Chinese culture, sharing baby pictures or videos is a means for Chinese parents to express their happiness and parental pride in witnessing their babies' growth and progress. In American culture, personal pictures or videos are generally considered as privacy, which people feel hesitant to share with the public. In addition, American parents feel that they might be biased in viewing their own children and others might not think the same way. One of the posts in BabyCenter mentioned, "I know I'm biased, but her gorgeous smile…"

Postpartum Recovery. Postpartum recovery was a topic of concern in the Chinese website; however, this topic was rarely discussed in the American website. The coverage on postpartum recovery reflects a significant cultural difference in maternal care. According to the Chinese tradition, women must keep warm and stay at home within one month after delivery. They should be taken good care of by their family members and avoid any heavy house chores. It is believed that many chronic diseases, especially, arthritis, are caused by poor care during the first month after delivery. The crucial recovery period is called "Zuo Yuezi." Most Chinese women observe this tradition strictly. However, in American culture, it is common to see women go outside, and even go to work, within a week of their delivery.

The Chinese posts on postpartum recovery include such issues as baby blue, vaginal tear, and breastfeeding. A typical post is exemplified as such,

"I had episiotomy when I gave birth to my son. His head is too big! It has been two months after my delivery. I can still feel the pain when I sit! Is this normal? How long does it take to recover? Anyone had similar experiences? Thanks for any suggestions!"

Taking Baby Back to China. One topic that was unique to the Chinese website was issues on taking baby back to China. This topic covered a variety of issues, such as looking for travel partners back to China, how to take care of babies living with grandparents in China, and travelling documents required for grandparents taking babies back to China. Typical examples are constructed as follows,

Jennifer: "Anyone flying back to China in October? I am taking my two-year old son back to China, and would like to find a travel partner in our online community. Please reply this message if interested. Thanks."

Eileen: "Is the immunization schedule in China the same as here? Where should I send my baby for immunization shots in Zhoushan? Any suggestions?"

Taking baby back to China becomes a concern for overseas Chinese for several reasons. First, most overseas Chinese parents either work or study in their host countries. The busy schedule leaves them little time to take care of their babies. Second, Chinese culture values extended families. It is common to see three generations living together in China. The retired grandparents take care of their grandchildren while the parents go to work. Therefore, some parents choose to send their babies back to China and take the babies back when they are ready for day care or school.

Social Support Types and Behaviors. Among the five categories of social support, information support, tangible assistance, esteem support, network support, and emotional support, information support was the most frequently sought or given social support type in both Dear Baby message board (n=328, 65.6%) and BabyCenter message board(n=281, 56.2%). Information support provides information about the problem itself or how to deal with it. Flanagin and Metzger's (2001) study on individuals' use of Internet in the contemporary media era indicates that "the Internet was the most highly used for getting information, over other technologies such as newspapers, television, books, and magazines" (p. 174). Not surprisingly, the analysis of posts on BabyCenter message board and Dear Baby message board shows that women seek information heavily on the message boards, which might be problematic, as information on the Internet is usually provided by nonexperts and might be unreliable and even false. This may also imply that both overseas Chinese women's and USAmerican women's information needs can not be fully met by the health practitioners.

Although overseas Chinese women and USAmerican women share a great extent of similarities in using the Internet to satisfy their information needs, they show great differences in listening, a type of emotional support. There were significantly more posts on listening support on BabyCenter message board (n=22, 4.4%) than those on Dear Baby message board (n=7, 1.4%). Posts coded as listening seek attentive comments. Those posts normally include long narratives followed by sentences such as:

"Thanks for letting me get it out!"

"Thank you for reading and I am sorry it is so long."

"Sorry, I have to vent……"

According to Moody (2001), "individuals who spend more time online are more likely to have higher rates of emotional loneliness" (p. 395). In the individualist American culture, American women may have weaker relational ties with people around them and feel difficult to find someone to listen to them. The online community, which is different and might be far away from the community people live in, becomes a safe place for women to share their stories that they may feel reluctant to share in real life. Venting online could be an effective cure of the emotional loneliness women suffer in real life. Although overseas Chinese women may not have as many social networks in their host countries as those of USAmerican women, influenced by Chinese collectivist culture, overseas Chinese women may develop a small but close community in which they feel comfortable to share their life stories. Therefore, fewer overseas Chinese women need the Internet to satisfy their emotional needs.

Furthermore, the quantity of posts on companion on the BabyCenter website (n=121, 24.2%) was more than three times of that on Dear Baby bulletin board (n=35, 15.6%). Companion is a type of network support that people seek/give reminders that other people are in the same boat or have been through the same thing. Posts coded as companion may include sentences such as:

"I am just wondering whether anyone with similar experiences would like to share."

"Does anyone else go through this before? Tell me I am not alone!"

USAmerican women had greater needs on companion on the Internet than overseas Chinese women. In many cases, when USAmerican women sought suggestions from members of the BabyCenter website, they tended to ask help from those who had similar experience. The suggestions that USAmerican women get from other women with similar experience may compliment the information they get from other sources.

Another interesting finding was that USAmerican women tended to include more emoticons and nonverbal cues such as "☺" "☹"and signature lines in their posts on the BabyCenter website, while fewer overseas Chinese women did so on the Dear Baby bulletin board. The nonverbal cues and signature lines in the messages revealed personality and beliefs of the individual who posted it.

CONCLUSION AND FUTURE RESEARCH DIRECTIONS

This research uses a binary, composite approach to analysis. While it is quite common for research to triangulate through the use of multiple methods, theories, researchers, or co-researchers, this analysis does so for a less-common reason. We do not maintain that multiple methods, derived from competing paradigms, can "point" to the same thing. Rather, methods that spring from different assumptions are likely to disclose different aspects of the things that are studied. Rather, we use multiple methods in order to speak to different persons or stakeholders: the positivist method speaks to the research community, while the interpretive approach speaks to the end user and to those who would want to understand things the way the persons in the study understood them. The hermeneutic stage of the binary method closes the gap between social-behavioral scientist and end-user.

Women went to the two pre- and post-natal sites with specific objectives in mind. While these objectives cannot be specified accurately for the "lurkers" who offered no posts, the researchers were able to paint a structural portrait of those who entered the on-line, asynchronous dialogue. Some of them quoted experts whom they had already consulted, reinforcing the literature that persons (primarily women) who go to health sites may go there for reinforcement and confirmation, reassurance and experiential certitude, more than for actual medical expertise. They may get their expertise elsewhere, or they may be told to do so in the case of the Chinese-language site. Some went to learn, others to advise.

It follows that health specialists who want to intervene in matters of women's health on-line should first determine the degree to which the women who come to post messages actually want medical expertise, as opposed to interpersonal and emotional assurances. By misreading the intended uses and gratifications of the on-line women, the interventions may miss their mark.

Whereas the common health approach to culture has been to identify characteristics of a segmented group of persons, and then to determine whether that segment experiences a disproportionate risk or exposure to medical crisis, the Internet may produce sites comprised of auto-segmented persons who interpretively define their own health needs. It may be necessary to leave the positivist mode of discovering and controlling, and to shift to a hermeneutic mode of observing, listening, and dialoguing. Medical experts may find it useful and gratifying to enter the conversations as a near-peer, someone with more than the usual expertise, but who will not be allowed to speak with the voice of absolute and final professionalization. By coming with the final word, they may not get even the first word.

It will be instructive to identify other health sites where the users auto-select their members, and to see if the structure of the conversations resembles the ones found for the baby posts. The degree of salience and risk may be important factors in determining the state and nature of postings, and advice giving and receiving. Rather than to simply accept the authors' explanations for the differences that were reported among the sites, it will be useful to confirm through further study which differences are culturally grounded, and which not. The collaboration among three authors helped to eliminate some of the most obvious misinterpretations of differences among the women studied, but it still produced explanations that were possibly more etic than emic. In the end, persons are persuaded by their own reasons more readily than by the reasons of outsiders.

REFERENCES

About BabyCenter. (n.d.). *About BabyCenter.* Retrieved on February 15, 2009, from http://hotjobs.yahoo.com/careers-500837-BabyCenter_LLC

About us (n.d.). *About us.* Retrieved on February 12, 2009, from http://docs.wenxuecity.com/aboutus/

Ahmad, F., Shik, A., Vanza, R., Cheung, A., George, U., & Stewart, D. E. (2004). Popular health promotion strategies among Chinese and East Indian immigrant women. *Women & Health, 40*(1), 21–40. doi:10.1300/J013v40n01_02

Albrecht, T. A., & Adelman, M. B. (1987). Communicating social support: A theoretical perspective. In Albrecht, T. A., & Adelman, M. B. (Eds.), *Communicating social support: A theoretical perspective* (pp. 18–39). Thousand Oaks, CA: Sage.

Alexander, B. K. (2008). Performance ethnography: The reenacting and inciting of culture. In Denzin, N. K., & Lincoln, Y. S. (Eds.), *Strategies of qualitative inquiry* (3rd ed., pp. 75–117). Thousand Oaks, CA: Sage.

Bernhardt, J. M., & Felter, E. M. (2004). Online pediatric information seeking among mothers of young children: Results from a qualitative study using focus groups. *Journal of Medical Internet Research*, 6(1), 7. doi:10.2196/jmir.6.1.e7

Blumler, J. (1979). The role of theory in uses and gratifications studies. *Communication Research*, 6, 9–36. doi:10.1177/009365027900600102

Boberg, E. W., Gustafson, D. H., Hawkins, R. P., Chan, C. L., Bricker, E., & Pingree, S. (1995). Development, acceptance, and use patterns of a computer-based education and social support system for people living with AIDS/HIV infection. *Computers in Human Behavior*, 11, 289–311. doi:10.1016/0747-5632(94)00037-I

Braithwaite, D. O., Waldron, V. R., & Finn, J. (1999). Communication of social support in computer-mediated groups for people with disabilities. *Health Communication*, 11, 123–151. doi:10.1207/s15327027hc1102_2

Camarota, S. (2007). Immigrants in the United States, 2007: A profile of America's foreign-born population. *The Center for Immigration Studies*. Retrieved on October 30, 2008, from http://www.cis.org/immigrants_profile_2007

Chan, B. (2006). Virtual communities and Chinese national identity. *Journal of Chinese Overseas*, 2(1), 1–32. doi:10.1353/jco.2006.0001

Cline, R. J. W. (1999). Communication in social support groups. In Frey, L., Gouran, D., & Poole, S. (Eds.), *Handbook of Small Group Communication* (pp. 516–538). Thousand Oaks, CA: Sage.

Cline, R. J. W., & Haynes, K. (2001). Consumer health information seeking on the Internet: The state of the art. *Health Education Research*, 16(6), 671–692. doi:10.1093/her/16.6.671

Company overview (n.d.). Company overview. Retrieved February 15, 2009, from http://www.BabyCenter.com/help-about-company

Culver, J. D., Gerr, F., & Frumkin, H. (1997). Medical information on the internet: A study of the electronic bulletin board. *Journal of General Internal Medicine*, 12, 466–470. doi:10.1046/j.1525-1497.1997.00084.x

Cutrona, C. E., & Suhr, J. A. (1992). Controllability of stressful events and satisfaction with spouse support behaviors. *Communication Research*, 19, 154–174. doi:10.1177/009365092019002002

Cutrona, C. E., Suhr, J. A., & MacFarlane, R. (1990). Interpersonal transactions and the psychological sense of support. In Duck, S., & Silver, R. (Eds.), *Personal relationships and social support* (pp. 30–45). London: Sage.

Denzin, N. K., & Lincoln, Y. S. (2008). The discipline and practice of qualitative research. In Denzin, N. K., & Lincoln, Y. S. (Eds.), *Collecting and interpreting qualitative materials* (3rd ed., pp. 1–45). Thousand Oaks: Sage.

Dutta, M. J. (2007). Communicating about culture and health: Theorizing cultural-centered and cultural sensitivity approaches. *Communication Theory*, 17, 304–328. doi:10.1111/j.1468-2885.2007.00297.x

Flanagin, A. J., & Metzger, M. J. (2001, January). Internet use in the contemporary media environment. *Human Communication Research*, 27(1), 153–181. doi:10.1093/hcr/27.1.153

Fox, S. (2009). Mobile could be a game-changer. But only for those who get in the game. Retrieved on April 28, 2009, from http://www.pewinternet.org/Commentary/2009/April/2--Mobile-could-be-a-gamechanger.aspx

Geist-Martin, P., Ray, E. B., & Sharf, B. F. (2003). Understanding health in cultural communities. In *P. Geist-Martin, B. Ray & B. F. Sharf, Communicating health: Personal, cultural, and political complexities* (pp. 54–94). Belmont, CA: Wadsworth/ Thomson Learning.

Ha, L., & James, E. L. (1998). Interactivity re-examined: A baseline analysis of early business Websites. *Journal of Broadcasting & Electronic Media, 42,* 457–474.

Harris, R. M., & Dewdney, P. (1994). Barriers to information: How formal help systems fail battered women. Westport, CN: Greenwood Press.

Hochschild, A. R. (1973). Communal life styles for the old. *Society, 10,* 50–57. doi:10.1007/ BF02698950

Jensen, K. B., & Jankowski, N. W. (1991). *A handbook of qualitative methodologies for mass communication research.* New York: Routledge. doi:10.4324/9780203409800

Johnson, J. L., Bootorff, J. L., Browne, A. J., Grewal, S., Hilton, B. A., & Clarke, H. (2004). Othering and being othered in the context of health care services. *Health Communication, 16,* 253–272. doi:10.1207/ S15327027HC1602_7

Jones, S. H. (2008). Autoethnography: Making the personal political. In Denzin, N. K., & Lincoln, Y. S. (Eds.), *Collecting and interpreting qualitative materials* (3rd ed., pp. 205–245). Thousand Oaks, CA: Sage.

Katz, E., Blumler, J. G., & Gurevitch, M. (1974). Utilization of mass communication by the individual. In Blumler, J. G., & Katz, E. (Eds.), *The use of mass communications: Current perspectives on gratifications research* (pp. 19–32). Thousand Oaks, CA: Sage.

Kreuter, M. W., & McClure, S. M. (2004). The role of culture in health communication. *Annual Review of Public Health, 25,* 439–455. doi:10.1146/ annurev.publhealth.25.101802.123000

Lupton, D. (1994). Toward the development of critical health communication praxis. *Health Communication, 6*(1), 55–67. doi:10.1207/ s15327027hc0601_4

Ma, G. X. (1999). Between two worlds: the use of traditional and western health services by Chinese immigrants. *Journal of Community Health, 24*(6), 421–437. doi:10.1023/A:1018742505785

Moody, E. J. (2001, November). Internet use and its relationship to loneliness. *Cyberpsychology & Behavior, 4*(3), 393–401. doi:10.1089/109493101300210303

Ruggiero, T. E. (2000). Uses and gratifications theory in the 21st century. *Mass Communication & Society, 3*(1), 3–37. doi:10.1207/ S15327825MCS0301_02

Salander, P. (2002). Using beliefs and magical thinking to fight cancer distress—A case study. *Psycho-Oncology, 9*(1), 40–43. doi:10.1002/ (SICI)1099-1611(200001/02)9:1<40::AID-PON429>3.0.CO;2-K

Schneider, S. J., & Tooley, J. (1986). Self-help computer conferencing. *Computers and Biomedical Research, an International Journal, 19,* 274–281. doi:10.1016/0010-4809(86)90022-4

Scott, W. A. (1955). Reliability of content analysis: The case of nominal scale coding. *Public Opinion Quarterly, 19,* 321–325. doi:10.1086/266577

Shaw, B. R., McTavish, F., Hawkins, R., Gustafson, D. H., & Pingree, S. (2000). Experiences of women with breast cancer: exchanging social support over the CHESS computer network. *Journal of Health Communication, 5,* 135–159. doi:10.1080/108107300406866

Singleton, Jr., & Straits, B. C. (2005). *Approaches to social research* (4th ed.). New York: Oxford University Press.

Starosta, W. J., & Chen, G.-M. (2009 forthcoming). Expanding the circumference of intercultural communication study. In Hulualani, R., & Nakayama, T. (Eds.), *Handbook of Critical Communication*. London: Blackwell.

Starosta, W. J., & Hannon, S. W. (1997). The multilexicality of contemporary history: Recounted and enacted narratives of the Mohawk incident in Oka, Québec. *The International and Intercultural Communication Annual, 20*, 141–165.

Suhr, J. A. (1990). *The development of the social support behavior code.* Unpublished master's thesis, University of Iowa, Iowa City.

Swanson, D. L. (1987). Gratification seeking, media exposure, and audience interpretations: Some directions for research. *Journal of Broadcasting & Electronic Media, 31*, 237–254.

Tardy, R. W., & Hale, C. L. (1998). Bonding and cracking: The role of informal, interpersonal networks in health care decision making. *Health Communication, 10*(2), 151–173. doi:10.1207/s15327027hc1002_3

Wandersman, L., Wandersman, A., & Kahn, S. (1980). Social support in the transition to parenthood. *Journal of Community Psychology, 8*, 332–342. doi:10.1002/1520-6629(198010)8:4<332::AID-JCOP2290080407>3.0.CO;2-H

Warner, D., & Procaccino, J. D. (2007). Women seeking health information: Distinguishing the Web user. *Journal of Health Communication, 12*, 787–814. doi:10.1080/10810730701672090

Williams, F., Rice, R. E., & Rogers, E. M. (1988). *Research methods and the new media.* New York: Free Press.

Yin, X. (2007). Diverse and transnational: Chinese (PRC) immigrants in the United States. *Journal of Chinese Overseas, 3*(1), 122–145. doi:10.1353/jco.2007.0037

Chapter 19
Culturally Unique Social Patterns in Computer-Mediated Social Networking

Devan Rosen
University of Hawaii, USA

Michael A. Stefanone
University at Buffalo, USA

Derek Lackaff
University of Texas at Austin, USA

ABSTRACT

People from distinct cultural backgrounds communicate and manage their interpersonal relations in systematically different ways. The current chapter utilizes a survey of young adults to examine the social patterns of culturally influenced differences in online behavior. Results show that individuals that identify with individualistic cultural backgrounds have larger networks of friends on social network sites (SNSs), have a larger proportion of these friends that they have not actually met face-to-face, and share more photos online, opposed to individuals that identify with less individualistic cultural backgrounds. The size of an individuals' offline social support network size was a significant predictor of satisfaction with life, while SNS network size was not. Findings suggest that individuals who identify with more individualistic cultural backgrounds tend to be better connected, self-promote, and are more satisfied with their social lives.

INTRODUCTION

As our communicative environment continues to be influenced by the introduction of new computer-mediated communication (CMC) applications, the effects of these applications are impacting the social world in complex ways. Communication technologies, such as social-networking sites (SNS), are being used in a number of ways to navigate and mediate the environment of personal identities and relationships. Since these applications are being used

DOI: 10.4018/978-1-61520-827-2.ch019

with increased frequency, using technologies like SNS has become an important skill when managing relationships online (Stefanone & Lackaff, 2009, Stefanone, Lackaff, & Rosen, 2008). As a result of the frequency and importance of CMC applications in our relationships, the instrumental decisions one makes when deciding how to behave in these mediated environments becomes an important element in managing our social world.

A unique aspect of these new computer-mediated technologies is that spatial and geographic boundaries are no longer barriers to interaction, allowing people from a diverse set of cultures to interact with each other with increased ease and frequency. Given that many of the new CMC applications require people to establish an online identity with personal profiles, earlier findings indicating that impressions formed in CMC environments can be more intense that offline (see Hancock & Dunham, 2004), it is important to understanding how individuals who identify with different cultures use the CMC platforms to present their identities. This chapter presents an investigation into the relationship between computer-mediated communicative behaviors and culture to explore whether culturally influenced behaviors normally associated with face-to-face communication emerge as patterned behavior in CMC.

In this chapter, literature on culture-specific communicative styles and behaviors frames an investigation into the use of specific Web 2.0 technologies: SNSs. Literature on broad cultural differences in behavior is reviewed, followed by a review of research on CMC technologies with emphasis on SNSs. The literature review concludes with hypotheses and research questions about the different uses of SNSs as related to culture. Methodological procedures will be discussed, followed by results, discussion of limitations and implications for future research.

LITERATURE REVIEW

Culture as Individualism and Collectivism

There are a number of distinct research streams investigating the various ways that culture can be categorized and conceptualized. Much research has been conducted in an effort to understand how people from different and distinct cultures behave in a plethora of situations, from which several seminal concepts were established. One of the most investigated areas of cultural differences relates to individualism and collectivism as associated with national cultures.

A principle amount of the initial conceptualization of cultural differences was done by Hofstede (1980), who defined four basic dimensions for characterizing cultures: power distance, uncertainty avoidance, masculinity, and individualism / collectivism. Hofstede defined decreased individualism as a tendency to place the needs of one's in-group above one's own needs, and increased individualism as the tendency to place one's own needs above the needs of one's in-group. Trandis and colleagues (Hui & Triandis, 1986; Triandis, 2001) have shown individualism to be multidimensional and identified key features of increased individualism like tendencies toward self-reliance, self-promotion, competition, emotional distance from in-groups and hedonism. Collectivism is also a complex construct and can be characterized by closeness to family, family integrity, and sociability.

National identity has been used to study cultural concepts such as individualism and collectivism and is associated with a diversified field of research, drawing some criticism and parallel methodologies, discussed below. Many researchers have established that individual nation states are broadly associated with a more or less individualistic culture, and have compared countries along the lines of individualism (Hofstede, 1980; Kim, Hunter, Miyahara, Horvath, & Bresnahan,

1994; Shavitt, Lalwani, Zhang & Torelli, 2006; Triandis, 2001). Trandis (2001) found that western societies are considered higher on the individualism scale, whereas Asian societies are considered lower on the individualistic scale.

Early research on individualism and collectivism treated the two as polar opposites at two sides of the same scale (Hofstede, 1980). However, recent findings have concluded that individualism and collectivism may indeed be related to different indicators, and should be investigated independent of each other due to several methodological issues. One issue relates to imbalanced keying in the scale producing within-subject standardization (Schimmack, Oishi, & Diener, 2005). Analyzing collectivism has created methodological issues, as well as national variation, whereas individualism has remained more constant through time. As a result of these issues, the research presented in this chapter conceptualizes differences between cultures as more or less individualistic, since this characteristic of culture is not theoretically attached to collectivism and is more stable on the national level.

Although there is much research using nations states as indicative of cultural identity, there is also some criticism of this practice. A meta-analysis by Oyserman, Coon, and Kemmelmeier (2002) suggests that there are problems with the measurement of individualism and collectivism using traditional scales, as there is a lack of convergent validity when comparing their construct findings with that of Hofstede. In response to Oyserman et al's analysis, Schimmack et al. (2005) present findings that contradict Oyserman et al, and propose that methodological issues with data collection, such as subjects having varied semantic understanding of wording in the scales. Additionally, the context that the data is collected in (e.g. work, home, university) produced widely different results across research findings. Schimmack et al. also point out that national differences in individualism have remained highly stable in the time since Hofstede (1980) first measured individualism, and that that

national differences in individualism will remain in the near future. Along the same lines, Hofstede (2001) updated his earlier findings and found that although individualism has risen over the past decades across the globe, the rank ordering of nations on individualism has remained stable.

In addition to cultural differences between countries, Green, Deschamps, and Páez (2005) found that a lack of consideration for within-country cultural variation could lead to an over-generalization of attributes. These findings stem from the composition of nations as made up of people from diverse national backgrounds. As such, the research presented in this chapter does not conceptualize all respondents as culturally similar if they are living in a specific country; rather, respondents were asked what ethnic and cultural background they identify themselves with, and to what extent they identify with that culture. As pointed out above, Schimmack et al. (2005) establishes that differences of culture have remained stable on the aggregate, national level, so garnering which culture one identifies with is likely to yield a valid measure of cultural identity. Further, Green et al. (2005) established that the most commonly reported results of within-country variation of individualism concerns gender differences, which controlled for in statistical models, and discussed in the methods section below.

Due to the methodological debate regarding the validity of individualism being measured at the individual level, the exploratory research presented in this chapter uses the more traditional conceptualization of the nation state as indicating a more or less individualistic culture.

There is little to no research on cultural identity and online networking behavior, with the few recent studies mostly related to learning contexts (Lapointe & Gunawardena, 2004). There is a shortage of research aimed at investigating new communication technologies, like SNSs, and the patterns of mediated relationships considering cultural differences regarding social networks and social support.

Social Support and Social Networks

Social network studies generally focus on the relationships between social entities and the analysis of systematic patterns of social relations between people (Scott, 2000). Social network studies that investigate patterns of interactions between individuals positioned in a network offer predictive abilities regarding individual behaviors and attitudes. Both social and behavioral sciences continue to become increasingly interested in the social network approach as the relation itself is utilized as the unit of analysis, as opposed to analyzing attribute data common in survey research. Social networks map out patterns of relationships which people use to assist a multitude of interpersonal exchange, and at their most basic level function as a mechanism for information transactions.

Similar many other social scientists, CMC researchers are increasingly framing their investigations in the context of social capital, and the relationship between social capital and CMC (for example, Ellison, Steinfield, & Lampe, 2007). Social capital can be an imprecise term, but generally refers to "the ability of actors to secure benefits by virtue of membership in social networks or other social structures" (Portes, 1989, p. 6). Social support is one such form of capital.

The value and qualities of mediated social support has emerged as an important research subject. Discussing earlier research, Bargh and McKenna (2004) argue that CMC appears to have little direct impact on meaningful social interaction with close friends and family, and that there is no apparent decrease in time spent with these strong ties due to Internet use. Rather than substituting for offline social interaction, Bargh and McKenna point to evidence that CMC is actually used to help maintain broader social networks (cf. DiMaggio, Hargittai, Neuman, & Robinson, 2001; Howard, Rainie, & Jones, 2001; Wellman, Haase, Witte, & Hampton, 2001).

Ellison, Steinfeld and Lampe (2007) looked at social capital in the framework of SNS use.

College students were surveyed about their use of Facebook and a range of behaviors were measured along with psychological traits and social capital. Results indicated a positive correlation between many forms of social capital and Facebook participation; while general Internet use did not predict access to social support (bonding social capital), Facebook use was a significant predictor. Ellison et al. (2007) noted that these finding necessitate the assessment of the particular types of online behaviors to explain the social outcomes.

In the present chapter, we suggest that systematic differences in SNS use result from different cultural identities. Specifically, people who identify with more individualistic cultures are likely to engage in more attention-seeking behaviors via SNS, opposed to those who identify with less individualistic cultures. A review of research on CMC and Web2.0 as applied culture is presented below, followed by hypotheses and research questions.

Computer-Mediated Communication and Web 2.0

There has been a wide range of research on communication technologies since the advent of the Internet (for a review of research see Walther & Parks, 2002), and much of this research has compared face-to-face (F2F) communication to CMC to better understand how the two forms of communication may differ. However, some research has concentrated on the social contexts created by CMC as uniquely different from F2F interaction. Spears and Lea (1992) found that the general social context in CMC could be seen as the actual subject matter of the interaction. They also differentiate personal identity and social identity, where personal identity is an individual's multifaceted understanding of their self and one's social identity derives from people's presentation of identity as part of group membership, or the taking on of a social role within the interaction. Thus, CMC can be treated as a medium that heightens consciousness of the social and socially constructed identities. Such added self-awareness produces differing results dependent upon the social context, and is particularly important to consider given the richness of emerging communication technologies, discussed below.

More recently, research attention has shifted towards use of CMC to support existing relationships, like weblogs (Stefanone & Jang, 2007) and social networking sites (boyd, 2007, Ellison, Steinfield, & Lampe, 2007, Kim & Yun, 2007). This parallels a shift in the way Internet users are afforded more opportunity to create and actively manage online content, often referred to as Web 2.0 (O'Reilly, 2005).

Traditionally media content has been the product of media companies, but new user-created and user-focused online platforms such as wikis, blogs, social networking sites and media sharing sites allow for an increased notion of individual media ownership, and thus personal investment in media content. Lenhart and Madden (2005), for example, found that over half of Internet-using teens are creating content in the form of blogs and are sharing photos and videos through a variety of other online services like Facebook, Flickr and YouTube.

SNSs such as Facebook and MySpace have emerged as a focal point for content creation and social interaction, and over 95% of college students have SNS profiles (PACS survey, 2007). boyd (2007, 2008) found that SNS users are modeling identity through social network profiles so that they can write themselves and their community into being in networked publics. More specifically, "[a process of] articulated expression supports critical peer-based sociality because, by allowing youth to hang out amongst their friends and classmates, social network sites are providing teens with a space to work out identity and status, make sense of cultural cues, and negotiate public life" (boyd, 2007, p.2). boyd's research frequently discussed notions of culture, and how SNSs allow users to both learn and perpetuate cultural norms and cues,

but has exclusively focused on subcultures such as youth or gay culture.

A SNS provides a multifunctional platform for personal online content creation, including photo and video sharing, text messaging, commenting on other users' content, blogging, and the main functionality, displaying with whom one is "friends." This so-called friending allows users to visualize their social network of connections in a photo-based display. SNS friends have access to the content of each other's personal profile, which is often not visible to non-friends through the use of privacy settings. The profile may contain photos, videos, personal messages "posted" by other friends, and other personal information such as interests and contact information.

Research interest in SNS use has grown recently, with topics including the study of online self-representation from a sociological perspective (boyd, 2007; Donath & boyd, 2004) and within specific cultural groups (Byrne, 2007; Kim & Yun, 2007). However, given the widespread international usage of many different SNSs, research on how different cultures utilize the large array of behavioral and communicative functionalities of SNS is called for.

Culture and CMC

Hecht, Warren, Jung, & Krieger's (2004) communication theory of identity posits that an individual's identity is not only projected through communication, but that the communication act is part of the self. Thus, communicative behavior should expose some of the uniqueness constituting cultural identity of the self, regardless of medium. Yet, there are few studies that investigate the impact of culture on SNS use. boyd and Ellison (2007) note that further work in the area of culture and SNS behavior is needed.

Systematic differences in language use due to cultural identity are consistent with previously outlined differences regarding the range of individualism in cultures (Ellis & Wittenbaum,

2000). In particular, the verbal endorsement of individuals differed depending on their self-perception. Ellis and Wittenbaum (2000) found a positive correlation between independent scores (which are similar to more individualistic tendencies) and self-promotion, and a negative correlation between interdependent scores (which are similar to les individualistic tendencies) and self-promotion. Broader analysis of computer-mediated communicative behavior has also found cultural differences.

Kim and Yun (2007) found that a Korean SNS reflected many of the collectivistic notions of Korean culture. The bulk of participants utilized the SNS to preserve close relationships with a small number of ties instead of creating new associations with people. Their results are similar to previous constructions of collectivistic culture. Conversely, maintaining large numbers of friends in SNS that one has not actually met in person, known as promiscuous friending (Stefanone, Lackaff, & Rosen, 2008) may characterize the aspiration to meet new people or be seen by many people, rather than purely to maintain relationships. Friending behavior of this type would be consistent with more individualistic cultural identities. Promiscuous friending sacrifices the privacy of the other friends and family in exchange for instrumental personal gains, thus representing a more self-focused behavior.

This evidence suggests that systematic differences in behavior that manifest online should be apparent among people from different cultures, and that these differences correspond to cultural identity. Considering that people from more individualistic cultures behave in more self-serving ways and are generally more likely to pursue attention, the following hypotheses are proposed:

H1. SNS users who identify with more individualistic cultures have larger networks of friends online, opposed to users who identify with less individualistic cultures.

H2. SNS users who identify with more individualistic cultures have larger proportions of friends not met online, opposed to users who identify with less individualistic cultures.

The following research question is included to address the impact of offline social network characteristics on online behavior:

RQ1: What is the relationship between traditional STN size and behavior on SNSs?

Because cultural identity should result in different structural properties of online social networks, it is likely that users will dedicate different levels of cognitive and temporal resources to these relationships. Yet, it is uncertain what the weight of SNS relationships may be considering many of these online "friends" may actually be strangers, consistent with H2. Thus, the following research question is proposed:

RQ2: What is the effect of identifying with a more or less individualistic culture on time spent maintaining profiles on SNSs?

Even though SNS users engage in friending behavior online, these CMC platforms also make possible photo sharing among ones network. Sharing photos online is a form of self-promotion, as it is a method for people to signal aspects of their identity and connection to others. It is expected that people that identify with more individualistic cultural identities are more likely to engage in this self-promotion (see Hui & Triandis, 1986). Thus,

H3. SNS users who identify with more individualistic cultures share more photos of themselves online, opposed to users who identify with less individualistic cultures.

Finally, the following research question is proposed to explore outcomes associated with social networks and SNS use. Taking into consideration Ellison et al.'s (2007) findings which suggest social benefits accrue to SNS users, the current study explores the comparative contributions of conventional, offline social support networks and networks mediated via SNSs as related to different cultural identities. Thus,

RQ3: What is the relationship between the online and traditional network characteristics and satisfaction of SNS users who identify with more individualistic cultures, opposed to users who identify with less individualistic cultures?

METHOD

Online surveys were voluntarily completed by a sample of university students (N=452), and the University Institutional Review Board for Human Subjects approved all materials. Data was obtained from two separate universities to obtain more authentic cultural identities from a larger variety of individuals. One of the universities was a large, multicultural university in the Pacific basin with a majority proportion of students representing Asian culture and identity, and the other was a large university in the northeastern United States with a majority population representing North American culture and identity. The student population at the pacific university resides in a city that is more that 50% Asian with a very strong Asian culture.

To garner cultural information, the participants were asked, "Which of the following BEST describes your ethnic or racial background?" The majority of participants identified their ethnic background as Caucasian (approximately 62%). About 16% were Asian, 6% were African-American, and 3% were Hispanic. The rest (about 13%) identified with a variety of other ethnicities. In terms of cultural identity, however, when asked "Which of the following best describes the cultural background you most identify with?," 319

participants identified with Mainland America (MNA), while only 96 participants identified with the Asia-Pacific Region (APR). To be consistent with cultural tendencies, respondents who identified with Japan, China, and the Philippines were selected to represent APR. The rest of the participants (n = 38) identified from a variety of other cultural backgrounds and were eliminated from the analyses. To check for the strength of participants' identity with their cultural backgrounds, they were asked on a 7-point likert scale, "To what extent do you identify with this cultural background?" (MNA, M=5.35, SD=1.62; APR, M=5.53, SD=1.49), indicating that participants were strongly associated with their cultural backgrounds. In a conservative approach to balance cell sizes for the analyses, a random sample of MNA cases were selected from the data. This resulted in MNA and APR group sizes of 98 and 96, respectively. Upon randomly sampling from the larger MNA population, approximately 60% of the sample was female; the average age of participants remained at 20.3 years (SD = 2.6). 58.5 per cent of participants identified their ethnic background as Caucasian. About 20% were Asian, 6% were African-American, and 3% were Hispanic. The rest (about 11%) identified with a variety of other ethnicities.

People have the capacity to accurately identify people they have frequent interaction with (Marsden, 1990), so offline (traditional) strong tie network STN size was measured using a single item that specifically explained the detailed uniqueness of strong tie affiliations. The question stated, "A strong tie is defined as a person you have known for a long time, have frequent communication with, and positive feelings for. Strong tie relationships include your immediate family members, as well as close friends. How many strong ties would you say you have?" SNS use was measured by asking participants to report the size of their online networks, the proportion of those SNS contacts not met, the number of photos of themselves shared, and how much time on an

Table 1. Correlations (means and standard deviations in parentheses along diagonal)

	Age	Gender	Edu	STN	SNS Size	Time	Not Met	Photo	Gen Sat	Soc Sat
Age	(20.1, 2.4)	0.06	0.64**	-0.04	-0.14**	-0.14*	0.10*	-0.18**	-0.06	-0.05
Gender		-	0.13**	-0.02	-0.08*	-0.15*	0.00	-0.22**	-0.23**	-0.15**
Education			(1.4, 1.0)	-0.02	-0.03	-0.15*	0.06	0.04	0.03	0.10*
STN				(9.0, 6.3)	0.21**	-0.08	0.07	0.18**	0.19**	0.23**
SNS Size					(248.9, 217.1)	0.14*	0.16**	0.52**	0.13**	0.10*
Time Online						(56.3, 51.1)	0.09*	0.12*	-0.06	0.01
Prop. Not Met [log]							(1.0, .58)	0.01	-0.05	-0.08*
Photo [log]								(1.6, .79)	0.23**	0.22**
General Satisfaction									(4.4, 1.2)	0.63**
Social Satisfaction										(4.6, 1.2)

Note: * = p<.05; ** = p < .01

average day they spend online managing their SNS profiles (in hours and minutes). Satisfaction with social life (Deiner, Emmons, Larsen, & Griffin, 1985) assesses the extent to which individuals feel they have adequate communication with friends and family, and was measured with 5 items (Cronbach's α = .76), and Deiner et al.'s (1985) general satisfaction with life scale (4 items) demonstrated a reliability of .74.

Results

Correlations, means, and standard deviations for all items are available in Table 1. Participants also indicated having an average of 248.9 (SD = 217.1) SNS friends, spent an average of 56.3 minutes per session (SD = 51.1) logged into their accounts, and reported that 11 percent (SD = .20) of their SNS friends had not been met in person. This variable was heavily skewed to the right and was log transformed to normalize the distribution for analysis (transformed M = 1.02, SD = .59). For the traditional STN variable, participants reported an average of 9.0 strong tie contacts (SD = 6.3). Finally, the photo-sharing

variable was greatly skewed right (M = 71.9, SD = 68.6) and was log transformed to normalize the distribution (transformed M and SD = 1.57 and .79, respectively).

T-tests were used to determine whether participants from both cultural groups were comparable in terms of age and education; these tests resulted in non-significant differences. MNA participants reported a mean age of 20.5 (SD = 2.9) and educational level of 1.6 (SD = 1.0), and APR participants reported a mean age of 19.9 (SD = 1.6) and educational level of 1.1 (SD = 1.0). Cultural differences in social network structure were apparent, however, as MNA participants reported an average STN size of 10.1 (SD = 7.5) while APR participants claimed only 7.8 strong ties (SD = 6.1, t(194) = 4.74, p < .01). Further, APR participants reported significantly fewer SNS friends (M = 172.5, SD = 162.4) than did MNA participants (M = 310.5, SD = 237.2, t(194) = 2.70, p < .001).

Cultural differences regarding well being were apparent between groups in this study. MNA participants reported higher general satisfaction than APR participants (M = 4.6, SD = 1.2 vs. M

Table 2. Standardized betas for models predicting SNS behavior

	Model 1	Model 2	Model 3	Model 4
	Time Managing Profile	*SNS Network Size*	*Proportion not Met*	*Photo Sharing*
Age	-.112*	-.151**	.017	-.099*
Gender	-.153**	.079	-.033	-.196***
STN Size	-.085	.167**	.044	.097*
Cultural Identity	.080	-.291***	-.274***	-.362***
F (4, 194), Adj. R²	3.91, .04**	14.27, .15***	7.53, .06***	24.17, .20***

*Note: * =p≤.05, ** = p≤.01, *** = p≤.001. For Gender, F=1, M=2; Cultural Identity, 1=MNA, 2=APR.*

= 4.2, SD = 1.1, t(194) = 2.93, p < .01) and with their social lives in particular (M = 4.8, SD = 1.2 vs. M = 4.5, SD = 1.1, t(194) = 2.68, p < .01). Finally, the cultural groups exhibited differences in their use of social web applications. MNA participants indicated that 14.7% of their listed "friends" on social network sites have not been met in person, in contrast to the 5.7% of unmet friends in APR participants' friend lists (t(194) = 3.42, p < .001).

To test the hypotheses and address the research questions, a series of ordinary least squares (OLS) regression models were calculated to control for a set of demographic variables including age, gender and STN size (or, traditional social support network). Results for both sets of analyses are presented in Tables 2 and 3.

Results presented in table 2 suggest that although MNA participants do not spend more time managing their profiles, providing results to answer research question 2, they do have significantly larger mediated networks (β = -.291, p < .001), and have larger proportions of those network relationships not actually met face-to-face (β = -.274, p < .001). Both models predicting time management and SNS size were significant, and

Table 3. Standardized Betas for models predicting satisfaction

		General Satisfaction with Life		Satisfaction with Social Life	
		Traditional	*SNS*	*Traditional*	*SNS*
Age		-.064	-.053	-.105*	-.125*
Gender		-.261***	-.259***	-.202***	-.206***
Cultural Identity		-.168***	-.125*	-.117**	-.121*
Network Size		.127***	.069	.193***	.005
F (4, 194), Adj. R²		14.65, .13***	8.70, .09***	12.58, .11***	5.83, .06***

Note: * =p≤.05, ** = p≤.01, *** = p≤.001. For Gender, F=1, M=2; Cultural Identity, 1=MNA, 2=APR

explained 4 and 15 percent of variance, respectively. Both hypotheses 1 and 2 were supported. In this model cultural identity functions as a unique predictor of friending behavior online; this variable demonstrated a significant relationship with the dependent variable in three out of four models presented in table 2. Further, younger participants spend significantly more time managing their networks, have larger networks and engage in photo sharing to a greater extent than older participants.

Research question 1 addressed the relationship between offline networks and behavior on SNSs. The results suggest that larger STN networks are not significantly related to time spent online managing SNS profiles (β = -.085, ns), but positively related to SNS network size (β = .167, p < .01) and photo sharing (β = .097, p < .05). STN network size did not have a significant relationship with the proportion of friends not met on SNSs.

Results in Table 2 also suggest that participants who identify with more individualistic cultures share significantly more photos online, as hypothesis 3 predicted (β = -.362, p < .001). This model explained 20 per cent of the variance in photo sharing via SNSs.

Table 3 reports standardized betas for OLS regression models predicting two dimensions of participants' satisfaction. These models were calculated to address research question 3 and differentiate between general satisfaction in life and satisfaction with one's social life, as well as social resources accessible via either traditional STNs (i.e., offline friends) and relationships facilitated by SNSs between SNS users who identify with more individualistic cultures, opposed to users who identify with less individualistic cultures.

The models in Table 3 suggest that STN size had the strongest relationship with both general satisfaction (β = .127, p < .001) and satisfaction with social life (β = .193, p < .001). These models explained 13 and 11 percent of the total variance respectively. Interestingly, SNS network size was not significant in either model. MNA

participants reported higher satisfaction in each model, as well.

DISCUSSION

Results presented in this chapter show that there are indeed differences in the way that people who identify with different cultures handle their communicative behaviors within SNSs. All hypotheses were supported and several significant findings help to better understand these cultural differences.

Several hypotheses were offered regarding SNS friending behavior. Hypothesis 1, which proposed that SNS users who identify with more individualistic cultures have larger networks of friends online, opposed to users who identify with less individualistic cultures, was supported. The support of hypothesis 1 indicates that people who identify with more individualistic cultures maintain larger available pools of mediated ties. Individualistic cultures tend to place greater importance on individual achievement, and the maintenance of a larger network catalyzes an increased ability to leverage resources.

The behavior of SNS friending behavior of promiscuous friending, i.e. the proportion of friends not met, has emerged as a unique communicative behavior largely enabled by SNSs. Many people keep in touch with large numbers of their friends and family in a variety of ways (which would be represented by the raw number of friends online), but until communication technologies became more common it was far less common to share directed contact and private information with people that one had not met in person. Further, the measure of promiscuous friending in this study is a proportion, and therefore controls for network size.

To address the promiscuous friending behavior, hypothesis 2 proposed that SNS users who identify with more individualistic cultures have larger proportions of friends not met online in contrast to those who identify with less individualistic cultures, and was supported. When friending people that one does not know, SNS users are sacrificing the personal privacy of anyone in their SNS network that does not have the maximum privacy setting on their profile. These behaviors can be understood as promoting an individualistic objective by increasing the size of the personal social network at the expense of the collective by exposing the existing personal network to unknown and potentially unwelcome social contacts. With most SNSs, one cannot view the contents of someone's personal profile unless friended by them, or sharing a mutual friend; general browsing does not result in access to personal profile contents.

Findings in support of hypotheses 1 and 2 indicate that earlier research on the cultural tendency of more individualistic cultures to engage in personal self-promotion in offline contexts has been mirrored online. SNS users in the current study who identify with more individualistic cultures engaged in personal self-promotion through large friendship networks as well as more promiscuous friending. A potential explanation of these findings is that personal self-promotion is closely related to creating ties with unknown people. On the other hand, it also make sense that people who identify with less individualistic cultures, valuing family and in-group ties, are less likely to sacrifice their in-groups' private information to extend their online network.

Hypothesis 3, which indicated that SNS users who identify with more individualistic cultures share more photos of themselves online, opposed to users who identify with less individualistic cultures, was supported. This finding indicates that individuals who identified with mainland American culture made use of Web 2.0 technology to engage in more self-promotion than those that identified with Asian culture. Online photo sharing is a form of self-promotion and established a great personal presence amongst networked contacts. Paired with the findings from H1 and H2, this finding established an understanding of online

cultural behavior that supports earlier theory and research on individualistic cultures. People that identify with more individualistic cultures tend to engage in self-promotion, are more likely to place the needs of the self above the needs of the in-group for the purpose of resource attainment.

Research question 1 queried the relationship between traditional STN size and behavior on SNSs, since one of the main goals of the current research is to investigate the degree to which offline behaviors persist online. The main finding is that SNS users who maintain larger offline strong-tie networks have larger online networks, indicating that their F2F networking behavior is indicative of their use of networking Web 2.0 technologies. These findings are in line with research on social capital, but expand our understanding of people's use of communication technologies to network their resources. Online social interactions are not simply scaled-up representations of individuals and ties, and do not unconditionally reflect offline behavior (Garton, Haythornthwaite, & Wellman, 1997). It is important for both information technology developers and researchers to understand how offline relations affect online relations, and how computer-mediated communication may or may not change behavior. SNS represent one of the most widely used networking tools to emerge in recent years, and it is an interesting finding that SNS users online network size is positively related to their STN size. It certainly could have been reasonable to expect that people who retain larger offline networks would not seek larger online ones, as they already have a rich access to resources, but this was not the case.

Research question 2 addresses the amount of time one spends maintaining SNS profiles regarding cultural differences. There were no cultural differences, but significant difference between the genders, a finding that warrants further research.

Research question 3 queried the relationship between SNS users' online and traditional network characteristics, and satisfaction. STN size was only predictor of both general satisfaction as well as social satisfaction, which is in line with prior social network research that indicates better-connected people are more successful in their relationships, life, and business. What is also interesting is that those who identify with North American (MNA) cultures were more satisfied that those who identify with Asian or Pacific Rim (APR) cultures. SNS network size was not significant which suggests that face-to-face contacts are more significant to satisfaction than computer-mediated social contacts. Online social support is indeed a very important and fitting use of this technology, but given a general life context, offline networks seem to be more important that online networks. Regarding satisfaction with social life both STN and culture were significant. MNA respondents were more satisfied than APR ones, and those with larger STN were more satisfied, which is consistent for both traditional as well as SNS network sizes.

The research presented in this chapter was exploratory and possesses several limitations that we hope to address in future research. The equivalence of identifying with a national background with having more or less individualistic cultural values, while present in scholarly cultural analyses, represents a somewhat rough categorization of a nuanced phenomenon. The measurement of culture using the more complex constructs advocated by Triandis and others (Triandis, 2001; Triandis & Gelfand, 1998) may yield more nuanced results. Yet, as presented in the literature section, there are several methodological issues with many of the more specific measures of culture as well. Further, the cultural identities of others in the social network should be taken into account: Facebook remains a predominantly North American social networking site, in contrast to other platforms such as CyWorld and Orkut, which may have unique technical structures leading to different behaviors. Additionally, using a greater number of measures used to determine SNS behavior will strengthen future research. Ellison et al.'s (2007)

Facebook Intensity Scale provides an interesting example of an effort to summarize the very broad range of behaviors and attitudes that may point to the intensity of SNS use. Finally, individuals' offline behaviors may differ from their online behaviors, and using self-report data only allows for inferences to be made regarding the association between the two contexts.

Cultural differences can manifest in many forms, and the research in this chapter has found that people who identify with different cultural orientations behave and communicate differently. The current research investigated the extent to which cultural norms, such as individualistic cultures, persist in online behavior. Findings presented in this chapter maintain the notion that people of different cultures do indeed behave in different ways when using communication technologies like social networking sites.

REFERENCES

Bargh, J. A., & McKenna, K. Y. A. (2004). The Internet and social life. *Annual Review of Psychology, 55*, 573–590. doi:10.1146/annurev. psych.55.090902.141922

boyd, d. (2007). Why youth (heart) social network sites: The role of networked publics in teenage social life. In D. Buckingham (Ed.) *MacArthur Foundation series on digital learning- Youth, identity, and digital media* (pp. 119-142).Cambridge, MA: MIT Press .

boyd, d. (2008). Facebook's privacy trainwreck: Exposure, invasion, and social convergence. *Convergence, 14* (1), 13-20.

boyd, d., and Ellison, N.. (2007). Social network sites: Definition, history and scholarship.*Journal of Computer-Mediated Communication, 13*(1), article 11.

Byrne, D. N. (2007). Public discourse, community concerns, and civic engagement: Exploring black social networking traditions on BlackPlanet.com. *Journal of Computer-Mediated Communication, 13*(1), 16.

Diener, E., Emmons, R. A., Larsen, R. J., & Griffin, S. (1985). The satisfaction with life scale. *Journal of Personality Assessment, 49,* 71–75. doi:10.1207/s15327752jpa4901_13

DiMaggio, P., Hargittai, E., Neuman, W. R., & Robinson, J. P. (2001). Social implications of the Internet. *Annual Review of Sociology, 27,* 307–336. doi:10.1146/annurev.soc.27.1.307

Donath, J., & boyd, d. (2004). Public displays of connection. *BT Technology Journal, 22,* 71–82. doi:10.1023/B:BTTJ.0000047585.06264.cc

Ellis, B., & Wittenbaum, G. M. (2000). Relationships between self-construal and verbal promotion. *Communication Research, 27,* 704–722. doi:10.1177/009365000027006002

Ellison, N. B., Steinfield, C., & Lampe, C. (2007). The benefits of Facebook "friends:" Social capital and college students' use of online social network sites. *Journal of Computer-Mediated Communication, 12*(4). doi:10.1111/j.1083-6101.2007.00367.x

Garton, L., Haythornthwaite, C., & Wellman, B. (1997). Studying online social networks. *Journal of Computer-Mediated Communication, 3*(1).

Green, E. G. T., Deschamps, J.-C., & Páez, D. (2005). Variation of Individualism and Collectivism Within and Between 20 Countries. *Journal of Cross-Cultural Psychology, 36,* 321–339. doi:10.1177/0022022104273654

Hancock, J. T., & Dunham, P. J. (2004). Impression formation in computer-mediated communication revisited: An analysis of the breadth and intensity of impressions. *Communication Research, 28,* 325–347. doi:10.1177/009365001028003004

Hecht, M. L., Warren, J., Jung, J., & Krieger, J. (2004). Communication theory of identity. In Gudykunst, W. B. (Ed.), *Theorizing about intercultural communication* (pp. 257–278). Newbury Park, CA: Sage.

Hofstede, G. (1980). *Culture consequences: International differences in work-related values.* Thousand Oaks, CA: Sage.

Hofstede, G. (2001). *Culture's consequences* (2nd ed.). Thousand Oaks, CA: Sage.

Howard, P. E. N., Rainie, L., & Jones, S. (2001). Days and nights on the Internet. *The American Behavioral Scientist, 45,* 383–404.

Hui, C. H., & Triandis, H. C. (1986). Individualism–collectivism: a study of cross-cultural researchers. *Journal of Cross-Cultural Psychology, 17,* 225–248. doi:10.1177/0022002186017002006

Kim, K. H., & Yun, H. (2007). Cying for me, Cying for us: Relational dialectics in a Korean social network site. *Journal of Computer-Mediated Communication, 13*(1), 15.

Kim, M. S., Hunter, J. E., Miyahara, A., Horvath, A., & Bresnahan, M. (1994). Individual vs. culture-level dimensions of individualism and collectivism: Effects on preferred conversation styles. *Communication Monographs, 63,* 29–49. doi:10.1080/03637759609376373

Lapointe, D. K., & Gunawardena, C. A. (2004). Developing, testing, and refining a model to understand the relationship between peer interaction and learning outcomes in computer-mediated conferencing. *Distance Education, 25,* 83–106. doi:10.1080/0158791042000212477

Lenhart, A., & Madden, M. (2005). *Teen content creators and consumers.* Washington, DC: Pew Internet & American Life Project. Retrieved April 2, 2008, from http://www.pewinternet.org/PPF/r/166/report_display.asp

Marsden, P. V. (1990). Network data and measurement. *Annual Review of Sociology*, *16*, 435–463. doi:10.1146/annurev.so.16.080190.002251

O'Reilly, T. (2005). What is Web 2.0? Design patterns and business models for the next generation of software. Retrieved October 29, 2007, from http://www.oreillynet.com/pub/a/oreilly/tim/news/2005/09/30/what-is-web-20.html

Oyserman, D., Coon, H. M., & Kemmelmeier, M. (2002). Rethinking individualism and collectivism: Evaluation of theoretical assumptions and meta-analyses. *Psychological Bulletin*, *128*, 3–72. doi:10.1037/0033-2909.128.1.3

Portes, A. (1989). Social capital: Its origins and applications in modern sociology. *Annual Review of Sociology*, *24*, 1–24. doi:10.1146/annurev.soc.24.1.1

Profile of the American College Student (PACS) Survey. (2007). Profile *of the American College Student: University of Missouri-Columbia*. Columbia, MO: Institutional Research, UMC. Retrieved April 3, 2008 from http://ir.missouri.edu/reports-presentations.html

Schimmack, U., Oishi, S., & Diener, E. (2005). Individualism: A valid and important dimension of cultural differences between nations. *Personality and Social Psychology Review*, *9*(1), 17–31. doi:10.1207/s15327957pspr0901_2

Scott, J. (2000). *Social network analysis: A handbook*. Thousand Oaks, CA: Sage.

Shavitt, S., Lalwani, A., Zhang, J., & Torelli, C. (2006). The horizontal/vertical distinction in cross-cultural consumer research. *Journal of Consumer Psychology*, *16*, 325–342. doi:10.1207/s15327663jcp1604_3

Spears, R., & Lea, M. (1992). Social influence in CMC. In Lea, M. (Ed.), *Contexts of computer-mediated communication* (pp. 30–65). London, UK: Harvester Wheatsheaf.

Stefanone, M. A., & Jang, C. Y. (2007). Writing for friends and family: The interpersonal nature of blogs. *Journal of Computer-Mediated Communication*, *13*(1), 123–140. doi:10.1111/j.1083-6101.2007.00389.x

Stefanone, M. A., & Lackaff, D. (2009). Reality television as a model for online behavior: Blogging, photo and video sharing. *Journal of Computer-Mediated Communication*, *14*(4), 964–987. doi:10.1111/j.1083-6101.2009.01477.x

Stefanone, M. A., Lackaff, D., & Rosen, D. (2008). We're all stars now: Reality television, Web 2.0, and mediated identities. In *Proceedings of ACM's Hypertext, Culture and Communication*. New York: Association for Computing Machinery (ACM).

Triandis, H. C. (2001). Individualism-collectivism and personality. *Journal of Personality*, *69*, 907–924. doi:10.1111/1467-6494.696169

Triandis, H. C., & Gelfand, M. J. (1998). Converging measurement of horizontal and vertical individualism and collectivism. *Journal of Personality and Social Psychology*, *74*, 118–128. doi:10.1037/0022-3514.74.1.118

Walther, J. B., & Parks, M. R. (2002). Cues filtered out, cues filtered in: Computer-mediated communication and relationships. In Knapp, M. L., & Daly, J. A. (Eds.), *Handbook of Interpersonal Communication* (3rd ed., pp. 529–563). Thousand Oaks, CA: Sage.

Wellman, B., Quan-Haase, A., Witte, J., & Hampton, K. (2001). Does the Internet increase, decrease, or supplement social capital? *The American Behavioral Scientist*, *45*, 436–455. doi:10.1177/00027640121957286

Chapter 20

The Representation of National Political Freedom on Web Interface Design:
A Comparative Study of Government-Based and Business-Oriented Web Sites

Rowena Li
Bayside High School Library, New York

ABSTRACT

The purpose of this chapter is to explore the representation of national political freedom on Web interface design by using power distance, one of the culture dimensions identified by Geert Hofstede, as a measurement. It also aims to determine if there are any differences between government-based Web sites and business-oriented Web sites in representing national political freedom. This study applied seven indicators validated from previous study (Li, 2009) in coding 312 Web sites selected from 39 countries and analyzed national political freedom represented on these Web sites with content analysis method. The result of two-way analysis of variance (ANOVA) indicated that large differences exist in Web interface design, which in turn reflects the aforementioned national political freedom. The research showed that the mean effect of freedom level between free-country group, partly-free-country group and not-free-country group was statistically significant ($p = .003$). So was the mean effect of Web site type between government-based and business-oriented Web sites ($p = .000$). Furthermore, the interaction between the freedom level and Web site type was also significant ($p = .041$). Therefore, we conclude that Web interface design correlates with a country's political freedom level and government-based Web sites embody more of a nation's authority and supremacy than business-oriented Web sites do. It is expected that this study furthers our exploration in culture dimensions on Web interface design and advances our knowledge in sociological and cultural studies of the Web.

DOI: 10.4018/978-1-61520-827-2.ch020

INTRODUCTION

With the rapid increase of global communication and economic exchange on the Internet, various regions and communities across the globe are now connected using this technology. The Internet has become one of the most important vehicles of communication by which we express our opinions and thoughts. A Web page, especially the homepage, is one of the most popular means for an organization or a business entity to disseminate its information to the public. It also has become the most important channel through which the organization establishes its own existence and value. As a result, the Web page has grown to be one of the most dependable resources for information-seeking endeavors.

As computer-based communication has taken its lead in global information exchange, Web developers and researchers have become aware of the inevitable impact of local culture traits on user interface design. In fact, Web interfaces not only reflect the linguistic aspects (language, date, and time formats) of the country, but also represent the culture characteristics (values, morals, and ethics) of the norm (Ford & Gelderblom, 2003). Therefore, it has become necessary to identify fundamental international cultural dimensions, with which local cultural characteristics can be analyzed and compared. In this way, Web designers and analysts are able to design user interfaces in such a way that the interfaces coordinate with local cultures in order to achieve the Web site's optimal effects.

Language has been considered one of the most powerful means for interpersonal, international, and intercultural communications. Several studies have explored the relationships between language, culture, reality, and thought, laying a solid theoretical foundation for the study of cultural representation in user interface design. Ludwig Wittgenstein's Picture Theory of Meaning states that language reflects reality and mirrors the world (1953, 2003). The theory of Semiotics, led by Swiss linguist Ferdinand de Saussure and American philosopher Charles Sanders Peirce, claims that language, one of the forms of a "sign," not only represents reality, but also bears its own social convention and cultural elements (Chandler, 2002; Eco, 1976; Jakobson, 1971; Ogden & Richards, 1923; Peirce, 1931-58; Saussure, 1966). Furthermore, the Sapir-Whorf Hypothesis asserts that the structure of language reflects and even determines our way of thinking and viewing the world. Language is the symbolic guide to culture. By studying language, the cultural elements embedded within will be revealed (Sapir, 1963, 1964; Whorf, 1988).

In response, several cultural models have been developed in culture studies during the past decade (Hall & Hall, 1989; Hofstede, 2001; Hofstede & Hofstede, 2005; Hoft, 1996; Stewart & Bennett, 1991; Trompenaars & Hampden-Turner, 1998). Among these models, after analyzing surveys conducted in 72 countries, Geert Hofstede developed five primary cultural dimensions to assist in differentiating cultures. The five cultural dimensions are *power distance*, *collectivism versus individualism*, *femininity versus masculinity*, *uncertainty avoidance*, and *long-term versus short-term orientation*. Subsequently, Marcus and Gould (2000) extended Hofstede's (2001) cultural theory to Web interface design. Their study illustrated how each of Hofstede's five cultural dimensions is represented on Web pages through examples from several different countries. Gould, Zakaria, and Yusof (2000) compared culture orientations and design preferences of Malaysian and U.S. Web sites with Hofstede's cross-cultural model and Marcus's (Marcus & Gould, 2000) Web application theory. N. Singh, Kumar, & Baack (2005) and N. Singh, Zhao, & Hu (2003, 2005) in recent years have also applied Hofstede's (2001) cultural dimensions with Marcus and Gould's (2000) vision in their pragmatic research for the purpose of validating cultural value framework and analyzing cultural content on various country Web sites.

While we examine the cultural and social attributes characterized on a Web site, one of the most important areas to consider is its power/authority representation. Since power and authority create a special social feature for a society's culture, the dominant groups in the society influence all cultures to some extent. Therefore, power becomes one of the aspects of culture. As power and culture are the two inseparable fundamentals in the study of a society, the analysis of a culture is associated with the examination of power relations within a society. The Web page, a communicative form of the language, inevitably represents, constructs, and reproduces both social and cultural inequality. As a result, *power distance*, one of the five cultural dimensions defined by Geert Hofstede, has received a great amount of interest by researchers.

Since Marcus and Gould (2000) first defined seven indicators on Web interface design representing Hofstede's (2001) *power distance*, Gould, Zakaria, and Yusof (2000) also concluded three other *power distance* indicators from Malaysian Web sites. Consequently, N. Singh, Zhao, and Hu (2003, 2005) presented six cultural categories in their research. Later on, Li's study (2009) distilled 10 *power distance* indicators from these studies and systematically and statistically validated these indicators. It concluded that seven indicators might be used in the future study as the defining indicators for representing national political freedom on Web interface design.

In this research, these validated indicators were applied to substantiate whether national political freedom is represented on Web interface design. This research also intends to determine if government-based Web sites and business-oriented Web sites represent national political freedom on the same level. Previous studies have involved business-oriented Web sites in the study of cultural dimensions to investigate the effectiveness and customers' response on cross-

cultural marketing and advertisement. However, no study has made an effort to explore the differences among various types of Web sites and their unique representations of cultural dimensions. The comparison between government-based Web sites and business-oriented Web sites on national political freedom representation in this study serves as the first to explore the differences among diverse Web site sectors of cultural representation on Web interface design. It is believed that a government agency represents the power of its government and a business entity aims to provide goods or services to its customers. Thus, the purpose of a government-based Web site is to introduce its officials and its policy to the public and to reflect the authority of the agency, while the function of a business-oriented Web site is to sell its merchandise and introduce its services to customers. Therefore, the construction of these two types of Web sites may not be the same. Based on this assumption, this research intends to find out whether these two different types of Web sites respond the same in representing national political freedom. A close cross-sectional examination of the Web interface design from 39 countries with 312 government-based and business-oriented Web sites was conducted to fulfill this purpose.

By examining national political freedom represented on the Web page, this study not only provides an insight into culture dimensions and Web interface design, but also extends the study of cross-cultural communication to the field of human-computer interaction and their usability within culture. Furthermore, the Web analysis of this cultural framework extends to 39 countries as well as to 2 Web site sectors. Through this analysis, this research will provide a framework for future investigations in evaluating cultural dimensions in different Web site sectors, such as university/college Web sites, news and media Web sites, entertainment Web sites, sports Web sites and so on. Web interface designers will be able to consider validated *power distance* indicators in designing culturally adapted Web sites for their international users. Information scientists, sociologists, and anthropologists will also find this research helpful in promoting understanding between cultures by examining Web page's characteristics.

Research Questions

By employing *power distance* as a measurement for national political freedom, this research focuses on the following questions:

- To what extent is a country's political freedom represented on Web interface design?
- Does any statistical difference exist between a country's government-based Web sites and its business-oriented Web sites in representing its political freedom?

REVIEW OF THE LITERATURE

With the intention of introducing background information and related research to support this study, this section presents the fundamental theories gathered from other related research fields, as well as current research development trends in the same area. It starts with the discussion of linguistic and philosophical theories on language, culture, and reality, including Wittgenstein's picture theory of meaning, the theory of Semiotics and the Sapir-Whorf Hypothesis. These postulations explore in great depth the relationships between culture and its representation in language. In addition, this section gives an overview of the main concepts and theories in cross-cultural communication by providing an outline of the major works in this area. More research on culture and user interface design, especially Geert Hofstede's model on cultural dimensions, is presented towards the end of the section.

Language, Reality, and Culture: Philosophical, Psychological, and Linguistic Interpretations on their Interrelations

The interrelations between language, reality, and culture have been explored in a great depth from philosophical, psychological, and linguistic perspectives. Wittgenstein's Picture Theory of Meaning and his subsequent language game theory, the theory of Semiotics, and Sapir-Whorf Hypothesis have elaborated the relations from three different viewpoints.

Wittgenstein (2003) stated that sentences in language, or mental representations, are pictures of facts. In his view, the logical structure of words corresponds to the actual structure in reality. In his unique way, Wittgenstein provided us with a view that language (linguistic representation) not only reflects pictures (mental representation), but also mirrors all the aspects of reality. However, in his later works, Wittgenstein (1953, 1958) realized that the function of language alone could not mirror the reality. He augmented his earlier theory by saying that language cannot simply be perceived as a one–to-one mapping to the object in the world. Instead, it should be understood and perceived from the social context in which it is situated.

On the other hand, the theory of Semiotics views the relationship between language, thought and reality from a psychological perspective. It examines how reality is reflected and interpreted in a human mind and how the interpretation of the reality is influenced by experience and prior knowledge. Saussure (1966) stated that linguistic sign unites two elements: concept (signifier) and sound/image (signified). A signifier refers to the concept the sign indicates; a signified refers to the image or sound reflected in a human mind when he/she reads the sign. He stated that the creation and interpretation of the new signified and signifier come from the individual's interpretation of previous signs, which is influenced by his/her past experiences and cultural environment.

Further advanced by Eco (1990), his theory of "unlimited semiosis" states that triadic model could lead to a series of successive interpretants. Since every sign has an interpretant, which in turn is the representamen of another sign, semiosis is successive and unlimited. Therefore, in the process of making signs, culture elements have been programmed into the codes. At the same time, the process of decoding signs is also socially and culturally conditioned. It is inevitable that cultural conventions have penetrated and become interwoven into the production and interpretation of the codes. As we study the patterns and relationships underneath these codes, specific cultural patterns surface. Furthermore, the understanding of high amount of abstract concepts in language depends greatly on the classification and categorization of the related concepts, and this mental process is determined once again by the social conventions and cultural heritage (Chandler, 2002).

Furthermore, the Sapir-Whorf hypothesis looks at the relations of reality and language from a linguistic perspective. This hypothesis contains two associated propositions: one is that the world is experienced and viewed distinctly within different language communities (linguistic relativity); and the other is that language determines these differences (linguistic determinism) (Cole & Scriber, 1974). Sapir (1963) defined language as a guide conditioning our thoughts. He claimed, "Language is a guide to 'social reality.' ... It powerfully conditions all our thinking about social problems and processes" (p.162). Whorf furthered his predecessor's theory by saying it is through language that culture influences an individual's view of the world. Whorf (1988) stated

The background linguistic system (in other words, the grammar) of each language is not merely a reproducing instrument for voicing ideas but rather is itself a shaper of ideas, the program and guide for the individual's mental activity, for his analysis of impressions, for his synthesis of his

mental stock in trade. (p. 212)

In conclusion, Ludwig Wittgenstein's earlier Picture Theory of Meaning, together with his later language game theory, has provided us with a solid theoretical underpinning for the examination of cultural elements represented in language on web content and interface design. The theory of Semiotics has also provided us with a profound philosophical and psychological foundation for decoding and analyzing cultural and social elements in language representation. The Sapir-Whorf hypothesis is based on the premises that language is part of culture. Therefore, the study of language leads to the unraveling of the cultural elements situated in language, including web interface design on the webpage. Its attraction lies both in the study of cultural differences and cultural relativity, as well as in the relation of culture to linguistic structure and language translatability. As the Internet has become a new means of language representation, the impact of this hypothesis extends beyond to the study of cultural representation on web content and interface design.

Language and Representation

Language is regarded as the primary means by which each generation receives its cultural heritage, whether in oral or written form. As language bears both its structural and semantic aspects, it is certain that we study not only the phonology and syntax of the language, but also its "self-contained systems of meanings" (Hoijer, 1974, p. 123). Since language is the foundation of social and cultural experiences, it is regarded as the mirror of the reality, reflecting the culture, power structure, and shared values of a society. With the analysis of language patterns, certain culture essences will be revealed. Therefore, language is a valuable source of cultural and social analysis.

Representation means "a symbol or image, or the process of presenting to the eye or the mind"

(Williams, 1983, p. 269). It is through language, in the form of sounds, words, images, or objects that a representational system is built to convey our thoughts, ideas, and feelings. As Hall (2003) once stated, "Representation is the production of the meaning of the concepts in our minds through language. It is the link between concepts and language which enables us to refer to either the 'real' world of objects, people or events, or indeed to imaginary worlds of fictional objects, people and events" (p. 17). O'Connor (1996) expanded on the definition of representation as "the set of means by which one thing stands for another. ... Representation is a complex web of attributes of disparate objects and concepts, idiosyncratic and socially constructed codes and agreements, and neurological abilities" (p. 11). Here he includes social codes and conventions into the concept of representation.

Moreover, images, a special form of representation, can also bring in a variety of visual dimensions depending on the depth, orientation, and arrangement of objects represented in the pictures. Although images are the reproduction of reality, they are not simply copies of the reality, but rather the creation of the photographer's view of seeing the world. Thus, images can be a photographer's way of expressing his/her own perspectives, which carry his/her cultural and social morals. Berger (1977) powerfully expressed this idea in the following passage:

Every image embodies a way of seeing. Even a photograph. For photographs are not, as is often assumed, a mechanical record....The photographer's way of seeing is reflected in his choice of subject. (p. 9-10)

Cultural Dimensions and Cross-Cultural Theories

Hofstede (2001) defined culture as "the collective programming of the mind that distinguishes the members of one group or category of people from another" (p. 9). In recent years, an increasing number of studies in information systems have focused on the role of culture on information architecture worldwide. Cultural models have been developed and tested by several researchers. Stewart and Bennett (1991) established their cultural model in two basic aspects: objective culture and subjective culture. Numerous cultural analysts have also used the iceberg model (Hoft, 1995) to view culture dimensions, which states that explicit artifacts only consist of 10% of the iceberg above the water while the rest of implicit cultural features submerge under the surface, not easily identified. Hall and Hall (1989) uncovered seven dimensions of cross-cultural communication patterns, which include *speed of messages, high context versus low context, space, time, information flow, interfacing,* and *action chains*. Trompenaars and Hampden-Turner (1998) established the onion model consisting of three layers: an explicit layer with artifacts and products, a middle layer reflecting norms and values, and a core of basic assumptions about human existence.

In spite of the existence of a wide range of cultural models, Hofstede's cultural dimension theory has become the most quoted in cross-cultural and Web usability studies. Between 1967 and 1973, Hofstede conducted two large surveys with the employees in the subsidiaries of multinational IBM Corporation in 20 languages, 38 occupations, and 72 countries. Altogether there were more than 116,000 questionnaires collected with over 100 questions in each (Hofstede, 2001). A correlation and factor analysis of the answers to the survey gathered from all these countries revealed several cultural fusions. These are the common variables, which can be used to measure cultural differences:

1. *Power distance* measures how subordinates respond to power and authority. It measures the degree of equality or inequality between people in a society.

2. *Collectivism versus individualism* measures the relationship among individuals. In individualistic culture, individuals value more on individualism; while in collectivist culture, individuals view more on community and society;

3. *Masculinity versus femininity* measures the degree to which a culture views its gender roles. Masculine cultures tend to view males as tough conquerors and females as tender homemakers, while feminine cultures tend to reduce these gender differences;

4. *Uncertainty avoidance* measures the extent people feel about uncertain situations (Marcus, 2005).

In 1980, Geert Hofstede and Michael Harris Bond from Chinese University of Hong Kong conducted a new questionnaire survey, the Chinese value survey. With 100 students (50 men and 50 women) selected from each of the 23 countries, the Chinese value survey yielded the fifth cultural dimension, *long-term versus short-term orientation* (Hofstede & Hofstede, 2005). Since then, these five cultural dimensions have been used as a basic framework to assess various cultural aspects in culture studies.

Recent Development on the Study of Cultural Dimensions

Cultural dimensions, particularly Geert Hofstede's (2001) five cultural dimensions and Edward T. Hall's dimension (Hall & Hall, 1989) of high-context versus low-context communication have been applied to a variety of research fields, especially cross-cultural marketing and advertising research. De Mooij's (2000) study used Hofstede's (2001) five cultural dimensions as independent variables against data on the change of product consumption of mineral water, cars, and Internet usage in 15 European countries over 20 years. He concluded that national cultures influence consumer behavior and that the future of international marketing is

quite predictable. As Internet and communication technology have permeated into all aspects of society, several studies focused on culture's impact on Internet and technology diffusion.

La Ferle, Edwards, and Musuno (2002) examined the impact of Hofstede's four dimensions on Internet diffusion in Japan and the United States. They found that cultural factors affect the degree of Internet growth. After an examination of the relationship between Hofstede's dimensions and Internet adoption rate of 62 countries, Nath and Murthy (2004) confirmed that the degree of *uncertainty avoidance* and *masculinity* in a country correlates to its rate of Internet adoption. Furthermore, Zakour (2004), based on Hofstede's cultural dimensions, established a technology acceptance model in his research. In the most recent study, S. Singh (2006) employed four of Hofstede's dimensions to national cultures to examine the adoption patterns of new products and the innovative and imitative behavior of consumers.

In addition, Hofstede's (2001) cultural dimension model has been used to examine information process (Steinwachs, 1999), the concept of the Internet as a virtual cultural region (Johnston & Johal, 1999), Internet portal (Zahir, Dobing, & Hunter, 2002), and e-gaming (Kale, 2006). A similar study, conducted by Burgmann, Kitchen, and Williams (2006), employed two of Hofstede's cultural dimensions *power distance* and *uncertainty avoidance* to explore the impact of culture on graphical user interface (GUI) design with comparative content analysis. The results showed that culture, at least partially, influenced graphical user interface design.

Furthermore, Hofstede's and Hall's cultural variables have established foundations in empirical research on Web-based communication and user-interface design as well. Marcus's study made great contributions to cross-cultural study by applying Hofstede's cultural dimension theory to a new area: Web interface design (Marcus, 2005; Marcus & Gould, 2000). Marcus (2005) asserted that user-interface has five components:

metaphors, mental models, navigation, interaction, and appearance. He mapped Hofstede's five cultural dimensions to each of these user interface components and defined cultural indicators for these user interface components.

Specifically, Marcus and Gould (2000) pointed out that *power distance* may influence several aspects of user-interface design, such as symmetric layout, information highly structured, hierarchies in mental model, nationalism or religion, focus on authority, official stamp, restricted security and restrictions to access, and restricted managerial sections. At the same time, Gold, Zakaria, and Yusof (2000) examined three Malaysian and three US Web sites in their study and concluded that prominent organizational charts, special title on members of the organization, and information arranged according to the management hierarchy are strong *power distance* indicators.

Recently, the most influential application of Hofstede's cultural dimension theory to Web content is those of Nitish Singh's (N. Singh, Kumar, & Baack, 2005; N. Singh, Zhao & Hu, 2003, 2005). In the past three years, N. Singh, with his colleagues, used content analysis method to investigate cultural content as well as cultural adaptation on Web site design. N. Singh, Zhao, and Hu (2003) compared 40 U.S-based company Web sites with their Chinese Web sites to investigate their cultural adaptation. They (2005) also conducted a cross-national comparison of China, India, Japan, and US. Later, N. Singh advanced his research into the investigation of e-commerce firms (N. Singh, Kumar, & Baack, 2005). All of the three studies revealed that Web content and design reflect local cultural values. Moreover, Li (2009) builds on these previous researches by focusing on the validation of national political freedom indicators. Two coders performed content analysis on 156 college/university Web sites selected from 39 countries. One-way analysis of variance (ANOVA) was applied to analyze each of the proposed ten indicators in order to detect statistical significant differences among three

freedom groups. The results indicated that six out of the ten proposed indicators could be used to measure a country's national political freedom on Web interface design. They are, *special title conferred on members of the organization, monumental building, authority figure, symbol of nationalism or religion, link to information about the leaders of the organization, information arranged according to the management hierarchy.* The seventh indicator, *symmetric layout,* demonstrated a negative correlation between the freedom level and the Web representation of *power distance.* The rest three proposed indicators, *official stamp or logo, security barrier not accessible,* and *manager section forbidden for access,* failed to show any significant differences among the treatment means and there are no clear trend patterns for the treatment means of the three freedom groups.

However, the study of cultural value representation on Web interface design remains to be an unfamiliar field. Very few studies have extended cultural dimensions to the study of cultural content on Web interface design and there are not enough studies exploring what types of Web sites best represent each of the cultural dimensions mentioned in Hofstede's (2001) and Hall and Hall's (1989) studies through Web content and design analysis. This research is to explore if national political freedom is in fact represented on Web interface design by using *power distance,* one of the culture dimensions identified by Geert Hofstede, as a measurement. It is also the intention of this study to determine if there are any differences in representing national political freedom on government-based Web sites and business-oriented Web sites.

RESEARCH DESIGN

By employing *power distance* as a measurement for national political freedom, this study focuses on following questions:

1. To what extent is a country's national political freedom represented on Web interface design?
2. Does any statistical difference exist between a country's government-based Web sites and its business-oriented Web sites in representing national political freedom?

Dependent Variable

The dependent variable for this research is the Web representation of *power distance*. It is the sum of the scores derived from content analysis on each Web site for seven *power distance* indicators. These indicators have been verified in Li's study (2009) and they are:

1. Symmetric layout
2. Special title conferred on members of the organization
3. Monumental building
4. Authority figure
5. Symbol of nationalism or religion
6. Link to information about the leaders of the organization
7. Information arranged according to the management hierarchy

Independent Variables

Two independent variables are involved in this research: Web site types (government-based and business-oriented) and freedom levels (Free-country Group, Partly-free-country Group, and Not-free-country Group).

The variable, Web site type, is determined according to the origination and functionality of the Web site. Government-based Web sites include any Web sites designed officially for offices and institutions, which belong to and work for the government of a country. However, personal Web sites for government officials, such as the official Web site of a president, are not included in this category, since the design of a personal Web site

is different from that of an institutional Web site. Business-oriented Web sites consist of any company Web sites. The company can be owned by an individual or by a board of trustees. However, the company's Web site has to be a local company Web site, not a Web site developed for an international audience. For instance, if Sony Corporation's Web site is included in business-oriented Web site category, only the Web site designed for the Japanese at http://www.sony.co.jp/ can be considered for this research, since only this Web site represents best the culture of Japan. Other Sony Web sites, SONY USA or SONY Canada, may be designed to customize other cultures.

The variable, freedom level, is determined by a conceptual variable: Freedom. The conceptual variable Freedom is measured in Appendix A provided by Freedom House.

Freedom House is an independent non-profit and non-partisan institution, which advocates for the expansion of democracy and freedom around the world. Freedom House has become a leading activist in promoting democratic values through its international programs and publications, and its standard annual publications include Freedom in the World, Freedom of the Press, Nations in Transit, and Countries at Crossroads (Freedom House, 2006a). Conducted by analysts and senior-level academic advisors, *Freedom in the World: Independent Countries 2007* has gone through comprehensive process of analysis and evaluation, covering the period from December 1, 2005 to December 31, 2006 for 193 countries and territories. Each country is classified by the status of "Free," "Partly Free," or "Not Free" according to its combined average rating of political rights and civil liberties. Free-country Group includes countries with combined average ratings of 1.0, 1.5, 2.0, and 2.5; Partly-free-country Group consists of countries with combined average ratings of 3.0, 3.5, 4.0, 4.5, and 5.0; and Not-free-country Group comprises countries with combined average ratings of 5.5, 6.0, 6.5 and 7.0 (Freedom House, 2006b). Countries with the same combined average ratings are grouped together alphabetically under each level.

Since its publication in 1972, this freedom rating has well been established as one of the two most widely used measures for political freedom and democracy across countries. It remains as the standard in cross-nation democracy evaluations (Huber & Solt, 2004; McClintock & Lebovic, 2006) and is one of the two lists, which place the level of democracy of a country on an ordinal scale (Foweraker & Krznaric, 2002).

Sample Size

Purpose of study, population size, sampling error, and confidence level determine the sample size for a research. In this study, a simplified formula is used to calculate sample size (Yamane, 1973, p. 1088; Israel, 1992), where n is the sample size, N the population size and e the level of precision:

$$n = \frac{N}{1 + N(e)^2}.$$

(1)

We get:

$$n = \frac{193}{1 + 193(.05)^2} = \frac{193}{1 + 0.4825} \approx 130$$ (Samples).

Here, N equals 193 countries listed in the *Freedom in the World: Independent Countries 2007* with 95% of confidence level and 5% precision. As the second research question is to determine if any statistical difference exists between a country's government-based Web sites and its business-oriented Web sites in representing national political freedom, the sample size of 130 is then doubled to 260.

Since there are 13 freedom levels on the list and an equal proportion of freedom levels should be presented in the research, this research

selected three countries from each of the 13 levels and conducted a content analysis of four government-based and four business-oriented Web sites from each country. This brings the sample size for this research up to 312, with 96 Web sites in Free-country Group, 120 Web sites in Partly-free-country Group, and 96 Web sites in Not-free-country Group. In order to balance the sample size for the three freedom groups, which is one of the criteria to run an ANOVA test for interval variables, the sample size for Partly-free-country Group was reduced to 96 at the analysis stage by eliminating 24 Web sites in Level 4 (the middle level). Therefore, 314 Web sites went through content analysis and 288 Web sites went into the final analysis stage. The ANOVA test was repeated subsequently by randomly eliminating Web sites in Partly-free-country Group with the intent to justify the first elimination method.

Country Selection

This research randomly selected three countries from each of the 13 freedom levels by using Research Randomizer, an online pseudo-random number generator at http://www.randomizer.org/form.htm. The Randomizer generated numbers individually for each level. As countries are listed alphabetically within each freedom level and the country selection is based on the random number generator, each country has an equal opportunity to be selected for this research. As a result, 12 countries selected under Category Free (Level 1.0 to 2.5) formed Free-country Group. Partly-free-country Group included 15 countries selected from Level 3.0 to 5.0. The last 12 countries drawn from Level 5.5 to 7.0 became Not-free-country Group. However, in the process of data analysis, three countries (Level 4.0) in Partly-free-country Group were eliminated in order to balance the sample size for the three freedom groups.

Web Site Selection

This study selected four government-based Web sites and four business-oriented Web sites from each country. The four government-based Web sites were selected based on Yahoo! and Google regional searches at http://dir.yahoo.com/Regional/Countries/ and http://directory.google.com/Top/Regional/ respectively. The search went further into specific countries and then the government directory. One or two official Web sites from national agencies were included for each country depending on their availability. In addition, the list contained official Web sites from city/state agencies and embassies. Since some of the countries do not have Web sites in these specific categories, the selection expanded to include other government agency Web sites as well.

The four business-oriented Web sites consist of the top four largest local-based business companies for each country listed. These Web sites were selected first from The *Global 2000* company list (Forbes.com Inc., 2007a) and The *Asian Fab 50* company list (Forbes.com Inc., 2007b). If there were not enough companies listed on these two lists for a country, Google and Yahoo! business searches were conducted. This selection method is used due to the belief that those companies listed on *Global 2000* and *Asian Fab 50* have enough resources in information technology to develop and maintain their Web sites while representing their local cultures. These two lists also represent a mix of industry sectors. If multiple companies are listed for a country, the top four companies from various industry sectors were considered to seek a better balance in industry variations. The list was then re-arranged alphabetically by the names of the Web sites before it was distributed to the coders, keeping the knowledge of the Web site's freedom level undisclosed.

Content Analysis

This research used a content analysis method to collect data from Web sites. The analysis was carried out mainly on the homepage with extensions to the second and third level Web pages through. With some companies setting up their introductory pages with flash software, the next page was considered as the homepage. The seven *power distance* indicators were evaluated on each Web site on a 0 (not present) to 4 (present to the most extent) scale. Since some of the Web sites might be written in languages other than English, native speakers were consulted to translate those Web sites into English if possible. If a Web site was presented in both English and its country's native language, the coding was mainly based on the Web site in its native language, since culture elements are best presented in their native languages. In some cases, Web sites in English were selected for coding, only under the condition that the English Web site had the same layout as its native language Web site, and the English Web site was merely the translation of its native language Web site, rather than a Web site with different construction designed for an international audience.

Data Collection

As the content analysis method has been used to collect data in this research, quantitative research method was employed to analyze the data collected. The two college graduates who conducted the content analysis for this research was trained in Li's study (2009). They have performed an inter-coder reliability test in Li's study and their agreement level is reached at .87. For this research, these two coders received one coding sheet (Appendix B) for each Web site, which was developed and revised according to Li's study. The coders were also given a Web site list with 312 Web sites listed in alphabetical order. During the period of March 21, 2008 to May 6, 2008, the two coders coded these Web sites independently based on the

Table 1. Map of the two-way 2 x 3 ANOVA

	Free-country Group	Partly-free-country Group	Not-free-country Group	Total
Government	Free-country Government ($n = 48$)	Partly-free-country Government ($n = 48$)	Not-free-country Government ($n = 48$)	Government Mean ($n = 144$)
Business	Free-country Business ($n = 48$)	Partly-free-country Business ($n = 48$)	Not-free-country Business ($n = 48$)	Business Mean ($n = 144$)
Total	Free-country mean ($n = 96$)	Partly-free-country mean ($n = 96$)	Not-free-country mean ($n = 96$)	Grand Mean ($N = 288$)

coding sheet. The final scores used in this data analysis were based on the agreement of the scores from the two coders. If disagreement occurred between the two coders, the researcher acted as the third coder. After reviewing and evaluating the Web site, a majority rule was used to decide the final coding. Subsequently, the Statistical Package for the Social Sciences (SPSS) software was used to perform the second-stage quantitative data analysis.

Two-Way Analysis of Variance

Since one dependent variable (Web representation of *power distance*) and two independent variables (freedom level and Web site type) are involved in this research design, a multi-level two-way analysis of variable was conducted to examine both the main effects of and the interaction between the two independent variables (three freedom levels and two Web site types). There is no covariate involved in this research.

This study intends to discover if freedom level, Web site type, and freedom level by Web site type interaction have effects on Web interface design. The basic research questions can be divided into the following:

1. Is there a main effect of freedom level? Do free-country Group, Partly-free-country Group, and Not-free-Country Group differ significantly in representing national political freedom on Web interface design?

2. Is there a main effect of Web site type? Do government-based Web sites and business-oriented Web sites differ significantly in representing national political freedom on Web interface design?

3. Is there a freedom level by Web site type interaction? Is there any statistical significance between the combinations of Free-country Group, Partly-free-country Group, and Not-free-country group on government-based and business-oriented Web sites?

The first question was evaluated by comparing the row marginal means while the second was calculated by comparing the column marginal means (see Table 1). However, the third question was answered by comparing the cell means of the factorial combination of freedom level and Web site type. The first question answers Research Question 1 and the last two questions answer Research Question 2. Table 1 maps out the concept of this two-way 2 x 3 ANOVA.

Null Hypothesis

First, a null hypothesis ($H_{0(A)}$) is established that the means of the three freedom groups (Free-country Group, Partly-free-country Group and Not-free-country Group) are not significantly different (α

= .05). That means

$$H_{0(A)}: \mu_{A1} = \mu_{A2} = \mu_{A3}$$

Where

$H_{0(A)}$ = the null hypothesis for the three freedom groups,

μ_{A1} = the mean of Free-country Group,

μ_{A2} = the mean of Partly-free-country Group, and

μ_{A3} = the mean of Not-free-country Group

In this hypothesis, $N = 288$ (the total number of Web sites under study). $n_1 = n_2 = n_3 = 96$ (the number of Web sites selected from Free-country Group, Partly-free-country Group, and Not-free-country Group respectively). If the null hypothesis is rejected, it indicates that statistically differences exist among freedom groups.

Secondly, a null hypothesis ($H_{0(B)}$) is established that the means of the two Web site types (government-based Web sites and business-oriented Web sites) are not significantly different ($\alpha = .05$). That means

$$H_{0(B)}: \mu_{B1} = \mu_{B2}$$

Where

$H_{0(B)}$ = the null hypothesis for the two Web site types,

μ_{B1} = the mean of government-based Web sites, and

μ_{B2} = the mean of business-oriented Web sites

In this hypothesis, $N = 288$ (the total number of Web sites under study). $n_1 = n_2 = 144$ (the number of government-based Web sites and business-oriented Web sites respectively). If the null hypothesis is rejected, it indicates that a statistically difference exists between government-

based Web sites and business-oriented Web sites in representing national political freedom on Web interface design.

Third, a null hypothesis ($H_{0(C)}$) is established that interaction effects do not exist between the two independent variables to influence scores on the dependent variable ($\alpha = .05$). That is

$$H_{0(c)}: \mu_{C1} = \mu_{C2}, \mu_{C1} = \mu_{C3}, \cdots \mu_{C5} = \mu_{C6}$$

Where

$H_{0(c)}$ = the null hypothesis for the interaction effects,

μ_{c1} = the mean of government-based Web sites in Free-country Group,

μ_{c2} = the mean of business-oriented Web sites in Free-country Group,

μ_{c3} = the mean of government-based Web sites in Partly-free-country Group,

μ_{c4} = the mean of business-oriented Web sites in Partly-free-country Group,

μ_{c5} = the mean of government-based Web sites in Not-free-country Group, and

μ_{c6} = the mean of business-oriented Web sites in Not-free-country Group

Here, $N = 288$ (the total number of Web sites under study) and $n_1 = n_2 = n_3 = n_4 = n_5 = n_6 = 48$ (the number of Web sites for each corresponding group).

According to the combination formula, where n is the total number of objects, k is the number to be chosen:

$$C_k^n = \binom{n}{k} = \frac{n!}{k!(n-k)!}$$

$$C_k^n = \binom{n}{k} = \frac{n!}{k!(n-k)!} \quad 0 \leq k \leq n \quad 0 \leq k \leq n$$

$$(2)$$

We get:

$$C_2^6 = \binom{6}{2} = \frac{6!}{2!(6-2)!} = 15 \text{ (Comparisons)}.$$

Since there are total of six means to compare ($\mu_{c1} \dots \mu_{c6}$) and two means to compare each time, the combination results in 15 comparisons. If the null hypothesis is rejected, it indicates that freedom level and Web site type interact with each other to influence the representation of national political freedom on the Web site interface design.

Statistical Test

The variables involved in this research are measured in an interval scale while the two independent variables are completely independent. With the intent of using the most powerful test to reject $H_{0\,(A)}$, $H_{0\,(B)}$ and $H_{0\,(C)}$, a two-way ANOVA is selected to perform data analysis for the total score. Afterward, post hoc multiple comparison tests examine the locations of the differences found in the ANOVA analysis. A plot graph of freedom levels * Web site types interaction is presented to show the interaction between the two independent variables. Towards the end, this study uses Cronbach's alpha to validate the internal consistency of the results.

DATA ANALYSIS

This section concentrates on analyzing data collected from March 21, 2008 to May 6, 2008. Altogether 312 sample Web sites were coded using content analysis method based on the Coding Sheet (Appendix B). Among them, 288 Web sites went into this analysis stage. First, 24 Web sites from Freedom Level 4.0 in Partly-free-country Group were excluded in order to equalize the number of Web sites among the three freedom groups. Subsequently, 24 Web sites were randomly taken out from Partly-free-country Group instead of those

from Freedom Level 4.0 and a two-way ANOVA analysis was re-run to ensure that the first run produced the same result as the second run. The findings showed that the first run, with the exclusion of Freedom Level 4.0, reached the same result as the second run with the random exclusion of the Web sites from Partly-free-country Group, although some slight fluctuations occurred.

Before the ANOVA test was conducted, three assumptions had to be checked and satisfied: independent observations, normal distribution, and homogeneity of variance (Ho, 2006). The first assumption suggests that the observations are all independent of each other. The second assumption requires that the dependent variable in the ANOVA analysis have a normal distribution. The third assumption expects equal variances of the dependent variable remain constant across the levels of the independent variables (Ho, 2006; Meyers, Gamst, & Guarino, 2006).

In this study, the first assumption has been satisfied since the two coders examined the Web sites independently and the Web sites under this study are individual Web sites, independent with each other. There were no repeated measures involved.

The second assumption, normal distribution of the dependent variable is confirmed by running a histogram generated by SPSS statistic program. In this study, the dependent variable is Web representation of *power distance*, which is the sum of the scores derived from the content analysis on each Web site for the seven *power distance* indicators. The result showed that with 288 sample Web sites, the mean total score equals to 13.17 in a range of 0 to 28 with a standard deviation of 6.938 (see Figure 1). With total points on the X-axis, Figure 1 provides a graphical display of how many Web sites scored in each 1.66-point range of values. It is concluded from Figure 1 that the dependent variable (total score - Web representation of *power distance*) has a near perfect normal distribution.

As required by the third assumption, each of the three freedom groups (Free-country Group, Partly-free-country Group, and Not-free-country

Figure 1. Histogram of distribution of total scores for sample websites

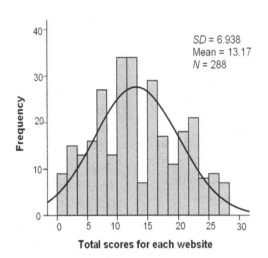

Group) should have approximately equal variances on the two dependent variables (freedom level and Web site type). This can be verified by applying Levene's Test for homogeneity of variances. Before Levene's test, a null hypothesis was established for this study that the variances were all equal. This means there is no significant difference between the groups' mean scores. In this research, the samples are in equal size between each freedom group and Web site type. As a result, the Levene statistic is $F(5, 282) = 2.042$ and the corresponding level of significance is large ($p = .073$, which is greater than $\alpha = .05$). Therefore, we failed to reject the null hypothesis that the variances are all equal. Since there is enough evidence that the assumption of homogeneity of variance has been met in this research (with random and independent samples), the two-way ANOVA test might be continued.

Results

Great differences exist in Web site design reflecting national political freedom

At the first stage of investigation, 156 government-based Web sites and 156 business-oriented Web sites were analyzed for each of the seven

power distance indicators. It appears that great differences exist in Web site design when Web sites are measured by these indicators.

Consulate of Equatorial Guinea in Romania Web site (Not-free-country Group, Level 6.5) was scored among the highest in content analysis, totaling 28 (see Figure 2). The layout of the homepage is completely symmetrical from left to right (scored 4). The second indicator, *monumental building*, is coded according to the Web page level on which a monumental building is displayed (homepage, second level Web page, or third level Web page), and whether it is the focus of the Web site or is used as a background in a picture. The findings indicate that more monumental buildings appear on Not-free- country Group Web sites as the focus of the homepage, usually situated at the center of the Web page, while Free-country Group Web sites show fewer monumental buildings or the buildings are placed as the background of an event. On this Web site, a picture of a monumental building is located on the homepage as one of the main pictures (scored 4).

Symbol of nationalism includes any national flags and/or country maps appeared on the Web site. Religious remarks, pictures, paintings, and Web links to external religious Web sites are con-

Figure 2. Consulate of Equatorial Guinea in Romania homepage. Freedom level 6.5, at http://www. ecaligiuri.com/index2.php

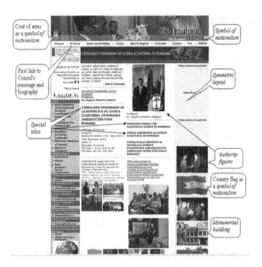

sidered as symbols of religion. The basic coding criterion for this indicator is focused on the Web site level on which the symbol appears. It is easy to find on this Web site a national flag and a coat of arms on the top banner to represent symbols of nationalism throughout the homepage and all the subsequent second level and third level Web pages (scored 4).

This study is also designed to code any information on organizational charts, titles and ranks of the administrators according to their location and transparency on the Web site. It aims to find out the importance the Web designers (or rather the administrators) have placed on the leaders (or administrators themselves). It is believed that a Web site's navigation scheme is achieved through the proper arrangement of the links on and between Web pages. The information placed on the homepage is usually the most important of all. This study intends to examine this feature horizontally (the arrangement of the administration information on the navigation bar of the homepage) and vertically (the Web site level it is placed on). The indicator, *information arranged according to management hierarchy*, is coded to examine the link arrangement on the navigation

bar of the homepage. Navigation bars, in most cases, are placed on the left side, at the top and/ or at the bottom of the Web page. Sometimes, two navigation bars appear on the same page. Since the vertical navigation bar bear the same weight in importance as the horizontal navigation bar, this study weights the two bars the same in the coding theme. Generally, links on a navigation bar are arranged according to their importance from left to right or from top to bottom. It is the intention of this study to find out how important the Web designers (or the administrators) view the information on leaders by examining the location of the *Administration* link on the navigation bar of the homepage. If the *Administration* link is not presented directly on the homepage, any link providing information on administrators or any link to *Administration* is considered as the link to be examined for this purpose. Generally, *Home* link points back to the homepage and is placed as the first on the navigation bar. It is simply a navigation tool, instead of an authoritative indicator. Therefore, it is not counted as one of the links displayed before the *Administration* link in this study. On this Web site, it is easy to find that three out of eight links (except *Home* link)

Figure 3. Cathay financial homepage (Taiwan). Free-country group, level 1.5, http://www.cathayhold-ings.com.tw/new/eng/index.htm

on the horizontal navigation bar are dedicated to the Consul, carrying his personal message as well as introducing his career and educational background. They are named as *El Cónsul, Carrera,* and *Short CV. El Cónsul,* carrying the Consul's message and personal biography. *El Cónsul* is the first link on the navigation bar (scored 4 for *information arranged according to management hierarchy*). Furthermore, Consul's message, biography, and CV are arranged on the second level Web page with direct links to the homepage. These links appear on each Web page, as they are part of the designed navigation bar (scored 4 for *link to information about the leaders*). Usually this information can be found under *Administration, About,* or *Introduction* links.

The indicator, *authority figure,* is evaluated in this study by the frequency of its appearance and the Web page level on which it is displayed. *Authority figures* include administrators and any prominent visitors. These authority figures can usually be found on the homepage, in the *News* section and/or the *Administration* section. They can also be found in the *Introduction* section, under the *History* link, which introduces former administrators of the organization. Several authority figures can be found on the homepage of Consulate of Equatorial Guinea in Romania. The picture of

Consul Eugenio Roberto Caligiuri is displayed in the middle of the homepage (scored 4).

A *special title* placed in front of a person's name usually shows a certain degree of respect from others and represents the importance of his/her social status. It can be of religion, political party, or social class, including but not limited to titles such as Honorable, H.E., His/Her Majesty, His/Her Excellency, His/Her Highness, Rev., Leader, and so forth. However, academic titles, such as Dr., President, and Dean, are not considered in this category. Several *special titles* appeared on this homepage, such as Consulado Honorario and Cónsul Honorario (scored 4).

On the other hand, Cathay Financial (Figure 3) from Taiwan (Level 1.5 in Free-country Group) scores very low on its coding sheet (scored 4). It features an unsymmetrical layout (scored 0) without any monumental buildings (scored 0) shown on any of its Web pages. There is no symbol of nationalism or religion found on the Web site, either (scored 0). A link to the company's organization chart and board of directors is arranged as the second link on the horizontal navigation bar (scored 3) and shown on the second level Web page (scored 1). There is no authority figure (scored 0) and special title (scored 0) found on this Web site.

Table 2. Table of means

	Free-country Group	Partly-free-country Group	Not-free-country Group	Total
Government	15.63	18.83	19.58	18.01
Business	7.98	8.38	8.65	8.33
Total	11.80	13.60	14.11	13.17

From these two Web site examples, it is clear that differences exist in Web interface design when Web sites are measured by these *power distance* indicators. In other words, national political freedom is represented in a wide spectrum on these three freedom group Web sites.

There is a main effect of freedom level. That is, free-country Group, Partly-free-country Group, and Not-free-Country Group differ significantly in representing national political freedom on Web interface design.

At the analysis stage, a multi-level two-way analysis of variance was conducted to investigate the data collected. There were 288 Web sites included in the analysis stage with 96 Web sites in each of the three freedom groups. Table 2 reveals that there are differences between the cell means (government: 15.63 vs. 18.83 vs. 19.58; business: 7.98 vs. 8.38 vs. 8.65), as well as the marginal means (total: 11.80 vs. 13.60 vs. 14.11) for the three freedom level groups across the two Web site types.

An advance ANOVA test was conducted to examine the statistical significance. As a result, the ANOVA Summary Table (Table 3) calculated the differences of the means for these freedom groups and indicated that they are statistically significant. The output indicated that the F_A statistic for the freedom level main effect is 6.026 with 2 and 282 degrees of freedom and with observed significance level at .003. Since p-value of .003 < .05, the null hypothesis that there is no statistical difference between the three freedom groups is rejected. There is enough evidence to conclude that the main effect for freedom level is statistically significant at $\alpha = .05$ significance level and there are differences among the freedom levels in mean value of the Web sites, although the differences are small (partial eta squared = .041). Thus, it is concluded that a nation's political freedom level has an influence on Web interface design. This main effect is the result of evaluating the differences among the three marginal means (11.80 vs. 13.60 vs. 14.11 shown in Table 2) associated with the freedom levels.

Moreover, the cell means and the marginal means for freedom groups showed a general increase in the government sector, the business sector and the overall scores (Table 2). It indicated that on both government-based Web sites

Table 3. ANOVA summary table - tests of between-subjects effects

Source	Type III Sum of Squares	df	Mean Square	F	Sig.	Partial Eta Squared
Freedom Level	283.382	2	141.691	6.026	.003*	.041
Sectors	6747.347	1	6747.347	286.957	.000*	.504
Freedom Level *Sectors	151.799	2	75.899	3.228	.041*	.022
Error	6630.792	282	23.513			

* The mean difference is significant at the .05 level.

Figure 4. Estimated marginal means of total

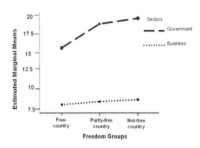

and business-oriented Web sites, the number of *power distance* indicators increased as the freedom level decreased. Figure 4 shows this trend in graph format.

Post hoc approach is usually used after ANOVA test has detected the differences among group means. Generally, ANOVA test intents to detect if there are any differences among the sample means, while post hoc approach aims to test "all possible pairwise comparisons of between-group means" to find out where these differences exist (Meyer, Gamst, & Guarino, 2006, p. 426). These comparisons "compare each group with every other group" (Meyer et al., p. 426) and Tukey (honestly significant difference - HSD) test is one of the popular options (Ho, 2006). Since the differences have been detected among the freedom levels, a Tukey post hoc test is performed in this research to determine where the differences lie among the three freedom groups. The results (Table 4) indicated that Free-country Group score mean was significantly higher than Partly-free-country Group score mean ($p = .028 < .05$) and Not-free-country Group mean ($p = .003 < .05$). However, there was no significant difference between Partly-

free-country Group and Not-free-country Group means ($p = .746 < .05$). Thus, with 95% of confidence, Free-country Group yielded higher mean values in representing national political freedom via Web design compared to Partly-free-country Group and Not-free-country Group. Therefore, it is concluded that Free-country Group exhibited fewer *power distance* indicators on its Web sites and consequently demonstrated more national political freedom.

There is a main effect for Web site type. That is, government-based Web sites and business-oriented Web sites differ significantly in representing national political freedom. Government-based Web sites scored much higher than business-oriented Web sites.

Among the 288 Web sites studied in the analysis stage, there are 144 Web sites in government sector and 144 in business sector. As shown in Table 2, the cell means (Free-country Group: 15.63 vs. 7.98; Partly-free-country Group: 18.83 vs. 8.38; Not-free-country Group: 19.58 vs. 8.65) as well as the margin means (Total: 18.01 vs. 8.33) for these two Web site types suggested that differences exist across the three freedom groups. An advance

Table 4. Multiple comparisons between freedom groups: Tukey HSD

(I) Freedom Groups	(J) Freedom Groups	Mean Difference (I-J)	Sig.
Free-country	Partly-free-country	-1.80	.028*
	Not-free-country	-2.31	.003*
Partly-free-country	Not-free-country	-.51	.746

* The mean difference is significant at the .05 level

ANOVA analysis confirmed the difference between the two sectors (Table 3). The output of the ANOVA test indicated that the F_B statistic for the Web site type main effect is 286.975 with 1 and 282 degrees of freedom and with the observed significance level at .000. Since the p-value of .000 is less than .05, the null hypothesis that there is no difference between the means of these two Web site types is rejected. So it is concluded that the main effect for Web site type is statistically significant at the $\alpha = .05$ significance level, which indicates that there is a significant difference between Web site types in mean value for the representation of *power distance* indicators on Web interface design. In addition, the partial eta squared score revealed that the difference is moderate (partial eta squared = .504). Furthermore, as shown in Table 2, the mean scores of government-based Web sites more than doubled those of business-oriented Web sites across the three freedom levels. Therefore, we concluded that government-based Web sites embed more *power distance* indicators than business-oriented Web sites do.

There is a freedom level by Web site type interaction.

The purpose of evaluating freedom level by Web site type interaction is to identify if the effect of freedom level on Web representation depends on Web site type or vice versa. Since there are three freedom levels and two Web site types, 15 interactions are examined in this study (see Equation 2). The ANOVA test results (Table 3) indicated that the freedom level by Web site type interaction is significant, F_{AB} (2, 282) = 3.228, p = .041 at $\alpha = .05$ significance level. This interaction can also be identified in Figure 4, in which the two lines for government-based Web sites and business-oriented Web sites are not in parallel position. This significance of the freedom level by Web site type interaction indicates that overall the effect of freedom level on Web representation of national political freedom depends on Web site type or vice versa. In other words, the interaction of freedom level and Web site type has an effect

on deciding a country's national political freedom level represented on Web interface design. It also means that certain Web sites, depending on their country's *power distance* level and their Web site type (government-based or business-oriented), may represent more of a country's national political freedom on Web interface design, while others may not. However, the ANOVA test did not indicate where the differences were, i.e., between what kind of Web site and in which freedom group. To identify specific Web sites, Tukey post hoc multiple comparisons were conducted. The results showed that 11 out of 15 pairs of means are statistically different (Table 5).

The results are further illustrated in Figure 5, which showed that Web site type has a great influence on the significance level, since each pair of means between the government-base Web sites and business-oriented Web sites is statistically significant. The only four pairs of means, which are not significant, are located within the same Web site type. On the other hand, no statistical significance in means was found among Free-country Group business-oriented Web sites, Partly-free-country Group business-oriented Web sites, and Not-free-country Group business-oriented Web sites. That means business-oriented Web sites did not show much of the freedom indicators on Web interface design across the three freedom groups. This indicates that Web site type influences the significance level between the freedom groups. Moreover, both freedom level and Web site type have a significant interaction effect on mean value of Web interface design.

Reliability and Replicability

In order to assess the reliability of the measuring instrument used in this research and to examine the stable behavioral relations between dependent variable and independent variables, it is necessary to verify the external and internal consistency of the results of all the items. Generally, a reliability test is to assess whether a test will produce identi-

Table 5. Multiple comparisons for freedom level by website type interaction

(I) Group(J) GroupMean Difference (I-J)Sig.Free-Country-Group – government		
Free – business	7.646	.000*
Partly-free – government	-3.208	.017*
Partly-free – business	7.250	.000*
Not-free – government	-3.958	.001*
Not-free – business	6.979	.000*
Free-Country-Group – business		
Partly-free – government	-10.854	.000*
Partly-free –business	-.396	.999
Not-free – government	-11.604	.000*
Not-free – business	-.667	.985
Partly-free-Country-Group – government		
Partly-free –business	10.458	.000*
Not-free – government	-.750	.974
Not-free – business	10.188	.000*
Partly-free-Country-Group –- business		
Not-free – government	-11.208	.000*
Not-free – business	-.271	1.000
Not-free-Country-Group – government		
Not-free – business	10.938	.000*

*$p < .05$

cal results over repeated tests if identical samples are applied in the same setting.

External consistency measurement refers to the procedure of comparing two test results to verify the reliability of the measure. It usually includes test-retest method and parallel forms of the same test method (Ho, 2006). Test-retest method checks reliability by comparing two sets of results gathered from the same group of samples at two different times. Parallel forms of the same test method checks reliability by evaluating two sets of results collected from equivalent but different groups of samples (Ho). This research applied parallel forms of the same test method to

Figure 5. Means not statistically significant between these two groups

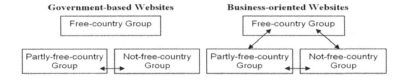

determine its external reliability. After the first run of the ANOVA with 288 Web sites (24 Web sites from Freedom Level 4.0 in Partly-free-country Group were excluded), the second run took place with the same number of Web sites but instead, randomly excluding 24 Web sites from the same country group. The initial intention of eliminating these 24 Web sites is to balance the number of Web sites among the three freedom groups involved in the research, which is the requirement for running an ANOVA test. However, this second run also satisfies the requirement of checking the external consistency and reliability of the research, as the two runs yield the same findings although slight difference in statistics occurred.

Internal consistency measurement intends to examine if all the items in the test are consistent in measuring the phenomenon investigated (Ho, 2006). Cronbach's alpha is the most widely used method for measuring internal consistency (George & Mallery, 2008). It can be interpreted as the mean of all possible split-half correlation coefficients (α) within a test. Cronbach's alpha formula (Cronbach, 1951, p. 321) is defined as follows:

$$\alpha = \frac{n}{n-1}\left(1 - \frac{\sum V_{subtests}}{V_{test}}\right). \qquad (3)$$

Where n is the number of subtests/items, $\sum V_{subtests}$ is the sum of the variances for the n individual subtests/items, and V_{test} is the variance for the sum of all the subtests/items. Generally, Alpha results range between 0 and 1. The closer the alpha is to 1.00, the greater internal consistency is achieved by the measuring instrument.

In this study, Cronbach's alpha was calculated with SPSS software. Of the total sample of 288 Web sites, all data were processed in the analysis for the seven *power distance* indicators ($n = 7$). The reliability output showed that Cronbach's alpha coefficient equals to .733 for these seven items, which indicated good overall internal consistency

of the measurement scales constructed for this research. In addition, Item-Total Statistics table shows the statistics of Cronbach's alpha if item deleted. The numbers shown under this column are the result of alpha if one of the seven items (on the left) has ever been deleted. Out of the seven items, only statistics for *symmetric layout* in this column reaches .738, which is greater than Cronbach's alpha (.733). Although deleting this item will increase the overall consistency correlation coefficient, the increase, however, is small and the item is much needed as an indicator for national political freedom on Web interface design. For this reason, this item is retained in this research.

This section detailed the process of analyzing 288 sample Web sites. The results of two-way ANOVA test have led to some interesting observations focusing on the two research questions. Furthermore, Tukey post hoc comparisons were carried out to locate the differences among the three freedom levels. Cronbach's alpha coefficient was also calculated to measure the internal consistency of the research. The next section will offer a discussion of the findings and draw inferences from data analysis. Recommendations for further research will be provided at the end.

DISCUSSIONS AND CONSIDERATIONS

This study has furthered our understanding of how national political freedom is represented on Web interface design. It has also advanced our knowledge of the differences between government-based Web sites and business-oriented Web sites in representing political freedom levels. This section will discuss the findings of this study, make inferences from data analysis, reflect on the implication of the study, and offer recommendations for further research.

Discussion

This study has focused on two research questions. They are:

1. To what extent is a country's national political freedom represented on Web interface design?
2. Does any statistical difference exist between a country's government-based Web sites and its business-oriented Web sites in representing national political freedom?

In data analysis phase, Research Question 1 has been reiterated as:

Is there a main effect of freedom level? Do free-country Group, Partly-free-country Group, and Not-free-Country Group differ significantly in representing national political freedom on Web interface design?

Several approaches have been taken to address this research question. A multi-level two-way ANOVA was applied to describe the means and standard deviations of each group, to analyze the statistical significance among the three freedom groups, as well as to measure the strength of the relationships between the groups. Further Tukey post hoc comparisons were performed to locate the differences. After an analysis of the data generated from the tests, it is concluded that significant differences exist among the three freedom groups (Table 3) and fewer *power distance* indicators are shown on Web sites in free-country Group than in Partly-free-country Group and Not-free-country Group (Figure 4). This indicates that a country's national political freedom level represented on Web interface design coordinates with its freedom level found through other traditional means of surveys, questionnaires, and interviews. In this way, it suggests that a country's national political freedom level can be assessed by analyzing *power distance* indicators represented on Web interface

design. However, after a thorough examination of the coding scores for each Web site, it is evident that not all Web sites in the same freedom level scored in a close range. As the freedom level decreases from *free* to *not free*, the coding scores show an increase for both Web site types and total scores. Nonetheless, the increase is not a steady one. A box plot is constructed to display the distribution and the percentiles of the total score collected from the sample Web sites (see Figure 6). It shows that there is some variation in the total scores of the three freedom groups. Although the median and the range showed some increases from Free-country Group to Not-free-country Group, the difference is not so obvious between the median of Partly-free-country Group and that of Not-free-country Group. In addition, the lower quartile of Partly-free-country Group almost has the same range as that of Not-free-country Group. In addition, most of their inter quartile ranges overlap with each other. This means some of the Web sites in the lower quartile of Partly-free-country Group scored very close to some of the Web sites in the lower quartile of Not-free-country Group. If we happen to sample the Web sites located in these two quartiles, it would be a challenge to find any statistical differences between the treatment means of these two groups. Therefore, a country's national political freedom cannot be determined just by the examination of a few Web sites. It is necessary to increase the sample size to at least 10% of the population in order to get an accurate freedom level assessment for a country in a research project.

Note: Illustration adapted from SPSS for Windows: Step by Step, by D. George and P. Mallery, 2008, 8th ed., New York: Pearson, p. 81.

Research Question 2 can be divided into two sub-questions:

1. Is there a main effect of Web site type? Do government-based Web sites and business-oriented Web sites differ significantly in representing national political freedom on Web interface design?

Figure 6. Box plot for three freedom groups: total score

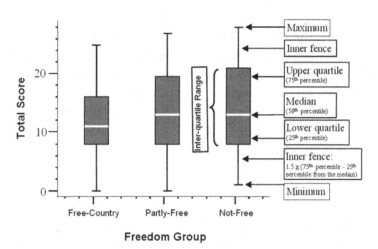

2. Is there a freedom level by Web site type interaction? Is there any statistical significance between the combinations of Free-country Group, Partly-free-country Group, and Not-free-country group on government-based and business-oriented Web sites?

The first sub-question explores the differences of freedom representation between government-based Web sites and business-oriented Web sites by using freedom indicators as a measurement. The result of the two-way ANOVA test indicates that there is statistical significance between the means of government-based Web sites and that of business-oriented Web sites (Table 3). In addition, it is clear that the mean scores of government-based Web sites more than doubled the mean scores of business-oriented Web sites for each freedom level (Table 2). In the initial process of choosing sectors to examine freedom representations on the Web, government-based Web sites became the first choice, since they function as official government Web portals. Besides, the government usually oversees the construction of its official Web site. The ideals, the power, and the mental structure of the government are fully represented on its government-based Web sites, whether the government is people-oriented or power-centered. On the

contrary, governments have limited controls over business-oriented Web sites, which renders these Web sites free from any government restrictions. Majority of companies establish their Web sites with the intent of introducing themselves to the public in order to gain trust from their customers. The rationale of selecting these two opposite Web site sectors in the designing phase is to examine if the freedom representation on Web interface design would prove to be at the same level across different Web site types. The results of the ANOVA test indicate that both government-based Web sites and business-oriented Web sites represent a country's political freedom level, since the mean scores for both sectors increased as the freedom level decreased (Table 2). However, there is a huge difference between the mean scores of these two sectors (government-based Web sites, $M = 18.01$; business-oriented Web sites, $M = 8.33$). These findings reveal that government-based Web sites represent more of freedom indicators and they are easier to use for locating a country's political freedom level. Apparently, not all Web site types reflect national political freedom at the same level. National political freedom level may not be easily detected depending on the selection of Web site sectors. Therefore, Web site type plays an important part in investigating national political freedom level on Web interface design.

The second sub-question aims to detect freedom level and Web site type interaction. While Research Question 1 and Sub-question 1 compare the marginal means of freedom groups and Web site types respectively, Sub-question 2 compares one-by-one the cell means between freedom groups and Web site types. The ANOVA test shows that the overall interaction is statistically significant (Table 3). In addition, the results from the Tukey post hoc comparisons conducted afterwards indicate that only 4 of the 15 pairs of comparisons do not show any statistical significance (Table 5). These four pairs are located between freedom levels within the same Web site types (Figure 5). Examining the location of these four pairs reveals that in business sector, the mean scores of the three freedom groups are not statistically significant, indicating that there is not much of a difference on business-oriented Web sites between the three freedom levels in representing national political freedom. Although the overall mean scores are significantly different among the three freedom groups, this result may depend on the relatively large difference between the mean scores of government-based Web sites. Therefore, it is obvious that business sector is not an effective sector to detect national political freedom level on Web interface design. This echoes the conclusion made from Sub-question 1.

In summary, main conclusions from this research can be summarized into three aspects. First, great differences exist in Web interface design for representing national political freedom. Secondly, a country's national political freedom level can be detected by analyzing Web interface design with effective freedom indicators. Third, Web site type influences the outcome of the study. The first two findings are consistent with Marcus and Gould (2000) theory of cultural dimensions represented on Web interface design and have supported his theory with statistical analysis. The third finding was not anticipated at the beginning of the research. It is, however, conceptually

informative and has advanced our knowledge in this research field.

In addition to the above conclusions found under a close examination of data analysis, further observations have also been made during this data analysis process. In the course of evaluating cultural impact on Web interface design, we realize that culture is only one of the variables affecting Web interface design. Other variables, such as financial resources, technology advancement, and software architecture, contribute to the similarity and dissimilarity of Web interface design as well.

An organization's financial resources determine its technology development and its software availability and accessibility. They have a tremendous impact on software selections and the technical skills of Web designers. Therefore, a company's overall financial situation certainly should not be overlooked in the examination of Web representations. While compiling the sample Web site lists for this research, the researcher came across some difficulties in fulfilling the required number of Web sites for some countries in Partly-free-county Group, especially in Not-free-country Group. In addition, in Not-free-country Group, interface designs for some Web sites are found too simple. From the overall design of these Web sites, it is easy to see that this minimalism is not the intention of the Web site designer, but the consequence of lacking necessary resources in information technology. Some Web sites have established their Web links to the administrators, but their pictures are not properly uploaded or the Web pages are still under construction. Because of the technological limitations in some nations, certain *power distance* indicators were not displayed on their Web sites and the coding scores for these nations appeared lower than they might be. Therefore, a country's technological advancement should be considered in future Web interface analysis as a covariate, which has substantial correlation with the coding scores and is regarded as an adjustment to the results of differences among the freedom groups (George & Mallery, 2008).

Furthermore, because of software functionality, some interface elements may be maximized or limited. Since Web designers usually follow the pre-designed functions embedded in the software, this mimetic aspect of software design has made Web interface design more similar than different. As a result, software functionality becomes one of the factors influencing cultural representation on the Web.

Limitations of the Study

This study confines itself to analyzing national political freedom from Web sites selected from 39 countries based on the country listing *Freedom in the World: Independent Countries 2007* provided by Freedom House, although there are other published listings, which may not assign the freedom levels for these countries in the same way. The criteria variables (*power distance* indicators) are based on the previous studies conducted by Li (2009).

This study randomly selects three countries from each of the 13 freedom levels and conducted data analysis of 288 Web sites (excluding 24 Web sites from Level 4.0) based on the country listing *Freedom in the World: Independent Countries 2007*. It defines a culture by its country, despite the fact that diverse ethnicity and cultural groups exist within a country boundary, and that some cultural groups may exist across countries. Nevertheless, as the purpose of this study intends to measure a nation's political freedom represented on its Web site design, the boundary set for national culture also serves its purpose well. In addition, the visits to each Web site for data collection purposes are limited to a specific period. Because of the constant modifications on Web sites' content and design features, changes may occur before or after the data collection period.

Web site selection for this research is guided strictly by the selection guidelines defined in the Research Design section. However, the researcher found it difficult at times to locate enough Web sites for certain countries in Not-free-country Group. As a result, replacements have been made for some countries in the initial list. In this way, some of the countries are left out of the study because of their technology disadvantages. Additionally, it is found that Web designs for some Web sites in Not-free-country Group exhibit only basic features without levels and navigation bars. It is evident that some freedom indicators were not present on the Web site, not because of Web designers' mental models, but because of the country's limitations in technology. As a result, a country's freedom level represented on these Web interface designs may have been elevated due to its technology deficiency. Therefore, a country's technology level should be taken into consideration in future studies on Web interface design. Much more research is necessary to clarify the correlations of Web representation of political freedom with a country's technology level.

Recommendations for Further Research

The findings from this study have confirmed that national political freedom is represented on Web interface design. As *power distance* is only one of the five culture dimensions identified by Hofstede, it is necessary to extend this statistical validation to the other four culture dimensions, *individualism versus collectivism, masculinity versus femininity, uncertainty avoidance*, and *long-term time orientation versus short-term time orientation*. Marcus (2005) has identified corresponding Web indicators for these four dimensions and these identified Web indicators need to be analyzed and validated. Moreover, with technology transformation, the diffusion of innovations, and globalization and localization of the Web, new indicators may have emerged and need to be identified and mapped to culture dimensions. Coding sheets should be developed to customize the special features of each dimension. Furthermore, more Web site types should be tested to find out the best ones to represent each culture dimension on Web interface design. Future study may also focus on the evaluation of different Web site sectors in representing national cultural dimensions. These Web site sectors may include but not limited to college/university Web sites, news/media Web sites, entertainment Web sites, sports Web sites, postal office Web sites, museum Web sites, and so on. In this way, a new framework for evaluating culture dimensions on Web interface design will be established.

As indicated in this research, a country's technology level may influence the examination of its Web representation of national political freedom. A country's technology level, therefore, should be considered as a covariate in the future studies of Web site examinations. Further research may also concentrate on investigating the correlation of a country's technology level with its freedom level represented on Web interface design.

The validated freedom indicators might also be used to investigate the impact of localization on Web interface design in representing political freedom by comparing organizations' local Web sites targeting their national audience with their mirror Web sites designed for their international audience. It is necessary to find out if localization has played a role on Web interface design in representing cultural dimensions.

Throughout the research, two coders manually conducted the coding process. Automated search tools will help to speed this content analysis process. Computer programs need to be developed to search designated Web sites automatically and to locate cultural indicators on the Web. They may also be used to facilitate coding analysis, although photo analysis has to be accomplished manually at this stage.

Furthermore, a longitudinal study of the impact of technology on Web representation of freedom may also be conducted. It would be interesting to find out whether a country's Web sites will

maintain its cultural elements at the same level after 5 or 10 years of technology advancement and the diffusion of innovation.

Implication of the Research

First, based on Hofstede's cultural dimension theory and Marcus' extension of these cultural dimensions into Web interface design, this research has provided some basic culture elements for designing, interpreting, and managing Web sites. Marketers and Web designers may use these culture elements to promote global communication in their localization approach. As more organizations are interested in building their Web sites for an international audience, in countries where cultures are dominated by high *power distance*, customers are used to the hierarchical form of communication and always look for authoritative indicators on Web pages to confirm the Web site's legitimacy. It would be recommended that authority figures or role models be displayed visually on the Web sites built for Not-free-country Group. It is equally important to establish Web links for the high authorities and display these links as the first group on the navigation bar. These are the essential elements for building commercial Web sites for companies in high *power distance* countries, since customers in those countries seek these indicators to boost their confidence before ordering merchandise online. Therefore, applying or excluding these specific freedom indicators according to a country's freedom level will enhance Web sites' comprehensibility, usability, and interactivity, which will increase a company's competitive advantages in this global market. Overall, culturally adapted Web sites will result in more business activity and productivity. Web designers may also avoid cultural taboos when designing Web sites for a specific country.

In addition, as an exploratory study, this research provides a cultural validating framework. It is the first attempt to compare cultural representation on different Web site types. As *power distance* is one of the five cultural dimensions stated in Hofstede's cultural model, this research method and the construction of the coding sheet will stand as an example for future studies to substantiate other cultural variables articulated in Hofstede's cultural dimensions and in other cross-cultural theories. Since this research has assessed cultural variables on an interval scale, it will serve as a starting point for future studies in the area of cultural analysis for Web interface design.

Furthermore, the results of this study show clear evidence that future research in national freedom and democracy should focus on the study of government-based Web sites. This research compared government-based Web sites with business-oriented Web sites regarding to their differences in Web representation of national political freedom. The result shows that government-based Web sites represent national political freedom better than business-oriented Web sites do. Therefore, Web designers may consider different Web design strategies for these two types of Web sites according to the features stated. Those validated freedom indicators might be used to evaluate the efforts of localization made by countries and Web sites. Current communication strategies should be evaluated and new strategies need to be developed to meet the new challenge.

Finally, this study has confirmed that local Web sites embed cultural values and they are culturally sensitive. This supports previous studies of N. Singh, Kumar, and Baack (2005), and N. Singh, Zhao, and Hu (2003, 2005). In its own way, this study has provided a better understanding for those who study the essence of cross-cultural interface design. It certainly helps researchers gain insights into the cultural characteristics of a particular nation. Moreover, this Web analysis of national political freedom enables general Web users to understand not only their own cultures but also other cultures from the perspective of Web interface design. In this way, this study has increased the awareness among general Web users of cultural elements represented on Web interface design.

Furthermore, it also has led their understanding of cultures into a completely new field.

ACKNOWLEDGMENT

This chapter is based on my dissertation, which will be included in ProQuest Dissertation and Theses database. My sincere thanks go to my mentors, Virgil Blake, Jiangping Chen, Samantha Hastings, and especially, Brian O'Connor, for their inspiration and advice.

REFERENCES

Berger, J. (1977). *Ways of seeing*. New York: Penguin Books.

Burgmann, I., Kitchen, P. J., & Williams, R. (2006). Does culture matter on the Web? *Marketing Intelligence & Planning*, *24*(1), 62–76. doi:10.1108/02634500610641561

Chandler, D. (2002). *Semiotics: The basics*. New York: Taylor and Francis. Retrieved May 4, 2006, from http://www.netlibrary.com

Cole, M., & Scribner, S. (1974). *Culture and thought: A psychological introduction*. New York: John Wiley & Sons.

Cronbach, L. J. (1951, September). Coefficient alpha and the internal structure of tests. *Psychometrika*, *16*(3), 297–334. doi:10.1007/BF02310555

De Mooij, M. (2000). The future is predictable for international marketers: Converging incomes lead to diverging consumer behaviour. *International Marketing Review*, *17*(2), 103–113. doi:10.1108/02651330010322598

Eco, U. (1976). *A theory of semiotics*. Bloomington, IN: Indiana University Press.

Eco, U. (1990). *The limits of interpretation.* Bloomington, IN: Indiana University Press.

Forbes.com Inc. (2007a, March). *The global 2000.* Retrieved April 29, 2009, from http://www.forbes.com/lists///_07forbes2000_The-Global-2000_Counrty.html

Forbes.com Inc. (2007b, September). *The Asian fab 50.* Retrieved April 29, 2009, from http://www.forbes.com/////_07fab50_Asias-Fab-50-Companies_land.html

Ford, G., & Gelderblom, H. (2003). The effects of culture on performance achieved through the use of human computer interaction. In *Proceedings of SAICSIT* (pp. 218-230).

Foweraker, J., & Krznaric, R. (2002). The uneven performance of third wave democracies: Electoral politics and the imperfect rule of law in Latin America. *Latin American Politics and Society, 44*(3), 29–60. doi:10.2307/3177046

Freedom House. (2006a). *Freedom House: About us.* Retrieved April 29, 2009, from http://www.freedomhouse.org/template.cfm?page=2

Freedom House. (2006b). *Freedom House: Methodology.* Retrieved April 29, 2009, from http://www.freedomhouse.org/.cfm?page=35&year=2006

George, D., & Mallery, P. (2008). *SPSS for Windows step by step: A simple guide and reference 13.0 update* (8th ed.). New York: Pearson.

Gould, E. W., Zakaria, N., & Yusof, S. A. (2000, September 24). Applying culture to website design: A comparison of Malaysian and US websites. In *Proceedings of 2000 joint IEEE international and 18th annual conference on computer documentation (IPCC/SIGDOC 2000).* Symposium conducted at Professional Communication Conference, Cambridge, MA. Retrieved February 10, 2009, from IEEEXplore database. (SPEC Accession Number: 6762865)

Hall, E. T., & Hall, M. R. (1989). *Understanding cultural differences: Germans, French and Americans.* Yarmouth, ME: Intercultural Press.

Hall, S. (2003). The work of representation. In Hall, S. (Ed.), *Representation: Cultural representations and signifying practices* (pp. 13–74). Thousand Oaks, CA: Sage Publications.

Ho, R. (2006). *Handbook of univariate and multivariate data analysis and interpretation with SPSS.* New York: Taylor & Francis Group. doi:10.1201/9781420011111

Hofstede, G. (2001). *Culture's Consequences: Comparing values, behaviors, institutions, and organizations across nations* (2nd ed.). Thousand Oaks, CA: Sage Publications.

Hofstede, G., & Hofstede, G. J. (2005). *Cultures and organizations: Software of the mind.* New York: McGraw-Hill.

Hoft, N. (1996). Developing a cultural model. In del Galdo, E. M., & Nielsen, J. (Eds.), *International user interfaces* (pp. 41–73). New York: John Wiley & Sons.

Hoft, N. L. (1995). *International technical communication: How to export information about high technology.* NY: John Wiley & Sons.

Hoijer, H. (1974). The Sapir-Whorf hypothesis. In Blount, B. G. (Ed.), *Language, culture, and society* (pp. 120–131). Cambridge, MA: Winthrop.

Huber, E., & Solt, F. (2004, October). Successes and failure of neoliberalism. *Latin American Research, 39*(3), 150–164. doi:10.1353/lar.2004.0049

Israel, G. D. (1992, November/December). *Determining sample size.* Retrieved April 29, 2009, from http://edis.ifas.ufl.edu///.pdf

Jakobson, R. (1971). Language in relation to other communication systems. In Selected writings (Vol. 2, pp. 570-9). The Hugue: Mouton.

Johnston, K., & Johal, P. (1999). The Internet as a "virtual cultural region": Are extant cultural classification schemes appropriate? *Internet Research: Electronic Networking Applications and Policy*, *9*(3), 178–186. doi:10.1108/10662249910274566

Kale, S. H. (2006). Designing culturally compatible Internet gaming sites. *UNLV Gaming Research & Review Journal*, *10*(1), 41–49.

La Ferle, C., Edwards, S. M., & Mizuno, Y. (2002). Internet diffusion in Japan: Cultural considerations. *Journal of Advertising Research*, *42*(2), 65–79.

Li, R. (2009). The representation of national political freedom on Web interface design: The indicators. *Journal of the American Society for Information Science and Technology*, *60*(6), 1222–1248. doi:10.1002/asi.21046

Marcus, A. (2005). User interface design and culture. In Aykin, N. (Ed.), *Usability and internationalization of information technology* (pp. 51–78). Mahwah, NJ: Lawrence Erlbaum Associates.

Marcus, A., & Gould, E. W. (2000, July/August). Crosscurrents: Cultural dimensions and global Web user-interface design. *Interaction*, *7*(4), 32–46. doi:10.1145/345190.345238

McClintock, C., & Lebovic, J. H. (2006). Correlates of levels of democracy in Latin America during the 1990s. *Latin American Politics and Society*, *48*(2), 29–59. doi:10.1353/lap.2006.0021

Meyers, L. S., Gamst, G., & Guarino, A. J. (2006). *Applied multivariate research*. Thousand Oaks, CA: Sage.

Nath, R., & Murthy, N. V. (2004). A study of the relationship between Internet diffusion and culture. *Journal of International Technology and Information Management*, *13*(2), 123–132.

O'Connor, B. (1996). *Explorations in indexing and abstracting: Pointing, virtue and power*. Englewood, CO: Libraries Limited.

Ogden, C. K., & Richards, I. A. (1923). *The meaning of meaning: A study of the influence of language upon thought and of the science of symbolism*. New York: Harcourt, Brace and Company.

Peirce, C. S. (1931-58). In Hartshorne, C., Weiss, P., & Burks, A. W. (Eds.), *Collected papers of Charles Sanders Peirce*. Cambridge, MA: Harvard University Press.

Sapir, E. (1963). *Selected writings of Edward Sapir in language, culture and personality* (Mandelbaum, D. G., Ed.). Berkeley, CA: University of California Press. (Original work published 1949)

Sapir, E. (1964). Conceptual categories in primitive languages. In Hymes, D. (Ed.), *Language in culture and society: A reader in linguistics and anthropology* (pp. 128–140). New York: Harper & Bow.

Saussure, F. D. (1966). *Course in general linguistics* (Bally, C., Sechehaye, A., & Riedlinger, A., Trans.). New York: McGraw-Hill Book.

Singh, N., Kumar, V., & Baack, D. (2005). Adaptation of cultural content: Evidence from B2C e-commerce firms. *European Journal of Marketing*, *39*(1/2), 71–86. doi:10.1108/03090560510572025

Singh, N., Zhao, H., & Hu, X. (2003). Cultural adaptation on the Web: A study of American companies' domestic and Chinese Web sites. *Journal of Global Information Management*, *11*(3), 63–80.

Singh, N., Zhao, H., & Hu, X. (2005). Analyzing the cultural content of Web sites: A cross-national comparison of China, India, Japan, and US. *International Marketing Review*, *22*(2), 129–146. doi:10.1108/02651330510593241

Singh, S. (2006). Cultural differences in, and influences on, consumers' propensity to adopt innovations. *International Marketing Review, 23*(2), 173–191. doi:10.1108/02651330610660074

Steinwachs, K. (1999). Information and culture - the impact of national culture on information processes. *Journal of Information Science, 25*(3), 193–204.

Stewart, E. C., & Bennett, M. J. (1991). *American cultural patterns: A cross-cultural perspective* (Rev. ed.). Yarmouth, ME: Intercultural Press.

Trompenaars, F., & Hampden-Turner, C. (1998). *Riding the waves of culture: Understanding diversity in global business* (2nd ed.). New York: McGraw-Hill.

Whorf, B. L. (1988). *Language, thought, and reality: Selected writings of Benjamin Lee Whorf* (Carroll, J. B., Ed.). 18th ed.). Cambridge, MA: The M.I.T. Press. (Original work published 1956)

Williams, R. (1983). *Keywords: A vocabulary of culture and society*. London: Fontana.

Wittgenstein, L. (1953). *Philosophical investigations* (Anscombe, G., Trans.). New York: Macmillan.

Wittgenstein, L. (1958). *The blue and brown books: Preliminary studies for the 'Philosophical Investigations*. NY: Harper & Row.

Wittgenstein, L. (2003). *Tractatus logico-philosophicus* (Ogden, C., Trans.). New York: Taylor & Francis.

Yamane, T. (1973). *Statistics: An introductory analysis* (3rd ed.). New York: Harper & Row.

Zahir, S., Dobing, B., & Hunter, M. G. (2002). Cross-cultural dimensions of Internet portals. *Internet Research: Electronic Networking Applications and Policy, 12*(3), 210–220. doi:10.1108/10662240210430892

Zakour, A. B. (2004). Cultural differences and information technology acceptance In *Proceedings of the 7th Conference of the Southern Association for Information Systems*. Retrieved April 29, 2009, from http://sais.aisnet.org/2004/Zakour.pdf

ADDITIONAL READING

Blair, D. C. (1990). *Language and representation in information retrieval*. New York: Elsevier Science.

Boas, F. (1995). Introduction to the Handbook of American Indian Languages. In Blount, B. G. (Ed.), *Language, culture, and society: A book of readings* (pp. 9–28). Long Grove, Illinois: Waveland Press.

Cyr, D., & Trevor-Smith, H. (2004). Localization of Web design: An empirical comparison of German, Japanese, and United States Web site characteristics. *Journal of the American Society for Information Science and Technology, 55*(13), 1199–1208. doi:10.1002/asi.20075

Drucker, J. (1995). *The alphabetic labyrinth: The letters in history and imagination*. New York: Thames and Hudson.

Gwartney, J., Lawson, R., & Holcombe, R. (1999). Economic freedom and the environment for economic growth. *Journal of Institutional and Theoretical Economics, 155*(4), 643–663.

Krippendorff, K. (1980). *Content analysis: An introduction to its methodology*. Thousand Oaks, CA: Sage Publications.

Krippendorff, K. (2007, June 1). *Computing Krippendorff's alpha-reliability*. Retrieved April 29, 2009, from http://www.asc.upenn.edu/usr/krippendorff/Webreliability.doc

Lombard, M., Snyder-Duch, J., & Bracken, C. C. (2005, June 13). Practical resources for assessing and reporting intercoder reliability in content analysis research projects. In *Intercoder reliability in content analysis*. Retrieved April 29, 2009, from http://www.temple.edu/sct/mmc/reliability/

Mainwaring, S., & Perez-Linan, A. (2003, November). Level of development and democracy: Latin American exceptionalism, 1945-1996. *Comparative Political Studies, 36*(9), 1031–1067. doi:10.1177/0010414003257068

Marr, D. (1982). *Vision: A computational investigation into the human representation and processing of visual information.* San Francisco: W. H. Freeman and Company.

McCulloch, R., & Pezzini, S. (2002). *The role of freedom, growth and religion in the taste for revolution.* Retrieved April 29, 2009, from http://repec.org/res2003/Pezzini.pdf

Robbins, S. S., & Stylianou, A. C. (2003). Global corporate Web sites: An empirical investigation of content and design. *Information & Management, 40*(3), 205–212. doi:10.1016/S0378-7206(02)00002-2

Singh, N., & Pereira, A. (2005). *The culturally customized web site: Customizing web sites for the global marketplace.* Burlington, MA: Elsevier Butterworth-Heinemann.

Tylor, E. B. (1970). *The origins of culture.* Gloucester, MA: Peter Smith. (Original work published 1958)

Weber, R. P. (1990). Basic content analysis (2nd ed.). Quantitative applications in the social sciences. Thousand Oaks, CA: Sage Publications.

Zahedi, F., Van Pelt, W. V., & Song, J. (2001). A conceptual framework for international Web design. *IEEE Transactions on Professional Communication, 44*(2), 83–103. doi:10.1109/47.925509

Zhao, W., Massey, B. L., Murphy, J., & Fang, L. (2003). Cultural dimensions of Web site design and content. *Prometheus, 21*(1), 75–84. doi:10.1080/0810902032000051027

APPENDIX A. FREEDOM IN THE WORLD: INDEPENDENT COUNTRIES 2007

FREE

1.0030

Andorra

Australia

Austria

Bahamas

Barbados

Belgium

Canada

Cape Verde

Chile

Costa Rica

Cyprus

Czech Republic

Denmark

Dominica

Estonia

Finland

France

Germany

Hungary

Iceland

Ireland

Italy

Kiribati

Latvia

Liechtenstein

Lithuania

Luxembourg

Malta

Marshall Islands

Micronesia

Nauru

Netherlands

New Zealand

Norway

Palau

Poland

Portugal

Saint Kitts and Nevis

Saint Lucia

San Marino

Slovakia

Slovenia

Spain

Sweden

Switzerland

Tuvalu

United Kingdom

United States

Uruguay

1.5

Belize

Bulgaria

Ghana

Greece

Grenada

Israel

Japan

Mauritius

Monaco

Panama

St. Vincent and the Grenadines

South Korea

Taiwan

2.0

Antigua & Barbuda

Argentina

Benin

Botswana

Brazil

Croatia

Dominican Republic

Mali

Mongolia

Namibia

Romania

Samoa

Sao Tome & Principe

South Africa

Suriname

Trinidad and Tobago

Vanuatu

2.5

El Salvador

Guyana

India

Indonesia

Jamaica

Lesotho

Mexico

Peru

Senegal

Serbia

Ukraine

PARTLY FREE

3.0

Albania

Bolivia

Bosnia-Herzegovina

Colombia

Ecuador

Georgia

Honduras

Kenya

Macedonia

Montenegro

Nicaragua

Niger

Papua New Guinea

Paraguay

Philippines

Seychelles

Turkey

3.5

Comoros

East Timor

Guatemala

Liberia

Madagascar

Malawi

Moldova

Mozambique

Sierra Leone

Solomon Islands

Tanzania

Zambia

4.0	Singapore	Kazakhstan
Bangladesh	Uganda	Maldives
Burkina Faso	**5.0**	Oman
Guinea-Bissau	Afghanistan	Pakistan
Kuwait	Bahrain	Quatar
Malaysia	Djibouti	Russia
Nigeria	Ethiopia	Rwanda
Sri Lanka	Fiji	Tajikistan
Tonga	Gabon	Thailand
Venezuela	Yemen	Togo
4.5	**NOT FREE**	Tunisia
Armenia	**5.5**	United Arab Emirates
Burundi	Algeria	**6.0**
Central-African Republic	Angola	Cameroon
Gambia	Azerbaijan	Chad
Haiti	Bhutan	Iran
Jordan	Brunei	Iraq
Kyrgyzstan	Cambodia	Swaziland
Lebanon	Congo (Brazzaville)	Vietnam
Mauritania	Congo (Kinshasa)	6.5
Morocco	Egypt	Belarus
Nepal	Guinea	China

Cote d'Ivoire	**7.0**	Turkmenistan
Equatorial Guinea	Burma	Uzbekistan
Eritrea	Cuba	
Laos	Libya	
Saudi Arabia	North Korea	
Syria	Somalia	
Zimbabwe	Sudan	

From Combined Average Ratings: Independent Countries 2007, by Freedom House. Retrieved May 6, 2009 from http://www.freedomhouse.org/template.cfm?page=366&year=2007. © 2007 Freedom House, Inc. Used with permission.

APPENDIX B. CODING SHEET

Please examine each Web page carefully and circle the correspondent "yes."

	Present ------> Not present				
Code	4	3	2	1	0
Symmetric layout (homepage only)					
The Web page is *100%* symmetric	yes				
The Web page is *75%* symmetric		yes			
The Web page is *50%* symmetric			yes		
The Web page is *25%* symmetric				yes	
The Web page is *not* symmetric					yes
Monumental building					
On the *homepage* as the focus?	yes				
in the background?		yes			
On a *2nd* level Web page as the focus?		yes			
in the background?			yes		
On the *3rd* level Web page/pages or beyond				yes	
On *none* of the Web pages					yes
Symbol of nationalism or religion					
on *homepage and beyond*	yes				
on *homepage only*		yes			
on the *2nd* level page/pages			yes		
on the *3rd* level Web page/pages or beyond				yes	
on *none* of the Web pages					yes

Link to information about the leaders					
on *every* Web page	yes				
on *homepage and 2nd* level Web pages		yes			
on *homepage* only			yes		
on the *2nd* level Web page/pages and beyond				yes	
No such link is found					yes
Information arranged according to the management hierarchy. Home link is not counted.					
On navigation bar, is the Administration link					
the *first* link or in the first group of links?	yes				
the *2nd* link or in the second group of links?		yes			
the *3rd* link or in the third group of links?			yes		
the *4th* link or in the fourth group of links?				yes	
no such link found					yes
Authority figure					
More than one on the *homepage*	yes				
One on the *homepage*		yes			
More than one on the *2nd* level Web page/pages		yes			
One on a *2nd* level Web page			yes		
On the *3rd* level Web page(s) and/or beyond				yes	
on *none* of the Web pages					yes
Special title conferred on members (religious or political, like Rev., Majesty, Honorable)					
More than one on the *homepage*	yes				
One on the *homepage*		yes			
More than one on the *2nd* level Web page(s)		yes			
One on the *2nd* level Web page			yes		
More than one on the *3rd* level Web page(s)			yes		
One on the *3rd* level Web page and/or beyond				yes	
on *none* of the Web pages					yes

Chapter 21
Sharing Usability Information:
A Communication Paradox

Paula M. Bach
Pennsylvania State University, USA

Hao Jiang
Pennsylvania State University, USA

John M. Carroll
Pennsylvania State University, USA

ABSTRACT

In this chapter, we investigate the social and communication challenges surrounding usability information sharing. Our objective is to investigate a communication paradox: software development teams, consisting of usability engineers, software developers, and project managers, chose communication channels to use every day that are not channels they prefer to use. This paradox was discovered in a survey and explored further in interviews with software development teams. Results indicated that challenges with common ground and work coupling affect the extent to which the affordances of different communication channels can be taken advantage of. The value of this study highlights and explains the paradox from a time-space perspective and provides insight to usability information sharing among software engineering teams. Future work includes investigating the effect of social capital on communication channel preference along with understanding how important usability issues can be discussed in complex teams.

INTRODUCTION

Cooperative aspects of complex teamwork include communicating through various communication channels about important issues. Software development teams work together to solve problems of various types, regularly communicating with co-workers in different job roles (usability engineers, software developers, and project managers). They communicate about issues and share information across a variety of communication channels (email, chat, web tools, bug trackers, face-to-face meetings, casual face-to-face interactions). Thus, software development is a form of complex teamwork. Historically, usability teams have had challenges with integrating their activities into software engineering processes (Boivie, Gulliksen, & Goransson, 2006) making communication and information sharing particularly challenging for usability issues. Software engineering groups are responsible for

DOI: 10.4018/978-1-61520-827-2.ch021

designing and implementing the system taking special care that the software is free of errors and works according to specification. In contrast, usability groups are responsible for designing and evaluating interactive systems taking special care to create a desirable user experience.

In this chapter, we investigate the social and communication challenges surrounding usability information sharing. Our objective is to investigate a communication paradox where software development teams consisting of usability engineers, software developers, and project managers chose communication channels they used every day as the opposite of what they preferred to use. This paradox is investigated using a survey and interviews with software development teams.

BACKGROUND

In this section we overview background literature on information sharing in software development and prior literature on information sharing in teams to demonstrate the challenges and benefits of information sharing in groups. We also overview the affordances and constraints of various communication channels available for teams to use and share information.

Information Sharing

Sharing usability information across interactive system development teams is essential for communicating and understanding the needs of each team member's activities when working together to produce the system. Personal connections and interactions that transcend organizational boundaries, such as the separation between development teams and usability specialist teams, support the flow of information (Salvador & Bly, 1997). The idea is to package information so that many different people can use it. For example, developers need usability information to understand the designs they are coding (Poltrock et al., 2003). Ko et al.

(2007), found that such information needs include answers to the following questions: What is the program supposed to do? Is this problem worth fixing? What are the implications for this change? These needs connect to usability information because changes could affect the user experience. Thus, indicating where code changes might affect usability would be more easily addressed via communication channels that enhanced information sharing. In addition, software design teams consisting of members across different job functions, including managers, project coordinator, usability engineers, developers, and visual designers, have collective information needs including identifying information needs, formulating information queries, retrieving relevant information, and communicating about information needs (Poltrock et al., 2003). Furthermore, teams use different channels for communication. Yet they have a tendency to choose informal face-to-face communication, such as walking in others' offices or chatting in the hallway (Bach et al., 2008). Development, management, and usability teams have a variety of information needs that can be accomplished through various communication channels.

Prior research investigates the social effects of information sharing. Because psychological costs exist for asking about information, individuals follow the law of least effort (Daft & Lengel, 1986). For example, if a manager is concerned about making a deadline he might ask a developer how technical a usability fix is to implement. On one hand, he could wait until the team meeting or send an instant message to the developer to get a quick answer. The manager might be concerned however, that he must explain the details of the rationale in order for the developer to fully understand the fix. This is a psychological cost of information sharing. Contrary to psychological costs of information sharing is the benefit of shared experiences. Shared experiences in information sharing benefit teams by several mechanisms. One such mechanism, the common knowledge effect, states that an item of information will have more influence on the judgment of a group when it is shared (Gigone & Hastie, 1993). For example, when developers, usability experts, and managers all share a certain piece of information about a usability issue, that piece is deemed more important if it is shared. Another mechanism, shared context, proposes that developing a shared interpretive context helps groups lacking substantial history (Zack, 1993). Therefore, a shared context, such as a common development methodology or motivation to solve particular usability issues should provide a better information-sharing context for interdisciplinary teams with varying backgrounds. Finally, a resource for beneficial information sharing is the need for dense social networks (Sonnenwald & Pierce, 2000). These networks promote frequent communication among team members about work context and arising situations. Iverson & Lee (2006), in a study of information sharing in online spaces, found that participants' willingness to share information in online spaces varies according to how they perceive the information will be used. Furthermore, they found that how much individuals trusted each other affected their willingness to share information. This has potential impact on teams with diverse backgrounds, not knowing or trusting how or if a team member will understand or be able to use shared information effectively, or even correctly. In addition, Barua et al., (2007) also found trust effects in information sharing, especially when groups do not have knowledge of each other's information processing capacity. They also found that performance goals played a role as an incentive for cooperation which benefited information sharing. These social aspects of information sharing can impact the quality of information sharing and account for breakdowns or successes.

In addition to the impact of social aspects on information sharing, communication channels also impact information sharing. Miranda and Saunders argue that information sharing is a conduit for intersubjective interpretation (Miranda & Saunders, 2003). In their study, they found several

implications of socially constructed meaning during information sharing that was reflected in the channels used for information sharing. Construction of meaning was more productive during face-to-face information sharing sessions than with electronic ones. Their finding shows that low social presence media limits depth of sharing. Yet, benefits for information sharing of electronic media include task closure and promoted breadth of sharing. Furthermore, Zack found that a shared context can substitute for bandwidth and social presence (Zack, 1993). Thus teams can benefit from using electronic media if they have a shared context.

Given that costs and benefits exist for information sharing among various communication channels, teams use the various communication channels despite their costs. Team member preference for communication channels may point to which channels have more benefit than cost and why the given channel is beneficial. As such different communication channels affect the flow of usability information.

Communication

Communication between developers and usability experts can be compromised in many ways. The communication breakdowns have ramifications for common ground (Clark, 1996). Reaching a joint understanding, or common ground, is difficult not only because of different perspectives and goals of usability experts, developers, and managers, but also because of distancing effects (Wellens, 1986) and media richness (Daft & Lengel, 1986). Therefore different information channels have consequences for effective information sharing. Information sharing through different channels in situated problem solving can have drastically different results. For example, the same time aspect of chat may be useful for such problem solving, but it might be better for the developers and usability experts to sit next to each other and work on a usability problem together, if at all possible.

The degree to which usability and software engineering are integrated affects whether information sharing is most effective through a given communication channel, for example, face-to-face or through common information spaces. This topic, the affordances and constraints of various media/channels is widely studied in computer-mediated communication, notably Clark and Brennan (1991) and McCarthy and Monk (1994) with respect to common ground.

As stated above, the research is important because usability teams and software development teams face challenges with cooperation and information sharing. Therefore, the research presented here not only contributes to the literature on integrating usability and software engineering, but also the literature in information sharing, particularly in software development, and generally in teamwork especially with respect to the effects of communication channel use and information sharing.

COMMUNICATION CHANNELS IN USABILITY INFORMATION SHARING

In a preliminary data analysis of a study on usability information sharing across different roles, we found a paradox in the channels participants used and preferred for usability information sharing (Bach et al., 2008). We have continued this study with further data analysis as reported below.

The broader scope of our research agenda includes a study of the integration of usability activities into interactive system development. In this chapter we report on how software development teams use various communication channels for usability information sharing and explain a paradox in how teams use the various channels and what they prefer to use as well as the frustrations encountered with usability information sharing. The research setting is a large (80,000 employees and 440 products) technology company. We do not name the company to preserve anonymity. The rationale for choosing this company is that the types of products the company produces and software development work in the company are diverse with teams consisting of different combinations of project manager, developer, tester, and usability practitioner. The diversity of products meant that different arrangements of tasks and goals existed and enhanced the diversity of usability information sharing activities. Each team had a project manager, developer, and tester, but may or may not have had a usability practitioner as part of the team. Different combinations of usability membership include, having no usability members on the team to having a ratio of one usability member to twelve developers. For example, some products have usability experts depending on the size of the project, whereas other smaller projects have access to usability experts, but are not directly related to the project. This means that usability is not considered much on small teams, especially if a limited budget exists. Therefore the diversity of the teams is wide and information sharing across different disciplines tends to be difficult. As such, studying usability information sharing across the different disciplines in this setting was motivated by an opportunity to examine instances of information sharing challenges, particularly for usability experts.

Usability experts collect information from several inputs: best practices, customer support channels, sales and marketing, customer service, on-sight fieldwork, and competitive analysis of the market. These experts share the information with other members of the usability team and with members of the development team, including the project manager(s). The usability experts conduct user research, design mockups and prototypes, conduct usability testing, and work with developers and product managers to ensure users are represented throughout the development of a product.

Method

To explore usability information sharing as a function of communication channels, we used data from an exploratory survey and open-ended interviews. The data was collected from May to August 2007.

Survey

The exploratory survey was designed to elicit information about the importance and challenges of integrating usability into interactive system development. This included information sharing related to usability in general, and the different channels used and preferred for various usability activities. The survey had 21 questions in total, and for this study we used data from the four questions that revealed the paradox about usability information sharing.

The usability information sharing questions asked participants about which communication channel they used to share usability information, which channels they preferred to use, their reason for their preference, and what frustrates them most about usability information sharing. Usability information sharing is measured by asking participants about discussing usability issues. The following were the four survey questions.

1. Which of the following do you use to discuss usability issues? (Please check all that apply.)
2. What is the preferred way for you to discuss usability issues? (Please choose one.)
3. Why is this the preferred way of discussing usability issues effective? (Open-ended question.)
4. What is the most frustrating problem when discussing usability issues? (Open-ended question.)

The two open-ended questions were coded and as such we used qualitative methods to analyze these questions and quantitative methods to analyze the other questions and we merged both of the analyses (Creswell & Plano Clark, 2007). The open-ended questions were analyzed using an emergent coding process (Strauss & Corbin, 1998) to explore the range of rationales for channel preference and frustrating problems experienced during usability discussions. Two of the researchers developed an initial coding frame based on a first pass of the responses to the open-ended questions. Next the researchers discussed the coding frame and coded the responses. After several iterations and discussions with the research team, the coding frame was finalized and a last coding pass was made on each question with an inter-rater reliability of 98% for the question about rationale for preferred way to discuss usability issues and 84% for the question about frustrating problems.

The channels explored include informal (stopping by someone's office) and formal (team meetings) face-to-face, instant messaging (IM), email, web tools (e.g. wiki, Content Management System, or blog), and bug tracker. We piloted the survey with three employees to check for face validity of the questions and ensure the wording reflected organizational culture.

Interviews

Interviews were open-ended with the goal of exploring usability discussions and interactions among the different members of various software development teams. The interviews were recorded and transcribed by members of the research team. After discovering the communication channel and information sharing paradox, we looked for specific evidence in the interview data that would help explain the paradox. This approach is similar to theoretical sampling where researchers gain a deeper understanding of analyzed cases (Strauss & Corbin, 1998). As such we deduced an explanation of the paradox found in the survey data.

Figure 1. Types of projects represented in the survey

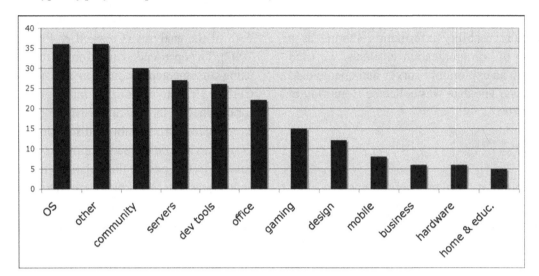

Participants

We wanted a wide coverage of projects to account for usability activities within the diversity of projects produced by the company, and the arrangement of development teams, management teams, and usability teams within the company. A representation of the diversity of projects survey respondents worked on is shown in figure 1.

Most of the projects are system software related as well as large applications. Many of the smaller projects are listed as *other*, and make up a just over 35% of the projects. *Other* projects include knowledge management websites, community websites, and internal tools, for example. Participants were project managers, usability experts, and developers.

Twelve hundred participants were chosen from the corporate email address book by job title, e.g. usability expert, project manager, developer. To choose the 1200, we downloaded the entire corporate address book of 80,000, filtered and separated by job title, and for each job title randomly chose 400 email addresses. Because the company is global, some participants were from different parts of the world, but most were from the main corporate office. Participants who responded to a request for

participation and completed the survey were entered into a draw for a $500 gift certificate to a popular online store. The survey collected a 19% response rate (n=229). The breakdown of roles included, 39% of the respondents had functions in the usability area; 34% had functions as a developer; and 27% were project managers. For the interviews, a question at the end of the survey asked participants if they were interested in a follow-up interview. Of the 229 survey respondents, 101 responded to the question about follow-up. Thirty-eight people responded to the initial contact and eleven participants were interviewed, with breakdown of four usability practitioners, four developers, and three project managers. The interviews were conducted at the main corporate office.

The interviews lasted from 25 to 90 minutes. Using the open-ended interview protocol, interview participants were asked about their job role, how usability discussions fit into their role, and, where possible, to reconstruct various discussions about usability issues. This reconstruction of usability sharing incidents allowed participants to share rich stories where the participant "recalls and recounts a relevant story" (Lutters & Seaman, 2007) that captures accounts of usability information sharing challenges.

Figure 2. Communication channels used for usability information sharing

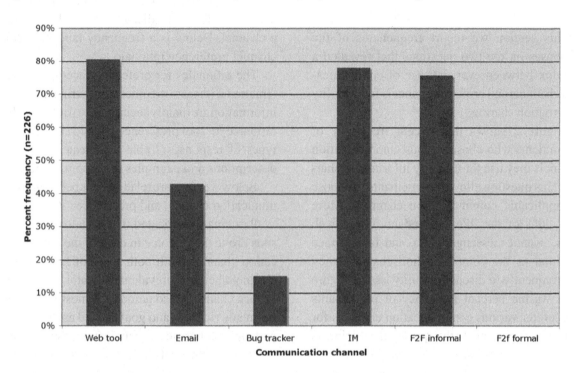

Figure 3. Communication channels preferred for usability information sharing

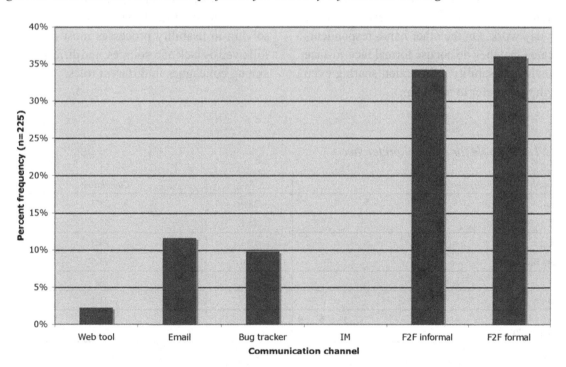

Results

In this section we report frequencies of the responses on the two questions that revealed a paradox between everyday use of communication channels and preferred channels for usability information sharing.

Figure 2 shows the percent frequency of respondents who chose various communication channels they use for usability information sharing. This question allowed participants to choose all applicable communication channels. More than 70% of the 226 respondents chose web tools, instant messenger (IM), and face-to-face informal as the communication channels they use frequently to discuss usability issues. Figure 3 shows the percent frequency of participants who prefer various communication channels for information sharing. In this question, participants chose one communication channel. The results show that close to 35% of the 225 respondents to this question prefer to use face-to-face channels, either formal or informal. This is in stark contrast to the channels used. Respondents chose to prefer formal and informal face to face rather than web tools and IM, which they actually use most in their everyday work. On the other hand, respondents indicated that they do not use formal face-to-face channels for usability information sharing even though they prefer to use them.

The relationship between channel and rationale for preference indicates possible benefit for a channel. Below is a frequency table for each channel preference rationale.

The rationales for preferring face-to-face interaction with team members for sharing usability information are mainly social and goal related. The rationale for tool preference yielded six different types of responses. Table 2 indicates category descriptions and examples of response types.

Below we compare relationships between communication channel and preference rationale.

Participants indicated that social-related reasons drove their choice in each of the communication channels with both types of face-to-face channels being a prevalent indicator. The face-to-face channels also gained the most responses for media richness and goal-related as the reason participants chose to communicate via the channel. The tool was the right choice for many respondents who chose email and bug tracker as their preferred channel for communicating usability issues.

Frustration about usability issue discussions yielded seven categories. Table 3 indicates descriptions and examples of response types.

Participants found issues related to problem solving in usability processes most frustrating, followed by lack of resources, and differing views among colleagues in different roles.

Table 1. Rationale for channel preference

Rationale for channel preference	*%*	*Cumulative %*
Social	38.7	38.7
Goal	25.1	63.8
Tool	16.1	79.9
Media Richness	13.6	93.5
Time	3.5	97
Usability Issue	3	100
N = 1 9 9 **Missing = 30**		

Table 2. Category descriptions for rationale

Category	Definition	Example
Tool related	Functions provided by channels or usability of tools, such as tracking, logging, and ease of use.	"It retains a copy of all the discussions about the issue which, if not recorded, can easily be forgotten."
Time related	Channel allows an increased response time or gets message to receiver quickly.	"Gives people the ability to think, rather than be time-pressured to think in f2f meetings."
Goal related	Channel aids with reaching objectives, such as solution, communication, and decision.	"More efficient to discuss large [numbers] of issues and get through them quickly."
Social related	Channels support interaction, information sharing among people, and bring different perspectives.	"Because all relevant parties can be present -- (hopefully) all disciplines (PM, Dev, Test, Usability, UE, etc) are present"
Media richness	The capacity of a communication channel that can convey social cues and amount of information. For example, face-to-face communication has highest media richness.	"There's a lot of nuance in usability issues that's lost in electronic communication."
Usability issue related	Usability issues are treated the same as bugs (normalization) or are formal and important issues (formalization).	"Because it's the same way that the rest of the product issues are discussed. This makes it clear that usability bugs are just like all other bugs."

Discussion

The data show a paradox for usability information sharing across different channels. When asked which communication channels they used, participants chose web tools, instant messaging, and face-to-face informal. Yet they did not choose face-to-face formal. When asked about which communication channel they preferred most, however, most participants chose face-to-face formal. In addition, respondents did not choose instant messaging at all as a preferred channel to share

Figure 4. Comparison of rationale for communication channel and preference

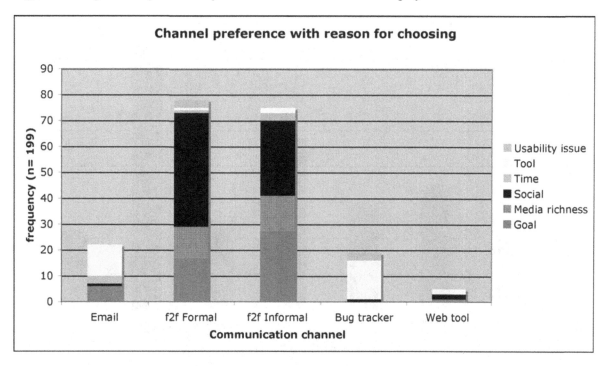

Table 3. Category descriptions for frustrating problems when discussing usability issues

Category	Definition	Example
Resources	(Lack of) Resource, such as time, people, expertise, or data, which contribute to discussion, decision making of usability issues.	"Not getting enough time to include a fix in the dev schedule."
Subjectivity	Decisions and/or arguments for usability change are made based on personal opinions, feelings, or taste	"There is no right answer, and when someone has as strong opinion, it is hard to back that up with fact or to refute it with fact."
Usability process	(Difficulties in) Identifying the problem, knowing what the best solution is, how to arrive at the best solution (through process), or agreeing what the best solution is, or that the problem exists	"Discussing the same problem again that you believed was fixed by a previous change. (I.E. it was either re-introduced, a regression, or the fix did not address the problem.)"
Users	(Lack of) Knowledge or information about target users	"Balancing the needs of the users of a particular thing"
Priority	(Lower) priority of usability issues compared with other issues, such as code defect.	"With the current amount of functionality defects, usability ranks very low."
Differing views	Different perspectives based on differing roles on the project, leading to breakdowns of communication, shared understanding of usability issues, etc.	"Different frames of reference for different team members. Dev, Test, PM, PdM, UX all look at problems in different ways. Finding a way to overcome this difficulty is the most important issue."
Communication	(Breakdowns of) Sharing usability information for understanding, keeping focus in meetings, or dissemination to key people	"Few people on the team share even a common vocabulary for discussing usability issues."

Figure 5. Frustrating problems when discussing usability issues

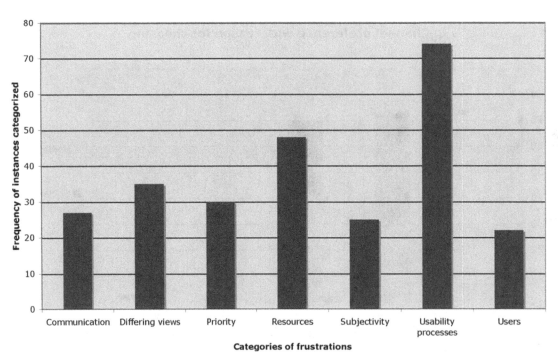

Table 4. time-place matrix, a communication channel view

	Same place (co-located)	Different place (remote)
Same time (synchronous)	IM (not intended) f2f formal f2f informal	IM
Difference time (asynchronous)	Email Web tools Bug tracker	Email Web tools Bug tracker

usability information, and very few (2%) chose web tools, even though over 80% chose web tools as one of the communication channels they used to discuss usability issues. These results are curious for the following reasons. First, we wonder why teams are not meeting to discuss usability issues. A first issue is that the teams are not co-located. We can conclude, however, that at least two of the team members are meeting face-to-face informally to discuss usability issues because 75% of them chose face-to-face as a communication channel. It could mean that not all of the team members are co-located, and therefore are not available to have a face-to-face formal meeting to discuss usability issues. Or it could mean that teams that are meeting face-to-face formally don't discuss usability issues at the formal meetings. Second, while instant messaging is a popular communication channel for discussing usability issues, it is not the preferred channel at all because none of the respondents chose it. If respondents don't prefer instant messaging then why are they using it? Use may be related to institutional norms (Handel & Herbsleb, 2002; Isaacs et al., 2002), that is, they use IM because everyone else does. Third, web tools are used frequently for sharing usability information, but are preferred by very few. This contrast could be due to use of or redundant secondary channels and organizational requirements. For example, usability specialists are required to use a content management system to store their field studies and usability reports but they discuss salient aspects of these reports with other team members in person.

If we view the communication channels on the time-place matrix shown in Table 4, we see that the synchronous channels (IM and f2f formal) showed the most distinct differences in the data, while the asynchronous channel, web tools, showed some distinction between use and preference.

The matrix indicates that both face-to-face channels and IM have same time and place affordances. Same place or co-located needs further distinction because various face-to-face situations may or may not be available for some team members. Face-to-face indicates that team members are in the same room and can see each other's gestures and hear each other speak. Day-to-day place, however, may not include team members sitting in the same room. Other orientations of co-located are *a few seconds away, same hallway, same floor, same building, same building cluster*, or *same metro area*. One could imagine face-to-face informal meetings happening frequently, where team members meet one-on-one when they are a few seconds away in the same hallway, just to drop in and ask a quick question. However, team members from all co-located orientations would be able to meet face-to-face for a formal meeting by walking down the hall or driving to a meeting room. Instant messaging is also available for all same time and place configurations in addition to same time, different place. Yet, while at same time and place, if respondents choose to ask a quick question via IM, the affordances limit the richness of a face-to-face channel. Given these differences in affordances between face-to-face and IM, and the preference for face-to-face chan-

415

nels, particular characteristics of sharing usability information might be driving the preference for face-to-face channels.

Distance Still Matters

Taking a close look at these channels, we found there are different constraints that can influence the choice of usability information sharing/communication channels in varied situations. This resonates with Olson and Olson's (2000) four conditions for success of collaboration tools. They are 1) common ground, which suggests that interlocutors should have or build shared understanding in order for the communication to be successful; 2) coupling of work, which denotes the complexity and the degree of intertwining of subtasks of a given task. A higher degree of coupling will impose more challenges for success of collaboration tools; 3) collaboration readiness, indicating the degree to which collaborators are ready to collaborate. This emphasizes sharing within group members and/or the readiness to cooperate; and 4) technology readiness, which refers to the technology skills required to use collaboration tools.

With these four concepts in mind, we went through the interview transcripts, and found issues that potentially hampered smooth communication and usability information sharing. Most are due to lack of common ground and complex coupling of work. It is not surprising that technology readiness is not a salient obstacle in our study setting, because the participants in this study were all from a software development company. However, lack of common ground and complex coupling of work can further diminish sharing among team members.

The interview data made clear the paradox between preference of communication channel and the actual tools used. From our analysis, we found that lack of common ground and complex coupling of work are major concerns for participants when they discussed their experiences related to sharing usability information and collaboration with other team members. Lack of common ground among team members was pervasive and covered factors related to usability knowledge/expertise/information. One participant said the following:

You have to recognize that the people you deal with are smart. If they are talking about something that seems stupid to you, there is a reason. It's either because you don't get it, or it's because they really don't get it, or it's because you are talking about totally different things and they don't realize it.

Interview and survey data revealed that team members with different roles not only differed in their understanding of usability, but also talked about usability differently. For example, when a usability issue emerged, team members prioritized problems differently; when approaching a usability issue, different knowledge sets may have reduced the effectiveness of information sharing and problem-solving; qualitative usability data presented to team members was not always understood; discrepancy about making decisions about usability design issues arose; and subjectivity usually lead to vacillation. Although the frustrations with usability discussions (differing views, priority, and subjectivity) from Table 3 are different in detail, they suggest an overall lack of common ground. Different roles and their implied responsibilities and foci restricted communications and usability information sharing.

The interviews revealed the importance and effects of building necessary common ground. For example, one participant mentioned the following:

There is storming where the productivity goes down and conflict goes up and then they start understanding ahhh now I understand what you are talking about and here is how I can collaborate and talk with you and so the trajectory goes up and now they're performing.

This quote shows that collaboration readiness contributes to usability information sharing.

As mentioned, software engineering is a very complex process, or using Olson and Olson's (2000) terminology, the coupling of work is close. Usability engineering work itself is highly coupled. A usability issue can come from different sources: a tester, user feedback, fieldwork, usability experiments, and so on. To resolve usability issues, different roles can be involved. For example, a usability issue can be a bug in the system, which leads to a system crash, but it can also be an improvement in the positioning of a button. To decide if a usability issue is a real problem, if it needs to be fixed in the current version or next, and how to fix it usually brings many people into the discussion and its final resolution depends on implementation by developers. The highly coupled work demands rich communication channels.

In the survey data, respondents mentioned many instances where they needed to share rich information with other teammates, especially with decision making about usability issues, such as discussing new designs or adding new features. In those situations, because (sub) tasks are interrelated and difficulty arises for stakeholders to understand the depth of issues related to usability, face-to-face communication, especially formal meetings, becomes a desired channel. We suspect because of informal face-to-face conversations and the absence of formal meetings, that the cost of formal meetings is too high. Informal conversations, however, occur amongst various key people.

In terms of collaboration readiness, lacking common ground in usability expertise and issues, such as differing attitudes toward usability, reduces the willingness to collaborate. For example, if a developer deems a usability fix unimportant, he might not want to spend time coding it. Considering the paradox we found from the previous study, these constraints partially explain the developer situation. Software development work in general and usability engineering in particular are complex

and highly coupled. As such, communication/information sharing channel choice is related to the degree of coupling and how much a task can be decomposed. Part of the work, after it is uncoupled, can be supported by particular types of communication technology. Ways of communicating and sharing information are determined by how coupled the work is.

Most of my strategies for communication is identifying the audience that needs to communicate and what it is gonna be used for, and how they are gonna need to use it.

That's one off or there is something I have to get to someone may not be connected to the network. Email is the right the vehicle. Emailing a document is ok thing to do, in that situation. However, if there is something where I am gonna need to refer to on and on basis, I need to put it some place where they can get out of it, and then I need to investigate and think about who are they that need to get out of it. So, a classic example, I have a team website that has multiple sets of document library, places where you stash different documents.

However, there are still many complex (sub) processes that are highly coupled even after decomposition. Our interviews and open-ended questions in the survey revealed that many processes are still highly coupled and the technologies are still unable support those processes. For example, when discussing a concrete usability design, engaging a team member with artifacts to be discussed is considered the most effective way of communicating usability information. But this is not possible beyond face-to-face channels.

Value of this Study

The value of this study relates to how usability knowledge and information are critical for successful team collaboration and communication.

In our previous study (Bach et al., 2008), we explored how job roles play a role in sharing and handling usability information among software development teams. In this chapter, we further analyzed usability information sharing practices and explained the usability information sharing channel paradox.

The different channels we investigated in this study have different features that benefit different situations, considering the time-space matrix. The paradox we found highlights the tension between practical needs and actual affordances provided by available technologies. Our analysis shows that some issues, many of which are rooted deeply in social context, need to be addressed in software development and usability engineering practices to be effective. Those issues are, for example, different or even contradict attitudes towards usability, which compounds information sharing and cooperation among different team members; also, common ground at various levels needs to be built in order to enhance communication. These call for a *place* or a *space* where team members can negotiate values, views, and understanding. However, the absence of using formal face-to-face communication to share usability information in practice may come from the fact, for example, that teams are distributed, so formal meetings are impossible and that scheduling/organizing meetings for every stakeholder to attend may be costly. In this sense, exploring common ground, collaboration readiness and supporting highly coupled work with technology will be of great value for information and communication technology researchers. However, we are not arguing all the issues can or should be solved with technologies; instead, the issues we highlighted here will need both technical as well as organizational/social remedies.

FUTURE RESEARCH DIRECTIONS

Our study provides starting points for future research. Common ground in complex social processes needs to be built more effectively. Also for complex coupling of work, we did not explore in detail the (de-) coupling work. In practice, people use existing technology to communicate when formal face-to-face meetings are not available. The division of labor in terms of task dependencies relies in part on job responsibility. It is valuable to see how people handle situations where for example worldviews clash but still need to collaborate. Differences in worldviews have been contributing factors in this research.

Collaboration readiness is also a factor in this research context. Common ground has an impact on collaboration readiness by bridging different worldviews of team members with different backgrounds. It is possible that high collaboration readiness can help overcome some obstacles of collaboration. Orlikowski (1992) showed that the same technology could be used differently in different social/organizational contexts and have different effects. Research from social psychology and sociology can shed some light on this. For example, intergroup behavior research discovered that putting people into different groups could lead to certain types of intergroup behavior. For example, people will favor the group they belong to and dislike outside group members. People usually see inner-group members as more consistent. Another possible direction is social capital. Recent research in knowledge management (KM) has begun to look at KM practices from a social capital perspective. Social capital is considered a resource that eases collaboration (Fukuyama, 2001) and knowledge/expertise sharing (Huysman & Wulf 2004; 2006; Wasko & Faraj, 2005).

CONCLUSION

We have presented a study investigating the affordances of communication channels used for sharing usability information. We investigated a particular paradox between chosen and preferred communication channels in a previous study. Upon further investigation with additional data we found that the effectiveness of usability information sharing is entangled in a complex web. This web poses challenges for work coupling and common ground. These issues are embedded in a complexity of social issues that teams must navigate while attending to usability issues. We have seen that the business of software development results in a complex social environment that is complicated by communication technologies and that in order for communication of usability information to be entirely successful, organizational changes such as building social capital amongst diverse and sometimes opposing teams is essential for successful use of communication technologies.

REFERENCES

Bach, P. M., Jiang, H., & Carroll, J. M. (2008). *Sharing usability information in interactive system development.* Paper presented at the 2008 international Workshop on Cooperative and Human Aspects of Software Engineering CHASE '08, Leipzig, Germany.

Barua, A., Ravindran, S., & Whinston, A. B. (2007). Enabling information sharing within organizations. *Information Technology and Management, 8,* 31–45. doi:10.1007/s10799-006-0001-7

Boivie, I., Gulliksen, J., & Goransson, B. (2006). The lonesome cowboy: A study of the usability designer role in systems development. *Interacting with Computers, 18*(4), 601–634. doi:10.1016/j.intcom.2005.10.003

Clark, H. H. (1996). *Using language.* New York: Cambridge University Press. doi:10.1017/CBO9780511620539

Clark, H. H., & Brennan, S. E. (1991). Grounding in communication. In Resnick, L., Levine, J. M., & Teasley, S. D. (Eds.), *Perspectives on socially shared cognition* (pp. 127–149). Washington, DC: APA. doi:10.1037/10096-006

Creswell, J. W., & Plano Clark, V. L. (2007). *Designing and conducting mixed methods research.* Thousand Oaks, CA: Sage.

Daft, R. L., & Lengel, R. H. (1986). Organizational information requirements, media richness and structural design. *Management Science, 32*(5), 554–571. doi:10.1287/mnsc.32.5.554

Fukuyama, F. (2001). Social capital, civil society and development. *Third World Quarterly, 22*(1), 7–20. doi:10.1080/713701144

Gigone, D., & Hastie, R. (1993). The common knowledge effect: information sharing and group judgement. *Journal of Personality and Social Psychology, 65*(5), 959–974. doi:10.1037/0022-3514.65.5.959

Handel, M., & Herbsleb, J. (2002). What is chat doing in the workplace? In [New York: ACM Press.]. *Proceedings of CSCW, 2002,* 1–10.

Huysman, M., & Wulf, V. (2004). *Social capital and information technology.* Cambridge, MA: MIT Press.

Huysman, M., & Wulf, V. (2006). IT to support knowledge sharing in communities, towards a social capital analysis. *Journal of Information Technology, 21*(1), 40–51. doi:10.1057/palgrave.jit.2000053

Isaacs, E., Walendowski, A., Whittaker, S., Schiano, D. J., & Kamm, C. (2002). The character, functions, and styles of instant messaging in the workplace. In *Proceedings of ACM CSCW Conf* (pp. 11–20). New York: ACM.

Ko, A. J., DeLine, R., & Venolia, G. (2007). Information Needs in Collocated Software Development Teams. In *Proceedings of the 29th international Conference on Software Engineering* (May 20 - 26, 2007). ICSE. IEEE Computer Society, Washington, DC\.

Lutters, W. G., & Seaman, C. B. (2007). Revealing actual documentation usage in software maintenance through war stories. *Information and Software Technology, 49*(6), 576–587. doi:10.1016/j.infsof.2007.02.013

McCarthy, J. C., & Monk, A. F. (1994). Measuring the quality of computer-mediated communication. *Behaviour & Information Technology, 13*(5), 311–319. doi:10.1080/01449299408914611

Miranda, S. M., & Saunders, C. S. (2003). The social construction of meaning: an alternative perspective on information sharing. *Information Systems Research, 14*(1), 87–106. doi:10.1287/isre.14.1.87.14765

Olson, G. M., & Olson, J. S. (2000). Distance matters. *Human-Computer Interaction, 15*(2/3), 139–179. doi:10.1207/S15327051HCI1523_4

Orlikowski, W. (1992). Learning from notes: Organizational issues in groupware implementation. In *Proceedings of the Conference on Computer Supported Cooperative Work*, (pp.362–369). New York: ACM.

Poltrock, S., Grudin, J., Dumais, S., Fidel, R., Bruce, H., & Pejtersen, A. M. (2003). *Information Seeking and Sharing in Design Teams*. Paper presented [New York: ACM.]. *Group, 03*, 239–247.

Razavi, M. N., & Iverson, L. (2006, November 4-8). *A Grounded Theory of Information Sharing Behavior in a Personal Learning Space*. Paper presented at the CSCW '06, Banff, Canada.

Salvador, T., & Bly, S. (1997). *Supporting the flow of information through constellations of interaction*. Paper presented at the ECSCW'97, 269-280, Springer.

Sonnenwald, D. H., & Pierce, L. G. (2000). Information behavior in dynamic group work contexts: interwoven situational awareness, dense social networks and contested collaboration in command and control. *Information Processing & Management, 36*, 461–479. doi:10.1016/S0306-4573(99)00039-4

Strauss, A., & Corbin, J. (1998). *Basics of oualitative research* (2nd ed.). Thousand Oaks, CA: Sage Publications.

Wasko, M. M., & Faraj, S. (2005). Why should I share? Examining social capital and knowledge contribution in electronic networks of practice. *Management Information Systems Quarterly, 29*(1), 35–57.

Wellens, R. A. (1986). Use of a psychological distancing model to assess differences in telecommunication media. In Parker, L. A., & Olgren, O. H. (Eds.), *Teleconferencing and Electronic Communication*. Madison, WI: University of Wisconsin Extension.

Zack, M. H. (1993). Interactivity and communication mode choice in ongoing management groups. *Information Systems Research, 4*(3), 207–239. doi:10.1287/isre.4.3.207

Compilation of References

Adelman, M. B., Parks, M. R., & Albrecht, T. L. (1987). Beyond close relationships: Support in weak ties. In Albrecht, T. L., & Adelman, M. B. (Eds.), *Communicating social support* (pp. 105–125). Beverly Hills, CA: Sage.

Adler, P. A., & Adler, P. (2007). The demedicalization of self-injury: From psychopathology to sociological deviance. *Journal of Contemporary Ethnography, 36*(5), 537–570. doi:10.1177/0891241607301968

Adler, P. A., & Adler, P. (2008). The cyber worlds of self-injurers: Deviant communities, relationships, and selves. *Symbolic Interaction, 31*, 33–56. doi:10.1525/si.2008.31.1.33

Afifi, T. D., Olson, L. N., & Armstrong, C. (2005). The chilling effect and family secrets: Examining the role of self protection, other protection, and communication efficacy. *Human Communication Research, 31*, 564–598. doi:10.1093/hcr/31.4.564

Afifi, W. A., & Caughlin, J. P. (2006). A close look at revealing secrets and some consequences that follow. *Communication Research, 33*, 467–488. doi:10.1177/0093650206293250

Afifi, W. A., & Guerrero, L. K. (2000). Motivations underlying topic avoidance in close relationships. In Petronio, S. (Ed.), *Balancing the secrets of private disclosures* (pp. 165–180). Mahwah, NJ: Lawrence Erlbaum Associates.

Afifi, W. A., & Lucas, A. A. (2008). Information seeking in the initial stages of relationship development. In Sprechter, S., Wenzel, A., & Harvey, J. (Eds.), *Handbook of Relationship Initiation* (pp. 135–152). New York: Psychology Press.

Ahmad, F., Shik, A., Vanza, R., Cheung, A., George, U., & Stewart, D. E. (2004). Popular health promotion strategies among Chinese and East Indian immigrant women. *Women & Health, 40*(1), 21–40. doi:10.1300/J013v40n01_02

Ahmed, S., & Stacey, J. (2001). *Thinking through skin.* London, UK: Routledge.

Ahuja, M. K., & Galvin, J. E. (2003). Socialization in virtual groups. *Journal of Management, 29*(2), 161–185. doi:10.1177/014920630302900203

Akrich, M. (1987). Comment décrire les objets techniques? *Technology and Culture, 9*, 49–64.

Albrecht, T. A., & Adelman, M. B. (1987). Communicating social support: A theoretical perspective. In Albrecht, T. A., & Adelman, M. B. (Eds.), *Communicating social support: A theoretical perspective* (pp. 18–39). Thousand Oaks, CA: Sage.

Albrecht, T. L., & Goldsmith, D. J. (2003). Social support, social networks, and health. In Thompson, T. L., Dorsey, A. M., Miller, K. I., & Parrott, R. (Eds.), *Handbook of health communication* (pp. 263–284). Mahwah, NJ: Lawrence Erlbaum Associates.

Alexander, B. (2008, July/August). Games for education: 2008. *EDUCAUSE* Review, *43*(4), 64-65. Retrieved July 10, 2008, from http://www.educause.edu/ir/library/pdf/ERM0849.pdf

Alexander, B. K. (2008). Performance ethnography: The reenacting and inciting of culture. In Denzin, N. K., & Lincoln, Y. S. (Eds.), *Strategies of qualitative inquiry* (3rd ed., pp. 75–117). Thousand Oaks, CA: Sage.

Althaus, S. (1997, July). Computer-mediated communication in the university classroom: an experiment with on-line discussions. *Communication Education, 46,* 158–174. doi:10.1080/03634529709379088

Althusser, L. (1971). Ideology and ideological state apparatuses (B. Brewster, Trans.). Lenin and Philosophy, and other Essays. New York: Monthly Review Press.

Annese, S. (2005). Processi di negoziazione e posizionamenti identitari in una comunità di pratiche. *Ricerche di Psicologia, 28*(3), 33–63.

Anonymous,. (1998). To reveal or not to reveal: A theoretical model of anonymous communication. *Communication Theory, 8,* 381–407. doi:10.1111/j.1468-2885.1998.tb00226.x

Antaki, C., Ardévol, E., Núñez, F., & Vayreda, A. (2005). 'For she who knows who she is': Managing accountability in online forum messages. *Journal of Computer-Mediated Communication, 11*(1), article 6. Retrieved February, 2009, from http://jcmc.indiana.edu/vol11/issue1/antaki.html

Anton, C. (2001). *Selfhood and authenticity.* Albany, New York: State University of New York Press.

Anton, C. (2002). Discourse as Care: A Phenomenological Consideration of Spatiality and Temporality. *Human Studies, 25,* 185–205. doi:10.1023/A:1015552526781

Anton, C. (2005). Early western writing, sensory modalities, and modern alphabetic literacy: On the origins of representational theorizing. *Explorations in Media Ecology: The Journal of the Media Ecology Association, 4*(2), 99–122.

Anton, C. (2005). Presence and interiority: Walter Ong's contributions to a diachronic phenomenology of voice. In Farrell, T. J., & Soukup, P. (Eds.), *Ong and media ecology: Essays in communication, composition, and literary studies.* Hampton Press.

Appadurai, A. (2002). Disjuncture and difference in the global cultural economy. In Xavier Inda, J., & Rosaldo, R. (Eds.), *The anthropology of globalization: A reader* (pp. 46–64). Malden, MA: Blackwell Publishers.

Arbaugh, J., Cleveland-Innes, M., Diaz, S., Garrison, R., Ice, P., Richardson, J., & Swan, K. (2008). Developing a community of inquiry instrument: Testing a measure of the community of inquiry framework using a multi-institutional sample. *The Internet and Higher Education, 11*(3-4), 133–136. doi:10.1016/j.iheduc.2008.06.003

Argamon, S., Koppel, M., Pennebaker, J. W., & Schler, J. (2007). Mining the Blogosphere: Age, gender and the varieties of self-expression. *First Monday, 12.* Retrieved April 7, 2008, from http://outreach.lib.uic.edu/www/issues/issue12_9/argamon/

Aries, E. (1996). *Men and women in interaction: Reconsidering the differences.* New York: Oxford University Press.

Aries, E. (1998). Gender differences in interaction: A reexamination. In Canary, D., & Dindia, K. (Eds.), *Sex differences and similarities in communication: Critical essays and empirical investigations of sex and gender in interaction* (pp. 65–82). Mahwah, NJ: Lawrence Erlbaum Associates.

Aristotle,. (1981). *On Poetics.* Pennsylvania: The Franklin Library. [translated by Ingram Bywater]

Arreguin, C. (2007). Reports from the field: Second Life community convention 2007 education track summary. *Global Kids Series on Virtual Worlds Report.* Retrieved March 23, 2008, from http://www.holymeatballs.org/pdfs/VirtualWorldsforLearningRoadmap_012008.pdf

Au, W. J. (2008). *The making of Second Life: Notes from the new world.* New York: Collins.

Aviv, R., Zippy, E., Ravid, G., & Geva, A. (2003). Network Analysis of Knowledge Construction in Asynchronous Learning Networks. *JALN, 7*(3), 1–23.

Awonusi, S. (2004). "Little Englishes" and the law of energetics: A sociolinguistic study of SMS text messages as register and discourse. In Awonusi, S., & Babalola, E. A. (Eds.), *The domestication of English in Nigeria* (pp. 45–62). Lagos, Nigeria: University of Lagos Press.

Bach, P. M., Jiang, H., & Carroll, J. M. (2008). *Sharing usability information in interactive system development.* Paper presented at the 2008 international Workshop on Cooperative and Human Aspects of Software Engineering CHASE '08, Leipzig, Germany.

Badiou, A. (2005). *Being and event.* New York: Continuum.

Baker, A. (1998). Cyberspace couples finding romance online then meeting for the first time in real life. *CMC Magazine*, July 1998. Retrieved May 2009, from http://www.december.com/cmc/mag/1998/jul/baker.html

Bakhtin, M. (1973). *Problems of Dostoevsky's Poetics* (Emerson, C. (Trans. Ed.)). Manchester, England: Manchester University Press.

Bakhtin, M. M. (1981). *The dialogic imagination* (pp. 259–300). (Emerson, C., & Holquist, M., Trans.). Austin, TX: University of Texas Press.

Baltes, B. B., Dickson, M. W., Sherman, M. P., Bauer, C. C., & LaGanke, J. S. (2002). Computer-mediated communication and group decision making: A meta-analysis. *Organizational Behavior and Human Decision Processes*, *87*, 156–179. doi:10.1006/obhd.2001.2961

Balthazard, P. A., Potter, R. E., & Warren, J. (2004). Expertise, extraversion and group interaction styles as performance indicators in virtual teams. *The Data Base for Advances in Information Systems*, *35*, 41–64.

Barak, A. (2005). Sexual harassment on the Internet. *Social Science Computer Review*, *23*, 77–92. doi:10.1177/0894439304271540

Barbieri, F. (2008). Patterns of age-based linguistic variation in American English. *Journal of Sociolinguistics*, *12*(1), 58–88. doi:10.1111/j.1467-9841.2008.00353.x

Bargh, J. A., & McKenna, K. Y. A. (2004). The Internet and social life. *Annual Review of Psychology*, *55*, 573–590. doi:10.1146/annurev.psych.55.090902.141922

Bargh, J. A., McKenna, K. Y. A., & Fitzsimons, G. M. (2002). Can you see the real me? Activation and expression of the "true self" on the Internet. *The Journal of Social Issues*, *58*, 33–48. doi:10.1111/1540-4560.00247

Bar-Lev, S. (2008). "We are here to give you emotional support": Performing emotions in an online HIV/AIDS support group. *Qualitative Health Research*, *18*(4), 509–521. doi:10.1177/1049732307311680

Barnes, S. (2003). *Computer-mediated communication: Human-to-human communication across the Internet.* Boston, MA: Allyn & Bacon.

Barnes, S. (2003). Cyberspace: Creating paradoxes for the ecology of self. In L. Strate, R. L. Jacobson, & S. Gibson (Eds.), Communication and cyberspace: Social interaction in an electronic environment (2nd. ed., pp. 229-253). Cresskill, NJ: Hampton Press.

Baron, D. (1999). From pencils to pixels: The stages of literacy technologies. In Hawishier, G., & Selfe, C. (Eds.), *Passions, pedagogies, and 21st century technologies* (pp. 15–33). Logan, UT: Utah State UP.

Baron, N. S. (2004). See you online: Gender issues in college student use of instant messaging. *Journal of Language and Social Psychology*, *23*, 397–423. doi:10.1177/0261927X04269585

Barrios, B. (2005). Blogs: A primer: A guide to weblogs in the classroom and in research for compositionists, rhetoricians, educators, &c. *Computers and composition online.* Retrieved February 24, 2009, from http://www.bgsu.edu/departments/english/cconline/bap/

Barua, A., Ravindran, S., & Whinston, A. B. (2007). Enabling information sharing within organizations. *Information Technology and Management*, *8*, 31–45. doi:10.1007/s10799-006-0001-7

Bastian, M. L. (1999). Nationalism in the Virtual Space, Immigrant Nigerians on the Internet. *West African Review 1.* Retrieved November 13, 2008, from http://www.westafricareview.com/vol1.1/bastian.html

Baym, N. K. (1995). From practice to culture on Usenet. In Star, S. L. (Ed.), *The cultures of computing* (pp. 29–52). Oxford, UK: Blackwell.

Baym, N. K. (1998). The emergente of Online Community. In Jones, S. G. (Ed.), *Cibersociety 2.0. Revising Computer-Mediated Communication and Technology* (pp. 35–68). Thousand Oaks, CA: Sage.

Baym, N. K., Zhang, Y. B., & Lin, M. (2004). Social interactions across media: Interpersonal communication on the internet, telephone, and face-to-face. *New Media & Society*, *6*(3), 299–318. doi:10.1177/1461444804041438

Bayne, S. (2005). Deceit, desire and control: the identities of learners and teachers in cyberspace. In Land, R., & Bayne, S. (Eds.), *Education in cyberspace* (pp. 26–42). London: Routledge Falmer.

Beckerman, Z. (2001). Constructivist perspectives on language, identity, and culture: Implications for Jewish identity and the education of Jews. *Religious Education (Chicago, Ill.)*, *96*(4), 462–473. doi:10.1080/003440801753442375

Beebe, S. A., & Masterson, J. T. (2006). *Communicating in Small Groups: Principles and practices* (8th ed.). Boston, MA: Pearson Education, Inc.

Beebe, S. A., Beebe, S. J., & Ivy, D. K. (2009). Communication Principles for a Lifetime: *Vol. 3. Communicating in groups and teams* (2nd ed.). Boston, MA: Pearson Education, Inc.

Belz, J. (2002). Social dimensions of telecollaborative foreign language study. *Language Learning & Technology*, *6*(1), 60–81.

Benne, K. D., & Sheats, P. (1948). Functional roles of group members. *The Journal of Social Issues*, *4*, 41–49.

Bente, G., Ruggenberg, S., Kramer, N. C., & Eschenburg, F. (2008). Avatar-mediated networking: Increasing social presence and interpersonal trust in net-based collaborations. *Human Communication Research*, *34*, 287–318. doi:10.1111/j.1468-2958.2008.00322.x

Berard, T. (2005). On multiple identities and educational contexts: Remarks on the study of inequalities and discrimination. *Journal of Language, Identity, and Education*, *4*(1), 67–76. doi:10.1207/s15327701jlie0401_4

Berger, B., & Berger, P. (1983). *The War over the Family*. London: Hutchinson.

Berger, C. R. (1979). Beyond initial interaction: Uncertainty, understanding, and the development of interpersonal relationships. In Giles, H., & St. Clair, R. N. (Eds.), *Language and social psychology* (pp. 122–144). Oxford, UK: Basil Blackwell.

Berger, C. R. (1987). Communicating under uncertainty. In Roloff, M. E., & Miller, G. R. (Eds.), *Interpersonal processes: New directions in communication research* (pp. 39–62). Newbury Park, CA: Sage.

Berger, C. R. (1997). Producing messages under uncertainty. In Greene, J. (Ed.), *Message Production: Advances in Communication Theory* (pp. 221–244). Mahwah, NJ: Lawrence Erlbaum Associates.

Berger, C. R. (2005). Interpersonal communication: Theoretical perspectives, future prospects. *The Journal of Communication*, *55*, 415–447. doi:10.1111/j.1460-2466.2005.tb02680.x

Berger, C. R., & Calabrese, R. J. (1975). Some explorations in initial interaction and beyond: Toward a developmental theory of interpersonal communication. *Human Communication Research*, *1*, 99–122. doi:10.1111/j.1468-2958.1975.tb00258.x

Berger, J. (1977). *Ways of seeing*. New York: Penguin Books.

Berger, P., & Luckmann, T. (1966). *The social construction of reality*. Harmondswarth, UK: Penguin.

Berkman, L. F. (2000). Social support, social networks, social cohesion and health. *Social Work in Health Care*, *31*(2), 3–14. doi:10.1300/J010v31n02_02

Bernhardt, J. M., & Felter, E. M. (2004). Online pediatric information seeking among mothers of young children: Results from a qualitative study using focus groups. *Journal of Medical Internet Research*, *6*(1), 7. doi:10.2196/jmir.6.1.e7

Berscheid, E., & Peplau, L. (1983). The emerging science of relationships. In Kelly, H. H., Huston, T. L., & Leaving, G. (Eds.), *Close Relationships* (pp. 1–19). New York: Freeman.

Berscheid, E., Dion, K., Walster, E., & Walster, G. W. (1971). Physical attractiveness and dating choice: A test of the matching hypothesis. *Journal of Experimental Social Psychology*, *7*, 173–189. doi:10.1016/0022-1031(71)90065-5

Bersheid, E., & Reis, H. T. (1998). Attraction and close relationships. In S. Fiske, D. Gilbert, & G. Lindsey (Eds.), Handbook of social psychology (4th ed., Vol. 2), pp. 93-281. NewYork: McGraw-Hill.

Bersin, J. (2004). *The blended Learning Book. Best Practices, Proven Methodologies, and Lessons Learned.* London: Wiley Publishers.

Bertinetto, P. M. (1979). 'Come vi pare'. La ambiguetà di 'come' e I rapporti tra paragone e metafora. In Leoni, A., & Piglliasco, M. (Eds.), *Retorica e scienze dil linguaggio* (pp. 131–170). Roma: Bulzoni.

Biggs, M. (2006). Comparison of student perceptions of classroom instruction: Traditional, hybrid, and distance education. *Turkish Online Journal of Distance Education*, *7*(2), 46–58.

Bijker, W. E., Hugues, T., & Pinch, T. (1987). *The social construction of technological Systems. New Directions in the Sociology and History of Technology.* Cambridge, MA: MIT Press.

Birchmeier, Z., Joinson, A. N., & Dietz-Uhler, B. (2005). Storming and forming a normative response to a deception revealed online. *Social Science Computer Review*, *23*, 108–121. doi:10.1177/0894439304271542

Birnie, S. A., & Horvath, P. (2002). Psychological Predictors of Internet Social Communication. *Journal of Computer-Mediated Communication, 7*(4). Retrieved May 14, 2009, from http://jcmc.indiana.edu/vol7/issue4/horvath.html

Bischoping, K. (1993). Gender differences in conversation topics, 1922-1990. *Sex Roles*, *28*, 1–18. doi:10.1007/BF00289744

Black, M. (1966). *Modelos y metáforas*. Madrid, Spain: Editorial Tecnos.

Black, R. W. (2006). Language, culture, and identity in online fanfiction. *E-learning*, *3*(2), 170–184. doi:10.2304/elea.2006.3.2.170

Blaskovich, J. L. (2008). Exploring the effect of distance: An experimental investigation of virtual collaboration, social loafing, and group decisions. *Journal of Information Systems*, *22*(1), 27–46. doi:10.2308/jis.2008.22.1.27

Bloch, J., & Crosby, C. (2008). Blogging and academic writing development. In Zhang, F., & Barber, B. (Eds.), *Handbook of research on computer-enhanced language acquisition and learning* (pp. 36–47). Hershey, PA: Information Science Reference.

Blood, R. (2002). *The weblog handbook: Practical advice on creating and maintaining your blog*. Cambridge, MA: Perseus Publishing.

Blood, R. (2004). How blogging software reshapes the online community. *Communications of the ACM*, *47*(12), 53–55. doi:10.1145/1035134.1035165

Blumer, H. (1969). *Symbolic Interactionism: Perspective and Method*. Berkeley, CA: University of California Press.

Blumler, J. (1979). The role of theory in uses and gratifications studies. *Communication Research*, *6*, 9–36. doi:10.1177/009365027900600102

Boase, J., & Wellman, B. (2006). Personal relationships: On and off the Internet. In Vangelisti, A., & Perlman, R. (Eds.), *The Handbook of Personal Relations* (pp. 709–723). Cambridge, UK: Cambridge University Press.

Boberg, E. W., Gustafson, D. H., Hawkins, R. P., Chan, C. L., Bricker, E., & Pingree, S. (1995). Development, acceptance, and use patterns of a computer-based education and social support system for people living with AIDS/HIV infection. *Computers in Human Behavior*, *11*, 289–311. doi:10.1016/0747-5632(94)00037-I

Boivie, I., Gulliksen, J., & Goransson, B. (2006). The lonesome cowboy: A study of the usability designer role in systems development. *Interacting with Computers*, *18*(4), 601–634. doi:10.1016/j.intcom.2005.10.003

Boler, M. (2002). The new digital Cartesianism: Bodies and space in online education. In the Philosophy of Education Society (ed.), Philosophy of Education (pp.331-340). Urbana, IL: Studies in Philosophy and Education.

Boling, E., Castek, J., Zawilinski, L., Barton, K., & Nierlich, T. (2008). Technology in literacy education collaborative literacy: Blogs and Internet projects. *The Reading Teacher, 61*(6), 504–406. doi:10.1598/RT.61.6.10

Bolter, J. D. (2001). *Writing space: Computers, hypertext, and the remediation of print* (2nd ed.). Hillsdale, NJ: Erlbaum Associates.

Boneva, B., Kraut, R., & Frohlich, D. (2001). Using e-mail for personal relationships: The difference gender makes. *The American Behavioral Scientist, 45*, 530–549. doi:10.1177/00027640121957204

Bonk, C. J., & Grahm, C. R. (2006). *Handbook of blended learning: global perspectives, local designs.* San Francisco: Pfeiffer.

Bortree, D. S. (2005). Presentation of self on the Web: An ethnographic study of teenage girls' weblogs. *Education, Communication, and Information Journal, 5*(1), 25–40.

Bott, E. (1971). *Family and social network.* New York: Free Press.

Bourdieu, P., & Wacquant, L. (1992). *An invitation to reflexive sociology.* Chicago: University of Chicago Press.

Boyd, D. (2006, October 2). The Significance of Social Software. *BlogTalks Reloaded.* Vienna, Austria.

Boyd, D. (2007). Why youth (heart) social network sites: The role of networked publics in teenage social life. In D. Buckingham (Ed.) *MacArthur Foundation series on digital learning- Youth, identity, and digital media* (pp. 119-142).Cambridge, MA: MIT Press .

Boyd, D. (2008). Facebook's privacy trainwreck: Exposure, invasion, and social convergence. *Convergence, 14* (1), 13-20.

Boyd, D., and Ellison, N.. (2007). Social network sites: Definition, history and scholarship. *Journal of Computer-Mediated Communication, 13*(1), article 11.

Braithwaite, D. O., Waldron, V. R., & Finn, J. (1999). Communication of social support in computer-mediated groups for people with disabilities. *Health Communication, 11*(2), 123–151. doi:10.1207/s15327027hc1102_2

Brennan, P. F., Moore, S. M., & Smyth, K. A. (1992). Alzheimer's disease caregivers' uses of a computer network. *Western Journal of Nursing Research, 14*(5), 662–673. doi:10.1177/019394599201400508

Bretag, T. (2006). Developping 'Third Space' interculturality Using Computer-Mediated Comunication. *Journal of computer-Mediated Communication, 11*(4), 981-1011, article 5. Retrieved February, 2009, from http://jcmc.indiana.edu/vol11/issue4/bretag.html

Bridge, K., & Baxter, L. (1992). Blended friendships: Friends as work associates. *Western Journal of Communication, 56*, 200–225.

Brock, A. (2007). *Race, the Internet, and the hurricane: A critical discourse analysis of black identity online during the aftermath of Hurricane Katrina.* Unpublished doctoral dissertation, Library and Information Studies, University of Illinois at Urbana-Champaign.

Bruckman, A. (1998). Community support for constructionist learning. *Computer Supported Cooperative Work: The Journal of Collaborative Computing, 7*, 47–86. doi:10.1023/A:1008684120893

Bruckman, A. (2006). Analysis of log file data to understand behavior and learning in an online community. In Weiss, J. (Eds.), *The international handbook of virtual learning environments* (pp. 1449–1465). New York: Springer. doi:10.1007/978-1-4020-3803-7_58

Bruner, J. (1996). *The Culture of Education.* Cambridge, MA: Harvard University Press.

Buber, M. (1957). Elements of the interhuman. *Psychiatry, 120*, 105–113.

Bucholtz, M. (2000). Language and youth culture. *American Speech*, 75(3), 280–283. doi:10.1215/00031283-75-3-280

Bucholtz, M. (2003). Sociolinguistic nostalgia and the authentication of identity. *Journal of Sociolinguistics*, 7(3), 398–416. doi:10.1111/1467-9481.00232

Bugeja, M. (2005). *Interpersonal divide: The search for community in a technological age.* New York: Oxford University Press.

Burgmann, I., Kitchen, P. J., & Williams, R. (2006). Does culture matter on the Web? *Marketing Intelligence & Planning*, 24(1), 62–76. doi:10.1108/02634500610641561

Burkhaler, B. (1999). Reading race online. In Smith, M. A., & Kollock, P. (Eds.), *Communities in Cyberspace* (pp. 60–75). London: Routledge.

Burleson, B. R., & MacGeorge, R. L. (2002). Supportive communication. In Knapp, M. L., & Daly, J. A. (Eds.), *Handbook of interpersonal communication* (pp. 374–424). Thousand Oaks, CA: Sage.

Burnett, G., & Buerkle, H. (2004). Information exchange in virtual communities: A comparative study. *Journal of Computer-Mediated Communication*, 9(2).

Burrell, N., Donohue, W., & Allen, M. (1988). Gender-based perceptual biases in mediation. *Communication Research*, 15, 447–469. doi:10.1177/009365088015004006

Buunk, B. P., & Gibbons, F. X. (1997). *Health, coping and well-being.* Mahwah, NJ: Lawrence Erlbaum Associates.

Byrne, D. (1971). *The attraction paradigm.* New York: Academic Press.

Byrne, D. N. (2007). Public discourse, community concerns, and civic engagement: Exploring black social networking traditions on BlackPlanet.com. *Journal of Computer-Mediated Communication*, 13(1), 16.

Byrne, R., & Findlay, B. (2004). Preference for SMS versus telephone calls in initiating romantic relationships. *Australian Journal of Emerging Technologies and Society*, 2(1), 48–61.

Camarota, S. (2007). Immigrants in the United States, 2007: A profile of America's foreign-born population. *The Center for Immigration Studies.* Retrieved on October 30, 2008, from http://www.cis.org/immigrants_profile_2007

Canary, D. J., & Stafford, L. (1994). Maintaining relationships through strategic and routine interaction. In D. J. Canary & L. Stafford's (Eds.), Communication and relational maintenance (pp. 3-22). San Diego, CA: Academic Press, Inc.

Canary, D. J., Stafford, L., Hause, K. S., & Wallace, L. A. (1993). An inductive analysis of relational maintenance strategies: Comparisons among lovers, relatives, friends, and others. *Communication Research Reports*, 10, 5–14. doi:10.1080/08824099309359913

Carpenter, E. (1973). *Oh, what a blow that phantom gave me!* New York: Bantam Books.

Caughlin, J. P., & Afifi, T. D. (2004). When is topic avoidance unsatisfying? Examining moderators of the association between avoidance and dissatisfaction. *Human Communication Research*, 30, 479–513. doi:10.1093/hcr/30.4.479

Caughlin, J. P., Afifi, W. A., Carpenter-Theune, K. E., & Miller, L. E. (2005). Reasons for, and consequences of, revealing personal secrets in close relationships: A longitudinal study. *Personal Relationships*, 12, 43–59. doi:10.1111/j.1350-4126.2005.00101.x

Cerulo, K. A. (1997). Identity construction: New issues, new directions. *Annual Review of Sociology*, 23, 385–409. doi:10.1146/annurev.soc.23.1.385

Chambers, J. K. (2003). *Sociolinguistic theory: Linguistic variation and its social significance.* Oxford, UK: Blackwell.

Chan, B. (2006). Virtual communities and Chinese national identity. *Journal of Chinese Overseas*, 2(1), 1–32. doi:10.1353/jco.2006.0001

Chandler, D. (2002). *Semiotics: The basics.* New York: Taylor and Francis. Retrieved May 4, 2006, from http://www.netlibrary.com

Chayko, M. (2002). *Connecting, how we form social bonds and communities in the Internet age*. Albany, NY: State University of New York Press.

Chen, D. (2008a). Boke xiezuo tezheng jiqi shuangchongxiaoying yanjiu (The writing style of blogging and its dual effects). *Journal of Henan Normal University, 35*(4), 197–199.

Chen, D. (2008b). Boke: yizhong xinxingde wanluo xiezuo xingshi (Blogging: a newly emerged online writing). *Lilun chuangxin tanqiu (Theoretical Innovation Inquiry)*, 178-180.

Cherny, L. (1999). *Conversation and community: Chat in a virtual world*. Stanford, CA: CSLI Publications.

Chesebro, J. W., & Bonsall, D. G. (1989). *Computer mediated communication: Human relationships in a computerized world*. Tuscaloosa, AL: University of Alabama Press.

Chidambaram, L., & Bostrom, R. P. (1996). Group development (I): A review and synthesis of development models. *Group Decision and Negotiation, 6*, 159–187. doi:10.1023/A:1008603328241

Chiluwa, I. (2008). SMS Text-Messaging and the Nigerian Christian Context: Constructing Values and Sentiments. *The International Journal of Language Society and Culture, 24*, 11-20. Retrieved August 30, 2008, from http://www.educ.utas.edu.au/users/tle/JOURNAL/issues/2008/24-2.pdf

Cho, H., Trier, M., & Kim, E. (2005). The Use of Instant Messaging in Working Relationship Development: A Case Study. *Journal of Computer-Mediated Communication, 10*(4), 17.

Chretien, K., Goldman, E., & Faselis, C. (2008). The reflective writing class blog: Using technology to promote reflection and professional development. *Journal of General Internal Medicine, 23*(12), 2066–2070. doi:10.1007/s11606-008-0796-5

Christian, A. (2005). Contesting the myth of the 'wicked stepmother': Narrative analysis of an online stepfamily support group. *Western Journal of Communication, 69*(1), 27–47. doi:10.1080/10570310500034030

Clark, H. H. (1996). *Using language*. New York: Cambridge University Press. doi:10.1017/CBO9780511620539

Clark, H. H., & Brennan, S. E. (1991). Grounding in communication. In Resnick, L., Levine, J. M., & Teasley, S. D. (Eds.), *Perspectives on socially shared cognition* (pp. 127–149). Washington, DC: APA. doi:10.1037/10096-006

Clerc, S. (1996). Estrogen brigades and "Big Tits" threads: Media fandom online and off. In Cherny, L., & Weise, E. (Eds.), *Wired women* (pp. 73–97). Seattle, WA: Seal Press.

Cline, R. J. W. (1999). Communication in social support groups. In Frey, L., Gouran, D., & Poole, S. (Eds.), *Handbook of Small Group Communication* (pp. 516–538). Thousand Oaks, CA: Sage.

Cline, R. J. W., & Haynes, K. (2001). Consumer health information seeking on the Internet: The state of the art. *Health Education Research, 16*(6), 671–692. doi:10.1093/her/16.6.671

Coates, J. (1993, 2004). Women, men, and language: A sociolinguistic account of gender differences in language. Harlow, UK: Pearson Longman.

Cohen, A. P. (1985). *The Symbolic Construction of Community*. London: Tavistock. doi:10.4324/9780203323373

Cohen, S., & Wills, T. A. (1985). Stress, social support, and the buffering hypothesis. *Psychological Bulletin, 98*(2), 310–357. doi:10.1037/0033-2909.98.2.310

Cole, M. (1996). *Cultural Psychology*. Cambridge, MA: Harvard University Press.

Cole, M., & Scribner, S. (1974). *Culture and thought: A psychological introduction*. New York: John Wiley & Sons.

Coleman, J. (1990). *Foundations of social theory*. Cambridge, MA: Belknap Press of Harvard University Press.

Colley, A., & Todd, Z. (2002). Gender-linked differences in the style and content of e-mails to friends. *Journal of Language and Social Psychology, 21*, 380–392. doi:10.1177/026192702237955

Colley, A., Todd, Z., Bland, M., Holmes, M., Khanom, N., & Pike, H. (2004). Style and content in e-mails and letters to male and female friends. *Journal of Language and Social Psychology, 23*, 369–378. doi:10.1177/0261927X04266812

Collins, M. (1992). *Flaming: The relationship between social context cues and uninhibited verbal behavior in computer mediated communication.* Retrieved February 13, 2009, from http://www.emoderators.com/papers/flames.html

Colomb, G. G., & Simutis, J. A. (1996). Visible conversation and academic inquiry: CMC in a culturally diverse classroom. In Herring, S. C. (Ed.), *Computer-mediated communication: Linguistic, social and cross-cultural perspectives* (pp. 203–222). Philadelphia: John Benjamins.

Company overview (n.d.). Company overview. Retrieved February 15, 2009, from http://www.BabyCenter.com/help-about-company

Connery, B. A. (1997). IMHO: Authority and egalitarian rhetoric in the virtual coffeehouse. In Porter, D. (Ed.), *Internet Culture* (pp. 161–180). New York: Routledge.

Conrad, D. L. (2002). Engagement, excitement, anxiety, and fear: Learners' experiences of starting an online course. *American Journal of Distance Education, 16*(4), 205–226. doi:10.1207/S15389286AJDE1604_2

Cook, H. M. (2001). Particles. In Duranti, A. (Ed.), *Key terms in language and culture.* Malden, MA: Backwell.

Cornetto, K. M., & Nowak, K. L. (2006). Utilizing usernames for sex categorization in computer-mediated communication: Examining perceptions and accuracy. *Cyberpsychology & Behavior, 9*, 377–387. doi:10.1089/cpb.2006.9.377

Coulson, N. S. (2005). Receiving Social Support Online: An Analysis of a Computer-Mediated Support Group for Individuals Living with Irritable Bowel Syndrome. *Cyberpsychology & Behavior, 6*(8), 580–585. doi:10.1089/cpb.2005.8.580

Coulson, N. S., Buchanan, H., & Aubeeluck, A. (2007). Social support in cyberspace: A content analysis of communication within a Huntington's disease online support group. *Patient Education and Counseling, 68*, 173–178. doi:10.1016/j.pec.2007.06.002

Coupland, N. (2001). Language, situation, and the relational self: Theorizing dialect-style in sociolinguistics. In Eckert, P., & Rickford, J. R. (Eds.), *Style and sociolinguistic variation* (pp. 185–210). Cambridge, UK: Cambridge University Press.

Coupland, N. (2007). *Style: Language variation and identity.* Cambridge, UK: Cambridge University Press.

Coupland, N., Coupland, J., & Giles, H. (1991). *Language, Society, and the Elderly: Discourse, Identity, and Ageing.* New York: Wiley Blackwell.

Craig, D. (2004). Instant messaging: The language of youth literacy. *Essays from the program in writing and rhetoric at Stanford University* (pp. 116-133). Retrieved January 1, 2009, from http://www.stanford.edu/group/pwr/publications/Boothe_0203/PWR%20Boothe-Craig.pdf

Craig, E. A. (2008). *"New to site and needing advice!": A content analysis examining role strain and social support in an online support group for childless stepmothers.* Unpublished doctoral dissertation, The University of Oklahoma, Norman.

Crawford, I., Allison, K., Zamboni, B., & Soto, T. (2002). The influence of dual-identity development on the psychosocial functioning of African American gay and bisexual men. *Journal of Sex Research, 39*(3), 179–189. doi:10.1080/00224490209552140

Cresswell, J. (2003). *Research design: Qualitative, quantitative, and mixed methods approaches.* Thousand Oaks, CA: Sage.

Creswell, J. W. (1998). *Qualitative inquiry and research design: Choosing among five traditions.* Thousand Oaks, CA: Sage.

Creswell, J. W., & Plano Clark, V. L. (2007). *Designing and conducting mixed methods research.* Thousand Oaks, CA: Sage.

Cronbach, L. J. (1951, September). Coefficient alpha and the internal structure of tests. *Psychometrika, 16*(3), 297–334. doi:10.1007/BF02310555

Cross, J. (2007). *Informal learning: Rediscovering the natural pathways that inspire innovation and performance.* San Francisco: Pfeiffer.

Crystal, D. (2001). *Language and the Internet.* Cambridge, UK: Cambridge University Press.

Crystal, D. (2006). *Language and the internet* (2nd ed.). Cambridge, UK: Cambridge University Press. doi:10.1017/CBO9780511487002

Culnan, M. J., & Markus, M. L. (1987). Information technologies. In Jablin, F. M., Putnam, L. L., Roberts, K. H., & Porter, L. W. (Eds.), *Handbook of organizational communication: An interdisciplinary perspective* (pp. 420–443). Newbury Park, CA: Sage.

Culver, J. D., Gerr, F., & Frumkin, H. (1997). Medical information on the internet: A study of the electronic bulletin board. *Journal of General Internal Medicine, 12*, 466–470. doi:10.1046/j.1525-1497.1997.00084.x

Curtis, P. (1997). Mudding: Social phenomena in text-based virtual realities. In Kiesler, S. (Ed.), *Culture of the Internet* (pp. 121–142). Mahwah, NJ: Lawrence Erlbaum.

Cutrona, C. E., & Suhr, J. A. (1992). Controllability of stressful events and satisfaction with spouse support behaviors. *Communication Research, 19*, 154–174. doi:10.1177/009365092019002002

Cutrona, C. E., Suhr, J. A., & MacFarlane, R. (1990). Interpersonal transactions and the psychological sense of support. In Duck, S., & Silver, R. (Eds.), *Personal relationships and social support* (pp. 30–45). London: Sage.

Daft, R. L., & Lengel, R. H. (1984). Information richness: A new approach to managerial behavior and organization design. *Research in Organizational Behavior, 6*, 191–233.

Daft, R. L., & Lengel, R. H. (1986). Organizational information requirements, media richness and structural design. *Management Science, 32*(5), 554–571. doi:10.1287/mnsc.32.5.554

Daft, R., & Lengel, R. (1984). Information richness: A new approach to managerial behavior and organization design. *Research in Organizational Behavior, 6*, 191–233.

Daft, R., & Lengel, R. (1986). Organizational information requirements, media richness, and structural design. *Management Science, 32*, 544–571. doi:10.1287/mnsc.32.5.554

Dainton, M., & Aylor, B. (2002). Patterns of communication channel use in the maintenance of long-distance relationships. *Communication Research Reports, 19*(2), 118–129.

Danet, B. (1995). Playful expressivity and artfulness in computer-mediated communication. *Journal of Computer-Mediated Communication, 1*(2). Retrieved February, 2009, from http://jcmc.indiana.edu/vol1/issue2/genintro.html

Danet, B. (1996, February). *Text as mask: Gender and identity on the Internet.* Paper presented at the conference, Masquerade and gendered identity; Venice, Italy. Retrieved (n.d.), from ttp://atar.mscc.huji.ac.il/~msdanet/mask.html

Danet, B. (1998). Text as mask: Gender, play and performance on the Internet. In Jones, S. G. (Ed.), *Cybersociety 2.0: Computer-mediated communication and community revisited* (pp. 129–158). Thousand Oaks, CA: Sage.

Danet, B. (1998). Text as Mask: Gender, Play, and Performance on the Internet. In Jones, S. G. (Ed.), *Cybersociety 2.0 revising Computer-Mediated Communication and Community* (pp. 129–158). Thousand Oaks, CA: Sage.

Danet, B., Ruedenberg, L., & Rosebaum-Tamari, Y. (1994). "Smoking dope" at a virtual party: Writing, play, and performance on Internet Relay Chat. In Rafaeli, S., Sudweeks, F., & McLaughlin, M. (Eds.), *Network and Netplay: Virtual Groups on the Internet.* Cambridge, MA: MIT Press.

Darrington, A. (2008). Six Lessons in e-Learning: Strategies and Support for Teachers New to Online Environments. *Teaching English in the Two-Year College, 35*(4), 416–421.

Davidson, K. P., Pennebaker, J. W., & Dickerson, S. S. (2000). Who talks? The social psychology of illness support groups. *The American Psychologist, 55*, 205–217. doi:10.1037/0003-066X.55.2.205

Davies, B., & Harrè, R. (1990). Positioning: the discursive production of selves. *Journal for the Theory of Social Behaviour, 20*, 43–63. doi:10.1111/j.1468-5914.1990.tb00174.x

Davies, P., & Lipsey, Z. (2003). Ana's gone surfing: A look at the disturbing rise of pro-anorexic websites. *The Psychologist, 16*(8), 424–425.

de Freitas, S. (2008). Emerging trends in serious games and virtual worlds. *Becta: Emerging Technologies for Learning, 3*, 57-72. Retrieved April 10, 2008, from http://partners.becta.org.uk/upload-dir/downloads/page_documents/research/emerging_technologies08_chapter4.pdf

De Mooij, M. (2000). The future is predictable for international marketers: Converging incomes lead to diverging consumer behaviour. *International Marketing Review, 17*(2), 103–113. doi:10.1108/02651330010322598

de Pillis, E., & Furumo, K. (2007). Counting the cost of virtual teams: Studying the performance, satisfaction, and group dynamic of virtual and face-to-face teams. *Communications of the ACM, 50*(12), 93–95.

Dede, C. (2005). Planning for neomillennial learning styles. *EDUCAUSE Quarterly, 28*(1), 7-12. Retrieved October 31, 2008, from http://www.educause.edu/ir/library/pdf/eqm0511.pdf

del-Teso-Craviotto, M. (2008). Gender and sexual identity authentication in language use: The case of chat rooms. *Discourse Studies, 10*, 251–270. doi:10.1177/1461445607087011

Denegri-Knott, J., & Taylor, J. (2005). The labeling game: A conceptual exploration of deviance on the Internet. *Social Science Computer Review, 23*, 93–107. doi:10.1177/0894439304271541

Denning, D. (2001). Activism, hacktivism and cyberterrorism: the Internet as a tool for influencing foreign policy. In J. Arquilla & D. Ronfeldt (Eds,), Networks and netwars: The future of terror, crime and militancy (pp. 239-288). Arlington, VA: Rand Corporation.

Denzin, N. K., & Lincoln, Y. S. (2008). The discipline and practice of qualitative research. In Denzin, N. K., & Lincoln, Y. S. (Eds.), *Collecting and interpreting qualitative materials* (3rd ed., pp. 1–45). Thousand Oaks: Sage.

Derlega, V. J., & Winstead, B. A. (2001). HIV infected persons' attributions for the disclosure and nondisclosure of the seropositive diagnosis to significant others. In Manusov, V., & Harvey, J. H. (Eds.), *Attribution, communication behavior, and close relationships* (pp. 266–284). New York: Cambridge University Press.

Derlega, V. J., Lovejoy, D., & Winstead, B. A. (1998). Personal accounts of disclosing and concealing HIV-positive test results. In Derlega, V. J., & Barbee, A. P. (Eds.), *HIV and social interaction* (pp. 147–164). Newbury Park, CA: Sage.

Derlega, V. J., Metts, S., Petronio, S., & Margulis, S. T. (1993). *Self-disclosure.* Newbury Park, CA: Sage Publications.

Derlega, V. J., Winstead, B. A., & Folk-Barron, L. (2000). Reasons for and against disclosing HIV-seropositive test results to an intimate partner: A functional perspective. In Petronio, S. (Ed.), *Balancing the secrets of private disclosures* (pp. 53–69). Hillsdale, NJ: Lawrence Erlbaum Associates.

Derlega, V. J., Winstead, B. A., & Greene, K. (2008). Self-disclosure and starting a close relationship. In Sprecher, S., Wenzel, A., & Harvey, J. (Eds.), *Handbook of relationship beginnings* (pp. 153–174). New York: Psychology Press.

Derlega, V. J., Winstead, B. A., Greene, K., Serovich, J., & Elwood, W. N. (2004). Reasons for HIV disclosure/nondisclosure in close relationships: Testing a model of HIV-disclosure decision making. *Journal of Social and Clinical Psychology*, *23*, 747–767. doi:10.1521/jscp.23.6.747.54804

Derlega, V. J., Winstead, B. A., Mathews, A., & Braitman, A. L. (2008). Why does someone reveal highly personal information? Attributions for and against self-disclosure in close relationships. *Communication Research Reports*, *25*, 115–130. doi:10.1080/08824090802021756

Derlega, V. J., Winstead, B. A., Wong, P. T. P., & Greenspan, M. (1987). Self-disclosure and relationship development: An attributional analysis. In Roloff, M., & Miller, G. (Eds.), *Interpersonal processes: New directions in communication research* (pp. 172–187). Newbury Park, CA: Sage.

Diener, E., Emmons, R. A., Larsen, R. J., & Griffin, S. (1985). The satisfaction with life scale. *Journal of Personality Assessment*, *49*, 71–75. doi:10.1207/s15327752jpa4901_13

Dietz-Uhler, B., & Bishop-Clark, C. (2001). The Use of computer-mediated communication to enhance subsequent face to face discussion. *Computers in Human Behavior*, *17*, 269–283. doi:10.1016/S0747-5632(01)00006-1

Dietz-Uhler, B., Bishop-Clark, C., & Howard, E. (2005). Formation of and adherence to a self-disclosure norm in an online chat. *Cyberpsychology & Behavior*, *8*, 114–120. doi:10.1089/cpb.2005.8.114

Dillard, J., & Witteman, H. (1985). Romantic relationships at work: Organizational and personal influences. *Human Communication Research*, *12*, 99–116. doi:10.1111/j.1468-2958.1985.tb00068.x

DiMaggio, P., Hargittai, E., Neuman, W. R., & Robinson, J. P. (2001). Social implications of the Internet. *Annual Review of Sociology*, *27*, 307–336. doi:10.1146/annurev.soc.27.1.307

Dindia, K. (2003). Definitions and perspectives on relational maintenance communication. In Canary, D. J., & Dainton, M. (Eds.), *Maintaining relationships through communication* (pp. 1–28). Mahwah, NJ: Lawrence Erlbaum Associates, Publishing.

Dindia, K., & Allen, M. (1992). Sex-differences in self-disclosure: A meta-analysis. *Psychological Bulletin*, *112*, 106–124. doi:10.1037/0033-2909.112.1.106

Dirkx, J., & Smith, R. (2004). Thinking out of a bowl of spaghetti: Learning to learn in online collaborative groups. In Roberts, T. (Ed.), *Online collaborative learning: Theory and practice* (pp. 132–159). Hershey, PA: Information Science Publishing.

Doering, A. (2006). Adventure Learning: Transformative hybrid online education. *Distance Education*, *27*(2), 197–215. doi:10.1080/01587910600789571

Donath, J. S. (1998). Identity and deception in the virtual community. In Kollock, P., & Smith, M. (Eds.), *Communities in Cyberspace* (pp. 29–59). London: Routledge.

Donath, J., & boyd, d. (2004). Public displays of connection. *BT Technology Journal*, *22*, 71–82. doi:10.1023/B:BTTJ.0000047585.06264.cc

Doostadar, A. (2004). 'The vulgar spirit of blogging': On language, culture, and power in Persian weblogestan. *American Anthropologist*, *104*(4), 651–662. doi:10.1525/aa.2004.106.4.651

Douglas, K. M., McGarty, C., Bliuc, A., & Lala, G. (2005). Cyberhate: Social competition and social creativity in online white supremacist groups. *Social Science Computer Review*, *23*, 68–76. doi:10.1177/0894439304271538

Dreyfus, H. L. (2001). *On the Internet*. New York: Routledge.

Driscoll, M. (2002). Blended Learning: Let's get beyond the hype. *E-learning*, 54.

Drotlet, A. L., & Morris, M. W. (2000). Rapport in conflict resolution: Accounting for how face-to-face contact fosters mutual cooperation in mixed-motive conflicts. *Journal of Experimental Social Psychology*, *36*, 25–50.

Drzewiecka, J., & Nakayama, T. (1998). City Sites: Postmodern Urban Space and the Communication of Identity. *The Southern Communication Journal, 64*(1).

Dube, L., & Robey, D. (2008). Surviving the paradoxes of virtual teamwork. *Information Systems Journal, 19*, 3–30. doi:10.1111/j.1365-2575.2008.00313.x

Dube, S. (2009, January 14). Online verification: Who can you trust in the virtual world? *Business Week Online*, Retrieved January 31, 2009, from Business Source Premier Database.

Dubey, G. (2001). *Le lien social à l'ère du virtuel.* Paris: Presses Universitaires de France.

Duck, S. (1994). Steady as (s)he goes: Relational maintenance as a shared meaning system. In Canary, D. J., & Stafford, L. (Eds.), *Communication and relational maintenance* (pp. 45–60). San Diego, CA: Academic Press, Inc.

Dunham, P. J., Hurshman, A., Litwin, E., Gusella, J., Ellsworth, C., & Dodd, P. W. D. (1998). Computer-mediated social support: Single young mothers as a model system. *American Journal of Community Psychology, 26*(2), 281–306. doi:10.1023/A:1022132720104

Duthler, K. W. (2006). The politeness of requests made via email and voicemail: Support for the hyperpersonal model. *Journal of Computer-Mediated Communication, 11*(2), article 6. Retrieved May, 2009, from http://jcmc.indiana.edu/vol11/issue2/duthler.html

Dutta, M. J. (2007). Communicating about culture and health: Theorizing cultural-centered and cultural sensitivity approaches. *Communication Theory, 17*, 304–328. doi:10.1111/j.1468-2885.2007.00297.x

Dyer, R., Green, R., Pitts, M., & Millward, M. (1995). What's the flaming problem? or Computer mediated communication—Deindividuating or disinhibiting? In A. J. Dix, J. E. Finlay, & M. A. R. Kirby (Eds.), *People and computers X: Proceedings of HCI'95 conference* (pp. 289-302). Cambridge, UK: Cambridge University Press.

Dziuban, C., & Moskal, P. (2001). Evaluating distributed learning in metropolitan universities. *Metropolitan Universities, 12*(1), 41–49.

Eagly, A. H. (1995). The science and politics of comparing women and men. *The American Psychologist, 50*, 145–158. doi:10.1037/0003-066X.50.3.145

Eckert, P. (2000). *Linguistic variation as social practice: The linguistic construction of identity in Belten High.* Oxford, UK: Blackwell.

Eckholm, E. (1984). Emotional outbursts punctuate conversation by computer. Retrieved January 22, 2009, from http://query.nytimes.com/gst/fullpage.html?res=9 B0CEFDD123BF931A35753C1A962948260

Eco, U. (1976). *A theory of semiotics.* Bloomington, IN: Indiana University Press.

Eco, U. (1990). *The limits of interpretation.* Bloomington, IN: Indiana University Press.

EDUCAUSE Learning Initiative. (2008, June 11). 7 things you should know about Second Life. *EDUCAUSE.* Retrieved June 13, 2008, from http://www.educause.edu/ir/library/pdf/ELI7038.pdf

Edwards, J. (1985). *Language, society and identity.* Oxford, UK: Basil Blackwell.

Edwards, J. (2005). A short history of online discussion groups. Retrieved January 2, 2009, from http://www.lib.jmu.edu/edge/archives/Spring2005(1)/Article3.asp

Edwards, S. L., Watson, J., Nash, R., & Farrell, A. (2005). Supporting explorative learning by providing collaborative online problem solving (COPS) environments. *Proceedings of the OLT-2005 Conference: Beyond delivery* (pp. 81-89). Brisbane, Australia, Retrieved January 15, 2008, from http://eprints.qut.edu.au/archive/00002146/

Eggins, S., & Slade, D. (1997). *Analyzing casual conversation.* New York: Continuum.

Eichhorn, K. C. (2008). Soliciting social support over the Internet: An investigation of online eating disorder support groups. *Journal of Computer-Mediated Communication, 14*(1), article 3.

Elbow, P. (2002). Closing my eyes as I speak: An argument for ignoring audience. In Johnson, T. R., & Morahan, S. (Eds.), *Teaching composition: Background readings* (pp. 197–218). Boston: Bedford/St. Martin's.

Ellis, B., & Wittenbaum, G. M. (2000). Relationships between self-construal and verbal promotion. *Communication Research, 27,* 704–722. doi:10.1177/009365000027006002

Ellison, N. B., Steinfield, C., & Lampe, C. (2007). The benefits of Facebook "friends:" Social capital and college students' use of online social network sites. *Journal of Computer-Mediated Communication, 12*(4). doi:10.1111/j.1083-6101.2007.00367.x

Ellison, N., Heino, R., & Gibbs, J. (2006). Managing impressions online: Self-presentation processes in the online dating environment. *Journal of Computer-Mediated Communication, 11*(2), article 2. Retrieved May, 2009, from http://jcmc.indiana.edu/vol11/issue2/ellison.html

Ellison, N., Heino, R., & Gibbs, J. (2006). Managing impressions online: Self-presentation processes in the online dating environment. *Journal of Computer-Mediated Communication, 11,* 415–441. doi:10.1111/j.1083-6101.2006.00020.x

Emig, J. (2001). Embodied learning. *English Education, 33*(4), 271–280.

Engleberg, I. N., & Wynn, D. R. (2007). *Working in Groups* (4th ed.). Boston, MA: Houghton-Mifflin Company.

Erdman, J. (2007). Reference in a 3-D virtual world: Preliminary observations on library outreach in "Second Life." *The Reference Librarian, 47*(2), 29–39. doi:10.1300/J120v47n98_04

Erickson, T. (1999). Persistent conversation: An Introduction. *Journal of Computer-mediated Communication, 4.* Retrieved July 18, 2007, from http://jcmc.indiana.edu/vol4/issue4/ericksonintro.html

Erikson, E. (1956, 2008). The problem of ego identity. In D. L. Browning (Ed.), Adolescent identities: A collection of readings (pp. 223-240). New York: The Analytic Press.

Estrada, M., & Vayreda, A. (2007). Support online? Computer-mediated social support and solidarity for people with bipolar web disorder. In *Proceedings of the IADIS Press Publishes Conference.*

Etzioni, A., & Etzioni, O. (1999). Face-to-face and computer-mediated communities: A comparative analysis. *The Information Society, 15*(4), 241–248. doi:10.1080/019722499128402

Facebook. (2009) *Press room: Statistics.* Retrieved February 15, 2009, from http://www.facebook.com/press/info.php?statistics

Faigley, L. (1986). Competing theories of process: A critique and a proposal. *College English, 48*(6), 527–442. doi:10.2307/376707

Fanderclai, T. L. (1995, January 1). MUDs in education: New environments, new pedagogies. *Computer-mediated Communication Magazine, 2*(1). Retrieved Spring 23, 2008, from http://www.ibiblio.org/cmc/mag/1995/jan/fanderclai.html

Fanderclai, T. L. (1996). Like magic, only real. In Cherny, L., & Weise, E. (Eds.), *Wired women: Gender and new realities in cyberspace* (pp. 224–241). Seattle, WA: Seal Press.

Ferber, R. (1995). Is speakers' gender discernible in transcribed speech? *Sex Roles, 32,* 209–223. doi:10.1007/BF01544789

Ferrara, K., Brunner, H., & Whittemore, G. (1991). Interactive written discourse as an emergent register. *Written Communication, 8*(1), 8–34. doi:10.1177/0741088391008001002

Ferriter, M. (1993). Computer aided interviewing and the psychiatric social history. *Social Work & Social Sciences Review, 4,* 255–263.

Festinger, L. A. (1954). A theory of social comparison processes. *Human Relations, 7,* 117–140. doi:10.1177/001872675400700202

Festinger, L., Schachter, S., & Back, K. (1950). *Social pressures in informal groups: A study of human factors in housing.* New York: Harper.

Field, J. (2003). *Social capital*. New York: Routledge.

Finch, E. (2003). What a tangled web we weave: Identity theft and the Internet. In Jewkes, Y. (Ed.), *Dot.cons: Crime, deviance, and identity on the Internet* (pp. 86–104). Portland, OR: Willan.

Fitze, M. (2006). Discourse and participation in ESL face-to-face and written electronic conferences. *Language Learning and Technology, 10*(1), 67-86. Retrieved January 3, 2009, from http://llt.msu.edu/vol10num1/fitze/

Fitzgerald, M. (2007, February). Only the money is real. *Inc. Magazine,* 80-85.

Fitzpatrick, L. (2008, August 12). Making an arguement for misspelling. *Time,* Retrieved (n.d.), from http://www.time.com/time/world/article/0,8599,1832104,00.html

Flanagin, A. J., & Metzger, M. J. (2001, January). Internet use in the contemporary media environment. *Human Communication Research, 27*(1), 153–181. doi:10.1093/hcr/27.1.153

Fleiss, J. L. (1981). *Statistical methods for rates and proportions*. New York: John Wiley.

Flichy, P. (2001). *L'imaginaire d'Internet*. Paris: Édition la Découverte.

Flower, L. (2003). Cognition, context, and theory building. In Villanueva, V. (Ed.), *Cross-talk in comp theory: A reader* (2nd ed., pp. 739–771). Urbana, IL: National Council of Teachers of English.

Flower, L., & Hayes, J. (1981). A cognitive process theory of writing. *College Composition and Communication, 32*(4), 365–387. doi:10.2307/356600

Forbes.com Inc. (2007a, March). *The global 2000*. Retrieved April 29, 2009, from http://www.forbes.com/lists///_07forbes2000_The-Global-2000_Counrty.html

Forbes.com Inc. (2007b, September). *The Asian fab 50*. Retrieved April 29, 2009, from http://www.forbes.com/////_07fab50_Asias-Fab-50-Companies_land.html

Force, W. R. (2005, February). There are no victims here: Determination versus disorder in pro-anorexia. Paper presented at the *Couch-Stone Symposium of the Society for the Study for Symbolic Interaction,* Boulder, CO.

Ford, G., & Gelderblom, H. (2003). The effects of culture on performance achieved through the use of human computer interaction. In *Proceedings of SAICSIT* (pp. 218-230).

Foss, S. K., & Griffin, C. L. (1995). Beyond persuasion: A proposal for an invitational rhetoric. *Communication Monographs, 62,* 2–18. doi:10.1080/03637759509376345

Foweraker, J., & Krznaric, R. (2002). The uneven performance of third wave democracies: Electoral politics and the imperfect rule of law in Latin America. *Latin American Politics and Society, 44*(3), 29–60. doi:10.2307/3177046

Fox, A. B., Bukatko, D., Hallahan, M., & Crawford, M. (2007). The medium makes a difference: Gender similarities and differences in instant messaging. *Journal of Language and Social Psychology, 26,* 389–397. doi:10.1177/0261927X07306982

Fox, A., B., Bukatko, D., Hallahan, M., & Crawford, M. (2007). The medium makes a difference: Gender similarities and differences in instant messaging. *Journal of Language and Social Psychology, 26,* 389–397. doi:10.1177/0261927X07306982

Fox, S. (2009). Mobile could be a game-changer. But only for those who get in the game. Retrieved on April 28, 2009, from http://www.pewinternet.org/Commentary/2009/April/2--Mobile-could-be-a-gamechanger.aspx

Fraser, B. (1996). Pragmatic markers. *Pragmatics, 6*(2), 167–190.

Frattaroli, J. (2006). Experimental disclosure and its moderators: A meta-analysis. *Psychological Bulletin, 132,* 823–865. doi:10.1037/0033-2909.132.6.823

Freedman, Debra, Striedieck, Iris, & Shurin, L. (2007). Not Without My Body: Embodied Learning With/In the Online Learning Environment. In S. Springgay & D. Freedman (Eds.), *Curriculum and the Cultural Body* (pp.39-49). New York: Peter Lang.

Freedom House. (2006a). *Freedom House: About us*. Retrieved April 29, 2009, from http://www.freedomhouse.org/template.cfm?page=2

Freedom House. (2006b). *Freedom House: Methodology.* Retrieved April 29, 2009, from http://www.freedomhouse.org/.cfm?page=35&year=2006

Fukuyama, F. (2001). Social capital, civil society and development. *Third World Quarterly, 22*(1), 7–20. doi:10.1080/713701144

Fulkerson, R. (2004). Composition at the turn of the twenty-first century. *College Composition and Communication, 56*(4), 654–687.

Furst, S., Blackburn, R., & Rosen, B. (1999). Virtual team effectiveness: a proposed research agenda. *Information Systems Journal, 9,* 249–269. doi:10.1046/j.1365-2575.1999.00064.x

Gal, S. (1995). Language, gender, and power: An anthropological review. In Hall, K., & Bucholtz, M. (Eds.), *Gender articulated* (pp. 169–182). New York, NY: Routledge.

Gall, M., Gall, J., & Borg, W. (2007). *Educational research: An introduction* (8th ed.). New York: Pearson.

Garcia, A. C., & Jacobs, J. B. (1998). The interactional organization of computer mediated communication in the college classroom. *Qualitative Sociology, 21,* 299–317. doi:10.1023/A:1022146620473

Garcia, A. C., & Jacobs, J. B. (1999). The eyes of the beholder: Understanding the turn-taking system in quasi-synchronous computer-mediated communication. *Research on Language and Social Interaction, 32,* 337–367. doi:10.1207/S15327973rls3204_2

Garnham, C., & Kaleta, R. (2002). Introduction to hybrid courses. Teaching with Technology Today. *8*(6). Retrieved (n.d.), from http://www.uwsa.edu/ttt/articles/garnham.htm

Garrison, D. R. (2000). Theoretical challenges for distance education in the 21st century: A shift from structural to transactional issues. *International Review of Research in Open and Distance Learning, 1*(1), 1-17. Retrieved June 15, 2007 from http://www.irrodl.org/index.php/irrodl/article/viewFile/2/22

Garrison, D. R., & Anderston, T. (2003). *E-learning in the 21st century*. New York: RoutledgeFalmer. doi:10.4324/9780203166093

Garrison, D. R., & Kanuka, H. (2004). Blended learning: Uncovering its transformative potential in higher education. *The Internet and Higher Education, 7*(2), 95–105. doi:10.1016/j.iheduc.2004.02.001

Garrison, D. R., Anderson, T., & Archer, W. (2000). Critical inquiry in a text-based environment: Computer conferencing in higher education. *The Internet and Higher Education, 2*(2-3), 87–105. doi:10.1016/S1096-7516(00)00016-6

Garrison, D. R., Anderson, T., & Archer, W. (2001). Critical thinking, cognitive presence, and computer conferencing in distance education. *American Journal of Distance Education, 15*(1), 7–23. doi:10.1080/08923640109527071

Garton, L., Haythornthwaite, C., & Wellman, B. (1997). Studying online social networks. *Journal of Computer-Mediated Communication, 3*(1).

Geist-Martin, P., Ray, E. B., & Sharf, B. F. (2003). Understanding health in cultural communities. In *P. Geist-Martin, B. Ray & B. F. Sharf, Communicating health: Personal, cultural, and political complexities* (pp. 54–94). Belmont, CA: Wadsworth/Thomson Learning.

George, D., & Mallery, P. (2008). *SPSS for Windows step by step: A simple guide and reference 13.0 update* (8th ed.). New York: Pearson.

Gergen, K. J. (1985). The social constructionist movement in modern psychology. *The American Psychologist, 40,* 266–275. doi:10.1037/0003-066X.40.3.266

Gergen, K. J. (2000). The self in the age of information. *The Washington Quarterly, 23*(1), 201–214. doi:10.1162/016366000560656

Gergen, K. J., & Shotter, J. (1989). *Texts of identity: Inquiries in social construction.* Newbury Park, CA: Sage.

Gersick, C. J. G. (1988). Time and transition in work teams: Toward a new model of group development. *Academy of Management Journal, 31,* 9–41. doi:10.2307/256496

Gibbs, J. L., Ellison, N. B., & Heino, R. D. (2006). Self-presentation in on-line personals: The role of anticipated future interaction, self disclosure, and perceived success in internet dating. *Communication Research, 33*, 152–177. doi:10.1177/0093650205285368

Gibson, C. (2003). Learners and learning: The need for theory. In M. Moore W. & Anderson (Eds.), Handbook of distance education (pp. 147-160). Mahwah, NJ: Lawrence Erlbaum.

Gigone, D., & Hastie, R. (1993). The common knowledge effect: information sharing and group judgement. *Journal of Personality and Social Psychology, 65*(5), 959–974. doi:10.1037/0022-3514.65.5.959

Gilbert, S. J. (1976). Self-disclosure, intimacy and communication in families. *The Family Coordinator, 25*, 221. doi:10.2307/582335

Gilbertson, J., Dindia, K., & Allen, M. (1998). Relational continuity constructional units and the maintenance of relationships. *Journal of Social and Personal Relationships, 15*, 774–790. doi:10.1177/0265407598156004

Glenn, C., Goldthwaite, M. A., & Connors, R. (2003). *The St. Martin's guide to teaching* (5th ed.). Boston: Bedford St. Martin's.

Goertzen, P., & Kristjánsson, C. (2007). Interpersonal dimensions of community in graduate online learning: Exploring social presence through the lens of Systemic Functional Linguistics. *The Internet and Higher Education, 10*(4), 212–230. doi:10.1016/j.iheduc.2007.06.005

Goffman, E. (1959). *The presentation of self in everyday life*. New York: Doubleday & Company.

Goffman, E. (1967). *Interaction ritual: Essays in face-to-face behavior*. Chicago: Aldine Pub. Co.

Goldsborough, R. (2005). Keeping e-mail in top form. *Black Issues in Higher Education, 22*(3), 39.

Goldsmith, D. J. (2004). *Communicating social support*. New York: Cambridge University Press.

Gong, W., & Ooi, V. B. Y. (2008). Innovations and motivations in online chat. In Kelsey, S., & St.Amant, K. (Eds.), *Research handbook on computer mediated communication* (*Vol. 1*, pp. 917–933). Hershey, PA: Information Science Reference.

Gooden, R. J., & Winefield, H. R. (2006). Breast and prostate cancer online discussion boards: A thematic analysis of gender differences and similarities. *Journal of Health Psychology, 12*, 103–114. doi:10.1177/1359105307071744

Gopal, Y., & Melkote, S. (2007). New work paradigms: Implications for communication and coordination in cross cultural virtual teams. In Hinner, M. B. (Ed.), *The Role of Communication in Business Transactions and Relationships*. Frankfurt, Germany: Peter Lang.

Gottlieb, B. H. (1981). *Social networks and social support*. Beverly Hills, CA: Sage.

Gould, E. W., Zakaria, N., & Yusof, S. A. (2000, September 24). Applying culture to website design: A comparison of Malaysian and US websites. In *Proceedings of 2000 joint IEEE international and 18th annual conference on computer documentation (IPCC/SIGDOC 2000)*. Symposium conducted at Professional Communication Conference, Cambridge, MA. Retrieved February 10, 2009, from IEEEXplore database. (SPEC Accession Number: 6762865)

Graham, C. R. (2003). A model of norm development for computer-mediated teamwork. *Small Group Research, 34*, 322–352. doi:10.1177/1046496403034003003

Graham, C. R. (2006). Blended Learning Systems: Definition, Current Trends, and Future Directions. In Bonk, C. J., & Graham, C. R. (Eds.), *Handbook of blended learning: Global perspectives, local designs*. San Francisco: Pfeiffer Publishing.

Graham, C. R., Allen, S., & Ure, D. (2003). *Blended learning environments: A review of the research literature*. Unpublished manuscript, Provo, UT.

Graner Ray, S. (2004). *Gender inclusive game design: Expanding the market*. Hingham, MA: Charles River Media.

Granovetter, M. S. (1973). The strength of weak ties. *American Journal of Sociology*, *78*(6), 1360–1380. doi:10.1086/225469

Green, E. G. T., Deschamps, J.-C., & Páez, D. (2005). Variation of Individualism and Collectivism Within and Between 20 Countries. *Journal of Cross-Cultural Psychology*, *36*, 321–339. doi:10.1177/0022022104273654

Greene, K. (2000). Disclosure of chronic illness varies by topic and target: The role of stigma and boundaries in willingness to disclose. In Petronio, S. (Ed.), *Balancing the secrets of private disclosures* (pp. 123–135). Mahwah, NJ: Lawrence Erlbaum Associates.

Greene, K. (2009). An integrated model of health disclosure decision-making. In Afifi, T. D., & Afifi, W. A. (Eds.), *Uncertainty and information regulation in interpersonal contexts: Theories and applications* (pp. 226–253). New York: Routledge.

Greene, K., & Faulkner, S. L. (2002). Self-disclosure in relationships of HIV-positive African American adolescent females. *Communication Studies*, *54*, 297–317.

Greene, K., Checton, M. G., Banerjee, S. C., Magsamen-Conrad, K., Venetis, M. K., & Bagdasarov, Z. (November, 2009). *Assessing information and relationships in disclosure decisions: testing an integrated model of disclosure decision-making.* Paper presented at the Annual conference of the National Communication Association, Chicago, IL.

Greene, K., Derlega, V. J., & Mathews, A. (2006). Self-disclosure in personal relationships. In Vangelisti, A., & Perlman, D. (Eds.), *Cambridge handbook of personal relationships* (pp. 409–427). New York: Cambridge University Press.

Greene, K., Derlega, V. J., Yep, G. A., & Petronio, S. (2003). *Privacy and disclosure of HIV in interpersonal relationships: A sourcebook for researchers and practitioners*. Mahwah, NJ: Lawrence Erlbaum Associates.

Greenwald, A. G. (1988). A social-cognitive account of the self's development. In Lapsley, D., & Power, F. (Eds.), *Self, ego, identity: Integrative approaches* (pp. 30–42). New York: Springer-Verlag.

Greist, J. H., Klein, M. H., & VanCura, L. J. (1973). A computer interview by psychiatric patient target symptoms. *Archives of General Psychiatry*, *29*, 247–253.

Grice, H. P. (1975). Logic and conversation. In Cole, P., & Morgan, J. (Eds.), *Syntax and semantics* (*Vol. 3*, pp. 41–58). New York: Academic Press.

Grodin, D., & Lindlof, T. (1996). *Constructing the Self in a Mediated World*. Thousand Oaks, CA: Sage.

Groom, C. J., & Pennebaker, J. W. (2005). The language of love: Sex, sexual orientation, and language use in online personal advertisements. *Sex Roles*, *52*, 447–461. doi:10.1007/s11199-005-3711-0

Grossen, M., & Apothéloz, D. (1999). Positions and position markers in conversational episodes containing sensitive topics. In J. Verschueren (Ed.), *Selected papers from the 6th International Pragmatics Conference* (pp. 181-188). Antwerp, Belgiium: International Pragmatics Association.

Guadagno, R. E., & Cialdini, R. B. (2002). Online persuasion: An examination of gender differences in computer-mediated interpersonal influence. *Group Dynamics*, *6*, 38–51. doi:10.1037/1089-2699.6.1.38

Guadagno, R. E., & Cialdini, R. B. (2007). Persuade him by email, but see her in person: Online persuasion revisited. *Computers in Human Behavior*, *23*, 999–1015. doi:10.1016/j.chb.2005.08.006

Gubrium, J. F., & Holstein, J. A. (1997). *The new language of qualitative method*. New York: Oxford University Press.

Guiller, J., & Durndell, A. (2006). 'I totally agree with you': Gender interactions in educational online discussion groups. *Journal of Computer Assisted Learning*, *22*, 368–381. doi:10.1111/j.1365-2729.2006.00184.x

Guiller, J., & Durndell, A. (2007). Students' linguistic behavior in online discussion groups: Does gender matter? *Computers in Human Behavior*, *23*, 2240–2255. doi:10.1016/j.chb.2006.03.004

Gumbrecht, M. (2004). *Blogs as "protected space"*. Paper presented at the Workshop on the Weblogging Ecosystem: Aggregation, Analysis, and Dynamics: WWW 2004.

Gunawardena, C., Wilson, P., & Nolla, A. (2003). Culture and online education. In Moore, M., & Anderson, W. (Eds.), *Handbook of distance education* (pp. 753–775). Mahwah, NJ: Lawrence Erlbaum.

Gupta, A., & Ferguson, J. (1997). Beyond "culture": Space, identity, and the politics of difference. In Gupta, A., & Ferguson, J. (Eds.), *Culture, Power, Place: Explorations in Critical Anthropology* (pp. 33–51). Durham, NC: Duke University Press.

Gurak, L. J. (2001). *Cyberliteracy: Navigating the Internet with awareness*. New Haven, CT: Yale University.

Gurak, L. J., Antonijevic, S., Johnson, L., Ratliff, C., & Reyman, J. (2005). Introduction: Weblogs, rhetoric, community, and culture. In L. J. Gurak, S. Antonijevic, L. Johnson, C. Ratliff, & J. Reyman (Eds.), *Into the blogosphere: Rhetoric, community, and culture of weblogs*. Retrieved December 17, 2008, from http://blog.lib.umn.edu/blogosphere/introduction.html

Ha, L., & James, E. L. (1998). Interactivity reexamined: A baseline analysis of early business Websites. *Journal of Broadcasting & Electronic Media, 42*, 457–474.

Hall, E. T., & Hall, M. R. (1989). *Understanding cultural differences: Germans, French and Americans*. Yarmouth, ME: Intercultural Press.

Hall, S. (2003). The work of representation. In Hall, S. (Ed.), *Representation: Cultural representations and signifying practices* (pp. 13–74). Thousand Oaks, CA: Sage Publications.

Halliday, M. (1994). *An introduction to functional grammar* (2nd ed.). London: Edward Arnold.

Hampton, K., & Wellman, B. (2001). Long distance community in the network society. *The American Behavioral Scientist, 45*, 476–495. doi:10.1177/00027640121957303

Hancock, J. T., & Dunham, P. J. (2004). Impression formation in computer-mediated communication revisited: An analysis of the breadth and intensity of impressions. *Communication Research, 28*, 325–347. doi:10.1177/009365001028003004

Handel, M., & Herbsleb, J. (2002). What is chat doing in the workplace? In [New York: ACM Press.]. *Proceedings of CSCW, 2002*, 1–10.

Hanna, B. E., & de Nooy, J. (2003). A funny thing happened on the way to the forum: Electronic discussion and foreign language learning. *Language Learning & Technology, 7*(1), 71–85.

Hannerz, U. (2002). Notes on the global ecumene. In (J. X. Inda and R, Rosaldo, Eds.), The anthropology of globalization: A reader (pp. 37-45). Malden, MA: Blackwell Publishers.

Haraway, D. (1991). A Cyborg Manifesto: Science, Technology, and Socialist-Feminism in the Late Twentieth Century. In *Simians, Cyborgs and Women: The Reinvention of Nature* (pp. 149–181). New York: Routledge.

Hardin, A. M., Fuller, M. A., & Valacich, J. S. (2006). Measuring group efficacy in virtual teams: New questions in an old debate. *Small Group Research, 37*(1), 65–85. doi:10.1177/1046496405284219

Harrè, R., & Van Langenhove, L. (1991). Varieties of positioning. *Journal for the Theory of Social Behaviour, 21*, 393–408. doi:10.1111/j.1468-5914.1991.tb00203.x

Harris, R. M., & Dewdney, P. (1994). Barriers to information: How formal help systems fail battered women. Westport, CN: Greenwood Press.

Harris, T. E., & Sherblom, J. C. (2005). *Small Group and Team Communication* (3rd ed.). Boston, MA: Pearson Education, Inc.

Harrison, S. (1998). Email discussions as conversation: moves and acts in a sample from a listserv discussion. *Linguistik Online, 1/98*. Retrieved July 30, 2008, from http://www.linguistik-online.de/harrison.htm

Harrison, S. (2004, June) *Turn Taking in Electronic Environment*, Paper presented at *Inter*-Varietal Applied Corpus Studies Conference, Belfast, UK.

Harwood, J. (2000). Communication media use in the grandparent-grandchild relationship. *The Journal of Communication, 50*(4), 56–78. doi:10.1111/j.1460-2466.2000.tb02863.x

Hayles, N. K. (2002). Flesh and metal: Reconfiguring the mindbody in virtual environments. *Configurations*, *10*(2), 297–320. doi:10.1353/con.2003.0015

Hayne, S. C., & Rice, R. E. (1997). Attribution accuracy when using anonymity in group support systems. *International Journal of Human-Computer Studies, 47*, 429–450. doi:10.1006/ijhc.1997.0134

Haynes, C. (1998). Help! There's a MOO in this class! In Haynes, C., & Holmevik, J. R. (Eds.), *High wired: On the design, use, and theory of educational MOOs* (pp. 161–176). Ann Arbor, MI: University of Michigan Press.

Hays, R. T. (2005, November). *The effectiveness of instructional games: A literature review and discussion.* Technical Report. Naval Air Warfare Center Training Systems Division. Orlando, Florida. Retrieved April 11, 2008, from http://adlcommunity.net/file.php/23/Groove-Files/Instr_Game_Review_Tr_2005.pdf

Haythornthwaite, C. (2001). Introduction: The internet in everyday life. *The American Behavioral Scientist, 45*(3), 363–382. doi:10.1177/00027640121957240

Haythornthwaite, C., Kazmer, M., Robins, J., & Shoemaker, S. (2000). Community development among distance learners: Temporal and technological dimensions. *Journal of Computer-Mediated Communication, 6*(1).

Hazen, K. (2001). Teaching about dialects. *Eric clearinghouse on language and linguistics Washington DC.* Retrieved February 9, 2009, from http://permanent.access.gpo.gov/websites/eric.ed.gov/ERIC_Digests/ed456674.htm

Hecht, M. L., Warren, J., Jung, J., & Krieger, J. (2004). Communication theory of identity. In Gudykunst, W. B. (Ed.), *Theorizing about intercultural communication* (pp. 257–278). Newbury Park, CA: Sage.

Helgeson, V. S., & Mickelson, K. D. (1995). Motives for social comparison. *Personality and Social Psychology Bulletin, 21*, 1200–1209. doi:10.1177/01461672952111008

Henley, S., & Kramarae, C. (1991). Gender, power and miscommunication. In Coupland, N., Giles, H., & Wiemann, J. (Eds.), *Miscommunication and problematic talk* (pp. 18–43). Newbury Park, CA: Sage Publications.

Herek, G. M., & Capitanio, J. P. (1996). "Some of my best friends": Intergroup contact, concealable stigma, and heterosexuals' attitudes toward gay men and lesbians. *Personality and Social Psychology Bulletin, 22*, 412–424. doi:10.1177/0146167296224007

Heritage, J. (1984). *Garfinkel and ethnomethodology.* Cambridge, UK: Polity Press.

Hermans, H. J. M. (1996). Voicing the self: From information processing to dialogical interchange. *Psychological Bulletin, 119*(1), 31–50. doi:10.1037/0033-2909.119.1.31

Hermans, H. J. M. (2001). The dialogical self: Toward a theory of personal and cultural positioning. *Culture and Psychology, 7*, 243–281. doi:10.1177/1354067X0173001

Hermans, H. J. M., & Kempen, H. J. G. (1993). *The dialogical self: meaning as movement.* San Diego, CA: Academic Press.

Hermans, H. J. M., Kempen, H. J. G., & Van Loon, R. J. P. (1992). The Dialogical Self: Beyond Individualism and Rationalism. *The American Psychologist, 47*(1), 23–33. doi:10.1037/0003-066X.47.1.23

Herring, S. (1994). Gender differences in computer-mediated communication: Bringing familiar baggage to the new frontier. *CPSR newsletter, 18*(1). Retrieved January 15, 2009, from http://cpsr.org/issues/womenintech/herring/

Herring, S. (1994, June). *Gender differences in computer-mediated communication: Bringing familiar baggage to the new frontier.* Keynote talk at the American Library Association Annual Convention. Miami, FL. Retrieved May 2, 2000 from http://www.cpsr.org/cpsr/gender/herring.txt

Herring, S. (1999). Interactional coherence in CMC. *Journal of Computer-Mediated Communication, 4*(4). Retrieved May 4, 2003, from http://www.ascusc.org/jcmc/vol4/issue4/herring.html

Herring, S. (1999). The rethorical dynamics of gender harassment on-line. *The Information Society, 15*(3), 151–167. doi:10.1080/019722499128466

Herring, S. (2000). Gender differences in CMC: Findings and implications. *Computer Professionals for Social Responsibility Newsletter, 18*(1). Retrieved (n.d.), from http://www.cpsr.org/publications/newsletters/issues/2000/winter2000/herring/htm

Herring, S. (2001). Computer-Mediated Discourse. In Schiffrin, D., Tannen, D., & Hamilton, H. E. (Eds.), *The handbook of discourse Analysis* (pp. 612–634). Nalden, MA: Blackwell Publishers.

Herring, S. C. (1993). Gender and democracy in computer-mediated communication. *Electronic Journal of Communication, 3*(2). Retrieved April 16, 2008, from http://ella.slis.indiana.edu/~herring/ejc.txt

Herring, S. C. (1994). Politeness in computer culture: Why women thank and men flame. In M. Bucholtz, A. Liang, L. Sutton, & C. Hines (Eds.), *Cultural Performances: Proceedings of the Third Berkeley Women and Language Conference* (pp. 278-94). Berkeley, CA: Berkeley Women and Language Group.

Herring, S. C. (1999). Interactional coherence in CMC. *Journal of Computer Mediated Communication, 4* (4). Retrieved December 23, 2008, from http://jcmc.indiana.edu/vol4/issue4/herring.html

Herring, S. C. (2002). Computer-mediated communication on the Internet. *Annual Review of Information Science & Technology, 36*, 109–168. doi:10.1002/aris.1440360104

Herring, S. C. (2003). Gender and power in online communication. In Holmes, J., & Meyerhoff, M. (Eds.), *The Handbook of language and gender* (pp. 202–228). Oxford, UK: Blackwell. doi:10.1002/9780470756942.ch9

Herring, S. C. (2003). Gender and power in online communication. In J. Holmes and M. Meyerhoff (Eds.), *The handbook of language and gender* (pp. 202-228). Oxford: Blackwell Publishers. Retrieved April 16, 2008, from http://ella.slis.indiana.edu/~herring/gender.power.pdf

Herring, S. C. (2004). Computer-mediated discourse analysis: An approach to researching online behavior. In Barab, S. A., Kling, R., & Gray, J. H. (Eds.), *Designing for virtual communities in the service of learning* (pp. 338–376). Cambridge, UK: Cambridge University Press.

Herring, S. C. (2004). Computer-mediated discourse analysis: An approach to researching online behaviour. In S. A. Barab, R. Kling, & J. H. Gray, (Eds.), Designing for Virtual Communities in the Service of Learning (pp. 338-376). New York: Cambridge University Press. Retrieved (n.d.), from http://ella.slis.indiana.edu/~herring/cmda.pdf

Herring, S. C. (2004). Content analysis for new media: Rethinking the paradigm. In *New research for new media: Innovative research methodologies symposium working papers and readings* (pp. 47–66). Minneapolis, MN: University of Minnesota School of Journalism and Mass Communication.

Herring, S. C. (2004). Slouching toward the ordinary: Current trends in computer-mediated communication. *New Media & Society, 6*, 26–36. doi:10.1177/1461444804039906

Herring, S. C. (2007). A faceted classification scheme for computer-mediated discourse. *Language@Internet, 4*(1). Retrieved February, 2009, from http://www.languageatinternet.de/articles/2007/761

Herring, S. C. (2008). Web content analysis: Expanding the paradigm. In Hunsinger, J., Allen, M., & Klastrup, L. (Eds.), *The international handbook of internet research*. Berlin: Springer Verlag.

Herring, S. C. (Ed.). (1996). *Computer-mediated communication: Linguistic, social and cross-cultural perspectives*. Philadelphia: John Benjamins.

Herring, S. C., & Martinson, A. (2004). Assessing gender authenticity in computer-mediated language use: Evidence from an identity game. *Journal of Language and Social Psychology, 23*, 424–446. doi:10.1177/0261927X04269586

Herring, S. C., & Nix, C. (1997). *Is "serious chat" an oxymoron?* Academic vs. social uses of Internet Relay Chat. Paper presented at the American Association of Applied Linguistics, Orlando, FL.

Herring, S. C., & Nix, C. G. (1997, March). Is "serious chat" an oxymoron? Pedagogical vs. social uses of Internet Relay Chat. *Paper presented at the American Association of Applied Linguistics Annual Conference,* Orlando, FL.

Herring, S. C., & Paolillo, J. C. (2006). Gender and genre variation in weblogs. *Journal of Sociolinguistics, 10*(4), 439–459. doi:10.1111/j.1467-9841.2006.00287.x

Herring, S. C., & Paolillo, J. C. (2006). Gender and genre variation in weblogs. *Journal of Sociolinguistics, 10,* 439–459. doi:10.1111/j.1467-9841.2006.00287.x

Herring, S. C., Scheidt, L. A., Wright, E., & Bonus, S. (2005). Weblogs as a bridging genre. *Information Technology & People, 18,* 142–171. doi:10.1108/09593840510601513

Herring, S., & Martinson, A. (2004). Assessing gender authenticity in computer mediate language use: Evidence from an identity game. *Journal of Language and Social Psychology, 4*(4), 424–446. doi:10.1177/0261927X04269586

Herring, S., Johnson, D., & DiBenedetto, T. (1995). This discussion is going too far! In Hall, K., & Bucholtz, M. (Eds.), *Gender articulated* (pp. 67–96). New York: Routledge.

Hewitt, J. (2001). Beyond threaded discourse. *International Journal of Educational Telecommunications, 7*(3), 207–221.

Hian, L. B., Chuan, S. L., Trevor, T. M. K., & Detenber, B. H. (2004). Getting to know you: Exploring the development of relational intimacy in computer-mediated communication. *Journal of Computer-Mediated Communication, 9.* Retrieved February 13 2009, from http://www3.interscience.wiley.com.proxy.libraries.rutgers.edu/cgi-bin/fulltext/120837925/HTMLSTART

Hian, L. B., Chuan, S. L., Trevor, T. M. K., & Detenber, B. H. (2004). Getting to Know You: Exploring the Development of Relational Intimacy in Computer-mediated Communication. *Journal of Computer-Mediated Communication, 9*(3). Retrieved May 14, 2009, from http://jcmc.indiana.edu/vol9/issue3/detenber.html

Hill, C. T., Rubin, Z., & Plepau, L. A. (1976). Breakups before marriage: The end of 103 affairs. *The Journal of Social Issues, 32,* 147–168.

Hiltz, S. R., & Turoff, M. (1993). *The Network Nation* (Revised Edition). Cambridge, MA: MIT Press.

Hinduja, S., & Patchin, J. W. (2008). Cyberbullying: An exploratory analysis of factors related to offending and victimization. *Deviant Behavior, 29,* 129–156. doi:10.1080/01639620701457816

Hine, C. (2000). *Virtual ethnography.* Thousand Oaks, California: Sage.

Hinterberger., et al. (2004, September). From hybrid courses to belended learning: A case study. International Conference on New Educational Environments (ICNEE) Switzerland: University of Neuchatel.

Ho, R. (2006). *Handbook of univariate and multivariate data analysis and interpretation with SPSS.* New York: Taylor & Francis Group. doi:10.1201/9781420011111

Hochschild, A. R. (1973). Communal life styles for the old. *Society, 10,* 50–57. doi:10.1007/BF02698950

Hodgson, J. (2009). New media scholars, old media students: A complicating of the guard. *Rocky Mountain Communication Review, 6*(1), 66–70.

Hoffman, M. A. (1996). *Counseling clients with HIV disease: Assessment, intervention, and prevention.* New York: Guilford.

Hofstede, G. (1980). *Culture consequences: International differences in work-related values.* Thousand Oaks, CA: Sage.

Hofstede, G. (2001). *Culture's Consequences: Comparing values, behaviors, institutions, and organizations across nations* (2nd ed.). Thousand Oaks, CA: Sage Publications.

Hofstede, G., & Hofstede, G. J. (2005). *Cultures and organizations: Software of the mind*. New York: McGraw-Hill.

Hoft, N. (1996). Developing a cultural model. In del Galdo, E. M., & Nielsen, J. (Eds.), *International user interfaces* (pp. 41–73). New York: John Wiley & Sons.

Hoft, N. L. (1995). *International technical communication: How to export information about high technology*. NY: John Wiley & Sons.

Hogan, R. (1991). Engendered autobiographies: The diary as a feminine form. *Prose Studies: History, Theory. Criticism, 14*(2), 95–107.

Hoijer, H. (1974). The Sapir-Whorf hypothesis. In Blount, B. G. (Ed.), *Language, culture, and society* (pp. 120–131). Cambridge, MA: Winthrop.

Holladay, S. J., & Seipke, H. L. (2007). Communication between grandparents and grandchildren in geographically separated relationships. *Communication Studies, 58*(3), 281–297. doi:10.1080/10510970701518371

Holland, F. (2007). *An essay on AfroSpear nomenclature: What we call ourselves and why*, Francis Hollander blog. Retrieved July 13, 2007, from http://francislholland.blogspot.com/2007/06/essay-of-afrospear-nomenclature-what-is.html.

Holland, S., & Harpin, J. (2008). "It's only MySpace": Teenagers and social networking online. In Holland, S. (Ed.), *Remote relationships in a small world* (pp. 117–136). New York: Peter Lang.

Holt, R., Court, P., Vedhara, K., Nott, K. H., Holmes, J., & Snow, M. H. (1998). The role of disclosure in coping with HIV infection. *AIDS Care, 10*, 49–60. doi:10.1080/09540129850124578

Honeycutt, C. (2005). Hazing as a process of boundary maintenance in an online community. *Journal of Computer-Mediated Communication, 10*(2), article 3. Retrieved May, 2009, from http://jcmc.indiana.edu/vol10/issue2/honeycutt.html

Hotep, U. (2007). Retreived January 26, 2009, from http://www.blackperspective.net/index.php/the-jena-march-and-the-debate-over-protest-politics-pt2/

Howard, P. E. N., Rainie, L., & Jones, S. (2001). Days and nights on the Internet. *The American Behavioral Scientist, 45*, 383–404.

Howard, P. E. N., Rainie, L., & Jones, S. (2001). Days and nights on the internet: The impact of a diffusing technology. *The American Behavioral Scientist, 45*(3), 383–404.

Hu, Y., Wood, J. F., Smith, V., & Westbrook, N. (2004). Friendships through IM: Examining the Relationship between Instant Messaging and Intimacy. *Journal of Computer-Mediated Communication, 10*(1), Article 6.

Huang, A. H., & Yen, D. C. (2003). Usefulness of instant messaging among young users: Social vs. work perspective. *Human Systems Management, 22*, 62–72.

Hubbler, M. T., & Bell, D. C. (2003). Computer-mediated humor and ethos: Exploring threads of constitutive laughter in online communities. *Computer and composition, 20*(3), 277-294.

Huber, E., & Solt, F. (2004, October). Successes and failure of neoliberalism. *Latin American Research, 39*(3), 150–164. doi:10.1353/lar.2004.0049

Huberman, A. M., & Miles, M. B. (1994). Data management and analysis methods. In Denzin, N. K., & Lincoln, Y. S. (Eds.), *Handbook of qualitative research* (pp. 428–444). Thousand Oaks, CA: Sage.

Huckin, T. (1992). Context-sensitive text analysis. In Kirsch, G., & Sullivan, P. A. (Eds.), *Methods and methodology in composition research* (pp. 84–104). Carbondale, IL: Southern Illinois UP.

Hudson, B., Hudson, A., & Steel, J. (2006)... *British Journal of Educational Technology, 37*(5), 733–748. doi:10.1111/j.1467-8535.2006.00552.x

Huerta, G., & Flemmer, L. (2005). Identity, beliefs and community: LDS (Mormon) pre-service secondary teacher views about diversity. *Intercultural Education, 16*(1), 1–14. doi:10.1080/14636310500061615

Huffaker, D. A. (2005). The educated blogger: Using weblogs to promote literacy in the classroom. *Advancement of computing in education journal, 13*(2), 91-98.

Huffaker, D. A., & Calvert, S. L. (2005). Gender, identity, and language use in teenage blogs. *Journal of computer-mediated communication, 10*(2), retrieved February 20, 2009 from http://jcmc.indiana.edu/vol10/issue2/huffaker.html

Hughes, J. A., O'Brien, J., Randall, D., Rouncefield, M., & Tolmie, P. (2001). Some 'real' problems of 'virtual' organisation. *New Technology, Work and Employment, 16*, 49–64. doi:10.1111/1468-005X.00076

Hughes, R. Jr, & Hans, J. D. (2001). Computers, the internet, and families: a review of the role new technology plays in family life. *Journal of Family Issues, 22*, 778–792. doi:10.1177/019251301022006006

Hui, C. H., & Triandis, H. C. (1986). Individualism–collectivism: a study of cross-cultural researchers. *Journal of Cross-Cultural Psychology, 17*, 225–248. doi:10.1177/0022002186017002006

Hutchins, E. (1995). *Cognition in the Wild.* Cambridge, MA: MIT Press.

Huysman, M., & Wulf, V. (2004). *Social capital and information technology.* Cambridge, MA: MIT Press.

Huysman, M., & Wulf, V. (2006). IT to support knowledge sharing in communities, towards a social capital analysis. *Journal of Information Technology, 21*(1), 40–51. doi:10.1057/palgrave.jit.2000053

Hwang, P. (2008). Linguistic characteristics in synchronous and asynchronous CMC. *English Language & Literature Teaching, 14*(2), 47–66.

Ifukor, P. (2008, October). *Face Claims on Weblogs.* Paper presented at First Conference of the International Society for the Linguistics of English, Freiburg, Germany.

Ihde, D. (1983). *Existential technics.* Albany, NY: State University of New York Press.

Ihde, D. (1986). A phenomenology of voice. In *Consequences of phenomenology* (pp. 27–48). Albany, NY: State University of New York Press.

Internet World Stats. (n.d.). *Internet World Stats.* Retrieved October 9, 2008 from http://www.internetworldstats.com/stats.htm

Isaacs, E., Walendowski, A., Whittaker, S., Schiano, D. J., & Kamm, C. (2002). The character, functions, and styles of instant messaging in the workplace. In *Proceedings of ACM CSCW Conf* (pp. 11–20). New York: ACM.

Ishiyama, F. I. (1989). Understanding foreign adolescents' difficulties in cross-cultural adjustment. *Canadian Journal of School Psychology, 5*, 41–56.

Ishiyama, F. I. (1995a). Use of validationgram in counseling: Exploring sources of self-validation and impact of personal transition. *Canadian Journal of Counselling, 29*(2), 134–146.

Ishiyama, F. I. (1995b). Culturally dislocated clients: Self-validation and cultural conflict issues and counseling implications. *Canadian Journal of Counselling, 29*(3), 262–275.

Israel, G. D. (1992, November/December). *Determining sample size.* Retrieved April 29, 2009, from http://edis.ifas.ufl.edu///.pdf

Jaffe, J. M., Lee, Y.-E., Huang, L.-N., & Oshagan, H. (1999). Gender identification, interdependence, and pseudonyms in CMC: Language patterns in an electronic conference. *The Information Society, 15*, 221–234. doi:10.1080/019722499128385

Jakobson, R. (1971). Language in relation to other communication systems. In Selected writings (Vol. 2, pp. 570-9). The Hugue: Mouton.

James, D., & Clarke, S. (1993). Women, men, and interruptions: A critical review. In Tannen, D. (Ed.), *Gender and conversational interaction* (pp. 231–280). New York: Oxford University Press.

James, D., & Drakich, J. (1993). Understanding gender differences in amount of talk: A critical review of research. In Tannen, D. (Ed.), *Gender and conversational interaction* (pp. 281–312). New York: Oxford University Press.

Janofsky, A. I. (1970). Affective self-disclosure in telephone versus face-to-face interviews. *Journal of Humanistic Psychology*, *10*, 93–103.

Janssen, J., Erkens, G., Kirschner, P. A., & Kanselaar, G. (2009). Influence of group member familiarity on online collaborative learning. *Computers in Human Behavior*, *25*, 161–170. doi:10.1016/j.chb.2008.08.010

Jenkins, C. A. (2004). The virtual classroom as ludic space. In Haythornthwaite, C. A., & Kazmer, M. M. (Eds.), *Learning, culture and community in online education* (pp. 163–176). New York: Peter Lang.

Jensen, K. B., & Jankowski, N. W. (1991). *A handbook of qualitative methodologies for mass communication research*. New York: Routledge. doi:10.4324/9780203409800

Johansen, R., Vallee, J., & Vian, K. (1979). *Electronic meetings*. Reading, MA: Addison–Wesley.

Johnson, A. J., Haigh, M. M., Becker, J. A. H., Craig, E. A., & Wigley, S. (2008). College students' use of relational management strategies in email in long-distance and geographically close relationships. *Journal of Computer-Mediated Communication*, *13(2)*, 381–404. doi:10.1111/j.1083-6101.2008.00401.x

Johnson, A. J., Wright, K. B., Craig, E. A., Gilchrist, E. S., Lane, L. T., & Haigh, M. M. (2008). A Model for Predicting Stress Levels and Marital Satisfaction for Stepmothers Utilizing a Stress and Coping Approach. *Journal of Social and Personal Relationships*, *25*(1), 119–142. doi:10.1177/0265407507086809

Johnson, J. L., Bootorff, J. L., Browne, A. J., Grewal, S., Hilton, B. A., & Clarke, H. (2004). Othering and being othered in the context of health care services. *Health Communication*, *16*, 253–272. doi:10.1207/S15327027HC1602_7

Johnson, S. D., Suriya, C., Yoon, S. W., Berrett, J. V., & La Fleur, J. (2002). Team development and group processes of virtual learning teams. *Computers & Education*, *39*, 379–393. doi:10.1016/S0360-1315(02)00074-X

Johnston, B. (2003). *Values in English language teaching*. Mahwah, NJ: Lawrence Erlbaum.

Johnston, K., & Johal, P. (1999). The Internet as a "virtual cultural region": Are extant cultural classification schemes appropriate? *Internet Research: Electronic Networking Applications and Policy*, *9*(3), 178–186. doi:10.1108/10662249910274566

Joinson, A. N. (1998). Causes and implications of disinhibition on the Internet. In Gackenbach, J. (Ed.), *The psychology of the internet* (pp. 43–60). New York, NY: Academic Press.

Joinson, A. N. (1999). Anonymity, disinhibition, and social desirability on the Internet. *Behavior Research Methods, Instruments, & Computers*, *31*, 433–438.

Joinson, A. N. (1999). Social desirability, anonymity, and internet-based questionnaires. *Behavior Research Methods, Instruments, & Computers*, *31*, 433–438.

Joinson, A. N. (2001). Self-disclosure in computer-mediated communication: The role of self-awareness and visual anonymity. *European Journal of Social Psychology*, *31*, 177–192. doi:10.1002/ejsp.36

Joinson, A. N. (2003). *Understanding the psychology of Internet behaviour, virtual worlds, real lives*. Basingstoke, UK: Palgrave-Macmillan.

Joinson, A. N. (2005). Deviance and the Internet: New challenges for social science. *Social Science Computer Review*, *23*, 5–7. doi:10.1177/0894439304271527

Joinson, A. N., & Dietz-Uhler, B. (2002). Explanations for the perpetration of and reactions to deception in a virtual community. *Social Science Computer Review*, *220*, 275–289.

Jonas, H. (1966). *The phenomenon of life*. New York: Dell Publishing Co., Inc.

Jones, S. G. (1995). Understanding community in the information Age. In Jones, S. G. (Ed.), *Cibersociety: Computer-Mediated Communication and Community* (pp. 10–35). Thousand Oaks, CA: Sage.

Jones, S. G. (1998). *Cibersociety 2.0. Revising Computer-Mediated Communication and Technology*. Thousand Oaks, California: Sage.

Jones, S. H. (2008). Autoethnography: Making the personal political. In Denzin, N. K., & Lincoln, Y. S. (Eds.), *Collecting and interpreting qualitative materials* (3rd ed., pp. 205–245). Thousand Oaks, CA: Sage.

Joseph, D. (2005). Hybrid Design Enables Individualized Learning Experience. *Distance Education Report, 9*(5), 6.

Joseph, J. (2003). Cyberstalking: An international perspective. In Jewkes, Y. (Ed.), *Dot.cons: Crime, deviance, and identity on the Internet* (pp. 105–125). Portland, OR: Willan.

Journal of Computer-Mediated Communication. *10 (2).* Retrieved March 23, 2009, from http://www3. interscience.wiley.com/cgi-bin/fulltext/120837938/ HTMLSTART

Kahn, R., & Kellner, D. (2004). New media and internet activism: From the 'Battle of Seattle' to blogging. *New Media & Society, 6*(1), 87–95. doi:10.1177/1461444804039908

Kale, S. H. (2006). Designing culturally compatible Internet gaming sites. *UNLV Gaming Research & Review Journal, 10*(1), 41–49.

Kalichman, S. C. (1995). *Understanding AIDS: A guide for mental health professionals.* Washington, DC: American Psychological Association. doi:10.1037/10497-000

Kandell, D. B. (1978). Similarity in real life adolescent friendship pairs. *Journal of Personality and Social Psychology, 36*, 306–312. doi:10.1037/0022-3514.36.3.306

Kane, C. M., Maguire, K., Neuendorf, K., & Skalski, P. (2009). *Nonverbal displays of self presentation and sex differences in profile photographs in Myspace.com.* Unpublished manuscript.

Kang, H.-S., & Yang, H.-D. (2006). The visual characteristics of avatars in computer-mediated communication: Comparison of internet relay chat and instant messenger as of 2003. *International Journal of Human-Computer Studies, 62*, 1173–1183. doi:10.1016/j.ijhcs.2006.07.003

Karlsson, L. (2006). Acts of reading diary weblogs. *Human IT, 8*(2), 1–59.

Katz, E., Blumler, J. G., & Gurevitch, M. (1974). Utilization of mass communication by the individual. In Blumler, J. G., & Katz, E. (Eds.), *The use of mass communications: Current perspectives on gratifications research* (pp. 19–32). Thousand Oaks, CA: Sage.

Kavanaugh, A., Carroll, J. M., Rosson, M. B., Zin, T. T., & Reese, D. D. (2005). Community Networks: Where Offline Communities Meet Online. *Journal of Computer-Mediated Communication, 10*(4), article 3.

Keating, E. (1993). Correction/repair as a resource for co-construction of group competence. *Pragmatics: Quarterly Publication of the International Pragmatics Association, 3*, 411–423.

Keifer-Boyd, K. (2007). Body Interfaces in Curriculum. In Springgay, S., & Freedman, D. (Eds.), *Curriculum and the Cultural Body* (pp. 51–60). New York: Peter Lang.

Kellerhals, J., Troutot, P. Y., &, Lazega, E. (1984). *Microsociologie de la famille.* Paris: Presses Universitaires de France.

Kelley, J. E., Lumley, M. A., & Leisen, J. C. C. (1997). Health effects of emotional disclosure in rheumatoid arthritic patients. *Health Psychology, 16*, 331–340. doi:10.1037/0278-6133.16.4.331

Kelly, A. E. (2002). *The psychology of secrets.* New York: Kluwer Academic/Plenum.

Kelly, A. E., & McKillop, K. J. (1996). Consequences of revealing personal secrets. *Psychological Bulletin, 120*, 450–465. doi:10.1037/0033-2909.120.3.450

Kelly, A. E., Klusas, J. A., von Weiss, R. T., & Kenny, C. (2001). What is it about revealing secrets that is beneficial? *Personality and Social Psychology Bulletin, 27*, 651–665. doi:10.1177/0146167201276002

Kelly, A. E., Otto-Salaj, L. L., Sikkema, K. J., Pinkerton, S. D., & Bloom, F. R. (1998). Implications of HIV treatment advances for behavioral research on AIDS: Protease inhibitors and new challenges in HIV secondary prevention. *Health Psychology, 17*, 310–319. doi:10.1037/0278-6133.17.4.310

Kelly, P., Gale, K., Wheeler, S., & Tucker, V. (2007). Taking a stance: promoting deliberate action through online postgraduate professional development. *Technology, Pedagogy and Education, 16*(2), 153–176. doi:10.1080/14759390701406760

Kendall, L. (2002). *Hanging out in the virtual pub: Masculinities and relationships online.* Berkeley, CA: University of California Press.

Kendall, L. (2007). Shout into the wind, and it shouts back. In *Identity and interactional tensions on LiveJournal. First Monday, 12. Retrieved April 7, 2008, Kroger, J. (2007). Identity development: Adolescence through adulthood* (2nd ed.). Thousand Oaks, California: Sage Publications.

Kennedy, H. (2006). Beyond anonymity, or future directions for Internet identity research. *New Media & Society, 8*, 859–876. doi:10.1177/1461444806069641

Kim, H., Kim, G. J., Park, H. W., & Rice, R. E. (2007). Configurations of Relationships in Different Media: FtF, Email, Instant Messenger, Mobile Phone, and SMS. *Journal of Computer-Mediated Communication, 12*(4), article 3.

Kim, K. H., & Yun, H. (2007). Cying for me, Cying for us: Relational dialectics in a Korean social network site. *Journal of Computer-Mediated Communication, 13*(1), 15.

Kim, M. S., Hunter, J. E., Miyahara, A., Horvath, A., & Bresnahan, M. (1994). Individual vs. culture-level dimensions of individualism and collectivism: Effects on preferred conversation styles. *Communication Monographs, 63*, 29–49. doi:10.1080/03637759609376373

King, S. (1994). Analysis of electronic support groups for recovering addicts. *Interpersonal Computing and Technology, 2*(3).

Kinney, S., & Dennis, A. (1994, January). *Reevaluating media richness: Cues, feedback, and task.* Paper presented at the twenty-seventh annual Hawaii International Conference on System Sciences, Kihei, Maui, HI.

Kirscner, P. A., & Lai, K.-W. (2007). Online communities of practice in education. Special issue in *Technology. Pedagogy and Education., 16*(2), 127–131. doi:10.1080/14759390701406737

Knapp, M. L., & Daly, J. A. (2002). *Handbook of interpersonal communication.* Thousand Oaks, CA: Sage Publications.

Ko, A. J., DeLine, R., & Venolia, G. (2007). Information Needs in Collocated Software Development Teams. In *Proceedings of the 29th international Conference on Software Engineering* (May 20 - 26, 2007). ICSE. IEEE Computer Society, Washington, DC\.

Koch, S. C., Mueller, B., Kruse, L., & Zumbach, J. (2005). Constructing gender in chat groups. *Sex Roles, 53*, 29–41. doi:10.1007/s11199-005-4276-7

Kolb, D. A. (1984). *Experiential learning experience as a source of learning and development.* Upper Saddle River, NJ: Prentice Hall.

Kolko, B. E. (1995). Building a World With Words: The Narrative Reality of Virtual Communities. *Works and Days, 13*(1-2), 105–126.

Kolko, B. E., & Reid, E. (1998). Dissolution and fragmentation: problems in On-line Communities. In Jones, S. G. (Ed.), *Cybersociety 2.0 revising Computer-Mediated Communication and Community* (pp. 212–230). Thousand Oaks, CA: Sage.

Kollock, P. (1999). The economics of online cooperation: gifts and public goods in cyberespace. In Smith, M. Ä., & Kollock, P. (Eds.), *Communities in Cyberespace* (pp. 220–239). London: Routletge.

Kraut, R., Mukhopadhyay, T., Szczypula, J., Kiesler, S., & Scherlis, B. (2000). Information and communication: Alternative uses of the Internet in households. *Information Systems Research, 10*, 287–303. doi:10.1287/isre.10.4.287

Kress, G. (2003). *Literacy in the new media age.* London: Routledge. doi:10.4324/9780203164754

Kreuter, M. W., & McClure, S. M. (2004). The role of culture in health communication. *Annual Review of Public Health*, *25*, 439–455. doi:10.1146/annurev.publhealth.25.101802.123000

Krippendorff, K. (2004). *Content analysis: An introduction to its methodology*. Thousand Oaks, CA: Sage.

Kristjánsson, C. (2003). *Whole-person perspectives on learning in community: Meaning and relationships in teaching English as a second language*. Unpublished doctoral dissertation. University of British Columbia, Vancouver, Canada.

Kristjánsson, C. (2006, June 17-20). *Projections of presence and perceptions of identity: Dynamics and dilemmas in online MA TESOL*. Paper presented at the joint AAAL and ACLA/CAAL Conference, Montreal, Canada.

Kristjánsson, C. (2007). The word in the world: So to speak (a Freirean legacy). In Smith, D., & Osborn, T. (Eds.), *Spirituality, Social Justice and Language Learning* (pp. 133–153). Charlotte, NC: Information Age Publishing.

Kristjánsson, C. (2008, May 29-31). *Language, identity, and pedagogy for adult immigrants*. Workshop presented at the TESL Canada 2008 Conference, Moncton, Canada.

Kroger, J., & Adair, V. (2008). Symbolic meanings of valued personal objects in identity transitions of late adulthood. *Identity: An International Journal of Theory and Research*, *8*(1), 5–24.

Krohn, F. B. (2004). A generational approach to using emoticons as nonverbal communication. *Journal of technical writing and communication, 34*(4), 321-328.

Kroskrity, P. V. (1999). Identity. *Journal of Linguistic Anthropology*, *9*(1-2), 111–114. doi:10.1525/jlin.1999.9.1-2.111

Kumar, R., Novak, J., Raghavan, P., & Tomkins, A. (2004). Structure and evolution of blogspace. *Communications of the ACM*, *47*(12), 35–39. doi:10.1145/1035134.1035162

Kurzweil, R. (2005). *The singularity is near: When humans transcend biology*. New York: Viking.

Kvasny, L., & Igwe, F. (2008). An African American weblog community's reading of AIDS in Black America. *Journal of Computer-Mediated Communication*, *13*(3), 569–592. doi:10.1111/j.1083-6101.2008.00411.x

La Ferle, C., Edwards, S. M., & Mizuno, Y. (2002). Internet diffusion in Japan: Cultural considerations. *Journal of Advertising Research*, *42*(2), 65–79.

Lakoff, G., & Johnson, M. (1980). *Metaphors We Live By*. Chicago: Chicago University Press.

Lampe, C., Ellison, N., & Steinfield, C. (2006). A Face(book) in the crowd: Social searching vs. social browsing. In [New York: ACM Press.]. *Proceedings, CSCW-2006*, 167–170.

Lane, J. D., & Wegner, D. M. (1995). The cognitive consequences of secrecy. *Journal of Personality and Social Psychology*, *69*, 237–253. doi:10.1037/0022-3514.69.2.237

Lapointe, D. K., & Gunawardena, C. A. (2004). Developing, testing, and refining a model to understand the relationship between peer interaction and learning outcomes in computer-mediated conferencing. *Distance Education*, *25*, 83–106. doi:10.1080/0158791042000212477

Larkin-H., T. (2001, October). *On-line discussions: a key to enhancing student motivation and understanding*? Paper presented at the 31st Frontiers in Education Conference, Reno, NV.

Larson, D. G., & Chastain, R. L. (1990). Self-concealment: Conceptualization, measurement, and health implications. *Journal of Social and Clinical Psychology*, *9*, 439–455.

Latest GMI poll reveals Second Life's potential for virtual consumer marketing and branding. (2007, April 23). *GMI*. Retrieved March 20, 2008, from http://www.gmi-mr.com/gmipoll/release.php?p=20070423

Lave, J. (1991). Situated Learning in Communities of Practice. In Resnick, L., Levine, J., & Teasley, S. (Eds.), *Perspectives on Socially Shared Cognition* (pp. 63–82). Washington, DC: American Psychological Association. doi:10.1037/10096-003

Lave, J. (1993). The practice of learning. In Chaiklin, S., & Lave, J. (Eds.), *Understanding Practice* (pp. 3–32). Cambridge, UK: Cambridge University Press. doi:10.1017/CBO9780511625510.002

Lave, J., & Wenger, E. (1991). *Situated learning. Legitimate Peripheral Participation*. Cambridge, UK: Cambridge University Press.

Lawler, S. (2008). *Identity: Sociological perspectives.* Cambridge, UK: Polity.

Le Page, R. B., & Tabouret-Keller, A. (1985). *Acts of identity: Creole-based approaches to language and ethnicity.* Cambridge, UK: Cambridge University Press.

Lea, M., & Spears, R. (1991). Computer-mediated communication, de-individuation and group decision-making. *International Journal of Man-Machine Studies, 34*, 283–301. doi:10.1016/0020-7373(91)90045-9

Lea, M., & Spears, R. (1992). Paralanguage and social perception in computer-mediated communication. *Journal of Organizational Computing, 2*, 321–341. doi:10.1080/10919399209540190

Lea, M., & Spears, R. (1995). Love at first byte? Building personal relationships over computer networks. In Wood, J., & Duck, S. (Eds.), *Under-studied relationships: Off the beaten track* (pp. 197–233). Thousand Oaks, CA: Sage.

Lea, M., & Spears, R. (1995). Love at first byte? Building personal relationships over computer networks. In Wood, J. T., & Duck, S. (Eds.), *Understudied relationships: Off the beaten track* (pp. 197–233). Thousand Oaks, CA: Sage.

Lea, M., Spears, R., & de Groot, D. (2001). Knowing me, knowing you: Anonymity effects on social identity processes within groups. *Personality and Social Psychology Bulletin, 27*, 526–537. doi:10.1177/0146167201275002

Leary, M. R., & Kowalski, R. M. (1990). Impression management: A literature review and two-component model. *Psychological Bulletin, 107*, 34–47. doi:10.1037/0033-2909.107.1.34

Leder, D. (1990). *The absent body.* Chicago: The University of Chicago Press.

Lee, C. (2008). 2008 Wallace foundation distinguished lecture. The centrality of culture to the scientific study of learning and development: How an ecological framework in education research facilitates civic responsibility. *Educational Researcher, 37*(5), 267–279. doi:10.3102/0013189X08322683

Lee, E.-J. (2004). Effects of gendered character representation on person perception and informational social influence in computer mediated communication. *Computers in Human Behavior, 20*, 779–799. doi:10.1016/j.chb.2003.11.005

Lee, S., Hwang, T., & Lee, H. H. (2006). Corporate blogging strategies for the Fortune 400 comapnies. *Management Decision, 44*(3), 316–334. doi:10.1108/00251740610656232

Lengel, R. H., & Daft, R. L. (1988). The selection of communication media as an executive skill. *The Academy of Management Executive, 2*, 225–232.

Lenhart, A., & Madden, M. (2005). *Teen content creators and consumers.* Washington, DC: Pew Internet & American Life Project. Retrieved April 2, 2008, from http://www.pewinternet.org/PPF/r/166/report_display.asp

Lepore, S. J., & Smyth, J. M. (Eds.). (2002). *The writing cure: How expressive writing promotes health and emotional well-being.* Washington, D.C.: American Psychological Association. doi:10.1037/10451-000

Lepore, S. J., Greenberg, M. A., Brunjo, M., & Smyth, J. M. (2002). Expressive writing and health: Self-regulation of emotion-related experiences, physiology, and behavior. In Lepore, S. J., & Smyth, J. M. (Eds.), *The writing cure: How expressive writing promotes health and emotional well-being* (pp. 99–117). Washington, D.C.: American Psychological Association. doi:10.1037/10451-005

Lepore, S. J., Ragan, J. D., & Jones, S. (2000). Talking facilitates cognitive-emotional processes of adaptation to an acute stressor. *Journal of Personality and Social Psychology, 78*, 499–508. doi:10.1037/0022-3514.78.3.499

Li, Q. (2006). Cyberbullying in schools: A research of gender differences. *School Psychology International, 27*(2), 157–170. doi:10.1177/0143034306064547

Li, R. (2009). The representation of national political freedom on Web interface design: The indicators. *Journal of the American Society for Information Science and Technology, 60*(6), 1222–1248. doi:10.1002/asi.21046

Lie, M., & Sorenson, K. H. (1996). *Making technology our own? Domesticating technologies into every day life.* Oslo, Norway: Scandinavian University Press.

Lifton, R. J. (1993). *The Protean Self: Human Resilience in an Age of Fragmentation.* New York: Basic Books.

Ligorio, M. B. (in press). Dialogical relationship between identity and learning. *Culture and Psychology.*

Ligorio, M. B., & Sansone, N. (2009). Structure of a Blended University Course: Applying Constructivist principles to blended teaching. In (Ed.), Carla R Payne. Information Technology and Constructivism in Higher Education: Progressive Learning Frameworks. Hershey, PA: IGI Global.

Ligorio, M. B., & Spadaro, P. F. (2005). Digital positioning and online communities. In Oles, P. K., & Hermans, H. J. M. (Eds.), *The Dialogical Self: Theory And Research.* Lublin, Poland: Wydawnictwo KUL.

Ligorio, M. B., & Veermans, M. (2005). Preface: Perspectives and patterns in developing and implementing international web-based Collaborative Learning Environments. *Computers & Education, 45*(3), 271–275. doi:10.1016/j.compedu.2005.04.007

Ligorio, M. B., Annese, S., Spadaro, P. F., & Traetta, M. (2008). Building intersubjectivity and identity in online communities. In Varisco, B. M. (Ed.), *Psychological, pedagogical and sociological models for learning and assessment in virtual communities of practice* (pp. 57–91). Milan: Polimetrica.

Ligorio, M. B., Cacciamani, S., & Cesareni, D. (2006). *Blended Learning: dalla scuola dell'obbligo alla formazione adulta.* Rome: Carocci.

Limandri, B. J. (1989). Disclosure of stigmatizing conditions: The discloser's perspective. *Archives of Psychiatric Nursing, 3,* 69–78.

Lin, C. A., & Atkin, D. J. (2007). *Communication technology and social change.* Mahwah, NJ: Lawrence Erlbaum Associates.

Linden Lab. (2008, November). *Second Life virtual economy demographic summary information through November 2008.* San Francisco: Linden Research, Inc. Retrieved January 14, 2009, from http://static.secondlife.com/economy/stats_200811.xls

Linden, P. (2009, January 1). Looking to the New Year. Message posted to SLED electronic mailing list. Retrieved (n.d.), from https://lists.secondlife.com/pipermail/educators/2009-January/028481.html

Lindlof, T. R. (1995). *Qualitative communication research methods.* Thousand Oaks, CA: Sage.

Linehan, C., & McCarthy, J. (2000). Positioning in practice: Understanding participation in the social world. *Journal for the Theory of Social Behaviour, 30,* 435–453. doi:10.1111/1468-5914.00139

Lizcano, E. (2006). *Metáforas que nos piensan. Sobre ciencia, democracia y otras poderosas ficciones.* Madrid, Spain: Ediciones Bajo Cero.

Lo, S.-K. (2008). The nonverbal communication functions of emoticons in computer-mediated communication. *Cyberpsychology & Behavior, 11*(5), 595–587. doi:10.1089/cpb.2007.0132

Lockard, J. (2007). Manifesto for Democratic Education and the Internet. In Lockard, J., & Pegrum, M. (Eds.), *Brave New Classrooms: Democratic Education and the Internet* (pp. 285–310). New York: Peter Lang.

Lombard, M., & Ditton, T. (1997). At the heart of it all: The concept of presence. *Journal of Computer-Mediated Communication, 3*(2). Retrieved May 14, 2009, from http://jcmc.indiana.edu/vol3/issue2/lombard.html

Long, Y., & Wang, X. (2008). Shilun boke yuyande tedian ji chenyin (Characteristics of blog language and their contributing factors). *Yuwen xuekan (Journal of Chinese Language)*(1), 163-165.

Lou, C. (2008). Shilun wangluoxiezuozhong yuyanyunyongde tedian (Features of language use in online writing). *Yuwen xuekan (Journal of Chinese Language)* (2), 87-88.

Luo, L. (2005). *A systemic functional perspective on native and non-native English speaking students' online discussion in a mixed-mode graduate seminar.* Unpublished doctoral dissertation. University of British Columbia, Vancouver, Canada.

Lupton, D. (1994). Toward the development of critical health communication praxis. *Health Communication, 6*(1), 55–67. doi:10.1207/s15327027hc0601_4

Lutters, W. G., & Seaman, C. B. (2007). Revealing actual documentation usage in software maintenance through war stories. *Information and Software Technology, 49*(6), 576–587. doi:10.1016/j.infsof.2007.02.013

Ma, G. X. (1999). Between two worlds: the use of traditional and western health services by Chinese immigrants. *Journal of Community Health, 24*(6), 421–437. doi:10.1023/A:1018742505785

Mabry, E. A. (1998). Frames and flames: The structure of argumentative messages on the Net. In Sudweeks, F., McLaughlin, M., & Sheizaf, R. (Eds.), *Network & Netplay: Virtual groups on the Internet* (pp. 13–26). Menlo Park, CA: AAAI Press.

Mabry, E. A. (2002). Ambiguous self-identification and sincere communication in CMC. In L. Anolli, R. Ciceri, & G. Riva (Eds.), Say not to say: New perspectives on miscommunication (pp. 247-264). Amsterdam, NL: IOS Press.

Madden, M., & Raine, L. (2003). *America's online pursuits: The changing picture of who's online and what they do.* Pew/Internet. Retrieved January 10, 2009, from http://www.pewinternet.org/PPF/r/106/report_display.asp

Madlock, P. E., & Westerman, D. (2009). *Cyberteasing as a component of cyberbullying in romantic relationships: Who's LOL?* Unpublished manuscript.

Majchrzak, A., Rice, R. E., King, N., Malhotra, A., & Ba, S. L. (2000). Computer-mediated inter-organizational knowledge-sharing: Insights from a virtual team innovating using a collaborative tool. *Information Resources Management Journal, 13*, 44–53.

Maltz, T. (1996). Customary law and power in internet communities. *Journal of Computer-Mediated Communication, 2*(1). Retrieved May, 2009, from http://jcmc.indiana.edu/vol2/issue1/custom.html

Mantovani, G. (1995). *Comunicazione e identità.* Bologna, Italy: Il Mulino.

Marcus, A. (2005). User interface design and culture. In Aykin, N. (Ed.), *Usability and internationalization of information technology* (pp. 51–78). Mahwah, NJ: Lawrence Erlbaum Associates.

Marcus, A., & Gould, E. W. (2000, July/August). Crosscurrents: Cultural dimensions and global Web user-interface design. *Interaction, 7*(4), 32–46. doi:10.1145/345190.345238

Markel, S. L. (2001). Technology and Education Online Discussion Forums: It's in the Response. *Online Journal of Distance Learning Administration, 4*(2). Retrieved January 5, 2009, from http://www.westga.edu/~distance/ojdla/summer42/markel42.html

Markman, K. M. (2005). To send or not to send: Turn construction in computer-mediated chat. In C. Sunakawa, T. Ikeda, S. Finch & M. Shetty (Eds.), *Proceedings of the twelfth annual Symposium About Language and Society-Austin* (Vol. 48, pp. 115-124). Austin, TX: Texas Linguistic Forum.

Markman, K. M. (2006). *Computer-mediated conversation: The organization of talk in chat-based virtual team meetings.* Unpublished doctoral dissertation, The University of Texas at Austin.

Markman, K. M. (2009). "So what shall we talk about?": Openings and closings in chat-based virtual meetings. *Journal of Business Communication, 46*(1), 150–170. doi:10.1177/0021943608325751

Marková, I., Linell, P., Grossen, M., & Salazar Orvig, A. (2007). *Dialogue in focus groups: Exploring socially shared knowledge*. London: Equinox.

Marsden, P. V. (1990). Network data and measurement. *Annual Review of Sociology, 16*, 435–463. doi:10.1146/annurev.so.16.080190.002251

Martin, J. R., & White, P. R. R. (2005). *The language of evaluation: Appraisal in English*. New York: Palgrave Macmillan.

Martin, R. (1997). "Girls don't talk about garages!" Perceptions of conversation in same- and cross-sex friendships. *Personal Relationships, 4*, 115–130. doi:10.1111/j.1475-6811.1997.tb00134.x

Martinez, A., Dimitriadis, Y., Gomez, E., Jorrin, I., Rubia, B., & Marcos, J. A. (2002). Studying participation networks in collaboration using mixed methods. *International Journal of Computer-Supported Collaborative Learning, 1*(3), 383–408. doi:10.1007/s11412-006-8705-6

Maslow, A. (1982). *Toward a Psychology of Being* (2nd ed.). Princeton, NJ: Van Nostrand.

Mason, R. (2003) Global education: Out of the ivory tower. In M. Moore W. & Anderson (Eds.), Handbook of distance education (pp. 743-752). Mahwah, NJ: Lawrence Erlbaum.

Matthew, S. (2007). Assessing Online Discussion Forum Participation. *International Journal of Information and Communication Technology Education, 3*(3), 39–46.

Matusov, E. (2001). Intersubjectivity as a way of informing teaching design for a community of learners class. *Teaching and Teacher Education, 17*, 383–402. doi:10.1016/S0742-051X(01)00002-6

Mayes, C. (2001). Cultivating spiritual reflectivity in teachers. *Teacher Education Quarterly, 28*(2), 5–22.

Maynor, N. (1994). The language of electronic mail: Written speech? In Montgomery, M., & Little, G. D. (Eds.), *Centennial usage studies* (pp. 48–54). Tuscaloosa, AL: Alabama UP.

Maznevski, M. L., & Chudoba, K. M. (2000). Bridging space over time: Global virtual team dynamics and effectiveness. *Organization Science, 11*, 473–492. doi:10.1287/orsc.11.5.473.15200

Mazzoni, E. (2005). La Social Network Analysis a supporto delle interazioni nelle comunità virtuali per la costruzione di conoscenza. *TD. Tecnologie Didattiche, 35*(2), 54–63.

Mazzoni, E. (2006). La Social Network Analysis: analisi strutturale delle comunità virtuali. In Calvani, A. (Ed.), *Rete, Comunità e conoscenza* (pp. 193–215). Trento, Italy: Edizioni Erickson.

Mazzoni, E., & Bertolasi, S. (2005). Software per analizzare le interazioni di gruppo: Cyram NetMiner e Ucinet. *TD. Tecnologie Didattiche, 35*(2), 64–69.

McArthur, J. A. (2009). Digital subculture: A geek meaning of style. *The Journal of Communication Inquiry, 33*(1), 58–70. doi:10.1177/0196859908325676

McCarthy, J. C., & Monk, A. F. (1994). Measuring the quality of computer-mediated communication. *Behaviour & Information Technology, 13*(5), 311–319. doi:10.1080/01449299408914611

McClintock, C., & Lebovic, J. H. (2006). Correlates of levels of democracy in Latin America during the 1990s. *Latin American Politics and Society, 48*(2), 29–59. doi:10.1353/lap.2006.0021

McCormick, N. B., & McCormick, J. W. (1992). Computer friends and foes: Content of undergraduate's e-mail. *Computers in Human Behavior, 8*, 379–405. doi:10.1016/0747-5632(92)90031-9

McCray, G. E. (2000). The hybrid course: Merging online instruction and the traditional classroom. *Information Technology and Management, 1*(4), 307–327. doi:10.1023/A:1019189412115

McCroskey, J. C., & Richmond, V. P. (1989). Bipolar scales. In Emmert, P., & Barker, L. (Eds.), *Measurement of communication behavior* (pp. 154–167). New York: Longman.

McCullagh, D., & Broache, A. (2007). Blogs turn 10 -- Who's the father? *CNET news*. Retrieved February 9, 2009, from http://news.cnet.com/2100-1025_3-6168681. html

McFadyen, R. G. (1996). Gender, status, and 'powerless' speech: Interactions of students and lecturers. *The British Journal of Social Psychology, 35*, 353–367.

McGann, R. (2004). The blogosphere by the numbers. *The ClickZ Network*. Retrieved September 29, 2008, from http://www.clickz.com/ showPage.html?page=3438891

McInnerney, J., & Roberts, T. (2004). Collaborative or cooperative learning? In Roberts, T. (Ed.), *Online collaborative learning: Theory and practice* (pp. 203–214). Hershey, PA: Information Science Publishing.

McKenna, K. Y. A. (2008). MySpace or your place: Relationship initiation and development in the wired and wireless world. In Sprechter, S., Wenzel, A., & Harvey, J. (Eds.), *Handbook of Relationship Initiation* (pp. 235–248). New York: Psychology Press.

McKenna, K. Y. A., & Bargh, J. A. (2000). Plan 9 from cyberspace: the implications of the Internet for personality and social psychology. *Personality and Social Psychology Bulletin, 4*, 57–75. doi:10.1207/S15327957PSPR0401_6

McKenna, K. Y. A., & Green, A. S. (2002). Virtual group dynamics. *Group Dynamics*, 116–127. doi:10.1037/1089-2699.6.1.116

McKenna, K. Y. A., Green, A. S., & Gleason, M. E. J. (2002). Relationship formation on the Internet: What's the big attraction? *The Journal of Social Issues, 58*, 9–31. doi:10.1111/1540-4560.00246

McKenna, K., & Bargh, J. (1998). Coming out in the age of the Internet: Identity 'demarginalization' through virtual group participation. *Journal of Personality and Social Psychology, 75*, 681–694. doi:10.1037/0022-3514.75.3.681

McKerrow, R. E. (1989, June). Critical rhetoric: Theory and praxis. *Communication Monographs, 56*.

McLaughtin, M. L., Osborne, K. K., & Smith, C. B. (1995). Standards of conduct on Usenet. In Jones, S. G. (Ed.), *Cybersociety: Computer-Mediated Communication and Community* (pp. 90–111). Thousand Oaks, CA: Sage.

McLoughlin, C., & Luca, J. (2003). Overcoming "process-blindness" in the design of an online environment: Balancing cognitive and psycho-social outcomes. In G. Crisp, D. Thiele, I. Scholten, S. Parker, and J. Baron, (Eds.), *Interact, integrate, impact: Proceedings of the 20th annual conference of the Australasian society for computers in learning in tertiary education*. Adelaide, 7-10 December 2003. Retrieved, March 20, 2006, from http://www.ascilite.org.au/conferences/adelaide03/docs/pdf/332.pdf

McLuhan, M. (1964). *Understanding media: The extensions of man*. Cambridge, MA: The M.I.T. Press.

McLuhan, M., & Fiore, Q. (1967). *The medium is the massage: An inventory of effects*. New York: Bantam Books.

McMillan, D. V., & Chavis, D. M. (1986). Sense of Community: A Definition and Theory. *Journal of Community Psychology, 14*, 6–23. doi:10.1002/1520-6629(198601)14:1<6::AID-JCOP2290140103>3.0.CO;2-I

McNamara, K., Dennis, A. R., & Carte, T. A. (2007). It's the thought that counts: The mediating effects of information processing in virtual team decision making. *Information Systems Management, 25*(1), 20–32. doi:10.1080/10580530701777123

Mead, G. H. (1934). Mind, Self and Society from the Standpoint of a Social Behaviorist. Chicago: The University of Chicago press.

Meadows, M. S. (2008). *I, avatar: The culture and consequences of having a second life*. Berkeley, CA: New Riders.

Mendoza-Denton, N. (2002). Language and identity. In Chambers, J. K., Trudgill, P., & Schilling-Estes, N. (Eds.), *The handbook of language variation and change* (pp. 475–499). Malden, MA: Blackwell Publishers.

Merleau-Ponty, M. (1962). *Phenomenology of perception* (Smith, C., Trans.). London: Routledge & Paul.

Merleau-Ponty, M. (1969). *The visible and the invisible*. Evanston, IL: Northwestern University Press.

Metzger, M. J. (2007). Communication privacy management in electronic commerce. *Journal of Computer-Mediated Communication*, *12*, 335–361. doi:10.1111/j.1083-6101.2007.00328.x

Meyerowitz, J. (1985). *No sense of place: The impact of electronic media on social behavior*. New York: Oxford University Press.

Meyers, L. S., Gamst, G., & Guarino, A. J. (2006). *Applied multivariate research*. Thousand Oaks, CA: Sage.

Min, S. (2007). Online vs. Face-to-Face Deliberation: Effects on Civic Engagement. *Journal of Computer-Mediated Communication*, *12*(4), 11. doi:10.1111/j.1083-6101.2007.00377.x

Mintzberg, H. (1980). Managerial work: Analysis from observation. In Leavitt, H., Pondy, L., & Boje, D. (Eds.), *Reading in managerial psychology* (pp. 551–559). Chicago, IL: Univ. of Chicago Press.

Miranda, S. M., & Saunders, C. S. (2003). The social construction of meaning: an alternative perspective on information sharing. *Information Systems Research*, *14*(1), 87–106. doi:10.1287/isre.14.1.87.14765

Mitra, A., & Watts, E. (2002). Theorizing cyberspace: the idea of voice applied to the internet discourse. *New Media & Society*, *4*(4), 479–498. doi:10.1177/146144402321466778

Mohan, B. (1986). *Language and content*. Reading, MA: Addison-Wesley Publishing Company.

Mohan, B. (2001). The second language as a medium of learning. In Mohan, B., Leung, C., & Davison, C. (Eds.), *English as a Second Language in the Mainstream: Teaching, Learning and Identity* (pp. 107–126). Harlow, UK: Pearson Education.

Mohan, B., & Luo, L. (2005). A systemic functional linguistics perspective on CALL. In Egbert, J. L., &

Petrie, G. M. (Eds.), *CALL research perspectives* (pp. 87–96). Mahwah, NJ: Lawrence Erlbaum.

Mondorf, B. (2002). Gender differences in English syntax. *Journal of English Linguistics*, *30*(2), 158–180. doi:10.1177/007242030002005

Monroe, B. (1999). Re-membering Mama: The female body in embodied and disembodied communication. In Blair, K., & Takayoshi, P. (Eds.), *Feminist cyberscapes: Mapping gendered academic spaces* (pp. 63–82). Stamford, CT: Ablex.

Moody, E. J. (2001, November). Internet use and its relationship to loneliness. *Cyberpsychology & Behavior*, *4*(3), 393–401. doi:10.1089/109493101300210303

Morahan-Martin, J., & Scumacher, P. (2003). Loneliness and social uses of the Internet. *Computers in Human Behavior*, *19*, 659–671. doi:10.1016/S0747-5632(03)00040-2

Mortara, B. (1988). *Manual de retórica*. Madrid: Alianza Editorial.

Much, N. (1995). Cultural Psychology. In Smith, J. A., Harré, R., & Van Langhenove, L. (Eds.), *Rethinking Psychology*. London: Sage.

Mulac, A. (1998). The gender-linked language effect: Do language differences really make a difference? In Canary, D., & Dindia, K. (Eds.), *Sex differences and similarities in communication: Critical essays and empirical investigations of sex and gender in interaction* (pp. 127–156). Mahwah, NJ: Lawrence Erlbaum Associates.

Muukkonen, H., Hakkarainen, K., & Lakkala, M. (1999). Collaborative Technology for Facilitating Progressive Inquiry: Future Learning Environment Tools. In C. Hoadley & J. Roschelle (Eds.), *Proceedings of the CSCL '99: The Third International Conference on Computer Support Collaborative Learning*, (pp. 406-415). Mahwah, NJ: Erlbaum.

Myers, D. (1987). "Anonymity is part of the magic": Individual manipulation of computer mediated contexts. *Qualitative Sociology*, *10*, 251–266. doi:10.1007/BF00988989

Na Ubon, A. (2005). *Social presence in asynchronous text-based online learning communities: A longitudinal study using content analysis*. Unpublished doctoral dissertation. The University of York, Heslington, York, UK. Retrieved, March 20, 2006, fromhttp://www.cs.york.ac.uk/ftpdir/reports/YCST-2005-08.pdf

Nakamura, L. (2002). *Cybertypes: race, ethnicity, and identity on the Internet*. New York: Routledge.

Nakamura, L. (2008). *Digitizing race: Visual cultures of the internet*. Minneapolis, MN: University of Minnesota Press.

Nardi, B. A., Schiano, D. J., & Gumbrecht, M. (2004). *Blogging as social activity, or, would you let 900 million people read your diary?* Paper presented at the 2004 ACM conference on computer supported cooperative work.

Nardi, B. A., Schiano, D. J., Gumbrecht, M., & Swartz, L. (2004). Why we blog. *Communications of the ACM*, *47*(12), 41–46. doi:10.1145/1035134.1035163

Nastri, J., Peña, J., & Hancock, J. T. (2006). The construction of Away Messages: a speech Act Analysis. *Journal of computer-Mediated Communication*, *11*(4), 1025-1045. Retrieved May, 2009, from http://jcmc.indiana.edu/vol11/issue4/nastri.html

Nath, R., & Murthy, N. V. (2004). A study of the relationship between Internet diffusion and culture. *Journal of International Technology and Information Management*, *13*(2), 123–132.

National Communication Association. (2002). *Definitions of communication*. Retrieved February 1, 2008, from http://www.natcom.org/nca/Template2.asp?bid=344

Newman, M. (2007, September 24). Jena, La, The New York Times Company (New York). RetrievedFebruary 2, 2008, from http://topics.nytimes.com/top/news/national/usstatesterritoriesandpossessions/louisiana/jena/index.html

Newman, M. L., Groom, C. J., Handelman, L. D., & Pennebaker, J. W. (2008). Gender differences in language use: An analysis of 14,000 text samples. *Discourse Processes*, *45*, 211–236. doi:10.1080/01638530802073712

Nordon, E. (1969). The Playboy Interview: Marshall McLuhan. *Playboy*. Retrieved December 14, 2005, from www.vcsun.org/~battias/class/454/txt/mclpb.html

Norton, B., & Toohey, K. (2002). Identity and language learning. In Kaplan, R. B. (Ed.), *The Oxford Handbook of Applied Linguistics* (pp. 115–123). Oxford, UK: Oxford University Press.

Nowak, K. L. (2003). Sex categorization in computer mediated communication (CMC): Exploring the utopian promise. *Media Psychology*, *5*, 83–103. doi:10.1207/S1532785XMEP0501_4

Nowak, K. L., Watt, J., & Walther, J. B. (2005). The influence of synchrony and sensory modality on the person perception process in computer-mediated groups. *Journal of Computer-Mediated Communication*, *10*(3), article 3. http://jcmc.indiana.edu/vol10/issue3/nowak.html

Nowson, S., Oberlander, J., & Gill, A. J. (2005). *Weblogs, genres, and Individual differences*. Paper presented at the 27th Annual Conference of the Cognitive Science Society. Retrieved September 13, 2007, from http://www.ics.mq.edu.au/ ~snowson/papers/nowson-cogsci.pdf

O'Barr, W., & Atkins, B. (1998). 'Women's Language' or 'Powerless Language. In Coates, J. (Ed.), *Language and gender* (pp. 377–387). Oxford, UK: Blackwell Publishers.

O'Brien, J. (1999). Writing in the body: gender (re) production in online interaction. In M. A. Smith, M., P. Kollock (Eds.), Communities in Cyberspace (pp.76-104). London: Routledge.

O'Connor, B. (1996). *Explorations in indexing and abstracting: Pointing, virtue and power*. Englewood, CO: Libraries Limited.

O'Keefe, B. J. (1988). The logic of message design: Individual differences in reasoning about communication. *Communication Monographs*, *55*, 80–103. doi:10.1080/03637758809376159

O'Neill, J., & Martin, D. (2003). Text chat in action. In *Proceedings of the 2003 international ACM SIGGROUP conference on Supporting group work* (pp. 40-49). New York: ACM Press.

O'Reilly, M., & Newton, D. (2002). Interaction online: Above and beyond requirements of assessment. *Australian Journal of Educational Technology, 18*(1), 57-70. Retrieved January 5, 2009, from http://www.ascilite.org.au/ajet/ajet18/oreilly.html

O'Reilly, T. (2005). What is Web 2.0? Design patterns and business models for the next generation of software. Retrieved October 29, 2007, from http://www.oreillynet.com/pub/a/oreilly/tim/news/2005/09/30/what-is-web-20.html

O'Sullivan, P. B. (1996, May). *A match made in cyberspace: interpersonal communication theory and interpersonal communication technology.* Paper presented at the Annual Meeting of the International Communication Association, Chicago, IL.

O'Sullivan, P. B. (2000). What you don't know won't hurt me: Impression management functions of communication channels in relationships. *Human Communication Research, 26*, 403–431. doi:10.1093/hcr/26.3.403

O'Sullivan, P. B., Hunt, S. K., & Lippert, L. R. (2004). Mediated immediacy: A language of affiliation in a technological Age. *Journal of Language and Social Psychology, 23*, 464–490. doi:10.1177/0261927X04269588

Oblinger, D. G., & Oblinger, J. L. (2005). Is it age or IT: First steps toward understanding the Net Generation. In D. G. Oblinger & J. L. Oblinger (Eds.), *Educating the net generation* (pp. 2.1-2.20). Retrieved March 1, 2008, from http://www.educause.edu/ir/library/pdf/pub7101c.pdf

Ochs, E. (1993). Constructing social identity: A language socialization perspective. *Research on Language and Social Interaction, 26*(3), 287–306. doi:10.1207/s15327973rlsi2603_3

Ofulue, C. I. Interconnectivity in "other tongues": A sociolinguistic study of SMS text messages in Yoruba. *Issues in Intercultural Communication, 2*(1), 1-12.

Ogden, C. K., & Richards, I. A. (1923). *The meaning of meaning: A study of the influence of language upon thought and of the science of symbolism.* New York: Harcourt, Brace and Company.

Ogilvie, D. M. (1987). The undesired self: A neglected variable in personality research. *Journal of Personality and Social Psychology, 52*, 379–385. doi:10.1037/0022-3514.52.2.379

Ojo, T. (2005). ICTs and the Construction of "Imagined African Communities" Online. In Brigitte, Hipfl & Theo Hug (Eds.) Media Communities. 167-188. Münster, Germany: Waxmann Verlag.

Olapiriyakul, K., & Scher, J. M. (2006). A guide to establishing hybrid learning courses: Employing information technology to create a new learning experience, and a case study. *The Internet and Higher Education, 9*, 287–301. doi:10.1016/j.iheduc.2006.08.001

Olson, G. M., & Olson, J. S. (2000). Distance matters. *Human-Computer Interaction, 15*(2/3), 139–179. doi:10.1207/S15327051HCI1523_4

Ondrejka, C. (2008). Education unleashed: Participatory culture, education, and innovation in Second Life. In K. Salen (Ed.), *The ecology of games: Connecting youth, games, and learning* (pp. 229-252). The John D. and Catherine T. MacArthur Foundation Series on Digital Media and Learning. Cambridge, MA: MIT Press. Retrieved April 3, 2008, from http://www.mitpressjournals.org/doi/pdfplus/10.1162/dmal.9780262693646.229

Ong, W. J. (1967). *The presence of the word: Some prolegomena for cultural and religious history.* New Haven, CT: Yale University Press.

Ong, W. J. (2002). Orality and literacy: The technologizing of the word (2nd ed.). New York: Routledge.Peters, J. D. (1999). Speaking into the Air: A History of the Idea of Communication. Chicago: University of Chicago Press.

Ooi, V. B. Y. (2002). Aspects of computer-mediated communication for research in Corpus Linguistics. In Peters, P., Collins, P., & Smith, A. (Eds.), *New frontiers of corpus research: Papers from the twenty first international conference on English language research on computerized corpora, Sydney 2000* (pp. 91–104). Amsterdam, New York: Rodopi.

Ooi, V. B. Y., Tan, P. K. W., & Chiang, A. K. L. (2007). Analyzing personal weblogs in Singapore English: the Wmatrix approach. *eVariEng (Journal of the Research Unit for Variation, Contacts, and Change in English), 2,* from http://www.helsinki.fi/varieng/journal/volumes/02/ooi_et_al/

Orestrom, B. (1983). *Turn-taking in English conversation.* Lund, Sweden: Gleerup.

Orlikowski, W. (1992). Learning from notes: Organizational issues in groupware implementation. In *Proceedings of the Conference on Computer Supported Cooperative Work,* (pp.362–369). New York: ACM.

Orlowski, A. (2003). Most bloggers "are teenage girls"-survey [Electronic Version]. *The Register.* Retrieved September 29, 2008, from http://www.theregister.co.uk/2003/05/30/most_bloggers_are_teenage_girls/

Osborn, T. (2006). *Teaching world languages for social justice: A sourcebook of principles and practice.* Mahwah, NJ: Lawrence Erlbaum.

Osman, G., & Herring, S. C. (2007). Interaction, facilitation, and deep-learning in cross-cultural chat: A case study. *The Internet and Higher Education, 10,* 125–141. doi:10.1016/j.iheduc.2007.03.004

Ostman, J. (1995). Pragmatic particles twenty years after. In Brita Warvick, Kaisa Tanskanen, and Risto Hiltunen (Eds.) Organization in discourse. 95-108. Turku, Finland: University of Turku.

Owen, J. E., Yarbrough, E. J., Vaga, A., & Tucker, D. C. (2003). Investigation of the effects of gender and preparation on quality of communication in Internet support groups. *Computers in Human Behavior, 19,* 259–275. doi:10.1016/S0747-5632(02)00068-7

Oyserman, D., Coon, H. M., & Kemmelmeier, M. (2002). Rethinking individualism and collectivism: Evaluation of theoretical assumptions and meta-analyses. *Psychological Bulletin, 128,* 3–72. doi:10.1037/0033-2909.128.1.3

Paccagnella, L. (1997). Getting the seats of your pants dirty: strategies for ethnographic research. *Journal of Computer mediated Communication, 3*(1). Retrieved February, 2009, from http://jcmc.indiana.edu/vol3/issue1/paccagnella.html

Pahran, A. A. (2004). Diaspora, Community and Communication: Internet Use in Transnational Haiti. *Global Networks, 4*(2), 199-217. Retrieved January 6, 2009, from http://jcmc.indiana.edu/vol9/issue1/panya_herring.html

Palloff, R., & Pratt, K. (2005). *Online learning communities revisited.* Paper presented at The 21st Annual Conference on Distance Teaching and Learning. The University of Wisconsin. Retrieved, March 20, 2006, from http://www.uwex.edu/disted/conference/Resource_library/proceedings/05_1801.pdf

Palomares, N. A. (2004). Gender schematicity, gender identity salience, and gender-linked language use. *Human Communication Research, 30,* 556–588. doi:10.1111/j.1468-2958.2004.tb00745.x

Palomares, N. A. (2008). Explaining gender-based language use: Effects of gender identity salience on references to emotion and tentative language in intra- and intergroup contexts. *Human Communication Research, 34,* 263–286. doi:10.1111/j.1468-2958.2008.00321.x

Panyametheekul, S., & Herring, S. C. (2003). Gender and turn allocation in a Thai chat room. *Journal of Computer-Mediated Communication, 9*(1). Retrieved April 3, 2004, from http://www.ascusc.org/jcmc/vol9/issue1/panya_herring.html

Park, J. (2007). Interpersonal and affective communication in synchronous online discourse. *The Library Quarterly, 77*(2), 133–155. doi:10.1086/517841

Park, Jung-ran (2007). Interpersonal and affective communication in synchronous online discourse. *Library Quarterly, 77*(2), (Special issue on Discourse Approaches to Information Seeking in Context), 133-155.

Parks, M. R., & Floyd, K. (1996). Friends in cyberspace: Exploring personal relationships formed through the Internet. *The Journal of Communication*, *46*, 80–97. doi:10.1111/j.1460-2466.1996.tb01462.x

Parsons, P., & Ross, D. (2002). Planning a campus to support hybrid learning. *Maricopa Center for Learning and Instruction*. Retrieved January 10, 2009, from http://www.mcli.dist.maricopa.edu/ocotillo/tv/hybrid_planning.html

Patchin, J. W., & Hinduja, S. (2006). Bullies move beyond the schoolyard: A preliminary look at cyberbullying. *Youth Violence and Juvenile Justice*, *4*(2), 148–169. doi:10.1177/1541204006286288

Pauley, P. M., & Emmers-Sommer, T. M. (2007). The impact of Internet technologies on primary and secondary romantic relationship development. *Communication Studies*, *58*(4), 411–427. doi:10.1080/10510970701648616

Paulus, T. M. (2007). CMC modes for learning tasks at a distance. *Journal of Computer-Mediated Communication*, *12*, 1322–1345. doi:10.1111/j.1083-6101.2007.00375.x

Pearce, C. (2004). Towards a game theory of game. In N. Wardrip-Fruin & P. Harrigan (Eds.), *First person: New media as story, performance and game*. Cambridge, MA: MIT Press. Retrieved June 2, 2008, from http://www.electronicbookreview.com/thread/firstperson/tamagotchi

Pecchioni, L. L., Wright, K. B., & Nussbaum, J. F. (2005). *Life-span communication*. Mahwah, NJ: Lawrence Erlbaum Associates.

Pedersen, S., & Macafee, C. (2007). Gender differences in British blogging. *Journal of Computer-Mediated Communication*, *12*(4). doi:10.1111/j.1083-6101.2007.00382.x

Peirce, C. S. (1931-58). In Hartshorne, C., Weiss, P., & Burks, A. W. (Eds.), *Collected papers of Charles Sanders Peirce*. Cambridge, MA: Harvard University Press.

Pennebaker, J. W. (1989). Confession, inhibition, and disease. *Advances in Experimental Social Psychology*, *22*, 211–244. doi:10.1016/S0065-2601(08)60309-3

Pennebaker, J. W. (1997). Writing about emotional experiences as a therapeutic process. *Psychological Science*, *8*, 162–166. doi:10.1111/j.1467-9280.1997.tb00403.x

Pennebaker, J. W., & O'Heeron, R. C. (1984). Confiding in others and illness rate among spouses of suicide and accidental death victims. *Journal of Abnormal Psychology*, *93*, 473–476. doi:10.1037/0021-843X.93.4.473

Pennebaker, J. W., & Seagal, J. D. (1999). Forming a story: The health benefits of narrative. *Journal of Clinical Psychology*, *55*, 1243–1254. doi:10.1002/(SICI)1097-4679(199910)55:10<1243::AID-JCLP6>3.0.CO;2-N

Pennebaker, J. W., Colder, M., & Sharp, L. K. (1990). Accelerating the coping process. *Journal of Personality and Social Psychology*, *58*, 528–537. doi:10.1037/0022-3514.58.3.528

Pennebaker, J. W., Kiecolt-Glaser, J. K., & Glaser, R. (1988). Disclosure of traumas and immune function: Health implications for psychotherapy. *Journal of Consulting and Clinical Psychology*, *56*, 239–245. doi:10.1037/0022-006X.56.2.239

Pennycook, A. (2001). *Critical applied linguistics: A critical introduction*. Mahwah, NJ: Lawrence Erlbaum Associates.

Petronio, S. (2000). The boundaries of privacy: Praxis in everyday life. In Petronio, S. (Ed.), *Balancing the secrets of private disclosures* (pp. 111–122). Hillsdale, NJ: Lawrence Erlbaum Associates.

Petronio, S. (2002). *The boundaries of privacy: Dialectics of disclosure*. Albany, NY: State University of New York Press.

Pew Internet & American Life Project. (2004). *The Internet and daily life: Many Americans use the Internet in everyday activities, but traditional offline habits still dominate*. Retrieved October 11, 2007, from http://www.pewinternet.org/

Pew Internet & American Life Project. (2006). *Bloggers: A portrait of the internet's new storytellers*. Retrieved January 15, 2009, from http://www.pewinternet.org/PPF/r/186/report_display.asp

Pew Internet & American Life. (2007, 3 March). Getting serious online: as Americans gain experience, they use the Web more at work, write e-mails with more significant content, perform more online transactions, and pursue more serious activities. Washington, DC: Pew Internet & American Life. Retrieved 4 March 2007, from http://www.pewinternet.org/

Pew Internet. (2009). *Demographics of Internet users.* Retrieved May 15, 2009, from http://pewinternet.org/Static-Pages/Data-Tools/Download-Data/~/media/Infographics/Trend Data/January 2009 updates/Demographics of Internet Users 1 6 09.jpg

Pierce, C. A., Byrne, D., & Aguinis, H. (1996). Attraction in organizations: A model of workplace romance. *Journal of Organizational Behavior, 17*(1), 5–32. doi:10.1002/(SICI)1099-1379(199601)17:1<5::AID-JOB734>3.0.CO;2-E

Pinch, T. (1996). The Social Construction of Technology: A review. In Fox, R. (Ed.), *Technological Change. Methods and Themes in the History of Technology* (pp. 17–36). Oxford, UK: Oxford University Press.

Pinch, T., & Bijker, W. E. (1987). The social construction of facts and artifacts: or how the sociology of science and the sociology of technology might benefit each other. In Bijker, W. E., Hugues, T. P., & Pinch, T. (Eds.), *The social construction of technology Systems* (pp. 17–50). Cambridge, MA: MIT Press.

Plag, I. (2003). *Word-formation in English.* Cambridge, UK: Cambridge University Press.

Poltrock, S., Grudin, J., Dumais, S., Fidel, R., Bruce, H., & Pejtersen, A. M. (2003). *Information Seeking and Sharing in Design Teams.* Paper presented [New York: ACM.]. *Group, 03*, 239–247.

Poole, A. (2005, December). *Black bloggers and the Blogosphere.* Paper presented at the Second International Conference on Technology, Knowledge and Society, Hyderabad, India.

Poole, M. S., Shannon, D. L., & DeSanctis, G. (1992). Communication media and negotiation processes. In Putnam, L. L., & Roloff, M. E. (Eds.), *Communication and negotiation: Sage annual reviews of communication research* (pp. 46–66). Thousand Oaks, CA: Sage.

Portes, A. (1989). Social capital: Its origins and applications in modern sociology. *Annual Review of Sociology, 24*, 1–24. doi:10.1146/annurev.soc.24.1.1

Poster, M. (1995). *CyberDemocracy: Internet and the public sphere.* Retrieved July 13, 2007, from http://www.uoc.edu/in3/hermeneia/sala_de_lectura/mark_poster_cyberdemocracy.htm

Poster, M. (1998). Virtual ethnicity: Tribal Identity in an Age of Global Communications. In S. G. Jones (Ed.) Cybersociety 2.0 revising Computer-Mediated Communication and Community (pp. (184-211). Thousand Oaks, CA: Sage.

Postmes, T., & Spears, R. (2002). Behavior online: Does anonymous computer communication reduce gender inequality? *Personality and Social Psychology Bulletin, 28*, 1073–1083. doi:10.1177/01461672022811006

Postmes, T., Spears, R., & Lea, M. (1998). Breaching or building social boundaries? *Communication Research, 25*(6), 689–715. doi:10.1177/009365098025006006

Postmes, T., Spears, R., & Lea, M. (2000). The formation of group norms in computer-mediated communication. *Human Communication Research, 26*(3), 341–372. doi:10.1111/j.1468-2958.2000.tb00761.x

Potter, R. E., & Balthazard, P. A. (2002). Virtual team interaction styles: Assessment and effects. *International Journal of Human-Computer Studies, 56*, 423–443. doi:10.1006/ijhc.2002.1001

Poulet, G. (1969). Phenomenology of reading. *New Literary History, 1*(1), 53–68. doi:10.2307/468372

Preece, J. (2000). *Online Communities.* Chichester, UK: John Wiley & Sons.

Preece, J. (2000). *Online communities: Designing usability and supporting sociability.* Hoboken, NJ: Wiley.

Prensky, M. (2001). *Digital game-based learning.* New York: McGraw-Hill.

Profile of the American College Student (PACS) Survey. (2007). Profile *of the American College Student: University of Missouri-Columbia.* Columbia, MO: Institutional Research, UMC. Retrieved April 3, 2008 from http://ir.missouri.edu/reports-presentations.html

Pruett, B. M. (1989). Male and female communication style differences: A meta-analysis. In Lont, C., & Friedley, S. (Eds.), *Beyond boundaries: Sex and gender diversity in communication* (pp. 107–120). Fairfax, VA: George Mason University.

Qiuyun, L. (2008). Student Satisfactions in Four Mixed Courses in Elementary Teacher Education Program. *The Internet and Higher Education, 11*(1), 53–59. doi:10.1016/j.iheduc.2007.12.005

Rabby, M. K. (1997, November). *Maintaining relationships via electronic mail.* Paper presented at the annual meeting of the National Communication Association, Chicago, IL.

Rabby, M. K., & Walther, J. B. (2003). Computer-mediated communication effects on relationship formation and maintenance. In Canary, D. J., & Dainton, M. (Eds.), *Maintaining relationships through communication* (pp. 141–162). Mahwah, NJ: Lawrence Erlbaum Associates, Publishing.

Rafaeli, S., & Sudweeks, F. (1998). Interactivity on the Nets. In Sudweeks, F., McLaughlin, M., & Rafaeli, S. (Eds.), *Network & Netplay: Virtual groups on the Internet* (pp. 173–190). Menlo Park, CA: AAAI Press.

Rafaeli, S., Sudweeks, F., Konstan, J., & Mabry, E. (1998). ProjectH oveview: A collaborative quantitative study of computer-mediated communication. In Sudweeks, F., McLaughlin, M., & Rafaeli, S. (Eds.), *Network & Netplay: Virtual groups on the Internet* (pp. 265–281). Menlo Park, CA: AAAI Press.

Rains, S. A., & Scott, C. R. (2007). To identify or not to identify: A theoretical model of receiver responses to anonymous communication. *Communication Theory, 17,* 61–91. doi:10.1111/j.1468-2885.2007.00288.x

Rains, S. A., & Scott, C. R. (2007). To identify or not to identify: A theoretical model of receiver responses to anonymous communication. *Communication Theory, 17,* 61–91. doi:10.1111/j.1468-2885.2007.00288.x

Ramirez, A. Jr, Zhang, S., McGrew, C., & Lin, S. (2007). Relational communication in computer-mediated interaction revisited: A comparison of participant-observer perspectives. *Communication Monographs, 74*(4), 492–516. doi:10.1080/03637750701716586

Ramirez, A., Walther, J., Burgoon, J., & Sunnafrank, M. (2002). Information-seeking strategies, uncertainty, and computer-mediated communication: Toward a conceptual model. *Human Communication Research, 26,* 213–228.

Rayson, P. (2003). Matrix: A statistical method and software tool for linguistic analysis through corpus comparison. Unpublished PhD thesis. Lancaster University.

Rayson, P. (2008). *Wmatrix: a web-based corpus processing environment: Computing Department.* Lancaster University.

Razavi, M. N., & Iverson, L. (2006, November 4-8). *A Grounded Theory of Information Sharing Behavior in a Personal Learning Space.* Paper presented at the CSCW '06, Banff, Canada.

Reckwitz, A. (2002). Toward a Theory of Social Practices. A development in culturalist theorizing. *European Journal of Social Theory, 5*(2), 245–265. doi:10.1177/13684310222225432

Redfern, S., & Naughton, N. (2002). Collaborative virtual environments to support communication and community in internet-based distance education. *Journal of Information Technology Education, 1,* 201–211.

Reeder, K., Macfadyen, L., Roche, J., & Chase, M. (2004). Negotiating cultures in cyberspace: Participation, patterns and problematics. *Language Learning & Technology, 8*(2), 88–105.

Reid, E. (1999). Hierarchy and power: social control in Cyberespace. In Smith, M. A., & Kollock, P. (Eds.), *Communities in Cyberespace* (pp. 107–133). London: Routledge.

Reid, E. M. (1994). *Cultural formations in text-based virtual realities.* Unpublished master's thesis, University of Melbourne, Melbourne, Australia.

Reid, S. A., Keerie, N., & Palomares, N. A. (2003). Language, gender salience, and social influence. *Journal of Language and Social Psychology, 22*, 210–234. doi:10.1177/0261927X03022002004

Reingold, H. (1993). *The virtual community.* New York: Addison-Wesley.

Remedios, L., Clarke, D., & Hawthorne, L. (2008). The silent participant in small group collaborative learning contexts. *Active Learning in Higher Education, 9*(3), 201–216. doi:10.1177/1469787408095846

Rheingold, H. (1993). *The virtual community: homesteading on the electronic frontier.* New York: HarperPerennial.

Rheingold, H. (1993). *Virtual Community. Homesteading on the Electronic Frontier.* Reading, MA: Addison-Wesley Publishing Company.

Rice, R. E. (1993). Media appropriateness: Using social presence theory to compare traditional and new organizational media. *Human Communication Research, 19*, 451–484. doi:10.1111/j.1468-2958.1993.tb00309.x

Rice, R. E., & Love, G. (1987). Electronic emotion: Socioemotional content in a computer-mediated communication network. *Communication Research, 14*, 85–108. doi:10.1177/009365087014001005

Richards, J. M., Beal, W. E., Seagal, J. D., & Pennebaker, J. W. (2000). Effects of disclosure of traumatic events on illness behavior among psychiatric prison inmates. *Journal of Abnormal Psychology, 109*, 156–160. doi:10.1037/0021-843X.109.1.156

Richardson, F. C., Rogers, A., & McCarroll, J. (1998). Toward a dialogical self. *The American Behavioral Scientist, 41*, 496–514. doi:10.1177/0002764298041004004

Richardson, J., & Swan, K. (2003). Examining social presence in online courses in relation to students' perceived learning and satisfaction. *JALN, 7*(1), 68–88.

Ridings, C. M., & Gefen, D. (2004). Virtual community attraction: Why people hang out online. *Journal of Computer-Mediated Communication, 10*(1). Retrieved June 28, 2005, from http://jcmc.indiana.edu/vol10/issue1/ridings_gefen.html

Riley, P. (2007). *Language, culture and identity: An ethnolinguistic perspective.* London: Continuum.

Rintel, E. S., & Pittam, J. (1997). "Strangers in a strange land": Interaction management on Internet relay chat. *Human Communication Research, 23*, 507–534. doi:10.1111/j.1468-2958.1997.tb00408.x

Rintel, E. S., Pittam, J., & Mulholland, J. (2003). Time will tell: Ambiguous non-responses on Internet relay Chat. *Electronic Journal of Communication, 13*(1). Retrieved January 13, 2004, from http://80-www.cios.org.content.lib.utexas.edu:2048getfile%5CRINTEL_V13N1

Riva, G. (2001). Communicating in CMC: Making order out of miscommunication. In Anolli, L., Ciceri, R., & Riva, G. (Eds.), *Say not to say: New perspectives on miscommunication* (pp. 204–230). Amsterdam: IOS Press.

Robinson, E. (2007, September 21). Drive time for the Jena 6, *Washington Post*, A19. Retrieved August 19, 2008, from http://www.washingtonpost.com/wp-dyn/content/article/2007/09/20/AR2007092001956.html

Robinson, J. D. (2006). Managing trouble responsibility and relationships during conversational repair. *Communication Monographs, 73*, 137–161. doi:10.1080/03637750600581206

Robinson, J. D., & Turner, J. (2003). Impersonal, Interpersonal, and Hyperpersonal Social Support: Cancer and Older Adults. *Health Communication, 15*(2), 227–234. doi:10.1207/S15327027HC1502_10

Robinson, R., & West, R. (1992). A comparison of computer and questionnaire methods of history taking in a genitourinary clinic. *Psychology & Health, 6*, 77–84. doi:10.1080/08870449208402024

Rodgers, S., & Chen, Q. (2005). Internet community group participation: Psychosocial benefits for women with breast cancer. *Journal of Computer-Mediated Communication, 10*(4), article 5. http://jcmc.indiana.edu/vol10/issue4/rodgers.html

Rodino, M. (1997). Breaking out of binaries: Reconceptualizing gender and its relationship to language in computer-mediated communication. *Journal of Computer-Mediated Communication, 3*(3). Retrieved August 22, 1999, from, http://www.ascusc.org/jcmc/vol3/issue3/rodino.html

Romaine, S. (2003). Variation in language and gender. In Holmes, J., & Meyerhoff, M. (Eds.), *The handbook of language and gender* (pp. 98–118). Malden, MA: Blackwell. doi:10.1002/9780470756942.ch4

Roszak, T. (1994). *Cult of Information*. Berkeley, CA: University of California Press.

Rothwell, J. D. (2006). *In Mixed Company: Communicating in small groups and teams* (6th ed.). Belmont, CA: Thompson Wadsworth.

Rovai, A. P. (2007). Facilitating online discussions effectively. *The Internet and Higher Education, 10*(1), 77–88. doi:10.1016/j.iheduc.2006.10.001

Rovai, A. P., & Jordan, H. M. (2004, August). Blended learning and sense of community: A comparative analysis with traditional and fully online graduate courses. *International Review of Research in Open and Distance Learning*. Retrieved February 12, 2009, from http://www.irrodl.org/content/V.S.2rovai-jordan.html

Ruggiero, T. E. (2000). Uses and gratifications theory in the 21st century. *Mass Communication & Society, 3*(1), 3–37. doi:10.1207/S15327825MCS0301_02

Ruhleder, K. (2004). Changing patterns of participation: Interactions in a synchronous audio+chat classroom. In Haythornthwaite, C. A., & Kazmer, M. M. (Eds.), *Learning, culture and community in online education* (pp. 229–242). New York: Peter Lang.

Rumbaugh, T. (2001). The development and maintenance of interpersonal relationships through computer-mediated communication. *Communication Research Reports, 18*, 223–229.

Rutowski, A. F., Vogel, D. R., van Genuchten, M., Bemelmans, T. M. A., & Favier, M. (2002). E-collaboration: The reality of virtuality. *IEEE Transactions on Professional Communication, 45*(4), 219–230. doi:10.1109/TPC.2002.805147

Sacks, H. A., Schegloff, E., & Jefferson, G. (1974). A simplest systematics for the organization of turn taking for conversation. *Language, 50*, 696–735. doi:10.2307/412243

Salander, P. (2002). Using beliefs and magical thinking to fight cancer distress—A case study. *Psycho-Oncology, 9*(1), 40–43. doi:10.1002/(SICI)1099-1611(200001/02)9:1<40::AID-PON429>3.0.CO;2-K

Salt, B., Atkins, C., & Blackall, L. (2008, October). *Engaging with Second Life: Real education in a virtual world*. Retrieved February 8, 2009, from http://slenz.files.wordpress.com/2008/12/slliteraturereviewa1.pdf

Salvador, T., & Bly, S. (1997). *Supporting the flow of information through constellations of interaction*. Paper presented at the ECSCW'97, 269-280, Springer.

Samp, J. A., Wittenberg, E. M., & Gillett, D. L. (2003). Presenting and monitoring a gender-defined self on the internet. *Communication Research Reports, 20*, 1–12.

Sapir, E. (1963). *Selected writings of Edward Sapir in language, culture and personality* (Mandelbaum, D. G., Ed.). Berkeley, CA: University of California Press. (Original work published 1949)

Sapir, E. (1964). Conceptual categories in primitive languages. In Hymes, D. (Ed.), *Language in culture and society: A reader in linguistics and anthropology* (pp. 128–140). New York: Harper & Bow.

Saranson, S. B. (1974). *The Psychological Sense of Community: Prospects for a Community Psychology*. San Francisco: Josses-Bass.

Sarch, A. (1996, November). *Keyboard encounters: Virtual sex and gendered identities.* Paper presented at the annual meeting of the Speech Communication Association, San Diego, CA.

Sassenberg, K., & Boos, M. (2003). Attitude change in computer-mediated communication: Effects of anonymity and category norms. *Group Processes & Intergroup Relations, 6,* 405–422. doi:10.1177/13684302030064006

Satchell, C., & Foth, M. (2008). The re-creation of identity in digital environments and the potential benefits for non-profits and community organizations. *3CMedia: Journal of community, citizens, and third sector media and communication,* 16-27.

Saussure, F. D. (1966). *Course in general linguistics* (Bally, C., Sechehaye, A., & Riedlinger, A., Trans.). New York: McGraw-Hill Book.

Savicki, V., Kelley, M., & Lingenfelter, D. (1996a). Gender and small task group activity using computer-mediated communication. *Computers in Human Behavior, 12,* 209–224. doi:10.1016/0747-5632(96)00003-9

Savicki, V., Kelley, M., & Lingenfelter, D. (1996b). Gender, group composition and task type in small task groups using computer-mediated communication. *Computers in Human Behavior, 12,* 549–565. doi:10.1016/S0747-5632(96)00024-6

Savicki, V., Kelley, M., & Oesterreich, E. (1999). Judgments of gender in computer-mediated communication. *Computers in Human Behavior, 15,* 185–194. doi:10.1016/S0747-5632(99)00017-5

Savicki, V., Lingenfelter, D., & Kelley, M. (1996c). Gender, language style and group composition in Internet discussion groups. *Journal of Computer-Mediated Communication, 2*(3). Retrieved August 22, 1999, from http://www.ascusc.org/jcmc/vol2/issue3/savicki.html

Schegloff, E. A. (1992). Repair after next turn: The last structurally provided defense of intersubjectivity in conversation. *American Journal of Sociology, 104,* 161–216.

Schegloff, E. A. (1997). Practices and actions: Boundary cases of other-initiated repair. *Discourse Processes, 23,* 499–545. doi:10.1080/01638539709545001

Schegloff, E. A. (2000). When 'others' initiate repair. *Applied Linguistics, 21,* 205–243. doi:10.1093/applin/21.2.205

Schegloff, E. A., Jefferson, G., & Sacks, H. (1977). The preference for self-correction in the organization of repair in conversation. *Language, 53,* 361–382. doi:10.2307/413107

Schiano, D. J., Nardi, B. A., Gumbrecht, M., & Swartz, L. (2004). *Blogging by the rest of us.* Paper presented at the Conference on Human Factors in Computing Systems (CHI 2004).

Schimmack, U., Oishi, S., & Diener, E. (2005). Individualism: A valid and important dimension of cultural differences between nations. *Personality and Social Psychology Review, 9*(1), 17–31. doi:10.1207/s15327957pspr0901_2

Schleppegrell, M. (2004). *The language of schooling: A functional linguistics perspective.* Mahwah, NJ: Erlbaum.

Schneider, B. (2002). Nonstandard quotes: Superimpositions and cultural maps. *College Composition and Communication, 54*(2), 188–207. doi:10.2307/1512145

Schneider, S. J., & Tooley, J. (1986). Self-help computer conferencing. *Computers and Biomedical Research, an International Journal, 19,* 274–281. doi:10.1016/0010-4809(86)90022-4

Schonfeldt, J., & Golato, A. (2003). Repair in chats: A conversation analytic approach. *Research on Language and Social Interaction, 36,* 241–284. doi:10.1207/S15327973RLSI3603_02

Schutz, W. (1966). *The interpersonal underworld.* Palo Alto, CA: Science and Behavior Books, Inc.

Scollon, S. (1999). Not to waste words or students: Confucian and socratic discourse in tertiary the classroom. In Hinkel, E. (Ed.), *Culture in second language teaching and learning.* New York: Cambridge University Press.

Scott, C. R. (1998). To reveal or not to reveal: A theoretical model of anonymous communication. *Communication Theory, 8*, 381–407. doi:10.1111/j.1468-2885.1998.tb00226.x

Scott, C. R. (1999). Communication technology and group communication. In L. R. Frey (Ed.), D. S. Gouran, & M. S. Poole (Eds.), The handbook of group communication theory & research (pp. 313-334). Thousand Oaks, CA: Sage.

Scott, C. R. (2007). Communication and social identity theory: Existing and potential connections in organization identification research. *Communication Studies, 58*(2), 123–138. doi:10.1080/10510970701341063

Scott, J. (1997). *Social Network Analysis. A Handbook.* London: Sage.

Scott, J. (2000). *Social network analysis: A handbook.* Thousand Oaks, CA: Sage.

Scott, M. (2009). *WordSmith Tools 5.0* (Version 5.0.0.140).

Scott, W. A. (1955). Reliability of content analysis: The case of nominal scale coding. *Public Opinion Quarterly, 19*, 321–325. doi:10.1086/266577

Second Life. (2008). *Economic statistics: raw data files.* Retrieved on February 2, 2009, from http://secondlife.com/statistics/economy-data.php

Selfe, C. C., & Meyer, P. D. (1991). Testing claims for on-line conferences. *Written Communication, 8*, 163–192. doi:10.1177/0741088391008002002

Sellers, R. M., Smith, M. A., Shelton, J. N., Rowley, S. A. J., & Chavous, T. M. (1998). Multidimensional model of racial identity: A reconceptualization of African American racial identity. *Personality and Social Psychology Review, 2*, 18–39. doi:10.1207/s15327957pspr0201_2

Serfaty, V. (2005). Cartographie d'Internet: Du virtuel à la reterritorialization. *Cercles, 13*, 83–96.

Sharf, B. F. (1997). Communicating breast cancer on-line: Support and empowerment on the Internet. *Women & Health, 26*(1), 65–84. doi:10.1300/J013v26n01_05

Shavitt, S., Lalwani, A., Zhang, J., & Torelli, C. (2006). The horizontal/vertical distinction in cross-cultural consumer research. *Journal of Consumer Psychology, 16*, 325–342. doi:10.1207/s15327663jcp1604_3

Shaw, B. R., McTavish, F., Hawkins, R., Gustafson, D. H., & Pingree, S. (2000). Experiences of women with breast cancer: exchanging social support over the CHESS computer network. *Journal of Health Communication, 5*, 135–159. doi:10.1080/108107300406866

Shedletsky, L. J. (1993). Minding computer-mediated communication: CMC as experiential learning. *Educational Technology, 33*(12), 5–10.

Sheffield, J. (1989). The effects of bargaining orientation and communication medium on negotiations in the bilateral monopoly task: A comparison of decision room and computer conferencing communication media. In *CHI '89 Conference proceedings: Human factors in computing systems* (pp. 43–48). New York: McGraw–Hill.

Shephard, E. R., & Williamson, L. K. (1996, November) *The niceties of netiquette: Gender patterns in computer-mediated communication.* Paper presented at the annual meeting of the Speech Communication Association, San Diego, CA.

Shetty, S., & Bellamy, E. J. (2000). Postcolonialism's archive fever. *Diacritics, 30*(1), 25–48.

Shneiderman, B. (2003). *Leonardo's laptop: Human needs and the new computing technologies.* Cambridge, MA: The MIT Press.

Shoffner, M. (2007). Preservice English teachers and technology: A consideration of weblogs for the English classroom. *Contemporay issues in technology and teacher education, 7*(4).Retrieved February 1, 2009, from http://www.citejournal.org/vol7/iss4/languagearts/article1.cfm

Short, J. A., Williams, E., & Christie, B. (1976). *The social psychology of telecommunications.* London: Wiley International.

Short, J. A., Williams, E., & Christie, B. (1976). *The social psychology of telecommunications.* Hoboken, NJ: Wiley.

Short, J., Williams, E., & Christie, B. (1976). *The social psychology of telecommunications*. London: Wiley.

Shotter, J., & Gergen, K. J. (1994). Social construction: knowledge, self, others, and continuing the conversation. In Deetz, S. A. (Ed.), *Communication yearbook* (pp. 3–33). Thousand Oaks: Sage.

Shultz Colbey, R., Colby, R., Felix, J., Murphy, R., Thomas, B., & Blair, K. (2005). A role for blogs in graduate education: Remediating the rhetorical tradition? *Computers and composition online,* retrieved February 13, 2009, from http://www.bgsu.edu/cconline/colbyetal/colbyetal.htm

Sierpe, E. (2005). Gender distinctiveness, communication competence, and the problem of gender judgments in computer-mediated communication. *Computers in Human Behavior, 21,* 127–145. doi:10.1016/j.chb.2003.11.009

Silverman, D. (1998). *Harvey Sacks: Social science and Conversation Analysis*. New York: Oxford University Press.

Simpson, J. (2005). Conversational floors in synchronous text-based CMC discourse. *Discourse Studies, 7,* 337–361. doi:10.1177/1461445605052190

Singh, N., Kumar, V., & Baack, D. (2005). Adaptation of cultural content: Evidence from B2C e-commerce firms. *European Journal of Marketing, 39*(1/2), 71–86. doi:10.1108/03090560510572025

Singh, N., Zhao, H., & Hu, X. (2003). Cultural adaptation on the Web: A study of American companies' domestic and Chinese Web sites. *Journal of Global Information Management, 11*(3), 63–80.

Singh, N., Zhao, H., & Hu, X. (2005). Analyzing the cultural content of Web sites: A cross-national comparison of China, India, Japan, and US. *International Marketing Review, 22*(2), 129–146. doi:10.1108/02651330510593241

Singh, S. (2006). Cultural differences in, and influences on, consumers' propensity to adopt innovations. *International Marketing Review, 23*(2), 173–191. doi:10.1108/02651330610660074

Singleton, Jr., & Straits, B. C. (2005). *Approaches to social research* (4th ed.). New York: Oxford University Press.

Skill, T., & Young, B. (2002). Embracing the Hybrid Model: Working at the Intersections of Virtual and Physical Learning Spaces. *New Directions for Teaching and Learning, 92,* 23–32. doi:10.1002/tl.76

Smith, P. (1988). *Discerning the subject*. Minneapolis, MN: University of Minnesota Press.

Smith, P. K., Mahdavi, J., Carvalho, M., Fisher, S., Russell, S., & Tippett, N. (2008). Cyberbullying: Its nature and impact in secondary school pupils. *Journal of Child Psychology and Psychiatry, and Allied Disciplines, 49*(4), 376–385. doi:10.1111/j.1469-7610.2007.01846.x

Smyth, J. M. (1999). Written disclosure: evidence, potential mechanism, and potential treatment. *Advances in Mind-Body Medicine, 15,* 179–184.

Smythe, M. J., & Schlueter, D. W. (1989). "Can we talk?" A Meta-analytic review of the sex differences. In Lont, C., & Friedley, S. (Eds.), *Beyond boundaries: Sex and gender diversity in communication* (pp. 31–48). Fairfax, VA: George Mason University.

Sohn, D., & Lee, B. (2005). Dimensions of Interactivity: Differential Effects of Social and Psychological Factors. *Journal of Computer-Mediated Communication, 10*(3), article 6.

Sonnenwald, D. H., & Pierce, L. G. (2000). Information behavior in dynamic group work contexts: interwoven situational awareness, dense social networks and contested collaboration in command and control. *Information Processing & Management, 36,* 461–479. doi:10.1016/S0306-4573(99)00039-4

Sorensen, E. K. (2004). Reflection and intellectual amplification in online communities of collaborative learning. In Roberts, T. (Ed.), *Online collaborative learning: Theory and practice* (pp. 242–261). Hershey, PA: Information Science Publishing.

Soukup, C. (2000). Building a theory of multimedia CMC: An analysis, critique and integration of computer-mediated communication theory and research. *New Media & Society, 2*, 407–425.

Spadaro, P. F. (2008). Grid for activity analysis (GAct). In Varisco, B. M. (Ed.), *Psychological, pedagogical and sociological models for learning and assessment in virtual communities of practice*. Milano, Italy: Polimetrica.

Spadaro, P. F., & Ligorio, M. B. (2007, August). *Perception of the self on ftf and online learning contexts*. Paper presented at the meeting of the EARLI, Budapest, Hungry.

Spears, R., & Lea, M. (1992). Social influence and the influence of the 'social' in computer-mediated communication. In Lea, M. (Ed.), *Contexts of Computer-Mediated Communication* (pp. 30–65). New York, NY: Harvester Wheatsheaf.

Spears, R., & Lea, M. (1992). Social influence in CMC. In Lea, M. (Ed.), *Contexts of computer-mediated communication* (pp. 30–65). London, UK: Harvester Wheatsheaf.

Spears, R., & Lea, M. (1994). Panacea or Panopticon? The hidden power in computer-mediated communication. *Communication Research, 21*(4), 427–459. doi:10.1177/009365094021004001

Spivak, G. C. (1988). Can the subaltern speak? In C. Nelson and L. Grossman, (eds.) Marxism and the interpretation of culture (p. 271-313). Urbana, IL: University of Illinois Press.

Springgay, S. (2005). Thinking through bodies: Bodied encounters and the process of meaning making in an e-mail generated art-project. *Studies in Art Education, 47*(1), 34–50.

Sproull, L., & Kiesler, S. (1985). Reducing social context cues: Electronic mail in organizational communication. *Managerial Science, 11*, 1492–1512.

Sproull, L., & Kiesler, S. (1991). *Connections: New ways of working in the networked organization*. Cambridge, MA: MIT Press.

Stafford, L. (2005). *Maintaining long-distance and cross-residential relationships*. Mahwah, NJ: Lawrence Erlbaum Associates, Publishing.

Stafford, L., Kline, S. L., & Dimmick, J. (1999). Home e-mail: Relational maintenance and gratification opportunities. *Journal of Broadcasting & Electronic Media, 43*(4), 659–669.

Stanton, A. L., Danoff-Burg, S., Cameron, C. L., & Snider, P. R. (1999). Social comparison and adjustment to breast cancer: An experimental examination of upward affiliation and downward evaluation. *Health Psychology, 18*, 151–158. doi:10.1037/0278-6133.18.2.151

Starosta, W. J., & Chen, G.-M. (2009forthcoming). Expanding the circumference of intercultural communication study. In Hulualani, R., & Nakayama, T. (Eds.), *Handbook of Critical Communication*. London: Blackwell.

Starosta, W. J., & Hannon, S. W. (1997). The multilexicality of contemporary history: Recounted and enacted narratives of the Mohawk incident in Oka, Québec. *The International and Intercultural Communication Annual, 20*, 141–165.

Stefanone, M. A., & Jang, C. Y. (2007). Writing for friends and family: The interpersonal nature of blogs. *Journal of Computer-Mediated Communication, 13*(1), 123–140. doi:10.1111/j.1083-6101.2007.00389.x

Stefanone, M. A., & Lackaff, D. (2009). Reality television as a model for online behavior: Blogging, photo and video sharing. *Journal of Computer-Mediated Communication, 14*(4), 964–987. doi:10.1111/j.1083-6101.2009.01477.x

Stefanone, M. A., Lackaff, D., & Rosen, D. (2008). We're all stars now: Reality television, Web 2.0, and mediated identities. In *Proceedings of ACM's Hypertext, Culture and Communication*. New York: Association for Computing Machinery (ACM).

Stefik, M. (Ed.). (1997). *Internet Dreams. Archetypes, Myths, and Metaphors*. Cambridge, MA: MIT Press.

Steinwachs, K. (1999). Information and culture - the impact of national culture on information processes. *Journal of Information Science, 25*(3), 193–204.

Stenström, A.-B., Anderson, G., & Hasund, I. K. (2002). *Trends in teenage talk: Corpus compilation, analysis and findings.* Philadelphia: Benjamins.

Stewart, E. C., & Bennett, M. J. (1991). *American cultural patterns: A cross-cultural perspective* (Rev. ed.). Yarmouth, ME: Intercultural Press.

Stiles, W. B. (1987). "I have to talk to somebody." A fever model of disclosure. In Derlega, V. J., & Berg, J. H. (Eds.), *Self-disclosure: Theory, research, and therapy* (pp. 257–282). New York: Plenum.

Stiles, W. B. (1995). Disclosure as a speech act: Is it psychotherapeutic to disclose? In Pennebaker, J. W. (Ed.), *Emotion, disclosure, and health* (pp. 71–91). Washington, DC: American Psychological Association. doi:10.1037/10182-004

Stiles, W. B., Shuster, P. L., & Harrigan, J. A. (1992). Disclosure and anxiety: A test of the fever model. *Journal of Personality and Social Psychology, 63,* 980–988. doi:10.1037/0022-3514.63.6.980

Stone, A. R. (1995). Sex and death among the disembodied: VR, Cyberespace, and the nature of academic discourse. In Star, S. L. (Ed.), *The culture of computing* (pp. 243–255). Oxford, UK: Blackwell.

Straus, E. W. (1966). *Phenomenological psychology* (Eng, E., Trans.). New York: Basic Books INC.

Strauss, A. (1987). *Qualitative analysis for social scientists.* New York: Cambridge University Press. doi:10.1017/CBO9780511557842

Strauss, A., & Corbin, J. (1990). *Basics of qualitative research: Grounded theory procedures and techniques.* Newbury Park, CA: Sage.

Strauss, A., & Corbin, J. (1998). *Basics of oualitative research* (2nd ed.). Thousand Oaks, CA: Sage Publications.

Suhr, J. A. (1990). *The development of the social support behavior code.* Unpublished master's thesis, University of Iowa, Iowa City.

Suler, J. (1999). *The psychology of cyberspace.* Retrieved February 13, 2009, from http://www.rider.edu/users/suler/psycyber/psycyber.html.

Sullivan, A. (2008). Why I blog. *The Atlantic,* (Nov. 2008). Retrieved Nov. 1, 2008, from http://www.theatlantic.com/doc/200811/andrew-sullivan-why-i-blog/4

Sullivan, C. F. (2003). Gendered cybersupport: A thematic analysis of two online cancer support groups. *Journal of Health Psychology, 8*(1), 83–103. doi:10.1177/1359105303008001446

Sunnafrank, M. (1986). Predicted outcome value during initial interactions: A reformulation of uncertainty reduction theory. *Human Communication Research, 13,* 3–33. doi:10.1111/j.1468-2958.1986.tb00092.x

Sunnafrank, M. (1988). Predicted outcome value in initial conversations. *Communication Research Reports, 5,* 169–172. doi:10.1080/08824098809359819

Sunnafrank, M. (1990). Predicted outcome values and uncertainty reduction theories: A test of competing perspectives. *Human Communication Research, 17,* 76–103. doi:10.1111/j.1468-2958.1990.tb00227.x

Sunnafrank, M. (1991). Interpersonal attraction and attitude similarity: A communication-based assessment. In Anderson, J. A. (Ed.), *Communication yearbook 14* (pp. 451–483). Newbury Park, CA: Sage.

Sussman, B. (2007, August 1). Teachers, college students lead a Second Life. *USA Today.* Retrieved January 20, 2008, from http://www.usatoday.com/news/education/2007-08-01-second-life_N.htm

Suzuki, R. (2004). Diaries as introspective research tools: From Ashton-Warner to blogs. *Teaching English as a second or foreign language, 8*(1). Retrieved December 13, 2008, from http://tesl-ej.org/ej29/int.html

Swanson, D. L. (1987). Gratification seeking, media exposure, and audience interpretations: Some directions for research. *Journal of Broadcasting & Electronic Media, 31,* 237–254.

Tabouret-Keller, A. (1997, 2000). Language and identity. In F. Coulmas (Ed.), The handbook of sociolinguistics (pp. 315-326). Oxford, UK: Blackwell Publishers.

Taiwo, R. (2008). Linguistic forms and functions of SMS Text Messages in Nigeria. In Kelsey, S., & St. Armant, K. (Eds.), *Handbook of research on computer mediated communication* (*Vol. 1*, pp. 969–982). Hershey, PA: Information Science Publishing.

Taiwo, R. (2009, July). *Discursive forms and functions of flaming in Nigerian online forums.* Paper presented at The International Conference on Linguistic Politeness and Rudeness, Lancaster, UK.

Tannen, D. (1990). *You just don't understand: Women and men in conversation.* New York: Ballantine Books.

Tannen, D. (2001). *Talking from 9-5.* New York: Quill/Harper Collins.

Tapanes, M., Smith, G., & White, J. (2009). Cultural diversity in online learning: A study of the perceived effects of dissonance in levels of individualism/collectivism and tolerance of ambiguity. *The Internet and Higher Education*, *12*(1), 26–34. doi:10.1016/j.iheduc.2008.12.001

Tardy, R. W., & Hale, C. L. (1998). Bonding and cracking: The role of informal, interpersonal networks in health care decision making. *Health Communication*, *10*(2), 151–173. doi:10.1207/s15327027hc1002_3

Taylor, S. F., & Lobel, M. (1989). Social comparison activity under threat: Downward evaluation and upward contacts. *Psychological Review*, *96*, 569–575. doi:10.1037/0033-295X.96.4.569

Taylor, T. L. (1999). Life in virtual worlds: Plural existence, multimodalities, and other online research challenges. *The American Behavioral Scientist*, *43*(3), 436–449. doi:10.1177/00027649921955362

Teich, A., Frankel, M. S., Kling, R., & Lee, Y.-C. (1999). Anonymous communication policies for the internet: Results and recommendations of the AAAS conference. *The Information Society*, *15*, 71–77. doi:10.1080/019722499128538

ten Have, P. (2000). Computer-mediated chat: Ways of finding chat partners. *M/C: A Journal of Media and Culture, 3*(4). Retrieved May 5, 2003, from http://journal.media-culture.org.au/0008/partners.php

Ten Have, P. (2000). Computer-Mediated Chat: Ways of Finding Chat Partners. *M/C: A journal of Media Culture, 3*(4). Retrieved May, 2009, from http://journal.media-culture.org.au/0008/partners.php

Teubert, W. (2005). My version of corpus linguistics. *International Journal of Corpus Linguistics*, *10*(1), 1–13. doi:10.1075/ijcl.10.1.01teu

Thomas, M. J. W. (2002). Learning within incoherent structures: the space of online discussion forums. *Journal of Computer Assisted Learning*, *18*, 351–366. doi:10.1046/j.0266-4909.2002.03800.x

Thomas, W. I. (1923). *The Unadjusted Girl.* Boston: Little, Brown, and Co.

Thompson, N. (2003). *Communication and language: A handbook of theory and practice. Basingstoke.* Hampshire, UK: Palgrave MacMillan.

Thomson, R. (2006). The effect of topic of discussion on gendered language in computer-mediated communication discussion. *Journal of Language and Social Psychology*, *25*, 167–178. doi:10.1177/0261927X06286452

Thomson, R., & Murachver, T. (2001). Predicting gender from electronic discourse. *The British Journal of Social Psychology*, *40*(2), 193–208. doi:10.1348/014466601164812

Thomson, R., Murachver, T., & Green, J. (2001). Where is the gender in gendered language? *Psychological Science*, *12*, 171–175. doi:10.1111/1467-9280.00329

Tidwell, L. C., & Walther, J. B. (2002). Computer-mediated communication effects on disclosure, impressions, and interpersonal evaluations: Getting to know one another one bit at a time. *Human Communication Research*, *28*, 317–348. doi:10.1111/j.1468-2958.2002.tb00811.x

Timmerman, C. E. (2002). The moderating effect of mindlessness/mindfulness upon media richness and social influence explanations of organizational media use. *Communication Monographs, 69,* 111–131. doi:10.1080/714041708

Tönnies, F. (2001). *Community and Civil Society.* Cambridge, MA: Cambridge University Press.

Treleaven, L. (2004). A new taxonomy for evaluation studies of online collaborative learning. In Roberts, T. (Ed.), *Online collaborative learning: Theory and practice* (pp. 160–180). Hershey, PA: Information Science Publishing.

Triandis, H. C. (2001). Individualism-collectivism and personality. *Journal of Personality, 69,* 907–924. doi:10.1111/1467-6494.696169

Triandis, H. C., & Gelfand, M. J. (1998). Converging measurement of horizontal and vertical individualism and collectivism. *Journal of Personality and Social Psychology, 74,* 118–128. doi:10.1037/0022-3514.74.1.118

Trompenaars, F., & Hampden-Turner, C. (1998). *Riding the waves of culture: Understanding diversity in global business* (2nd ed.). New York: McGraw-Hill.

Tu, C., & McIsaac, M. (2002). The relationships of social presence and interaction in online classes. *American Journal of Distance Education, 16*(3), 131–150. doi:10.1207/S15389286AJDE1603_2

Tuckman, B. (1965). Developmental sequence in small groups. *Psychological Bulletin, 63,* 384–399. doi:10.1037/h0022100

Tuckman, B. W. (1965). Developmental sequence in small groups. *Psychological Bulletin, 65*(6), 384–399. doi:10.1037/h0022100

Tuckman, B., & Jensen, M. C. (1977). Stages of small-group development revisited. *Group & Organizational Studies, 2,* 419–427. doi:10.1177/105960117700200404

Turkle, S. (1995). *Life on the screen.* New York: Simon & Schuster.

Turner, J. C., Hogg, M. A., Oakes, P. J., Reicher, S. D., &

Wetherell, M. (1987). *Rediscovering the social group: A self-categorization theory.* Oxford: Blackwell.

Unsworth, L. (2000). *Researching language in schools and communities: Functional linguistic perspectives.* Washington, DC: Cassell.

Valacich, J. S., George, J. F., Nunamaker, J. F. Jr, & Vogel, D. R. (1994). Physical proximity effects on computer-mediated idea generation. *Small Group Research, 25,* 83–104. doi:10.1177/1046496494251006

Valley, K. L., Moag, J., & Bazerman, M. H. (1998). A matter of trust: Effects of communication on the efficiency and distribution of outcomes. *Journal of Economic Behavior & Organization, 34,* 211–238. doi:10.1016/S0167-2681(97)00054-1

van der Meij, H. (2007). What research has to say about gender-linked differences in CMC and does elementary school children's e-mail use fit this picture? *Sex Roles, 57,* 341–354. doi:10.1007/s11199-007-9270-9

van Dijck, J. (2004). Composing the self: Of diaries and lifelogs. *Fibreculture, 3.* Retrieved May 11, 2008, from www.journal.fibreculture.org /issue3/issue3_vandijck. html van Doorn, N., van Zoonen, L., & Wyatt, S. (2007). Writing from experience: Presentations of gender identity on weblogs. *European Journal of Women's Studies, 14*(2), 143-158.

Vandrick, S. (1997). The role of hidden identities in the postsecondary ESL classroom. *TESOL Quarterly, 31*(1), 153–157. doi:10.2307/3587980

Vangelisti, A. L. (1997). Gender differences, similarities, and interdependencies: Some problems with the different cultures perspective. *Personal Relationships, 4,* 243–253. doi:10.1111/j.1475-6811.1997.tb00143.x

Vangelisti, A. L., & Caughlin, J. P. (1997). Revealing family secrets: The influence of topic, function, and relationships. *Journal of Social and Personal Relationships, 14,* 679–705. doi:10.1177/0265407597145006

Vangelisti, A. L., & Timmerman, L. (2001). Criteria for revealing family secrets. *Communication Monographs, 68,* 1–28. doi:10.1080/03637750128052

Varghese, M., Morgan, B., Johnston, B., & Johnson, K. (2005). Theorizing language teacher identity: Three perspectives and beyond. *Journal of Language, Identity, and Education*, *4*(1), 21–44. doi:10.1207/s15327701jlie0401_2

Vaughan, G. M., & Hogg, M. A. (2005). Introduction to social psychology (4th ed.). Frenchs Forest, Upper Saddle River, NJ: Prentice Hall.

Vayreda, A., & Antaki, Ch. (in press). Unsolicited Advice in an Online Bipolar Disorder Forum: a Conversation Analysis of the "Matching Hypothesis". *Qualitative Health Research*.

Vayreda, A., & Estalella, A. (2007). Software social: ¿teoría social? In F. Tirado & and M. Doménech (Eds.), Lo Social y lo virtual. Nuevas formas de control y transformación social (p. 78-92). Barcelona, Spain: Editorial UOC.

Vayreda, A., Estrada, M., Balasch, B., & Tomàs, S. (2007). Redes virtuales de apoyo social y de autoayuda: análisis de un caso. In C. Guillen, & R. Guil (Eds.). *X Congreso Nacional de Psicología social. Psicología Social: un encuentro de perspectivas*. Cádiz, Spain: Asociación de profesionales de la Psicología Social.

Venetis, M. K., Greene, K., Banerjee, S. C., & Bagdasarov, Z. (2008, May). *Comparing private and secret information in disclosure decisions*. Paper presented at the annual meeting of the International Communication Association, Montreal, Canada.

Visser, J. (2003). Distance education in the perspective of global issues and concerns. In M. Moore W. & Anderson (Eds.), Handbook of distance education (pp. 793-810). Mahwah, NJ: Lawrence Erlbaum.

Voos, R. (2003). Blended learning--What is it and where might it take us? *Sloan-C View*, *2*(1), 2–5.

Vygotskij, L. S. (1972). Apprendimento e sviluppo intellettuale nell'età scolare. In Vygotskji, L. S., Luria, A., & Leont'ev, A. N. (Eds.), *Psicologia e Pedagogia*. Rome: Editori Riuniti.

Wajcman, J. (2007). From women and technology to gendered technoscience. *Information Communication and Society*, *10*(3), 287–298. doi:10.1080/13691180701409770

Wallace, P. (1999). *The psychology of the internet*. Cambridge, MA: Cambridge University Press.

Wallace, P. (1999). The psychology of the Internet. New York: Cambridge.

Walther, J. (1996). Computer-mediated communication: Impersonal, interpersonal, and hyperpersonal interaction. *Communication Research*, *23*, 3–43. doi:10.1177/009365096023001001

Walther, J. B. (1992). Interpersonal effects in computer mediated interactions: A relational perspective. *Communication Research*, *19*, 52–90. doi:10.1177/009365092019001003

Walther, J. B. (1992). Interpersonal effects in computer-mediated interaction: A relational perspective. *Communication Research*, *19*, 52–90. doi:10.1177/009365092019001003

Walther, J. B. (1994). Anticipated ongoing interaction versus channel effects on relational communication in computer mediated interaction. *Human Communication Research*, *20*, 473–501. doi:10.1111/j.1468-2958.1994.tb00332.x

Walther, J. B. (1995). Relational aspects of CMC: experimental observations over time. *Organization Science*, *6*, 186–203. doi:10.1287/orsc.6.2.186

Walther, J. B. (1996). Computer-mediated communication: Impersonal, interpersonal, and hyperpersonal interaction. *Communication Research*, *23*(1), 1–43. doi:10.1177/009365096023001001

Walther, J. B. (1997). Group and interpersonal effects in international computer-mediated collaboration. *Human Communication Research*, *23*, 342–369. doi:10.1111/j.1468-2958.1997.tb00400.x

Walther, J. B., & Bunz, U. (2005). The rules of virtual groups: Trust, liking, and performance in computer-mediated communication. *The Journal of Communication, 58*(4), 828–846. doi:10.1111/j.1460-2466.2005.tb03025.x

Walther, J. B., & Parks, M. R. (2002). Cues filtered out, cues filtered in: Computer-mediated communication and relationships. In Knapp, M. L., & Daly, J. A. (Eds.), *Handbook of Interpersonal Communication* (3rd ed., pp. 529–563). Thousand Oaks, CA: Sage.

Wandersman, L., Wandersman, A., & Kahn, S. (1980). Social support in the transition to parenthood. *Journal of Community Psychology, 8*, 332–342. doi:10.1002/1520-6629(198010)8:4<332::AID-JCOP2290080407>3.0.CO;2-H

Wang, Z., Walther, J. B., & Hancock, J. T. (2009). Social identification and interpersonal communication in computer-mediated communication: What you do versus who you are in virtual groups. *Human Communication Research, 35*(1), 59–85. doi:10.1111/j.1468-2958.2008.01338.x

Wang, Z., Walther, J. B., Pingree, S., & Hawkins, R. P. (2008). Health information, credibility, homophily, and influence via the Internet: Web sites versus discussion groups. *Health Communication, 23*, 358–368. doi:10.1080/10410230802229738

Waring, H. Z. (2005). The unofficial business of repair initiation: Vehicles for affiliation and disaffiliation. In Tyler, A., Takada, M., Kim, Y., & Marinova, D. (Eds.), *Language in use: Cognitive and discourse perspectives on language and language learning* (pp. 163–175). Washington, DC: Georgetown University Press.

Warner, D., & Procaccino, J. D. (2007). Women seeking health information: Distinguishing the Web user. *Journal of Health Communication, 12*, 787–814. doi:10.1080/10810730701672090

Warschauer, M. (2000) Language, identity, and the Internet. B. Kolko, L. Nakamura, & G. Rodman(Eds.), Race in Cyberspace, (pp. 151-170) New York: Routledge.

Warschuer, M., & De Florio-Hansen, I. (2003). Multilingualism, identity, and theInternet. In Hu, A., & De Florio-Hansen, I. (Eds.), *Multiple identity and multilingualism* (pp. 155–179). Tübingen, Germany: Stauffenburg.

Waseleski, C. (2006). Gender and the use of exclamation points in computer-mediated communication: An analysis of exclamations posted to two electronic discussion lists. *Journal of Computer-Mediated Communication, 11*(4), article 6. Retrieved May, 2009, from http://jcmc.indiana.edu/vol11/issue4/waseleski.html

Wasko, M. M., & Faraj, S. (2005). Why should I share? Examining social capital and knowledge contribution in electronic networks of practice. *Management Information Systems Quarterly, 29*(1), 35–57.

Wasserman, S., & Faust, K. (1994). *Social Network Analysis. Methods and Applications*. Cambridge, UK: Cambridge University Press.

Watt, R. J. C. (2004). Concordance (Version 3.2.0.212).

Watts, S. A. (2007). Evaluative Feedback: Perspectives on Media Effects. *Journal of Computer-Mediated Communication, 12*(2), article 3.

Weber, S., & Mitchell, C. (2008). Imaging, keyboarding, and posting identities: Young people and new media technologies. In Buckingham, D. (Ed.), *Youth, identity, and digital media* (pp. 25–47). Cambridge, MA: The MIT Press.

Weinberg, N., Schmale, J. D., Uken, J., & Wessel, K. (1995). Computer-mediated support groups. *Social Work with Groups, 17*(4), 43–54. doi:10.1300/J009v17n04_04

Weisband, S., & Kiesler, S. (1996, April). *Self disclosure on computer forms: Meta-analysis and implications*. Paper presented at the meeting of the Conference on Human Factors in Computing Systems, Vancouver, BC.

Wellens, R. A. (1986). Use of a psychological distancing model to assess differences in telecommunication media. In Parker, L. A., & Olgren, O. H. (Eds.), *Teleconferencing and Electronic Communication*. Madison, WI: University of Wisconsin Extension.

Wellman, B. (1999). *Networks in the global village: Life in contemporary communities.* Boulder, CO: Westview Press.

Wellman, B. (2001). Physical place and cyber place: the rise of personalized networks. *International Journal of Urban and Regional Research, 25*(2), 227–252. doi:10.1111/1468-2427.00309

Wellman, B. (2001). *The Persistence and Transformation of Community: From Neighbourhood Groups to Social Networks.* Toronto, Canada: Report to the Law Commission of Canada.

Wellman, B., Haase, A. Q., Witte, J., & Hampton, K. (2001). Does the Internet increase, decrease, or supplement social capital? *The American Behavioral Scientist, 45*, 436–455. doi:10.1177/00027640121957286

Wellman, B., Quan-Haase, A., Witte, J., & Hampton, K. (2001). Does the Internet increase, decrease, or supplement social capital? *The American Behavioral Scientist, 45*, 436–455. doi:10.1177/00027640121957286

Wells, G. (1993). Intersubjectivity and the Construction of Knowledge. In C. Pontecorvo (a cura di), La Condivisione della Conoscenza, (pp. 353-380). Rome: La Nuova Italia.

Wenger, E. (1998). *Communities of Practice: learning, Meaning, and Identity.* Cambridge, UK: Cambridge University Press.

Werry, C. C. (1996). Linguistic and interactional features of Internet Relay Chat. In S. C. Herring (Ed.), Computer-mediated communication: Linguistic, social and cross-cultural perspectives (pp. 47-63). Philadelphia: John Benjamins.

Westerman, D., Van Der Heide, B., Klein, K. A., & Walther, J. B. (2008). How so people really seek information about others?: Information seeking across internet and traditional communication channels. *Journal of Computer-Mediated Communication, 13*, 751–767. doi:10.1111/j.1083-6101.2008.00418.x

Whitty, M. (2005). The realness of cybercheating: Men's and women's representations of unfaithful internet relationships. *Social Science Computer Review, 23*, 57–67. doi:10.1177/0894439304271536

Whitty, M., & Gavin, J. (2001). Age/sex/location: Uncovering the social cues in the development of online relationships. *Cyberpsychology & Behavior, 4*, 623–639. doi:10.1089/109493101753235223

Whorf, B. L. (1988). *Language, thought, and reality: Selected writings of Benjamin Lee Whorf* (Carroll, J. B., Ed.). 18th ed.). Cambridge, MA: The M.I.T. Press. (Original work published 1956)

Wilkins, H. (1991). Computer talk: Long distance conversations by computer. *Written Communication, 8*, 56–78. doi:10.1177/0741088391008001004

Williams, D., Consalvo, M., Caplan, S., & Yee, N. (2009). Looking for gender (LFG): Gender roles and behaviors among online gamers. [from http://dmitriwilliams.com/LFGpaperfinal.pdf]. *The Journal of Communication, 59*(4), 700–725. Retrieved January 29, 2009. doi:10.1111/j.1460-2466.2009.01453.x

Williams, E. (1977). Experimental comparisons of face-to-face and mediated communication: A review. *Psychological Bulletin, 84*, 963–976. doi:10.1037/0033-2909.84.5.963

Williams, F., Rice, R. E., & Rogers, E. M. (1988). *Research methods and the new media.* New York: Free Press.

Williams, R. (1983). *Keywords: A vocabulary of culture and society.* London: Fontana.

Wingard, R. G. (2004). Classroom teaching changes in web-enhanced courses: A multi-institutional study. *EDUCAUSE Quarterly, 1*, 26–35.

Wise, K., Hamman, B., & Thorson, K. (2006). Moderation, response rate, and message interactivity: Features of online communities and their effects on intent to participate. *Journal of Computer-Mediated Communication, 12*(1), article 2. Retrieved (n.d.), from http://jcmc.indiana.edu/vol12/issue1/wise.html

Witmer, D. F., & Katzman, S. L. (1997). On-line smiles: Does gender make a difference in the use of graphic accents? *Journal of Computer Mediated Communication [on-line], 2(4)*. Retrieved (n.d.), from http://ascusc.org/jCMI/vol2/issue4/witmer1.html

Witmer, D., & Katzman, S. (1997). On-line smiles: Does gender make a difference in the use of graphic accents? *Journal of Computer-Mediated Communication, 2*(4). Retrieved August 23, 1999, from http://www.ascusc.org/jcmc/vol2/issue4/witmer1.html

Witt, H. (2007, September 17). Blogs help drive Jena protest, *Chicago Tribune (Chicago, IL)*. Retrieved January 26, 2009, from http://www.chicagotribune.com/news/nationworld/chi-jena_blog_web19,0,4309628.story

Wittgenstein, L. (1953). *Philosophical investigations* (Anscombe, G., Trans.). New York: Macmillan.

Wittgenstein, L. (1958). *The blue and brown books: Preliminary studies for the 'Philosophical Investigations*. NY: Harper & Row.

Wittgenstein, L. (2003). *Tractatus logico-philosophicus* (Ogden, C., Trans.). New York: Taylor & Francis.

Wolf, A. (2000). Emotional expression online: Gender differences in emoticon use. *Cyberpsychology & Behavior, 3*(5), 827–833. doi:10.1089/10949310050191809

Wood, J. T. (2000). *Relational communication: Continuity and change in personal relationships*. Belmont, CA: Wadsworth.

Wright, K. B. (2002). Social support within an on-line cancer community: An assessment of emotional support, perceptions of advantages and disadvantages, and motives for using the community from a communication perspective. *Journal of Applied Communication Research, 30*(3), 195–209. doi:10.1080/00909880216586

Wright, K. B. (2004). On-line relational maintenance strategies and perceptions of partners within exclusively internet-based and primarily internet-based relationships. *Communication Studies, 55*(2), 239–253.

Wright, K. B., & Bell, S. B. (2003). Health-related support groups on the Internet: Linking empirical findings to social support and computer-mediated communication theory. *Journal of Health Psychology, 8*(1), 39–54. doi:10.1177/1359105303008001429

Wynn, E., & Katz, J. E. (1997). Hyperbole over cyberspace: Self-presentation and social boundaries in Internet home pages and discourse. *The Information Society, 13*, 297–327. doi:10.1080/019722497129043

Xiao, S. (2008). Lun boke wentide yuyan xingshi shenmei tese (The aesthetic features of the linguistic styles in blogging). *Kaoshi zhoukan (Examination Weekly)14*, 204-205.

Xiao, W., & Wang, S. (2008). Lun wangluoyuyande qingnian yanwenhua tezheng (The youth subculture nature of internet Chinese). *Qingnian yanjiu (Youth Study)6*, 21-26.

Yamane, T. (1973). *Statistics: An introductory analysis* (3rd ed.). New York: Harper & Row.

Yates, S. J. (2001). Gender, language, and CMC for education. *Learning and Instruction, 11*, 21–34. doi:10.1016/S0959-4752(00)00012-8

Yildiz, S. (2009). Social presence in the web-based classroom: Implications for intercultural communication. *Journal of Studies in International Education, 13*(1), 46–65. doi:10.1177/1028315308317654

Yin, R. K. (2009). *Case study research: design and methods* (4th ed.). Thousand Oaks, CA: Sage.

Yin, X. (2007). Diverse and transnational: Chinese (PRC) immigrants in the United States. *Journal of Chinese Overseas, 3*(1), 122–145. doi:10.1353/jco.2007.0037

Young, J. (2002, March 22). Hybrid teaching seeks to end divide between traditional and online instruction [Electronic version]. *The Chronicle of Higher Education*. Retrieved January 10, 2009, from http://chronicle.com/free/v48/i28/28a03301.htm

Younge, G. (2007, September, 20). Jena is America, *The Nation (New York)*. Retrieved August 25, 2008, from http://www.thenation.com/doc/20071008/younge

Zack, M. H. (1993). Interactivity and communication mode choice in ongoing management groups. *Information Systems Research*, *4*(3), 207–239. doi:10.1287/isre.4.3.207

Zahir, S., Dobing, B., & Hunter, M. G. (2002). Cross-cultural dimensions of Internet portals. *Internet Research: Electronic Networking Applications and Policy*, *12*(3), 210–220. doi:10.1108/10662240210430892

Zakour, A. B. (2004). Cultural differences and information technology acceptance In *Proceedings of the 7th Conference of the Southern Association for Information Systems*. Retrieved April 29, 2009, from http://sais.aisnet.org/2004/Zakour.pdf

Zhang, J. (2007). A cultural look at information and communication technologies in Eastern education. *Educational Technology Research and Development*, *55*(3), 301–314. doi:10.1007/s11423-007-9040-y

Zitzen, M., & Stein, D. (2004). Chat and conversation: A case of transmedial stability? *Linguistics*, *42*, 983–1021. doi:10.1515/ling.2004.035

Zuccermaglio, C. (2002). *Psicologia Culturale dei Gruppi*. Rome: Carocci.

About the Contributors

Jung-ran Park is currently an assistant professor at the College of Information Science and Technol¬ogy at Drexel University. Her research areas are computer-mediated communication/online discourse and knowledge organization and representation, concentrating on metadata. She has published widely in these areas. Dr. Park is the principal investigator of a four-year (2006-2010) research project entitled Metadata Creation and Metadata Quality Control across Digital Collections: Evaluation of Current Practices from the Institute of Museum and Library Services (IMLS). As principal investigator, she has also been awarded an IMLS grant (2008-2010) for the research project entitled Modeling Interpersonal Discourse for Digital Information Service: Evaluation of the Question-Answering Service of the Internet Public Library. She is currently serving as editor-in-chief of the Journal of Library Metadata published by the Taylor & Francis Group. In addition to this edited book, Dr. Park has recently published Marking Discourse Coherence and Social-Interpersonal Meaning: Semantic Shifts and Functional Development of Discourse-Pragmatic Markers in Korean (LAP Lambert Academic Publishing AG & Co. KG ISBN 978-3-8383-0888-3). She is also working on a book entitled Metadata Applications in Digital Repositories and Libraries: Tools, Systems, and Architecture. This book is scheduled to be published by Chandos Publishing (Oxford) Limited in fall/winter 2011.

Eileen Abels is Masters' Program Director and Professor in the College of Information Science and Technology at Drexel University. Prior to joining the faculty at Drexel in January 2007, Dr. Abels spent more than 15 years at the College of Information Studies at the University of Maryland. She teaches courses in the areas of digital reference, information access, access in electronic environments, and business information. Her research focuses on digital reference education, remote reference services, and automated question answering services. She is involved in overseeing the Internet Public Library, a digital reference service and learning environment.

* * *

Mike Allen (Michigan State University) is Professor and Director of Graduate Studies in the Department of Communication at the University Wisconsin-Milwaukee. His work has appeared in Health Education and Behavior, Human Communication Research, Journal of Personal and Social Relationships, Law and Human Behavior, and Communication Education. He is co-author of Persuasion: Advances through Meta-analysis, Interpersonal Communication Research: Advances through Meta-analysis, and Classroom Communication and Instructional Processes: Advances through Meta-analysis.

Susanna Annese is a researcher in Social Psychology at University of Bari since 2001. She graduated in Psychology of Mass Communication in 1993 at University of Bari; she was research student at the Department of Social Psychology – Area Media and Communications – London School of Economics and Political Science in 1996; she obtained PhD in Psychology of Communication in 1998 at University of Bari and she had a research contract in Psychology of Computer Mediated Communication since 1999 to 2001 at University of Bari. Her current teaching in Group Psychology and Social Communication Psychology courses at University of Bari matches with her research interests: participation and identity dynamics in real, virtual and blended communities and the innovative methodological approaches to study them. Even her involvement in various interdisciplinary research projects aims at deepen these research interests.

Paula M. Bach is a PhD graduate of the College of Information Sciences and Technology at the Pennsylvania State University. Her areas of research include CSCW and HCI and she investigates how user-centered design happens in open source contexts. Generally she is interested in the social interactions surrounding software design and development. Other relevant research areas include community informatics and collaborative learning. She obtained her Bachelor's degree in English and Psychology from the University of British Columbia and Master's degree in Rhetoric and Technical Communication from Michigan Technological University. She has industry experience working at Microsoft, IBM, and startups.

Nancy A. Burrell (Michigan State University) is Professor and Chair of the Department of Communication at the University of Wisconsin-Milwaukee. Professor's Burrell's Research centers on managing conflict in family, workplace, and educational contexts. She is co-author of Interpersonal Communication Research: Advances through Meta-analysis, and Classroom Communication and Instructional Processes: Advances through Meta-analysis. She has published in Human Communication Research, Communication Monographs, and Management Communication Quarterly.

John M. Carroll is Edward Frymoyer Chair Professor of Information Sciences and Technology at the Pennsylvania State University. His research interests include methods and theory in human-computer interaction, particularly as applied to networking tools for collaborative learning and problem solving, and the design of interactive information systems. He has written or edited 14 books, including Making Use (MIT Press, 2000), HCI in the New Millennium (Addison-Wesley, 2001), Usability Engineering (Morgan-Kaufmann, 2002, with M.B. Rosson) and HCI Models, Theories, and Frameworks (Morgan-Kaufmann, 2003). He serves on 9 editorial boards for journals, handbooks, and series; he is a member of the US National Research Council's Committee on Human Factors and Editor-in-Chief of the ACM Transactions on Computer-Human Interactions. He received the Rigo Award and the CHI Lifetime Achievement Award from ACM, the Silver Core Award from IFIP, the Alfred N. Goldsmith Award from IEEE, and is an ACM Fellow.

Kate Magsamen-Conrad (MA, Illinois State University, 2005) is a doctoral candidate at Rutgers University. Her research focuses on disclosure and privacy, especially in relational and health contexts. She is specifically interested in the role of the partner in the process of disclosure, as well as in the experience of health and illness. Her publications and conference papers explore interpersonal communication, and she has received several top paper awards at conferences.

Brittany B. Cottrill is a Ph.D. candidate in Rhetoric and Writing. She has taught a variety of writing courses including introductory and intermediate writing at both two and four year institutions. In addition to this chapter, Brittany has published in the College English Association Forum and Computers & Composition Online. She currently holds the position of Virtual Classroom Section Editor for the journal Computers & Composition Online, is a facilitator for the Digital Mirror Camp at Bowling Green State University, and has presented at a number of national conferences.

Elizabeth A. Craig (Ph.D., University of Oklahoma, 2008) is an Assistant Professor in the Department of Communication at North Carolina State University. Her research interests include interpersonal communication, face-to-face and computer-mediated relational maintenance, stepfamily communication, and social aggression within friendship cliques. Her work appears in Journal of Social and Personal Relationships, Personal Relationships, Communication Quarterly, and Journal of Computer-Mediated Communication.

John Dowd is a PhD student in Communication at Purdue University. His research seeks to problematize overly instrumental, linear, and mechanistic conceptions of communication. To this end he is interested in unpacking the implications of various strands of educational discourse. Rather than conceiving of higher education in terms of specialized training, he hopes to reinvigorate notions of learning as a means of cultivating capacities for life-long growth and responsibility. In short, he seeks to articulate an ethics of education.

Wengao Gong obtained his Master's degree from National University of Singapore, and has recently completed his doctoral studies there. He is also an Associate Professor at the School of Foreign Studies of Yangtze University, Hubei, China. His research interests include internet-mediated communication, corpus linguistics, lexicography, English-Chinese biliteracy studies, and other SLA-related topics.

Kathryn Greene (Ph.D., University of Georgia, 1992) is an Associate Professor of Communication at Rutgers University. Her research and teaching focus on health communication, specifically on health decision-making. This health decision-making research has explored two paths: 1) she explores disclosure decision-making, with an emphasis on modeling information and relational influences on health disclosure and 2) she examines messages targeting adolescent risk-taking decision-making, focusing on involving adolescents in message processing. Dr. Greene also consults with HIV service organizations, school districts, and Health Departments regarding disclosure issues related to HIV and risk taking programs. Dr. Greene has published more than 60 chapters and articles, including one book. Her research has received numerous awards including national and international conference top paper awards.

Kayla Hales is a PhD candidate at the Pennsylvania State University's College of Information Sciences and Technology. She earned her Bachelor's degree in Information Technology from Rensselaer Polytechnic Institute. Ms. Hales' current research focuses on Computer-Mediated Communication (CMC) as it relates to interpersonal relationship maintenance. She examines interpersonal communication through the use of Information and Communication Technologies, such as instant messaging, text messaging, telephones, and other electronic media. She will explore the interaction among CMC and race, gender, class, relational stability, relational satisfaction, and other relationship features. More specifically, Ms. Hales' dissertation topic focuses on the use of CMC in pre-established, monogamous, non-platonic relationships. Her intention is to uncover the factors that influence whether the use of CMC has a positive or negative impact on particular types of interpersonal relationships.

Hao Jiang is a Ph.D student working in the human-computer interaction center at Pennsylvania State University, USA. His research targets design science, computer-supported collaborative work (CSCW), computer-supported collaborative learning (CSCL), and community informatics. He graduated from Beijing University in China, 2001, with a bachelor degree majoring in Library Science. He joined the computer-supported collaboration and learning (CSCL) lab in 2005, participating in several research and system development projects. He has a strong interest in exploring interactions between social factors (social capital, social networks, social identity, etc) and information technology in various levels of social interactions, and developing knowledge to enhance designing in society.

Carolyn Kristjánsson is an Associate Professor of Linguistics at Trinity Western University in British Columbia, Canada where she teaches in both face to face and online contexts. Her interest in diversity stems from living outside of North America for extended periods of time as well as learning other languages and teaching English to people from many locations around the globe. Her scholarly activities are broadly guided by an interest in 1) ecological perspectives of learning that encompass the interconnected nature of language, identity, and education in any given location, 2) interpersonal dimensions of learning communities (face to face and online) evidenced in discourse, and 3) the influence of teachers' and students' spiritual beliefs and values in the construction of teaching and learning.

Lynette Kvasny is an Associate Professor of Information Sciences and Technology at the Pennsylvania State University. Her research focuses on how and why historically underserved groups appropriate information and communication technologies (ICT). Her current research examines the performance of racial and ethnic identities in virtual communities, ICT education and workforce participation in the African Diaspora, and the influence of racial, class and gender identities on health information seeking and content creation. Her research has been published in The Information Society, Information Systems Journal, The DataBase for Advances in Information Systems, Journal of Computer Mediated Communication, and Information, Communication and Society.

Derek Lackaff is a doctoral candidate in the Department of Communication at the State University of New York at Buffalo. His research explores the impacts of technological mediation on communication processes and social structure. His present research focus is the effects of communication technology use on social support structures during a life transition.

Deborah Leiter is an Andrews Fellow and a doctoral student in Communication at Purdue University. In 2008 she was named a DeKruyter Graduate Scholar in Communication by the Gainey Center in Faith & Communication. Her research interprets the cultural, genre-related and rhetorical aspects of communication in and through a variety of environments, both face-to-face and mediated. Her fascinations with stories and narrative theories often leads her to focus on author and audience interactions with genres that are enacted through and across a variety of media, particularly the mystery genre. This allows her to unpack aspects of transmedial storytelling along with the affordances of media, culture, and genre.

Lynnette G. Leonard is an Assistant Professor whose research interests include human communication and new technology with a focus on collaboration and online identity. She has been active in Second Life since 2006 and has integrated Second Life into her communication research and classes since the spring of 2007. She developed the University of Nebraska at Omaha (UNO) School of Communication's Second Life campus. Dr. Leonard has presented on Second Life in Higher Education to the faculty at UNO, the Omaha (NE) Public School District, the Lincoln (NE) Public School district, and at regional and national conferences.

Rowena Li a school media specialist at Bayside High School in New York, received her doctoral degree in information science from the University of North Texas in 2008. Her Master Degree of Library and Information Science came from Queens College, CUNY, in 1997. She has worked in her current position as a school librarian for eight years. Prior to that, she worked as a senior reference librarian at Queens Borough Public Library in New York, a prospect researcher at Queens College Foundation, and a lecturer at Nankai University in China. Her research interests focus upon cross-lingual information retrieval, cultural dimensions of documentations and website designs.

Edward A. Mabry (Bowling Green State University) is Associate Professor, in the Department of Communication, at the University of Wisconsin-Milwaukee. His research and teaching focuses on: mediated communication in groups and organizations, implications of communication in distance education, and social interaction structure in group decision making. His work has appeared in Communication Monographs, Human Communication Research, Journal of Communication, and The Handbook of Group Communication Theory & Research.

Katheryn C. Maguire (Ph.D., University of Texas at Austin, 2001) is an Assistant Professor in the Department of Communication at Wayne State University where she teaches courses in communication theory, nonverbal communication, and family communication, among others. Her research centers on how individuals use communication to maintain relationships and cope with stressful situations in both mediated and face-to-face contexts. She has also studied the role of computer-mediated interactions in long-distance relationships, with a particular interest in how perceptions of social presence facilitate the accomplishment of both individual and relational goals. She has presented her work at national and international conferences and has published in a number of academic journals, including Communication Monographs and Communication Quarterly.

Yuping Mao is the Academic Developer of the Master of Arts in Communications and Technology program at University of Alberta in Canada. She teaches graduate courses on both qualitative and quantitative research methodologies and health communication. Yuping is expected to get her Ph.D. in organizing and relating from Ohio University in 2010. Yuping's research focuses on organizational communication and health communication. With her multi-cultural background, Yuping takes intercultural communication perspectives into some of her research. Yuping has presented her research in national and international conferences in both Canada and the U.S., and has published her work in Review of Communication, Teaching Ideas for the Basic Communication Course, Howard Journal of Communications, and Feminist Media Studies. Yuping also does consultation work for the City of Edmonton on public deliberation.

Kris M. Markman (Ph.D., 2006, The University of Texas at Austin) is an Assistant Professor in the Department of Communication at the University of Memphis. She teaches classes in computer-mediated communication, new media, and broadcasting, and conducts research on people's everyday uses of new communication technologies. She is particularly interested in examining language and social interaction in online groups and communities. A former public radio professional, she is also interested in how the internet is changing the way media content is produced and distributed, particularly by amateurs and fans, and has recently begun studying independent podcasters.

John A. McArthur is an Assistant Professor and the Director of Undergraduate Programs in the School of Communication at Queens University of Charlotte (NC). He earned a Ph.D. in Rhetorics, Communication, and Information Design at Clemson University (SC) and a M.Ed. at the University of South Carolina. His academic interests involve user-experience design, proxemics, and the role of technology and media design in society. Dr. McArthur's current research includes studies of user-experience design as it relates to the creation and use of documents in various media forms, mass media, and physical and virtual spaces.

Jessica L. Moore holds a Ph.D. in Communication Studies from the University of Texas at Austin and is an Assistant Professor in the Department of Communication at North Carolina State University. Dr. Moore's research explores the intersection of relational development, social influence, and new technology. She teaches undergraduate and graduate courses on interpersonal communication, persuasion, and computer-mediated communication.

Francesc Núñez Ph. D. in Sociology is a lecturer at the Arts and Humanities Department (Universitat Oberta de Catalunya, Barcelona, Spain) where he coordinates the area of philosophy. Hi also holds a BA in Philosophy. He belongs to the Institute of Sociological Research (ISOR) of the Universitat Autònoma de Barcelona (UAB) and he has carried out several research projects like "The meaning of love among young people", or the PhD thesis Secularized Priests. He is a member of the research group GRECS (Research Group in Cultural and Social Studies, IN3/UOC) and he has carried out several research projects on on-line sociability in everyday life. His current research is focused on the relation between emotions and subjective experience in consumer society. He is also co-editor of Digithum e-zine (http://digithum.uoc.edu/ojs/index.php/digithum/english).

Fay Cobb Payton Associate Professor of Information Systems at North Carolina State University, was recently named an American Council on Education Fellow for 2009-2010. She works extensively with The PhD Project and was recently featured in the June/July 2009 issue of Diversity/ Careers in Engineering and Information Technology. Her research focuses on healthcare informatics, data management and social exclusion. She has published in European Journal of Information Systems, Journal of the AIS, IEEE Transactions, Communications of the ACM, The Information Society, Health Care Management Review, Computer Personnel, and Information and Management. She is the co-editor of Adaptive Health Information Systems which was released in May 2009.

Yuxia Qian is an assistant professor in the Department of Communication Studies at Albion College. She teaches small group and organizational communication, intercultural communication, interpersonal communication, and introduction to human communication. Her primary research interest lies in organizational communication in the multicultural work environment. Her past work focused on social information processing and employee attitude toward organizational change. She is currently exploring online social support groups of patients in the field of health communication. She holds a doctorate from Ohio University. She has presented her research in both national and international communication conferences, and published her work in the Emerald journal Corporate Communications: An International Journal.

John C. Sherblom Ph.D., is a Professor at the University of Maine with research interests in organizational communication technology, work groups, and computer-mediated communication. He teaches graduate and undergraduate courses in communication and technology, research methods, and organizational communication, and has published more than 30 research articles and a text on Small Group and Team Communication. His current research interests focus on identity, presentation of self, and participation in group decision making in Second Life.

Michael A. Stefanone is an assistant professor in the Department of Communication at the State University of New York at Buffalo. His research focuses on the intersection of people, organizations, and technology. His current research explores how personality differences influence the ways people position themselves within social and task networks, how people's social context influence technology adoption and use, and the relationship between traditional mass media and new media use.

Devan Rosen (Ph.D., Cornell University) is an Assistant Professor of Speech at the University of Hawaii at Manoa, and has published on topics including social network analysis, self-organizing systems, and computer-mediated communication. His research focuses on decentralized communication networks, communication technology, and culture. He has also developed network analytic methods for the structural and content analysis of online communities and virtual worlds.

Paola Francesca Spadaro is research assistant at University of Bari from 2007. She collaborates at Educational Psychology and E-Learning Psychology courses at University of Bari (IT). In 2003 she graduated in Psychology at University Sapienza and in 2007 she obtained a PhD in Psychology: cognitive, emotional, and communicational processes at University of Bari with a titled "Intersubjectivity and Digital Activity Systems". In 2005 she obtained a "Marie Curie Research Training Grants" at School of Education - University of Leeds (UK). She collaborated to project and realize several local and national research projects regarding to the study of psychological processes involved in technological innovation in various contexts: SME, professional and university learning. She is editor in chief of scientific journal "Qwerty. Journal of education, culture, and technology".

William J. Starosta (Ph.D., Indiana U., 1973) is Graduate Director of the Department of Communication and Culture, Howard University, Washington, D.C. He is Founding Editor of The Howard Journal of Communications, and has published or edited over 100 works across several disciplines concerning culture and communication, rhetoric, or gender.

Sharon Stoerger is a doctoral candidate in the School of Library and Information Science at Indiana University, Bloomington. Her research interests include computer-mediated communication in learning environments and communities of practice. More specifically, she has been investigating virtual worlds, their use in formal and informal educational settings, and the ways in which visitors to these Web 2.0 spaces communicate with each other. Her current work examines continuing education courses in Second Life (SL) through an ethnographic approach, including participant observation and informal interviews. In addition, she has been using discourse analysis methods to better understand the interactions between students and instructors in virtual environments, as well as the learning potential of these worlds.

Rotimi Taiwo attended the University of Benin, Benin-City and Obafemi Awolowo University, Ile-Ife, Nigeria. He holds PhD in English and he has been teaching in the Department of English, Obafemi Awolowo University since 1997, where he is currently a senior lecturer. His main research focus over the last decade has been the application of (critical) discourse analytic theories to a wide range of discourse contexts, such as media, religion, popular culture, computer-mediated discourse and students' composition. He has co-edited two books: Perspectives on media Discourse and Towards the Understanding of Discourse Strategies. He is a member of the editorial boards of Ife Studies in English (Nigeria), Linguistik Online (Switzerland) International Journal of Language, Culture and Society (Australia). Rotimi Taiwo was a fellow of Alexander von Humboldt at the Englisches Seminar, Albert-Ludwigs University, Freiburg, Germany (September, 2008 – August 2009).

Marta Traetta is PhD student in Psychology: cognitive, emotional, and communicational processes at University of Bari (IT) since 2007. She is interested in psychosocial processes in communities of practices, especially of blended learning communities. She collaborates at Group Psychology and Social Communication Psychology at University of Bari, where she graduated in Psychology in 2006. She collaborates to plan and realize several local and national research projects about psychological processes involved in technological innovation in contexts such as professional and university learning ones. She is member of Collaborative Knowledge Building Group Association (CKBG) and of Association of Internet Researcher (AOIR). Furthermore she is qualified to psychology profession since 2008.

Stephanie Troutman is a Dual PhD Candidate in the departments of Curriculum & Instruction (Education) and Women's Studies (Liberal Arts) at The Pennsylvania State University. She earned her Master of Education degree from Stetson University in 2005. Over the past seven years, Ms. Troutman has taught in traditional, hybrid, and virtual/online environments at the middle school, high school, and college level. Her research interests include feminist theory, feminist pedagogy, learning through media, film analysis, media literacy curriculum, and cultural studies. She is currently writing her dissertation using Discourse analysis to explore how a particular media literacy curriculum as it relates to constructs and represents identity in accordance with stable (political) notions of race, class, and gender.

Agnès Vayreda is Lecturer at the Humanities Department of the Open University of Catalonia (UOC), where she coordinates the Social Psychology area. Her research interests concern computer-mediated communication, the emergence and construction of virtual communities, online identity and Internet utopias.

Lesley A. Withers is an Associate Professor with research interests in collaboration in virtual worlds and the "dark side" of communication. Her personal interest in new technologies led her to try Second

Life; she has been active in this virtual world since April 2006 and has taught and conducted research in Second Life since Spring 2008. She has presented demonstrations and short courses on teaching in Second Life at the local, regional, and national levels. With Leonard and Sherblom, Withers has co-authored book chapters on communication in Second Life that explore issues of identity, collaboration, and pedagogical potential in Second Life.

Index

C

W